The Information Resources Policy Handbook

edited by
Benjamin M. Compaine
William H. Read

The Information Resources Policy Handbook

Research for the Information Age

The MIT Press
Cambridge, Massachusetts
London, England

This book was set in Times New Roman by Asco Typesetters, Hong Kong.
Printed and bound in the United States of America.

Library of Congress Cataloging-in-Publication Data

The Information resources policy handbook : research for the
  information age / edited by Benjamin M. Compaine, William H. Read.
    p. cm.
  Includes bibliographical references and index.
  ISBN 0-262-03264-3 (hc : alk. paper)
  1. Information resource management—Handbooks, manuals, etc.
  I. Compaine, Benjamin M. II. Read, William H.
  T58.64.I5335 1999
  658.4′038—dc21   98-48229
                                                           CIP

This book is dedicated to Anthony G. Oettinger, who founded the Program on Information Resources Policy, which for a quarter of a century has provided insightful, competent, and impartial research on controversial matters of continuing relevance about the evolution of the age of information.

Contents

Foreword: Into the Age of Information

An Age of Information has its modern base in the Age of Science and Technology that has characterized the twentieth century. Previously, technology and invention came along as human supplements for human activities in moving and exercising: the wheel and its mechanization for locomotion; energy conversion such as the steam engine and distributed electricity, dynamos, and motors. But the analogs in communication—the printing press, the telegraph, the telephone—were complements to other activities in the thinking and doings of people. Similarly, these special qualities of human action are reflected in the Babbage machines, the electrical relays of Stibitz, the ENIAC of Eckert and Mauchly, and von Neumann's conceptions.

Professor Anthony Oettinger of Harvard University was among the very few who recognized that major parts of the surging science and technology of the early twentieth century would converge with inventive design and conceptual uses of knowledge. This was happening especially in the cataclysmic struggles of the mid-century leading to the structuring of knowledge to be called "information."

Thus, as systems of telecommunications and logic machines coevolved, Dr. Oettinger saw that societies, economies, and industries, as well as governments, were likely to seek deeper understanding and implementation of how information could be organized and processed. A major advance was Claude Shannon's theorems and concepts that the elements of logic (that is, a binary state of yes-or-no, plus or minus, north or south) were central to communications techniques. Another step in comprehending that telephone switching systems could have universal meanings for the coding of information were the principles of Nyquist and his associates (somewhat like the dots and dashes with which electric telegraphy functioned). As television and, to a lesser extent, enhanced telephony, magnified its requirements, telecommunications companies sought higher and higher frequencies for broader bandwidths in their networks. We worked in our laboratories with a growing electronics technology but suffered from the inadequate capacities and reliability of a technology dominated by de Forest's and Arnold's vacuum tubes.

Ultimately came the discovery of the transistor and a vast range of its derivatives. We were aided by the dramatic advance in materials for all sorts of mechanical and electrical systems, including rocketry and satellites, as well as the spread of quantum theoretic insight into crystals and condensed matter. This was at the same time that Shannon's insights into information content and the structure of messages and signaling were illuminating cryptography and cryptanalysis and related issues crucial to victory in World War II. Their value was even more decisive in the dangerous confrontation with the nuclear threats of the Cold War.

Dr. Oettinger's keen interest in creativity and novelty had, in due course, associated him with Professor Howard Aiken's work on computers for cryptanalysis for the National Security Agency. And his connoisseur's concern with how the telecommunications system could serve a global video and universal telephonic economy stirred his interest in solid-state circuitry. Soon Dr. Oettinger saw that the transistor and the solid-state diode would enable digital circuitry responsive to Shannon's units.

Dr. Oettinger also early exhibited a keen instinct for how commercial uses could grow if information was recognized as a supplement to labor and personal skills, or a complement to human capabilities. He thus foresaw the reality of the expectations reported to the Engineer's Joint Council on the "Nation's Engineering Research Needs."[1] That report said that the traditional role of the engineer and technologists, as well as most other sorts of specialists (such as physicians, journalists, brokers, and bankers), would be recast in their services to society. That report stated:

This recasting will be discussed as taking primarily the form of vastly reducing the routine actions of handling and applying information for designs, maintenance, and operation (whether of manufactures, of vehicles or of people). There is accordingly the possibility of restoring large elements of personal independence and ingenuity to the specialized manpower of the nation, a quality which has been progressively reduced in the first half of this century by the necessary proliferation of rigid and standard practices which accompany the great growth of industrial and public systems.

Dr. Oettinger quantified how much of this reformation in human function could occur. Within a decade he had established the Harvard Program on

Information Resources Policy. This originated and remains the most sapient source of how the enduring creativity of information science and engineering have interacted with people in the second half of the twentieth century.

Accordingly, it is striking that Dr. Oettinger recognized that, in the Age of Information, science and technology would become concurrent rather than leading-edge elements of commercial, governmental, and social applications. This is in contrast to what is now happening in the life sciences, and has traditionally occurred in energy and vehicular systems. What is now being called the cybereconomy is nevertheless not even half of the proportion of the gross domestic product represented by the health care industry. Specifically, by 1998 "information" products were about $900 billion or 8 percent of the gross domestic product. This was roughly 50 percent higher than in 1992 and employed about five million Americans. Much of this growth has been concentrated in software, itself a $100 billion industry, forecast to employ 3.5 million in the United States by 2005, or about 3 percent of the total work force. Already, and somewhat astonishingly to many of us, the population of the United States is now spending more on computers than on TV sets (although the number of TV sets remains far greater).

The Harvard program recognized these trends long before they became obvious. Insights such as Dr. Oettinger's can be seen in the factors that permit the multitrillion dollar operations of the world's currency markets that is now a routine exercise. Oettinger identified forces and trends very early that are consistent with subsequent data, such as the data documenting that banks that processed about 265 checks an hour in 1971, by 1986 processed over 1000 such units with the benefits of information technology. This rate pales further with today's digital funds transactions.

This little foray into economic impacts could be extended into many other realms beyond the entertainment and communications of daily life. Thus, even though, in 1998, bytes per day of telephone traffic in the United States was about 30 times that of Internet traffic and will double in a fairly short time, Internet traffic was expected to triple annually through 2002 or 2003. These volume gains have been accompanied by striking innovations that confirm the seeming outsized predictions of only a few years ago. Thus, the prediction of usage in a report at the 100th anniversary of the Ericsson Company in Stockholm in 1976, while extreme at the time, has now largely been achieved and bypassed by ever-more effective capabilities.[2]

Indeed, while these particular services are largely telecommunications-based, compilations such as *The Second Information Society Index* (ISI) have surveyed more important or more extensive information age activities, such as books, newspapers, and periodicals.[3] The study was characterized as the "world's first measurer of the country's capacity to access, absorb, and utilize information and information technologies." This study concluded that the United States has about a 35 percent overall lead over the second national capacity, that of Finland, with the United Kingdom and Japan coming out tenth and eleventh, behind the Scandinavian countries. Perhaps not surprisingly, in 1998 the Asia-Pacific region nevertheless included ten of the fourteen fastest-growing information societies. It was this sort of potential which Oettinger perceived during the quarter-century evolution of the Harvard program.

A purpose of this crude sampling of the scope of the Oettinger pathway into the information age is also to indicate the coherence of how mechanized scientific principles in both the hardware and software are used. Hence, the Harvard program recognized the likelihood of a steady advance, in comparison to the rather erratic, though creative, inventions of the century before.

The Harvard Program on Information Resources Policy, identified with a major era of science and engineering, is generally associated with an orientation toward industry, with concurrent experience in government and with national security. The program's perspective, dominated by science and technology, is consistent with our personal sense of a proper introduction to an age of information.

However, the program should also be credited for its place in the philosophy and sociology of the era. There remains a need for humility when it comes to understanding the wider recognition of human knowledge—the philosopher's realm. Several modern authors are increasingly dealing with the vast influence of technology on information, from Marshall McLuhan to Esther Dyson and her contemporaries.[4] Nonetheless, before we discard the industrial model like an old shoe, we should recall that the principal science and technologies involved in creating the mechanisms for the information age originated in industrial laboratories.

I remarked above that Oettinger and his associates from the start were aware of how machines have liberated humankind from the drudgery and burdens of energy-using labor. Now, through computers and communications, we will be liberated from the narrow constraints of reacting to only the small body of information that is ordinarily available. We can partake of the macrocosmos of thought and knowledge, called by the philosopher Teilhard de Chardin, the "Anoösphere." About this, Sir Julian Huxley has said,

This covering of the earth's sphericity with a thinking envelope, whose components are interacting with a steadily rising intensity, is now generating a powerful psychosocial pressure favouring a solution of least effort, by way of integration in a unitary organization of ideas and beliefs.... When we look at the whole sweep of man's history on earth, as now revealed by the labours of historians, archaeologists, and anthropologists, we see that everything that properly deserves to be called progress has depended on new knowledge and new organizations of knowledge in the shape of ideas.... We have discovered that each advance may lead us into difficulties, but also that evolution is a dialectic or cybernetic process operating by feedback, in which new difficulties can be surmounted, but only with the aid of new discoveries and new applications of knowledge. During the past three centuries the most powerful agency for providing new knowledge has been Science.... In place of separate subjects each with their own assumptions, methodology and technical jargon, we must envisage networks co-operative investigation, with common methods and terminology, all eventually linked up in a comprehensive process of enquiry. This, of course, will mean a radical reorganization of scientific teaching and research.

Now Dr. Oettinger has related a singular sense of these deeper meanings to the operations of telecommunications and computers. Some of us were convinced that what he eventually termed "compunications" were intrinsic to the evolution of telephone as early as 1967,[5] which lead to the research with packet switching that was well underway in our laboratories by 1978.[6] By then the need for the articulation of new degrees of sociotechnical articulation became compelling. Dr. Oettinger's program produced it in unsurpassed form.

W. O. Baker
Bell Laboratories—Lucent Technologies

Notes

1. Engineer's Joint Council, "A Nation's Engineering Research Needs," May 26, 1962, 153–172.

2. "Telephone Communications in the Future," Stockholm, May 5, 1976.

3. International Data Corporation and the World Times, Inc.

4. Here I am thinking of Dyson's *Release 2.0: A Design for Living in the Digital Age* (New York: Broadway Books, 1997).

5. *ISA Transactions* 6 (April 1967): 87–93.

6. *Signal* (Falls Church, Va.: AFCE Association, Sept. 1980).

Preface

Benjamin M. Compaine and William H. Read

Our motivations for compiling this volume were twofold. We think it useful for readers to know the context for this book.

The immediate impetus was the seventieth birthday of Anthony Oettinger, the cofounder and intellectual force behind the Program on Information Resources Policy. In 1995, Anne Branscomb, a friend as well as colleague of Tony's, suggested to a group of friends and associates of his that it would be appropriate to celebrate Tony's seventieth birthday in 1999 with several events: a conference, a dinner, and a book. The two of us volunteered to edit a book in that spirit.

The timing was right, as we had been talking about doing a book together. This was the second "fold." Each of us has taught courses under titles such as "Strategic Issues in the Management of Technology" or "Information Technology and Policy" for which we could not find an appropriate basic text for our students. We had to pull together collections of articles into "course packets," at considerable cost and time. We knew there were other faculty in the same position. We also knew that there were many other professionals in the management, regulation or analysis of information companies who could use both a nonengineer's understanding underlying the digital world and insights into its implications for corporate and government policymakers.

This, then, is the book that we fashioned to be both a tribute to Tony Oettinger's work and a comprehensive primer on information resources policy. We believe that the two objectives are complementary.

Organization of the Book

The contents of this book are principally from research that spans nearly two decades of the Harvard Program on Information Resources Policy. They are supplemented with original chapters written by prominent professionals and academics. In a still-developing discipline, some contemporary judgments regarding the resources of the information age are certain to change. Others are more stable. To strike a balance between the two, which implicitly means a balance between abstract concepts of enduring value and writings on particular subjects illustrated with specific examples, the editors have resorted to partitioning.

Thus, the first chapter in each section of the book is what we have dubbed an "Evergreen" work. Whether newly written or authored years ago, these chapters contain perspective and principles that are not nor are likely to get outdated. Some of the remaining chapters are also contemporary; others have an enduring quality. But, over time, we expect that the Evergreen chapters will stay consistent from edition to edition, while the "contemporary" chapters will be changed as topics become resolved and new ones become current.

This approach further explains what may strike readers as a curious artifact in some of these articles: the relatively ancient data cited in some of the chapters. In a few cases, tabular data may be no more current that the early 1980s. While our first impulse was to update these, we made a decision to reprint these articles as they were originally written. We judged that the analyses, forces, or trends that these data were provided to support when written have held true up to the time of this publication, even as the details may have changed.

The Program on Information Resources Policy

Since its founding at Harvard by Anthony G. Oettinger and his associate John LeGates in 1972, the Program on Information Resources Policy has been monitoring and analyzing developments in a variety of fields that it has defined (admittedly loosely) as the "information industries." Defining the nature and scope of the information industries—an area marked by ambiguity and turmoil—has been a continuing problem for the program, for policymakers, and for the information industries themselves. While many of the program's research projects over the years have focused on developments within a specific traditional information industry, such as broadcasting, telephone, or cable TV, the program has continually emphasized the interaction among the different information technologies, markets, and types of government intervention. The program's principals speak frequently, therefore, about merging technologies and new conflicts among traditional industries.

In organizing the Harvard Program on Information Resources Policy, Oettinger and LeGates sought to create knowledge, both competent and impartial, on controversial information-related matters. Their idea of success was that this new knowledge would be of high quality and that it would be trusted by any party to a controversy, anyone with stakes in the outcome of the controversy, or, for that matter, any bystander.

Combining competence and impartiality is not easy. But Oettinger, LeGates, and their colleagues have done it with great success for a quarter century—and the two of us are pleased to have been involved in a small measure—and their impact and influence has been global in scope. Central to their objective of not only stating their impartiality in the policy realm but maintaining the *appearance* of impartiality, the program has created a unique funding mechanism. Because it dealt in areas of high stakes of corporate and political self-interests, it successfully sought out a broad base of financial support. Competing industries and competitors within those industries are contributors. The program has never undertaken a specific study at the behest of any contributor, done any proprietary research, nor allowed an organization or industry to fund a specific research project. It did not allow any player to contribute a sum large enough to cripple the program should that sum of funding be withdrawn for any reason.

Not all players bought into this procedure. But enough did see the merit in having a policy "think tank" whose output could always be viewed as impartial by any standard. This book stands as a testimony to what has been achieved.

As changes in technology markets and public policy reshape the traditional information industries, these industries must be viewed as part of a larger world, one that the program has termed the "information business." That is why this is but the first edition of the *Information Resources Policy Handbook*.

A Map of the Information Business

The information business is a complex of companies and government agencies involved in the acquisition, packaging, processing, storage, transmittal, and distribution of information. The size and scope of the business in economic terms is the subject of chapter 11.

The information business map in figure P-1 is a less conventional approach to describing the complex of organizations that make up the information business. It displays the operating boundaries of players in the information business along product–service and form–substance axes. The map has been useful for

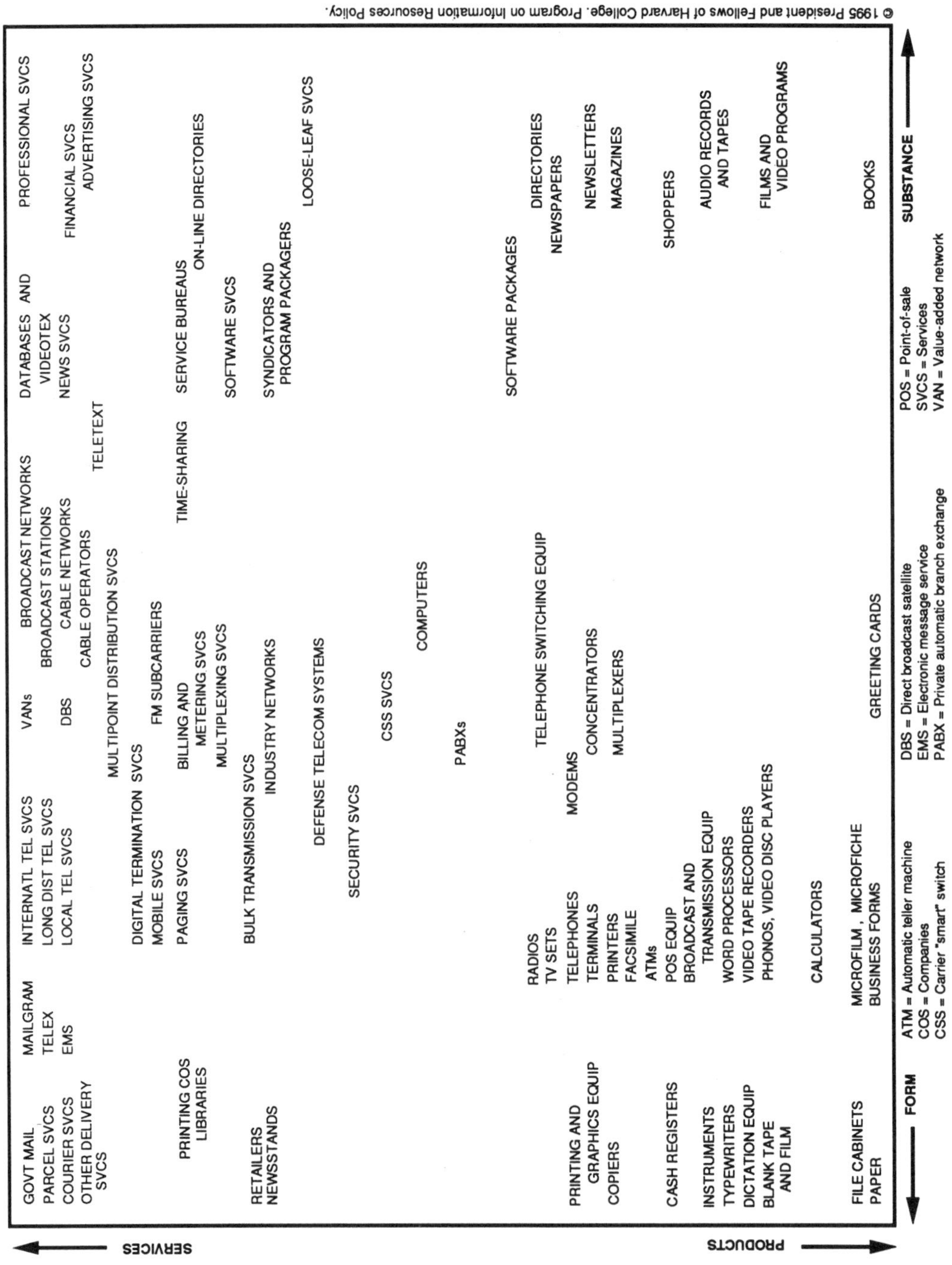
The Information Business
GOVT MAIL
PARCEL SVCS
COURIER SVCS
OTHER DELIVERY SVCS
PRINTING COS
LIBRARIES
RETAILERS
NEWSSTANDS
PRINTING AND GRAPHICS EQUIP
COPIERS
CASH REGISTERS
INSTRUMENTS
TYPEWRITERS
DICTATION EQUIP
BLANK TAPE AND FILM
FILE CABINETS
PAPER
MAILGRAM
TELEX
EMS
RADIOS
TV SETS
TELEPHONES
TERMINALS
PRINTERS
FACSIMILE
ATMs
POS EQUIP
BROADCAST AND TRANSMISSION EQUIP
WORD PROCESSORS
VIDEO TAPE RECORDERS
PHONOS, VIDEO DISC PLAYERS
CALCULATORS
MICROFILM, MICROFICHE
BUSINESS FORMS
INTERNATL TEL SVCS
LONG DIST TEL SVCS
LOCAL TEL SVCS
DIGITAL TERMINATION SVCS
MOBILE SVCS
PAGING SVCS
BULK TRANSMISSION SVCS
DEFENSE TELECOM SYSTEMS
SECURITY SVCS
MODEMS
VANs
DBS
MULTIPOINT DISTRIBUTION SVCS
FM SUBCARRIERS
BILLING AND METERING SVCS
MULTIPLEXING SVCS
INDUSTRY NETWORKS
CSS SVCS
PABXs
TELEPHONE SWITCHING EQUIP
CONCENTRATORS
MULTIPLEXERS
GREETING CARDS
BROADCAST NETWORKS
BROADCAST STATIONS
CABLE NETWORKS
CABLE OPERATORS
TELETEXT
TIME-SHARING
COMPUTERS
DATABASES AND VIDEOTEX
NEWS SVCS
SERVICE BUREAUS
ON-LINE DIRECTORIES
SOFTWARE SVCS
SYNDICATORS AND PROGRAM PACKAGERS
SOFTWARE PACKAGES
PROFESSIONAL SVCS
FINANCIAL SVCS
ADVERTISING SVCS
LOOSE-LEAF SVCS
DIRECTORIES
NEWSPAPERS
NEWSLETTERS
MAGAZINES
SHOPPERS
AUDIO RECORDS AND TAPES
FILMS AND VIDEO PROGRAMS
BOOKS
SERVICES
PRODUCTS
FORM
SUBSTANCE
ATM = Automatic teller machine
COS = Companies
CSS = Carrier "smart" switch
DBS = Direct broadcast satellite
EMS = Electronic message service
PABX = Private automatic branch exchange
POS = Point-of-sale
SVCS = Services
VAN = Value-added network
© 1995 President and Fellows of Harvard College. Program on Information Resources Policy.

Figure P.1 The Harvard information business map

illustrating the corporate and regulatory churning that has been under way in the information business in recent years, and serves to highlight areas that invite further attention from financial analysts, public policymakers, and corporate strategists.

The mapping technique (see chapter 10) can be used to illustrate a variety of relationships and developments in the information business, including:

1. the jurisdictional boundaries of regulatory agencies;
2. the strategic positioning of companies in the information business in relation to regulatory boundaries and competitors' positions;
3. operations and planning within individual organizations;
4. some basic forces and trends driving changes in the information business; and
5. the historical evolution of the information business.

The information business map is not a fixed matrix, but a dynamic model, and will continue to evolve in response to changes in the information business. *Mapping the Information Business* was one of the seminal research projects of the research program, which is why we introduce it here and include a chapter on the subject (see chapter 10).

Although Tony Oettinger has been the guiding intellectual force behind this work, he has attracted over the years a cadre of collaborators, associates, reviewers, and support staff. We have already referred to John LeGates, who has been the managing director of the program since its inception. We hesitate to name names as there are so many, and so few could be mentioned. But a short list would include John McLaughlin and Oswald Ganley, as long-time program directors. Claire Merola was there at the start as Tony's secretary and emerged as the program's administrator. We are all also saddened that the moving force behind this volume, Anne Wells Branscomb, died in 1997, just as the plans she initiated were starting to take shape.

We are grateful for the opportunity to assemble a unique body of work that addresses the question, "In the age of information, what should an educated person understand about the resources that are involved in the worldwide shift toward information-intensive economies and societies?" We trust that the knowledge in this book will be useful to our readers in either your personal lives or in your institutional roles, as the Age of Information continues to evolve.

Introduction: Information Resources: Knowledge and Power in the 21st Century

Anthony G. Oettinger

By widening the range of possible social "nervous systems," the continuing growth of information resources is upsetting the world order, just as the Industrial Revolution upset it by widening the range of physical modes of production. Where this will lead is as hard to foretell now as predicting today's world was when the steam engine was invented. However, the timeless truth that knowledge is power once again needs reinterpretation because of newly abundant, varied, and versatile modes of gathering, storing, processing, transmitting, and exploiting information that contrast with ever scarcer and costlier materials and energy. Why this is so is illustrated first by showing how changing prices of the services delivered by the computer-and-communications ("compunications") infrastructure have almost literally changed the shape of the United States.

The Changing "Compunications" Infrastructure

Nineteen seventy-six marked the centennial of the telephone; the telegraph is a generation older. The birth of radio early in the twentieth century and of television in midcentury are other notable milestones in the evolution of the electronic communications technologies. Computer and other digital electronic information technologies flowered during and after World War II.

Wholly unprecedented is our still rapidly developing engineering mastery over the microscopic information processes embodied in devices such as large-scale integrated (LSI) circuits and microcomputers. The digital technologies underlying such devices are a merger of computer and communications technologies into a common stream that I have called *compunications technologies*.

Coincident with the unfolding of compunications technologies, political decisions began to be made in the late 1960s that awoke competition in the telecommunications industry where it had been dormant for half a century; in the same period, the boundary between the telecommunications and computer industries blurred. The resulting price changes have changed the shape of the United States. Figure I.1a is a familiar geographic map of the United States marked with distances from Jefferson City, a place at about the center of Missouri. The less familiar maps of Figure I.1 (b–d) are telephonic maps. Whereas the geographic map shows actual shapes with the circles showing miles, the telephonic maps show costs, not distances, from Jefferson City.

Similar politico-economic-technological changes in our perceptions of distance—and of time—continued globally over the next decade, along with domestic and international battles over how the resulting benefits and burdens are to be shared among advanced or developing nations, big or little businesses, urban or rural households, and different types of uses such as the traditional and dominant voice services from mouths to ears or the new and growing digital transmission services to and from communications terminals at work or at home.

Concomitant changes in industrial organizations also can already be discerned behind a still-stable facade of traditional labels.

What comes of that turmoil clearly matters to the numerous protagonists— such as AT&T, IBM, the U.S. Postal Service, Exxon, Chase Manhattan, Dun and Bradstreet, McGraw-Hill, the *Washington Post*, and numerous other enterprises, large and small, public and private—in the United States and abroad— who are redefining themselves and their missions in the light of technological changes that lifted the traditional barriers among themselves and among their markets.

Beyond the stakes of particular corporations, some see the changing patterns of prices of information and of access to information as likely to entail pervasive and profound social transformation, just as the advent of mechanized industry and the subsequent rise of the bourgeoisie transformed Western societies once before. Hence such labels as the "information revolution," the "information society," or the "post-industrial society."

It is generally recognized how significant changing modes of transportation are in commercial terms of access to raw materials, energy, labor, and markets, or in terms of the projection of military power. Since it is less widely understood, the significance of changing modes of information resources is next described in similar terms.

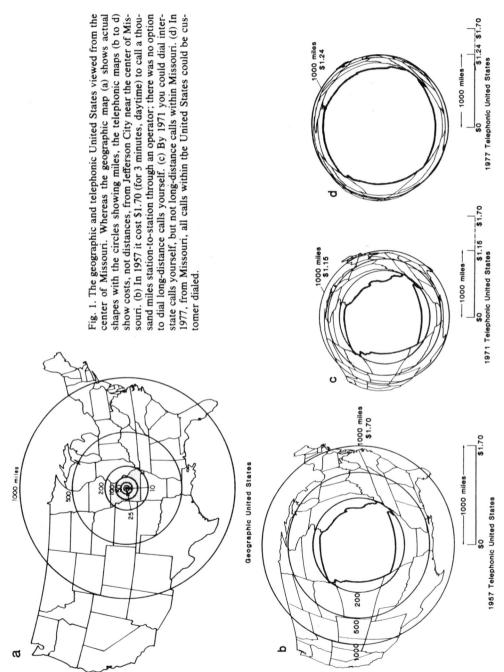

Fig. 1. The geographic and telephonic United States viewed from the center of Missouri. Whereas the geographic map (a) shows actual shapes with the circles showing miles, the telephonic maps (b to d) show costs, not distances, from Jefferson City near the center of Missouri. (b) In 1957 it cost $1.70 (for 3 minutes, daytime) to call a thousand miles station-to-station through an operator; there was no option to dial long-distance calls yourself. (c) By 1971 you could dial interstate calls yourself, but not long-distance calls within Missouri. (d) In 1977, from Missouri, all calls within the United States could be customer dialed.

Figure I.1 The geographic and telephonic United States. From Anthony G. Oettinger, "Information Resources: Knowledge and Power in the 21st Century," *Science* 209 (July 4, 1980): 192.

Information Resources and Post-Industrial Society

Every society is an information society, and every organization an information organization, just as every organism is an information organism. Information is necessary to organize and to run everything from a cell to General Motors or the Pentagon. Large organizations get information and use it through formalized functions that military commanders call "intelligence" and "command-and-control," and that civilian managers refer to as "staff assimilation of information for line management." If an organism is taken as a metaphor for a group, corporation, military service, country, or society, then, metaphorically, intelligence is the function of the outward senses, and command-and-control encompasses all other functions of the nervous system, including the inward senses. In organizations as in organisms the scope of these functions and the means for executing them range from the rudimentary to the highly elaborate.

Motor functions, those of muscles, weapons systems, or assembly lines, are, of course, essential to doing anything; they depend on materials and on energy, and without materials there is nothing and without energy nothing happens. But without information, nothing has meaning: Materials are formless, motion is aimless. Contrasting an information society to an industrial society therefore does not imply, as is often mistakenly supposed, that the intrinsic importance of motor functions is diminishing. It merely shifts focus from motor functions or physical actions to the nervous systems that direct the senses, thought, and physical action. The contrast also reflects a proportion of information-related activities greater in modern societies than before.

Nowadays, major and rapidly growing industries either produce, distribute, store, or process information as their main product, or else supply others with the means for doing so. Almost half of the U.S. labor force is already engaged in information occupations. Although highly visible institutions, most notably public libraries and commercial television, continue to foster the illusion that information is a free good, information resources do in fact cost something. These resources are also essential for planning, directing, and monitoring the purposive activities of organisms and organizations.

Like materials and energy, then, information is a basic resource; and the critical questions about any resource also apply to information: Who has it, who wants it, how can you get it, and what are the terms of trade? These questions are timeless; changing information technologies are changing only the answers.

Signs of the increasingly abundant fruits of modern information technologies are now all around us; witness, for instance, the many new and relatively cheap consumer products that are parts of a "computer society."

The growing variety and versatility of information resources are masked by lingering traditional ties between specific kinds or purposes of information and specific means of dealing with them. Stereotypically, for example, news went with ink on paper and legmen, rewrite men, heroic editors with green eye-shades, massive presses, and little merchants staggering around the block under a Sunday's load. Mass entertainment was live hoofers on sawdust stages in the 1920s, silver halide images on celluloid projecting motion onto the screens of art deco movie palaces in the 1930s and 1940s, and phosphorescent images with commercials on the tubes in "home entertainment centers" since the 1950s. Personal communication for many still means ink, paper, envelopes, licking stamps, and the ring of the postman; for others, it's now mainly a finger in the dial or on the beeping buttons, the ring of the telephone and a voice at the other end. Dickens's Bob Cratchit and Uriah Heep are ancestors both of the key-punchers of yesterday's clerical warrens in banks and insurance companies and of the word processors sought in today's want ads. Digital compunications technologies are already versatile enough to discharge all of the above functions, certainly in part, perhaps entirely: All the different kinds of information can be represented in digital format, processed by computers, and transmitted electronically.

The term "information" appears to cover too much that seems distinctive: knowledge, data, information in a narrow sense that some treat as synonymous with data, news, intelligence, and numerous other colloquial and specialized denotations and connotations. However, the distinctions implied by oppositions such as observations/theories, data/knowledge, raw intelligence/finished intelligence, accounting details/management information are secondary, not fundamental, in characterizing information resources. They reflect only relative judgments. For instance, one person's knowledge is often another's raw data. What a vice president for marketing, production, or finance thinks he knows is just data to the chief executive officer's staff. What a scientist thinks he knows about the merits of a flu vaccine or the safety of a nuclear reactor is just data for presidential policy and politics. Data or knowledge are just types of information content—of greater or lesser value, of greater or lesser cost.

Furthermore, information content comes to us in many readily interchangeable forms—pictures, words, speech, writing. These forms are representations of information content, as in the spoken representations of the word "car" in southern or in Yankee dialects, or the representations of "car" in cursive or block letters or in Morse code. And then there are formats of information content, the physical tokens that embody it: toe marks traced in the sand, gouges chiseled in stone, ink marks on paper, glowing phosphor patterns on television screens, electrical currents in telegraph or telephone wires, electromagnetic waves from satellites to Earth stations, magnetic bubbles in computer memories, laser beams in glass fibers. The processes of gathering, storing, manipulating, transmitting, evaluating, and using information content in various formats are mediated by physical processors such as pen and paper, printing presses, computers, and human brains.

It is only tradition that associates specific kinds of information content or purpose with specific representations, formats, and processors. In contrast, the generic concept of information resources encompasses any information content represented in any way, embodied in any format, and handled by any physical processor. It encompasses any information processor for any content in any representation and any format, run within any public or private organizational structure. Adopting this generic concept enables us, as indicated above, to ask about information resources the same basic questions that we ask about any other resource. It also enables us, as with other generic resources, to select specific modes for greatest effectiveness, efficiency, esthetic value, or any other criterion in order to get the most out of the potential of the vast panoply of information technologies now at our disposal.

I *Ageless Issues*

1   Telling Ripe from Hype in Multimedia: The Ecstasy and the Agony

Anthony G. Oettinger

The ecstasy I refer to in the title is the ecstasy felt by myself and by others who live at the frontiers of the applications of computer and communications technologies. This ecstasy stems from observing that the marvelous cornucopia of smaller, faster and cheaper information hardware devices that electro-optical digital technologies have filled to overflowing in the course of the last half-century or so still keeps brimming over with fresh flowers and fruits; or, to switch the figure of speech, this ecstasy stems from a continuing vision of the dawn of a new information age or information society coming just ahead. In practice, indeed, the fact that hardware has gotten so much smaller, faster and cheaper in so few decades often more than compensates for the fact that the software needed for complete systems has simultaneously been getting larger and dearer.

In many realms of application, this has made things better for buyers as well as for sellers by changing an economy of scarcity, which stresses efficiency over effectiveness, into an economy of plenty, which stresses effectiveness over efficiency. We have experienced that kind of transition with pads of paper. In the 17th century, when Newton corresponded with Leibniz, both of them filled up every tiny corner of the paper, front and back, to use that scarce paper efficiently. In contrast to Newton's outlook, think about all the pads of paper each of us owns, all the books on our shelves, all the telephones and all the telephone directories in our offices, all the cars we drive, all of them unused most of the time: Once things get convenient enough and cheap enough, the effectiveness of abundance (erstwhile wastefulness) overwhelms the efficiency of high load factor (latter-day miserliness). Commercial airlines, by way of contrast, still live or die in the late 20th century by their load factors, namely, by how efficiently they use their expensive capital equipment. In the era of the PC, this transition from stressing efficiency to stressing effectiveness is well under way for computers and, with the spread of optical fiber and LANs (local area networks), it is beginning to happen to telecommunications. So, many buyers, if not ecstatic, are at least satisfied for many of their purposes.

The agony is from the simultaneous observation that the public, myself among them, is usually slower to smell all those flowers or slower to bite all those apples than entrepreneurs and technologists wish they would; that many of the fruits that look so ripe are only hype; or, to switch figures of speech again, that it's not a new information age we see dawning, but just the flashing neon signs advertising yet another wave of the "new ages" or "new societies" that seem to churn over us with apparently increasing speed and turmoil, most of them to wash out on some beach where both prospective buyers and prospective bankruptcy yawn at them. In less poetic terms, its inventors may love a new system even while the marketplace sees it as merely another gadget, not a better product or service.

What accounts for simultaneous ecstasy and agony? For one thing, just as beauty is in the eye of the beholder, so are ecstasy and agony in the perceptions of each participant in the evolution of technologies and of markets. Buyers and sellers, among other categories of beholders, naturally see things differently: As the saying goes, "where you stand depends on where you sit."

Here, I aim to clarify the root causes of the differing perceptions of buyers, sellers and others—such as referees, policemen or catalysts from governments. In essence, I'll sketch as competently and impartially as I can some fundamental forces and trends that I think underlie all the perceptions. My hope is that this will clarify how each of us, whatever our stakes in the future, might better steer a safer course through those successive swirling, churning information ages. Interactive multimedia, for which enthusiasm was so widespread in the early 1990s, will serve as a concrete example.

So, whence spring whose ecstasy and whose agony today, in our own fin de siècle era?

The effects of smaller, faster and cheaper electro-optical digital technologies are already extensive after fifty years of evolution. Fundamentally, smaller, faster and cheaper electro-optical digital technologies have already vastly increased the range of alternative information products and services that sellers can dream up, develop and bring to market, and that buyers of information products and services can choose from. Where once a few large sellers plus a very few large buyers were in control, the buyers in control have grown ever larger in numbers and ever smaller in size. No sphere of human endeavor has remained untouched by evolving electro-optical digital technologies.[1] In many endeavors, like airline, bank and even retail operations, normal functioning is no longer conceivable without computers and communications. In many other endeavors, like most manufacturing, operations would seriously degrade at the very least.

There's ecstasy in the early 1990s among the sellers of information products and services because huge markets have developed that didn't exist fifty, ten, or even five years ago, and some even less than that. There is agony in the early 1990s among these same sellers because, as their markets have become huge, they have also tended to become both highly competitive and increasingly fragmented.[2] Nowadays, the buyer is in the saddle, controlling the markets and eroding the sellers' margins in increasingly competitive declining cost markets, not just in such perennially dog-eat-dog precincts of the information businesses as the consumer electronics industry, but even in such genteel-for-a-while information businesses as the newspaper, broadcasting, computer, and tele-communications industries where monopoly, near-monopoly and monopoly margins had become the comfortable norm of the previous few decades and had conveniently quenched memories of the dog-eat-dog beginnings of those businesses.

The agonies of "old line" computer companies like IBM are highly visible in the early 1990s. The divestiture of American Telephone and Telegraph Company (AT&T) in the United States in 1984 and the worldwide and ongoing reregulations, privatizations and restructurings of telephone monopolies in the early 1990s are widely appreciated, at least among cognoscenti. Simultaneous but less visible and less widely appreciated is the fundamental restructuring from the bottom up implied by unregulated marketplace phenomena like the rapid growth of personal computers and of LANs in the early 1990s. In spite of efforts by some traditional managers and government regulators, especially in telecommunications, to hold on to traditional ways, all information businesses, those engaging in telecommunications functions prominently among them, are looking more and more like the consumer electronics, book-publishing and apparel industries and less and less like government Postal, Telegraph and Telephone authorities (PTTs).

There's ecstasy in the early 1990s among the buyers of information products and services because of the continually widening range of choices that buyers are offered by increasing numbers of competitors among more or less better information products and services with which to fulfill their institutional and personal responsibilities or desires. There is agony in the early 1990s among these same buyers because, as the range of their choices has become huge, that very abundance of choices—often where no choice at all existed before—has also become the source of indigestions (oh, so unreliable; oh, what lack of integrity of records, etc.) and frustrations (what is "better"? oh, that uninstalled software; oh, those "the computers are down" blues; oh, those claims of actually decreased productivity after computerization; and oh, what terrible things TV and video arcades are doing to the young, etc., etc.) and, I think most significant of all, the source of renewed and profound instability in the cycle of learning and experimentation that binds information skills and tools together into the bundles that we call literacy, numeracy, and artistic sensibility, bundles which make up a controlling element of the information infrastructure at least as critical as any information distribution systems. Distribution systems—old fashioned, or information superhighways to the field of dreams, or anywhere in between—are necessary for leading the water to the horse. But they are not sufficient to make the animal drink.

I think that the best and the worst are yet to come. The most exquisite of ecstasies and agonies still lie ahead. The mainstream killer applications of electro-optical digital technologies to date have done in a more efficient way the mental tasks which humanity has done from the beginning of literacy, numeracy, and art, and mostly the menial tasks at that. The full potential is yet to be realized.

An historical parallel is the transition at the start of the 20th century from horse-drawn carriages to horseless carriages that had buggy whips and running boards mounted on them. Still ahead lay the automobile, the suburbs and the shopping malls that blossomed from the 1950s on. In the institutional mainframe world, the equivalent of using horseless carriages has been automating and globalizing the routine tasks of business and government—airline reservations, financial transactions, moon-trip and missile Newtonian ballistics, and so on. In the individual PC world this has meant writing (word processors), mathematics (math packages), accounting (spreadsheets, tax preparation and review programs), keeping track (data bases), and representing (graphics). Especially in the world of individuals by the millions (contrasted with the world of institutions by the thousands), there is still growth ahead in these buggy-whip-and-running-board applications, such as linking them, and making them portable, easier to use, cheaper, more capacious, and the like.

Fundamental change is beginning to happen in earnest in the early 1990s, as it has happened at only a few previous milestones of recorded history. Our exploiting the fruits of faster, smaller, cheaper electro-optical digital technologies—whether packaged as computers, as telecommunications systems, as music synthesizers, as fuel injection controllers, as video-arcade games or as brilliant weapons guidance systems—is having two major catalytic effects of central concern here:

First, we are dissolving away the cords that tie together the traditional bundles of information conventions and skills we call literacy, numeracy and artistic sensibility, bundles we had come to live by in their present forms only since about the middle of the 19th century when they began to be born of the necessities and the possibilities of steam-driven technologies and societies.[3] This is divergence, not the convergence that seems to be fashionable in the early 1990s.[4]

Second, we are embarking on a voyage of trials and errors of unpredictable length and unknowable destination. By fashioning new tools that exploit interactivity, virtuality, and multiple information modes (words, music, pictures, etc.) on a scale unprecedented in human history because they rely intimately on the necessities and on the possibilities of electro-optical digital technologies, we are discovering possibilities for entirely new information conventions and skills. These new conventions and skills encompass traditional 19th century-born literacy, numeracy and artistic sensibility but they also go beyond them in ways and extents as yet only barely fathomed, although we'll sample some of them up ahead infra. Whether there's convergence or divergence in the marketplace remains to be seen. On the seller side, in any case, much mutual fear and loathing were evident in the early 1990s, as for instance between Hollywood and Silicon Valley working folks, whatever alliances their board rooms might have contrived.

The new information conventions and skills then in their turn enable us to imagine new tools with which to apply the conventions and exercise the skills more efficiently and, mostly, more effectively. This puts new demands on the existing tools and stimulates imagining and building newer tools yet. Eventually the newest tools once again loosen the ties that bound the very bundles of information conventions and skills that shaped the demand for those newest tools. This triggers yet another evolutionary cycle, and so on. Meanwhile, several generations of information conventions and skills coexist in uneasy anarchy, dominated at the start by the traditional information conventions and skills but increasingly disordered by the waxing and the waning of numerous alternatives undergoing trial and error.[5]

There not only is interactivity between the user and the tool at any instant, but both are redefining each other as they go. Although user skills and tools redefining one another is a process with numerous historical antecedents,[6] there are three new elements here:

- the tools in question are tools for mental, not physical, work or play;
- the duration and the rapid pace of redefinition are unprecedented because of the unprecedented and enormous malleability and speed of computers;
- and the process is endless in principle, because there is no end to complexity.

No matter how complex a process, just repeating it makes another process that's more complex—and that pattern is just a most elementary example. Increasing complexity would be self-defeating, were it not that complexity under the hood, so to speak, can make the tool look and feel simple to the driver. Just as the self-starter, when it replaced the hand crank, made automobiles safe for men's arms and jaws and usable by women unassisted, so software packages of ever increasing under-the-hood complexity can make it look easier to the "driver" at the keyboard, mouse, and screen. We don't care about the "inefficiency" if the resulting product or service is both more useful and cheaper than alternatives. This is one of the key ways in which faster, smaller, cheaper electro-optical digital technologies can make products or services better in a relatively clear-cut sense, although what this really means for workers and workplaces is a question addressed mainly by ongoing trial and error in businesses and other organizations to the accompaniment of a Greek chorus of falsehoods from economists and platitudes from business schools.

This anarchic, apparently tail-chasing, yet evolutionary process, when as rapid as it has been in the 1980s and as it promises to be through the 1990s, helps to account in substantial part for both the ecstasies and the agonies. The heroic and dedicated early adopters who dwell at the frontier outposts of innovation combine new tools, new information conventions, and new skills to create apparent wonders. The entrepreneurial imaginations fired up by the wonders of the early adopters promise those wonders to the prosaic, fickle old-time dwellers of the comfortable hinterlands as a wealth of new applications that never could have existed within the old confines. Hence the ecstasy. But some products and services will be ripe, others only hype. Some products and services will be ripe but unwanted. Others will be seen as too complex; still others as too simple. And the ones successful at the expense of someone else's market often enrage the losers into political action that changes the rules of the marketplace. Hence the agony.

"What is ripe?" in any given period is therefore a key question for would-be sellers and would-be buyers alike to ask. But, alas, the answer is usually forthcoming only from hindsight and not beforehand, so the question is one to which only a soothsayer would claim a valid answer with which to solidify the entrepreneur's or the early adopter's necessary faith.

Fortunately, "What is ripening?" and "By what process is it ripening?" are questions that can be addressed with some hope for realistic and useful illumination of the choices available to buyers and to sellers and to the referees, the policemen, and the catalysts of the marketplaces as they make their decisions.

In the myths of the ancient Greeks, the goddess Athena sprang instantly and full-grown from the brow of the supergod Zeus. In the real world, true innovations usually reach big markets only after lengthy gestation involving considerable trial and error among a few early adopters, unless the innovation happened to plug right in, so to speak, to fulfill an already familiar function in a familiar environment in about the same familiar way.

Some apparent counter-examples, like the rapid emergence of the facsimile in the 1980s, are just that: *apparent* counter-examples. The following lament sounds contemporary:

The probable simplification of the facsimile [sic] system of Caselli, by which an exact copy of anything that can be drawn or written may be instantaneously made to appear at a distance of hundreds of miles from the original; and the countless other applications of electricity to the transmission of intelligence yet to be made,—must sooner or later interfere most seriously with the transportation of letters by the slower means of post.

Its source, however, is the *Annual Report of the Postmaster-General of the United States* for 1872.[7] The poor man scared himself half to death at least 100 years too soon. All the necessary ingredients got ripe enough in the eyes of all the relevant beholders only at the turn of the 1980s when personal fax machines began to take off, much to the chagrin of the Federal Express company, which had just bet on a market for facsimile offices from which mechanical delivery by courier or post would fan out to the ultimate destinations.

Other apparent counter-examples illustrate that gestation and trial and error can take place in just a few years if there are entrepreneurs and early adopters willing to defy the conventional wisdom *and* if the innovation can be useful standing alone rather than embedded in an environment many aspects of which must evolve to simultaneous ripeness. A story vouched to me to be true has it that IBM once commissioned a consultant study of the market for dry copying which concluded that carbon paper would more than adequately meet all foreseeable market needs. IBM consequently lost interest in the fledgling company then called Haloid Xerox. However, familiar copying in a familiar enough way (with the complexity of the new-fangled technology hidden under the hood, so to speak) vastly expanded because of the significantly greater net ease of doing so with the new products.

The continuing complaints of the older set about the difficulties of using TV remote controllers and the continuing evolution of that gadget illustrate an intermediate case.

Although no one is quite sure what anyone else means specifically when they talk of interactive multimedia in the early 1990s, the common generic element in usage of the term seems to cover expressions using, more or less simultaneously, spoken, written, pictorial, musical, or any other form of human expression about real or virtual or imaginary worlds.

Interactivity is hardly new. All of us, and our ancestors back beyond the dawn of history, have had what we might call "innate interactivity" thanks to the speech format, the most ancient human information format we know of. Although highly interactive, speech lacked durability: once said, gone with the wind, except for what remained in the heads of speakers and listeners for their brief time in the sun. That is because, until Edison invented the phonograph in the last century, speech relied entirely on formats born inside our heads, issuing out of our mouths, going through the air to the ears of anyone within earshot and hence to their brains. Although fixed by physics and evolutionary biology, this format has always lent itself to very real, albeit space-and-time limited possibilities of what we nowadays refer to as creating open-ended structures as you go along and interacting with and controlling information. That's where languages as we know them were born and keep evolving.

By providing not only durability which frees the speech format from limitations of time and space but also unprecedented means for speech synthesis (relatively easy) and for speech analysis (from merely difficult to impossible, depending on what's asked for), electro-optical digital technologies have made ancient speech a modern glamour format of the early 1990s, with plenty of ecstasy at the renewed interest in speech's capacity for creating open-ended structures as you go along and interacting with and controlling information, but also increasing agony as the realities of multiple perceptions of ripeness along multiple dimensions once again take their toll and markets expand by meandering inches rather than by leaps and bounds.

Digitally synthesized or at least digitally controlled speech, for instance, is nowadays routinely heard in airport announcements, in instructions for credit card phone calls, and in voice-mail systems. Speech analysis has produced devices that enable handicapped people to operate computers with spoken instructions rather than by hand, although the process is still too cumbersome and expensive for routine common use. But the availability of voice-actuated and voice-responding tools in the workplace holds out the opportunity or the threat—depending on the beholder—of spoken "literacy" reclaiming not the exclusive hold it had before the upstarts writing and print came along, but at least some greater share than it holds now of the workaday human communications load. Whatever their intentions, advocates of universal literacy like Barbara Bush and Hillary Rodham Clinton seem unaware that they are helping the continuing enshrining of the 19th century in schooling investments without a forward glance to what the 21st might want.[8] The access to contemporary technology envisaged by proponents of a "national information infrastructure," "information superhighway," "infobahn" or the like is a beginning, but only a beginning, for reasons that I develop further ahead.

The invention of writing brought us *practical* durability throughout an age reckoned in mere thousands of years. But writing also diminished interactivity, relative to the innate interactivity of speech, since handwriting formats in the West were initially manipulated only by the servants of the elites. Only later did writing become a job-related necessity for the elites themselves and for the masses when the so-called Industrial Revolution sparked a need for clerical skills that outran the world's supply of noble second sons and favored serfs, formerly the menial custodians of a menial skill. As writing gained in dominance, we conveniently forgot the upstart character of writing that had one of Plato's protagonists look down his nose at it, just the way the literary snobs of the late 20th century look down their noses at speech, video games, and PCs:

Socrates But there remains the question of propriety and impropriety in writing, that is to say the conditions which make it proper or improper. Isn't that so?

Phaedrus Yes.

. . . .

Socrates ... when it came to writing Theuth said "Here, O king, is a branch of learning that will make the people of Egypt wiser and improve their memories: my discovery provides a recipe for memory and wisdom." But the king answered and said "O man full of arts, to one is it given to create the things of art, and to another to judge what measure of harm and of profit they have for those that shall employ them. And so it is that you, by reason of your tender regard for the writing that is your offspring, have declared the very opposite of its true effect. If men learn this, it will implant forgetfulness in their souls: they will cease to exercise memory because they rely on that which is written, calling things to remembrance no longer from within themselves, but by means of external marks; what you have discovered is a recipe not for memory, but for reminder. And it is no true wisdom that you offer your disciples, but only its semblance; for by telling them of many things without teaching them you will make them seem to know much, while for the most part they know nothing; and as men filled, not with wisdom, but with the conceit of wisdom, they will be a burden to their fellows."[9]

As the king points out, writing is not an interactive format, but essentially a static format, what we would call a ROM (read-only memory) in the early 1990s, though obviously not a CD-ROM. Once committed to paper, writing stays put ever after, namely, until the paper disintegrates. Anyone who remembers using an eraser, even on pencil marks, knows how poorly reusable paper is, or even a slate or a blackboard. Of great merit for books of accounts and for archives, this property of the paper format precluded our using it to create open-ended structures as you go along and interacting with and controlling information except by a laborious process of manual drafting and redrafting which was convenient relative to working in stone but which, by the early 1990s, had been almost totally displaced among the upscale younger generation by the PC or laptop word-processing software. Still, with the advent of the universal prepaid post, the writing format, as letters, became a major mode of delayed-interactive (in contrast to instantaneous-interactive) communication for the world's people until supplanted in the industrialized nations by the telephone within the last decade or two. Whether the massive investment nations make in teaching handwriting in the schools remains a sensible one is an urgent question for the mid 1990s. The zenith of handwriting lives on in the novels of Charles Dickens, but its sun may be setting in the real industrialized world of keyboards, mice, and rudimentary speech recognition.[10] On the other hand, the continuing popularity of greeting cards and the birth of email and voice mail suggest that people often prefer delayed-interactive communication over instantaneous-interactive communication.

Print, like writing, is essentially a noninteractive, static format of good durability which brought pre-electro-optical but digital formats and processes into ascendancy in all industrialized nations. The analog formats of speech, music and pictures became the province of the fine arts, while literature and business built on the digital formats. In any case, the print formats, like writing before and concurrently, were static ROMs unsuited for creating open-ended structures as you go along and interacting with and controlling information, except to a limited extent by elites called authors tied in to businesses called publishers. The era in the West that followed immediately after Gutenberg's development of the movable type press did not differ all that markedly from the preceding manuscript-copying era: reading remained an elite skill. Only in the mid-19th century when the steam era and the resulting migrations from the countryside to the "dark satanic mills" created a need for widespread "readin', writin' and 'rithmetic" skills in the new industrial work force did print become democratized and today's conventional literacy enshrined as a state-sanctioned and state-financed bundle of skills. Since the economic and political conditions that brought forth conventional literacy, numeracy and artistic sensibility have long since been overtaken by new realities, it seems timely to reconsider the merits of the conventions rather than merely attempt to recast them into the mold of new technologies.

As digital print was reaching its zenith in the West, analog pictures came on the scene first as movies and later as TV. Although a mode of personal expression for their producers, until the 1980s the high price of production technology for movies and TV meant that most watching was bound to be as passive as the term "couch potato" evokes. The summit of ecstasy in classical movie/video marketing at the turn of the 1990s was the prospect of choosing which from among 500 or more movies to watch. But movies mark the birth of dynamic virtuality. Traditional paintings and sculptures epitomize static virtuality. They are virtually real, they represent reality, in a way that words are not and do not, even though words strung together do denote reality.[11] But paintings and sculptures stand still, while reality moves.

Movies captured moving reality for the first time in history, hence dynamic virtuality. But a traditional movie, bound up on its film or its analog videotape, is not easily malleable in the way that computers have already accustomed us to smithing words and numbers with great ease and great speed and low cost. However, faster, smaller, cheaper electro-optical digital technologies are enabling computers to give pictures and music the same malleability, the same simultaneous interactivity as words; and those faster, smaller, cheaper electro-optical digital technologies are putting that power within reach of not only the Steven Spielbergs, the Walt Disneys, the research hospitals, and the militaries of the world but, increasingly, within reach of the small business and, eventually, of the individual.

This possibility is entirely unprecedented; even the video arcade fan of the early 1990s does not yet personally control the palette, so to speak, that the Spielbergs and so on have at their disposal today. And what would he or she do with it? While Henry David Thoreau ultimately proved to be wrong in his sarcastic assessment of the value of Maine linking up telegraphically with Texas ("What does Maine have to say to Texas?"), it did take a while to get there. Hence while ecstasy over the possibilities runs highest in this realm of image multimedia, so does the agony over the barriers on the way to realizing dreams.[12] The agony is not entirely technological and commercial. The cultures of words, pictures and music have evolved in large measure apart from one another, so it is unlikely that shaking them all up with a computer will produce instant nirvana except among some of the avant-garde.

But seedlings of the interactive multimedia future abound in the outposts of the computer mainframe world, even as that world transforms itself into a world of parallelism and other approaches to supercomputing. For instance, they are visible—or at least easily visualizable—from the areas where pictorial experimentation is rife, sometimes in TV advertising and in other forms of noninteractive advertising, but especially with supercomputer and interactive high-resolution pictorial facilities as, for example, in medical imaging systems —such as ultrasound, magnetic resonance imaging (MRI), computerized axial tomography scanning (CAT scans), and X-rays—sometimes coupled with telecommunications as in teleradiology and telepathology, which involve the transmission of radiological images and pathology slides, respectively, to remote sites, and in military applications such as aerial reconnaissance, defense map displays, cockpit displays, simulators, and large-screen displays for command centers.[13]

In the mid-1990s, the seedlings of the interactive multimedia future also grew increasingly visible not only in video arcades but on home game-playing devices and PCs. Professional industrial design, Hollywood blockbuster movie animation, and musical synthesizer instruments appear to be in transition from upscale institutional buyers to upscale personal buyers.

Both the firm rooting of interactive multimedia in the past and the potential for growth into the future are evident in the following scenario taken from a study of the High-Definition-Television (HDTV) fever of the turn of the 1990s by my associate Robert Tirman:

Scenario events

On Monday morning, Jane Smith rises and prepares for her work day. While she and her eighteen-year-old daughter, Jackie, eat their wheat toast and oat bran cereal with strawberries, they watch the "Today Show" coverage of the latest pictures of Neptune sent to Earth from the *Voyager* spacecraft. After they part at the door of their town house, Jackie walks down the street and takes the number 3 bus to her high school, noticing the advertisement on the side of the bus for the latest style of "Guess" jeans. Jane stops at a newsstand to pick up the copy of *Time Magazine* celebrating the 200th Anniversary of the French Revolution before taking a taxi to the airport to meet an out-of-town client. At the airport, Jane scans the large-screen display for the latest flight information on her client's arrival and pauses to watch the commercial for the new Lancia Dedra before heading to Gate 12.

My interpretation of portentous events

watching synthetic "real reality" is opening up into watching real "synthesized reality"

Back at her office, while her client meets the rest of her staff, Jane sits at her computer workstation putting the finishing touches on the multimedia presentation she has prepared. In addition to the overview of her company with the usual graphs and financial data, Jane adds a video "walk-through" of one of the buildings she has just designed and decorated and goes off to make the presentation. At Millard Fillmore High School, Jackie is researching the life and works of Monet from the video encyclopedia on the personal computer in the school library in preparation for the class trip to the Fine Arts Museum that afternoon. She then attends her lunchtime meeting of the Young Physicians' Club where she, and 30 other pre-med hopefuls with strong stomachs, view a videotape of a heart bypass procedure while munching their sandwiches.

"working within structures" is opening up into "creating open-ended structures as you go along"

"receiving information" is opening up into "interacting with and controlling information"

After her presentation and a quick lunch at the hot dog stand on the corner, Jane takes the subway across town to meet with one of her fabric suppliers. Hurrying from the subway entrance, she ruefully eyes the Pepto-Bismol advertisement on the billboard across the street. Inside the conference room of her supplier, Jane previews the color and weave of some new fabrics—by videoconference—with the supplier's manufacturer in Singapore. After placing an order in anticipation of concluding a deal with today's client, Jane stops at the clinic to get the results of the blood test she had taken

"exchanging information" is opening up into "taking informed action"

yesterday. The receptionist tells her that her doctor finished reviewing the blood sample with the pathologist each in their respective offices that morning and the results were negative. With that good news, Jane returns to her office to finish her afternoon's work.

Meanwhile, Jackie and her classmates are comparing the live exhibit of Monet's works at the Fine Arts Museum with a televised exhibit of Renoir's paintings currently on display in another city. The director of the museum points out the minute differences in the brush strokes and the subtle color values of the respective Impressionist painters. On its way out of the museum, the class stops to watch a computer artist create a full-motion 3-D rendering of a futuristic automobile for the museum's coming exhibit on commercial art.

Flushed with the excitement and success of their day, Jackie and Jane decide to treat themselves to dinner and a movie that evening. They make reservations at the new Video Theater, where they enjoy a meal while watching *Indiana Jones and the Last Crusade* on the 23-foot screen. On their way out, Jane makes reservations for the following Saturday to see the Rolling Stones concert to be broadcast live to the theater. Mother and daughter then return home, turn on the TV, yawn, and promptly fall asleep on the couch. Another typical Monday comes to an end.

"time proportional to distance" is opening up into "time independent of distance"

What the portentous events in the scenario have in common, of course, is a newly felt influence of maturing faster, smaller, cheaper electro-optical digital technologies: *the capacity for individuals to interact instantaneously and at their own volition either with themselves or with other individuals by transparent means, namely, means that do not significantly interfere with the desired functions of the interactions.*

The independence of time from distance has, of course, been experienced by people of all ages and in all ages but to significantly lesser degrees than today and tomorrow. Every child is conscious of his or her ability to shout to someone out there to go after a ball about to get lost down the hill and therefore to get the ball retrieved a lot faster, if at all, than by running after it themselves. We've had that capacity as long as there have been people. The telegraph in the middle of the last century gave global reach, but without instantaneity (although the speed-up was near-miraculous by the perceptions of those times) and with considerable interposition by intermediaries who could both snoop on and garble the messages. And message transfer was about as far as capabilities went.

By the yardstick of the telegraph, the telephone was a miracle of instantaneity (at least once you got connected) and of directness and privacy of communication, at least once you could be sure you were connected without the operator or the secret police listening in. But you were limited to what you could *say* or *sing*, with no chance to draw, except in the dreams of Caselli and the nightmares of the postmaster general. In the mid 1990s, as far as the electro-optical digital science and the electro-optical digital technology of it are concerned and except for touching and feeling, everything you can do by way of communicating with people in a room with you can do as instantaneously and, in principle, as privately with people anywhere on earth or in modest orbits around it.[14]

Of course not all the capabilities are ripe today! Sorting what you think is ripe from the hype even in the limited domain of telecommunications needs doing along *all* the following dimensions that sellers see: scientific, technological, economic, political, legal and marketplaces (customers). And then there are the dimensions the buyers see: price and effectiveness. What we do at the Harvard Program on Information Resources Policy is, indeed, to look at all these dimensions. But there's no time here to say more than "ripeness is very different along all these dimensions for different products and services."

Taking informed action instead of merely exchanging information with the aid of tools built from new-fangled electro-optical digital technologies by now has a long history as histories go in this young realm, reaching back all the way to the use of radar in World War II. The steady ripening among early institutional adopters is evident in many realms, as for example in currency trading and other high-value, high-volume financial transactions and military intelligence, command and control. Even here, however, the ripening is uneven and often not very far advanced; some of the failures mixed in with the successes of the U.S. military in the 1991 Persian Gulf War attest to that, often in areas where the interface of electro-optical media deviated from the customary print-on-paper look and feel to take advantage of new capabilities.[15] There's a price to pay for eliminating the buggy-whip holder and the running board too soon. But the scenario illustrates hopes for diffusing the capacity to take informed actions into much broader markets, like purchasing agents—not even speaking, yet, of the general public.

Watching real "synthesized reality" begins to take advantage of the results of the wholly unprecedented processing capabilities of electro-optical digital technologies. But those results are mostly presented in a familiar format. A picture of Neptune synthesized by computer from signals sent to Earth by the onboard sensors of the *Voyager* spacecraft is tolerated even with its synthetic colors. Who on Earth, after all, has seen Neptune with their own eyeballs? However, accepting synthetic pictures of Earth itself in synthetic colors is something still done mostly by professionals like astronomers, weather forecasters, and pilots. The general public sees the skies as blue, has seen them that way on the occasional TV shots beamed down from Earth orbits, and gets them that way in all the synthesized products exhibited on the nightly TV weather forecast and even in the Hollywood adventure, cartoon and horror productions created on mainframes. Even those high points of current more widespread synthesized realities, the icons and cellular L-shapes used in PC menus and in spreadsheets, stick very closely to the familiar born of the older information technologies.

It is the acts of creating open-ended structures as you go along and interacting with and controlling information that lie at today's frontiers with only the half-forgotten lessons of spoken interactivity to guide us in the exploitation of entirely novel capabilities. "Interactivity" is the mostly unprecedented capability that contemporary faster, smaller, cheaper, electro-optical digital technologies are, for the first time in human history, moving from the rarefied reaches of the institutional early adopters to the earthy and wide-open spaces of the (hopefully) mass markets of individual purchasers. What ecstasy!

But where interactivity is concerned, ripeness is in question in all dimensions but the scientific. The technological, economic, political, legal, marketplaces and customers dimensions are all still problematical. What agony! The moves in the advanced industrialized nations exemplified in the United States by Vice President Gore's long-time advocacy for getting the electronic superhighways of the future from pipe dreams to paid-for glass pipes exemplify one dimension of the ecstatic hopes and the agonizing frustrations in the early 1990s. The electronic highways in place are practically global for speech and for writing. They are as yet but cowpaths for interactive digital pictures, so the question is, who will pay how fast for the field of dreams?

Indeed, the symptoms of ecstasy and agony, exhibited only privately among friends in the early days of the cresting interactive multimedia wave of the early 1990s, had gone shamelessly public by the mid 1990s. "MEDIA MANIA," headlined *Business Week* on July 12, 1993. *Digital. Interactive. Multimedia. The rush is on. Warning: not everyone will win*, the subhead specified. On July 14, 1993, the *Wall Street Journal* brought interactive multimedia out of the closet in its lead article under the headline *Vague New World* with subheads *Digital Media Business Takes Form as a Battle of Complex Alliances* and *Partnerships Across Industries Coalesce in Chaotic Race to Establish a Market* and with the following headline-supporting quotes from industry leaders:

"People know what the skeleton looks like, but they don't know what the muscles look like," says Frank Biondi, chief executive of cable operator Viacom Inc. Intel Corp. Chief Executive Andrew Grove says that when speculating about what will be a hit, "I don't know what the hell I'm talking about, really. . . . We'll know the truth when we get there."

Judging ripeness is indeed no easy task. In what remains, I offer some fundamentals for use in judging ripeness in the hope of leaving you with a considerably sharper image than when you came in, as well as with tools for better understanding of the present and for at least improving our odds as we forge ahead in our own enterprises, commercial, political, or scholarly.

Where there is interactivity, ripeness is a moving target. Why is ripeness a moving target? Because, except for the heroes among us, we buyers only rarely perceive effectiveness (an essential aspect of ripeness along with price) absent transparency: It's too much trouble to use a tool if that tool is not transparent but instead interferes with performing the desired functions. And transparency requires familiarity, which comes from stability—or at least the stability of enough familiar elements perceptible to the user. To the extent that it makes unfamiliar processes perceptible to us, gives us control over them, and leads us to the unexpected—which, after all, is the point of interactivity—interactivity breeds unfamiliarity. Facing the unfamiliar or unexpected, we are forced to keep learning continually, and that can be a source of discomfort for most of us in most workaday situations, even though it is pleasurable in games. This is why mere access to technology is only a beginning.

In his paper *Computers and Literacy: Redefining Each Other*,[16] my associate Martin Ernst sketches the basis for that observation as follows:

The computer industry, tumultuous even in its calmest times, showed signs in the early 1990s of being at an evolutionary watershed. The symptoms of structural death and structural birth seemed to be swirling in a melée of stark contrasts. . . .

. . . The primary source of the turmoil has been a major transition that only recently got underway and is moving us in new directions for the sources of future growth and toward new paradigms for the future roles of PCs. In the process, the transition will redefine not just computing but also the nature of future literacy—and what it will mean to be, and take to become, literate in a meaningful way.

Computers have already redefined themselves many times, and, as they did, they redefined many of the ways people work with information and even work in general. . . .

Except for a handful of pioneers, the general public has stayed in the buggy-whip-holder-and-running-board era of computer applications. In the early 1990s, even the tools to help collective work, and the means to find and use information more effectively, as by means of programs that can help search for, filter, prioritize, and link materials, and the means for integrating multiple types of media in a single computer product for work, education, or pleasure remain traditionalist, with icons, screen buttons, whizzing spacecraft and projectiles, stylized heroes and villains and the like at the outer limits. So far, in brief, the ways people work with information and even work in general have, throughout the turmoil and at considerable collective effort and cost in training and retraining, remained the "readin', writin' and 'rithmetic" of the 19th century, with a bit of doodling and pointing thrown in but with the basic investment in schooling intact. That already keeps taking considerable learning, almost like learning a new language a month. The learning entailed in traveling into the altogether uncharted territory of simultaneous interactivity with moving visual material still lies ahead.

The potential widespread availability of faster, smaller, cheaper means for creating open-ended structures as you go along and interacting with and controlling information puts in question all prior investment in literacy, numeracy, and artistic sensibility. If the investment stays as it is, the buggy-whip holders and running boards will be with us as long as it takes for the postmaster general's fax nightmare to come to pass—which could be a long time, given that the post offices of the world are still alive and mostly well, thank you. If the investment is shifted too soon, we may be lost in limbo. If the investment is shifted too late, those who happen to find themselves first and faster than you can say "Xerox" in an information world better than the one we're accustomed to will have an advantage.

What is it that's so all-fired fundamental about faster, smaller, cheaper means for

- creating open-ended structures as you go along; and
- interacting with and controlling information?

In old-fashioned terms, creating open-ended structures as you go along means nothing less ambitious than making up your own languages as you go along or, as we go along, making up even more general means of expression than languages as we now pretend to use them.[17] The already evident explosion of PC applications programs is ample testimony to the enormous potential this unleashes for both convenience and confusion, power, and impotence, ecstasy and agony.

The last time a similar opportunity is said to have occurred, it is said to have had the following consequences, probably because someone aspired to have their operating system become the world's standard:

Now the whole world had one language and a common speech. [2]As men moved eastward, they found a plain in Shinar and settled there.

[3]They said to each other, "Come, let's make bricks and bake them thoroughly." They used brick instead of stone, and tar for mortar. [4]Then they said, "Come, let us build ourselves a city, with a tower that reaches to the heavens, so that we may make a name for ourselves and not be scattered over the face of the whole earth."

[5]But the Lord came down to see the city and the tower that the men were building. [6]The Lord said, "If as one people speaking the same language they have begun to do this, then nothing they plan to do will be impossible for them. [7]Come, let us go down and confuse their language so they will not understand each other."

[8]So the Lord scattered them from there over all the earth, and they stopped building the city. [9]That is why it was called Babel—because there the Lord confused the language of the whole world. From there the Lord scattered them over the face of the whole earth. [18]

A more contemporary and thoroughly practical assessment is Mitchell Kapor's observation that "there are only two problems with computers: they're impossible to program and impossible to use." More ecstasy and more agony.

In old-fashioned terms, interacting with and controlling information means mostly nothing outside the realm of speech: mostly our past is that of passive couch potatoes, taking it all in from the outside—or at least reading and watching only what we want to hear—but with little going back out, at least in writing or in pictures. About the only agents we could interact with and control were our own minds and maybe those of a relative or a friend or two. Now, even in print—but dynamic interactive print—we communicate with people and with computers around the world with new means like electronic bulletin boards and with new usage patterns, as with email in the mushrooming electro-optical digital networks (like the Internet) for which there are no evident precedents and to which aficionados refer as cyberspace. The earlier advent of other "retail" information technologies (like VCRs) has already vastly changed the reach of individuals, with truly global political as well as economic consequences already evident. [19]

More important, perhaps, but far less widely understood, let alone appreciated, is the fact that when we use computers we still communicate mostly with ourselves, but in ways that we can tailor at will to our own predilections. The tensions between efficiency and effectiveness for such solitary purposes, which point toward idiosyncratic choices of linguistic and other expressive information conventions and efficiency and effectiveness for collective purposes, which point toward universal compatibility if not standardization, set up a dynamic that infuses intense contemporary relevance into the ancient story of the Tower of Babel.

What it all boils down to is that faster, smaller, cheaper electro-optical digital technologies have put in our hands enormously powerful and varied yet increasingly practical and economical means for information processing, means that stimulate us to reexamine everything we do to information and with information and then choose to do nothing, to reinforce the old ways, to modify them, or to abandon them altogether in favor of altogether new ways. Enthusiasm for corporate reengineering is one early '90s reaction to this stimulus in one particular realm with a long history of earlier buggy-whip-holder-and-running-board imitations But fundamentally, throughout the realm of information itself, the stimulus is for reexamining what we mean by literacy, numeracy, and artistic sensibility.

To reexamine effectively, we need concepts expressive enough to say what we want to say without being tied to the past and without mortgaging our ideas to futures that may not materialize. Substance, format, and process are the immutable conceptual pillars of information products and services. Substance is the subject matter, the stuff of interest to the ultimate user. Format is the embodiment of the substance, as in voice in the air, ink on paper, pixels on a screen, bits and bytes traveling on a glass fiber or stored in a computer's memory. Process is what happens to substance-embodied-in-format as it wends its way from producer to consumer. While substance, format, and process are distinct concepts, they are intimately linked in practice in the specification of information products and services as bundles of substance, process, and format.[20]

To illustrate the significance of the linkages, the introduction of printing made it possible to produce books with consistent pagination; before then, the substance (or contents) of individual pages (for the same total document substance) differed from one scribe or copy to another, making pagination relatively futile. With effective pagination, tables of contents, indices, references, cross references, and other positional information could be used, changing the nature of legal practice as well as of scholarship and aiding books in the competition with scroll formats. All that is relatively easy to see with hindsight.[21]

With mere foresight at their disposal and no omniscience, Messrs. Biondi and Grove are realistically vague. Whatever the degree of their control over the dimensions of ripeness that sellers see, their degree of control (or anyone's) over the dimensions of ripeness near and dear to buyers is far less because buyers are engaged in the intensive and recurrent bouts of learning I described above. Hence the realistic tone of their blank predictions of the future marketplace. Very few as yet know much about the dynamics set in motion by the new possibilities for creating, outside of speech, open-ended structures as you go along and for interacting with and controlling information.

There's ecstasy in contemplating the many attractive new and open roads ahead. There's agony in choosing among them. In organizations accustomed to planning with a high probability of being on mark in not-so-long-ago stable and controllable environments, the notion of gambling on the future takes getting used to for managements, boards, legislatures, financiers, and referees alike. Deep pockets are an asset only if they aren't mortgaged to the past. It's often their big anchors to the past that allow big enterprises to be overtaken by upstarts. But placing bets is the best we can do. I believe, however, that it helps to be smart; and I believe that knowing a little bit more is better, on the average, than knowing a little bit less, because it can help you to improve the odds in your favor. You also need to be lucky.

Notes

1. My associate Martin Ernst has identified the information activities most profoundly affected to date as: correct-integrate, link-find, examine, analyze, interpret, sense. Ernst, Martin L. *Computers and Literacy: Redefining Each Other.* Research Report, P-94-5, Cambridge, Mass.: Harvard University, Program on Information Resources Policy, 1994. Table 4-3 "Computer-Aided Capabilities to Support Improved Use of Information."

2. Classical telecommunications voice transmission products and services have been fragmented on economic and political grounds through elaborate systems of differential costing and pricing, as detailed in Weinhaus, Carol L., and Anthony G. Oettinger. *Behind the Telephone Debates.* Norwood, N.J. Ablex, 1988. From the standpoint of customers, as from a scientific or technological standpoint, telephony took sound from mouths and conveyed it to distant ears. These functional traits of the service made it as stable and as homogeneous a commodity as they come, given that the statistical distribution of mouth and ear characteristics is genetically determined, hence very stable (and, after a century of study, extremely well understood, at least for transmission purposes); and that the evolution of the arbitrary conventions of human vernaculars is slowed by the very fact that languages must have

some stability to remain effective as tools of communication. By contrast, end-user data applications are highly idiosyncratic, inherently fragmented by occupations, therefore presenting niche markets with clear commonalities only at very high levels of abstraction corresponding at the highest levels to commodities such as transport of uninterpreted bits. Even the statistical characteristics of bit streams are unstable and not well known at the turn of the 1990s. Unity or fragmentation of markets, however, is not causally linked to unified or fragmented industry structure, as Derrick Huang shows in his March 1994 computer science doctoral thesis at Harvard University, "A Bang or a Whimper: Key Issues and Implications of Alternative Telecommunications"; in his *Up in the Air: New Wireless Communications.* Cambridge, Mass. Harvard University, Program on Information Resources Policy, 1992; and in his *Managing the Spectrum: Win, Lose, or Share.* Cambridge, Mass.: Harvard University, Program on Information Resources Policy, 1993.

3. How the bundles were tied in the first place is detailed for England by Clanchy, Michael T. *From Memory to Written Record, England 1066–1307*, 2nd ed. Oxford, U.K.; Cambridge, Mass.: Blackwell, 1993; and by Altick, Richard D. *The English Common Reader: A Social History of the Mass Reading Public 1800–1900.* Chicago: Univ. of Chicago Press, 1957; and for the United States by Boorstin, Daniel J. *The Americans.* Vol. 3, *The Democratic Experience.* New York: Random House, 1973.

4. The only clear-cut convergence is the convergence of the science and the technology of all information devices and systems into the science and the technology of electro-optical digital devices and systems, as I've noted in Oettinger, Anthony G., "Compunications in the National Decision-Making Process." In *Computers, Communications and the Public Interest*, edited by M. Greenberger, Baltimore: Johns Hopkins University Press, 1971 (with discussion by Ithiel Pool, Alain Enthoven, David Packard). This has no *necessary* consequences for industry structure, politics, markets or any other dimension of the evolution of information products or services.

5. These processes are exemplified both in the design of any one spreadsheet system and by the evolution of spreadsheets since the original Visicalc; they are detailed in Ernst op.cit. Note 1, and in the following earlier publications: Ernst, Martin. *Users and Personal Computers: Languages and Literacy, Costs and Benefits.* Cambridge, Mass.: Harvard University, Program on Information Resources Policy, 1993; Ernst, Martin L. *The Personal Computer: Growth Patterns, Limits, and New Frontiers.* Cambridge, Mass.: Harvard University, Program on Information Resources Policy, 1991; Ernst, Martin L. *Electronic–Print Competition: Determinants of the Potential for Major Change.* Cambridge, Mass.: Harvard University, Program on Information Resources Policy, 1989.

6. Various facets of the diffusion of new technologies are described by Cowan, Ruth Schwartz. *More Work for Mother: The Ironies of Household Technology from the Open Hearth to the Microwave.* New York: Basic Books, 1983; Basalla, George. *The Evolution of Technology.* New York: Cambridge University Press, 1989; Petroski,

Henry. *The Pencil: A History of Design and Circumstances.* New York: Knopf, 1990, and *The Evolution of Useful Things.* New York: Knopf, 1992.

7. *Annual Report of the Postmaster-General of the United States* for 1982. The Fiscal Year Ended June 30, 1872. Washington, D.C.: Government Printing Office, 1872. The historian Jonathan Coopersmith gives a more thorough account of facsimile's tortuous road to universality in his "Facsimile's False Starts." *IEEE Spectrum,* February 1993, 46–49.

8. The question of ripeness needs asking repeatedly, to reduce the odds of going unawares from the premature scare of the postmaster general to the belated recognition of the value of dry electrostatic copying. In following the question in this realm over several decades, I've found negative answers until now, but the tools are getting better! My prior assessments are in Oettinger, Anthony G. *Proceedings of a Symposium on Digital Computers and Their Applications.* Annals of the Computation Laboratory of Harvard University, vol. 31, Cambridge, Mass.: Harvard University Press, 1962 (general editor, and contributor of the "The Geometry of Symbols"); "The Uses of Computers in Science." *Scientific American* 215, no. 3, September 1966, 160–172; in *Run, Computer, Run: The Mythology of Educational Innovation.* Cambridge, Mass.: Harvard University Press, 1969; and in "The Semantic Wall," in *Human Communication: A Unified View,* edited by E. E. David, Jr., and Peter B. Denes. New York: McGraw Hill, 1972.

9. Hackforth, Richard, trans. *Plato's Phaedrus.* Cambridge: Cambridge University Press, 1952, 156.

10. A presentation I made in this vein on July 18, 1981, to a meeting of the Business– Higher Education Forum at the Harvard Faculty Club in Cambridge, Mass., met with total disbelief on the part of the assembled industrialists and academics. Judging contemporary ripeness is left to the reader. The history of prior transitions is recounted in Altick, in Boorstin, and in Clanchy, Note 10. That ripeness of this idea *may* have increased is evidenced by the publication in 1993 of Aufderheide, Patricia (rapporteur). *Media Literacy: A Report of the National Leadership Conference on Media Literacy.* Washington, D.C.: The Aspen Institute, 1993; but—alas—the media-literacy movement seems to take current television as its main image of "media" and interprets literacy as the ability to tell TV lies and propaganda from truth, a stance useful perhaps if not mere political smoke, but limited in its scope in any case.

11. Much of this is still difficult to express, even for professional art historians and philosophers of art. The gaps in our understanding of the fundamentals of non-alphabetic representations may be discerned from such philosophical works as Putnam, Hilary. *Representation and Reality.* Cambridge, Mass.: MIT Press, 1988; Gombrich, E. H. *Art and Illusion: A Study in the Psychology of Pictorial Representation.* First Princeton/Bollingen paperback edition, Princeton, N.J.: Princeton University Press, 1969; and Goodman, Nelson. *Languages of Art: An Approach to a Theory of Symbols.* Indianapolis: Hackett Publishing Company, 1976.

12. Examples of trial and error by creators in this realm are in the July 1993 issue of the professional journal *Communications of the ACM* under the headline "Computer Augmented Environments: Back to the Real World"; and in Gelernter, David Hillel. *Mirror Worlds, or The Day Software Puts the Universe in a Shoebox: How It Will Happen and What It Will Mean.* New York: Oxford University Press, 1991. *Scientific American* carried my earlier version of such dreams nearly three decades ago (Note 8); much of the latter has since been realized.

13. The examples and the scenario that follows are drawn from Appendix H of Tirman, W. Robert. *The Elephant and the Blind Men: The Phenomenon of HDTV and Its Would-Be Stakeholders* P-91-3, Cambridge, Mass.: Harvard Program on Information Resources Policy, 1991.

14. The technologies to guarantee communications privacy through cryptography and other precautions exist. In most countries, however, what is to be kept private from the government (and also within the government) is the subject of continuing controversies. Some of the issues are outlined in Knauf, Daniel J. *The Family Jewels: Corporate Policy on the Protection of Information Resources.* Cambridge, Mass.: Harvard University, Program on Information Resources Policy, 1991.

15. Additional details are given in Coakley, Thomas P. *Command and Control for War and Peace.* Washington D.C.: National Defense Univ. Press/Superintendent of Documents, U. S. Government Printing Office, 1992; and in *Seminar on Intelligence, Command, and Control: Guest Presentations.* Nine volumes from Spring 1980 through Spring 1991 [the seminar was not held during 1983]. Cambridge, Mass.: Harvard University, Program on Information Resources Policy. By 1994 a vast and still-growing literature had become available detailing the events of the 1991 war in the Persian Gulf, often tagged as the first "information war."

16. Op. cit. Note 1.

17. We pay lip service to "correct" grammar, diction and spelling, but all of us have our little pet words at home and collectively do pretty well at inventing local and professional jargons, slang raps, acronyms and so on. Only the French formalize their hypocrisy with the insistence of the Académie Française on keeping the language "pure." Evolution and cross-fertilization, not fossilization, are the observed conditions of all living languages. Not even de Gaulle could stop "franglais" from its incursions into French, though he tried, even as the Balladur government kept on trying, in 1994, to pass laws prohibiting the use of English at scientific meetings in France. The late Léon Dostert, who was Eisenhower's interpreter in World War II, told me the following story of a meeting between Eisenhower and de Gaulle, who pretended not to understand English and refused to speak it on political grounds. When de Gaulle requested permission to use his Free French troops instead of Americans in operations in Eastern France, Eisenhower turned to Dostert and said: "Tell the son of a bitch he can't do it." Dostert turned to de Gaulle and rendered this in polite and unemphatic language, whereupon de Gaulle retorted to Dostert: "Monsieur, vous adoucissez!" (Sir, you are softening it!)

18. Genesis 11:1–9.

19. Examples are treated extensively in the following: Ganley, Gladys D. Unglued Empire: The Soviet Experience with Communications Technologies. Norwood, N.J. Ablex, 1996. Ganley, Gladys D. *The Exploding Political Power of Personal Media.* Norwood, N.J. Ablex 1992. Ganley, Oswald H., and Gladys D. Ganley. *To Inform or To Control? The New Communications Networks.* 2nd ed. Norwood, N.J. Ablex 1989. Ganley, Gladys D., and Oswald H. Ganley. *Global Political Fallout: The VCR's First Decade.* Norwood, N.J. Ablex, 1987.

20. Details on these concepts and their practical applications are given in McLaughlin, John F., with Anne Louise Antonoff. *Mapping the Information Business.* Cambridge, Mass.: Harvard University, Program on Information Resources Policy, 1986 and in this volume, Chapter 7 ("The Information Evolution: Building Blocks and Bursting Bundles") and Chapter 8 ("Publishing as a Creature of Technology").

21. Adapted from Ernst, Martin. *Computers and Literacy: Redefining Each Other.* Op. cit. Note 1.

2 Will Computer Communication End Geography?

Vincent Mosco

Many people have said that developments in transportation and especially in communications have led to the decline of geography as a factor in industry and government. This study examines what is known about this development and what differences it makes. Specifically, how have organizations made use of smaller, faster, cheaper, and better computer and communications products and services to eliminate or, at least, reduce the constraints of space and time on their activities?

The study concludes that, much as with transportation, as computer communication approaches ubiquity, it increasingly diminishes the influence of physical geography and expands the choices available to decisionmakers. Nevertheless, rather than just attenuate geography, computer communication transforms it by creating new and expanded spatial terrains on which organizations can operate.

Computer communication appears to be following the pattern historians document for the process of electrification. Electricity began as a spectacle featured in every "Great White Way" that lit the night in cities across America. As with most technologies, its unique value as spectacle gave way to routine when the real process of electrifying society took place, as electricity powered enormous gains in productivity, transformed social relations, and widened choice everywhere. All this occurred even as electricity literally and figuratively vanished into the woodwork.

Taking up the lessons electrification offers for the contemporary spectacle of the Information Superhighway, this chapter concludes by examining the factors likely to grow in importance as computer communication shifts from spectacle to become a very powerful resident in today's woodwork.

Transportation Shrinks the Map

A large body of research documents the impact of technological change in transportation on the speed of travel. For most of human history, transportation was slow and inefficient and the cost of attenuating geography prohibitively high. By the end of the eighteenth century, with the exception of a few stagecoaches and ships, vehicles could not move faster than a person could walk.[1] Until the turn of the nineteenth century, the means of travel differed little from what prevailed in biblical times: "shanks mare and draft animals on land, oar and sail on water."[2]

As Pool has documented, this meant little significant change in the geography of cities, as the city, dependent on pedestrian traffic, grew from a radius of four miles to the eight-mile radius of the horse-using city but little further.[3] Geographers have described the changes brought about by technological innovation over the last two centuries (see figure 2.1). The nineteenth century saw the application of steam power as a means of propulsion and the use of iron and steel for ocean-going vessels, trains, and track. The twentieth century introduced the gasoline-powered internal combustion engine, which made truck and automobile travel widely available. Large, ocean-going "superfreighters," containerization, and commercial jet aircraft reduced travel times further (see figure 2.2).[4]

In their attempt to comprehend the significance of transportation-based changes, Malone and Rockart (1991) identify three orders of effects. The first order substitutes new technologies for old, when people ride steam trains and later cars, rather than horses and horse-drawn carriages. Improvements in technology lead to the emergence of a second-order effect, that is, people travel more, whether to work every day, to visit distant friends, or to attend business meetings. Finally, a third-order effect is marked by the rise of new transportation-intensive social patterns, which include principally suburbanization; shopping malls; and, more recently, the global, "edge," or "100–mile" city.[5]

The rate of change in what geographers refer to as *time-space convergence* is worth reflection.[6] For example, assuming a foot speed of three miles per hour, until the sixteenth century the effective distance between Portland, Maine, and San Diego, California, was two years. Horseback reduced this distance to eight months by the seventeenth century. By the mid-nineteenth century, the stagecoach and wagon halved that distance to four months; and, by the turn of the next century, trains made the trip in four days. By 1950, air travel reduced that

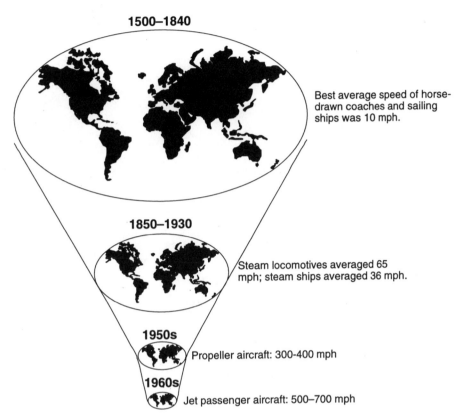

1500–1840

Best average speed of horse-drawn coaches and sailing ships was 10 mph.

1850–1930

Steam locomotives averaged 65 mph; steam ships averaged 36 mph.

1950s

Propeller aircraft: 300-400 mph

1960s

Jet passenger aircraft: 500–700 mph

Figure 2.1   The shrinking world: The impact of transportation technology on effective distance. From Vincent Mosco, *Will Computer Communication End Geography?* (Cambridge, Mass.: Program on Information Resources Policy; P-95-4, 1995; p. 3 figure 1. Originally: "Global Shrinkage," from Peter Dicken, *Global Shift* (New York: Harper Collins, 1986); reprinted with permission. Based on J. McHale, *The Future of the Future* (New York: George Braziller, 1969), figure 1.

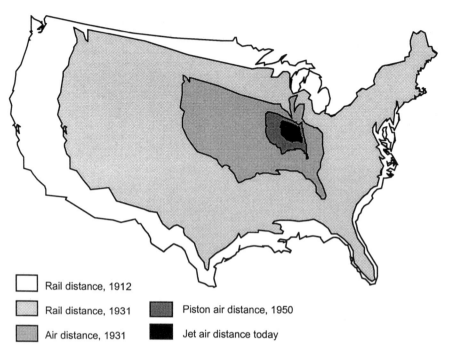

Rail distance, 1912

Rail distance, 1931   Piston air distance, 1950

Air distance, 1931   Jet air distance today

Figure 2.2   The shrinking United States: Transportation and effective distance, 1912–1970. From John C. Lowe and S. Moryadas, *The Geography of Movement* (Boston: Houghton Mifflin, 1975), 51.

distance to 10 hours, and today it is 5. According to Lowe and Moryadas (1975), San Diego is, in effect, 15 miles from Portland. Alternatively, in terms of transcontinental or intermetropolitan area travel time, the United States is now as large as a medium-size state, New York now closer to Tokyo than it was to Philadelphia in colonial times.[7] Similarly, innovations in vehicle and road technologies reduced the distance between London and Edinburgh from 2,000 minutes by stagecoach in 1658, to 2,500 by the modernized stage of 1840, to 800 minutes by rail in 1850 (400 in 1950), and down to 200 by air in 1970, for an annual rate of convergence between the two cities of about 29 minutes a year, though with each innovation in transportation, locations converge at a decreasing rate. Since 1840, when the best average speed of horse-drawn coaches and sailing ships was 10 miles per hour, the speed of transportation has increased 70 times with jet passenger aircraft.[8]

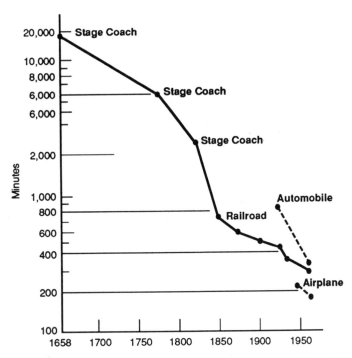

Figure 2.3 Time–space convergence between Edinburgh and London, 1685–1966. From John C. Lowe and S. Moryadas, *The Geography of Movement* (Boston: Houghton Mifflin, 1975), 52.

Communication Shrinks the Map and Expands Choice

Until electricity and mechanics combined brought the telegraph in the nineteenth century, transportation and communication were effectively conjoined, because information could only move as fast as transportation systems could take it. Pred (1973) has documented and mapped the time necessary for information to circulate both within the United States and between it and foreign centers in the pre-telegraph era (see figures 2.5, 2.6, and 2.7). Although he notes significant advances, these depended entirely on improvements in transportation technologies. For example, the postal act of 1836, which supported "express" mail routes, coupled with the growth of steamboat traffic, decreased the public information time lag between Cincinnati and New York from nineteen to seven days.

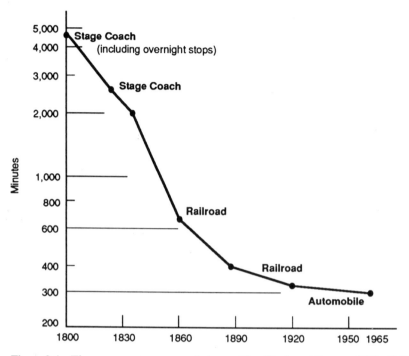

Figure 2.4 Time–space convergence between New York and Boston, 1800–1965. From Donald G. Janelle, "Global Interdependence and its Consequences," in *Collapsing Space and Time: Geographic Aspects of Communication and Information*, edited by Stanley D. Brunn and Thomas R. Leinbach (London: Harper Collins Academic, 1991), 50.

Although semaphore, bonfire, and smoke signals offered earlier transport-independent (but not weather-independent) means of communication, the telegraph and the submarine cable are chiefly responsible for severing the link between transportation and communication, with significant consequences for geography. No longer would it be necessary to use rail or ship to send a message across the country or across the seas. Telegraphy enabled a message to cross the country instantly; undersea cable took messages across oceans. Chandler's (1977) research demonstrates how communication and transportation systems worked together to lay groundwork for the modern American business system: The telegraph extended the reach of timely price information, and the railroad sped the product to market. Along with them came organizational innovations, required to run railroad companies, and new "transac-

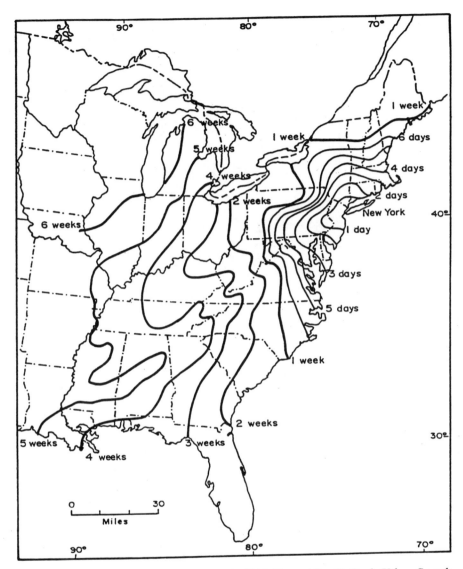

Figure 2.5 Rates of travel from New York, 1800. From Allan R. Pred, *Urban Growth and the Circulation of Information: The United States System of Cities, 1790–1840* (Cambridge, Mass.: Harvard Studies in Urban History, Harvard University Press, 1973), 176.

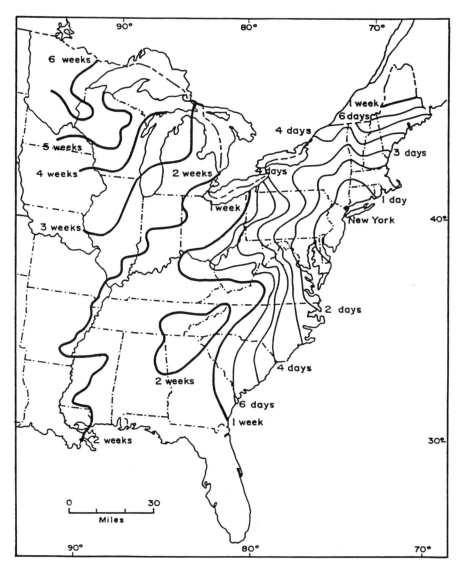

Figure 2.6 Rates of travel from New York, 1830. From Allan R. Pred, *Urban Growth and the Circulation of Information: The United States System of Cities, 1790–1840* (Cambridge, Mass.: Harvard Studies in Urban History, Harvard University Press, 1973), 177.

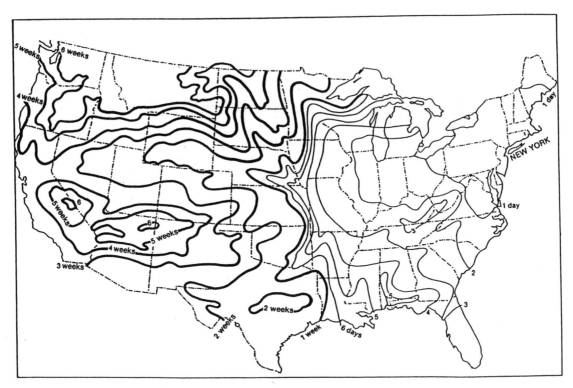

Figure 2.7 Rates of travel from New York, 1857. From Alfred D. Chandler, Jr., *The Visible Hand: The Managerial Revolution in American Business* (Cambridge, Mass.: Harvard University Press, 1977), 85.

tion" jobs, for example, commodity dealer, wholesale jobber, retailer, that tied together networks formed out of the extended reach of new transport-communication systems.[9] Today transportation and communication systems are integrated to improve the flows of people and vehicles that grew with innovations in transport technologies.[10]

Geographers have applied the idea of time–space convergence to map the impact of communication. For example, it took fourteen minutes to carry a voice message from San Francisco to New York City in 1920. Improvements in network structure and technology reduced that to less than thirty seconds by 1970, a standard that now applies to much of the world and amounts to near-perfect time–space convergence.[11] The difference between advances in network structure and technology describe the difference between improvements in

Table 2.1 Speeds of information transfer mechanisms

670,000,000 mph	Electronic: telegraph, telephone, radio
670,000,000 mph	Visual: semaphore, bonfires, smoke signals
660 mph	Sonic: drums, horns, whistles
100–600 mph	Aircraft
60 mph	Carrier pigeon
30–60 mph	Vehicle: motorcycle, automobile, truck, railroad
15–30 mph	Ship
9 mph	Horse: postrider, coach
6 mph	Man

Source: Stephen H. Lawrence, *Centralization and Decentralization: The Compunications Connection* (Cambridge, Mass.: Harvard University, Program on Information Resources Policy, Incidental Paper, July 1983, I-83-2), A1-3.

system speed—or the organization of people, institutions, and technologies—and in the speed of *technology*—or what the technology alone can accomplish (see tables 2.1 and 2.2).[12]

Research has also taken up time–space convergences for specific types of information. For example, Pred (1980) examined spatial biases in the circulation of specialized economic information in the United States from the colonial period. He found that during that time New York City had become central both as entry point and as dissemination node for such information. Information moved more rapidly and frequently between New York, Philadelphia, Boston, and Baltimore than between any of the latter three cities and almost all hinterland locations. In additional, economic information flowed more rapidly and frequently to and from New York and the southern ports of New Orleans, Richmond, Charlestown, and Mobile than among the those four cities (see table 2.3 and figure 2.8).

Since by the 1990s communication has trivialized, if not entirely flattened, most graphs of time against distance, geographers have turned to more interesting dimensions of the measure, such as *cost–space convergence*, that is, the cost of moving a message over a given distance. Janelle[13] describes the declining cost of a telephone connection between San Francisco and New York from more than $15 in 1920 to less than $1 today. Oettinger (1980) mapped telephone cost–space convergence from the geographical center of the United States, and Neuman (1991) adapted Abler's research to describe general telephone price convergence.

Table 2.2 Development of information transmission systems

500 B.C.	Persian Empire	Postrider	9 mph
0–500 A.D.	Roman Empire	Postrider	9(+) mph
1305–early 1800s A.D.	von Taxis (Europe)	Coach	4 mph (summer)
			3.5 mph (winter)
Early 1500s A.D.	Aztec Empire	Runner	11 mph
Late 1500s A.D.	Elizabethan England	Coach	7 mph (summer)
1627 A.D.	d'Medici (Florence-Rome)	Semaphore	5 mph (winter)
Late 1700s A.D.	British Postal Service	Coach	9 mph
1800 A.D.	French Empire	Tachygraphe	120 mph
1860 A.D.	United States	Postrider	8.6 mph
1850 A.D.	United States	Telegraph	670,000,000 mph
			(between telegraphers)
1900 A.D.	United States	Telephone	670,000,000 mph

Source: Stephen H. Lawrence, *Centralization and Decentralization: The Compunications Connection* (Cambridge, Mass.: Harvard University, Program on Information Resources Policy, Incidental Paper, July 1983, I-83-2), A1-5.

Table 2.3 Mean public information time lags for New York, 1817 and 1841 (in days)

Public-information source	1817	1841	Percentage decrease
Charleston	8.2	5.5	32.9
Savannah	10.2	6.3	38.2
Cincinnati	19.0	7.0*	63.2
Detroit	18.0	7.5*	58.3

*"Since eastbound and westbound mails were of equal frequency, and since both Cincinnati and Detroit possessed daily papers in 1841, New York-to-Cincinnati and New York-to-Detroit time lags were presumably not significantly different from delays in the opposite direction."

Sources: Allan R. Pred, *Urban Growth and the Circulation of Information: The United States System of Cities, 1790–1840* (Cambridge, Mass.: Harvard Studies in Urban History, Harvard University Press, 1973), 56: *New York Evening Post*, 1817, *New York Daily Tribune*, 1841.

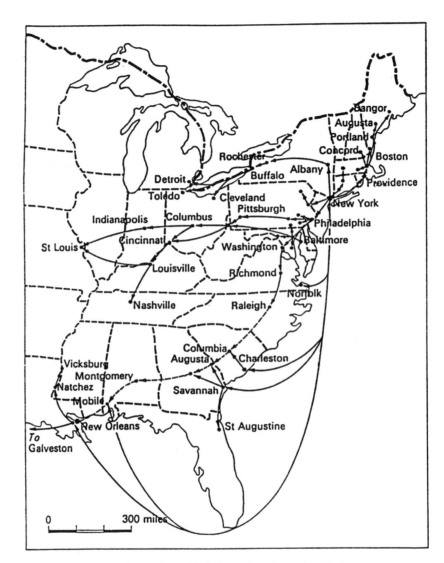

Figure 2.8 Flows of pre-telegraphic information from New York newspapers to the rest of the country. From Allan R. Pred, *Urban Growth and the Circulation of Information: The United States System of Cities, 1790–1840* (Cambridge, Mass.: Harvard Studies in Urban History, Harvard University Press, 1973), 33.

The development in the 1960s of the geosynchronous-orbiting satellite provided the technological means to remove the friction of distance in the determination of communication costs, leading researchers to conclude that in terms of time *and* cost geographical distance is less and less meaningful for communication and information purposes (see figures 2.9, 2.10, and 2.11).[14]

Malone and Rockart (1991) extend their analysis of orders of effect in transport technology to communication, or what they call "coordination technology." A first-order impact of reducing communication costs is the substitution of information technology for human coordination, which occurs when computer systems eliminate clerks in the back offices of banks and insurance firms and directory-assistance operators from telephone companies. Declining communication costs have a second-order effect of increasing the overall amount of communication used to manage activities. As a result, travel agents can more easily consider a wider range of travel options for their customers, and airlines can offer a wider range of fares. Otis Elevator uses highly trained, multilingual operators who process trouble calls from a national toll-fee number, record problems in a database, and electronically dispatch local repair personnel.

Third-order effects emerge with the shift to communication-intensive structures. These include intrafirm structures, such as at Frito-Lay, where some ten thousand route sales personnel, using hand-held computers, record all sales of each of two hundred grocery items even as they also deliver products to customers. Every night the information is summarized for forty senior executives, who can make quick price, product, and marketing adjustments. Communication-intensive structures cut across firms to link a chain of, for example, textile suppliers, manufacturers, and retailers into an interfirm network committed to reducing inventory and responding to changing fashions. The Benetton company pioneered the application of inventory-reducing just-in-time controls to the clothing industry.[15] These networks can bring together competitors, as in the Rosenbluth International Alliance, an electronic consortium of travel agencies that share customer records, services, and software.

Researchers have developed measures of *social space* to denote the number of social contacts over a specific territory, one variation of which, the mean information field (MIF), measures the probability of communication against the distance between communicators.[16] For example, for a sample of telephone calls in a region, the log of the number of calls can be plotted against the distance over which the calls move. The result suggests a general decline in the density of communication with distance, and defines, for that region, the MIF.

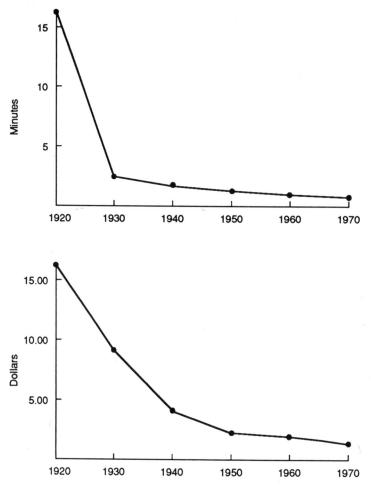

Figure 2.9 Telephone time–space and cost–space convergences. From Ron Abler, Donald G. Janelle, Allen Philbrick, and John Sommer, *Human Geography in a Shrinking World* (Belmont, Calif.: Wadsworth, 1975), 39, 40.

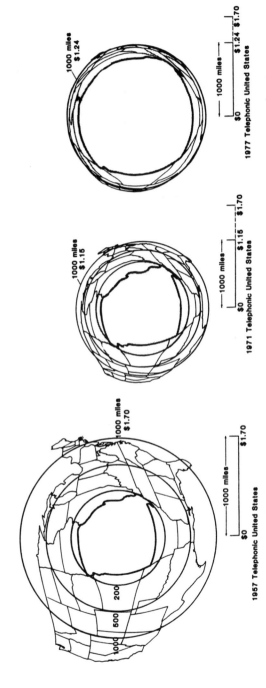

Figure 2.10 Telephone cost distances from Missouri, 1957–1977. From Anthony G. Oettinger, "Information Resources: Knowledge and Power in the 21st Century," *Science* 209 (July 4, 1980), 192.

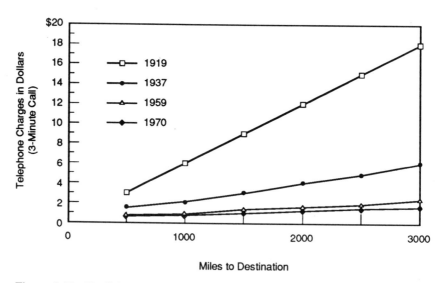

Figure 2.11 Declining costs of long-distance communication. From W. Russell Neuman, *The Future of the Mass Audience* (New York: Cambridge University Press, 1991), 58.

The slope of the MIF in simple societies is steep, indicating that most communication occurs over short distances, and it is shallower in complex, mobile societies. For some of today's heavy users of electronic networks like the Internet, the slope of the MIF is reversing from its historical downward tendency because the community of interest extends over great distances. Measures of social space are used most in research on patterns of innovation and diffusion to measure the time required, for example, for a new technology to move from one area to another.

In addition to these objective measures of time–space convergence, geographers take into account the *perceptual* or cultural dimension of convergence. In fact, Abler suggests that

what people *think* about distance and space is more important in the long run than the "real" nature of space and distance. Even if time- and cost-, and N-space convergence succeed in producing a functionally dimensionless world, people will continue to have strong feelings about places and what they perceive to be distance.[17]

While in one sense convergence means the end of geography, in another it means that we pay greater attention to the intensity and immediacy of communication, qualities that, admittedly, are more difficult to measure than time– or cost–space convergence. Convergence measures vary with the individual's place within society. Although agreeing that time–space and cost–space convergences demonstrate that places are generally moving closer together, Abler suggested in 1975 that "for those possessing lesser means, time–space convergence may be negligible. In fact, there is reason to believe that convergence contributes to the polarization of the 'haves' and 'have nots.'"[18] He cites research suggesting that, in large U.S. cities, for example, the average distance between home and work decreased for whites but increased for blacks. More recently, McLaughlin (1992) suggested that convergence may be creating a growing gap within the corporate world, dividing businesses that, owing to management practices or to regulatory policies of their host nations, are either more or less able to take advantage of computer communication.

The research literature offers a number of general conclusions. The declining price–performance ratio of transportation and communication technologies has contributed to spatial convergence.[19] The extent of the convergence is widespread but varies with cultural, social, and political conditions. Cultural conditions include the values embedded in specific places and in the distances between them. For example, a person based in Akron, Ohio, headed for New York City has a different perception of New York and the distance from Akron depending on whether the trip is viewed as a chance to visit the center of civilized life or as a descent into barbarism. Social variations include an individual's place in various economic, educational, and social status hierarchies that can either make convergence a taken-for-granted reality or, at the other extreme, practically unthinkable. Finally, politico-economic decisions about transportation (what is the condition of Akron's airport? which, if any, carriers, fly between Akron and New York, and what is the fare?) and communication (the quality and price of mail, facsimile, and telephone between the two cities) influence the nature of convergence.

Rather than contribute to what O'Brien (1992) calls "the end of geography," convergence transforms geography by increasing the spatial flexibility of those who can take advantage of smaller, faster, cheaper, and better computer communication technology and by underscoring the significance of nontechnical factors that can enhance or impede convergence. As Abler puts it, "A world without distance will not be an undifferentiated, isotropic sphere; because it would allow preference free rein, such a world would be immensely varied and differentiated."[20]

The Analogy to Electricity, or the Information Superhighway Meets the Great White Way

Who now writes about electricity in the language of this reporter, impelled to hyperbole by the lighting display at the 1894 Chicago World's Fair?

Look from a distance at night, upon the broad space it fills, and the majestic sweep of the searching lights, and it is as if the earth and sky were transformed by the immeasurable wands of colossal magicians and the superb dome of the structure that is the central jewel of the display is glowing as if bound with wreaths of stars. It is electricity! When the whole casket is illuminated, the cornices of the palaces of the White City are defined with celestial fire—the thunderbolts are harnessed at last.[21]

For the brief period when it held out most promise and before it moved into the relative obscurity brought about by universality and mundane function, as one historian put it, "Electrification was placed quite consciously at the apex of an evolutionary framework."[22] This "spectacle" phase of the new technology lasted for a few decades. In 1880 a crowd gaped at one arc light in a shop window, and in 1885 another was drawn to gawk at a lighted mansion. But with the first lighted signs of the 1890s, the novelty began to wear thin. Soon, lighting took a back seat, even at the great fairs. By 1901 attendees of the Buffalo fair paid more attention to the design of lighting than to the sheer amount of light, and at the 1915 San Francisco fair the lights were hidden in order to focus attention on the buildings and objects illuminated. By 1925, Nye concludes, lighting had shifted from a spectacular device designed to attract crowds to world fairs to an essential part of business and of life on the street. In that process, as historians describe, electrification opened a wide range of opportunities in business, the military, and social and cultural life, even as its spectacle value diminished.[23] The major payoff in electrification arrived when it ceased to be considered the wonder of the century and became, instead, the full-time preoccupation of small groups of experts who electrified transportation, communication, and lighting in factories, offices, homes, streets, and highways. It came long after people had lost a sense of rapture in the face of many Great White Ways, those heavily lit main streets that publicity-conscious lighting companies created in cities across America. The irony of electrification, as with many new technologies, is that its full power was unleashed only after it was seen as a particular spectacle and after it had become taken for granted as integral to systems, such as transportation, which it has enhanced in, yes, spectacular ways.

The history of electrification contains food for thought about computer communication, specifically for the debate about the Information Superhighway. Some of the questions posed about the development of electricity are relevant today. What were the political and economic factors contributing to the construction, ownership, management, and spatial distribution of the electricity infrastructure? What were the implications of these historical choices for the spatial organization of social and economic life? Following Nye's analogy, computer communication is in its spectacle phase, with the Superhighway its Great White Way. Although people are beginning to think about the integration of microprocessors in cars, dishwashers, and watches, etc., they persist in viewing computer communication, particularly the computer itself, as a discrete marvel. Computers are still advertised with the indiscreet charms of power and sexuality once bestowed on an earlier spectacle technology, the automobile. Computers elicit the same kinds of promises as those proffered by electrical boosters, who saw the Brush arc light and its successors ending crime and night's other terrors when what they called this new "white magic" led to the "electrical millennium."[24]

In the 1990s, computers in general are far from ordinary features of daily life. But, if technological history is any guide, a time will come when few write of computers in the hyperbolic language of the journalist celebrating the vision of the Chicago World's Fair. People may someday ask, as scholars now do about electricity's Great White Way, who now writes about the Information Superhighway? History suggests, as computers are becoming sufficiently commonplace to be banal, their real power—the power to enhance systems, enable people, and breed choice—is growing. Reflections on the Information Superhighway may soon be reserved to historical accounts of a time when the computer was spectacle, when, like electricity, "it provided a visible correlative for the ideology of progress."[25] This is no small accomplishment. Visions of progress are important levers to pry open societies reluctant to embrace new technologies. Admittedly, the Great White Way helped to electrify America, but it also contributed to mobilizing a policy apparatus behind a wide range of schemes that, among other things, amounted to creating literal monopolies of power. Will the Information Superhighway, which is arguably spreading the word about computer communication, also offer a case of, in the words of baseball philosopher Yogi Berra, "déjà vu all over again"?

After the Spectacle: Computer Communication Breeds Choice in Business Location

When deciding where to locate a business, few ask, "How close are we to the electrical grid?"[26] Although once this was an important question, constraining the search for sites, just as proximity to a body of water once limited location, proximity to electricity or water plays little role today in decisions about where to set up shop. Proximity to telecommunications networks still matters; but that, too, is declining in importance as networks access the hinterland. Again, if the history of electrification can serve as a guide, computer communication will fade in salience to locational decisionmaking, even as it grows in power as a breeder of choice. As a result, like electrification before it, it will make other locational factors more important. What is known about these other factors?

Beyond academic jargon and methodological hairsplitting, research on the significance of geography for organizations has primarily contributed useful checklists of factors that managers need to take into consideration when determining where to locate. Raymond Vernon, a long-time student of the field, noted that most scholars recognize that the phenomenon of locational choice is far more enigmatic than the literature and its theoretical approaches have been able to address.[27]

The systematic study of location began with ideas pulled together first in 1909 in the work of Alfred Weber.[28] Weber and his followers aimed to help businesses determine the least-cost location for factories and offices. To that end, they calculated transportation, manufacturing—particularly labor—and marketing costs, which they used to identify the least expensive site. Weber's major discovery was that businesses benefited from concentrating plants and offices in one location, what is now referred to as *agglomeration economies*. The next generation of location scholars, influenced by Weber's work, added to the traditional concern with making and moving goods the costs of making and moving information.[29]

The most useful research in the field provides different types of lists that firms should consider in making locational choices. For example, Hepworth and Ducatel (1992) identify factors, including the cost of information, over the range of business activities: planning, purchasing, manufacturing, storage and distribution, and marketing (see figure 2.12). Greenhut (1956) put together demand, cost, and personal factors (table 2.4); and Townroe (1976) organized determinants along geographical lines: regional, community, and site (table 2.5).

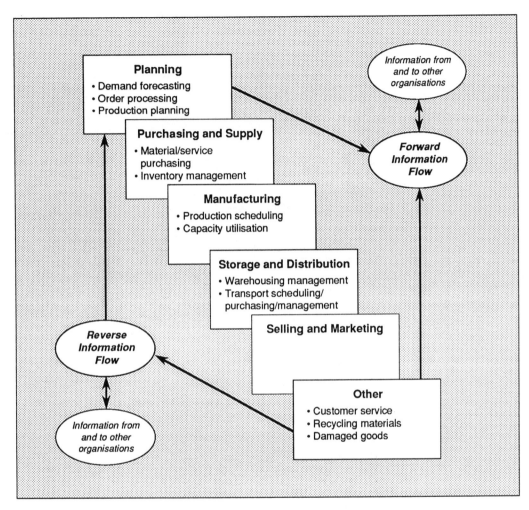

Figure 2.12   Locational factors by business activity. From Mark Hepworth and Ken Ducatel, *Transport in the Information Age: Wheels and Wires* (London: Belhaven Press; Transnet, the London Transport Technology Network, 1992), 56.

Table 2.4 Demand, cost, and personal considerations in the location decision

Demand factors

1 The shape of the demand curve for a given product

2 The location of competitors, which in turn partially determines

   (a) the magnitude of the demand, and

   (b) the cross-elasticity of demand at different places.

3 The significance of proximity, type of service, and speed of service; predjudices of consumers.

4 The relationship between personal contacts and sales.

5 The extent of the market area, which itself is partially determined by cost factors and pricing policies.

6 The competitiveness of the industry in location and price; certainty and uncertainty.

Cost factors

2 The cost of land, which includes

   (a) the rent of land;

   (b) the tax on land;

   (c) the availability of capital, which partially depends upon

       (i)   the banking facilities and financial resources, and

       (ii) personal contacts;

   (d) the cost of capital, which is also partially dependent upon

       (i)   the banking facilities and financial resources and

       (ii) the type of climate;

   (e) the insurance rates at different sites, which in turn partially depend upon

       (i)   the banking facilities and financial resources,

       (ii)   the police and fire protection, and

       (iii) the type of climate;

   (f) the cost of fuel and power, which is partially dependent upon

       (i)   natural resources,

       (ii)   topography, and

       (iii) climate.

2 The cost of labor and management, which is influenced by

   (a) the health of the community, the park and education facilities, housing facilities, wage differences, etc., and

   (b) state laws.

3 The cost of materials and equipment, which is partially determined by

   (a) the location of competitors (sellers and buyers),

   (b) the price system in the supply area, (f.o.b. mill, equalizing or other forms of discriminatory delivered prices),

Table 2.4 (continued)

    (c) the extent of the supply area, which in turn is partially dependent upon

        (i) personal contacts and

        (ii) price policy.

4 The cost of transportation, which is partially determined by

    (a) the topography

    (b) the transport facilities and

    (c) the characteristics of the product.

Purely personal factors

1 the importance of psychic income (size of plant),

2 environmental preferences, and

3 the security motive.

Source: Melvin L. Greenhut, *Plant Location in Theory and in Practise: The Economics of Space* (Chapel Hill: University of North Carolina Press, 1956), 279–281.

Table 2.5 Locational factors by region, community, and site

Key regional factors

1 Government regional policy

2 Strategic communications

3 Labour relations

4 Markets

Key community factors

1 Transport and communications

2 Ties with parent plant

3 Labour/supply/cost/training

4 Supplies of materials and components

5 Access to services

6 Local and central govenment services

7 Amenity

Key site factors

1 Intra-urban locaton

2 Physical characteristics

3 Tenure

4 The availability of buildings

5 Access to services and utilities

6 Price

Source: Based on data in Peter M. Townroe, *Planning Industrial Location* (London: L. Hill, 1976), Ch. 4.

Research has slowly turned to the role of computer communication in locational decisions. Studies typically elaborate on the general conclusion that technology expands on the possible locations available to organizations, because it overcomes the need to be physically near information resources. Transportation and power technologies once lessened the need to locate near bodies of water; now the spread of computer communication networks around the world has reduced the need to choose a specific location because of its proximity to telecommunications networks. According to an AT&T executive, locational decisions are increasingly based on the view that people can communicate reasonably well from anywhere to anywhere. Decisions are therefore based on the remaining opportunities and constraints, such as labor force, customers, and environmental considerations.[30]

Those who look closely at the issue of computer communication in locational decisions focus on the likely mix of technologies and systems to hasten distance insensitivity. According to Carol C. Knauff, who oversees research on global business video services for AT&T, one of the critical steps in overcoming the barrier of distance in business is to integrate video services with the personal computer.[31] Knauff anticipates that this integration will take place for large and medium-size businesses by the end of the 1990s. Access to live video extends the physical presence of the communicators beyond the text. One of the keys is the development of inexpensive digital video-compression techniques. Although many large businesses now use general digital video extensively, they are just beginning to integrate digital video into computer terminals. The next wave will be the application of digital video to medium-size firms. According to Knauff's research, as might be expected, people collaborate most effectively once a relationship based on face-to-face contact has been established. As might not be expected, people care more about the quality of the audio and its synchronization with the video than about the quality of the video. They can tolerate degraded, even jerky video but not poor audio or a bad sync. Further, they respond well to multilocation meetings situated in a room that looks like a face-to-face meeting room.

Centralization or Dispersal: Choose Both, Wisely

Early studies of the impact of transportation and communications considerations on the locational choice of corporate headquarters found two prominent patterns. First, firms tended to locate either near their manufacturing facilities or close to other corporate headquarters. For example, Leone distinguished between the advantages of a New York City location "given the proximity to the financial community, access to the educational and legal establishment, and so on." However, "In the past these advantages have frequently been counterbalanced by the diseconomies of separating control functions from operating functions."[32] Drawing on this research, Lavey (1974) noted a growing tendency for firms to locate in large cities, even when doing so put some distance between headquarters and manufacturing operations. He speculated that "this evidence supports the importance of face-to-face communication" in the choice of headquarters location.

Recent assessments confirm the tendency to separate the headquarters location from manufacturing facilities.[33] The steel company Armco is a typical case. In 1990 Armco moved its top management from Middletown, Ohio, to Parsippany, New Jersey. According to its chairman and CEO, Robert Boni, the firm moved the fifty-nine top managers to New Jersey to get them away from the company's roots and make it easier for them to gain the "strategic objectivity" necessary to expand the company's steelmaking and other facilities around the world.[34] Specifically, the relocation would "separate the executives from the town steelworks, the retired Armco executives at the country club, and from the local press focus on hometown responsibilities." More positively, according to Boni, it placed Armco managers "into the midst of their major corporate peers," including bankers, investment counselors, and sources of premier corporate directors.[35]

Partly as a result of advances in computer communication, interest is growing in moving the corporate world headquarters of U.S. firms offshore (see table 2.6).[36] The principal reason cited is that the risk of losing control is offset by proximity to major customers and competitors in fast-changing markets far from home. According to an analyst with McKinsey & Co., businesses increasingly "recognize that they can't rule the world from one single location," leading to the prediction that, by the year 2005, half or so of the Fortune 500 companies will make the move.[37] Among the companies that have already done so is AT&T, which moved the headquarters of its corded telephone business from New Jersey to France.

Additional case research supports the view that advances in transportation and especially in communication make it easier for firms to operate at a distance and thereby take advantage of benefits enjoyed in locations that were once not cost-effective.[38] More specifically, according to Sassen the dispersal of

Table 2.6 Multinational firms moving headquarters abroad. Moving the home base to foreign soil: some multinational corporations moving global headquarters of major business units overseas

Company	Home country	New location	Operation shifted	Year moved
AT&T	U.S.	France	Corded telephones	1992
Du Pont	U.S.	Japan	Electronics	1992
Hyundai Electronics Industries	South Korea	U.S.	Personal computers	1992
IBM	U.S.	U.K.	Networking systems	1991
Siemens	Germany	U.K.	Air-traffic management	1991
Siemens	Germany	U.S.	Ultrasound equipment	1991
Du Pont	U.S.	Switzerland	Agricultural products, and parts of fibers and polymers businesses	1991
Hewlett-Packard	U.S.	France	Desktop personal computers	1990
Siemens	Germany	U.S.	Nuclear-medicine products and radiation-therapy equipment	1989
Cadbury Schweppes	U.K.	U.S.	Beverages	1987*
Du Pont	U.S.	Switzerland	Lycra business	1987

* Moved back to London in 1991.
Source: From Joann S. Lubin, "Multinational Firms Moving Headquarters Abroad," *The Wall Street Journal*, Dec. 9, 1992, B1. Reprinted by permission of *The Wall Street Journal* © 1992 Dow Jones & Co., Inc. All rights reserved worldwide.

work "was a result of the introduction of new technologies designed to separate low-wage, routine tasks from highly skilled tasks therewith maximizing locational options."[39] New technologies have enabled the *decentralization* or dispersal of work in manufacturing, the office, and retail services over a wide range of locations. Both GM and Ford use computer-aided tools to design, source, and manufacture components in different countries.[40] Credit card companies have relocated to South Dakota and Delaware because these states are among the most liberal about credit card fees and interest rate regulation.[41] Both Canadian and U.S. customer-service and telemarketing firms have moved to rural New Brunswick and Manitoba, where a low-wage, bilingual work force provides the major incentive.[42]

Computer hardware and software companies have moved to Bangalore and other parts of India to take advantage of labor-cost savings. As a result,

Bangalore-based software engineers working for Texas Instruments have customized the automated inventory system of Dayton Hudson Corp.'s Target chain of U.S. discount stores, developed a new digital-signal processor for Ericsson of Sweden, and produced a tailor-made programmable chip for AT&T. One Indian project manager refers to the "globalization of software" where "the user is in one country, the developer in another place, the project manager in another."[43] A major reason for relocating software engineering is to save on personnel costs. At Motorola in Bangalore a mid-level engineer earns $800 a month.[44] Similarly, Nippon Telegraph and Telephone (NTT) Data Communications, the largest computer systems integrator in Japan, has identified Beijing and Shanghai as prime locations for a software production center in China, on the expectation that the new facility will reduce personnel costs.[45] General Electric has relocated technical drafting departments to computer-aided design facilities in India and Eastern Europe.[46] Other large companies have found the Philippines an inexpensive haven for everything from data-input to software design.[47] Research suggests that firms are increasingly able to save on labor costs by eliminating, as well as dispersing, labor. For example, when it took over the Bank of New England, the Fleet Street Bank increased its investment in computer communication. By 1992, it had become the largest bank in New England, with $44 billion in assets. In the process, its work force dropped from seven thousand to four thousand. Using technology, the company reduced from twenty-four to three the number of its check-processing offices, from eighteen to one the number of data centers, and its annual back-office budget from $180 million to $90 million.[48]

Considerable research also supports the view that communication and information technologies have facilitated the choice to *centralize* corporate functions. The first studies of centralization focused on manufacturing by pointing to the tendency of small, specialized firms to group together in new industrial zones.[49] For example, several hundred small factories concentrated in the Emilia Romagna region in northern Italy serve as flexible subcontractors to manufacturers around the world. Studies have shown that by remaining small they can respond more flexibly to changes in global demand. Territorial concentration enabled them to form loose associational networks for joint research, investment, and marketing, which make it possible for groups of firms to act like and enjoy some of the scale economies of larger firms. Cohen and Zysman describe the dynamics of these firms:

Manufacturers, facing increased labor costs and restricted ability to manage flexibly inside their plants, took to subcontracting production.... These subcontractors often began to innovate themselves and to produce new production equipment and products. An entire sector of smaller firms sprang up.... Eventually, these small producers broke loose from their subcontracting role to begin a different pattern of dynamic flexibility. They have become innovative suppliers in world markets.[50]

This tendency suggests that some parts of the economy may take on the look of an earlier family-farm economy, in which relatively small farms supplied and sold to large organizations, such as railroad, seed, and grain companies. Focusing on transnational firms, a 1993 study carried out by McKinsey & Co. concluded that the most successful global firms "tend to centralize their international decisionmaking in every area except new-product development."[51]

New Wave in Location: The Growth of Producer Services

Increasingly, research has turned to centralization in the producer services sector, that is, services produced for organizations, including private and public sectors, rather than for final consumers.[52] These technically "intermediate outputs" cover financial, legal, and management services, as well as advertising, communication, wholesale distribution, insurance, accounting, and professional associations.[53]

Firms specializing in producer or consumer services tend to follow different locational patterns. There is a stronger tendency for consumer service firms to locate on the basis of the size of the market for final consumers.[54] Communication technology has abated this tendency, as demonstrated by the geographical dispersal of telemarketing firms. Yet evidence strongly supports the hypothesis that consumer service firms are more evenly distributed than those in producer services.[55] Consumer services lack a strong contrast between central and peripheral locations.

On the other hand, producer services firms tend to concentrate particularly in the major international cities of New York, London, and Tokyo, central points for the coordination and control of economic processes.[56] According to this view, as these places lost their manufacturing bases, they also surrendered their importance as sites of production and took on the role of coordinator of services for production activities taking place elsewhere. In the 1990s, observers view global cities as *production* sites, though not, as in the past, principally for manufactured goods or for final consumer services. Rather, they are primarily organized for the production of *specialized services* that organizations require to run spatially dispersed networks of factories, offices, and consumer service outlets. International cities are responsible for the production of financial instruments and innovations and for making markets—both essential for the health of the financial services industry.[57]

According to that research, the high density of producer services activity concentrated in the central business districts of global cities and their increasingly disproportionate share of all financial transactions challenge the contention that agglomeration and density decline as global communications make possible resource and population dispersal. The spatial dispersion of manufacturing production and consumer services, including their internationalization, has contributed to the growth of centralized nodes for the production of management, regulation, and control functions necessary for coordination of globally dispersed economies.

Why do producer services firms concentrate in global city locations? Research tends to focus on the particular characteristics of such firms' production and markets. Unlike consumer services, producer services do not depend on proximity to final consumers. For them, it is more important to be close to other firms producing key inputs or providing opportunities for joint production of services. For example, consulting and accounting firms benefit from proximity to law firms, marketing companies, and computer programmers. Thrift found that financial services firms are likely to locate in world cities, because they need to be near clients, including the headquarters of banking and industrial firms, as well as government departments.[58] In addition, financial services companies need to be close to markets, many of which work out of fixed exchanges. Finally, they need to tap into information on both clients and markets rapidly and efficiently.

In general, major business transactions require the organized participation of numerous specialized companies that provide financial, legal, accounting, management consulting, media and public relations, and other services. Research in different national settings confirms this conclusion.[59] For example, according to Moulaert, Chikhaoui, and Djellal (1991), French high-technology consultancy firms tend to concentrate in Paris (and, to a lesser extent, in Rhônes-Alpes and Provence) because of "the sector's need for both backward and forward linkages." These linkages include access to higher levels of decision-making in clients' organizations and proximity to the high-technology industry. Ettinger and Clay (1991), in their examination of national occupational data over the period from 1983 to 1988, noted the tendency for "high-order corporate services" to concentrate in major metropolitan areas, while routine services, such as data entry and related clerical work, have been dispersed to peripheral regions.[60] Research shows that the urban concentration of producer or corporate services has multiplier effects which deepen the tendency. For example, further concentration arises out of the needs and expectations of higher-income workers employed by corporate services firms who prefer the cultural and lifestyle amenities within global cities.[61]

One source of confusion in the analysis of dispersal and concentration lies in the definition of a central location. For example, some researchers distinguish between metropolitan centers and "edge cities," sites located thirty or so miles away that have grown out of office parks and shopping malls.[62] Those making this distinction identify dispersal with movement from a central to an edge location, such as the movement of the research divisions of NEC, Samsung, Matsushita Electronics, Hitachi, and Toshiba to Princeton, New Jersey (dubbed Video Valley for its focus on high-definition television research). One reason for the move, however, is proximity to the metropolitan centers of New York and Philadelphia (as well as Washington, D.C.), to Princeton University, and to one another, so that the move might be regarded as a form of metropolitan agglomeration. One Matsushita executive noted that the company passed up less expensive sites precisely in order to take advantage of geographical synergies.[63]

Telecommunications has advanced the dispersal of some organizational activities, primarily manufacturing and, increasingly, consumer services. Partly because of relative ease and partly because of cost savings, organizations have tended to disperse more routine functions. Although telecommunications has multiplied the products or corporate services available, these have not been dispersed. Some maintain that the process of dispersal in manufacturing and consumer services has itself intensified the need to coordinate and control these functions in centralized locations. Analysts such as Sassen and O'Brien conclude that dispersal and centralization are part of the process comprising the structural transformation of contemporary economic geography. According to Sassen, writing in 1991, "the spatial dispersion of production and the reorganization of the financial industry over the last decade have created new forms of centralization in order to manage and regulate the global network of production sites and financial markets."[64] Writing specifically about financial services, O'Brien (1992) identifies two counterforces at work under "end-of-geography" conditions. On the one hand, because communication enables experts to work together electronically, a case can be made for the decline of financial centers. Even the City of London is no longer confined to the Square Mile. On the other hand, communication makes it possible to take advantage of scale economies and concentrate markets in one location, selling the same product from one center across an even greater area.

Yet the durability of this pattern of dispersal and centralization remains an open question. Organizations have applied telecommunications to speed the dispersal of manufacturing and, more recently, consumer services. When, and with what consequences, will telecommunications be applied to the entire complex of managerial and professional services at the top of organizational hierarchies? This depends on both technological and social considerations.

The nature of producer services work requires both close coordination and flexibility among a wide range of professionals, activities that benefit from the physical proximity that brings easy access to people and their information resource networks. Current research on the tools to produce virtual proximity, such as advanced videoconferencing, aims to apply telecommunications to what may be the last friction barrier to overcoming geographical constraints but has not yet had much impact.[65]

The social consideration is rooted in the ability to sustain tendencies toward polarization in the labor force of global cities that mark a deepening division between the professionals, managers, brokers, and others at the command centers of producer services and, at the other extreme, those who fall into the growing category of low-wage, part-time, temporary workers whose jobs are readily subject to automation and relocation.[66] The automation and dispersal of manufacturing and some services work have led to the decline of the middle class, whose income and job security helped purchase the social stability that contributed to social order. Now, the same commentators speculating on the growing pattern of homelessness in global cities employing increasing numbers of high-income professional workers wonder how long the pattern of dispersal and centralization can sustain what appears to be a changing social structure. This suggests the need for the advanced economies to rethink industrial economic development strategies.

Redrawing the Map and Rethinking the Organization

Computer communication is not the only factor that leads decisionmakers to redraw industry maps and rethink their firms. The growth of a well-educated middle class in parts of the developing as well as the advanced economies, and the universal spread of English as an international language of business, make it possible to loosen the traditionally rigid hierarchies once necessary to manage global firms. Nevertheless, research confirms the significance of computer communication as companies redraw their organizational maps to encompass global markets. Effective telecommunications is replacing organizational restructuring as a central factor in the success of firms changing locations. In a 1993 study, the management consultants McKinsey & Co. showed that the most successful international firms shared several common traits. Superior international performance appears to require widespread use of telecommunications to "link international managers with global electronic networks, such as video-conferencing and electronic mail," considered far more important than altering a company's international organizational structure through creation of global divisions, centers of excellence, and international business units.[67] According to an executive with a successful international firm, although communication has expanded the geographical reach of the span of control, with people reporting from Singapore, Sidney, Tokyo, Toronto, and Nashville, the persistence of the hierarchical reporting structure itself has not been challenged.[68] Though the McKinsey study was limited to forty-three large U.S. consumer companies, it does suggest that, in an international environment, telecommunications may play a more important role than organizational change in determining the success of a firm in overcoming distance constraints.

Studies suggest that when telecommunications changes the geography of firms, it leads managers to rethink production. For example, Pine's (1992) research on the process of production shows that multilocale companies linked by computer communication can shift from mass to specialized production or to *"mass customization."* Pine distinguishes three types of transition from mass production to mass customization, starting with a slow, incremental shift, typified by Toyota. The second type transforms the business in a short period of time, exemplified by Motorola, which, under strong competitive pressure, revamped the production of its pagers with a fully automated production process. Orders for customized pagers are transmitted to the Motorola plant in Florida, where they are manufactured, tested, and readied for delivery in less than two hours. Finally, some companies create new businesses geared to produce customized products at mass produced prices, for example, the on-demand CD. Furthermore, research on the process of production used to relegate transportation and communication to the distributional function, ancillary to the central act of making a good or service. Thinking is changing as, in Hall's view, companies "extend the concept of the integrated production line to include the wide-area transportation and communication network which supports that production line."[69]

Changes in the ways managers think about the relationship between location and production are connected to changes in their thinking about the location of labor, leading researchers to look at new forms of work dependent on advances in telecommunications. These include pure forms of telecommuting, in which workers carry out full-time jobs from computer communication links in the home. According to Mokhtarian, research on this pure form raised doubts about its long-range prospects, because the benefits did not outweigh the negative impacts, "including the psychological and professional need for face-to-face interaction, the desirability of a buffer between work and home, the importance of visibility to professional advancement."[70] Recent research responds to these concerns by rethinking the pure form of telecommuting. For example, though computers facilitate telecommuting, much of the information-related work completed in the home is done with plain old pen, paper, and telephone. Telecommuting, however, is rarely a full-time occupation, but, more often, a formalization of the practice of bringing work home from the office, or simply a part-time job. It is part of a generally recognized trend toward a more flexible workplace, including more part-time workers, and what a recent report referred to as a "contingency work force."[71] Finally, studies point to the growth of telecommuting work centers located outside but close to the home. These provide the employer with greater confidence in worker productivity, greater control over liability risks, and higher levels of security. For the worker, they offer opportunities for interaction, a work space away from home, and shared access to facilities and services not available at home. For example, the advertising agency Chiat/Day includes numerous mobile or virtual offices that provide professional staff with temporary work spaces, conference rooms, and portable telephones, fax machines, and computers, etc., for work locations that shift throughout the day. Chiat/Day executives resist calling their work reorganization telecommuting, because, "Rather than a suite in a skyscraper, a den at home or even the front seat of a car, proponents of the virtual office see it as a bubble of information created by new technologies."[72]

In general, computer communication, and the instantaneous linkages and delinkages it can provide, is leading businesses to question the boundaries between firms. For example, companies have used computer communication to tighten connections between retail companies and their producers and suppliers. Kmart linked its computer system with those of its top two hundred suppliers to provide warehouse and sales information on-line in return for faster, more frequent deliveries. As a result, suppliers can more easily forecast demand, and Kmart is able to strengthen its supply network. Similar linkages connect airlines to travel agents, manufacturers to terminals in the truck cabs of their distributors, and governments to customers seeking access to data. For some analysts, these new interdependencies signal a new "co-operative competitiveness" as firms share resources, such as banks operating over the same financial networks, to improve their individual competitive positions *and* to strengthen the overall position of the industry.[73] Aside from their admitted usefulness, terms like *cooperative competitiveness* suggest that computer communication is compelling a rethinking, perhaps a redefinition, of the firm.

Computer communication is leading to a rethinking of sovereignty or the appropriate boundaries in governance. Vernon and Spar (1989) and Wriston (1992a; 1992b) conclude that developments in computer communication hold profound implications for the location of sovereignty. The former see it as a fundamental driving force in the growth of interstate alliances, a qualitative change, they contend, in international political and economic relations:

This spectacular decline in the cost of moving goods, people, and—especially—information across national borders has left governments with little room for unilateral action and little choice but to find changed forms of mutual accommodation. With facsimile and telex facilities on tap in such far-off places as Beijing and Monrovia, with the containerization of sea and air freight available to all, international economic relations differ in kind as well as in volume from those of the 1950s.[74]

They anticipate a period of tension, because governments are not yet prepared to give up control over their traditional domain. Wriston, concentrating on the declining ability of governments to control flows of finance, concludes that these developments amount to the "twilight of sovereignty." Contrasting the present to a time, not too long ago, when a finance minister could declare that the nation was not satisfied with the rules of the international financial game and opt out, Wriston concludes, "Today, the new information standard is far more draconian than any previous arrangement, such as the gold standard or the Bretton Woods system, since there is no way for a nation to opt out."[75]

Conclusion: Computer Communication Breeds Locational Choice

First transportation and now computer communication are shrinking geographical space and expanding choice. One by one, temporal, economic, social, and cultural barriers have fallen to new waves of technology. The introduction of computer communication technology is similar to the process of electrification, beginning as a unique spectacle and evolving into an ordinary feature empowering practically all of life. The Great White Ways gave way to a powerful, if unspectacular, resource for breeding choice. Computer communication is still a distinct spectacle, the burgeoning Information Superhighway our Great White Way, but it, too, is on the way to normalization. If this pattern holds, computer communication will expand opportunities across the full range of social activities as it fades into the woodwork. The importance for decision-makers of proximity to communication networks will recede, just as proximity to water for transportation and power receded, and then the electrical grid. The process of normalization includes the integration of technologies into day-to-day life, enrichment of those systems infused with computer communication, the general expansion of choice, and the growth of factors other than tele-communications in decisionmaking about business location. The last includes labor costs, proximity to markets, suppliers, and competitors, as well as environmental considerations.

Smaller, faster, cheaper, and better computer communication technologies have not only diminished the importance of geography for business, they have also transformed it. In particular, telecommunications has advanced the dispersal of some organizational activities, primarily manufacturing and, increasingly, consumer services. Partly because of relative ease and partly because of cost savings, organizations have tended to disperse their more routine functions. Though telecommunications has multiplied the products or corporate services available, these have not been dispersed. The process of dispersal in manufacturing and consumer services has intensified the need to coordinate and control these functions in centralized locations. In essence, dispersal and centralization are part of the same process, making up the structural transformation of contemporary economic geography. How long this pattern can be sustained depends on how long it will take for computer communication to produce the virtual proximity needed to achieve the coordination and control that producer services require. It also depends on the social consequences of tendencies toward a deepening division between the professionals, managers, brokers, and others at the command centers of producer services and, at the other extreme, those who fall into the growing category of low-wage, part-time, temporary workers, whose jobs are readily subject to automation and relocation.

Much of the policy debate surrounding the introduction of new computer communication technologies has focused on the Information Superhighway. It has contributed to attracting wider attention to computer communication, but not always the right attention. The Great White Way drew people to electrification, but, as historians have shown, it also skewed public policy to emphasize electricity as a unique spectacle. Similarly, public policy about computer communication ought to mean more than maintaining the spectacle of the contemporary version of the Great White Way, because progress depends not on maintaining the distinct spectacle but on eliminating it, so that computer communication can grow into obscurity.

References

Abler, Ron, John S. Adam, and Peter Gould. *Spatial Organization*. Englewood Cliffs, N.J.: Prentice-Hall, 1971.

Abler, Ron, Donald Janelle, Allen Philbrick, and John Sommer. *Human Geography in a Shrinking World*. Belmont, Calif.: Wadsworth, 1975.

Beniger, James. *The Control Revolution*. Cambridge, Mass.: Harvard Univ. Press, 1986.

Best, Michael. *The New Competition: Institutions of Industrial Restructuring*. Cambridge: Mass.: Harvard Univ. Press, 1990.

Blainey, Geoffrey. *The Tyranny of Distance: How Distance Shaped Australia's History*. Melbourne: Sun Books, rev. ed., 1982.

Brauchli, Marcus W. "Bangalore Takes on Tasks a World Away: Foreign Companies Flock to India's High-Tech Capital." *Wall Street Journal*, Jan. 6, 1993.

Brunn, Stanley D., and Thomas R. Leinbach, eds. *Collapsing Space and Time: Geographic Aspects of Communication & Information*. London: HarperCollins Academic, 1991.

Castells, Manuel. *The Informational City: Information Technology, Economic Restructuring, and the Urban-Regional Process*. Oxford: Basil Blackwell, 1989.

Chandler, Alfred D., Jr. *The Visible Hand: The Managerial Revolution in American Business*. Cambridge, Mass.: Harvard Univ. Press, 1977.

Chapman, Keith, and David Walker. *Industrial Location: Principles and Policies*. Oxford: Basil Blackwell, 1987.

Coakley, Thomas P. *Command and Control for War and Peace*. Washington, D.C.: National Defense Univ., 1992.

Cohen, Stephen S., and John Zysman. *Manufacturing Matters—The Myth of the Post-Industrial Economy*. New York: Basic Books, 1987.

Daniels, Peter W. *Service Industries: A Geographical Appraisal*. New York: Methuen, 1985.

Davenport, Thomas, H. *Process Innovation: Reengineering Work through Information Technology*. Boston: Harvard Business School Press, 1993.

Davidow, William H., and Michael S. Malone. *The Virtual Corporation*. New York: HarperBusiness, 1992.

Dicken, Peter. *Global Shift*. New York: HarperCollins, 1986.

Ernst, M. L., A. G. Oettinger, A. W. Branscomb, J. S. Rubin, and J. Wikler. *Mastering the Changing Information World*. Norwood, N.J.: Ablex Publishing Corp., 1993.

Ettinger, Nancy, and Bradley Clay. "Spatial Divisions of Corporate Services Occupations in the United States, 1983–88." *Growth and Change* 22 (Winter 1991): 36–53.

Fierman, Jaclyn. "The Contingency Work Force." *Fortune*, Jan. 24, 1994, 30–36.

Fine, Philip. "Telecom Gives Faltering Towns New Life: Firms Find That Distance Is No Barrier to Running Back-Office Operations." *The Globe and Mail Report on Telecommunication*, Sept. 8, 1992, C8.

Friedmann, John. "The World City Hypothesis." *Development and Change* 17 (1986): 69–84.

Ganley, Oswald H. "Rewards and Risks of the Communications-and-Information-Dependent Global Financial Services Industries." *PIRP Perspectives*. Cambridge, Mass.: Harvard Univ. Program on Information Resources Policy, June 1992.

Gargan, Edward A. "India Among the Leaders in Software for Computers." *New York Times*, Dec. 29, 1993, A1, A7.

Garreau, Joel. *Edge Cities*. New York: Doubleday, 1988.

Greenhut, Melvin L. *Plant Location in Theory and in Practice: The Economics of Space*. Chapel Hill, N.C.: Univ. of North Carolina Press, 1956.

Hagerstrand, Torsten. *Diffusion of Innovation*. Translated by Allan Pred. Chicago: Univ. of Chicago Press, 1968.

Hepworth, Mark. *Geography of the Information Economy*. London: Belhaven Press, 1989.

Hepworth, Mark, and Ken Ducatel. *Transport in the Information Age: Wheels and Wires*. London: Belhaven Press; Transnete, the London Transport Technology Network, 1992.

Heskett, Jim. *Managing in the Service Economy*. Boston: Harvard Business School Press, 1986.

Hoover, Edgar M. *Location Theory and the Shoe and Leather Industry*. Cambridge, Mass.: Harvard Univ. Press, 1937.

Hughes, Thomas P. *American Genesis: A Century of Invention and Technological Enthusiasm*. New York: Penguin, 1989.

Isard, Walter. *Location and Space-Economy: A General Theory Relating to Industrial Location, Market Areas, Land Use, Trade, and Urban Structure*. Cambridge, Mass.: Technology Press of the Massachusetts Institute of Technology; New York: Wiley, 1956.

Janelle, Donald G. "Global Interdependence and Its Consequences." In *Collapsing Space and Time: Geographic Aspects of Communication and Information*, edited by Stanley D. Brunn and Thomas R. Leinbach, 49–81. London: HarperCollins Academic; Routledge, 1991.

Kilborn, Peter T. "Small Towns Grow Lonelier as Bus Stops Stopping." *New York Times*, July 11, 1991, A14.

King, Ralph T., Jr. "Quiet Boom: U.S. Service Exports Are Growing Rapidly, But Almost Unnoticed." *Wall Street Journal*, April 21, 1993, A1.

Kirn, T. J. "Growth and Change in the Service Sector of the U.S.: A Spatial Perspective." *Annals Assoc. of Amer. Geographers* 77, 3 (1987): 353–372.

Langdale, John V. "The Geography of International Business Telecommunications: The Role of Leased Networks." *Annals Assoc. Amer. Geographers* 79, 4 (1989): 501–522.

Lavey, Warren. G. *Transportation/Communication Considerations in the Location of Headquarters for Multi-Establishment Manufacturing Firms*. Cambridge, Mass.: Harvard Univ. Program on Information Technologies and Public Policy, Working Paper 74–9, August 1974.

Lawrence, Stephen H. *Centralization and Decentralization: The Compunications Connection*. Cambridge, Mass.: Harvard Univ. Program on Information Resources Policy, Incidental Paper, July 1983, I-83–2.

Leone, R. *Location of Manufacturing Activity in the New York Metropolitan Areas*. New York: N.B.E.R., 1974.

Lotochinski, Eugene B. Transcript of seminar presentation. Cambridge, Mass.: Harvard Univ., Program on Information Resources Policy, March 11, 1992.

Lowe, John C., and S. Moryadas. *The Geography of Movement*. Boston: Houghton Mifflin, 1975.

Lublin, Joann S. "Firms Ship Unit Headquarters Abroad." *Wall Street Journal*, Dec. 9, 1992, B1.

———. "Study Sees U.S. Businesses Stumbling On the Road Toward Globalization." *Wall Street Journal*, March 22, 1993.

MacDonald, Lawrence. "Software Concerns Thrive in Philippines: Cheap Labor Makes Data-Input Firms Big Exporters." *Wall Street Journal*, May 10, 1991, B-3a.

Malone, Thomas W., and John F. Rockart. "Computers, Networks and the Corporation." *Scientific American* 265, 3 (1991): 128–136.

March, James G., and Herbert A. Simon. *Organizations*. New York: Wiley, 1958.

McLaughlin, John F. "Unequal Access to Information Resources among Corporations: Causes and Implications." Paper presented to the Ninth World Communications Forum, Tokyo, draft, Oct. 5, 1992.

Mokhtarian, Patricia L. "Telecommuting and Travel: State of Practice, State of the Art." *Transportation* 18 (1991): 319–342.

Moulaert, Frank, Youssef Chikhaoui, and Faridah Djellal. "Locational Behaviour of French High-Tech Consultancy Firms." *Int. J. Urban and Reg. Res.* 15 (1991): 5–23.

Neuman, W. Russell. *The Future of the Mass Audience*. New York: Cambridge, 1991.

Nye, David E. *Electrifying America: Social Meanings of a New Technology*. Cambridge, Mass.: MIT Press, 1990.

O'Brien, Richard. *Global Financial Integration: The End of Geography?* New York: Council on Foreign Relations Press, 1992.

Oettinger, Anthony G. "Building Blocks and Bursting Bundles." In Ernst et al., *Mastering the Changing Information World*. Norwood, N.J.: Ablex Pub. Corp., 1993.

———. "Information Resources: Knowledge and Power in the 21st Century." *Science* 209 (1980): 191–198.

O'hUallachain, B. "Agglomeration of Services in American Metropolitan Areas." *Growth and Change* 20, 34–49.

Patton, Phil. "The Virtual Office Becomes Reality." *New York Times*, Oct. 28, 1993, C1–C2.

Peterson, Iver. "New Companies Bring Research to 'Video Valley.'" *New York Times*, July 5, 1992, "Metro Report," 19, 21.

Pine, B. Joseph. *Mass Customization*. Boston, Mass.: Harvard Business School Press, 1992.

Piore, Michael, and Charles F. Sabel. *The Second Industrial Divide: Possibilities for Prosperity*. New York: Basic Books, 1984.

Pool, Ithiel de Sola. *Forecasting the Telephone: A Retrospective Technology Assessment of the Telephone*. Norwood, N.J.: Ablex Pub. Corp., 1983.

Pred, Allan R. *Urban Growth and City-Systems in the United States, 1840–1860*. Cambridge, Mass.: Harvard Univ. Press, 1980.

————. *Urban Growth and the Circulation of Information: The United States System of Cities, 1790–1840*. Cambridge, Mass.: Harvard Univ. Press, 1973.

Sassen, Saskia. *The Global City: New York, London, Tokyo*. Princeton, N.J.: Princeton Univ. Press, 1991.

Saunders, Anthony. "New Communications Technologies, Banking, and Finance." In *New Directions in Telecommunications Policy*, edited by Paula R. Newberg, 266–289. Durham, N.C.: Duke Univ. Press, 1989.

Saunders, John. "GM's Just-in-Time Delivery Gives Union More Leverage." *The Globe and Mail Report on Business*, Sept. 7, 1992, B1.

Schnaar, Steven P. *Megamistakes: Forecasting and the Myth of Rapid Technological Change*. New York: The Free Press, 1989.

Scott, Allen J. *Metropolis: From the Division of Labor to Urban Form*. Berkeley: Univ. of California Press, 1988.

Solomon, Julie. "Corporate Elite Leaving Home Towns for Headquarters in Faraway Places." *Wall Street Journal*, Feb., 21, 1990, B1, B9.

Sudjic, Deyan. *The 100 Mile City*. London: Harper Collins, 1992.

Tapscott, Don. "Brain Storming: Creating the Company without Borders." *The Globe and Mail Report on Business*, Nov. 17, 1992, B24.

Tapscott, Don, and Art Caston. *Paradigm Shift: The New Promise of Information Technology*. New York: McGraw-Hill, 1993.

Thrift, Nigel, and Andrew Leyshon. "'The Gambling Propensity': Banks, Developing Country Debt Exposures and the New International Financial System." *Geoforum*, 19, 1 (1988): 55–69.

Townroe, Peter M. *Planning Industrial Location*. London: L. Hill, 1976.

Vance, James E., Jr. *Capturing the Horizon: The Historical Geography of Transportation*. New York: Harper & Row, 1986.

Vernon, Raymond. "Cities of the Next Century." *APA Journal* (Winter 1991): 3–6.

Vernon, Raymond, and Debora L. Spar. *Beyond Globalism: Remaking American Foreign Economic Policy*. New York: The Free Press, 1989.

Wheeler, J. O. "The Corporate Role of Large Metropolitan Areas in the United States." *Growth and Change* 19 (1989): 75–86.

Woytinsky, W. S., and E. S. Woytinsky. *World Commerce and Government: Trends and Outlook*. New York: Twentieth Century Fund, 1955.

Wriston, Walter. "The Decline of the Central Bankers." *New York Times*, Sept. 20, 1992a, 3–11.

―――. *The Twilight of Sovereignty*. New York: Scribner, 1992b.

Notes

1. Though a fresh wind might give them a best speed of six to seven knots, the English Pilgrims sailed to what became the United States in 1620 at an average of two miles per hour (Vance, 1986).

2. Woytinsky and Woytinsky, 1955: 306.

3. 1983: 45.

4. Dicken, 1986. Blainey's (1982) study of Australia's development provides some of the richest descriptive detail on the relationship between transportation and geography. Lawrence (1983) reminds us that it was not simply the speed of travel that attenuated geographical constraints but the regularity of service. For example, the development of packet ship service between New York and Liverpool was significant, because it regularized service, including message distribution service, between the two points.

5. Sassen, 1991; Garreau, 1988; Sudjic, 1992.

6. Janelle, 1991.

7. Woytinsky and Woytinsky, 1955.

8. It is hard to question the declining price–performance ratio of transportation technologies. Nevertheless, the curve does not travel in one direction for everyone who would travel. For example, recent attention has been directed to the impact on small towns of declining bus service (Kilborn, 1991).

9. Cf. Beniger, 1986.

10. Hepworth and Ducatel, 1992.

11. Abler, Janelle, Philbrick, and Sommer, 1975: 38–39.

12. Lawrence, 1983. For example, there is no difference between the speed of telephone message transmission in 1900 and 1994, but the system that brings people together in a telephone network has expanded over the years.

13. In Brunn and Leinbach, 1991.

14. According to McLaughlin (personal communication, 1993), however, despite the elimination of distance as a cost factor, people need to operate within reasonable proximity to major telecommunications networks. As networks expand, proximity will diminish as a problem.

15. General Motors (GM) learned the hard way that just-in-time inventory controls can have harmful consequences. These controls so tighten the network of producer-suppliers that in the event of a strike assembly plants close down more quickly. An August 1992 strike at the GM plant in Lordstown, Ohio, led almost immediately to plant shut-downs from Baltimore to Oklahoma. According to an industry consultant, "It just means you close it down in one day instead of two weeks" (Saunders, 1992). Ganley (1992) described the opportunities and challenges that telecommunications raise for networks of financial services companies.

16. Hagerstrand, 1968; Abler, Adam, and Gould, 1971.

17. 1975: 53.

18. 1975: 9.

19. Schnaar (1989) offers numerous examples of failed technological applications, what he calls "megamistakes," that document the need to focus on price–performance capabilities as an antidote to technological wanderlust.

20. 1975: 53. For example, much has been made of the likelihood that communication replaces transportation. But, for some, the reverse is likely to be the case, as the productivity gains from communication expand opportunities to travel, as communication broadens the range of social and economic relationships, and as it disperses residential settlements and deconcentrates businesses. Moreover, as the growth of transportation-based rapid-response systems demonstrates, electronic communication increases the productivity of transportation, i.e., call for a pizza over cooking dinner.

21. Cited in Nye, 1990: 38.

22. Nye, 1990: 35.

23. Hughes, 1981.

24. Nye, 1990: 66.

25. Nye, 1990: 35.

26. An aluminum plant is one among the exceptions.

27. Interview with the author, December 1992.

28. Chapman and Walker, 1987; Hoover, 1937; Isard, 1956.

29. March and Simon, 1958.

30. Interview by the author with John Petrillo, December 1992.

31. Interview with the author, March 1993.

32. Leone, 1974.

33. Solomon, 1990; Lublin, 1992.

34. Solomon, 1990.

35. Solomon concludes that relocation can also create disaffection. The Middletown plant erupted with its first strike the year top management moved and union members travelled to New Jersey to set up a picket line. Moreover, to overcome the feeling among corporate staffers in Ohio that they were "orphans" of a "caste system," Armco increased visits between Middletown and Parsippany and set up a staff newsletter.

36. Lublin, 1992.

37. Ibid.

38. Langdale, 1989.

39. 1991: 25.

40. Davenport, 1993: 53.

41. Saunders, 1989.

42. Fine, 1992: C8.

43. Brauchli, 1993: A4.

44. Gargan, 1993; Brauchli, 1993. Nevertheless, India's software firms have begun to worry that they may be stuck in the low value-added segments of the computer software industry.

45. *Japan Telescene*, Oct. 1, 1992.

46. King, 1993.

47. MacDonald, 1991.

48. *Boston Globe*, Nov. 22, 1992: 81.

49. Piore and Sabel, 1984; Scott, 1988.

50. 1987: 148. Offering a detailed analysis of what is now generally referred to as "the Third Italy," Best explains the value of geographical proximity for maintaining a sense of collective identity: "A carefully nurtured collective identity can potentially provide the social fabric which sustains cooperation in an industrial district as in

a corporation. Here again, the role of geographically concentrated small firms is important for an industrial district. For geographical proximity makes it possible for individuals to interact socially and politically as well as economically" (1990: 237–238).

51. Lublin, 1993: B4.

52. Sassen, 1991.

53. Sassen, 1991; see also Castells, 1989.

54. Daniels, 1985.

55. Daniels 1985; Sassen 1991.

56. Friedmann, 1986.

57. Castells, 1989; Sassen, 1991; O'Brien, 1992.

58. 1987: 208.

59. Hepworth, 1989; Sassen, 1991; Moulaert, Chikhaoui, and Djellal, 1991.

60. See also Kirn, 1987; O'hUallachain, 1989; Wheeler, 1988.

61. Sassen, 1991: 12.

62. Garreau, 1988.

63. Peterson, 1992.

64. 1991: 324.

65. The producers or marketers of technologies are not the only ones optimistic about the possibilities. According to a long-time student of business and cities, "High-definition TV and holographic processes promise to bring startlingly life-like quality to images projected on TV screens, perhaps enough to satisfy the needs of bankers negotiating with borrowers and auctioneers dealing with art buyers. It is possible that these developments will reduce the advantages of face-to-face communication sufficiently to weaken the centripetal pulls that have contributed to the growth of central business districts" (Vernon, 1991: 5).

66. Castells, 1989, Sassen, 1991, Sudjic, 1992.

67. Lublin, 1993.

68. Lotochinski, 1992.

69. Cited in Davidow and Malone, 1992: 137.

70. Mokhtarian, 1991: 320.

71. Fierman, 1994.

72. Patton, 1993: C2.

73. Tapscott and Caston, 1993; Heskett, 1986.

74. Vernon and Spar, 1989, 3.

75. 1992a: 11. In the same work, Wriston highlights the case of President François Mitterrand's Socialist government, which came to power in 1981: "The market took one look at his policies and within six months the capital flight forced him to reverse course."

II New Age Technology

3 A Convergence of Form and Function: Compunications Technologies

Anthony G. Oettinger

Once upon a time, people perceived computing and communications processes as distinct and independent from one another. After World War II, this view gradually shaded into a perception of computing and communications as bundled inextricably into computing-and-communications processes, compunications processes for short. The unity of computer and communications science and technology, a commonplace by the 1980s, was noteworthy years earlier. As I wrote in the late 1960s: "The spectacular growth of compunications fortunately has given us powerful tools and techniques for the quick handling of masses of data. (Computers and commmunications have long since become inseparable. It is time to reflect this union in the fusion of their names.)"[1]

A decade later it was widely understood that the unity of the scientific and technological base had implications for industry structure and that it had political overtones as well. In 1978, Simon Nora and Alain Minc wrote for the president of France: "This increasing interconnection between computer and telecommunications—which we will term 'telematics'—opens radically new horizons." Nora and Minc commented in a note that the neologism "telematics" "closely resembles the term used in the United States, 'compunication.'" They added: "The fact that the American term stresses the computer and ours the telecommunications aspect is not accidental. It expresses a set of power relationships that in France give the upper hand to the latter."[2]

In the 1940s, no one quite likely had seen even the basic unity itself. Claude Shannon, whose pioneering work did much to reveal that unity, described his seminal work as "a mathematical theory of communication." Wrote he: "The fundamental problem of communication is that of reproducing at one point either exactly or approximately a message selected at another point."[3]

The classical 1940s perception of computers shown in figure 3.1a saw them as bundles of five basic functions, none of them communications.

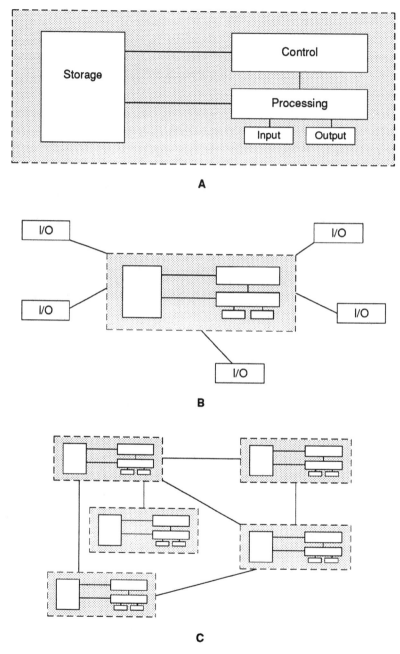

Figure 3.1   Evolving perceptions of computer systems

Processing is the computer's reason for being. Game playing, word processing, and number crunching are familiar examples of particular kinds of processing.

The built-in control function is what makes computers run automatically once someone has programmed them.

Storage plays two roles. Storage serves to remember the substance that is being processed. It also serves to remember the processing commands, the programmed commands that drive the control function. Storage, in short, is for both data and programs.

Even if capable of storing substance and of processing it under automatic control, a computer is worthless unless it can also get raw substance from its environment and put processed substance back into that environment. Hence the input function, as done by keyboards or joysticks, and the output function, as done by printers, monitors, even TV screens.

Figure 3.1a shows the processing, control, storage, input and output functions linked to symbolize the organic unity of these component functions of a computer.

That the links might also denote communications paths among the devices that do the five basic functions is at most an incidental perception in the classical view. The designer who worries about the innards of a machine might see communications paths. But communications paths are irrelevant to someone who is holding a common calculator in the palm of his or her hand or to someone who is looking at one of the dinosaur-sized early computers through the glass of a museum exhibit. The classical computer was self-contained except for the private communications between it and the fingers and the eyes of its owner. The communications function was inseparable from the computing function. It was, however, perceived as secondary if perceived at all. In the classical computer, the five functions all happen inside one box. That box fits in one hand or in one room. The hand or the room belong to one person or one organization. Under these circumstances, attention understandably focuses on computing, not on communications.

Computer-related communications became increasingly visible in the early 1950s, beginning with military systems. This perception diffused into the business and the academic worlds throughout the 1960s. Figure 3.1b suggests the focus of the newer perception. A computer mainframe, the classical computer of figure 3.1b, is seen as the center of the galaxy. Revolving around it are remote input/output devices of a kind that the 1980s came to call "dumb terminals." These satellites just accept input to the mainframe from a remote site and deliver output from the mainframe to the remote site.

All the smarts—the control functions—are in the mainframe, which is why it is the main frame. In this view, as it evolved through the 1960s, the terminals are perceived as doing no processing. Likewise, the communications links between the terminals and the mainframe are perceived as pure transmitters, like a splendidly caring, competent and inviolate postal service that transports an envelope and delivers it in precisely the mint condition in which it accepted it and, on the way, permits neither eyes nor hands to be laid on the letter inside. Another common figure of speech paints ideal communications links as technically totally transparent: The mainframe and the terminals see each other as if nothing more had come between them than when both of them were inside one box in the Eden of figure 3.1A. Institutionally, however, the mainframe and the terminals often have different owners. And the communications links are mostly supplied by one or more public utilities. Under these circumstances, attention begins to focus on communications as well as on computing, and the two are seen as belonging to different worlds.

By the 1970s the idea of distributed computing had become widespread (figure 3.1c). Many mainframes are linked to one another. Some of them are smart terminals. "Smart" only means that the terminals are less main than some other frames, the spectrum of available potency by now defying any neat dichotomy between smart mainframes and dumb terminals. Workload is shared among the sites in proportions that depend on the particulars of the services being rendered and of the prevailing costs or prices. Many more parties are involved than just the computer owners and the communications public utilities. Some are hybrids like Tymshare, a company which describes itself as having "since inception ... focused on practical timeshared use of computing, communications, and intricate online software to solve problems, manage information, and bring the intelligence of centralized data to a universe of users."[4] Others, like Dow Jones & Co., Inc., pull together under one corporate roof a variety of means for a variety of ends. Besides the *Wall Street Journal,* Dow Jones "publications and services include the computerized Dow Jones News/Retrieval ... [a] provider of electronically delivered business and financial information; Dow Jones News Service, which operates newswires and delivers information over radio, television and telephone; *Barron's* magazine, *American Demographics* and the *National Business Employment Weekly.*"[5] Planetwide and indeed galaxywide communications links have become essential system components.

Since the 1940s, the view from the communications standpoint has also changed. Classically, communications highlights the links in figure 3.1, while computing sees mainly the nodes that the links tie together. As late as 1980,

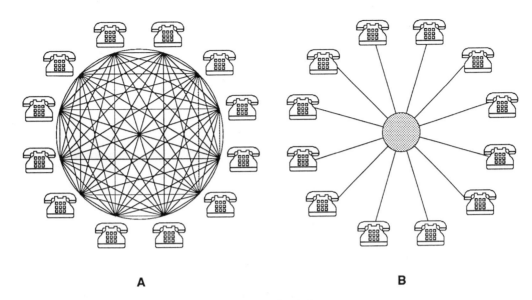

Figure 3.2 Communications links and switches

approximately 84% of the Bell System's annual telecommunications plant costs of some $40 billion were for links and only 16% for terminals.[6] But this understates and masks the importance of the role of the nodes within the system of links that ties together the terminals—the telephones, the computers, the answering machines—of the telephone companies' customers.

Coupling computing and communications within the telephone system makes it possible to avoid linking every customer directly to every other. For example, figure 3.2a shows the 66 lines it takes to connect each of 12 terminals directly to every other terminal. It would be economically absurd and physically impractical to hook up every telephone directly in this way to every other telephone. This would take ten million billion links just within the United States. Switches take care of this problem. Running one link from each of 12 terminals to a switch permits connecting any one terminal to any other (figure 3.2B) with only 12 links, 54 links fewer than the 66 links of figure 3.2a.

In its simplest conception, the switch of figure 3.2b allows only one conversation at a time. One trick in engineering real-life switches is to enable just enough conversations to go on simultaneously. If too few conversations are planned for, some customers trying to make calls don't even get a dial tone. Or, if the switch is overengineered, most of it will remain idle most of the time, adding an unnecessary cost for customers, stockholders or taxpayers to bear.

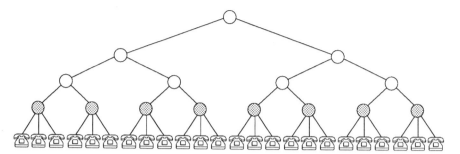

Figure 3.3 Link and switch patterns in actual telephone systems

As the number of telephones grows, and with it the amount of traffic and the distance between telephones, the single-switch arrangement of figure 3.2b rapidly gets uneconomical and impractical. Actual telephone networks use many switches interconnected as sketched in figure 3.3.[7]

In the early days of telephony, the switching took place literally on switchboards like that in figure 3.4. People named operators did the thinking to figure out which wire to plug into which hole to make the right connection. They also "forwarded calls to someone's likely location, took messages, and advised callers whom best to call for a solution to a plumbing or medical problem." To Almon Strowger, an undertaker in Kansas City, "these extra services reflected power that invited abuse, pure and simple. (He was not necessarily being paranoid. In the earlier years of phone service, there were many complaints of backtalk, biased service, and eavesdropping . . .)." This "drove Strowger to such a pitch of exasperation and inspiration that in 1889 he invented what he called the first 'girl-less, cussless telephone,' or, more neutrally, the automatic switch."[8] By 1980, the connections were made almost exclusively by automatic switches whose generic functions were precisely the generic functions of the classical computer of figure 3.1a.

The 1980s telephone switch differs from the 1980s mainframe or small terminal only in the specifics that define its mission as switching instead of game playing, word processing, air traffic controlling, number crunching, or what have you. Given a phone number as an input, the switching "computer" produces the right connection as its output. Seen in this light, the telephone network of figure 3.3 looks like a distributed computing system, and the distributed computing system of figure 3.1c looks like a communications network.

That there is a functional kinship of computing and communications as members of a common compunications species is made evident by figures 3.3

Figure 3.4   An early switch board

and 3.1C, either of which evokes the other; whether you see a distributed computing system or a communications network depends only on your mindset. That functional kinship is independent of the details of form. Once perceived, the functional kinship can be discerned as having been there all along, even when the only computers around were mechanical adding machines and when the control element of a switch was an operator's brain. But computing and communications are now kin in form as well as in function. Both sit on a common technological base of electro-optical digital formats and processes.

Notes

1. Oettinger, Anthony G. "Compunications in the National Decision-Making Process." In *Computers, Communications, and the Public Interest*, edited by Martin Greenberger. Baltimore: Johns Hopkins Univ. Press, 1971. For the record, the word

"compunications" was coined by my wife, Marilyn, when we were sitting in front of a fire in Harvard's Kendall House, on Sutton Island, Maine, in August of 1969.

2. Nora, Simon, and Alain Minc. *The Computerization of Society: A Report to the President of France.* Cambridge, Mass.: The MIT Press, 1980, 4, 178 n. 1.

3. Shannon, Claude E., and Warren Weaver. *The Mathematical Theory of Communication.* Urbana: University of Illinois Press, 1949, 3.

4. Tymshare Inc. Annual Report (1981), 5.

5. Dow Jones. Annual Report (1983), "Introduction."

6. Oettinger, Anthony G., and Carol L. Weinhaus. *Behind The Telephone Debates.* 3: *Federal/State Costing Methods: Who Controls the Dollars?* Cambridge: Program on Information Resources Policy, Harvard Univ., 1984.

7. Weinhaus, Carol L., and Anthony G. Oettinger. *Behind the Telephone Debates.* 1: *At the Heart of the Debates: Cost, Control and Ownership of the Existing Network.* Cambridge: Program on Information Resources Policy, Harvard Univ., 1985.

8. Hapgood, John. "The Connection." *Science '84* 5, 8 (Oct. 1984): 75.

4 Understanding Computers and Communications

Robert W. Lucky

Technology has been the enabling and driving force of the information age. It has created the opportunities, challenges, and problems that permeate this book. The purpose of this chapter is to discuss current trends in the technology of computer communications, and the implications of these trends on the world's telecommunications infrastructure.

It is difficult to write about technology in the abstract, as if it were something to be studied under a microscope, isolated, and grown in controlled cultures. More and more we have moved from the conception of technology as an independent thing to that of technology as an unfolding process, inextricably entangled with the social and economic fabrics of life.

The historic conception of technology as an isolated force was exemplified by the motto of the Century of Progress International Exposition held in 1933 in Chicago. This showplace of science and technology had a slogan that today sounds to us like a time capsule from a past civilization: "Science finds— industry applies—man conforms."

How quaint and simplistic this now seems! Certainly it is still true that science finds, although that phrase seems to suggest an aimless serendipity that today is less in evidence. Science finds where scientists are looking, and scientists look for the most part where they are paid to look.

It is also true that industry applies. However, the implication seems to be that industry has a compulsion to apply whatever science has found. We now realize that industry applications are not always a direct consequence of the findings of science. Industry chooses what it wishes to apply, and puts a spin on its applications—choices and spins dictated of necessity by the profit motive. Furthermore, industry often decides what it wishes science to find; these are not necessarily independent events.

The biggest disconnect with this 1933 slogan and today's environment is, of course, the last phrase—man conforms. What an antiquated phrase! The very idea today seems like a challenge. We do not conform! Technology offers many possibilities. We decide.

However, as quaint as the motto now sounds, there is a germ of underlying truth here. Technology cannot be undone, and there are many concepts of the digital world that force us inevitably to change our behavior, our laws, and ultimately, ourselves.

Technology Evolution

Billions of dollars of investment ride on being able to anticipate technological change and to understand its implications. Yet there seems to have been very little progress in our ability to make such predictions. Nearly every major technological revolution has been missed by the experts of the previous generation. Partly this is because of the vested interest that technologists have in their own existing areas of expertise, but it is also due to the chaotic nature of the market in which technology operates. Technological progress itself is inextricably interwoven with social and economic factors that often determine which technologies succeed and which fail.

It is often assumed that we cannot predict the future in technology because of the disruptions caused by unexpected, revolutionary inventions. Although these disruptive inventions do happen, the frequency is probably less often than people assume. Almost all the technology in telecommunications and computing today was known a decade ago. It is often said that "technology isn't the problem," or "we have all the technology we need." What is lacking is the ability to project the market acceptance of technologies and any semblance of insight into the future applications of these technologies.

Technology itself often follows a predictable path of progress. In telecommunications, the capacity of optical fibers follows a steady exponential expansion, while in computers and electronics, the size of memory, the clock speed, and the general capability of integrated circuit chips are entirely predictable.

Moore's Law

The single most important thing to know about the evolution of technology is Moore's Law. Most readers will already be familiar with this "law." However, it is still true today that the best of industry executives, engineers, and scientists fail to account for the enormous implications of this central concept.

Gordon Moore, a founder of Intel Corporation, observed in 1965 that the trend in the fabrication of solid state devices was for the dimensions of transistors to shrink by a factor of two every 18 months. Put simply, electronics doubles its power for a given cost every year and a half.

In the three decades since Moore made his observation, the industry has followed his prediction almost exactly. Many learned papers have been written during that period predicting the forthcoming end of this trend, but it continues unabated today. Papers projecting the end are still being written, accompanied with impressive physical, mathematical, and economic reasons why this rate of progress cannot continue. Yet it does.

Moore's Law is not a "law" of the physical world. It is merely an observation of industry behavior. It says that things in electronics get better, that they get better exponentially, and that this happens very fast. Some, even Gordon Moore himself, have conjectured that this is simply a self-fulfilling prophecy. Since all corporations know that progress must happen at a certain rate, they maintain that rate for fear of being left behind.

It is also possible that Moore's Law is much broader than it appears. Possibly it applies to all of technology, and has applied for centuries while we were unaware of its consequences or mechanisms. Perhaps it was only possible to be explicit about technological change in 1965 because the size of transistors gave us for the first time a quantitative measure of progress. If this is so, then we are embedded in an expanding universe of technology, where the dimensions of the world about us are forever changing in an exponential fashion.

The notion of exponential change is deceptively hard to understand intuitively. All of us are accustomed to linear projection. We seem to view the world through linear glasses—if something grows by a certain amount this year, it will grow an equal amount the next year. But according to Moore's Law, electronics that is twice as effective in a year and a half will be 16 times as effective in 6 years and over 1000 times as effective in 15 years. This implies periodic overthrows of everything we know. An executive in the telecommunications industry recently said that the problem he confronted was that the "mean time between decisions exceeded the mean time between surprises." Moore's Law guarantees the frequency of surprises.

Metcalfe's Law—Network Externalities

There is another "law" that affects the introduction of new technology—this time in an inhibiting fashion. Metcalfe's Law, also known to economists generally as the principle of network externalities, applies when the value of a new communications service depends on how many other users have adopted this service. If this is the case, then the early adopters of a given service or product are disincented, since the value they would obtain is very small in the absence of other users. In this situation, innovation is often throttled.

Metcalfe's Law often applies to communications services. A classic example, of course, is the videotelephone. There is no value in having the first videotelephone, and it only acquires value slowly as the population of users increases. If there are n users at a given time, then there are $n(n-1)$ possible one-way connections. Thus the value grows as the square of the number of users. The value starts slowly, then reaches some point where it begins to rise rapidly. It seems as if there needs to be a critical mass for takeoff, and that there is no way to achieve that critical mass, given the burden on initial subscribers.

Metcalfe's Law has defeated many technological possibilities, left stillborn at the starting gate of market penetration. Nonetheless, there are important examples of breakthroughs. For example, facsimile became a market success, but only after decades of technological viability. Even so, facsimile is a complex story, involving the evolution of standards, the inevitable progress of electronics, the equally inevitable progress in the efficiency of signal-processing algorithms, and the rise of the business need for messaging services.

Moore's and Metcalfe's laws make an interesting pair. In the communications field, Moore's Law guarantees the rise of capabilities, while Metcalfe's Law inhibits them from happening. Devices that appear to have little intrinsic value without the existence of a large networked community continue to diminish in cost themselves until they reach the point where the value and cost are commensurate. Thus Moore's Law in time can overcome Metcalfe's Law.

The Evolution of the World Wide Web

The most important case study in communications technology is the emergence of the World Wide Web. This revolutionary concept seemed to spring from nothingness into global ubiquity within the span of only two years. Yet its development was completely unforeseen in the industry—an industry that had pursued successive long and fruitless visions of videotelephony, home information systems, and video-on-demand, and had spent decades in the development of ISDN with no apparent application. It now seems incredible that no one had foreseen the emergence of the Web, but except for intimations in William Gibson's science fiction novel *Neuromancer*, there is no mention in either scientific literature or in popular fiction of this idea prior to its meteoric rise to popularity.

There is a popular notion that all technologies take 25 years from ideation to ubiquity. This has been true of radio, television, telephony, and many other technologies prevalent in everyday life. How, then, did the Web achieve such ubiquity in only a few years?

Well, the historians argue, the Web relied on the Internet, which in turn was enabled by the widespread adoption of personal computers. Surely this took 25 years. We might even carry this further. The personal computer would not have been possible without the microprocessor, which depended on the integrated circuit evolution, which itself evolved from the invention of the transistor, and so forth. By such arguments, nearly every development, it seems, could be traced back to antiquity.

Although the argument about the origin and length of gestation seems an exercise in futility, the important point is that many revolutions are enabled by a confluence of events. The seed of the revolution may not seem to lie in any individual trend, but in the timely meeting of two or more seemingly unrelated trends. In the case of the World Wide Web, the prevalence of PCs and the growing ubiquity of the Internet formed an explosive mixture ready to ignite. Perhaps no invention was really even required. The world was ready—it was time for the Web.

While this physical infrastructure was forming in the world's networks and on the desktops of users, there was a parallel evolution of standards for the display and transmission of graphical information. HTML, the hypertext markup language, and HTTP, hypertext transmission protocol, were unknown acronyms to the majority of technical people, let alone the lay public. But the definition of these standards that would enable the computers and networks to exchange rich mixtures of text and pictures was taking shape in Switzerland at the physics laboratory CERN, where Tim Berners-Lee was the principal champion.

The role of standards in today's information environment is critical, but often unpredictable. What is really important is that many users agree on doing something exactly the same way, so that everyone achieves the benefits of interoperability with everyone else. It is exactly the same concept of network externalities that is at work in Metcalfe's Law. An international standard can stimulate the market adoption of a particular approach, but it can also be ignored by the market. Unless users adopt a standard, it is like the proverbial tree falling in the forest without a sound. Standards are, for the most part, advisory. User coalitions or powerful corporations can force their own standards in a fascinating and ever-changing multiplayer game. Moreover, de facto standards often emerge from the marketplace itself.

So in the mid-1980s there was a prevalent physical infrastructure with latent capabilities and an abstract agreement on standards for graphics. One more development and two brilliant marketing ideas were required to jump-start the Web. The development was that of Mosaic at the National Center for Supercomputing Applications (NCSA) at the University of Illinois. Mosaic was the first browser, a type of program now known throughout the world for providing a simple point-and-click user interface to distributed information. Following the initial versions of Mosaic from NCSA, commercial browsers were popularized by Netscape and Microsoft, among others.

The revolutionary marketing ideas needed for the Web now seem obvious and ordinary. A decade ago, however, they were not at all obvious. One idea was to enable individual users to provide the content for the Web. The other idea was to give browsers free to everyone. Between these ideas, Metcalfe's Law was overcome. Even though browsers initially had almost no value, since there were no pages to browse, they could be obtained electronically at no cost. The price was directly related to the value. Thus browsers spread rapidly, just as their value began to build with the accumulation of Web pages.

Allowing the users to provide content was counter to every idea that had been held by industry. The telecommunications and computer industries had tried for a decade to develop and market remote access to information and entertainment held in centralized databases. This was the cornerstone of what were called "home information systems" that were given trials in many cities during the 1970s and 1980s with names like Prestel and Vientron. Later, the vision pursued by the industry was that of video-on-demand—the dream of providing access to every movie and television show ever made, like a giant video rental store, over a cable or telephone line. Virtually every large telecommunications company had trials and plans for video-on-demand, and the central multimedia servers required for content storage were being developed by Microsoft, Oracle, and others.

The Web exemplifies some powerful current trends—the empowerment of users, geographically distributed content, distributed intelligence, and intelligence and control at the periphery of the network. Another principle is that of open, standard interfaces that allow users and third parties to build new applications and capabilities upon a standardized infrastructure.

It is hard to criticize industry for pursuing the centralized approach. Imagine proposing the Web to a corporate board in 1985, and describing how browsers would be given away free, and how industry would depend upon the users to provide whatever content might appear. Even today many corporations wonder and worry about the business model for the Web, and few are making any profits at all.

The Evolution of Digital Telephony

Ironically, in 1876 when Alexander Graham Bell invented the telephone, there was already a nationwide, digital network in place. It was owned by Western Union, and it was the telegraph system.

Bell's invention was essentially the use of analog waves for the transmission of speech, rather than the dots and dashes used in Morse code for the transmission of text. The pressure waves caused by human speech in air were converted by a carbon microphone into an electrical wave, which was then transmitted over copper wires to a distant location.

Over the next century Bell's analog telephone replaced the telegraph as the chosen instrument of human communication. The telephone wires spanned the nation, a giant corporation came together and reigned as a monopoly, and the analog transmission and switching were progressively refined. The transmission medium, which began as copper wires, became microwave carrier, then coaxial cable, then partially satellite, and finally became primarily digital optical fiber. The switching, which began as manual patchcords, became rotary step-by-step switches, then electronically controlled relays, and finally centrally controlled digital switches.

The analog waves so naturally congruent to human speech were replaced gradually by their digital representation. With today's rise of the Internet, another revolution is now taking place in which the medium of exchange is not the bit itself, but a standardized envelope of bits known as a packet. In the succeeding sections we will follow the progress of the telephone infrastructure from waves to bits to packets. Why is the plant digital? Why packets? These are the questions we will seek to answer.

The Conception of Digital Telephony

The first big technological revolution after the telephone had spanned the nation was the digitization of the network. Curiously, the telephone infrastructure began its digitization about 1960, considerably before the concepts of the information age became popularly understood. When the world needed a digital infrastructure in later decades, the telephone system was already there—not because telephone engineers had foreseen the need for data, but rather because they had wanted a cheaper analog network for voice.

Just as the natural voice waveform is analog, so intrinsically are all transmission media. It takes an artificial discipline to impose a digital signal upon an analog world. As late as the mid-1950s, there seemed no reason to do this. The network was carefully crafted to convey a 3-kHz analog signal as the universal medium of exchange. The bandwidth of 3 kHz was calculated to be the smallest range of frequencies that would enable speech to seem perceptually unimpaired. This range of frequencies, roughly from 300 to 3000 Hz, would on a piano be the three octaves beginning at middle-C. Any more bandwidth was wasteful, while any less hurt the intelligibility of the speech. The scientific literature of that day had numerous studies of the "mean opinion score" of speech over a telephone connection, which was designed to be about a "4," where a "5" was equivalent to face-to-face conversation.

Pulse Code Modulation (PCM) was invented by Reeves of IT&T in 1939. In PCM the analog speech signal is converted to a stream of bits by sampling the signal at periodic intervals, and then representing the samples as digital approximations. As we shall see presently, the practice is to convert an analog voice signal into a 64-kilobit-per-second digital stream. In so doing, the bandwidth required for transmission becomes greatly expanded, and so engineers had little incentive to implement PCM for many years. The only application that seemed to call for PCM was that of encrypted speech during the war years immediately following Reeves' invention.

Analog to Digital Conversion

There is a famous theorem in communications technology, called the sampling theorem (Nyquist), that states that a bandlimited signal may be reconstructed exactly from samples taken at a rate of twice the highest frequency. So that if we assume on the safe side that speech has a 4-Hz bandwidth, then a sampling rate of 8000 samples per second could be used to reconstruct exactly the speech signal.

It may seem curious to the uninitiated that a signal can be reconstructed exactly from little snippets taken at regular intervals. Hasn't something been lost? What about the values of the signal in between the sampling instants?

The key here is the assumption that the signal is truly bandlimited. This means that the signal is constrained as to how fast it can change, since there are no "high frequencies" present. This implies a smoothness or predictability that enables the signal to be extrapolated between the sampling instants. In a sense this is a mathematical abstraction, since in theory no signal can be simultaneously time-limited and bandlimited. No matter—speech can be well reconstructed from samples taken at a rate of 8000 per second. There is no perceptible difference between the reconstructed and original signals.

After the speech signal has been sampled, it is translated into a stream of numbers. The next step is the approximation of these numbers as a sequence of bits. For example, the first sample might be 1.32956, or some such number. Transmitting the number exactly would require an infinite sequence of bits, but obviously no one is going to hear the difference if we truncate it somewhat. Even in everyday speech, the ambient noise in the room sets a lower threshold on how exactly the speech signal can be perceived.

Engineers determined that 8 bits were sufficient for intelligibility of speech. Thus every sample could ideally be represented as one of 256 possible values. It was found that the representation was better served by having a logarithmic spread of these values, so as to compress the extreme values and expand the smaller values. Again, the engineering of the network infrastructure was based entirely on the perceptual quality of speech transmission. In PCM the analog voice signal is converted to a stream of 8-bit numbers, occurring 8000 times a second, for a total of 64,000 bits per second. This is the standard digital representation of speech that is used in telephony today throughout the world.

The Philosophy of PCM

Now it is important to understand the implications of this conversion into a digital stream. We started with an analog signal that could be transmitted in a 3-kHz bandwidth. How much bandwidth does it now take to transmit the equivalent 64,000-bit-per-second digital stream? A rule of thumb is that it is possible to transmit a digital stream in a bandwidth of about half the bit rate. Thus the digital equivalent of the voice might require a bandwidth of 32 kHz—almost ten times what the original voice required! So why should anyone want to convert speech to digital format?

In the mid-1950s the answer to this question slowly permeated the scientific community. The reason why it was a good idea to convert the speech to bits was because, while an analog signal is fragile, bits are almost indestructible. This is one of the central tenets of the digital world. Since we know that a bit can only be a "1" or a "0," a "degraded" bit can be restored to its original perfection. In contrast, when an analog wave is degraded, there is no notion of how it can be restored.

Waves come and go, while bits are forever.

It seems miraculous that in the telephone network of the 1950s, voice signals were transmitted in analog form across the continent and around the world. Every source of noise or distortion during transmission would accumulate on this long path. Only the most careful design of equipment was able to convey intelligible speech at the other end of this long and tortuous pipe. If, on the other hand, the speech was converted to bits—even at the cost of greatly increased bandwidth—it was no longer necessary to carry the signal perfectly for long distances. Instead, it could be restored periodically before it had been seriously degraded. Again and again, the bit stream could be regenerated to its perfect original state.

The Digitization of the Telephone Infrastructure

In the first digital carrier system, commercialized in 1961, the digital voice signals were restored about every mile and a half. What a difference! Instead of having to traverse thousands of miles, the signal only had to travel a mile or so. Because it only had to negotiate such a short distance, many more voice channels could be transmitted over the same pair of wires—hence the economic argument for digitization.

The new digital carrier systems were rapidly installed in metropolitan areas, so that in the late 1970s most of the intracity transmission was digital. However, both the local loop and the long distance systems were still analog. The local loop—the last mile or two to the home—consisted of pairs of coppers wires, while intercity transmission was accomplished by modulated analog signals on coaxial cables and microwave carrier systems.

This was the point where one of the great disruptive inventions took place, when Corning announced that it had made an optical fiber sufficiently transparent to carry lightwave signals for about a mile. Very shortly thereafter, the telecommunications industry abandoned plans for more advanced microwave transmission systems, and concentrated fully on optical transmission. There were two important ramifications of this breakthrough. One was the startling promise of capacity that the fibers held—more than anyone at the time thought would ever be needed for any conceivable use of telecommunications. The other ramification of fibers was that they were inherently digital. The quality of analog transmission was so distorted that it seemed impossible to convey any degree of accuracy unless the signal was in the robust digital format. Incredibly, it was only a few short years later that AT&T wrote off its entire analog plant. The long distance network, thanks to fiber, had been suddenly digitized.

Thus the economics of voice telephony resulted in the central portion of the telecommunications network being digitized. This left, however, the local connections to the consumer still in analog format. The analog signals generated by the microphone in the telephone handset were transmitted over a pair of copper wires to the serving central office, usually a distance of one to three miles. At the central office the analog signal would be converted to a 64-kilobit-per-second digital signal, which would subsequently be interleaved in time with other digital streams for transmission over the long-haul facilities.

Although the end portion of the local connection to the home is essentially always analog, there has been a great penetration of a local digital carrier system, called *subscriber loop carrier*, which carries typically 24 interleaved digital streams into a neighborhood. At that neighborhood point the streams are converted into analog, and the copper wires fan out to serve a number of homes in the area. The effect is as if the central office had been moved closer to the home, but the ultimate connection at the subscriber is still an analog voice channel.

The Packet Revolution

The need for computer communications began to emerge in the late 1950s. At that time the goal was access to time-shared central computers. The telephone network had been designed solely for the transport of analog voice signals, so the only way to transport the computer data was to design apparatus to convert the data into voice-like analog signals. The units that did this conversion became known as modems. In this era only the Bell System was permitted to design and deploy equipment connected to the network, so the first modems were manufactured by Western Electric, and had a transmission speed of up to 300 bits per second. In the early 1960s progressively faster modems using better modulation formats were designed that provided transmission at 1200 and then 2400 bits per second.

Thus in the mid-1960s an increasing number of modems were being used to transmit computer data over the voice telephone network. At the same time, the interior network itself was being changed over to digital format. These two trends continued, so that in 1990 there were millions of modems connected to a network that was essentially entirely digital in its core. In spite of the digital network, the modems were still necessary to negotiate the two ends of the connection, which remain analog even today.

Consider when a home PC is connected to an Internet Service Provider (ISP). The bits generated by the PC for transmission are converted by the modem to an analog signal with voicelike bandwidth. This is done by very sophisticated techniques enabling transmission speeds of up to 33 kilobits per second. The modem's signal then travels about two miles to the serving central office, where it is sampled, quantized, and converted to a 64-kilobit-per-second digital stream. This stream is interleaved with many other streams, and transmitted as light pulses for long distances. Arriving at the distant central office, it is reconverted into an analog signal that closely resembles the original signal generated by the sending modem at the PC. This analog signal is sent the last mile or so to the ISP, where it is demodulated to regain the 33-kilobit-per-second digital information. It is ironic that the modems have to work so hard to realize only a fraction of the capacity of the digital stream that carries the signal through the long-haul network.

The newer technology of 56-kilobit modems is much more efficient in its use of the 64-kilobit network transmission. These modems rely on the Internet Service Provider having a digital connection directly to their computers, so that only the home PC end of the network is analog. In the downstream direction—from the ISP to the PC—a simpler and faster method of transmission is used that couples the high-speed data from the ISP directly onto the digital carrier.

While the access ends of an Internet connection are really a kluge of overlays to old technology, the backbone of the Internet is entirely different. It is there that a new paradigm for communications has taken shape—one that threatens to engulf and overwhelm the entire telecommunications infrastructure of the world. The Internet cloud itself—between ISPs and host computers—relies on the relaying of digital packets from one network node to another. The question now being asked everywhere is: Why shouldn't the entire network work this way?

Packet Switching

The conventional telephone network, called the PSTN (Public Switched Telephone Network), is analogous to the child's toy telephone where two tin cans are connected by a string. When a call is originated, the network predetermines a path that can be used to connect the caller A with called party B. Circuit switches are set so as to provide a full-time, two-way connection between the parties. Within the network each party has a 64-kilobit-per-second dedicated path to the other. The bits flow along this path whether or not the parties are actually talking to each other at the moment. It is as if the two parties had indeed installed a very long string between their tin can telephones.

Packet switching, originated by Paul Baran of Rand in 1964, uses a radically different philosophy. The analogy here is much like mailing information on postcards using the ordinary post office mail system. Each postcard has a place for an address, a return address, and a space for information. It is in effect an envelope of bits. If the message to be sent is larger than the space available on a single postcard, then it is broken up and sent in a series of postcards, each of which is numbered so that the recipient can reassemble the entire message. As the postcard (packet) is routed through the network, the address is read at each switching node, and placed in a queue for transmission to another node that is closer to the intended destination.

In packet switching there is nothing similar to the string connecting the tin cans. There is no predetermined, full-time path between the sender and receiver. The packets flow autonomously, each in ignorance of the progress of its fellow packets, each trying to wend its way towards its intended destination.

The efficiency and flexibility advantages of packet switching over circuit switching in the case of computer communications are large and obvious. Only as much of the transmission and switching capacity as is needed for a given communication is used. When no information is being sent, there are no packets, and other connections can use the common facilities. When, on the other hand, a great deal of information is required to be sent by a particular connection, then it can surge a great many packets onto the network to meet its sudden demand.

In packet switching the similarities to transportation systems are inescapable. Each packet of bits is like an automobile entering a highway. Network nodes are like interchanges. Rush hours and traffic jams are possible. Queues for entrance to the highway or to a particular exit can develop and build. None of this can happen, of course, with the circuit-switched PSTN. If you have dial-tone, then you are assigned a path and guaranteed your own private road. It is, however, an expensive and inflexible road that you own for the duration of your call.

Rules of the Road for Packets—TCP/IP

When the Department of Defense funded the development of ARPANET in the early 1970s to connect between large computer sites, the academic community (although corporations—Bolt Beranek and Newman in particular—also played key roles) designed the network from the beginning using packet switching. The early protocol that defined the rules for traffic flow of the packets was replaced in 1975 with a protocol known as TCP/IP (Transmission Control Protocol/Internet Protocol) written by Robert Kahn and Vinton Cerf. For many years thereafter the name "TCP/IP" was unknown to all but a few hundred academic designers. Today TCP/IP is the center of a multibillion dollar industry, and dominates networking technology everywhere. The last frontier is whether it takes over from the PSTN for voice telephony.

There is a particular genius in the conception of IP, seen clearly in the retro-spective vision from a quarter century after its origin. IP is the protocol for handling packets inside the network, whereas TCP is the end-to-end protocol that resides at the user and host sites at the periphery of the network. Crudely speaking, TCP cleans up any mess left by the inside protocol, IP. (Obviously, it does more than that!) The genius in IP is its utter simplicity: It defines the minimum set of features necessary to connect packets at a network node—no more, no less. Because of this simplicity, it has been possible through the years to use IP for many more purposes than were ever envisioned when it was designed, while maintaining interconnectivity between disparate networks.

A view that designers have of today's TCP/IP network is that of an hourglass. The wide bottom of the hourglass consists of all the physical media used for electrical and photonic transmission of bits—fibers, copper wires, microwave signals, etc. The wide top of the hourglass consists of all the applications that require communications—speech, video, email, file transfer, etc. The center of the hourglass—the narrow waist—is the restriction to IP inside the network. To pass through this point, all signals must be formatted in IP packets, no matter what application they represent or what media on which they flow.

There isn't very much to an IP packet. Basically, it is a blank postcard with designated spaces for intended and return addresses, as well as an expandable space for the information bits representing the payload. There are some other bits in the packet which are used for special purposes, such as "time to live" indicators that ensure packets get thrown away before they clog the network like dead letters. But IP packets can get lost, be ruined with errors, get out of sequence, get misdirected—whatever. IP itself doesn't care. Somebody else will have to worry about this later. This is a job for an end-to-end protocol such as TCP. If such features had been built into IP, as they were with some earlier protocols, it would have been at a cost of efficiency and flexibility.

In spite of the genius of IP, in a different world another protocol might have triumphed in the market. Other protocols were formulated and implemented through the years, including even a protocol adopted as a standard by the Department of Defense, called GOSIP. The success of TCP/IP has some similarity to that of the Web, in that early versions of it were given away free, and were integrated into the UNIX operating systems, which had achieved a great deal of academic popularity. UNIX itself achieved much of that popularity by being given free to universities by AT&T. Perhaps it comes down to the sign hung in one executive's office: Deployment wins.

The addressing scheme used in the Internet also differs conceptually from that used in the PSTN. In telephony, for historical reasons, the telephone number is related to a place, rather than a person. In the access network and switching system, the telephone number is something that is physically wired. Moreover, the telephone number is confined to something that can be dialed by the old rotary phones—usually a meaningless sequence of digits.

In the Internet, in contrast to the PSTN, the domain name address is alphanumeric, mnemonic, and not at all coupled to a geographical location. Adding a new customer, or changing an address, is a process of registration in a database, not rewiring. When a user sends an email or requests a Web page, say http://www.harvard.edu or www.bellcore.com, it is first necessary to translate this domain name address to an IP address that locates the recipient in the physical hierarchy of systems that comprise the vast Internet. The domain name is forwarded up the hierarchy of domain name servers, asking successive network servers if they know the translation to the actual address being requested. Ultimately, if lower level name servers are unable to supply the data, the request reaches the root server for the top level domain (.com in this example), which by definition knows all the next-lower translations within its domain. The network address, a sequence of digits, is returned to the user, and is applied to succeeding packets in the email or Web page.

With the meteoric rise of the Internet, the traffic on the telephone network that represents data, rather than speech, has been rising exponentially. Unfortunately, there is no reliable way to estimate the actual data traffic. However, it is believed that data and voice traffic are now about equal. While the voice traffic grows at the historical rate of 3–6%, the data traffic is growing at the alarming rate of roughly 300% annually. If the current growth rates maintain, the data traffic will overwhelm the speech traffic in the first years of the 21st century. The great majority of this data traffic originates in the TCP/IP protocol.

The Internet today rides as an overlay to the pre-existing voice telephone network. As such, it has been in some ways a parasite, living off the nourishment of its host. However, with the sudden and dramatic rise of Internet users and traffic, a new possibility has arisen. Is it possible that the parasite could eat the host? With this fear in mind, there is much discussion today about whether the telecommunications infrastructure should be entirely converted to the Internet model. This would be a complete reversal of the current paradigm. Instead of data riding on a voice network, we would have voice riding on a network designed for data.

The appeal of a packet-switched, Internet model is best dramatized by the comparison in size and economics between a packet router and a typical end office circuit switch, such as the Lucent ESS#5. The router looks like a desktop computer, while the circuit switch looks more like a small building. There is a visceral appeal to the former. Moreover, the idea of having one common format—the data packet—as the only traffic type in the network has both a practical and philosophical attraction. But the immediate question to resolve in the case of packet switching is its ability to handle voice traffic.

Circuit switching seems naturally adapted to voice. The speech signal is continuous and real time, and goes only in general to a single predetermined destination. In contrast, packet switching seems ill adapted to speech. The packets are asynchronous, unreliable, and suffer variable amounts of transmission delay. They can even arrive out of order at the receiver. Even today many telephone engineers argue that carrying voice by data packets simply doesn't make sense. Why do such an unnatural thing?

Today there is a small amount of voice traffic on the Internet. For the most part this is hobby traffic, like the Morse code transmissions of radio amateurs of a previous era. The quality of transmission is poor, and the ease of use is relatively awkward. Aside from the hobby appeal, there is only one compelling reason for voice on Internet today, and that is the evasion of the existing tariff structure, which imposes a usage-based access fee on all voice traffic except that from the Internet. This is an artificial inducement that cuts the price of communications by about half for domestic traffic and much more for international calls. While this might not be a lasting advantage, it has served to stimulate the technology of voice on the Internet.

Even though the reasons for voice over packets today are artificial, there are reasons why in the future packet switching might be a good way to carry voice. First, packet switching offers a considerable multiplexing advantage over circuit switching, possibly by as much as a factor of 30. For example, voice conversations typically are active in only one direction at a time, saving a factor of 2 in bandwidth for the use of as-needed packet switching. Additionally, there are pauses in conversation that further save bandwidth.

The big savings for voice over packets, however, is in the efficiency of speech coding itself. Since the voice standard of 64 kilobits per second was set for the telephone network, there have been almost 40 years of progress in speech coding. Today excellent quality speech can be coded at about 8 kilobits per second—a factor of 8 more efficient than was possible in 1960. Realizing the efficiency of modern speech coding is possible on the Internet because the coding is not fixed within the network, but can be arbitrarily chosen by the users at the periphery of the network—an important principle in the philosophy of the Internet.

In addition to bandwidth efficiency and less expensive switching, there are potential advantages in the flexibility of packet switching for voice. Since the users can choose their own coding, it is even possible to send high-fidelity, stereo speech. A more compelling advantage, however, is in the integration of speech with the data environment. Multimedia formats can be integrated with speech, and signaling (network control, such as call setup) can be embedded into the Internet connection carrying the speech. The entire environment can be integrated on the work desktop, and Internet domain name addresses can be used interchangeably with ordinary telephone numbers.

While there are certainly advantages to the integration of the voice and data networks, the original objections to sending voice with packets need to be discussed. It is still true that speech is continuous, while packets are sporadic. It is also true that the reliability of packet transmission is a problem for high-quality speech. Probably the worst problem is neither of these but the inherent delays in the transmission of packets over the Internet. We are very sensitive to delays of more than about one-quarter second in speech transmission, as most of us have experienced with satellite telephony. In typical PC-based systems for IP-telephony today the processing delays are considerably more than this critical value.

In spite of the difficulties of handling speech on a packet network, the problems are not insurmountable. A better quality of service on the Internet would help cure the network delay and lost packet difficulties. The delays inherent in today's PC client software for packet voice will be minimized in future systems. A number of companies are now making systems that work directly from one canonical "black" telephone to another, using Internet packet technology within the network. The advantage of this network-based solution is that it eliminates the PC software delay, and permits intelligent integration of the PSTN and Internet.

If today's trends continue, the network of the near future will be entirely packet switched. We will have accomplished the third of three great revolutions. First was the voice telephone network. Connecting the nation took about 50 years. Next was the digital revolution, which required perhaps 25 years. Most recently we have the packet revolution, which measured from the start of ARPANET has also taken about 25 years.

The Quest for Bandwidth

There is an historical trend in the consumption of bandwidth. Whatever bandwidth is available at a given time seems insufficient. Users demand more bandwidth, while communications designers insist that there must be a sufficiency for all foreseeable applications. The problem in the past has always been that the actual future applications were not in the foreseeable category. Nonetheless, the trend has always been evident—while we cannot predict the future uses of bandwidth, we know that more will always be required.

The backbone is always the most amenable portion of the network for upgrading. There is an economy of scale that enables technological solutions to bandwidth enhancement. When a user pays $20 a month to an ISP for Internet service, something like 50 cents or a dollar of this monthly fee goes to the backbone provider. Thus, for example, the backbone investment could be doubled with almost no impact on the price of service.

The backbone traffic is currently growing at an annual rate estimated at 250–1000%. If such a growth were to continue, it would imply that in about six years we would need a network almost a thousand times larger than that today. In other words, today's network would be almost irrelevant to the network in the near future. To some people this seems marvelous, to others impossible. The latter group argues that this growth rate cannot be maintained, that some Malthusian principle will limit the growth.

What are the components of today's traffic growth? First, we should note that the majority of this growth is from enterprise extranets—businesses implementing their own IP networks from leased digital circuits. New businesses and new users join the fray every day. In the Internet itself, the growth in hosts has maintained at 100% annual rate for more than a decade. (Recent measurements indicate that this rate may be slowing somewhat, however.) So there are more users, and those users are staying on longer, and are increasingly using applications that require more bandwidth.

Looking at potential increases, we might assume that the number of users continues to double annually. There are about 100 million users of the Internet today. While these users are spending more time on the Internet, in contrast to other activities such as television, the amount of time spent by an individual obviously cannot increase indefinitely. If the average Internet user spends an hour a day now, how much more is possible? Perhaps as much as a factor of 4, but more is hard to envision. Meanwhile, the applications might go from casual Web browsing to watching full-time video—perhaps a bandwidth increase of a few thousand bits per second to a megabit per second. Putting these factors together, we might see bandwidth increasing at a 300% annual rate for at least another half-dozen years. Moreover, history has shown us that it is dangerous to predict future uses of bandwidth. We have always been wrong in the past, and there is no reason to believe that pattern will not continue.

Inside the network a new technology, called dense wavelength division multiplexing (DWDM), is emerging at exactly the right time to satisfy today's enormous bandwidth demands. DWDM upgrades existing optical fiber transmission systems by allowing multiple wavelengths to be transmitted simultaneously, each wavelength carrying its own high-speed data stream. Wavelengths on the fiber are like colors in the visible spectrum, so that we might think of one data stream being carried by "red" light, another by "green," and so forth. (Since the actual wavelengths involved are in the infrared spectrum, they are not visible.)

In just the last two or three years the number of wavelengths that can be multiplexed on a single fiber has gone from 2 to 40. In addition the speed of transmission at each wavelength has increased by a factor of 4, going from 2.5 gigabits per second to 10 gigabits per second. Thus there has been almost a factor of 100 increase in the capacity of fiber systems in the last couple of years.

The new fiber technology has enabled new entrants to the long-distance telecommunications market to implement entirely new national and worldwide fiber networks quickly and at lower cost than that of existing carriers. Qwest and Level 3 are new companies that have already begun the rewiring of the world with DWDM. Meanwhile, the traditional long-distance carriers are upgrading their capacities, but in some cases are hampered by right-of-way issues or their own earlier investment decisions in the conduit space and number of strands allowed for future growth. The Internet traffic explosion has invalidated their previous network planning assumptions.

Aside from the better utilization of the fiber spectrum, bandwidth is also gained by the use of better compression technology. We have already noted that one of the advantages of packet voice is that it can use more modern speech coding technology—8 kilobits per second, as opposed to 64 kilobits per second in the standard PSTN encoding. In the transmission of images, the JPEG compression of bit-mapped images can save an order of magnitude in the number of bits required. In video transmission, MPEG2 has made digital video possible, giving many more channels to direct broadcast video systems. Improvements continue to be made, and there is a kind of Moore's Law curve in compression technology that buys us continually increased bandwidth relative to our needs.

There is much argument about whether in long-distance transmission there is a glut of capacity or a shortage. Are we bandwidth-rich or bandwidth-poor? On the side of rich, we have the huge increase in capacity offered by DWDM and the extensive new fiber networks being installed. On the side of bandwidth poor, we have the 300–1000% annual traffic growth in data, and the emergence of broadband, multimedia applications. So far it seems a close call, with capacity and need fairly well balanced. If the balance would begin to tip one way or the other, it would have serious implications to the business models of companies in the telecommunications field.

The real problem in the bandwidth demand is the access bottleneck. How do we get multimegabit streams to the home and the small office? Large offices are not an issue, since wherever there is an aggregated demand, as in a corporation, the economics allow the leasing of high-capacity fiber. But in the home and small office regime, there is no economy of scale; and regardless of the capabilities of technology, issues of expense dominate the arguments.

There are many technologies that can be used to enable broadband data to the home, including traditional copper pairs, fiber, coax, wireless, satellites, airships, and packet radio. The very existence of so many alternatives indicates that none of them is a clear winner. There are enthusiastic proponents and investors behind every one of these possibilities, with little likelihood of any shakeout in the near future.

In a preplanned world, fiber would be a logical choice for consumer access. A new fiber installation is possibly no more expensive than using copper, and it would offer a dedicated and almost limitless bandwidth for the future. The problem is that an extensive rewiring of neighborhoods for fiber access would require a large investment with a considerable associated risk and a long period for recovery. If in the meantime a new solution, such as wireless, should emerge, the investors could be stuck with the sunk cost of an unused fiber network.

Disincented to run fiber directly to the home itself, the telephone companies instead put fiber into neighborhood nodes, and now depend on the traditional copper wire pair for the final connection to the home. Depending on the length of this copper pair, it is possible to send data at rates as high as 52 megabits per second. More typical, however, would be a rate of 1.5 megabits per second over a loop length of 2 miles using a modem pair called ADSL (asymmetric digital subscriber loop). A number of different modem technologies are currently being developed with various acronyms. The family name "DSL" or "xDSL" is usually used to refer to the general technology of sending digits over the local copper loop.

DSL technology is currently the access method of choice for the operating telephone companies. Its advantages are a reasonably high data rate, dedicated per-subscriber capacity, and—most importantly—incremental investment. Moreover, since DSL brings packets directly into the central office, the traffic can bypass the existing circuit switch, and be sent to a router. Thus DSL would enable the evolution of the PSTN towards a packet network—an evolution which is greatly complicated by the preponderance of voiceband modems that depend on analog, circuit-switched connections.

Despite these considerable advantages, there are drawbacks for DSL technology. Most of these disadvantages directly bear on the economics. Most importantly, how expensive is it to provision DSL over the great variety of loops currently in existence? Some fraction of customers will be at the end of a loop that is too long or has poor performance for other reasons. Any custom engineering would require expensive attention, and at present there is not enough experience to be able to quantify this cost.

The DSL modems are still rather expensive, and there is no single standard that permits a mass, competitive market to emerge. However, both of these problems should be solved in the near future.

The best alternative to DSL today is the cable modem. The great majority of homes in the United States are already passed by coaxial cable. Modern cable systems have a gigahertz of bandwidth that is shared among several hundred homes in a neighborhood. That bandwidth can be allocated flexibly for both broadcast and two-way data channels. Cable modems have speeds of as much as 30 megabits per second in the downstream direction. However, this total rate is shared among all users in that branch of the system.

The advantages of cable modems are that it is a relatively low-cost add-on to the existing infrastructure. Unlike the telephone companies, the cable companies do not have other data services that might be cannibalized by the cable modem. To some degree, the fact that the cable modem uses a shared bandwidth is an advantage. This means that heavier users can take more as needed from the light users at a given time. However, the shared bandwidth brings disadvantages, centered around the possible deterioration of the environment through excess traffic or accumulated noise.

Other proposed broadband connection technologies involve wireless transmission, whether terrestrial, airship, or satellite. For each of these possibilities there are economic tradeoffs involving the total bandwidth and the number of users. Spot beams for the satellites and sectorized antennas in terrestrial systems allow the available spectrum to be reused among sets of users. At present, however, wireless systems have been predicated on voice traffic, so that permitting many data users at megabit speeds may be uneconomical in today's architectures. A number of companies are challenging the assumptions of wireless for data, so it would be premature to believe that broadband data will not be delivered by wireless technology in the future.

Conclusion—Back to Moore's Law

This chapter started with some comments about Moore's Law and the changing price/performance of silicon technology. We need now to recast the packet revolution in this light. While computers have been able to take advantage of Moore's Law, exponentially increasing their performance for a given price, it seems that communications has not followed suit. To highlight this disparity, people have often quoted in jest a similar law that says that communications doubles its cost-effectiveness every century. The question is: Can Moore's Law be applied to communications, and is packet switching the means of its application?

Clearly, the silicon chips inside switches and transmission equipment follow Moore's Law, doubling their cost-effectiveness at approximately 18-month intervals. However, there are many costly components that are not primarily silicon and do not follow Moore's Law, such as cabinets, power supplies, wiring, etc. Thus the cost-effectiveness of traditional circuit-switching equipment is doubling at about 80-month intervals—considerably slower than Moore's Law.

Packet switches, on the other hand, are progressing much more rapidly, with doubling periods of 10–20 months. While it is tempting to find some intrinsic technological reason why this is much better than the pace of circuit-switching progress, the truth is more likely to be simply that the world is now working on packet switches. If an army of people were put together to rethink circuit switches, they could probably match this pace, but that is not the case—packet switches are the fashion of today. Just as Moore's Law itself may be a self-fulfilling prophecy, the technologies that are in fashion at any given time show the most dramatic progress, and leave their competitors behind even as they gain more and more adherents.

There is another important consideration in the economics of packet switching, and that is the migration of cost and intelligence to the periphery of the network. One reason that the old circuit switches were so expensive is that they supported the dumbest terminal imaginable—the common telephone. All the intelligence was centralized in the network so that the peripheral devices could be very inexpensive. Since there were so many telephones on the periphery, this seemed like a good engineering choice.

In an IP network, on the other hand, there needs to be considerable intelligence at the periphery. In fact, we assume that there is a computer or its equivalent at the end of the network in order to execute the complexities of the transport protocols. A packet network may be envisioned as a very cheap network with a $2000 telephone, while a circuit-switched network is an expensive network connected to a $20 telephone.

Curiously, the economics of these two contrasting philosophies may be a standoff. The telephone plant in the United States today is said to represent a $300 billion investment. If, alternatively, the plant were free and there were 150 million computers connected at the periphery, the total cost would be almost the same. Of course, in the latter case, it is often argued that the computers have other uses, and that only a portion of their cost is attributable to telecommunications.

With packet switches showing exponential cost improvement and optical transmission following an even faster progress (about 12-month doubling), the equipment cost for telecommunications is plummeting. The capital cost per bit transmitted is rapidly approaching zero. At any given time, however, the mix of equipment in the telecommunications plant ranges from the latest technology to that which may be 30 to 40 years old. The average depreciation period of telecommunications equipment is more than a decade, which may not be appropriate for today's rapidly changing technology.

The dynamics of technology change have given the opportunity for many new entrants into the telecommunications business. At any given time the new technology is much more cost-effective than that used in the plants of the established companies. Start-ups can build entire infrastructures for a fraction of the cost spent by the incumbents. With the technology revolutions of today this causes an instability in the telecom business environment. Every six months it seems that a new company is bragging about rewiring the world and wiping out the existing carriers in the process.

Moore's Law, of course, only applies to the technology of communications. Most of the cost in traditional telecommunications is not in the capital equipment, but rather in the operational expense. The real expense in telecom is in maintenance, billing, customer care, provisioning, administration, and so forth.

These are people expenses, and the only way that these can be reduced is to steadily decrease the number of people required per access line. In fact, this reduction has occurred throughout this century, but on a pace much slower than that of progress in electronics.

Because of the dominance of operational costs in telecom, some people argue that a packet-switched network will ultimately be no less expensive than a circuit-switched plant. While this argument is far from resolved, there exist opportunities to lower the operational expense in the new networks. We have already noted, for example, that in the PSTN each new customer requires considerable labor, while in an IP network it is conceivable that the new terminal could be automatically recognized and registered electronically.

The economics of the new networks are also determined by innovative business plans, which may bear more on the cost of providing service than the actual technology. Today's long-distance service providers are burdened with high marketing costs. Carriers which sell exclusively to a small set of large industrial companies do not suffer this expense. Moreover, if the new companies do not bill by the minute and mile, they do not need the extensive infrastructure for measurement and processing of data that is required to render such bills.

After decades of relative stagnation, it now appears that telecommunications is indeed following Moore's Law. Bits are getting cheaper, and they are getting cheaper very fast. Going back to the motto of the Chicago Exposition, science has found a better way to communicate, industry has applied this technology, and now it remains for humankind to explore and innovate the wonderful new uses of plentiful bandwidth.

Bibliography

Brooks, J. *Telephone—The First Hundred Years*, Harper & Row, 1976.

Gilder, G. "Angst and Awe on the Internet." *Forbes ASAP*, Febrary 1996.

Gilder, G. "Fiber Keeps Its Promise." *Forbes ASAP*, April 1997.

Gilder, G. "Metcalfe's Law and Legacy." *Forbes ASAP*, September 1993.

Gilder, G. "The Bandwidth Tidal Wave." *Forbes ASAP*, December 1994.

Lucky, R. W. "New Communications Services—What Does Society Want?" *Proceedings of the IEEE* 85, no. 10:1536–1543.

Peterson, L. L., and Davie, B. S. *Computer Networks*, Morgan Kaufmann, 1996.

National Research Council. "Realizing the Information Future." National Academy Press, 1994.

Pierce, J. R., and Noll, A. M. *Signals*. Scientific American Library, 1990.

Schaller, R. R. "Moore's Law: Past, Present, and Future." *IEEE Spectrum* 34, no. 6:52–59.

Sevcik, P. J. "Why Circuit Switching Is Doomed." *Business Communications Review*, September 1997.

5 Understanding Digital

Anthony G. Oettinger

Analog and digital formats and processes are two distinctive ways of handling information substance. Both are age-old. Analog formats directly mimic substance. The drawing of a cat, an analog format, both looks like a cat and refers to it. Digital formats and processes mimic substance, if at all, only indirectly. The word "cat," a digital format, does not look like a cat at all but nonetheless refers to one.

Both the drawing and the word are meant to evoke a particular cat or the general idea of cats, but each does the job differently and each does it more or less faithfully. Neither an analog nor a digital format necessarily is what it evokes; either one just denotes, connotes, or represents, with all the frailties and ambiguities inherent in the tie between a sign and what it signifies.

The analog drawing of a cat and the digital word "cat" demonstrate that both analog and digital formats are familiar and ubiquitous. They have long been so, just as gravity, or rather its effects, was familiar and ubiquitous long before Isaac Newton explained it more profoundly and with greater practical import than anyone before him.

The contemporary attractiveness of digital formats stems in part from a self-conscious and deep understanding, reached only within the last half-century, of the properties of these formats. It stems also from the invention of practical electro-optical processors capable of putting digital formats through useful processes of increasing complexity, at increasing speed and with decreasing cost. The rest of this paper describes how that came about and why it is likely to go on for the foreseeable future. To pave the way, this section sketches familiar digital formats a bit more but not much more precisely than by pointing to the word for a cat and differentiating it from a picture of a cat. More specific detail about less familiar but increasingly important digital formats then follows.

All digital formats have in common their foundation of alphabets and arrays. This very text is in a digital format built on an alphabet that includes the familiar 26-letter roman alphabet, augmented by punctuation marks, spaces, ampersands and the like. The array of this text—or of any English text—is an imaginary endless sequence of imaginary empty slots. By convention each slot either is empty or else it has in it a single character drawn from the alphabet and nothing else. Anything else, like a smudge, is meaningless. In conventional and contemporary Western practice, the imaginary sequence, when filled for real, is broken up into horizontal line segments which are read from left to right and packed into pages which in turn are folded and bound into books. Israelis agree to read their arrays from right to left and Japanese from top to bottom. Scrolls, not folios, predominated under older Western technologies.

The way we write numbers is another familiar digital format. The set of ten familiar arabic numerals "$0, 1, 2, \ldots 9$" is the alphabet of a digital format built on an array that is an imaginary sequence of empty slots with names like "ones' place," "tens' place" and so on. If the sequence is cut into two pieces, one going to the left of a decimal point and the other going to the right, the integer places to the left of the decimal are named as above and the fraction places to the right are called "tenths' place," "hundredths' place," and so on.

The typewriter is a familiar mechanical digital processor designed to lay out, on sheets of paper, digital formats with slots filled by characters drawn from the literal and numeral alphabets available on its keyboard. The newer electronic word processor is like the typewriter and then some. Both the word processor and the typewriter supplanted or at least supplemented ball point pens, fountain pens, goose-quill pens, and other processors. But the format of English writing has always been essentially a digital format. For an example of a shift from analog writing to digital writing, one must reach back to the evolution of hieroglyphics from analog pictograms to digital abstract symbols for sounds.[1]

Analog and digital formats are often intermingled, as in analog and digital watches. Both kinds of watches mimic the flow of time. The conventional watch does this with a swinging pendulum or a flywheel driving an escapement. More modern watches do it with a vibrating quartz crystal.[2]

In a watch with a traditional analog readout, the time-mimicking process drives two or three hands. The angular position of each hand is analogous to time. For the short hand the dial is read in hours, for the longer hand the face is read in minutes, and for the longest hand the face is read in seconds. In a watch with digital readout, the time-mimicking process drives a digital counter that is faster and smaller than fingers or toes or than the beads of an abacus. Figure

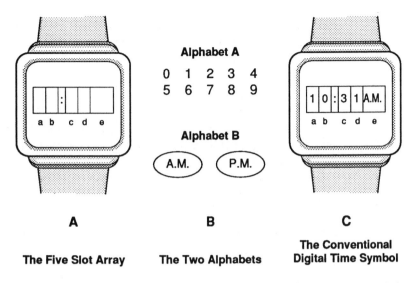

A

B

C

The Five Slot Array   **The Two Alphabets**   **The Conventional
Digital Time Symbol**

Figure 5.1   A digital watch readout. a. The five-slot array. b. The two alphabets. c. The conventional digital time symbol

5.1 shows the digital alphabets and arrays that portray a digital count on the watch's face.

Figure 5.1a shows the five-slot array of a simple digital watch face. Slots *a* and *b* are for numerals chosen from alphabet *A* in figure 5.1b. The prevailing convention is to read that pair of numerals as hours. Slots *c* and *d* are also for numerals from alphabet *A*, but the prevailing convention is to read that pair as minutes. The fixed ":" reminds us of the convention. Slot *e* is reserved for a symbol drawn from the two-symbol alphabet *B* (figure 5.1b). Figure 5.1c shows a complete conventional digital readout.

The combinations "A.M." and "P.M." are circled in figure 5.1b to underscore that each is essentially monolithic according to our watch-reading conventions. The components "A," "P," "M," and "." make each symbol self-explanatory at least for literate folks. Some digital watches tag mornings with a "*" and afternoons with a blank, or vice-versa. The "*," "blank" alphabet is not self-explanatory. Unlike the long-stable conventions for analog watch faces, digital watch-reading conventions were still fluid in the early 1980s; and both watch-setting and watch-reading conventions still varied confusingly from watch to watch, even for watches from one manufacturer.

Watches intermingle analog and digital formats and processes in yet another way. The traditional analog watch readout illustrates how. The angular positions of the hour, minute, and second hands are respectively analogous to hours, minutes, and seconds. But, looked at as a whole, the readout appears as a digital array of three slots: an hours' slot, a minutes' slot, and a seconds' slot or position. Instead of being strung out on a line like the letters in this sentence, these three slots are piled one on top of the other, and told apart mainly by the size and speed of their respective hands.

It is each position in this superimposed array that has an analog format. Instead of being filled by a symbol picked from some finite and discrete alphabet of letters or numerals, each position is filled by an infinitely and continously varying angular position of a hand. The hand position is analogous to the flow of time in units of hours, minutes, and seconds respectively. Ordinary writing occasionally plays similar tricks. In the linear digital arrays that name t-bar ski-lifts and that name the C-clamps that hold pieces of wood together while the glue dries, the letters *t* and *C* serve as analog pictograms and not as arbitrary digital symbols.

Perceptions of what is analog and what is digital are relative in still another sense. Typing, as mentioned earlier, is an essentially digital process. Symbols, picked from among the alphabet available on the keyboard, are strung out in a linear array on the page. But reproducing a typed page in a dry copier or by photography is an analog process. The copier or the camera is made to deliver shapes as exactly analogous to the original as possible. The copier and the camera treat doodles as faithfully as they treat typed words. Where the ink shapes on the page came from matters not when a newspaper is used to wrap up fish. It matters not when the printed page is a graphic object to be copied. It matters only when the printed page is used as a digital format for substance. What a printed page is at any given moment depends on what convention you follow when you look at it at that moment.

Pictorial analogies are often approximated by digital processes. The arrays of black dots and white blanks that make up the traditional half-tone pictures in newspapers are one example of digitized analogies. In a digital watch display or a digital calculator display, an analog of the shape of each conventional numeral is synthesized by turning on or off one or more of seven elements in the array shown in figure 5.2.

Laborious spacing, line-feeding, and key-pecking can produce a crude half-tone picture on a typewriter, a process few people have the patience to carry out. The process gets easier when computer driven. On October 24, 1965, a forgotten hero named H. P. Peterson cranked out "Mona by the Numbers," a half-tone Mona Lisa, at Control Data Corporation's Digigraphics Laboratories.

Figure 5.2   Digital array to synthesize shapes of numerals

Later on, anyone's picture by the numbers could be had for a few dollars in a few minutes at most any carnival or fair (figures 5.3a and 5.3b).

Digital formats themselves sometimes incorporate valuable analogies! Moving the decimal point in a conventional arabic numeral one place to the left is like dividing the named number by ten. Moving the decimal point one place to the right is like multiplying the named number by ten. The size of a number expressed in arabic notation is thus easier to estimate at a glance than the size of a number expressed in roman notation: where the leftmost nonzero digit sits relative to the decimal point tells the story.

Information substance is necessarily always embodied in some material format and processed by some energy-consuming processor. Historically, certain kinds of substance bundles have been linked up with certain format-and-process bundles—that is, with certain technologies. Figure 5.4 lists a sample of such bundles.

In its time, each of these bundles became attractive for some combination of economic, technical, esthetic, political, and other reasons. Whole industries, like the newspaper, radio, TV, movie, or record industries, were founded on particular associations of specific kinds of substance with specific kinds of technologies under specific economic, social, and political conditions.

The following sections sketch the reasons why electro-optical digital formats and processes have become so very attractive compared to other available formats and processes.

Abundance: Why Electro-Optical Digital Formats Are Better

The following claims—to increasing versatility and economic and other efficiencies—are substantiated in the remainder of this paper:

Figure 5.3a Mona by the numbers

Figure 5.3b Mona by the numbers: Digital detail of the smile

- Every intrinsically analog format is sharply limited in its range of application: It must resemble the substance it embodies. Intrinsically digital formats are based on arbitrary alphabets linked only by convention to what they embody. They are therefore in principle more versatile than analog formats. They can be built in arrays not limited to slots strung out indefinitely along a line, but laid out in two, three, or more conceptual dimensions. Such digital arrays can be devised to embody any substance whatever, as precisely as desired. Most especially, digital arrays can mimic analog formats as closely as desired.

- In practice, digital arrays can be handled by electro-optical digital compunications processors that have cost and performance characteristics superior to

| Substance | Format | | | |
| | Analog | | Digital | |
	Processor	Analogy	Processor	• Alphabet • Array
Time of day	Traditional watch	Angle of hand to minute or hour	Digital watch	• numerals and am/pm indications • four digit positions and one am/pm position
Ideas (musical)	Record player – – – – – – – – Cassette player	Depth or width of groove to loudness and pitch Strength of magnetization to loudness and pitch	Digital record player	• bits • positions in sequence
Ideas (verbal)	Person speaking	Amount of exertion of vocal chords on air to loudness and pitch	Person writing phonetic transcription Person writing script or print characters	• phonetic symbols • positions on line • letters, numerals and punctuation marks • positions on line
Ideas (pictorial realism)	Person painting	Disposition of pigment on canvas to real world color patterns	Newspaper half tone photo processor	• dot or no dot • two dimensional grid
Any type of substance	None	None	Compunications systems	• arbitary alphabet • multi-dimensional grid

Figure 5.4   Historical combinations of substance, format, and process

those of mechanical digital processors and to those of both mechanical and electronic analog processors.

The relative advantage of digital over analog formats and processors is likely to keep growing.

The arbitrary relationship that convention sets between substance and a digital format confers great versatility. A picture of a cat has to look like a cat or it won't work, at least not as an analog format. The convention that the word "cat" means cat is arbitrary. Some other digital format would serve as well, like "chat" in French or "Katze" in German.

It is far from self-evident that arbitrariness necessarily means useful versatility. The Tower of Babel story testifies to a contrary tendency. One problem is that arbitrary conventions have to be learned. A rose is a rose is a rose. The ability to identify a picture of a cat with a cat, once one has seen a cat, is either innate in people or learned in earliest childhood. But, although every normal child masters the arbitrary conventions or at least the rudiments of spoken language in his or her daily family setting, industrialized nations have had to invest heavily in literacy training.

Literacy training means, among other things, propagating the subtler conventions of standardized spoken language, hammering in the arbitrary convention that "c," "a," "t" is the written format for the spoken English word "cat," and sorting out the different sounds that convention arbitrarily links to the same letters in "although," "bough," and "tough." These tasks are not easy: witness the perennial controversies over why kids can't read and over how best to teach them. Industrialized nations invest less heavily, but still substantially, in teaching foreign languages, which means among other things clueing English speakers in on the alien conventions that "chat" means cat in French but "Katze" means cat in German.

The versatility that comes from arbitrary ties between a digital symbol and the substance it stands for is of net value only if it confers advantages that outweigh the bother of tieing and untieing arbitrary substance, format, and process bundles. Historical changes in ordinary language give evidence of one kind of recurring perception of a positive net value of versatility. The most frequently used words in all languages ultimately get the shortest strings of phonemes or of letters. The words "I," "the," "yes," "no," spoken or written, are English examples. The evolution of certain familiar conventional expressions from "horseless carriage" or "automobile" to "car" or "auto" and from "television" to "TV" illustrates how shifts in symbolic conventions mirror shifts in the frequency of reference to the symbolized substance.

In processes based on electro-optical digital formats, the costs of versatility in money or in convenience are down sharply from the costs of versatility in digital processes that rely on flesh-and-blood-brain formats or on mechanical formats.

One case in point is the user-friendly personal computers that began to get widely popular in the early 1980s. In part what made them friendly was exploiting the increasingly cheap versatility of microcomputers and their software. For example, someone could choose to name data or commands by such diverse alternative format-and-process combinations as touching a spot on a screen, pointing at the spot by moving a cursor by key, by "mouse," or even by voice, typing a name in full, using abbreviations, and so on, depending on personal predilections or the stage of developing skills. The machine, properly programmed, could effectively and affordably track shifts in conventions. Putting the burden of adaptation on the machine makes the shift to its formats as effective and as unselfconscious as the accommodation between one's feet and a really good, not to say foot-friendly, pair of new shoes.

There are three main reasons why electro-optical digital processes became more versatile and less costly than any others known in the 1980s:

First, electro-optical digital processes make it much easier and therefore more advantageous than mechanical or known biological processes, analog or digital, to switch from format to format for best effects at different stages of different processes. Depending on what the process does to the substance embodied in the format and depending on who or what the processor is, one format can make doing it easier, cheaper, faster, more reliable, more intelligible (or more of many other desirable properties) than some other format. Multiplying by 10 is easy in our conventional decimal digital notation, but the Mayan convention was better for multiplying by 5 or by 20. Switching back and forth between conventions is not something people like to do. But it's cheap and easy for electro-optical digital processors.

Second, the precision of analog formats is more severely limited by the laws of nature than is the precision of digital formats. Why this should be so is more apparent from the two formats for the number 3.34 in figure 5.5 than it is from the two formats for a cat. The arabic numeral "3.34" on the face of the digital calculator makes the value of the number evident at a glance. Estimating where the hairline is between the 3-mark and the 4-mark on the slide rule analog for-

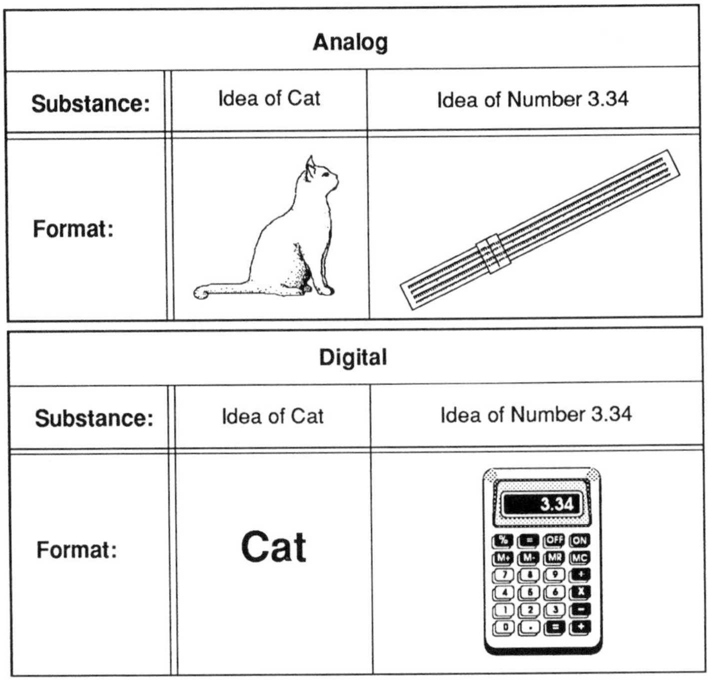

Analog		
Substance:	Idea of Cat	Idea of Number 3.34
Format:		

Digital		
Substance:	Idea of Cat	Idea of Number 3.34
Format:	**Cat**	

Figure 5.5   Analog and digital cats and numbers

mat is not so easy. One could put additional marks between the 3-mark and the 4-mark. If the size of the slide rule is fixed, that tactic quickly founders on how finely the lines can be engraved or, even if finely engraved, then on how finely they can be seen by the naked eye. In any case, lines finer than the molecular structure of the slide rule are impossible in this world. If, instead, the slide rule is made bigger and bigger, it quickly gets unwieldy.

There is no theoretical limit to the precision of the digital format. In principle, an infinite number of decimal places can be strung on both sides of the decimal point. In practice, too, the number of places can easily be enlarged: writing out a dozen or so decimal places is no great strain on either hand or paper. Practical slide rules are good for three or four places at most. In 1980, eight-place calculators had become common at less than $10, and slide rules had become obsolete. A picture may be worth a thousand words, but thousands of words come easily in both the digital spoken and the digital written ordinary language. Speaking another word—in an additional time slot—is easy and

Properties of formats		Electro-optical digital advantage
Analog	Digital	
Analogical relationship to substance	Arbitrary relationship to substance	Versatility
Precision limited in practice	Precision unlimited in practice	Precision and reliability
Linear processes needed to preserve analogy	Fundamentally nonlinear	Abundance and low cost

Figure 5.6   Advantages of electro-optical digital formats

cheap. Adding another page—additional slots—to a letter or to a manuscript is also easy and cheap.

The theoretically unlimited precision of digital formats has a more subtle but enormously important and practical value: Their precision enables the creation of digital processes of arbitrarily high reliability, almost independent of the reliability of the physical building blocks that might be used to carry out real digital processes on real material formats with real energy-consuming processors.

Digital processors are far more reliable in practice than analog processors partly because the real-world building blocks for digital tokens and for their digital processors are intrinsically reasonably reliable. Mostly, however, digital processors are so very reliable because of the understanding, developed after World War II, of how to build up large digital systems that are more reliable than any of their individual parts.

Third, realizing the potential versatility, precision, and reliability of digital processes is possible because digital formats and processes can be realized by exploiting so-called nonlinear materials. Contrasted to the so-called linear materials that are necessary for analog processors, nonlinear materials are vastly more abundant and cheap. In particular, the nonlinear silicon that's at the base of the electro-optical devices of the 1980s comes from a raw material that is found everywhere and that is literally dirt cheap—namely, sand.

The greater versatility, precision, reliability, abundance, and low cost of electro-optical digital formats are, as summarized in figure 5.6, the practical keys to unlocking the vast and versatile powers of electro-optical digital processes.

Dirt Cheap Is Spelled "Nonlinear"

Digital formats have always had one peculiar in-principle advantage over analog formats. This advantage accounts for why ordinary languages the world over ultimately evolved as digital phonemic and graphemic systems, and not as analog onomatopoeic or pictographic systems. But languages got that way by just growing. People have caught on explicitly to the digital advantage only within the last century. The source of this advantage is reliance by digital formats on a ubiquitous property of the physical materials and processes that happen to be at hand abundantly in this, the only universe we know. That very property of physical materials and processes also happens to be disastrous for analog formats.

The High Cost of Linearity

Analog formats and processes must rely on physical materials and processes that are linear in a sense that will be made plain shortly. But most of this world's physical materials and processes are nonlinear. Various tours-de-force can make them seem more linear than they are. But that is usually over a narrow range of usefulness and at relatively high expense. Digital formats and processes thrive on cheap nonlinearity.

Whether, at any given time and for some specific purpose, practical analog formats and processes are preferred over practical digital formats and processes or vice-versa depends on the relative costs of analog and digital systems over the desired range of performance. Theoretical understanding developed since the 1930s and electro-optical materials developed since the 1950s have tipped the balance increasingly in favor of digital systems.

Materials that can be fashioned into physical formats, or tokens, that are appropriately analogous to some given information substance, are not easy to find, not easy to fashion, and not easy to keep faithfully analogous. The history of representational painting from caveman to Leonardo da Vinci attests to that. Only within the last century have techniques been achieved for making sizeable magnifying glasses or eyeglass lenses that will not make straight lines look curved or white paper look like the rainbow. Some rather effective analog formats and processors have nonetheless been fashioned. Many have to work with more than one material and more than one process to do their job.

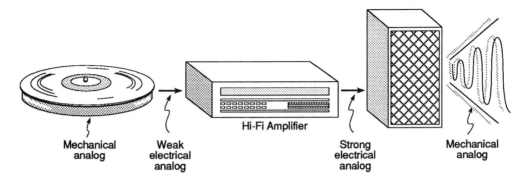

Figure 5.7 An analog transducer

Figure 5.7 depicts how a hi-fi system uses both mechanical and electrical analog tokens and processors. The aim is to preserve analogies so that the music from the loudspeaker is just like the music on the record, only audible. Evanescent sound-in-air is how the music was embodied at the moment when it was recorded as the more stable groove-in-disk token and how it must be embodied once again to be heard. A sound-in-air embodiment expresses substance—musical ideas—by variations in air pressure—compressions and rarefactions—around the normal resting state. A pattern of air-pressure variation over time is converted at the recording studio into a mechanical pattern in the grooves of the record, then by the hi-fi tone arm into an electrical pattern, both the latter analogous to the original pattern of pressure variation. If all goes well, what finally emerges from the loudspeaker sounds satisfactorily like what went into the recording.

The ultimate analogy is identity, when two patterns are one and the same. Identity is not only rare but also pretty useless in this instance. Music played loudly is not identical to music played softly. The weak electrical analog produced by a phono tone arm is not identical with the strong electrical analog that comes out of the hi-fi amplifier and is fed to the speakers. What makes the magnified image analogous to the picture seen without magnifying glass, the loud music analogous to the soft, the strong electrical signal analogous to the weak, and the electrical signal analogous to the sound-in-air is not identity but proportionality. The size of the picture or the size of the sound may change, but when everything is kept in exact proportion—even through several transmutations, as in going from sound-in-air to mechanical to electrical to sound-in-air—people perceive the result as the same picture, only bigger, or the same music, only louder—not as a different picture or a different music.

"Transducer" is the name for either an abstract process or else a concrete processor that converts one abstract format or its concrete token to another. The hi-fi amplifier in figure 5.7 is a transducer that turns weak electrical analog tokens into strong electrical analog tokens. Microphones are transducers that turn sound-in-air tokens into electrical tokens; speakers are transducers that do the reverse.

A not just high fidelity but perfect fidelity transducer would preserve proportions exactly, no matter what the circumstances: for picture small or large; in light bright or dim; for sound loud or soft; for bass drum or for piccolo. There is no such thing as perfect fidelity in the real analog world, not even at the most exorbitant hi-fi prices. The way our world happens to be built, there are, to the best of our knowledge, no materials suitable for making analog tokens and analog transducers that will faithfully preserve proportions under all but a limited range of conditions. A conceptual bridge that René Descartes built in the 17th century between Greek and Arabic ideas helps to explain why this is so.

What makes a three-inch square proportional to a one-inch square and keeps it looking like a square is that each side of the larger square is precisely three times the length of a side of the one-inch square. If the length of one side of the small square were multiplied by three and each of the others by something else, a cockeyed four-sided figure would ensue. The trick here, obscure to the Ancients, but casually evident to most educated Moderns, is to multiply everything exactly by three, the proportionality factor.

Proportionality as a geometric idea was well understood by the sculptors and the architects of ancient Greece. Euclid gave it formal elaboration. Multiplication is an arithmetic or algebraic idea. As a process applied to two numbers, multiplication is an algorithm from the Arabic culture. In linking the Greek geometric tradition to the Arabic arithmetic and algebraic tradition with his analytical geometry, Descartes also made explicit the following kinship among proportionality, multiplication, and smooth straight lines.

The distance that a car will travel at a constant speed is proportional to the time spent traveling. Traveling at 55 mph takes you 55 miles in one hour, 110 miles in two hours, and so on. Multiplying time on the road by speed, the proportionality constant, gives the distance traveled. In arithmetic and algebraic terms, Distance = Speed × Time.

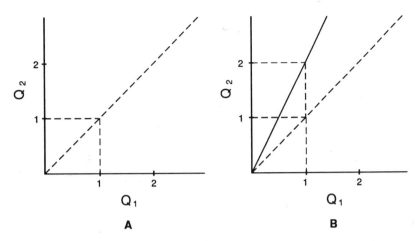

Figure 5.8 Proportionality and linearity

Figure 5.8 expresses this proportionality in terms of Cartesian analytical geometry. For speeds of 1 mph and 2 mph respectively, the Cartesian planes of figures 5.8a and 5.8b show smooth straight lines that plot how distance is related to time by speed, the proportionality constant. In figure 5.8a, Distance $= 1 \times$ Time to depict a speed of 1 mph. When the speed is 1 mph, the distance after one hour is one mile, as marked by the horizontal and vertical dashed lines in figure 5.8a. After two hours, the distance is two miles, and so on. The solid straight line in figure 5.8b plots how a speed of 2 mph relates distance to time. The formula is Distance $= 2 \times$ Time. After one hour, the distance traveled at 2 mph is two miles, not one. The greater proportionality constant gives a steeper straight line.

Arithmetic and algebra express the kinship between a quantity $Q2$ related to another quantity $Q1$ by a proportionality constant P by the multiplication $Q2 = P \times Q1$. This kinship is expressed geometrically in the Cartesian plane by a smooth straight line. The greater the proportionality constant P, the steeper the smooth straight line. The phrase "$Q2$ is linear in $Q1$" expresses the geometric aspect of the relationship between $Q2$ and $Q1$.

A nonlinear relationship is one where the change in $Q2$ is not proportional to the change in $Q1$ for at least some values of $Q1$. For instance, figure 5.9a plots what happens to $Q2$, $100 left in the bank at 10% a year compounded once a year at year's end, over the time $Q1$ that the money is kept in the bank. $Q2$ is not proportional to $Q1$, so the plot is called nonlinear even though it is made up

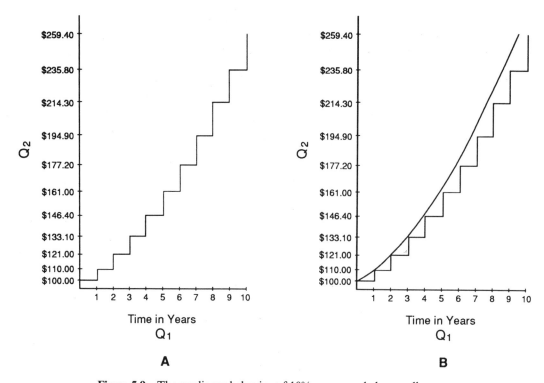

Figure 5.9 The nonlinear behavior of 10% compounded annually

of little choppy straight line segments. When interest is compounded continuously, the smooth but nonetheless nonlinear curve of figure 5.8b expresses the relationship between $Q2$ and $Q1$. Only a smooth straight line, as in figures 5.8a and 5.8b, expresses a direct proportionality and only a direct proportionality is expressible as a smooth straight line.

Euclid, visiting a Radio Shack today, might say that a transducer (figure 5.10a) has "perfect-fi" if its output is proportional to its input. Muhammad ibn-Musa Al-Khwarizmi, whose name lives on in "algorithm," might agree with Descartes that perfect-fi means that the transducer turns input into output by applying the following simple algorithm or recipe: Whatever the size of the input, multiply it by precisely the same constant number to get the output. Descartes might point to figure 5.10b and say that the output is a linear function of the input. To an engineer, figure 5.10b says that the transducer has a linear characteristic curve.

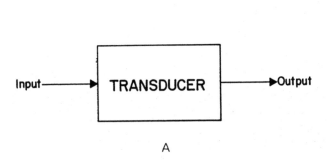

A

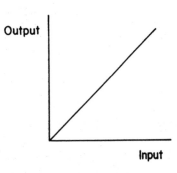

B

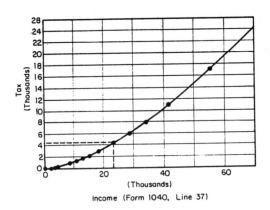

Income (Form 1040, Line 37)

C

1983 Tax Rate Schedules

Caution: You must use the Tax Table instead of these Tax Rate Schedules if your taxable income is less than $50,000 unless you use **Schedule G** (Income averaging), to figure

Schedule X
Single Taxpayers

Use this Schedule if you checked **Filing Status Box 1** on Form 1040—

If the amount on Form 1040, line 37 is: Over—	But not over—	Enter on Form 1040, line 38	of the amount over—
$0	$2,300	—0—	
2,300	3,400	........11%	$2,300
3,400	4,400	$121 + 13%	3,400
4,400	8,500	251 + 15%	4,400
8,500	10,800	866 + 17%	8,500
10,800	12,900	1,257 + 19%	10,800
12,900	15,000	1,656 + 21%	12,900
15,000	18,200	2,097 + 24%	15,000
18,200	23,500	2,865 + 28%	18,200
23,500	28,800	4,349 + 32%	23,500
28,800	34,100	6,045 + 36%	28,800
34,100	41,500	7,953 + 40%	34,100
41,500	55,300	10,913 + 45%	41,500
55,300	....	17,123 + 50%	55,300

D

Figure 5.10   Linear and nonlinear transducer characteristics

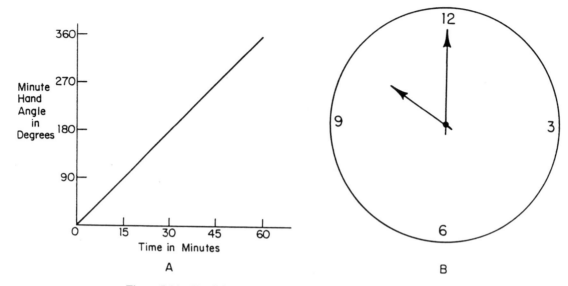

Figure 5.11   Traditional clock and its characteristic curve

Unfortunately, the real-world materials at hand for making real-world transducers generally have nonlinear characteristic curves in the vein of figure 5.10c. Aeons of ingenuity have brought forth relatively few workable analog transducers.

The output of a tranducer made from such materials is not proportional to the input. Rather, the effect is like that of a progressive income tax: The bite is not the same percent at each income level; the percent tax bite rises as income does. The nonlinear characteristic of the U.S. income tax is expressed by the nonlinear curve of figure 5.10c or, more conventionally, by the table of figure 5.10d. Both show how a $23,500 income (input) translates into a $4349 tax bite (output).

Figure 5.11a shows the characteristic curve desired of a conventional clock. The input is the flow of time itself. The output is the angle that a hand, in this instance the minute hand, makes with the high noon position (figure 5.11b). The conventional transducer was a mechanical clockwork, itself a miracle of the high technology of the 14th century, when it first appeared.[3]

Other historic analog transducers of time into readily visible manifestations of time include sand flowing in an hourglass, a form that survives in egg timers (figure 5.12). Historic analog transducers of time also include numerous varia-

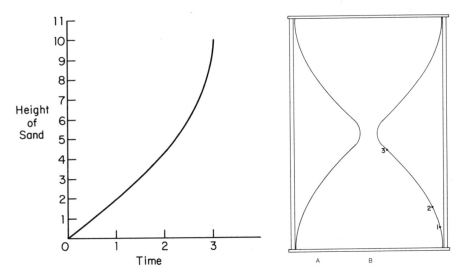

Figure 5.12   The egg timer

tions on the theme of water flowing through more or less elaborate races and containers.

The design of an egg timer is remarkably ingenious, reflecting the tours de force needed to make serviceable analog transducers. The amount of sand flowing through the constriction between the two reservoirs is linear in time (or proportional to time). But that amount can't be gauged on the fly by unaided human senses. What is visible is the height of the sandpile. But, for practical hourglass shapes, the height of the pile is nonlinear in time (figure 5.12a). It is the egg-timer craftsman who relieves the egg cooker of the burden of sorting that out in the kitchen before breakfast by calibrating the glass in minutes (figure 5.12b) before selling it. Finding a recipe for calibration was the craftsman's problem. Even so, the nonlinear calibration makes it hard to cook eggs precisely for durations other than whole minutes, a burden relieved by the modern microwave oven with its split-second electro-optical digital timer.

More generally, what still saves the day for the practicality of some analog processors is that some kinds of characteristic curves are more linear than others (figure 5.13). For instance, the characteristic curve of figure 5.13a is smoother than the characteristic curve of figure 5.13b. The smoother curve is also less nonlinear than the staircase curve in a sense that is visually evident and that 19th-century mathematicians nailed down formally. If you happen to be at

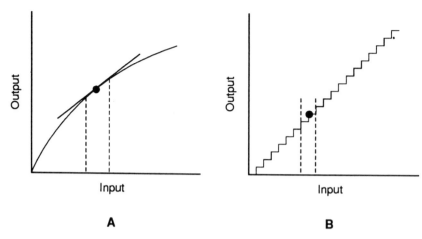

Figure 5.13   Degrees of nonlinearity

or near one of the corners of the staircase, it is impossible to approximate the characteristic curve of figure 5.13b by any straight line that is also faithful to the turning of the corner. With smooth curves like the one in figure 5.13a, however, the following is mathematically true: For a small enough distance around any point on such a smooth curve, a straight line is a reasonable approximation to the curve.

Although most materials that can be considered for building real-life analog tranducers or other analog information processors are nonlinear, enough of them are smooth like figure 5.13a to make some analog devices reasonably serviceable and affordable.

In audiophile terms, reasonable means that you can get hi-fi cheaply provided that you're willing to play it softly. The louder you want to play your hi-fi, the more it costs. Everyone has experienced this: A $10 portable transistor sounds tolerable, perhaps even good, if played softly enough. If figure 5.13a is the transistor's characteristic curve, "softly enough" means softly enough for the excursions around the heavy dot in figure 5.13a to stay within the bounds of reasonable approximation to linearity, for instance, between the two vertical dashed lines. Excursions beyond that run into the region of noticeable nonlinearity, sooner for musicians, later for tin ears.

Within the linear region of figure 5.14a, the output is proportional to the input. One unit of input gives two units of output. Once the input exceeds the threshold in either direction, the output stops being proportional to the input.

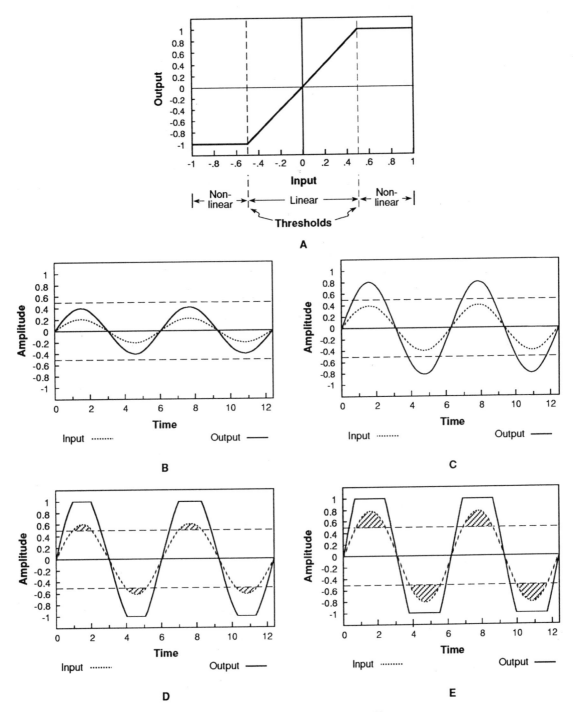

Figure 5.14 Effects of linear and nonlinear amplifiers

Indeed, in this extreme example, the output stays put at one no matter how big the input gets.

Figure 5.14 shows what an abrupt departure from linearity does to a pure tone.

In figures 5.14b and 5.14c, the maximum input amplitudes, 0.2 and 0.4 respectively, are below the 0.5 threshold. The outputs are therefore bigger than the inputs, but proportional throughout. The ear hears the output as a pure tone of the same pitch as the input, just louder.

In figures 5.14d and 5.14e, the maximum input amplitudes, 0.6 and 0.9 respectively, are above the 0.5 threshold. Both outputs are still bigger than the inputs, but they are no longer proportional throughout. It is as if the parts proportioned to the shaded portions of the inputs had been clipped off the outputs. The effect is of a loud and annoyingly rasping noise, not of a pure tone.

To put together apparatus that is reasonably linear over a wide dynamic range, namely that one can play loud and hi-fi as well as soft and hi-fi, is difficult but not impossible. Prices for the loud hi-fi that can range up to a hundred- or even a thousandfold the price of the soft-playing bargain reflect the difficulty.

The advent of practical digital processors has sharply cut down our dependence on the limited linearities available in nature. Instead, all digital formats and processes glory in the very nonlinearities, like those of figure 5.14b, that limit the scope of analog formats and processes.

Many humble but useful gadgets are nonlinear, like the light switch of figure 5.15a. When the switch is open, no current flows and the lamp is dark. When the switch is closed, current generated by the power source flows through the circuit and the lamp glows.

Figures 5.15b and 5.15c show what happens as the switch blade travels through positions where it keeps the circuit open to where it makes contact and closes the circuit. While the blade travels from the wide-open position *a* to the point *b* where it just makes contact, the circuit remains open, no current flows, and the light stays out. When contact is made, current flows and the light goes on as indicated by the abrupt transition from the lower *b* to the upper *b* in figure 5.15c. The pieces of a switch are flexible, so the blade will travel a bit further to *c*. However, since contact has already been made at *b*, there is no further increase in current flow. The arrows in figure 5.15c indicate that the reverse happens when the switch is opened.

The circuit of figure 5.15a is a transducer (figure 5.15d) that converts a mechanical input, switch-blade travel, into an electrical output, current flow,

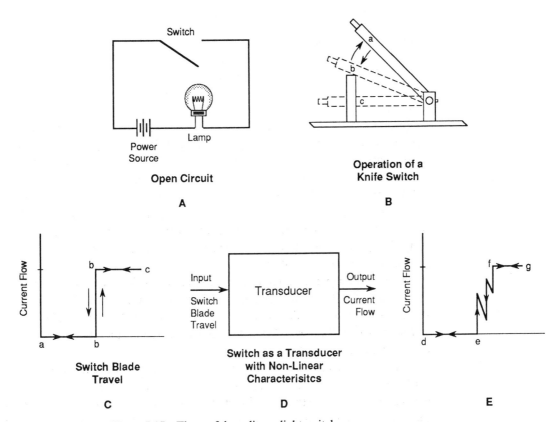

Figure 5.15 The useful nonlinear light switch

that is further transduced into light by the glowing lamp filament. This transducer has the very nonlinear characteristic curve of figure 5.15c.

Real-world switches do not behave precisely as in figure 5.15c. Instead, as shown in 5.15e, there is apt to be bouncing and jiggling as the blade makes contact or when it opens up. Dust or corrosion on the contacts might cause sparking or intermittent current flow. These accidents are indicated by the jagged transition from *e* to *f* in 5.15e. What makes the circuit valuable in spite of the messy transition is the presence of well-defined and stable positions where there is either no current (line *de* in figure 5.15e) or full flow of current (*fg* in figure 5.15e). Devices with such a characteristic curve are called "bistable" or "two-state."

Figure 5.16 illustrates a collection of two-state devices commonplace by the 1980s, the credit card. Imagine a spot on the card's magnetic stripe (figure 5.16a) to be magnetized, say in the south/north direction, and quietly sitting there. This state of affairs is depicted by the point marked "1" in figure 5.16b. Now suppose that a magnetizing force is applied, say, by a burst of electric current. The stripe stays magnetized precisely as before until, at point c, the magnetizing force reaches a strength specific to the particular magnetic material used in the stripe. The magnetization of the spot then flips from south/north to north/south as shown by the transition to d. Further increase of the magnetizing force causes no further change in the state of magnetization.

Like the switch, which may be opened and closed over and over again, the magnetizing process is reversible over and over again. The process differs from the switch in that the path is not retraced exactly. The magnetizing force has to be fairly strong in the opposite direction before anything happens; so the reversal occurs not at d but at f.

Real-world magnetic materials have sloppier transitions than in the idealized picture of 5.16b. The characteristic curve in 5.16c is more realistic. Allowing for the transitional indeterminacy, it still has the two well-defined and stable resting states shown by the heavy dots. This sharp definition and stability are what counts in making two-state devices.

Figure 5.17 depicts the workings of the vanishing punched card (figure 5.17a). Figure 5.17b, a characteristic curve relating percent holiness (output) to exerted cutter pressure (input), tells what happens when a cutter presses through the paper to make a hole. Nothing happens until enough pressure is applied. Then all at once the cutter tears through the cardboard and ejects a little rectangle, leaving a hole.

Once again the real-world way is neither quite so abrupt nor quite so clean. Figure 5.17c comes closer to reality.

In principle the process is reversible: One can imagine stuffing the little rectangles back in the holes and gluing them or taping them back in. Except in desperation, however, the process is one-directional, making the venerable punched card an example of what computer hackers now call a ROM, from Read-Only Memory. Once you've written (punched) in a card, you can only read it again and again, but not write into it anew. The reversible switches, magnets, and transistors can be erased and rewritten over and over again in more practical ways than stuffing little rectangles back into some holes and punching new ones.

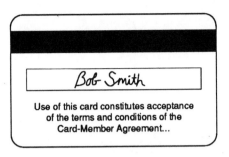

A

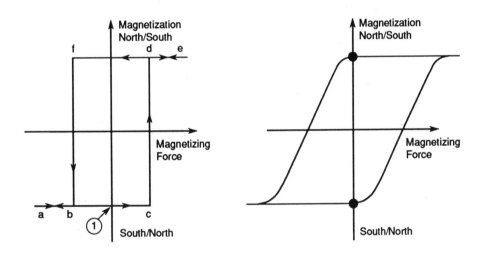

Magnetization of Stripe

B   **C**

Figure 5.16   The nonlinear two-state credit card

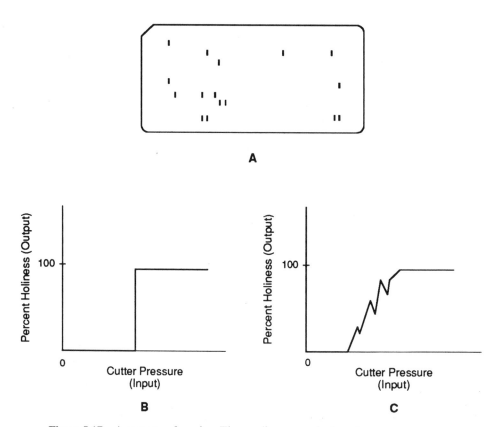

Figure 5.17   A century of service: The nonlinear punched card

Two-state devices abound in nature and in artifacts. Even with their region of slop or indeterminacy, they are readily exploited both as tokens for two-symbol alphabets and as processors for such tokens.

What makes these devices so useful is the fact, illustrated by figures 5.15, 5.16, and 5.17, that they are common and readily manipulated. Avoiding slop or indeterminacy and working only with the stable positions is much easier and cheaper in practice than seeking linearity.

Figure 5.18 shows only three of the infinity of possible ways of setting the conventions that associate two symbols with the stable states of two-state tokens. Column 1 shows a dot and a triangle as the associated symbols. Columns 2 and 3 show the possible ways of associating the symbols 0 and 1 with the two stable states.

	Two-State Token			Arbitrary Symbol		
Condition	**Electric Circuit**	**Magnetic Stripe**	**Punched Card**	**Column 1**	**Column 2**	**Column 3**
Stable State 2	Current Flow	North/ South Magnet	Hole	●	1	0
Region of Indetermincy				**Ignored**		
Stable State 1	No Current Flow	South/ North Magnet	No Hole	▲	0	1

Figure 5.18   Associating symbols with two-state tokens

There is nothing magical about using two-symbol or binary alphabets. The importance difference is between one and many. Two is just the least among many. Binary alphabets are used because two-state tokens will do, and because two-state tokens suitable for electronic digital processors happen to be handy in this universe and in this epoch. If and when multi-state tokens (figure 5.19) become readily available, multi-symbol alphabets will be used.

As in any relation between symbols and tokens, the choice of the symbol pair 0 and 1 is just an arbitrary convention. This convention is rooted in the historical accidents of the needs and the tastes of early computer designers, but has no deeper significance.

The punched card, although inherently binary, was mainly used decimally and alphabetically. Any one column could be used to hold one decimal digit as a punch in one of the rows designated $0, 1, 2, \ldots, 9$. Any one column could be used to hold a letter of the alphabet by double-punching it with combinations of two holes. This scheme best suited the electro-mechanical clunkers—literally—which processed punched cards in their heyday.

Transistors can be made to behave like the two-state mechanical switch, the two-state magnetic stripe, and the two-state punched card, only much, much faster, not in seconds, but in millionths or billionths of seconds. And transistors can be made much, much cheaper than mechanical two-state devices, at unit

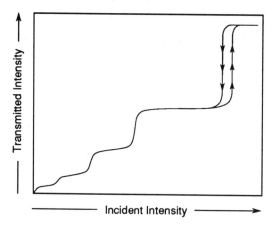

Figure 5.19 Multi-state optical tokens adapted from "The Optical Computer," by Eitan Abraham, Colin T. Seaton, and S. Desmond Smith. © 1983 by Scientific American, Inc. All rights reserved. Reprinted by permission.

costs reckoned not in dollars but in minute fractions of cents. They are usually in circuits that control the current flow through other transistors, not just in circuits that directly turn on a lamp or directly do some other useful thing. Webs of circuits where some circuits control other circuits that control still other circuits are the building blocks of electro-optical digital devices.

How Everything Can Be Said in Digital

It is easy to make a bigger collection of digital symbols from a smaller one. The trick is familiar. With a few letters you can make up many more words. With those words in turn you make up many more sentences. And so on. By playing with the positions and the combinations of holes in a punched card, the hole/no-hole pair can make up decimal numerals and alphabetic literals.

It is not so easy to make analog symbols from digital ones. But it is possible. The why and the how of that come later.

So, in principle, everything that can be done either with analog symbols or with a large collection of digital symbols can be built up from a small digital alphabet. An alphabet with two symbols, a binary alphabet, will do.

Figure 5.20 shows how it is done. The story begins with the bit. A bit is a slot or position that may be filled by, and only by, either of the two symbols in some

Number of Bits			
1 ☐	2 ☐☐	3 ☐☐☐	4 ☐☐☐☐
Number of Symbols Representable			
$2 = 2^1$	$4 = 2^2$	$8 = 2^3$	$16 = 2^4$
0 1	0 0 0 1 1 0 1 1	0 0 0 0 0 1 0 1 0 0 1 1 1 0 0 1 0 1 1 1 0 1 1 1	0 0 0 0 0 0 0 1 0 0 1 0 0 0 1 1 0 1 0 0 0 1 0 1 0 1 1 0 0 1 1 1 1 0 0 0 1 0 0 1 1 0 1 0 1 0 1 1 1 1 0 0 1 1 0 1 1 1 1 0 1 1 1 1

Figure 5.20 How little alphabets make big alphabets

chosen binary alphabet. A bit is just like the familiar decimal place or like the literal slots filled by the letters of this text. A bit slot differs from decimal slots or literal slots only in the size of the alphabet from which you choose the symbol that fills the slot.

Figure 5.20 makes explicit how the number of bits relates to the number of symbols you can build up from the bits. One bit can express either of two symbols. Since there are four ways of filling two bits, two bits can express any of four symbols (column 2, figure 5.20). And, in general, n bits can express up to and including $2n$ symbols.

Nothing stops us from using n bits to express fewer than $2n$ symbols. Judicious waste and gargantuan haste are what make for the profitable exploitation of the versatility of the arbitrary conventions whereby digital tokens and representations are associated with symbols.

For the moment, suffice it to say that it is possible to choose digital formats in ways that make this or that easier, cheaper, more convenient, or whatever

Representations of Decimals

Arabic Numeral	Pure Binary	Binary-Coded Decimal (BCD) Tens Place	Ones Place
0	0		0 0 0 0
1	1		0 0 0 1
2	1 0		0 0 1 0
3	1 1		0 0 1 1
4	1 0 0		0 1 0 0
5	1 0 1		0 1 0 1
6	1 1 0		0 1 1 0
7	1 1 1		0 1 1 1
8	1 0 0 0		1 0 0 0
9	1 0 0 1		1 0 0 1
10	1 0 1 0	0 0 0 1	0 0 0 0
11	1 0 1 1	"	0 0 0 1
12	1 1 0 0	"	0 0 1 0
13	1 1 0 1	"	0 0 1 1
14	1 1 1 0	"	0 1 0 0
15	1 1 1 1	"	0 1 0 1
16	1 0 0 0 0	"	0 1 1 0
17	1 0 0 0 1	"	0 1 1 1
18	1 0 0 1 0	"	1 0 0 0
19	1 0 0 1 1	"	1 0 0 1
20	1 0 1 0 0	0 0 1 0	0 0 0 0
21	1 0 1 0 1	"	0 0 0 1

Figure 5.21 Different strokes for different folks

else might be desired for any substance. This simple fact is the solvent eating up the boundaries between information industries. Figuring out precisely the what and how of making this or that easier, cheaper, or more convenient is what all the engineering, market research, experimentation, instant millionaires, and failures in the information businesses of the 1980s were all about.

Figure 5.21 shows two ways of putting decimal numerals in a binary format: One way is called "pure binary," the other "binary-coded decimal" (BCD). BCD keeps the familiar decimal slots. There is a ones' place, a tens' place, a hundreds' place, and so on, just as in the ordinary way of writing numerals. The difference is that, instead of using the ten familiar symbols of the arabic numeral alphabet in each of those places, BCD uses a binary representation of the ten arabic digits. Instead of using a single arabic numeral to fill a decimal place, BCD uses a four-bit byte to stand for a decimal digit. "Byte" is the term for a cluster of bits, a big position or slot made up of little slots.

Figure 5.21 illustrates why one would bother picking one representation over the other. People, for example, find BCD somewhat easier to decipher than a pure binary format. One need only memorize ten four-bit combinations in order to read BCD as if it were ordinary decimal notation. Deciphering the pure binary notation is harder for people to learn. But pure binary notation is more economical than BCD because it uses fewer bits. This suggests using BCD as a display format and pure binary for processing. But then translation is necessary from one to the other and back. And so on. By such picky tradeoffs are the minds of compunications engineers seized. The success or failure of these picky tradeoffs influences competitive costs and weights the wheel by whose spins fortunes are made or lost.

Figure 5.22 illustrates how the conventional 26-symbol alphabet may be formatted by five-bit bytes. Some waste is inherent here, since five bits could do 32 symbols.

Calling electro-optical digital processors "computers" is a hangover from their earliest limited forms. Specialized forms have gotten other names, like "word processor," but even the generic name masks the full generality of the generic power of digital processors. Together, figures 5.21 and 5.22 show why anything done not only in numbers but also in words can be formatted not only digitally—which the conventional decimal numerals and alphabetic literals already do—but more particularly in the binary alphabets which happen to be suitable for versatile and abundant electro-optical formats and processors. Thus, absolutely anything that can be said in numbers or words, in numerals or literals, can be formatted in binary digital formats and processed by electro-optical digital processors.

More remarkably, the same holds for sounds and pictures and indeed for any conceivable kind of substance, no matter how that substance might be represented according to prevalent conventions. Sounds and pictures can be digitized in distinctive ways, some of them of universal applicability but somewhat superficial, others more particular but also more profound. Whether or not a given kind of substance can be formatted in a particular as well as in a universal way affects costs, convenience, and the scope and practicality of the amorphous mass of processes lumped under the rubric of artificial intelligence.

An Encoded Alphabet					
Letters	Binary Coding with Five Bits				
A	0	0	0	0	1
B	0	0	0	1	0
C	0	0	0	1	1
D	0	0	1	0	0
E	0	0	1	0	1
F	0	0	1	1	1
G	0	1	0	0	0
H	0	1	0	0	1
I	0	1	0	1	0
J	0	1	0	1	1
K	0	1	1	0	0
L	0	1	1	0	1
M	0	1	1	1	0
N	0	1	1	1	1
O	1	0	0	0	0
P	1	0	0	0	1
Q	1	0	0	1	0
R	1	0	0	1	1
S	1	0	1	0	0
T	1	0	1	0	1
U	1	0	1	1	0
V	1	0	1	1	1
W	1	1	0	0	0
X	1	1	0	0	1
Y	1	1	0	1	0
Z	1	1	0	1	1

Figure 5.22 The alphabet in bits

To help illustrate diverse ways of digitizing sound, figure 5.23 shows what happens between a speaker's brain and a listener's brain. Telephone transducers are intermediaries here, but the intermediaries might be radio or television systems or some other artifact.

Not much is understood about what goes on in either brain. Whatever does go on in the speaker's brain is nowadays made manifest almost exclusively by the effects of the nerve impulses that actuate the vocal tract, which in turn pushes on the air to make the audible waves that we call sound. All else comes either from unreliable introspections and speculations or else from unusual and still very rudimentary laboratory experiments with electroencephalograms, implanted electrodes, and the like. Once sound-waves-in-air hit the listener's

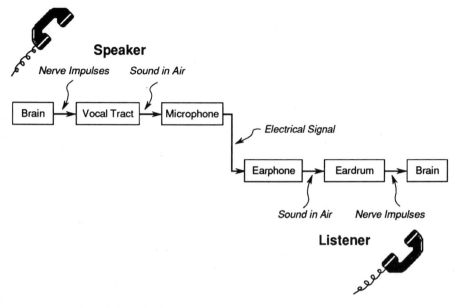

Figure 5.23   Speech from brain to brain

eardrum and get transduced into nerve impulses, the brain and its mysteries take over once again.

What people set forth explicitly in digital formats is not what concerns us right here. Writing is digital. So is typing. Written or typed substance comes out of the human brain, nerves, and muscles explicitly formatted in the 26-member alphabet and arrayed in the limitless sequence of digital slots. Music is no problem either when it issues forth from the brain and the hand in conventional musical notation. Staff, clefs, notes, and so on, make up a digital format. The mysteries of the composer's brain, nerves, and muscles have embodied musical substance in an explicitly digital format.

What the brain, nerves, and muscles put forth as speech, or as music whistled or hummed, is an altogether different matter. Speech, whistles, and hums as sound-in-the-air remain explicitly analog formats by the lights of the scientific understanding of the 1980s.

It is surmised that speech is inherently but implicitly digital. The evidence for this is disarmingly simple. If speech were inherently analog, it would be mostly unintelligible owing to the enormous variations among speakers and hearers that stem from sex, dialect, the condition of the speaker's nose or of the hearer's ear. No way is a word uttered by one man, woman, or child, Northern or Southern, healthy or racked by a cold, simply proportional to or analogous to the same word uttered by someone else, or even by the same person in a different sentence! The prevalent linguistic theory is that the speaker's brain produces—and the listener's brain recognizes—digital phonemes.

Phonemes are supposed to be elements of a small alphabet, not much larger than the alphabet of literals. The speaker produces phonemes and the listener interprets them unruffled by distortions, much as a reader recognizes "a" or "f," however distorted in diverse handwritings or in diverse type fonts. There are more phonemes than there are literals. For example, the "a" phoneme in "bad" is not the same as the "a" phoneme in "bathe." That the two sounds must be truly distinct and not just distinguished by their different contexts in "bad" and "bathe" is based on such evidence as the pair of words "tack" and "take." In "tack" and "take" what surrounds "a" is the same. The inference is that since "tack" and "take" are heard differently, the literal "a" stands for one phoneme in "tack" and for a different phoneme in "take."[4]

But all of this occurs, if at all, inside brains. Try as we might, the evidence for phonemes in speech as sound-in-the-air remains scant. A most convincing kind of evidence, the building of an artifact that would, if not understand speech, at least convert speech into its written equivalent, remains beyond our grasp. In the mid-1980s the results of research in speech recognition fall far short of that goal. Any successes hinge on techniques that do have their commercial possibilities—as in substituting ten spoken digits for the finger in the dial or on the beeping buttons—but that shed only a dim light on the supposed phonemic (digital) nature of speech. So, between brains, speech or music that started as sound-in-the-air—and not as phonemic or alphabetic transcription or as a musical score—must for the foreseeable future be dealt with as analog symbols. And the same applies to pictures.

It is not entirely self-evident that speech or music as sound-in-the-air, or visual images as light waves, or any other kind of sound or electromagnetic wave can in fact be given fully faithful digital expression under usefully benign and widely prevalent enough conditions. The familiar half-tone newspaper photo points the way. A half-tone, as illustrated in figure 5.3a, is made up of black and white dots or, if not so binary, of a limited alphabet of discrete shadings of gray. But the quality of the usual half-tone is not what one would choose to mean by a "fully faithful" digital expression. Major mathematical discoveries by Joseph Fourier in the 19th century and by Claude Shannon in the 20th century were necessary to unlock the way to fully faithful digital expressions of a universal but superficial kind.[5]

Not only is the theory far from self-evident, but the fact that Shannon's theoretical possibility could be realized in practice does not at all flow from the theory itself. It just happens—Bell System irredentists would add the aside "but not just by accident"—that the transistor and, later, its elaboration into increasingly complex and powerful integrated circuits of decreasing cost provided the practical means for carrying out Shannon's processes fast and cheaply enough to be of workaday value.

The story of fully faithful, universal, but superficial digital formats begins with Fourier's decomposition of complex waves, sound waves among them, into simple building blocks.

Some details about the nature of waves—sound waves in particular but other waves as well—help explain what Fourier and Shannon did that made fully faithful digital encoding of sound a theoretical possibility.

Imagine that you are looking through the glass of a fish tank at a stretch of open water, with your eyes at the level of the undisturbed water. That level is denoted by the horizontal straight line in figure 5.24. A wave is sweeping across the tank from left to right. At the instant when you are looking, the crests and troughs of the wave are as shown in figure 5.24. The pattern of crests and troughs is repetitive. The length of one unit or cycle in this repetitive pattern, shaded in figure 5.24, is the wave length l of the wave.

What you see in the tank as time goes by is sketched in figure 5.25. The snapshot of figure 5.24 is the 0 time line of figure 5.25. The last snapshot in figure 5.25 is taken at a time T. Intermediate snapshots taken at $\frac{1}{4}$, $\frac{1}{2}$, and $\frac{3}{4}$ of the time T are also shown. As time goes by, any particular crest, trough, or feature

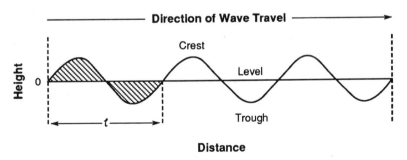

Figure 5.24   Water wave in a fish tank

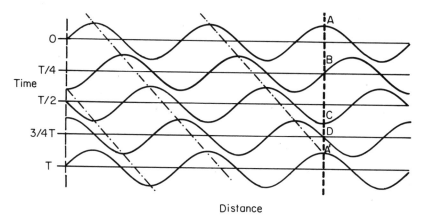

Figure 5.25   Wave motion as time goes by

in-between seems to move from left to right across the tank. The diagonal dashed lines in figure 5.25 suggest this motion of wave features.

If, instead of following a wave feature across the tank, the eyes stay fixed, they see the succession *ABCDA'* on the vertical dashed line in figure 5.25. A piece of duckweed sitting at point *A* just bobs up and down as the wave features appear to travel under it across the fishtank. The time *T* is the period of the wave, namely the time it takes for the duckweed to bob back to precisely where it was at time 0 and to be heading precisely the way it was heading at time 0. *A'* is exactly the same place as *A*.

Figure 5.26 plots the height of the piece of duckweed as it bobs down from *A* and back up to *A'* in a time interval equal to the period *T*.

The number of wave periods per unit time is called the frequency of the wave. For example, if the period of a wave is $\frac{1}{60}$ of a second, the frequency of the wave is 60 cycles per second, or 60 hertz, the frequency of household alternating current. If the period is 0.0000015 seconds (1.5 microseconds), the frequency is 650 kilohertz, the frequency of the radio waves emitted by AM radio station WNBC, 650 on your dial in New York. If the period is .000000011 seconds (11 nanoseconds), the frequency is 90 megahertz, the frequency of FM radio station WGBH, FM-90 in Boston.

Sound waves in the air behave similarly. A water crest is like a compression of the air molecules. A water trough is like a rarefaction where the air molecules are farther apart than in the undisturbed air. A pure tone sung by a singer travels from the singer's mouth to the listener's eardrum like the water waves

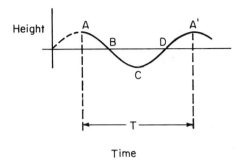

Figure 5.26   Duckweed motion as time goes by

traveling across figure 5.25. The effect on the listener's eardrum may be visualized as in figure 5.26. At a crest, the eardrum is pushed away from its resting position toward the inner ear. It then returns to its resting position, only to be drawn toward the outside of the ear as a rarefaction passes by. The resulting vibration of the eardrum thus is a mechanical analog of the compression/ rarefaction wave traveling through the air.

Figures 5.24, 5.25, and 5.26 depict a shape typical of many kinds of wave, including the wave shape of a pure tone of sound. Waves that convey pure tones are called sine waves. Shannon discovered additional properties of sine waves that underlie the methods now more and more widely used commercially for the fully faithful digital formatting of analog sound waves.

Sine waves are named after the sine of an angle. The sine of an angle of a right triangle is the ratio of the length of the side of the triangle opposite the angle to the length of the hypotenuse of the triangle, as in figure 5.27.

With the length of the hypotenuse taken as the unit of length, the value of the sine of the angle is just the height of the side opposite the angle, as indicated by the circled 1 in figure 5.28. As the unit hypotenuse turns counterclockwise and describes a circle, the sine takes on different values, as indicated by points 1, 2, 3, and 4 in figure 5.28.

Figure 5.29 shows intermediate values of sin a, the sine of a, as a goes from 0° to 360° or, equivalently, from 0 radians to 2π radians. Figure 5.29 also shows that the value of sine a ranges between +1 and −1. A sin a, which therefore ranges in value between $+A$ and $-A$, thus can represent pure tone waves of any amplitude A.

One additional arithmetic trick completes the adaptation of the trigonometric sine to the description of pure tones. By definition a pure tone goes

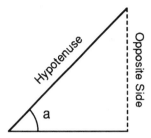

Figure 5.27   Sine equals opposite over hypotenuse

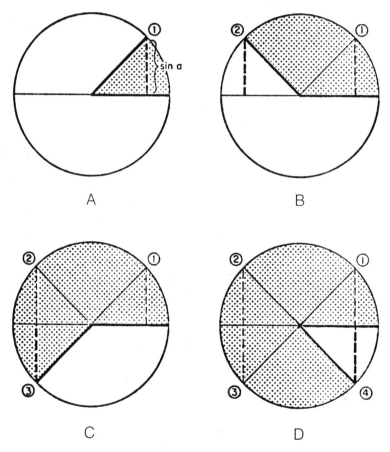

Figure 5.28   Four sine values

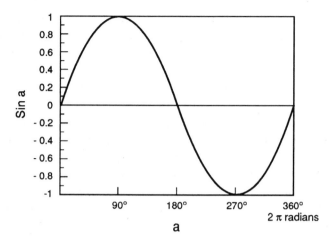

Figure 5.29   The sine waveform

through one cycle or period in a time interval T. Defining a as $\frac{2\pi t}{T}$, where t is elapsed time and T the period of the wave, is that trick. When $t = 0$, at the beginning of a period, $a = \frac{2\pi\phi}{T} = 0$ and $\sin a = 0$, as desired. When $t = T$, at the end of a T period, $a = \frac{2\pi T}{T} = 2\pi$ and $\sin a = 0$, as desired. Likewise at all intermediate values of t. The quantity $\frac{2\pi}{T}$ thus joins the period T and the frequency $f = \frac{1}{T}$ among convenient descriptors of pure tones.

Why pure tone waves happen to be sine-shaped has to do with linearity and with how natural vibrations happen in the springs of a harmonica, the strings of a violin, the air in an organ pipe, the membranes of kettle drums or of eardrums, the water in the fish tank, the pendulum of a clock, and so on.

Imagine a violin string that is displaced from its resting position, but not too far. "Not too far" here amounts to asking for enough linearity in the neighborhood of the resting state precisely as in figure 5.13a. The restoring force F that pulls the string back to its resting position is proportional to the displacement D, namely $F = \text{constant} \times D$, if only D is small enough. It then follows from Newton's laws of motion that a sine wave precisely describes the vibration of the violin string.

That remarkable conclusion may not impress any musician who knows that real strings or skins are not necessarily displaced just a little bit from their resting position. Indeed, what makes middle C on the violin differ from middle C on the piano is that in each instrument real fundamental notes or pure tones come with harmonics. These harmonics differ from instrument to instrument and give each instrument its unique tonality.

But the harmonics themselves can be thought of as pure tones of a pitch or frequency different from the fundamental pitch. True harmonics are of a frequency that's a multiple of the frequency of the fundamental pure tone. What Fourier discovered is that every periodic wave—and indeed much more general sound patterns—can be portrayed as made up of sine waves. In particular, such a wave is made up of a fundamental pure tone and various combinations of its pure harmonics.

Figure 5.30 shows how sine waves, added together in systematically different ways, can make up different shapes. The triangular shape is discernible by the third step in figure 5.30A, the square by the third step in figure 5.30B. After 60 steps, the only discernible action is all the sharp corners. The sine waves that make up another waveform are called the Fourier components of that waveform.

Describing a waveform by its Fourier components leads to simplifying insights of major practical import as well as of deep theoretical significance. It so happens that in this universe any linear transducer behaves very simply with inputs that are the sums of sine waves. What the linear transducer does to the sum of several sine waveforms is just the sum of whatever it does to each sine waveform by itself. So, if we know what a transducer does to a sine wave of any arbitrary frequency and if we know what sine waves the input is made up of, then the output of the transducer is just the sum of whatever the transducer would do to each of the component sine waves in isolation. In summary, once you know how a linear transducer treats one sine wave, you know how it treats any wave.

Turning these insights into practical schemes for fully faithful digital formats for sounds hinges on a trait already noted about the universe we happen to live in. Because they are linear enough only over a limited range (figure 5.13a), real-world transducers work well for only a limited range of harmonics. That's why hi-fi sets must have woofers for the low notes, tweeters for the high notes, and, when more expensive, some additional loudspeakers for in-between notes.

Our vocal tracts and our ears are transducers for sounds, the sound of speech and the sound of music among them. Like all materials, throats and ears can

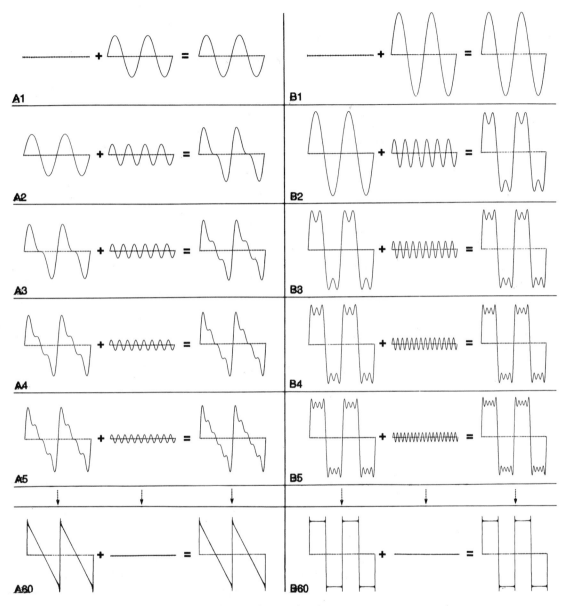

Figure 5.30   How sines make up triangles, squares, or you name it

handle only a limited range of frequencies. In particular, the ear cannot hear sounds pitched higher than about 20 kilohertz (20,000 cycles per second). Dogs do better than that, which is why we've invented ultrasonic dog whistles with a pitch that is beyond what we can hear but that dogs jump to. Indeed, most of us get anywhere near 20 kilohertz only in youth; as we grow older, we drop off toward 15 or perhaps even 12 kilohertz as the upper limit of our hearing range.

At the lower end of our hearing range, most of us can hear enough of the 60-hertz hum that fluorescent lamps make to get annoyed, but acuity drops off pretty fast below that.

The range of frequencies over which a transducer functions well enough by someone's lights is called the bandwidth of the transducer. Thus our ears have a bandwidth of about 12 to 20 kilohertz. The concept of bandwidth provides a good way of matching the makeup of waveforms with transducers—transmission channels among them—of just the right capacities.

Fourier analysis describes any waveform by listing the pure sine waves that make it up. The range between the frequency of the lowest-frequency sine wave in the waveform and the frequency of the highest-frequency sine wave in the waveform is the bandwidth of the waveform. A sound wave with lowest-frequency component near 60 hertz and highest-frequency component between 12 and 20 kilohertz has a bandwidth of about 12 to 20 kilohertz.

A waveform with, say, a 15-kilohertz bandwidth is best matched to a transmission channel of exactly that bandwidth. A transmission channel with less than 15 kHz bandwidth would not provide fully faithful reproduction because it would not pass through enough of the pure sine waves that make up the input waveform. A transducer with more than 15 kHz bandwidth would waste its capacity for handling sine waves that aren't in the waveform.

Matching a waveform's bandwidth to a transducer's bandwidth is the analog way to efficiency.

On a foundation of analog-bandwidth matching, Shannon built a scheme guaranteed to deliver a fully faithful digital format for any waveform of a specified bandwidth.

As a first step, Shannon discovered that just sampling a waveform of specific bandwidth W is good enough to define that waveform with full faithfulness.

Figure 5.31 illustrates this. The waveform of figure 5.31a is sampled at discrete intervals. Shannon discovered conditions under which transmitting only samples as shown in figure 5.31b and omitting everything else is good enough, in principle, to give fully faithful reproduction of the original signal at the receiving end.

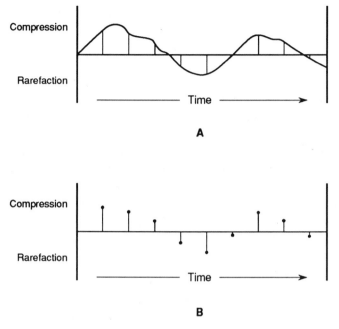

Figure 5.31 Sampling sounds for fully faithful reproduction

The bandwidth W of the original signal fixes the interval at which samples must be taken. Shannon found that the sampling interval cannot exceed $\frac{1}{2}W$ seconds for full faithfulness. For instance, if W equals 4 hertz, then $\frac{1}{2}W$ equals one eighth of a second. The samples must be taken no more than one eighth of a second apart. No faithfulness is lost if samples are taken at shorter intervals, but that's wasteful. If samples are taken at intervals longer than one eighth of a second, then reproduction will not be fully faithful.

The French have a saying "C'est simple, mais il fallait y penser," meaning, "It's simple, once you thought of it." As a colleague of mine in the early days of the Apollo moon-landing program put it, "This problem, when solved, will be easy." And so with the elegant simplicity of the Shannon sampling theorem. It is intuitively reasonable. A slowly varying waveform, oscillating no faster than four times a second, can be faithfully described by sampling it every one-eighth of a second. A fast-varying waveform, say one with a 20-kilohertz component at the limit of human hearing, would be described faithfully only if sampled every 25 millionths of a second.

Elegant, simple, but not at all practical when first thought of.

The practicality of digital telephones, digital records, and so on, turns on compromises that make a virtue of human limitations and that exploit cheap, fast electro-optical digital technologies.

The bandwidth of our throats and ears is in the 10 to 20 kilohertz range. The experience of the world's telephone companies, however, is that a bandwidth of three to four kilohertz is more than adequate for transmitting voices faithfully enough to keep their customers happy. A 4-kilohertz bandwidth makes speech intelligible. Moreover, speakers are recognizable and shades of inflection and intonation are discernible. As anyone knows who has listened to music-on-hold, 3 to 4 kilohertz is terrible for music. It is, however, an adequate and, in any case, widely adopted, standard for voice transmission. The tradeoff is between what it would cost to provide hi-fi telephone service to everyone at all times and what it costs to provide it to some—notably radio and TV networks —at some times.

In the world of real telephones, therefore, convention sets the Shannon bandwidth W equal to 4 kilohertz, or 4000 hertz. By that convention $\frac{1}{2}W$ equals $\frac{1}{8000}$ seconds as the interval not to exceed between samples for faithfulness no worse than that imposed by the 4-kilohertz bandwidth limit. This is 0.125 thousandths of a second, or 125 microseconds per interval. Eight thousand samples must be taken every second.

A requirement to take 8000 samples in one second may seem tight on a scale of seconds and just barely reasonable on a scale of microseconds. It may seem ample or even lavish on the scale of billionths of a second or nanoseconds: The interval between samples amounts to 125,000 nanoseconds. Counting nanoseconds was unthinkable in the practice of the 1930s and 1940s, when Shannon first proposed his sampling idea. By the 1980s, measuring time and taking samples by the nanosecond had become routine.

Some other hurdles had also been cleared by the 1980s. Were it necessary in practice as well as in principle to measure the heights of sample pulses (figure 5.31b) with absolute accuracy, Shannon's scheme would nonetheless have remained a mathematical curiosity devoid of practical impact.

Another compromise led closer to practicality. This compromise rests on yet another pragmatic observation. Just as our ears have a limited bandwidth, so our ears are also incapable of hearing very small jumps in loudness. The same kind of scientific and commercial observations that inspire reliance on a 4-kilohertz bandwidth as adequate for intelligible, recognizable, and marketable speech have led to the convention that speech with no more than 128 discrete levels of loudness is of adequate quality. Given that convention, measurements of sample heights can be rounded off to the nearest among those 128 discrete loudness levels.

There is just one more step to the end of this trail. A stream of sample pulses, coming 125,000 nanoseconds apart and each of a height chosen among 128 discrete levels, would still have to be amplified from time to time if it had to travel over more than hundreds of feet. The necessary analog amplifiers would have to be linear over the full range of 128 possible input levels or else the speech would be distorted. The trail could be at a dead end.

Fully faithful transmission of waveforms limited to a 4-kilohertz bandwidth and 128 discernible levels of loudness was achieved by shifting to a digital format that takes advantage of the nonlinearities of nature. Instead of trying to transmit 128 distinct pulse levels through analog amplifiers, the levels are converted to a binary code with a seven-bit byte per pulse.

That encoding is illustrated for eight levels in figure 5.32. Instead of having to find materials linear over the whole range of eight distinct and discrete levels, as in the first column of figure 5.32, the binary format of the second column can be

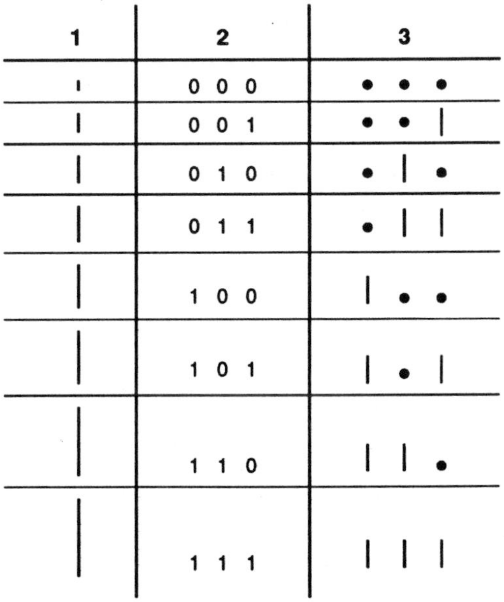

1	2	3
ı	0 0 0	• • •
I	0 0 1	• • |
|	0 1 0	• | •
|	0 1 1	• | |
|	1 0 0	| • •
|	1 0 1	| • |
|	1 1 0	| | •
|	1 1 1	| | |

Figure 5.32   Pulse-formatted speech

embodied as a stream of presences or absences of pulses of uniform height. Pulse/no-pulse tokens, as in the third column of figure 5.32, are readily handled by two-state devices of the kind illustrated earlier. A three-bit byte is enough for $8 = 2^3$ levels. A seven-bit byte is needed for $128 = 2^7$ levels.

What began as an electrical analog of the continuous compression and rarefaction stream in the air has now been transformed into binary digital tokens fully faithful to the original analog tokens. Nothing distinguishes binary tokens that came from a stream of speech or a snatch of music from tokens for the letters of some alphabet or for numbers. The demonstration that speech can be said in digital just as numbers and letters can be said in digital is now complete, at least in principle.

The digital tokens derived by subjecting speech to Shannon's scheme, now a routine scheme called "pulse code modulation," have no necessary relation to the hypothesized phonemic digital expression of speech in the brain. What that might be remains a mystery. A practical consequence is that the voice-actuated typewriter remains an elusive goal. Just digitizing the waveform does not help us get there from here. Only digitizing speech as phonemes would, if we could.

As of April 1984, the latest in decades of brave words was reported as follows:

... Research on continuous speech recognition has been largely dormant in this country; the sole exception is the ongoing effort at IBM's Thomas J. Watson Laboratories in Yorktown Heights, New York, where the goal is a real-time office dictation machine with a vocabulary of 5000 words. In Japan, however, the so-called "Fifth Generation" project has announced that one of its long-range goals will be a 10,000 word, speech-activated typewriter with the ability to understand hundreds of different speakers. Some observers in the United States believe that, with a substantial application of resources, a limited version of such a system could be available in the 1990's.[6]

In practice, using digital tokens for speech requires not only the initial analog to digital conversion. Eventually the digital bit stream must be turned back into a continuous stream of compressions and rarefactions that can move our eardrums. The formula that Shannon elaborated, when he discovered how to do the sampling, envisages restoring the original continuous speech waveform by a complicated process of weighted averaging of the samples. That process, like most aspects of Shannon's scheme, would have been impossible in practice at the time Shannon proposed his theory. Versatile and abundant electro-optical digital formats and processors have made it practical.

What can be done for speech can also be done for pictures, color and all. The not-so-faithful dot/no-dot two-state tokens used in the familiar half-tone pictures in newspapers thus foreshadow the more general Shannon process for practical, fully faithful, binary formatting of any analog symbols whatsoever.

Shaping Digital Formats for Efficiency

Although hardly ever a front-page headline matter, the search for formats that are efficient in various stages of business information processes is important to all information suppliers and consumers struggling for competitive advantage. Making it with profitable data bank services, for example, depends in part on finding format-and-process combinations that are more efficient than the competition's in delivering comparable substance to customers. Here, like anywhere else, the bottom line depends on both the product—the substance—and the process for making and selling it.

In the extreme, a format that is just dandy for substance undergoing one process may be worthless for another process. When standing next to me, you can tell me in plain spoken English that the British are coming by land or else by sea. But if I'm about to go farther away than your shouts will carry, plain shouted English won't do. We have to arrange for you to hold up one lantern in the Old North Church steeple for one message or two lanterns for the other. In this familiar early American epic, changing the format to accommodate the process was the key to conveying any substance at all.

There are cases in-between. If you are paying for a message by the word, as in the bygone days when telegrams were the only form of rapid communication at a distance, you might be quite interested in conveying any given substance with as few words as possible. To one familiar with New England, the message "New England winters are cold" at $10 a word might seem like the epitome of gouging for worthless substance. If you're about to board a plane in Sydney, Australia, bound for Boston, the message "The Soviets just nuked Boston" at $10 a word might seem more worthwhile. There is a strong intuitive sense that one of these messages conveys more substance and is of greater significance than the other. It therefore ought to cost less to send less substance.

No one has yet managed to capture in any formal, global, and also useful way all that we lump within the vague ideas of "amount of substance" and "appropriately matched format." There is one particular sense, however, in which the idea of amount of substance has been made explicit in a way that permits precise matching of substance and formats. Here again the theory was pioneered, in the 1940s and 1950s, by Claude Shannon. Shannon's way of measuring amount of substance starts with a universe of discourse. It builds on the notion that how much substance there is in some message is not an absolute, but depends on the universe of discourse from which that message is drawn.

Out of the many ways in which one might construe the common-sense notion of "universe of discourse," Shannon singled out one far less grandiose than the Universe of All Possible Discourse. How many messages are in a universe of discourse and how likely each message is to be sent fully describes a universe of discourse in Shannon's scheme. This simple idea is very useful in assessing the efficiency of digital formats.

Shannon's measure of substance serves the digital world the way bandwidth serves the analog world. Within this measure's limited sphere, it gives benchmarks for matching media with messages. This measure also sheds light on the relative costing and pricing of messages, again within its limited coverage of the scope of the intuitive idea of value of a message.

That is, let's say Shannon's universe U_1 has one message in it; U_2 has two messages in it; U_3 has three; and so on. The universe U_n has n messages in it. When each message is as likely as any other message in a universe, the universe is fully defined by that number of messages in it. How much substance a message conveys when drawn from one of these universes or another is fully defined, granted the following three propositions that Shannon enunciated about amount of substance.

The first proposition is that getting a message M from a universe of discourse U_1 in which M is the only possible message conveys no substance whatever. If this strikes you as paradoxical because you think that a message is a message and conveys substance no matter what, consider the following. Suppose you always cry wolf. Since that's the only message I ever get from you, I'll pay no attention to it and be none the worse off since your message is without substance. A message out of a universe of discourse with only one message in it is worthless.

If, on the other hand, we have agreed that no news is good news and you call me to tell me that the sky is falling, then this conveys some substance to me because there is an alternative. In this illustration, the universe of discourse has two messages in it. The format for the first message happens to be the English sentence "The sky is falling." The format for the second message happens to be your failing to send the first one by an agreed-upon time. "No communication" is used to convey substance in this instance in much the same way that Sherlock Holmes milked substance from observing that the dog did not bark.

In summary, just as the presence of a pulse and the absence of a pulse at a particular time are two possible tokens that may be used to format a binary alphabet (figure 5.32), so, in a specific context, the uttering of a sentence and the absence of any sentence may be the tokens for two messages.

Shannon's second proposition generalizes the foregoing observations. It asserts that if a message comes from a larger universe of discourse, say U_n with n messages in it, then that message conveys more substance than a message coming from a smaller universe of discourse, say $U_n - 1$ with $n - 1$ messages in it.

Together, the first two propositions rank the universes of discourse. In that ranking, the message from the universe with only one message in it conveys no substance, while a message selected from each succeedingly larger universe conveys increasingly more substance.

The third proposition looks a bit more complicated than the first two propositions because it focuses on the process for picking a message. The third proposition asserts that how a message is picked from its universe makes no difference in the amount of substance that the message conveys. Specifically, given a universe of discourse U_n, just picking a message and getting it over with conveys exactly the same substance as first coyly asserting that the selected message is among a group of i messages in U_n (hence not among the other $n - i$ messages in U_n), and only then telling which one it actually is among the i messages in the group.

Since the coyness could be repeated in picking the one message from among the group of i messages, this proposition clears away quite a bit of underbrush. It asserts that all that matters in this view of substance is the total quantity of messages from among which a particular message is drawn. The details of formats or processes do not affect the amount of substance that is conveyed. No matter how tortured or hidden my procedure for picking which one out of n messages I will send you, and no matter how plain or how bizarre the format of that message, the only thing that ultimately influences the amount of substance that this particular message conveys is that it is this particular message I sent to you from among the n messages in U_n, and not some other.

The image of the communication process implied by these propositions is somewhat as follows. You and I agree about a universe of discourse with some number n of messages in it. That sets up the conditions of communication, the context in which the messages are significant. It also fixes the amount of substance conveyed in this particular situation by one specific message out of the universe of discourse, hence the value of the message in the given context.

No. n of messages in universe U_n	H_n = Information per message Scale:							
	$\log_2$	$\log_3$	$\log_4$	$\log_5$	—	$\log_{10}$	—	$\log_{26}$
1	0	0	0	0	—	0	—	0
2	1	0.63	0.50	0.43	—	0.30	—	0.21
3	1.58	1	0.79	0.68	—	0.48	—	0.34
4	2	1.26	1	0.86	—	0.60	—	0.43
5	2.32	1.46	1.16	1	—	0.70	—	0.49
6	2.58	1.63	1.29	1.11	—	0.78	—	0.55
7	2.81	1.77	1.40	1.21	—	0.85	—	0.60
8	3	1.89	1.50	1.29	—	0.90	—	0.64
9	3.17	2	1.58	1.37	—	0.95	—	0.67
10	3.32	2.10	1.66	1.43	—	1	—	0.71
11	3.46	2.18	1.73	1.49	—	1.04	—	0.74
12	3.58	2.26	1.79	1.54	—	1.08	—	0.76
13	3.70	2.33	1.85	1.59	—	1.11	—	0.79
14	3.81	2.40	1.90	1.64	—	1.15	—	0.81
15	3.91	2.46	1.95	1.68	—	1.18	—	0.83
16	4	2.52	2	1.72	—	1.20	—	0.85
—	—	—	—	—	—	—	—	—
26	4.70	2.97	2.35	2.02	—	1.41	—	1

Figure 5.33   Information per message from universe U_n

The idea is that prior to receiving a specific message there is uncertainty about the state of the world. Receiving a message reduces that uncertainty or, in other words, conveys substance. In Shannon's approach, the amount of substance and the amount by which uncertainty is reduced are identical ideas. Both grow with the number of possible messages.

Remarkably, these three propositions determine a unique and useful numerical measure of the amount of substance conveyed by the sending and receiving of a particular message from a universe of discourse U_n with n messages in it. That measure H_n is the logarithm of the number of messages in U_n (figure 5.33).

If the number n of messages is 100, then, since $100 = 102$, the logarithm to the base 10 of 100, written as $\log_{10}100$, is 2. In general, if a number $n = bp$, then p, the power to which the base b is raised to gen n, is the logarithm to the base b of n. Figure 5.33 shows logarithms to bases 2, 3, 4, 5, 10, and 26, and universes with from 1 to 16 messages in them. The logarithms to the various bases are

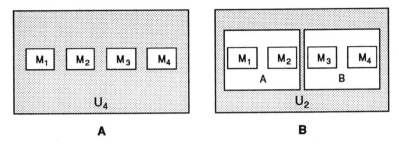

Figure 5.34   Alternative ways to pick a message

proportional to one another, so choosing a base is just choosing a convenient scale. For instance, the bold-face "1"s in figure 5.33 show that if there are b messages in a universe of discourse then, on the scale of logarithms to the base b, one message picked from that universe of discourse conveys one unit of substance. How message formats influence the choice of scale is touched on below.

Figure 5.33 shows how H_n satisfies the three propositions. H_n is 0 on every scale when $n = 1$, namely for the universe U_1. H_n increases as n increases. That takes care of the first two propositions, but any sequence of numbers that goes up from 0 would do that. The logarithmic measure also satisfies the third proposition and, although we don't prove that here, nothing but the logarithmic measure satisfies the third proposition.

Suppose, to make all this concrete, that instead of picking a message directly from the universe U_n with four messages in it (figure 5.34a), the message is picked in two steps. The first step picks group A or group B (figure 5.34b). The second step picks one message of the two in the selected group. The first step is visualized as selecting one of the two messages A and B in a universe U_2. Either message conveys 1, 0.63, 0.50, 0.43, 0.30, or 0.21 units of substance depending on the scale (figure 5.34). The second step, say if group A has been picked in the first step, consists of picking one of M_1 and M_2. Either way, this second selection is once again from a universe U_2, $A(U_2)$ in this example. The second selection therefore also conveys 1, 0.63, 0.50, 0.43, 0.30, or 0.21 units of substance depending on the scale (figure 5.34).

Fully elaborated, Shannon's third proposition asserts that the total substance conveyed is the sum of the substance conveyed at each step. In this instance the sum is 2, 1.26, 1, 0.86, 0.60, or 0.42 depending on the scale. But, as figure 5.33 makes plain, that sum is just the amount of substance conveyed by a message picked in one step from a universe A_4.

Although couched in terms of message selection, Shannon's third proposition can be translated into a guarantee that no substance need be gained or lost when encoding messages in the way that figure 5.20 illustrates. This opens the door to a wide range of choices of the formats for messages, while matching the substance-carrying capacity of the formats with the substance measure of the messages, just as, for analog signals, Fourier analysis gave a way of thinking about efficiency as the matching of a waveform's bandwidth to the bandwidth of a transducer.

For a concrete instance of those ideas, think once again of the universe of discourse U_4 with four messages in it. These four messages can be formatted in the two-bit formats "00," "01," "10," and "11," in the manner of figure 5.20. Each of these two-bit formats can also be seen as a sequence of two one-bit formats, but for what messages? Figure 5.34b suggests viewing "0" in the left (first) bit position as a format for, say, "the message is in group $A(U_2)$" and "1" in the first bit as a format for "the message is in group $B(U_2)$." The interpretation of the symbol in the right (second) bit depends on what is in the first bit. If there's "0" in the first bit, then the second bit is a format for either M_1 or M_2. If there's a "1" in the first bit, then the second bit is a format for either M_3 or M_4.

Each bit is a format for a message selected from a universe U_2. Figure 5.33 shows that the measure of the substance conveyed by a message from U_2 is 1 unit, 0.63 units, 0.50 units, and so on, depending on the choice of scale. Picking the $\log_2$ scale for U_2 gives a nice round number, namely 1 unit. Since one bit position has the capacity to format one out of two possible messages and such a message conveys 1 unit of information on the $\log_2$ scale, this unit is also called a bit. In our example, one bit position holds exactly one unit of substance.

It therefore seems natural to use "bit" for the name of the unit of substance on Shannon's logarithmic scale as well as for the name of a slot that can hold either of the two symbols in a two-symbol alphabet. One bit slot, in our example, holds one bit of substance. In this limited context, at least, that is the most efficient possible use of a bit slot.

At first blush, such maximum efficiency is the exception, not the rule. Figure 5.33 tells us that a message from a universe of discourse U_3 conveys only 1.58 bits of substance. Unfortunately, there is no such thing as 1.58 bit slots. One bit slot can format only one of two messages. Two one-bit slots are enough for one out of four messages. The obvious thing to do is to use only three of the four possible two-slot binary codes. The inefficiency of doing so is also evident: allowing two one-bit slots for only 1.58 bits of information uses only $\frac{1.58}{2}$ or 79% of the available capacity.

Figure 5.33 shows that the only 100% efficient binary formats are those for universes with a number of messages in them that is a power of 2. Decimal formats are fully efficient only for universes with numbers of messages that are powers of 10, and alphabetic formats only for powers of 26. The gaps between 100% efficient formats are smallest for binary formats so, in that limited sense, binary formats are more efficient than any other format. Along with the ubiquity of two-state devices noted previously, this fact helps to account for the popularity of binary formats for digital processors.

Why not for all processors? There are concepts of efficiency other than the one we have just explored that favor formats other than binary.

One way to format the n messages in U_n is by representing each of them by one distinct element chosen from an alphabet of n elements. That is straightforward enough.

In theory, it also maximizes efficiency by using exactly one format position for one unit of information. But it has two drawbacks. One is that in the absence of natural n-state devices, the n symbols of the alphabet themselves have to be built up from some alphabet based on whatever number-of-state-devices are economically available. In most instances this synthesis introduces inefficiencies; witness, in figures 5.21 and 5.22, the binary formats for the decimal digits and for the 26 letters of the conventional alphabet.

More important than these technical inefficiencies is the tradeoff for people, expressed as follows by the logician Willard Quine:

In logical and mathematical systems either of two mutually antagonistic types of economy may be striven for, and each has its peculiar practical utility. On the one hand we may seek economy of practical expression—ease and brevity in the statement of multifarious relations. This sort of economy calls usually for distinctive concise notations for a wealth of concepts. Second, however, and oppositely, we may seek economy in grammar and vocabulary; we may try to find a minimum of basics concepts such that, once a distinctive notation has been appropriated to each of them, it becomes possible to express any desired further concept by mere combination and iteration of our basic notations.[7]

Since people find it difficult to memorize large alphabets, we have evolved ways of avoiding large alphabets by synthesizing formats for each of the many messages in large universes as arrays of formats for smaller universes. The universe of all possible English sentences is formatted by representing each sentence not as a unique alphabetic symbol in one slot but as a collection of many slots filled by words drawn from the "alphabet" that is the English dictionary. Each word, even, is not formatted as one slot filled by a single alphabetic

M$_i$	1 P$_i$	2 P$_i$	3 P$_i$
M$_1$	1/4	1/2	1
M$_2$	1/4	1/4	0
M$_3$	1/4	1/8	0
M$_4$	1/4	1/8	0

M = Message
P = Probability

Figure 5.35 Messages with different probabilities

symbol unique to that word but as a collection of slots filled by letters drawn from the bedrock 26-member roman alphabet of conventional English writing.

So far we have assumed that each message is as likely as every other message in the particular universe of discourse. For the universe of discourse U_4 with four elements, this amounts to assuming that each message is selected with a probability of $\frac{1}{4}$, as shown in column 1 of figure 5.35.

Another possibility, illustrated in column 3, is that one of the symbols has probability 1 while all other symbols have probability 0. If this is not to make a mockery of Shannon's second proposition, then a useful extension of the logarithmic measure must give an amount of substance per message that, in this case, is precisely equal to the amount of substance per message in a one-message universe, namely a zero.

Figure 5.35, column 2, suggests the most common case, and figure 5.36 illustrates it. The letters of the alphabet do not occur with equal frequency in English texts, nor does only one letter occur to the exclusion of all others. Figure 5.36 displays the probabilities of letters in English text as estimated by Godfrey Dewey in 1923. Not suprisingly, $e, t, a, o, i,$ and n were the five most probable letters.

As we have noted, English sentences are not each formatted as a monolithic symbol. They are instead strung together with words which, in turn, are strung together with letters, the letters, in turn, being picked from the roman alphabet with the probabilities shown in figure 5.36. That way of formatting messages as

Letter	%	Occur rences	Items	Initial	Medial	Final	Word	Letter
e	12.68	55,465	9,493	2,123	32,472	20,870		e
t	9.78	42,815	5,366	17,182	15,210	10,423		t
a	7.88	34,536	5,352	9,477	22,791	148	2,120	a
o	7.76	33,993	4,305	7,764	21,608	4,617	4	o
i	7.07	30,955	6,058	6,691	23,094	15	1,155	i
n	7.06	30,902	5,480	2,317	20,521	8,064		n
s	6.31	27,642	6,069	6,119	9,508	12,015		s
r	5.94	26,051	5,569	2,165	17,734	6,152		r
h	5.73	25,138	1,634	4,916	17,772	2,450		h
l	3.94	17,261	3,668	2,118	12,155	2,988		l
d	3.89	17,046	3,394	2,756	4,227	10,063		d
u	2.80	12,285	2,448	1,214	10,278	793		u
c	2.68	11,747	3,148	4,327	7,170	250		c
f	2.56	11,199	1,164	4,037	2,550	4,612		f
m	2.44	10,678	1,916	4,010	5,198	1,470		m
w	2.14	9,396	712	6,839	1,604	953		w
y	2.02	8,837	1,189	1,454	971	6,412		y
g	1.87	8,191	2,079	1,588	3,588	3,015		g
p	1.86	8,162	2,154	3,476	4,213	473		p
b	1.56	6,838	1,207	4,788	2,006	44		b
v	1.02	4,481	907	537	3,944			v
k	0.60	2,610	526	436	1,373	801		k
x	0.16	687	214		626	61		x
j	0.10	421	117	256	165			j
q	0.09	403	122	171	232			q
z	0.06	284	131	15	265	4		z
Totals	100.00	438,023	74,422	96,776	241,275	96,693	3,279	
		674 28	159 9	17	644 25	13 3		

Figure 5.36 Probabilities of letters in English text. From Godfrey Dewey, *Relative Frequency of English Speech Sounds* (Cambridge, MA: Harvard University Press, 1923), Table D2. Reprinted by permission.

strings of elementary messages lends itself to ways of formatting that ultimately can approximate 100% efficiency as closely as desired. On the average, for instance, it is even possible to format messages strung together with symbols drawn with equal probability from a three-symbol alphabet so that precisely 1.68 bit slots are used per message on the average and not the inefficient 2 bit slots per message suggested earlier.

When messages have unequal probabilities, like the letters in figure 5.36, the amount of information to be matched with the capacity of a letter slot in an English text strung together with these letters is the weighted average of the amount of information per letter.

Shannon has shown that the amount of information per letter is $\log\frac{1}{p}$, where p is the probability of the letter. If all letters have equal probability, as in column 1 of figure 5.35, the weighted average is $p \cdot \log\frac{1}{p}$—the amount of information per letter weighted by the probability of the letter—multiplied by n, since all n letters have precisely the same probability. But, since p is just $\frac{1}{n}$, where all probabilities are equal, then $n \cdot p$ is $n \cdot \frac{1}{n} = 1$, so the average amount of substance per letter is just $\log\frac{1}{p}$ itself. In this instance, since $p = \frac{1}{4}$ hence $\frac{1}{p} = 4$, $\log\frac{1}{p} = \log 4$ or two bits of substance per message, the logarithm of the number of messages as before. Two bit slots match this exactly, as we already know.

When the probabilities are unequal, the weighted probabilities have to be added together one by one, as in $p_1 \cdot \log\frac{1}{p1} + p_2 \cdot \log\frac{1}{p2} + \cdots + p_n \cdot \log\frac{1}{pn}$. For $n = 2$, p_2 is $1 - p1$, so the average amount of substance per message is $H_2 = p \cdot \log\frac{1}{p} + (1 - p) \cdot \log\frac{1}{(1-p)}$. Figure 5.37 plots the values of H_2 as the probability of the first message ranges from 0 to 1. When the first message has probability 0, the second has probability 1; and for all practical purposes, this is like U_1, the universe with only one message in it. The amount of substance per message is 0. Likewise when the probability of the first message is 1. The average amount of substance per message grows as the probabilities get more nearly equal, coming to the not-unexpected maximum of one bit of substance per symbol as the probability of each of the two messages reaches $\frac{1}{2}$. It is intuitively satisfying that the amount of substance per message is greatest when either message is as likely as the other and that the amount decreases as the likelihood that one message will be forthcoming rather than the other increases.

Now, to make good on the promise to match fractional amounts of substance per symbol with symbol slots that come only in whole numbers:

In a literal sense, this is impossible. For example, a single message from a universe of discourse U_2 that conveys only a fraction of a bit of substance still must take up at least one bit slot. Bit slots come only in whole numbers.

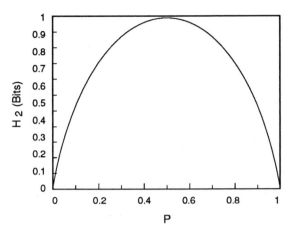

Figure 5.37   Average amount of substance per message in a two-message universe

However, on the average, fractional capacities can be made up to match fractional bits of substance. Figuring out how to do this took an explicit understanding and exploitation of a way to pick formats that is always informally at work in the evolution of ordinary language.

The very short formats that the informal evolution of English language conventions assigns to the very frequent articles and prepositions "a," "the," "in," "to," and so on, are consistent with the modern formal understanding. So is the assignment of the shortest Morse code symbols, dot and dash, to the most frequent letters "e" and "t" in the writings of North American and Western European countries.

The formatting scheme illustrated by figures 5.32, 5.33, and 5.34 does not take into account the probabilities of the messages in the universe of discourse being formatted. For a universe U_4 with messages M_1, M_2, M_3, and M_4 in it (figure 5.35), this approach uses the four two-bit formats "00," "01," "10," and "11" whether all four messages have equal probability $\frac{1}{4}$ or whether the probabilities $p(M_i)$ are different, say $p(M_1) = \frac{1}{2}$, $p(M_2) = \frac{1}{4}$, and $p(M_3) = p(M_4) = \frac{1}{8}$. But in the first instance two bits, the average amount of substance per message, is precisely equal to the number of bit slots and the formatting is as efficient as it can be. In the second instance, the average amount of substance per message, namely the quantity $p(M_i)\log\frac{1}{p(M_i)}$ summed over the four messages, is only 1.75 bits, or $\frac{1.75}{2}$ for 87.5% efficiency.

However, a different formatting scheme, invented by David Huffman in 1952, leads on an average to an exact match between substance per message and slots per message.[8] Huffman's method is a variation on the approach of figure 5.34. In the first step, the universe of discourse is divided into two parts selected to make the sum of the probabilities of the messages in each part as nearly equal as possible. In the example of figure 5.35, column 2, the partition is not as shown in figure 5.34, but rather into a universe U_1 with M_1 in it, for a total probability of $\frac{1}{2}$, and a universe U_3 with M_2, M_3, and M_4 in it, and probabilities that add up to $\frac{1}{2}$.

The one message in U_1, namely M_1, is assigned the first—and, it turns out, the only—format digit "1." All three messages in U_3, namely M_2, M_3, and M_4, are assigned the first format digit "0." For U_3, however, the process does not end, since it remains to tell M_2, M_3, and M_4 apart one from another. The partitioning process is, therefore, repeated for U_3. U_3 is divided into U_1 with M_2 in it and total probability $\frac{1}{4}$ and U_2 with M_3 and M_4 in it (and total probability also $\frac{1}{4}$). To the first format digit "0" which all messages in U_3 have in common this second partitioning adds the second format digit "1" for M_2 and the second format digit "0" for each of M_3 and M_4. Since M_3 and M_4 remain together in their U_2, they need a third format digit to tell them apart, say "1" for M_3 and "0" for M_4.

The outcome is a one-slot format "1" for M_1 with its probability $\frac{1}{2}$, a two-slot format "01" for M_2 with its probability $\frac{1}{4}$, and, for M_3 and M_4 with their probabilities of $\frac{1}{8}$ each, the three-slot formats "001" and "000" respectively. The average number of slots per format is 1.75, precisely the average amount of substance per message.

Formally, the possibility of the Huffman scheme is accounted for by a sharpening of Shannon's third proposition to take account of unequal message probabilities: The amount of substance per message in a one-step message selection is the weighted sum of the substance per message in each step of a two-step selection. Even where the probabilities aren't as neat as the $\frac{1}{2}$, $\frac{1}{4}$, $\frac{1}{8}$, and $\frac{1}{8}$ of the exemplary universe U_4, extensions of Huffman's process can fit slot capacity to amount of substance with an efficiency that, on the average, can be brought as close to 100% as desired.[9] The continual creation and testing of acronyms and abbreviations, only some of which make it into the mainstream of language, is one phenomenon that reflects the evolutionary equivalent of the Huffman process at work.

The match between format slot capacity and the amount of substance is only one measure of efficiency. There is also a tradeoff between the efficiency that comes from having a unique monolithic symbol for every message in a universe and the alternative efficiency that comes from building up each message as a sequence of more elementary messages. At the level of words as the universe of messages, Chinese is at the one extreme of this tradeoff and English is at the other extreme, among contemporary languages. The Chinese "alphabet" is hell to learn but economical in use, at least by people. The English alphabet is easier to learn, but it takes so many more characters in English than in Chinese to express a given message.

Identifying and expressing key efficiency measures for formats and for the tradeoffs among formats remains a lively challenge to the digital arts and sciences and to the world of competitive digital enterprises. The square off between the proponents of keyboards and mice in the microcomputer marketing world in the early '80s is but one example of the search for format-and-process efficiency in various contexts.

There is also a parallel search for effectiveness.

To be effective in real-world processors, real-world formats have to stay what they are meant to be and not become something else. If I wire a payment of $100, I don't want $1000 to be paid at the other end just because an extra "0" got put in the format. But accidents in real-world processors can change a collection of physical tokens in random or systematic but always unwelcome patterns. The effects of such accidents are generically called "noise." Noise degrades the effectiveness of formats.

"Effectiveness" here refers to the effectiveness of formats, not of substance. Substance might be graded from positive values, as in a timely warning not to step off the curb in front of a truck, through negative values, as in disinformation meant to make mischief, like a scurrilous rumor. Whatever the intrinsic quality of substance, its intended effect is not achieved if the format or formats intended to convey it fail to do their job. Noise is anything that leads to such a format failure.

Figure 5.38, where the signal gets noisier from left to right, gives an analog example that illustrates the origin of the noise metaphor. A pure tone, as we have already seen in figure 5.24, gives a sinusoidal trace, as shown on the left side of figure 5.38. What is heard when a pure tone is played next to a buzzer might look like the trace at the right of the diagram. Describing the signal at the right as noisy implies that the buzzing sound was unintended. Otherwise the trace at the right would itself be a good format. Like weedy lawns, or slops on a dinner plate, noisy formats are noisy in the mind of the beholder because they include something unwanted. Dandelion grown for salad is not a weed, the

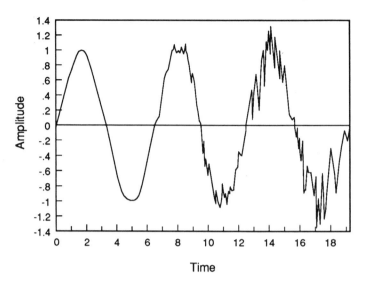

Figure 5.38 Analog signal and noise

buzzer announcing someone at the door is a signal not a noise, and the last mouthful is good food and not slops when you're still hungry. In a Bach cantata, the trace on the right would be noisy!

Noise is best avoided whenever possible. FM radio, for example, is inherently less vulnerable to the kinds of noise that afflict radio transmission than AM radio is. Even once it has intruded into analog signals, noise can often be eliminated from them, especially when the noise is random. Generally, a little noise, as in the middle of figure 5.38, is as tough to eliminate as a lot of noise, as on the right of figure 5.38. The Dolby circuit in expensive tape recorders is one widely known noise suppressor. Once again, however, digital trading on nature's nonlinearity makes noise control and even noise suppression relatively easier and cheaper in the digital world than in the analog world.

Figure 5.39a shows the characteristic of an amplifier for a digital format wherein no-pulse is the token for "0" and a pulse is the token for "1." Any input pulse lower than the threshold value .25 marked by the left-dashed vertical is output as no-pulse. Any input pulse higher than the threshold value .75 marked by the right-dashed vertical is output as a pulse. Figure 5.40b shows how perfect input pulses (lightly shaded) pass throught the transducer unaltered to become perfect output pulses (heavily shaded).

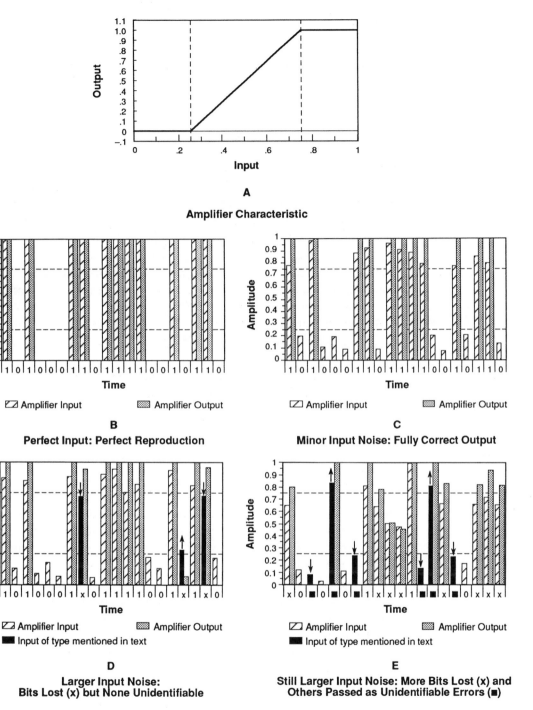

Figure 5.39 Digital signals and noise

In the digital world, a small amount of noise is as good as no noise at all. The input signals in figure 5.39c include some no-pulses that noise has perverted into palpable pulses. The input signals in figure 5.39c also include some pulses that noise has degraded to a fraction of their original height. But the former never get above the .25 threshold and the latter never get below the .75 threshold, so the effect of the nonlinear transducer characteristic is a perfect restoration of the intended signal, free of any noise.

But, as the noise level increases (figure 5.39d, e), more and more no-pulses creep up above the lower threshold and cannot be told apart from pulses that have crept down below the upper threshold. When there is good discrimination between perfect pulses and the degraded ones, as there happens to be in figure 5.39d, some digits are lost but no error creeps in undetected. In figure 5.39e, however, the noise level is high enough to make one no-pulse creep above the upper threshold and therefore be turned into what seems to be a perfect token for "1" when it is really a token for "0" gone wrong.

But even a degraded pulse masquerading as a perfect can be caught. In 1950 Richard Hamming systematized the design of digital formats that can detect and even correct errors.[10]

The relationship between digital formats and the substance they stand for is arbitrary. Different digital formats behave differently under noisy conditions. It is therefore possible to pick formats with behaviors more or less effective under various conditions.

Figure 5.40 shows a four-message universe with the messages $a, b, c,$ and d. These four messages are shown formatted in a two-bit-per-message format and also in a variable length format. The two-bit format is called a block code, because each message is formatted as a block of bits with the same number of bits in each block. The variable length formats are called prefix formats, because no format is the prefix of a longer format. Note, for example, that since the binary digit "1" formats the message "A," it does not occur as the first digit in any longer message. Neither does the two-bit combination "01" occur in any three-bit combination.

These different traits of block and prefix formats give them different behavior under noisy conditions.

Column 1 of figure 5.40b shows the message "BAD" formatted first in a block format and next in a prefix format. Column 2 shows the effect of a type of noise that makes the first bit get lost altogether. The effect on the message is quite different depending on the format. In the block format, the first two bits are paired to yield the erroneous message c, then the next two are paired to

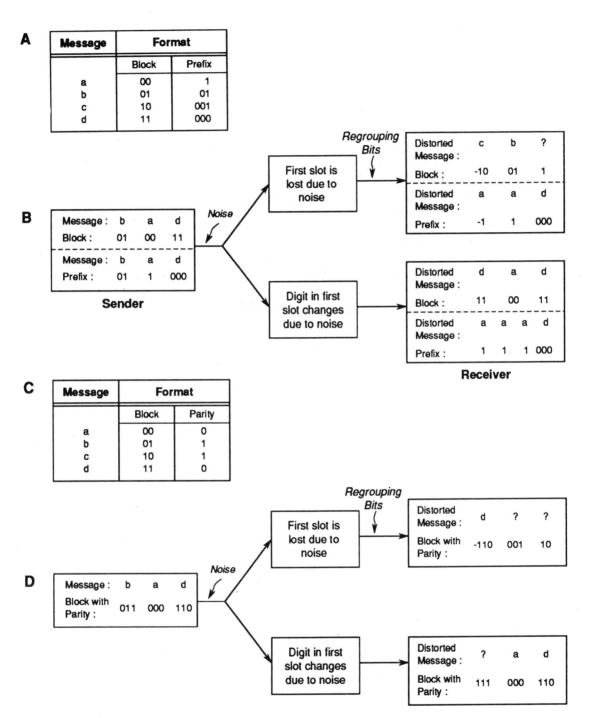

Figure 5.40 Effectiveness of binary formats

yield an erroneous *b*, but one bit is left over. That unpaired bit gives a clue that something is awry. In the prefix format, however, the first two "1"s are twice erroneously interpreted as "a," leaving the last three bits to be interpreted—as it happens correctly—as a "d." There is no clue that the message is in error. In column 3, the noise manifests itself as a reversal that puts a 1 where there was a 0. In this instance, both the block format and the prefix format yield erroneous messages. Neither gives a clue that an error has occurred.

We saw earlier that the prefix format is more efficient than the block format when not all the messages in a universe of discourse equal probabilities. Here we see that this efficiency is gained at a price. In no instance did the prefix-formatted text give any clue about an error. But in one out of three instances, the block-formatted text indicated that the message was in error. This hints at the possibility of tradeoffs between efficiency and effectiveness. These tradeoffs have been systematized over the years in an elaborate theory of formatting, called coding theory by its practitioners.

Coding theory systematizes an art which all people have unconsciously practiced over the centuries.[11] Told that "Noe ia thr yime fpr alk hood mwn ti cone to thw aud if tjeir partu" is supposed to be English, most every English speaker is instantly able to tell that if the text is English, then it must be egregiously misspelled. Almost as instantly, most people are able to correct the spelling errors, even without being told that each of them stems from a finger hitting a neighboring key on the typewriter instead of the intended one. This capability stems from the redundancy built into the formatting of English messages in the conventional 26-letter alphabet. The ability to detect errors stems from the fact that not every possible sequence of letters is used to format English words. It is therefore child's play to see that "thr" and "thw" are wrong, at least in ordinary text without chemical abbreviations or British or Canadian zip codes. There is a tradeoff here. A redundant format is not as efficient as one without redundancy. More messages could be represented in three alphabetic positions than actually are represented. It is wasteful to resort to four-letter words when three-letter combinations like "thr" and "thw" go unused.

Figure 5.40b shows one widely used way of systematizing the tradeoff between efficiency and effectiveness. Starting with the block format, a bit is added that makes the number of "ones" in each three-bit format an even number. This uses only four out of the eight possible three-bit combinations. The four other three-bit combinations, each with an odd number of ones in it, are unused.

Adding a parity bit changes behavior under noise. The loss of the first slot bit still lets an erroneous block-formatted message through, but the next block is recognized as incorrect since it is of odd parity and, as before, the two-bit block can be recognized as not a format at all. Under a digit change, the loss of parity is immediately recognizable, and the error is detected right where it occurs.

In general, a block format of any length with a single parity bit lends itself to the unfailing detection of a single reversal error. This follows from the fact that any single error in a parity bit block code changes the parity and thus leads to an unused bit combination.

Figure 5.41 shows a parity bit for single error detection added to the three-bit code used to represent the eight levels of quantization in a pulse code modulated voice signal of figure 5.32. The ASCII (American Standard Code for Information Interchange) format used by telephone companies and computer manufacturers worldwide to format numerals, letters, punctuation marks, and digitized speech is a seven-bit code with an eighth bit added for parity.

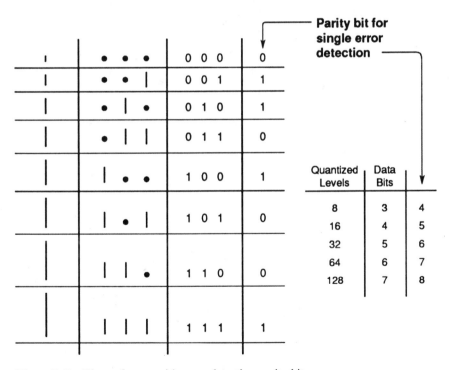

Figure 5.41   Binary format with error-detecting parity bit

That is, during a period of rapid technological change, relative understanding of these possibilities and of their economical applications is one of the many factors affecting the survival or the success of old and new competitors.

Digital Processes: What Hardware and Software Processors Do

Digital formats are useful because digitally formatted substance is amenable to electro-optical digital processing. "Digital processor" is not just a pretentious way of saying "computer" but rather a reflection of the protean capabilities of the technology. In contrast, "computer" has lost whatever generic connotation it once had, conveying far too narrow a picture of what digital processors do. "Computer" conjures up images of technicians fiddling with numbers, while the early 1980s saw many special tags put on computers specialized to particular tasks. A computer programmed to assist in secretarial work was called a "word processor." Detroit called computers that control fuel injection and other functions in an automobile engine "command control modules." No computers were in the U.S. Army, only "fire control subsystems." In short, electro-optical digital processors adapted to market niches or to legal quirks.

Digital processors are attractive in the first place because of certain theoretically unlimited capabilities. This attractiveness-in-principle keeps translating into attractiveness-in-practice because of the continuing increases in capabilities and decreases in costs of real-world electro-optical digital processors.

Two things account for the theoretically unlimited capability of digital processors. First, as set forth in the preceding sections, any substance can be represented in a digital format to as close a degree of approximation as one might wish. The only practical limit is the cost of digital formats and of digital processors, a cost which keeps coming down while most other costs keep going up. Digital formats cannot miraculously capture the unknown or the ineffable. But what is known and expressible in any format is expressible in some digital format. Second, any recipe for doing something to substance can be expressed as a recipe for doing it with a digital processor to a digital format for that substance.

Stipulating a recipe to be in hand is important.

For instance, there is no recipe for creative thinking. Although almost everything about research in artifical intelligence is racked by controversy, not even the most ardent AI advocates claim that digital processors can rival the entire gamut of human capacities for creative thinking.[12] Between trite recipes and impossibility there is a whole gamut of more or less successful attempts to capture expert knowledge and to computerize its application to medicine, chemistry, and warfare, among others.[13] There are also whole categories of mathematical problems for which it has been understood, since the work of Kurt Godel in the late 1930s, that no recipe can ever be found.[14] Within these boundaries, there is a lot of scope for useful recipes.

The aim here is not to detail how industry actually designs and builds digital processors. The main point is to explain why designing and building digital processors remains adventuresome and not cut-and-dried, why the former Data General engineer could reminisce to Tracy Kidder, in *The Soul of a New Machine*, that it was "a lot of fun, a lot of pressure, . . . a tremendous amount of team spirit. . . . It was decided that the Eclipse should have error-correction code. What was that? There wasn't that much written about it at that time. Tom went and learned about it and came up with how to do it."[15]

At the heart of the matter is the fact that it takes a huge number of building-block processes to make up useful workaday processes going on in concrete workaday electro-optical digital processors. For instance, the president of AT&T Bell Laboratories has said that 40 million building-block processes of a certain kind were used at the time of divestiture in January 1984 "in the local communications networks now run by the divested Bell companies, and in the long distance network run by AT&T Communications."[16] These building blocks made up programs to control switches, programs to help install and keep track of plant, and so on. Precisely what is being counted and precisely how much of it there is at this stage of the story is less important than the idea that whatever it is, it is literally counted in the millions of units, and that its cost is an increasingly dominant factor in the cost of electro-optical digital processing systems. Figure 5.42 shows how software costs have overwhelmed hardware costs in the last three decades.

There are two reasons for the ambiguity in what is being counted. First, big building blocks are made up of little building blocks, made up in turn of littler building blocks like the electrons and protons within the atoms within the molecules that make up a piece of cheese or a bird. How much you count depends on what layer you focus on. Second, there is much latitude—hence much opportunity for "now you see it, now you don't"—in realizing building blocks in either hardware or software, a point about which more later.

What matters at this juncture is that whatever level of building block is being counted and however that level might be realized, the right or wrong choice of the most elementary building blocks, the primitive building blocks,

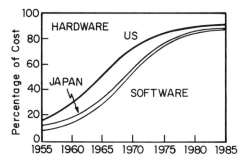

Figure 5.42   Relative hardware and software costs

has enormous consequences when multiplied by the large number of building blocks needed to make up a system that is useful in the workaday world. The choice of primitive processes and the decision as to what to synthesize and what to treat as a primitive are among the many scientific and engineering decisions made in this industry. Indeed, the search for new devices that might be more effective or efficient building blocks continues.

The most elementary building blocks or primitives of digital recipes are elementary processes on elementary statements. For a collection of elementary statements and elementary processes to be useful, combinations of these statements and processes must be sufficient to express any desired statement in a desired universe of discourse and any desired process on these statements. Logicians have assured the world that there are many possible collections of elementary statements and processes—primitives—that fit this bill for a wide variety of purposes.[17] The following examples build on a selection of primitives that happens to be particularly well matched to the binary formats based on the abstract binary representations that are so well matched in turn to the concrete binary tokens that happen to be so readily available in this universe at this time.

One widely used set of primitives or building blocks includes pairs of statements only one of which can be true at a time. Examples are such pairs as A, "The sun is shining today" and its negation A', "The sun is not shining today"; the pair B, "The fifth digit is '0'" and its negation B', "The fifth digit is not '0'," the latter equivalent to "The fifth digit is '1'" if the universe of discourse happens to be numbers in a binary format; and the pair C, "This customer gets the dunning letter" and its negation C', "This customer does not get the dunning letter." Here we take it on faith that statements useful in designing and using digital processors can be built up from these primitive pairs of statements.

NOT			AND and OR		
Input	Output		Inputs A B	AND Output A and B	OR Output A or B
0	1		0 0	0	0
1	0		0 1	0	1
			1 0	0	1
			1 1	1	1

Figure 5.43   Truth tables for primitive digital processor transducers

Words like "and," "or," and "not" are the cement that holds our primitive statements together in more complicated and more subtly expressive statements. "The debt is over $500" and "The time overdue is more than three months" may express the finer structure of "This customer gets the dunning letter." Once the arcane province of scholars, putting together such expressions has become the realm of the daily secretarial routine with word and list processors. Fortunes were made in the early 1980s with software products such as Lotus Development Corporation's Lotus 1-2-3 and Microsoft's MS-DOS and AT&T Bell Laboratories' UNIX that made such tasks easy for anyone to specify.[18]

Paired primitives are especially well suited to binary formatting, as by formatting "*A* is true" as "1" and "*A* is false" as "0." If *A* is true ($A = 1$) and *B* is true ($B = 1$), then their negations A' and B' are both false ($A' = B' = 0$), their conjunction "*A* and *B*" and their disjunction "*A* or *B*" are both true, and so on.

The process of transforming the truth values of statements into the truth value of their negation, conjunction, or disjunction can be looked at as the process done by a transducer which accepts as inputs all the possible combinations of truth values of the statements and delivers the truth value of the negation, conjunction, or disjunction as its output. Figure 5.43 shows the truth tables, as the "characteristics" of such logical transducers are called, for negation ("not"), conjunction ("and"), and disjunction ("or") transducers.

Although foreshadowed in the work of the English mathematician George Boole in the 19th century, all of this was of limited interest even to logicians until, in the late 1930s and early 1940s, first electrical relays and then vacuum tubes were used to build concrete transducers that actually behaved in accordance with the truth tables of figure 5.43 for pulse (1) and no-pulse (0) combinations. The transistor was invented in 1948 by John Bardeen and Walter

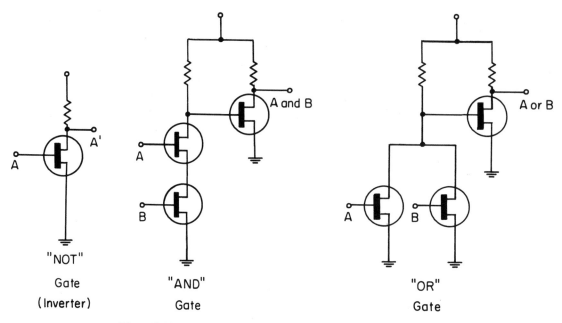

Figure 5.44   Transistor not, and, and or gates

Brattain, and later improved by William Shockley. All three got a Nobel Prize in 1956. After that, and-, or-, and not-gates, as digital people call the primitive transducers, were quickly realized in transistor technology. Figure 5.44 sketches how this is done.

Figure 5.44 shows that both "and" and "or" can be wired up as combinations of three transistors (the circles) and two resistors (the sawtooth shapes). In this instance, only the geometry of the connections differentiates the "and" gate from the "or" gate. One factor impacting the success of a firm that makes digital processors is the combination of competency and luck necessary to select the right primitive operations realizable with the right economies in manufacture to produce the intended product. Dissipating the heat generated by millions of operating gates and figuring out practicable ways of interconnecting them are the fundamental design problems for the creators of digital processor hardware. Even so elementary a circuit as an "and" gate or an "or" gate has at least 13 points that must be connected correctly and securely: the two terminals on each of the two resistors (four) plus the three terminals on each of the three transistors (nine). When transistors first appeared in the early '40s, this meant

Type	Model	Word size	Memory	Memory cycle time	I/O transfer rate	Price range (1984)
Micro computer	Apple II/II+	8 bits	16–64 kilobytes	300 nanoseconds		$2000
Mini computer	Digital Data Systems 315	16 bits	64–256 kilobytes	500 nanoseconds	1.7 NB/sec	$10,000
Mainframe computer	IBM 3083–B	32 bits	32,768–98,304 kilobytes	312 nanoseconds	24 NB/sec	$182,000

Figure 5.45   Number of primitives in real digital processors

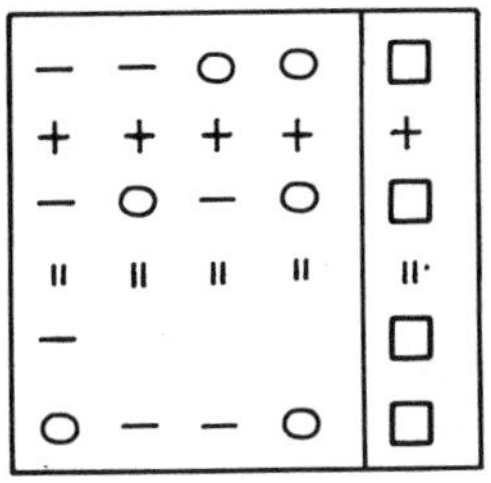

Figure 5.46   Substance: The binary adder

handling 13 individual wires. The technology that evolved since then has permitted enormous increases in the number of elements that can be interconnected effectively and economically.

Figure 5.45 summarizes the number of primitives of various kinds contained in some representative machines.

Figure 5.46 is a table that defines the process of adding together a pair of binary numbers, each only one bit long. The four possible input combinations to this one-place binary adder are shown in the second column. The equivalent decimal sum is shown in the first column. Two one-place binary numerals can generate a carry into the 2's place just as two one-place decimal numerals, when added together, can generate a carry into the tens' place (e.g., in decimal, $7 + 5 = 13$, where "3" is the sum digit and "1" the carry). This two-input device therefore also needs two outputs, one to produce the sum digit, the other to produce the carry digit when appropriate. The carry and sum digits are shown in the third and fourth columns, respectively.

A one-place binary adder can be synthesized from a combination of the three primitive functions of figure 5.43. An adder that handles enough binary places

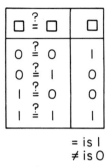

$$\square \overset{?}{=} \square \qquad \square$$

$$O \overset{?}{=} O \qquad I$$
$$O \overset{?}{=} I \qquad O$$
$$I \overset{?}{=} O \qquad O$$
$$I \overset{?}{=} I \qquad I$$

= is I
≠ is O

Figure 5.47 Process: The test for equality

to be useful can then be synthesized from one-place binary adders. A full-blown binary adder is just one element of a digital processor that might do useful computations. The art of designing digital processors thus entails contemplating the possible combinations of many such building blocks into a whole that will not only be technically harmonious but also economical to manufacture and to use. The trials and errors this entails give birth to strong emotions. As Tracy Kidder reports in *The Soul of a New Machine*:

Some computer engineers harbor strong feelings toward their new designs, like Cossacks toward their horses. Carl Alsing, a veteran engineer ..., told the fable of an engineer, who, being informed that his plans for a new machine had been scrapped by the managers of his company, got a gun and murdered a colleague whose design had been accepted. Alsing said he thought that such a murder really happened but that a woman was probably involved—yet it came, he said, to much the same thing.[19]

If adding a pair of numbers typifies building blocks for what a digital processor might usefully do to substance, the test for equality shown in figure 5.47 typifies building blocks for controlling the process itself. Testing for equality is one of the many ways in which digital processors use the outcome of earlier stages of processing to govern later stages of processing. If, for example, figures 5.46 and 5.47 came from earlier processes, one set of further processes might be followed if figure 5.46 is the same as figure 5.47 and another set of further processes might be followed if both figures are not the same. Built into a digital process, the test for equality is one of the many possible building blocks for choice.

The digital processor designer's agony and his venture capitalist's cliffhanging are compounded by interactions between substantive processing and process control, with consequences that may be manifest immmediately but that might also play themselves out only in some performance characteristic defined by many layers of building blocks made out of blocks made out of blocks made out of primitives. The fact that the equality test could be built from the primitive adder or vice versa illustrates this road to madness. Comparing the output column of the adder (figure 5.46) with the output column of the equality tester (figure 5.47) shows that either one is just the negation of the other: Wherever one of them has a "1" the other has a "0" and vice-versa. Hence, given an adder, one could make up an equality tester not by creating a new primitive, but by combining the primitive adder with the primitive negation process to synthesize the equality tester. Or, alternatively, a primitive equality tester, combined again with the primitive negation process, could serve to synthesize an adder. Either way, two primitives would do instead of three. Consequently there would be manufacturing savings, as in tooling up for fabricating the third primitive. But there would be assembly costs in putting together two primitives to synthesize the third process. And the synthezised process of figure 5.48 might be slower than a logically equivalent process realized as a primitive. Such decisions are far from cut and dried. They have a lot to do with style. As Tracy Kidder reports about one decision:

Looking into the VAX, West imagined he saw a diagram of DEC's corporate organization. He felt that VAX was too complicated. He did not like, for instance, the system by which various parts of the machine communicated with each other: for his taste there was too much protocol involved. He decided that VAX embodied flaws in DEC's corporate organization. The machine expressed that phenomenally successful company's cautious style. Was this true? West said it didn't matter, it was a useful theory. Then he rephrased his opinions. "With VAX, DEC was trying to minimize the risk," he said, as he swerved around another car. Grinning, he went on: "We're trying to maximize the win, and make Eagle go as fast as a raped ape."[20]

Although the details vary from digital processor to digital processor, the zillions of pieces described in figures 5.42 and 5.44 are organized into five principal functional units as illustrated in figure 5.48.

The operations or processing unit is in one sense the heart, if not the soul, of a new machine. That's what does whatever the machine is intended to do by way of useful processes on substance. The binary adder of figure 5.46 might be one of the elementary pieces inside an operations unit.

The control unit is what distinguishes an automatic digital processor from a processor that needs human intervention at every step of the way. How automatic a digital processor is perceived to be depends, as things so often do, on

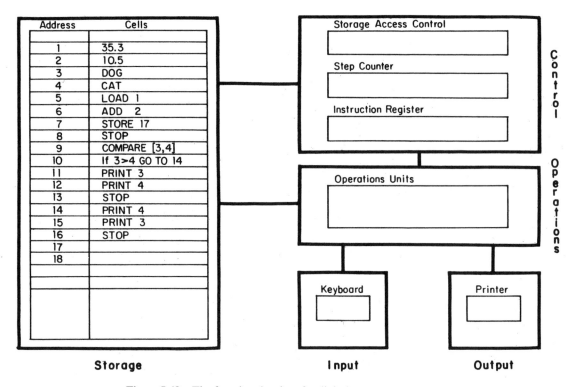

Address	Cells
1	35.3
2	10.5
3	DOG
4	CAT
5	LOAD 1
6	ADD 2
7	STORE 17
8	STOP
9	COMPARE [3,4]
10	If 3>4 GO TO 14
11	PRINT 3
12	PRINT 4
13	STOP
14	PRINT 4
15	PRINT 3
16	STOP
17	
18	

Storage Access Control

Step Counter

Instruction Register

Operations Units

Keyboard

Printer

Control

Operations

Storage   **Input**   **Output**

Figure 5.48   The functional units of a digital processor

who's looking and when. As seen by its user, the $5 hand-held four-function calculator is not at all automatic. However, from the standpoint of whoever designed the chip inside the box, there is a good deal of automatic control within what the user sees as a primitive operation, like an addition or a multiplication. Explicitly or implicitly, however, every digital processor has both some operations units and some mechanisms for controlling the process.

A digital processor with only control and operations units would be of little value if unable to communicate with the entire world. Hence, input and output units.

And, finally, in order to keep track of intermediate results, storage units.

Besides holding substance, the storage units can perform an additional and crucial function: They can also store the instructions, the program, that the digital processor will follow. Conceptually, this means that controlling information is substance just like the substance meant to be processed in the first place, so that digital processors can process their own control system and alter their own behavior. How much this possibility ultimately adds to the range of choice already afforded by devices like the equality test remains conjectural. In practice, substance and program-as-substance have been kept apart by designers in the Aiken architecture tradition who stress the reliability gained by not taking the risk of accidentally mucking up control information by mistaking it for substance to be processed. Substance and program-as-substance have been intermingled by designers in the Von Neumann architecture tradition who stress the economy afforded by having only one memory system used more efficiently than if two distinct memories are provided.

Figure 5.49 illustrates how all this works in either tradition. Specifically, it shows how the numbers 35.3 and 10.5, stored in cells 1 and 2 respectively (figure 5.49), are added together—by the instructions held in cells 5 through 8 (figure 5.49)—and their sum stored in cell 17.

Before the process begins, the special storage cells (registers) in the control and operations units are empty except for the step counter, which is assumed to have been set to 5, which is the cell number or address of the first instruction in the program. The "initial column" of figure 5.49 shows these conditions of the registers.

In the first of the 12 steps in figure 5.49, the first instruction is fetched from cell 5 and put in the instruction register. That first instruction is made up of two parts. One part, consisting of the letters "LOAD," tells the digital processor what to do. The other part, consisting of the numeral "1," tells the processor what to do it to, in this instance to whatever is in cell 1. For that purpose, the address "1" is stripped from the full instruction and also put in the storage access control register. The purpose of the instruction is to take whatever is in cell 1 and load it into the operations unit.

At the second step, the instruction in the instruction register is actually executed: The number held in the storage cell 1 is brought into the operations unit. Once an instruction has been executed, the control unit prepares itself to do the next one—assumed to be in the next cell of the processor's storage area—by incrementing the step counter, as shown in the third column of figure 5.49. An instruction is thus executed in a three-element cycle: fetching the instruction, executing it, and, by incrementing the step counter, getting ready to fetch and execute the next instruction. This cycle is repeated for the instruction held at address 6, then for that at address 7. The instruction at address 8 is a stop instruction which halts the process at mid-cycle in the fourth step.

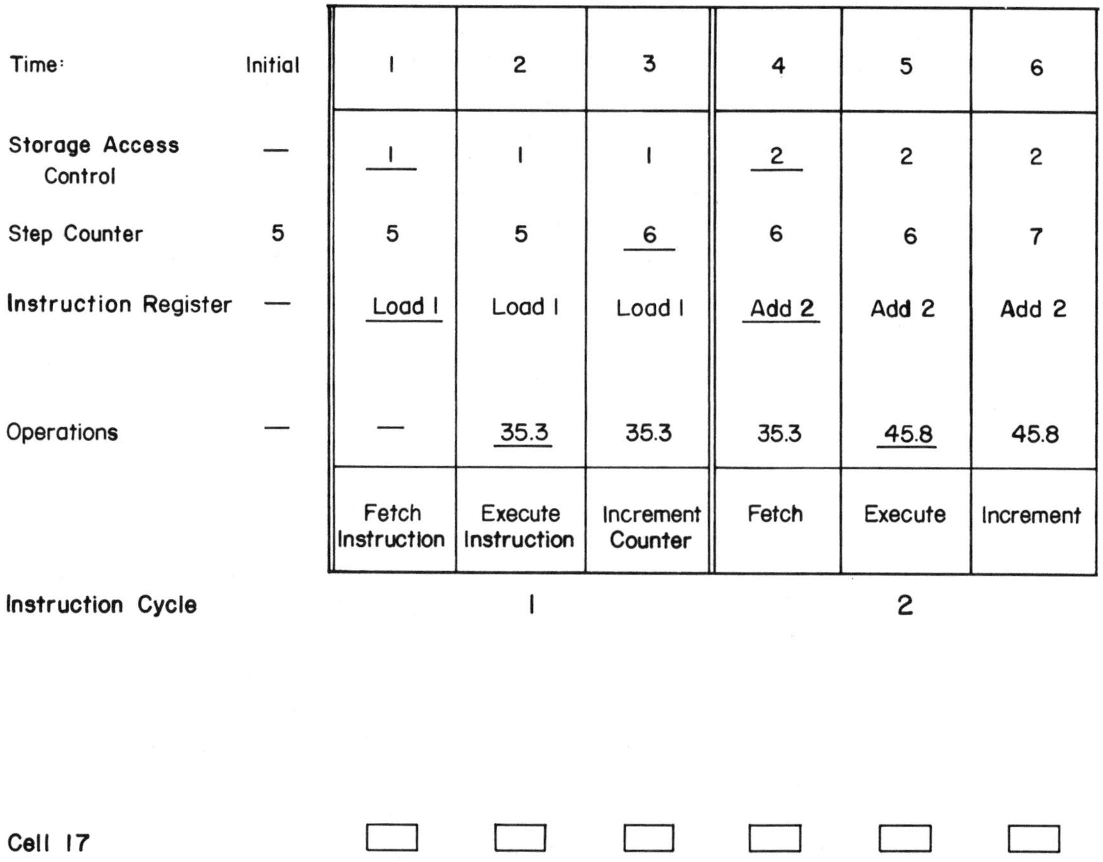

Time:	Initial	I	2	3	4	5	6
Storage Access Control	—	I	I	I	2	2	2
Step Counter	5	5	5	6	6	6	7
Instruction Register	—	Load I	Load I	Load I	Add 2	Add 2	Add 2
Operations	—	—	35.3	35.3	35.3	45.8	45.8
		Fetch Instruction	Execute Instruction	Increment Counter	Fetch	Execute	Increment

Instruction Cycle	I	2

Cell 17   ☐ ☐ ☐ ☐ ☐ ☐

Figure 5.49   Digital processor operation

Note that the capability for going through the three elements of the instruction cycle is here assumed to have been built into the digital processor's hardware. On the other hand, the specifics of the particular illustrative program are not built in the machine as hardware, but are inserted as software into the machine's storage or memory.

The distinction between hardware and software is real enough in the sense just illustrated: Hardware is the palpable stuff out of which a machine is built; software is information put in afterwards. What is not nearly so hard and fast is the assessment of the relative merits of what is wired into hardware and what is left to be put in or taken out ad lib after construction of the hardware has been

7	8	9	10	11	12
<u>17</u> 7 Store 17 45.8	17 7 Store 17 45.8	17 <u>8</u> Store 17 45.8	— 8 Stop 45.8	— 8 Stop 45.8	
Fetch	Execute	Increment	Fetch	Execute	Increment

| | 3 | | | 4 | |

☐   45.8   45.8   45.8   45.8   45.8

Figure 5.49 (continued)

completed. How much of a machine's "smarts" should be embodied in hardware? How much is left to be added afterwards as software? How much in between in various kinds of more or less "firmware"? These are matters for everlasting debates among digital processor designers, marketers, and users. For instance, the joystick used to control spaceships and their weapons on many a computer-controlled videogame usually has an activating trigger. An IBM Technical Reference had this to say about the trigger on the IBM Personal Computer's joystick: A trigger button is on each joy stick or paddle. These buttons default to an open state and are read as "1." When a button is pressed, it is read as "0." Software should be aware that these buttons are not debounced in hardware.

In other words, the design decision was made in this instance to assign to software rather than to hardware the responsibility for ignoring the switch until the bouncing shown in figure 5.15 had settled down. One can easily imagine military applications in which the decision would have gone the other way, and a hardware chip built into the joystick.

Whether realized as hardware, software, or firmware, or any other variants on those themes, the program in cells 5 through 8 has one glaring flaw: It is not worth writing at all. It clearly is easier to add 35.3 and 10.5—even in one's head, certainly on a hand calculator—to get 45.8 than to go through the bother of writing four instructions, let alone giving the explanation that went along with figure 5.49. Even if the processors themselves are fast and cheap, there is nothing to be gained by repeating, even fast and cheaply, something that had to be done in the first place by laborious human efforts.

The capability for avoiding this patent absurdity is itself the fruit of another set of key concepts devised in the early stages of the development of digital processors and elaborated in various ways ever since. These concepts are (1) branching, (2) looping, and (3) hierarchies of hardware, firmware, and software building blocks.

Branching, as triggered in this instance by an equality test such as that of figure 5.47, is illustrated in figure 5.50a and by the program in cells 9 through 16 of figure 5.48.

Figure 5.50a schematizes the generic characteristics of a branching instruction. The main provision is for testing for the truth or falsehood of whatever statement fills in the blank of "if _____ then." If "_____" is true, then the instructions denoted by block *A* are followed; otherwise the instructions denoted by the block *B* are followed instead.

Cells 9 through 16 of figure 5.48 illustrate one of the numerous ways in which specific branching instructions might be realized in specific processors. Again, the details of any specific approach to realization are all-important to the economics and the marketing of digital processors, although the underlying principle remains precisely what has already been described.

The objective of the program in cells 9 through 16 (figure 5.48) is to print out in alphabetic order the words "dog" and "cat" stored in cells 3 and 4. The instruction in cell 9 compares the contents of 3 and 4 to yield an indicator of whether 3 is earlier than 4 in alphabetic order, the same as 4 in alphabetic order, or later than 4 in alphabetic order. What primitives might be used to do this or whether the instruction "compare (3, 4)" is itself a primitive is among

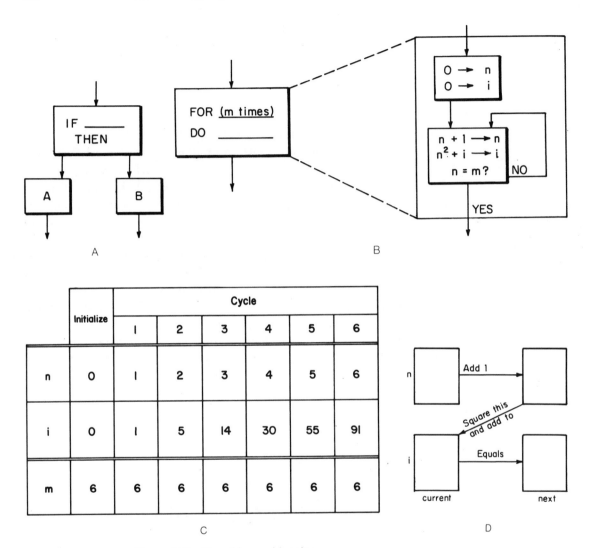

Figure 5.50 Branching and looping

the choices that might make or break a commercial venture. It is of no concern to us here. All that matters is that this instruction sets things up for the branching instruction in cell 10. That instruction is set to break the normal sequence of fetching the next instruction from cell 11, but only if the word in cell 3 is later in the alphabetic order than the word in cell 4. Since that is the case in this illustration, the flow of instructions jumps from cell 10 to cell 14. The latter holds an instruction to print the contents of cell 4, namely the word "cat." The next instruction then is one for printing the word in cell 3, namely "dog." Finally, the instruction in cell 16 instructs the machine to stop.

Had cell 3 held "cat" and cell 4 held "dog" then, at the time when the instruction in cell 10 is executed, the indicated condition would not hold and the instructions in cells 11, 12, and 13 would have been executed in the normal way. Either way, "cat" and "dog" are printed in alphabetic order.

Branching instructions clearly add useful power to the range of capabilities of digital processors. But, as in the earlier illustration, to set up a program remains so laborious a process as to raise doubts about the practical merits of going through all this nonsense. Rather, it is the looping capability, along with the intrinsically high speed and low cost of digital processor operations, which makes digital processors worth building for practical economic reasons.

The essentials of looping are schematized by the left block of figure 5.50b. In essence, a loop is a means for repeating a process a specified number of times. As a primitive or as a composite, the instruction "for so and so many times, do such and such" may be realized in numerous different ways, each with its own peculiar economic, technical, or other advantages. The mode illustrated in figure 5.50b explicitly synthesizes the loop out of more elementary operations, including the test for equality defined in figure 5.47.

Figure 5.50c illustrates what the loop does. In brief, it computes the sum of the squares of the first m integers. The specific illustration in 5.50c is for m equals 6. The right-hand block of figure 5.50b assumes that m has been set equal to 6 before the process is entered through the arrow at the top. When the loop itself is first entered, it is set up to a starting condition by setting the quantities n and i both equal to zero. This is illustrated in the "initialize" column of figure 5.50c. The number n is going to be each successive integer 1, 2, 3, 4, 5, 6. The number i is going to be the sums of the squares of these integers.

The first time that the loop proper is entered, 1 is added to the initial value (namely 0) of n and this new value replaces the old value of n. The resulting value of n is shown in column 1 of figure 5.50c. Then the square of the number in *n*—by now equal to 1—is added to the current value of *i*, namely its initial value 0, yielding the new value of *i*, again 1. Figure 5.50d schematizes this process. The third statement in the main loop then tests if *n*, currently equal to 1, is equal to *m*, preset to 6. Since *n* is equal to 1, the answer is no and the loop is traversed again for a second iteration.

The values of *n* and *i* as the digital processor traverses the loop through each successive iteration are shown in the successive columns of figure 5.50c. The process continues until it has happened six times. By then the value of *n* is itself 6 and equal to *m*. This time the equality test is positive and the digital processor leaves the loop.

For small values of *m*, it may still seem doubtful whether it's better to do the computation oneself or to go through the labor of building a digital processor and programming it. The potential for labor saving by digital processors is clearly apparent from this illustration only when the value for *m* is set large enough: For a fixed investment in a digital processor and in the programming of the loop illustrated in 50b, the computation may be carried out for any value of *m*—however large—at least in principle. Even in practice, looping on increasingly fast digital processors has enabled mathematical feats in the spirit of climbing Mount Everest because it's there. In 1949, ENIAC, one of the first vacuum tube computers, was used to compute π (3.14 ...) to 2037 decimal places in 70 hours. In 1959, 16,167 decimal places emerged in only 4. 3 hours; and, only two years later, more than 100,000 places in 8 hours 43 minutes. By 1976 the ante had been raised to millions of places.[21] The same capacity has led to wry observations about how marvelous it is that one computer can make a mistake in one millionth of a second that it would take a million people a million years to make.

Finally there is the capability to control the growth of complexity by turning lots of little building blocks into one bigger building block or, in other words, by creating new primitives out of simpler operations. Once the operations of figures 5.46 and 5.47 were synthesized out of more elementary operations, they could be used as primitives in the development of the loop of figure 5.50b which, once synthesized, could in turn be used as a building block or primitive in some larger program which, once synthesized, could be used as a building block, and so on and on and on. The operations controlled by pushbuttons in the automatic teller machines at banks and the instruction sets in "higher level languages," like the BASIC language supplied with many so-called home computers, are both examples of apparent primitives created from several layers of more basic primitives.

Association for Computing Machinery Special interest groups	Institute of Electrical and Electronics Engineers Computer society technical committees
Automata and computability theory	Computational medicine
APL	Computer architecture
Architecture of computer systems	Computer communications
Artificial intelligence	Computer elements
Business data processing	Computer graphics
Biomedical computing	Computer languages
Computers and the physically handicapped	Computer packaging
Computers and society	Computing and the handicapped
Computer and human interaction	Computers in education
Data communications	Database engineering
Computer personnel research	Design automation
Computer science education	Distributed processing
Computer uses in education	Fault-tolerant computing
Design automation	Mass storage systems
Systems documentation	Mathematical foundations of computing
Computer graphics	Microprogramming
Information retrieval	Microprocessors and microcomputers
Measurement and evaluation	Oceanic engineering and technology
Microprogramming	Office automation
Management of data	Operating systems
Numerical mathematics	Optical processing
Office automation	Pattern analysis and machine intelligence
Operating systems	Personal computing
Personal computing	Real-time systems
Programming languages	Robotics
Technical committee on Ada	Security and privacy
Security, audit, and control	Simulation
Symbolic and algebraic manipulation	Test technology
Simulation and modeling	VLSI
Small computing systems and applications	
Software engineering	
University and college computing services	

Figure 5.51   The growth of specialization. Source: Adapted from *Communications of the ACM*, no. b. 1983, and *Computer*, September 1983.

Whole departments or divisions of innovative organizations are necessary to transform a new idea into a marketable product. Figure 5.51 illustrates how the elaboration of the simple principles developed in the preceding pages occupies hosts of professional societies and subgroups within them. The specific choices made are matters of corporate life and death.

A given computer can be many things. Empty of all programs, it is like a blank piece of paper or an empty cash register: capable of much but worthless until animated by a user.

Digital processors can be deliverers of formal services, as illustrated by the mailgram and E-Com. Unlike books, however, databases are rarely sold outright. They are usually marketed by selling access to them. Portraying all of the potential variations on the theme of digital processor is potentially infinite.

The hardware/software distinction is quite irrelevant except as it affects the efficiency of a realization. Whether a particular manifestation of a digital processor is realized through hardware with elaborate software, or through hardware entirely, or through some mix of hardware, software, firmware, etc., is important in the same sense that the choice of wood pulp, rags, or reprocessed or recycled paper is of interest in the economics of papermaking. To someone who wishes to write, these details matter only insofar as they affect the price and the performance quality of the paper—or of the digital processor. They lie at the heart of the papermaker's or the computer manufacturer's trade.

Notes

1. The "Writing" entries in the *Encyclopaedia Britannica* and in the *Encyclopedia America* have as good a summary of the little that is known of the history of writing as may be found anywhere.

2. Landes, David S. *Revolution in Time: Clocks and the Making of the Modern World.* Cambridge: Harvard University Press, 1983, p. 12.

3. Ibid, p. 53.

4. Jakobson, Roman, and Morris Halle. *Fundamentals of Language.* The Hague, Holland: Mouton & Co., 1971.

5. Fourier, Joseph. *Analytical Theory of Heat.* Cambridge, England: The University Press, 1878; and Shannon, Claude E., and Warren Weaver. *The Mathematical Theory of Communication.* Urbana, Ill: The University of Illinois Press, 1949, p. 3.

6. "Natural Language Understanding." *Research News Science* 224, no. 4647 (April 1984): 373.

7. Quine, Willard Van Orman. *From a Logical Point of View: Logico-Philosophical Essays*. Cambridge, Mass.: Harvard University Press, 1953, p. 26.

8. Huffman, David. "Method for Construction of Minimum Redundancy Codes." *Institute of Radio Engineers—Proceedings* 40, no. 9 (September 1952): 1098–1101.

9. McEliece, Robert J. *The Theory of Information and Coding*. Reading, Mass.: Addison-Wesley Publishing Co., 1977, pp. 243–248.

10. Hamming, Richard. "Error Detecting and Error Correcting Codes." *The Bell System Technical Journal* 27, no. 2 (April 1950): 147–160.

11. Peterson, Wesley, and Edward Weldon. *Error-Correcting Codes*. Cambridge, Mass.: The MIT Press, 1972.

12. The flavor of the claims and counterclaims may be savored in such works as: Dreyfus, Hubert L., *What Computers Can't Do: The Limits of Artificial Intelligence*. New York: Random House, 1979, p. 197; Feigenbaum, Edward, and Pamela McCorduck. *The Fifth Generation: Artificial Intelligence and Japan's Computer Challenge to the World*. Reading, Mass.: Addison-Wesley Co., 1983; and Turkle, Sherry. *Computers and the Human Spirit*. New York: Simon and Schuster, 1984, p. 271.

13. For details on claims about expert systems, see Feigenbaum and McCorduck. Ibid., part 3.

14. Heijenoort, Jean Van. *From Frege to Godel: A Source Book in Mathematical Logic 1879–1931*. Cambridge, Mass.: Harvard University Press, 1967.

15. Kidder, Tracy. *The Soul of a New Machine*, Boston: Little Brown & Co., 1981, p. 52.

16. Ross, Ian M., AT&T Bell Laboratories. Personal communication, June 20, 1984.

17. Mendelson, Elliott. *Introduction to Mathematical Logic*. Princeton, N.J.: D. Van Nostrand Co., 1964, p. 25.

18. See "Lotus: The Next Act May Spotlight Apple," *Business Week*, November 19, 1984, p. 164; and "Computer Software: The Magic Inside the Machine," *Time*, April 16, 1984.

19. Kidder, p. 33.

20. Ibid., p. 32.

21. See Shanks, Daniel, and John W. Wrench, Jr. "Calculations of pi to 100,000 Decimals." *Mathematics of Compunication* 16, no. 77 (January 1962): 76–99; and Salamin, Eugene. "Computation of 11 Using Arithmetic-Geometric Mean." *Mathematics of Computation* 30, no. 135 (July 1976): 565–570.

6   Standards: The Rough Road to the Common Byte

Martin C. Libicki

Good information technology standards are common conventions for representing information as data so that finicky but increasingly indispensable machines may speak the common byte. Standards play a key though poorly understood role in the Information Era. Without them, the trillions of bytes on the Net would make little sense, intelligent machines would lose much of their brainpower, one type of equipment could not work with another, and all the data being so busily created would be accessible only to the creators.

In many ways standards are technical matters of little obvious significance; mention them and listeners' eyes glaze over. Most standards arise with little fuss, while others feature tedious Tweedledee–Tweedledum conflicts of no real import. Yet fights over the important standards matter, because the outcomes affect the architecture and politics of information. Standards require convergence on the correct question as well as the correct answer.

The fundamental issues of standards are reflected by the most basic information standard: human language. A good language has certain properties. It represents meaning efficiently and avoids unnecessary ambiguity but is robust against noise and error, ensures that a word can group like concepts, and, finally, remains alive, that is, flexible enough to absorb new meaning. Language has an architecture; it reflects and reinforces the ways by which societies construct human discourse. Thus results the extensibility of English, the logic of French, the lyricism of Italian, the fluid formality of Japanese, and the social range of Russian. Language can make particular concepts easy or difficult to convey. Life would be simpler if everyone spoke the same language, but they will not, and for good reasons.

Information technology standards exist to solve three problems. The first is interoperability, that is, getting systems to work with one another in real time (for example, telephone systems). Failure could prevent communication, but most of the time a kluge to glue systems together is sufficient. The second problem is portability, which permits software to work with heterogenous systems (for example, a consistent computer language). Again, failure could lead to closed systems, but most of the time software can be ported if more code is written to accommodate each system (or functions are dropped). The third problem is data exchange among different systems (for example, wordprocessing files). Failure could mean loss of access to information, but most of the time translators work, although with a cost in effort and dropped details. Successful standards share the ability to facilitate plug-and-play systems and induce competition among potential software and hardware providers, thus lowering costs and raising choices.

Interoperability, portability, and data exchange are usefully distinguished from one another when evaluating the need for and reach of specific standards or the consequences of their absence. Standards have costs. A convention that fits the general may be inefficient for the specific. When standards enable certain functions they inhibit others. A standard often limits efforts to extend and maintain what is standardized. The wait for standards may cause technologies to miss their markets.

All good standards go through two steps: invention and proliferation. Most are also formalized in standards bodies (sometimes prior to proliferation). Proliferation is usually more important than formalization (which is too often the focus of standards studies). De facto standards offer many of the virtues of de jure ones, particularly if the latter are a waste of time (or, worse, yet one more check-off in a government bid). But formalization has advantages: It opens the review process to outsiders (e.g., users, small vendors, and third parties), generally improves definition, and aids the inclusion of the standard in government purchases.

At the international level, communications standards come from two committees of a treaty organization, the International Telecommunications Union (ITU): the ITU-T for telecommunications and the ITU-R for radio. Computer standards come from the voluntary International Organization for Standards (ISO). NATO standards often subsume those of the United States Department of Defense (DOD).

At the national level, the American National Standards Institute (ANSI) charters committees, trade groups, and professional societies (such as the Institute of Electrical and Electronic Engineers [IEEE]) to write standards. Government standards are set by the National Institute of Standards and Technology (NIST). The DOD, the largest U.S. buyer of goods and services, is influential, as is the Federal Communications Commission (FCC), the spectrum regulator.

Often proliferation is driven by strong bandwagon effects. A standard that appears to be winning will garner more support in the form of software, training, expertise, and drivers. Potential winners offer users the possibility of interacting with an increasing number of other users. Growing sales mean lower costs for conforming products. All these make the standard more appealing and lengthen its lead. Accidents of birth or early support, by starting a virtuous circle, can make a large difference in a standard's success. Can a targeted government purchase constitute sufficient early support to drive the market toward convergence on a standard? In theory, yes, but it is risky. If the market pulls away from the government (e.g., Ada, OSI), government users may be stranded. Alternatively, convergence may be forced before the embedded technology has been proved superior.

Correct comprehensiveness, timing, and family relationships influence the success of a standard. Figure 6.1 shows some choices involved in choosing a standard's scope. A standard may cover only the core of a solution—that is, the functions supported by all vendors. In this case, proprietary ways of dealing with peripheral functions can frustrate interoperability for years. An overly comprehensive, perhaps anticipatory, standard, however, may cost too much to implement. By supporting alternatives ways of representing essentially similar functions, such a standard can frustrate unambiguous translation between two systems. An intermediate solution is to take a large problem and divide it into layers, standardizing each. This is easier said than done, particularly if, as with data communications, standard solutions at one layer and nonstandard solutions at another do not interact well.

When should standardization occur? Premature standardization leaves no time for the market to smooth the kinks and separate out nice-to-have from need-to-have features. Late standardization yields years of market confusion and the need to cope with a proliferation of variants that arise in the interim. If the technology matures before the market takes off (see figure 6.2), standardization can occur smoothly in between. What if the market threatens to take off before the technology matures? With image compression, technology keeps getting better; a premature standard may either forestall further progress or itself be swept away by better but nonstandardized solutions.

Figure 6.3 shows standards clustered in families. Because a member's takeoff often carries another along, a coherent standards strategy pushes related standards. In contrast, the federal government has promoted the Ada computer

Universe of Possible Functionality

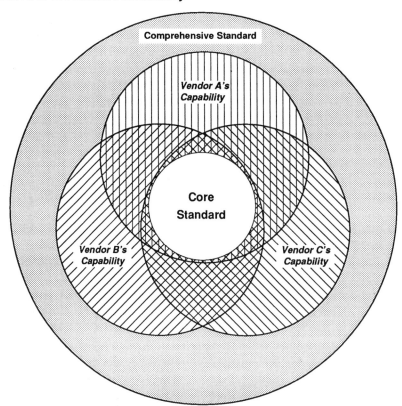

Figure 6.1   How comprehensive a standard? © 1994 President and Fellows of Harvard College, Program on Information Resources Policy.

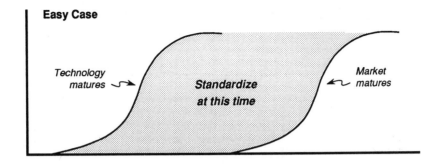

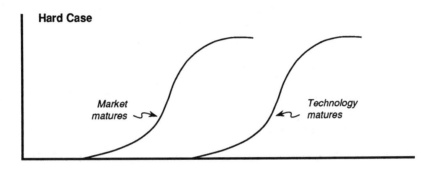

Figure 6.2   When should a technology be standardized? © 1994 President and Fellows of Harvard College, Program on Information Resources Policy.

language, the UNIX operating system, the OSI data communications model, and the Standard General Markup Language (SGML) text formatting system, all from competing families. Ada competes with the C computer language from the UNIX family; UNIX is strongly associated with a specific transport protocol (the transmission control protocol/Internet protocol [TCP/IP]) that conflicts with OSI's, while the OSI community is associated with an open document interchange format (ODIF) that competes with SGML.

Beyond technical issues, standards influence the architecture of information. A choice of computer languages implies a relationship of programmers to their managers and to one another. Compared with a top-down communications protocol, a bottom-up one facilitates different flows of information and different social relations. Standards that make it easy to exchange and annotate computer-aided designs are related to the status of manufacturing engineers relative to that of design engineers. Because the problems standards solve are

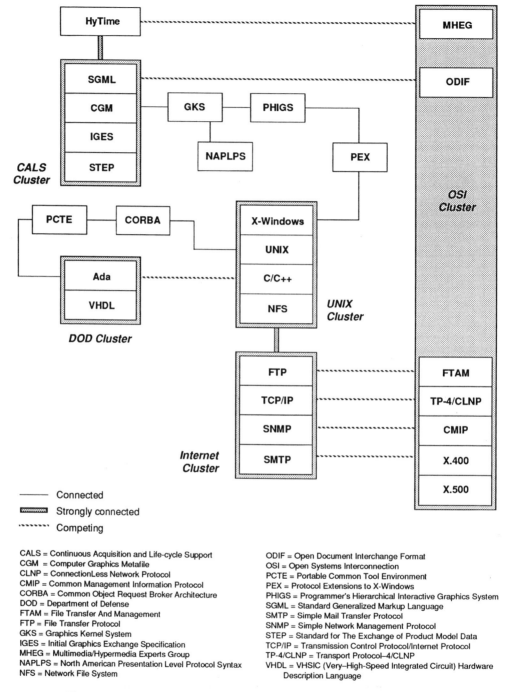

Figure 6.3 Families of standards. © 1994 President and Fellows of Harvard College, Program on Information Resources Policy.

not always perceived the same way, choices among solutions influence who is connected to whom, what is expressed easily and what requires effort, whose needs matter, and who exercises influence. Standards have been touted as a way to avoid the Scylla of chaos and the Charybdis of monopoly; they shape the struggles of competing vendors and their technologies and the power of vendor versus user.

Standards also affect larger issues:

- The timing, shape, and potential of the national (and international) information infrastructure
- The internal structure of organizations (for example, from hierarchical to horizontal) and their external relationships (for example, virtual corporations)
- Choices among systems designs, from tightly integrated (which tends to be efficient) to tightly interfaced (which needs standards but is more flexible)
- The form information is likely to be seen in—linear (such as text), linked (hypertext), or lateral (database)—with further effects on the changing roles of writer and reader in providing coherence
- The speed with which new technologies come into use
- The competitiveness of the U.S. software and systems integration sector

Indeed, there are very few information issues standards do *not* affect.

Each of the seven topics presented below illustrates a theme that sets the virtues of standards against obstacles to the realization of standards. The openness of UNIX (for example, source code in public domain), for instance, has made standardization difficult. Users rejected OSI in favor of a protocol with fewer features that worked by the time they needed a standard. The DOD's Continuous Acquisition and Life-cycle Support program is impeded, because its computer-aided design (CAD) standards attempt to bridge competing paradigms of spatial information. Ada was invented for managers but rejected by programmers. The narrowband integrated services digital network (ISDN) has a known architecture and slow-to-settle standards, while broadband versions are the opposite. Multimedia standards to bring together tomorrow's digital libraries have been called for, while the requisite technologies are still jelling. Five specialized standards (encryption, electronic chip design, machine tools, maps, and TRON) illustrate the weakness of public standards policy in the face of market forces.

The Open Road

Standard interfaces between layers of software—whether to run programs or to communicate data—permit the construction of systems from mix-and-match parts and free users from dominance by a single vendor. In the 1990s, all vendors pay lip service to open systems, but agreement ends there. The computer industry needs as many words for "open" as Eskimos need for snow

Is the PC DOS architecture open? Although its well-defined software and hardware interfaces and hundred-million-plus user base make it a proved mix-and-match technology, one company controls the operating system and another the microprocessor. Most applications markets are dominated by a single vendor, and software struggled for years against the (640K) memory limitation that resulted from early standardization. In some respects the Macintosh, whose box and operating system come from one company, Apple, is more closed than the PC DOS system, but a well-defined user interface freed customers to switch among competing software applications without sinking time into becoming familiar with each.

Even though IBM opened its mainframe architecture by the early 1980s to allow development of plug-compatible machines, third-party peripherals, and a robust software base, many defined open as any system that would get them out from under IBM's thumb. The UNIX operating system is available from open sources but comes in so many flavors that an era of mix-and-match software is still years away. Proponents consider OSI open because it was developed in a formal process in a public forum, yet the scarcity of applications in the United States forces users to pay a premium for conforming products. To advocates of high-definition television (HDTV), open means "capable of absorbing new technology within the standard," while to the federal government, open systems mean those that can be specified in a request for proposals (RFP) without the need to mention either specific vendors or branded products.

UNIX

Open and standard, although apparently synonymous, can conflict. Openness helped UNIX spread: UNIX was the first operating system in use not exclusive to any one brand of computer (antitrust rulings kept its parent, AT&T, from selling computers). That plus the availability of its source code made UNIX popular in universities, an environment where writing and sharing code are common. When the government needed an operating system to use as a test-bed for artificial intelligence (AI) and networking, UNIX (in the version refined at Berkeley) was there to benefit. As computer scientists and engineers flowed from academia into business, they brought with them their fondness for UNIX, opening a large market for UNIX-based minicomputers and workstations. By the mid-1980s UNIX was the dominant operating system on workstations and by the end of the decade had driven most proprietary minicomputer operating systems (and many of their vendors) out of the market. UNIX is poorly suited for mainframes and microcomputers, which make up two-thirds of the market, but it dominates the remainder: supercomputers, minicomputers, and workstations.

The features that made UNIX fun to play with led to a proliferation of dialects, inhibiting the creation of a mass applications market. Personal computer users enjoy a consistent applications binary interface (ABI) that lets any software run on any machine. The absence of a dominant architecture for workstations or minicomputers (or of any successful architecturally neutral distribution format [ANDF]) limits the odds of a shrink-wrapped UNIX software market. The standardization of UNIX can, at best, foster a common applications portability interface (API), so that when source code is compiled on different machines it will act in similar ways.

Formal UNIX API standards include POSIX from an official body (IEEE) and XPG from an unofficial body (X/Open, a consortium of vendors active in Europe). XPG is more comprehensive than POSIX, but POSIX, developed in a neutral forum, has been chosen by the federal government to define UNIX. POSIX compliance, however, can be claimed by many non-UNIX systems, which allows those system to compete for government contracts when UNIX is what is really wanted.

The search for a de facto common UNIX has been a busy mating dance. Through the mid-1980s UNIX was split between versions based on AT&T UNIX and Berkeley UNIX. In 1988 AT&T united with Sun (whose co-founder helped write Berkeley UNIX) to create what was hoped would be a standard UNIX. The rest of the industry, in opposition, formed the Open Software Foundation (OSF) to develop its own version. Although the new split stalled unification, it prompted each group to compete in complementing UNIX with graphical user interfaces, network file systems, distributed computing environments, and multiprocessing architectures. In 1993, under the threat of Microsoft's Windows NT, UNIX vendors banded to support a common open systems environment (COSE).

UNIX illustrates several themes in standards:

- Standards reflect the communities they come from. UNIX's growth among small machines and within the academic environment gave it enduring characteristics: well-understood building-block function calls, cryptic names, poor documentation (UNIX users do not need user-friendly), good communications, but generally weak operational and database security.

- A respected but disinterested developer makes becoming a standard more likely. AT&T played that role for UNIX. (MIT played it for X-windows, a machine-independent graphical user interface associated with UNIX.)

- A standard does well to start small. Vendors (or their consortia) can compete to add functionality; surviving features can later be massaged into standard form.

- The openness of a technology can be inimical to standardization if vendors can tweak the source code in different ways to meet specific needs.

If Windows NT makes UNIX extinct (a prospect that seemed more likely the year before Windows NT was released), UNIX's lack of standardization will have been a contributing factor. Otherwise, even though UNIX is not standard, it still hosts most work on the cutting edge of computer technology; it is the operating system on which even microcomputer operating systems are converging.

OSI

In contrast to UNIX, which started off in a corner, OSI saw life as a comprehensive reference model for data communications that only needed to be filled in by actual standards to thrive.

The OSI reference model breaks down the problem of data communication into seven layers; this division, in theory, is simple and clean, as shown in figure 6.4. An application sends data to the *application layer*, which formats them; to the *presentation layer*, which specifies byte conversion (e.g., ASCII, byte-ordered integers); to the *session layer*, which sets up the parameters for dialogue; to the *transport layer*, which puts sequence numbers on and wraps check-sums around packets; to the *network layer*, which adds addressing and handling information; to the *data-link layer*, which adds bytes to ensure hop-to-hop integrity and media access; to the *physical layer*, which translates bits into electrical (or photonic) signals that flow out the wire. The receiver unwraps the

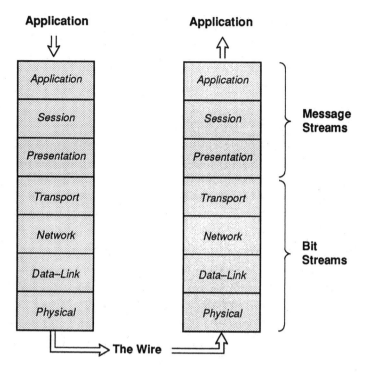

Figure 6.4 Open Systems Interconnection (OSI). © 1994 President and Fellows of Harvard College, Program on Information Resources Policy.

message in reverse order, translating the signals into bits, taking the right bits off the network and retaining packets correctly addressed, ensuring message reliability and correct sequencing, establishing dialogue, reading the bytes correctly as characters, numbers, or whatever, and placing formatted bytes into the application. This wrapping and unwrapping process can be considered a flow and the successive attachment and detachment of headers. Each layer in the sender listens only to the layer above it and talks only to the one immediately below it and to a parallel layer in the receiver. It is otherwise blissfully unaware of the activities of the other layers. *If* the standards are correctly written, the services and software of any one layer can be mixed and matched with no effect on the other six.

Intent on inventing an optimal protocol, OSI's developers ended up with something not so much optimal as invented. They created standards that detail a wealth of functionality, with little market feedback on what features were worth the cost in code or machine resources. OSI standards were a long time in the making, complex with options, difficult to incorporate into products, and a burden on system resources such as memory and clock cycles.

The standards took time to fill in. The IEEE provided local area network (LAN) standards; the ITU-T supplied both the X.25 standard for public packet switching and the X.400 electronic mail standard. The rest of the OSI standards were laboriously written during the early to mid-1980s.

Because many layers of the OSI model featured several OSI standards and because the standards were laden with options, profiles of standards (e.g., one from layer A, two from layer B) were needed to ensure interoperability within an OSI architecture. In the early 1980s General Motors sponsored a profile, the Manufacturing Applications Protocol (MAP), with a top layer that formatted instructions to automated factory equipment and two bottom layers that shuttled bits along a token bus factory LAN. Profiles were also developed for the electric utility industry and air-ground communicators. The most complete profile, shown in figure 6.5, is the government's OSI profile (GOSIP), which became mandatory for federal purchases after August 1990.

With a reference model, standards, and profiles in hand, advocates took their show on the road—or the promise of a show; what with late standards spelling later products, they entered a world many of whose needs had been met by other standards. Most were proprietary (e.g., IBM's Systems Network Architecture [SNA], introduced in 1974). OSI's most serious competition, however, came from another open suite, the Internet's, which covered core application functions (e-mail, file transfer, remote terminals) plus transport and address mechanisms. The standards process for the Internet was completely different from that for OSI. For every new problem engineers would hack together a solution and put it out on the Internet for users to try out. If the responses were favorable, the solution was a standard.

Thus the problem of transition strategies was born: how to build a new network protocol suite in place of, around, or between existing suites. Figure 6.6 illustrates four strategies: bridging, gateway, dual-host, and encapsulation, each serving a different function.

Bridging places feature-rich OSI application layer protocols atop proven TCP/IP networks. It works by slipping in a layer of code to translate OSI's application function calls into terms the transport layer understands.

Gateways allow existing networks to communicate with other networks in a lingua franca. For every X.400 native e-mail system, for instance, there are ten X.400 gateway translators to glue other e-mail systems together.

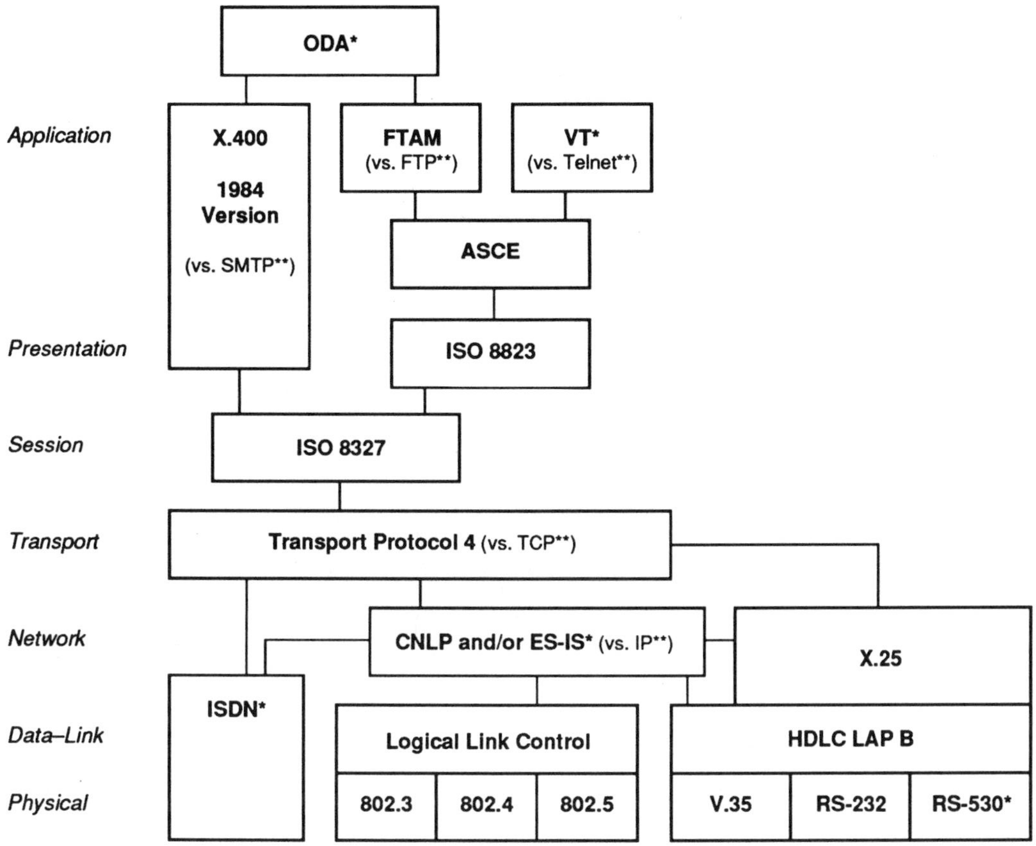

*Requirements of GOSIP 2, but not GOSIP 1. ODA, although not an ISO protocol, was included in GOSIP, because it provides services the OMB feels are required by federal agencies. Another protocol, CONS (connection-oriented network service, ISO 8878), is not shown, because it is *optional* and may be specified to link systems directly connected to X.25 WANs and ISDNs (and systems not GOSIP-compliant).

**Indicate Internet equivalents for some GOSIP standards.

ASCE = Association Service Control Element
CLNP = ConnectionLess Network Protocol
ES-IS = End System–Intermediate System
FTAM = File Transfer and Management
HDLC = High-level Data–Link Control
IP = Internet Protocol
ISDN = Integrated Services Digital Network
ISO = International Standards Organization
ODA = Open Document Architecture
SMTP = Simple Mail Transfer Protocol
TCP = Transmission Control Protocol
VT = Virtual Terminal

Figure 6.5 The GOSIP 2 Stack. © 1994 President and Fellows at Harvard College, Program on Information resources policy.

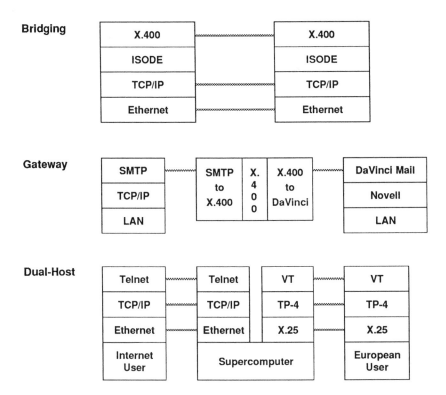

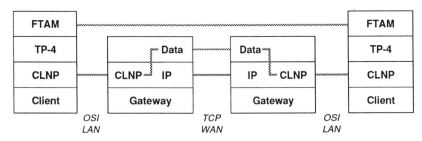

Figure 6.6 Infiltration strategies. © 1994 President and Fellows of Harvard College, Program on Information Resources Policy.

Dual-host (more commonly, multihost) computers permit machines on heterogenous networks to use their own protocols to access a common resource (such as a supercomputer).

Encapsulation lets machines on two OSI LANs talk to each other through a TCP/IP wide area network (WAN). OSI address and transport information is treated as raw bits by the TCP/IP network, which wraps its own envelope around the data.

The four, billed as transition techniques, became in practice accommodation techniques (or general glue methods for any two protocols). OSI appears valuable primarily for its e-mail and directory standards (X.400 and X.500). Of the four strategies, bridging and gateways will probably garner the most attention.

Most experts initially felt that the triumph of OSI, though slow, was inevitable. A study done in 1985 for the DOD, for instance, recommended a move to OSI not for technical reasons but because everyone else was headed there. Since about 1990 the tide has turned. Few believe OSI will do well in the U.S., and even Europe may reexamine its commitment.

What went wrong? First, contrary to theory, one size does not fit all. OSI was too heavy for personal computers and their networks but less efficient than IBM's SNA for supporting the mainframe as the data pump. OSI was left with the middle market and the glue market (sticking heterogenous platforms and networks together). The middle market went to UNIX, and thus to TCP/IP (which, for historical reasons, is free in most UNIX systems). The glue market might have gone to OSI, but when such needs surfaced in the late 1980s, OSI products were either late or too new to inspire confidence. The momentum built up by available, tested, and ready TCP/IP products and their presence on the growing Internet could not be overcome. Between 1989 and 1991 the big computer vendors, hitherto committed to OSI, backed away; by 1993 even the government was reconsidering its earlier exclusion of TCP/IP from GOSIP. The contest between rough-and-ready Internet standards and formally constructed OSI standards was repeated in network management (OSI's Common Management Interface Protocol [CMIP] versus the Internet's Simple Network Management Protocol [SNMP]) and path routing (OSI's Intermediate System to Intermediate System [IS-IS] protocol versus the Internet's Open Shortest Path First [OSPF] protocol), with much the same results.

Tomorrow's integrated data communications networks are likely to be a complex patchwork of proprietary protocols built around mainframes and servers (e.g., SNA and Novell's) plus Internet standards (for internetworking and systems management) and some OSI protocols (e.g., X.400 and X.500).

Had the major computer companies and the government thrown their weight behind TCP/IP rather than OSI, perhaps much of the complexity might have been avoided.

Front Line Manufacturing

During the 1980s the DOD took a hard look at how information technology could promote better software and hardware, and it concluded that standards would be the core of its approach. One set of standards, Continuous Acquisition and Life-cycle Support (CALS), was to govern the production of documentation associated with weapons systems, while another, Ada, would be the language in which defense software was written.

With standards as with any specification, the DOD always has three choices: (*i*) it can lead, by creating difficult but worthwhile challenges and supporting the search for their solution; (*ii*) it can lag, by scouting the commercial realm for good solutions and encouraging their adoption by the DOD's workers and suppliers; and (*iii*) it can mandate a separate convention that differs from what others do. The third choice is often the unintended result of seeking the first (leadership for improved interoperability) and laying claim to the second (taking standards stamped in commercial forums). Separate conventions are often worst, because they further divide the defense production base from the commercial production base. The DOD's leadership is also vitiated by mixed signals (its standards mandates compete with many more urgent internal mandates) and long development cycles (so that its standards are often out of date).

CALS

The CALS initiative, begun in 1985, specifies a set of standards used in formatting text (see next section) and images of technical data. CALS was intended to meet three goals. The first was to move from paper to write-once, read-many bytes. The second was to collect product data in CAD form for post-production support (i.e., recompeting, redesigning, and remanufacturing subsystems and spare parts). The third, concurrent engineering, was looked on as the most important goal. A common CAD file format would facilitate early and frequent exchange of information between prime contractors and their vendors, thereby injecting the considerations of manufacturing engineering into those of design—a way to raise quality and lower life-cycle costs.

Table 6.1 CALS standards

Standard	Purpose	IOC	Standardized
Raster	Images	Early 1990s	1980, 1984
CGM	Technical drawings	Late 1990s	1981–1986
IGES	CAD	Early 2000s	1979–1982
STEP	CAD/CAM	Maybe never	1984–1994

Table 6.1 shows the DOD's four-level schema to represent technical imagery; each level permits increasing abstraction. Raster standards are for pictures, computer graphics metafile (CGM) for technical illustration, Initial Geometric Exchange Specification (IGES) for CAD data, and Standard for the Exchange of Product (STEP) for CAD/CAM (computer-aided manufacturing) data.

CALS requirements slowly seeped into contracts; the DOD's project managers wanted digital data without the expense of mandating conformance to complex standards. Only programs started since the late 1980s (thus unlikely to yield fielded systems this century) will get delivery of data in IGES form; the rest will rely on less manipulable deliverables.

The DOD had several choices in specifying how it wanted CAD data. It could have mandated delivery of all CAD data either in a format that was de facto a standard (e.g., Autocad's DXF) or one from a selected vendor (e.g., Navy's systems commands buy all CAD stations from a single vendor). It could have specified two or three formats (e.g., GM's C4 program). It could have ignored the issue and purchased format-to-format translators as needed. Instead, it chose IGES, a standard labelled as commercial but one the DOD had actually sponsored in 1979.

IGES is generally disparaged by the DOD's customers. Although prime contractors respect the IGES mandate when dealing with the DOD, they rarely pass it down to their subcontractors, preferring to get data in the CAD format they themselves use. Failing that, translators are preferred. Only paper is less popular than IGES. IGES mandates almost never cross over from military to commercial operations of prime contractors, and IGES stands no chance of becoming any vendor's native file format.

Why has IGES done so poorly? In part because the standard was too broad and ambiguous. Internal loop tests (from a vendor's CAD format to IGES and back) drop a tenth of the data; external loop tests (one vendor's file format to another vendor's via IGES) drop a quarter. Thus, IGES requires the use of flavored CAD files—that is, files written with subsequent translation in mind. In addition, IGES files are ten times as large as native CAD files. Perhaps no neutral format could have worked. The underlying paradigm for CAD modeling is still evolving and therefore unsettled. IGES did not keep up.

Many observers, critical of IGES, aver that the STEP data will fix all of IGES's problems and more. At the very least, since the late 1980s the imminence of STEP inhibited the development of IGES. STEP is not just a better IGES, it is a completely new way to manage the data life-cycle of manufacturing, from design to production to maintenance. Advocates claim STEP avoids many specific mistakes of IGES and includes many general advances: built-in product conformance testing, the Express programming language (to ease building translators to CAD systems), and support for hierarchical decomposition of images. Most important, it supports object-oriented feature-based modeling. STEP represents a cement pipe differently from a shirt sleeve or a glass column, even though all are cylinders.

It would be easier to be optimistic about STEP if only it did not echo OSI. The standard has been ten years in the making but is still not a superset of IGES; its document exceeds 2,500 pages. Few products reify the technology STEP is supposed to standardize. Between the unpopularity of IGES and the vapor of STEP, it is difficult to see how CALS can promote concurrent engineering.

Since roughly 1990 the electronic delivery of technical data under CALS has been officially linked with the electronic delivery of business data under electronic data interchange (EDI). As a standard for business documents, the ANSI's X12 series has succeeded. When EDI was invented in the early 1970s, major buyers imposed their own proprietary forms, which were followed by forms developed by industry groups. The ANSI drew the best of these together so that, as the mid-1990s near, proprietary forms are nearly gone and applications for standard forms are now submitted by groups previously disinclined to merge their forms with those of truckers and grocers. X12, however, is a domestic standard; the international standard EDI For Administration, Commerce, and Transport (EDIFACT), little used in the U.S., is slated to supersede X12 starting in 1997.

The success of X12 may be ascribed to two factors. First, X12 did not try to solve everything at once. It started with a few forms and grew. Second, the paradigms for business data (e.g., invoices) are common and mature. Electronic representation follows closely from standard business forms. In promoting

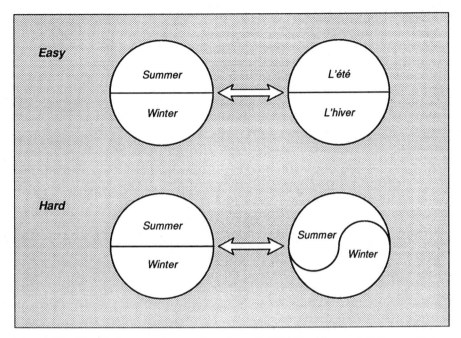

Figure 6.7 Translating notations and notions. © 1994 President and Fellows of Harvard College. Program on Information Resources Policy.

EDI, the DOD (thanks to restrictive contracting law) has not been a leader but seems, to its credit, to be following in well-plowed paths.

The contrast between the success of EDI standards and the difficulties of CAD standards illustrates the greater importance of common notions over common notations in predicting a standard's success. As figure 6.7 illustrates, translation between an Ottawan's "winter" and a Quebecois's "l'hiver" is easy if both refer to the same months. Similar translation between the experience of Houstonians (with their short winters) and Edmontonians (with their longer winters) is more difficult even though both use the same language.

Ada

The search for a standard computer language has been going on since the late 1950s, beginning with the development of three fundamental families. FORTRAN (formula translator) became a standard over time as the multitude of algorithms written by early users required later users to work with the language. Common Business-Oriented Language (COBOL) became a standard for business computation, in part because of federal pressure. Both FORTRAN and COBOL are based on old technology and have not spawned new languages in almost thirty years. Algol, an elegant language widely used only in Europe, spawned JOVIAL (an Air Force standard prior to Ada), Pascal (Ada's progenitor), and C and then C++, which in the 1990s is becoming the standard for applications development.

Ada was invented when the DOD found its software costs escalating partly because it was supporting more than three hundred computer programming languages. Rather than converge on an existing language, the DOD spent the eight years from 1975 to 1983 developing one of its own. Standardization followed in lock-step order.

Any analysis of Ada must address two questions: Was it a good language? Has it become a common one?

Ada was designed for the large, long-lived projects that characterize defense systems. It benefits from a solid analytical foundation and supports object-oriented design and strong type checking. But it is large, prolix, and ponderous; it produces object code that tends to run slowly and tax computer resources (although the problem is lessened with newer compilers).

Ada brought unique strengths to the realm of embedded systems. It featured exception handling (so that faults do not shut down all operations), concurrence, standard interrupt handling and protection against real-time bugs, and very high host-target portability (Ada code is often transported from development environments to weapons). The DOD hierarchy is generally satisfied with Ada's contribution to software engineering.

As a common language, the story is different. Ada's acceptance within the DOD was assured by about 1987. Many of those forced to use Ada grew to like it, and the DOD made it hard to get exceptions. Ada has also become the language of choice for non-Defense aerospace projects (e.g., the Federal Aviation Administration [FAA], the National Aeronautics and Space Administration [NASA], Boeing, Beechcraft). Outside that community it has spread poorly; advocates enumerate its users, a fact that speaks for itself.

What hurt Ada outside the DOD? Too much time was taken determining requirements, too little fieldtesting the desirability of its features. It was solidified just before object-oriented technologies caught on. Worse, Ada's model of programming was inimical to programmers. The language implicitly assumed that programmers never document code adequately, take too many short cuts, make too many sloppy errors, and look over everyone's shoulders. Managers might agree, but programmers are put off by the restrictions in the language prompted by such perceptions.

Ada's newest incarnation is Ada 9X, a mere six years in the making (1988–94). This time around, managers at least recognize the need to market Ada aggressively, exploit the established vendor base, and appeal to business users. The last focus stems from efforts to make Ada a standard language for business applications within the DOD. This is a less obvious need than supporting embedded systems; standard languages already exist in these areas (such as COBOL, or MUMPS for health applications), and Ada does not hook well to database languages and user interface tools common in such environments.

Ada's fate is in doubt. Computerdom is converging on C and its object-oriented descendent, C++. In contrast to supersafe Ada, C and C++ empower the programmers, some soaring to great heights while others crash. C is what programmers learned in school (partly because UNIX programs are written in it) and so like working in after they leave.

As the emerging standard, standard, C/C++ is the language that today's tools support, tomorrow's microprocessors are optimized for, and the global network objects of the future will be written in. Ada users, in contrast, will always be late getting new tools (e.g., computer-aided systems engineering [CASE]), new technologies (such as object-oriented programming), hooks to operating systems features (such as windows environments), and, in the thin times of the 1990s, new jobs in commercial enterprises. Ada's vendors are retreating, and the Ada mandate is being questioned more frequently at the military's highest levels.

To the Gigabit Station

The great promise of the National Information Infrastructure (NII) is the individual's ability to access all the information in the universe—data, text, image, audio, and video (both real-time and archived)—with only a computer and a telephone. The technology to realize this promise exists; its economics are not prohibitive (fiber to the home is neither necessary nor sufficient). Two types of standards are necessary for realization: those that specify how users are plugged into networks and those that format the information users receive.

As an indication of potential policy choices involved in construction of the NII, figure 6.8 illustrates capabilities that become available with increases in

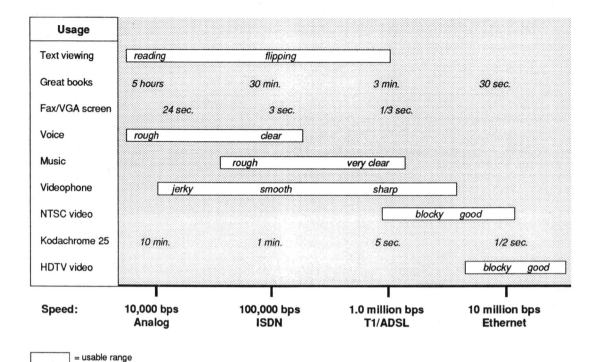

Figure 6.8   What various communications rates permit. © 1994 President and Fellows of Harvard College, Program on Information Resources Policy.

bandwidth, from today's analog telephones (equipped with a 14,400 bit per second [bps] modem), to dual-line ISDN phones (128,000 bps), to T1 rates (1.5 million bps), to Ethernet rates (10 million bps). Different uses require different bandwidths; even low-bandwidth digital networks (such as ISDN) enable powerful services.

ISDN

In the early 1980s the road to the gigabit station appeared obvious. Public telephone systems worldwide would install an integrated services digital network with circuits containing two 64,000-bps B lines (for voice, videotelephony, facsimile, and modems) and one 16,000-bps D line (for call-control information and packet-switched data).

ISDN could have been the second stage of the personal computer revolution. Its digital lines would have permitted major increases in data throughput. The D-channel services would have presented the nation's central office (CO) switches as just another personal computer device. The packet-switching capabilities of ISDN would have permitted remote command and control of the many smart machines that surround us. ISDN's compatibility with the nation's local loops makes it relatively inexpensive. The current cost of roughly $1,500 per connection (about $500 for each phoneset, CO-line card, and CO-switch software) could have dropped sharply had U.S. installations exceeded the present paltry rate of ten thousand a month.

As with many formal standards, ISDN took time. After a decade of discussion, in 1984 the ITU-T cobbled together enough specifications to make a standard. Implementation was to have followed quickly. In 1985, chipsets hit the market, then in 1986, ISDN-compatible CO switches, and in 1987, the first trials. On the heels of the trials surfaced the first reports of widespread incompatibilities among versions supported by the various CO vendors. The 1984 standard was too fuzzy, and, in its place, a tighter 1988 standard had to be specified. At about the same time, in 1987, Bellcore began to sponsor intensive discussions with individual switchmakers to develop compatible call control specifications. As Bellcore's ambitions were steadily pruned, in 1991 the talks resulted in the National ISDN-1 specification (demonstrated in installed switches a year later).

Yet ISDN has come to mean It Still Does Nothing. Progress remains slow, particularly in North America. Residential and small business services began only in 1992–93, and as yet there are few long-distance clear-channel lines. Corporate customers, which were expected to create initial volumes for ISDN deployment, could not wait, and they developed their own networks instead. Most D-channel services are now available on analog lines (although via a very complex user interface). Although ISDN may yet prevail in the absence of easy alternatives for user-driven digital communications devices, its success is hardly assured.

Its problems can be ascribed to two factors: mistargeted services and slow standardization. ISDN was sold on the basis of its services to very large customers (predominantly those with Centrex service), but their complex needs do not need ISDN to be satisfied. Instead, ISDN shines as a service for small and home offices, where workers rely on public infrastructure (rather than a corporate LAN). Phone companies ought to have thought of ISDN as wires and specs to link personal computers (for a fee) to the world; attic entrepreneurs of the sort that powered the personal computer revolution would do the rest.

Deliberately paced standards setting, although once appropriate for monopoly networks, was ill-suited to the far faster realm of computers. The divestiture of AT&T—erstwhile supplier of local service, long lines, switches, phonesets, and technology—deprived the standards community of its leader, whose mantle has only recently and not completely been assumed by Bellcore. The ISDN standard is extremely complex: providing B-line service was a snap; most of the difficulty was with the D-line switch-control functions (e.g., those targeted for large customers). The complexity of ISDN was also exacerbated by its goal of unifying phone systems around the world, yet ISDN calls require translations at many levels (trunk line speeds, analog-digital conversion, rate adaptation, interface levels) to cross the Atlantic.

The hoopla over the looming information highway has suggested to some that ISDN deployment might have been, at best, a brief rest stop on, and, at worst, a detour from that road. Broadband ISDN remains a mix of technologies, standards, and architectures that is far from convergent. In the early 1990s Bellcore demonstrated a technology, asymmetric digital subscriber line (ADSL), that, compared with ISDN, can transport more than ten times the bits (inbound only) on the same wires to the same distance (18,000 feet without signal regeneration) or, in its discrete multitone version, forty times as much to nearly the same distance (12,000 feet). Cable companies have the bandwidth to offer video-on-demand and even shared Ethernet-like services, although internal switching architectures and standard connections to long-distance services are still to be worked out.

For business communications ISDN defined the Primary Rate Interface (PRI), a 1.5 million-bps service. Lacking a standard way to synchronize lines (as AT&T's Accunet does in a proprietary implementation), PRI is a bundle of 64,000 bps straws (good for PBX traffic, which has low growth rates) rather than a single pipe (which is more appropriate for data traffic, which grows far faster).

Since the mid-1980s, business users have met their expanding needs for data communications by building private telephone systems from leased lines, notably T1 (at 1.5 million bps). Since 1991, quasi-public systems have been introduced to offer similar services. Two of them, frame relay and switched multimegabit data services (SMDS), were expected to take off, but their ascent has been slow, even though their standards processes, while leaving some holes, have been swift. Architectural issues plague acceptability. Frame relay is marketed as a virtual private system, and SMDS traffic is limited to single metropolitan areas. Neither frame relay nor SMDS effectively permits large data transfers outside predefined walls.

Broadband's great hope is a cell-switching technology, asynchronous transfer mode (ATM), which promises the ability to mix constant bit-rate voice, variable bit-rate video, and bursty data traffic. Its standards process has been very fast (once computer vendors perceived the LAN interconnect market and took over from the phone companies). The combination of hype (extreme even for the information industry), dozens of potential switch suppliers, a lack of serious interoperability testing among their switches, and the varied uses for which ATM is touted (campus LANs, private WAN interconnection, internets, telephone trunk lines, cable switching) warrant caution about its prospects.

If the NII can be defined by its services rather than by its switches, the Internet, whose standards became its architecture, has succeeded as a model by any measure. It reaches twenty million people on two million hosts in more than a hundred countries. To become the global information infrastructure, the Internet will need to overcome two deficiencies. First, its orientation to packet switching (coupled with nontrivial message delays and heterogeneous access rates) inhibits its support of real-time voice and video. Second, a system built to support subsidized academic and government uses is having difficulty coping with growth. New standards need to be created to expand its address space, enlarge its routing tables, and separate paying customers from free riders. To complete the circle, as Internet access becomes widely available to users outside institutions, it may drive a demand for ISDN-type access speeds and thus propel the ISDN along.

Narrowband ISDN had a settled architecture, but its standards were too long getting settled. The broadband version seems to have standardized faster, but its architecture remains in flux. Time—and success—will tell which, stable standards or settled architecture, matters more.

The Congress of Libraries

The standards that would organize the formatting, accessing, and compression of information within tomorrow's congress of libraries are in various states of repair; many are attempting to coalesce before the technology behind them has settled.

One problem is how to go past ASCII's standard for text in order to represent documents that also contain metatext (e.g., italics), hypertext (even footnotes), and images. Two approaches are possible. The first represents layout and other metatext directly; the second specifies a grammar to separate text and metatext (to be processed separately).

The DOD's CALS program selected the second approach, in the form of SGML, a standard way to define and mark nontext features. SGML technology has advantages for CALS beyond ensuring a consistent organization (and look) for DOD manuals and other publications. Formatted documents are essentially free-form databases; a marked-up document can be sliced and diced into a variety of reports. SGML also lends itself to hypertext, which many consider the best electronic expression of a maintenance manual.

By removing formatting decisions from authors, SGML supports many-to-one publishing well, but it supports peer-to-peer exchange of documents poorly. Because it is a metastandard, two systems must support a standard tag set to interchange documents. The DOD has an official tag set for technical manuals; book publishers, classicists, and airlines, among others, each have their own. All of these are different and not interoperable. Such differences may not matter initially (few classicists read tank-repair manuals), but interdomain exchange and software portability require a convergence of tag sets, something less likely with every new set invented. Documents must contain (or reference) not only the material itself but also the tag set and the output specifier (to convert markup into page-printing instructions) before they can be exchanged.

Widespread adoption of SGML, by making one cluster of functions easier, inhibits the rise of alternative standards to facilitate other clusters. A standard extended ASCII for metatext is likely to be preempted by Unicode, a 16-bit extension to represent every language's alphabets. Other methods of direct format representation include Microsoft's Rich Text Format (which primarily supports fonts), Adobe's Postscript page-description language, and its successor, the Portable Document Format. The last may achieve de facto status for representing pages (as unrevisable images), but its use requires purchasing Adobe's software. In the absence of a common format, direct translation among popular wordprocessing formats leaves much to be desired.

Query systems for the digital congress of libraries—or, at least, the fraction kept as databases—have been successfully standardized. Following the invention of the relational database in 1969, IBM released the specifications for its structured query language (SQL) in 1976, which it commercialized for mainframes in the early 1980s. Because IBM boxes ruled the corporate data warehouse, every other major vendor of database management software felt required to follow suit and support SQL, which they did between 1985 and 1988.

Like UNIX, SQL has continued to evolve with deeper and richer colors. In 1986, SQL received ANSI imprimatur, with subsequent versions appearing in 1989 and 1992. Each successive version is more complex—sometimes following and sometimes inducing corresponding features in products. Again like UNIX, the portability of SQL, never perfect, continues to improve for the core functions, as other functions, less well standardized, are added. In 1989, the SQL Access Group was formed to tighten the standard (X/Open and NIST, too, worked on the issue). The group also sought to promote SQL's companion in interoperability, remote database access (RDA), so that clients using one database management system could access data managed by another.

Image compression is necessary for the digital library, because the picture worth a thousands words needs fifty thousand words' worth of bytes to be transmitted. Technology permits lossless compression at ratios of 10:1, acceptable lossy compression at 30:1, and workable compression at higher rates. A surfeit, not a lack, of standards is the problem. Fax machines support two standards; videophones, one; still and motion pictures one each; television, several; and the list does not include either de facto standards or efficient but unstandardized approaches.

For real-time videophone compression, the ITU-S's H.261 standard provides least-common-denominator interoperability. Every major vendor of encoder-decoder (codec) boxes claims its proprietary algorithms can support twice the data rate H.261 does at the same level of quality. They will keep the video-conferencing market, while H.261 is expected to prevail on personal computer-based systems (where clarity is less an issue because video windows are smaller than full screen).

Official standards for still and motion picture image compression (JPEG and MPEG, respectively) are gathering support. Yet, newer technologies, wavelet and fractal compression schemes (both funded by the DOD's Advanced Research Projects Agency [ARPA]), are frequently better (because they produce less objectionable artifacts at high rates of compression). Other schemes, such as Intel's Indeo and Media Vision's Captain Crunch, are less efficient but work without a dedicated hardware chip. Standardization before the technology was fully developed may be premature.

The search for a television compression standard was buffeted by two unexpected developments. The FCC's 1989 dictate that HDTV signals must fit within the narrow spectrum now allocated for analog television effectively ended the front runner status of Japan's MUSE analog technology in favor of a digitally compressed signal. In 1992, aggressive cable companies announced they could use compression to offer five hundred channels (mostly for video on demand) along existing coaxial wiring. In contrast to terrestrial service, which uses many broadcasters (each of them necessarily using the same standard), neighborhoods tend to be served by a single provider that can impose a compression format on its subscriber base. Standards are not necessary, although they can keep costs down.

Lessons and Prognostications

The search for better standards (or better paths to what standards provide) continues. The quest can be summarized by looking at five areas that illustrate the limits of government standards policy, exploring a future for standards, and drawing some lessons.

Limits of Standards Policy

Although in theory public policy can promote growth in particular sectors by adroit backing of standards, in practice its influence is circumscribed. For example:

- As the major buyer and developer of encryption and digital-signature technology, the federal government can be expected to be a large influence on creating standards, but public policy has not resolved the tension between the government's desire to support commercial security and its desire to tap into private and foreign data streams. Thus, the government's standards efforts are increasingly suspect.

- The DOD financed an electronic CAD standard, the very-high-speed integrated circuit (VHSIC) hardware description language (VHDL), and mandated it for a certain class of chips, but the standard did not catch on. Unexpectedly, however, a private firm, Cadence, boosted its own proprietary language, Verilog, to de facto status. Cadence's competitors, in response, rallied 'round VHDL, available as a de jure standard, which then took off.

- The DOD has also supported development of a standard for machine tool controllers, in part to support machine tool builders competing with Japan, which had a single controller vendor. U.S. companies earlier unable to unite on a de facto standard, however, appear unable to unite on one supported by the DOD.

- As the world's largest collector and archiver of map data, the U.S. government ought to be able to set standards for its archived data and, by so doing, influence how everyone represents map data. The government's spatial data transfer standard (SDTS) was a trifle too long in the making. In the early 1990s private repackagers of geographical data began to use incompatible approaches based on older formats.

- Japan tried to counter U.S. dominance in microprocessors and operating systems by having electronic firms adopt a single standard, The Real-time Operating Nucleus (TRON). But a standard by itself appears unable to help Japanese producers in this area.

The Future of Standards

If microcomputer markets are any indication, the conflict between closed and open architectures may be settled by the rise of owned architectures (see figure 6.9). In a closed architecture (e.g., IBM or AT&T circa 1975) a single vendor defines and sells most of the basic systems on one side of the interface and the software on the other side. In an open architecture, the interfaces are externally defined, often in open forums, and vendors compete in the segments delineated by the interfaces. In an owned architecture, a single vendor sells all or most of a segment and by its dominance establishes an interface whose specifications are released to the public. Other vendors develop products that support that interface, and thus the interface becomes entrenched as the de facto standard. The architect nevertheless retains control, either by owning the technology needed to make the interface work (e.g., Adobe) or by using a deep knowledge of the interface to stay a generation ahead of rivals (e.g., Intel).

Sometimes the architect profits solely through its market clout in the basic segment (e.g., Hewlett-Packard in laser printers). Occasionally a vendor that dominates one segment uses knowledge of the interface to dominate another. Microsoft's knowledge of its Windows environment, for instance, allowed it to jump off to an early (and perhaps sustainable) lead in Windows-compatible applications software. In contrast, its knowledge of DOS provided no such advantage. Figure 6.10 suggests why Windows had a greater effect. Computer markets are typically shown as segmented by one-dimensional interfaces. The interface between DOS and an application tends to be short, that is, information-poor; applications write directly to the chip. The interface between Windows and typical applications is long, that is, information-rich (the applications make many calls on Windows functions). If Microsoft's object-linking

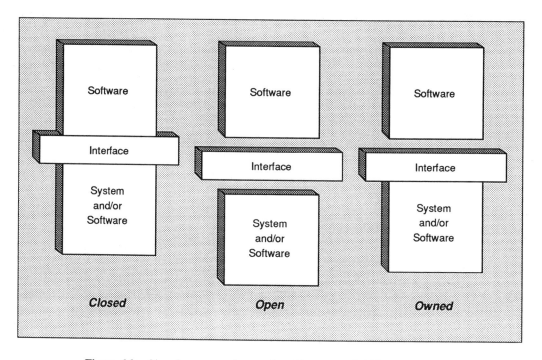

Figure 6.9 Closed, open, and owned architectures. © 1994 President and Fellows of Harvard College, Program on Information Resources Policy.

and embedding technology proves functional and popular, the interface will be richer yet. The richer the interface, the more difficult to master and thus more important to control. Other vendors compete with owners of dominant interfaces, not by breaking into the original architecture but by developing new uses—such as network operating systems or groupware—that establish alternative interfaces as more important.

How useful is the layer model for comprehending standards? The OSI's travails should have suggested that layers may be misleading. Perhaps software should be understood as clusters of objects—packages that combine data-structures, data, and operations defined on the data. Such packaging provides well-defined but extensible interfaces. Accessing these objects requires both standard ways to call them and standard ways to package them so they behave predictably. To this end, a consortium, the Object Management Group (OMG), developed a common object-request broker architecture (CORBA), which enjoys wide support but needs far more definition to be truly useful.

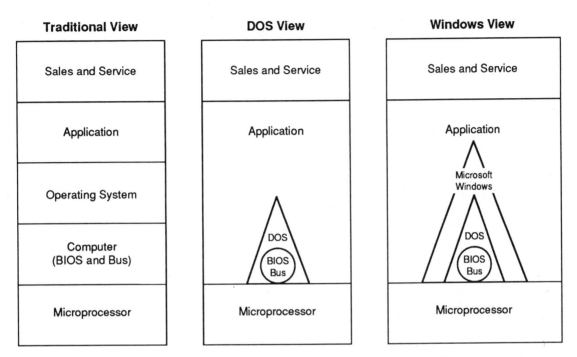

Figure 6.10   Altering the interfaces of the microcomputer world © 1994 President and Fellows of Harvard College, Program on Information Resources Policy.

Powering the challenge of integration is the increasing convergence of the entire information industry. The personal computer model of a lone user on a stand-alone machine running a single application is giving way to networked groups running applications that must work with one another (figure 6.11 shows a typical profile). The scale of integration is rising from the user to the office, the institution, and, sooner rather than later, the universe. With increases in scale comes a shift in the purposes of standardization, as figure 6.12 shows. For the lone user, standards provided familiarity with systems built from plug-and-play components made cheap through competition among clones. For the institution, familiarity matters less and interoperability more; standards help users knit heterogenous legacy systems into a functioning whole. At the global level, plug-and-play declines in importance, while political issues of architecture influenced by competing standards assume importance.

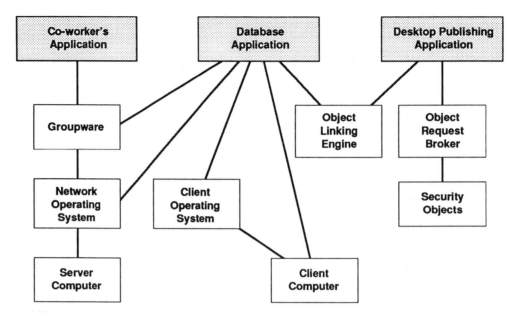

Figure 6.11 Objects rather than layers. © 1994 President and Fellows of Harvard College, Program on Information Resources Policy.

Interoperability is often understood as a way of making two parallel systems (e.g., workstations on two networks) talk to each other. Yet conversion or translation is always possible with enough work; what matters is how much. Rival products, each attempting to own an architecture, cover territory differently, and gluing them to create, say, an open database architecture may require varied methods: front-end APIs; gateways, structured and open; SQL routing; and database encapsulation. Each method emphasizes another standard, some more formal than others. The OSF melds suites in many ways at once—by incorporation, extension, hooks above, hooks below, and, if all else fails, by gateways and translation. Parts of this can always talk to parts of that, but which parts varies by case. Putting virtual layers (e.g., hardware abstraction layers) above real ones is another way standards can glue systems together. CASE, as another example, is looked to as a way to surmount problems caused by multiple computer languages, but its tools must be interoperable—calling for yet more standards (e.g., the portable common tools environment [PCTE] from Europe).

Standards become critical for the external systems integration necessary to building tomorrow's networks, which will unite users, instruments, sensors, and

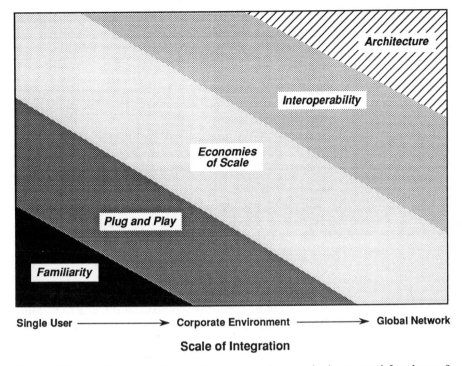

Figure 6.12 As the scale of integration grows, what standards are good for changes? © 1994 President and Fellows of Harvard College, Program on Information Resources Policy.

software with contributions from governments, corporations, and other institutions. One network might monitor the earth's environment, trading data and rules back and forth; another may do the same for personal health, linking medical sensors with monitoring stations, expert systems, and doctors. Microstandards are needed to ensure that data (the nouns and adjectives) are defined in mutually comprehensible ways while functions (the verbs) can interact predictably.

So Many Standards, So Little Time

The worth of or rationales for information technology standards are empirical: Do conventions work? Are they common? Are they sufficient to meld heterogenous applications, products, and systems smoothly?

For those who cannot tell the standards without a scorecard, tables 6.2–4 summarize standards in three ways: their status as common conventions, their origins and spread, and the influence of standards groups and the government on their development. Forty-one standards are classified according to whether they promote interoperability, portability, or data exchange, an imprecise trichotomy (many interoperability standards, for instance, promote software portability and data exchange).

Table 6.2 places standards in one of eight groups (largely on the basis of how they fare in North America). *Winners* are well-accepted conventions subdivided into *stable winners*, *unstable winners* (which may be overtaken, particularly by microcomputer conventions), and *chaotic winners* (which may spawn multiple versions at higher speeds). *Niche* standards are stable within a well-defined segment but failed to penetrate the entire market; some (e.g., Ada, ISDN, CMIP) may, for that reason, be considered *losers*. *Comers* are not well accepted but seem to be growing toward that status. *Babies* have yet to emerge strongly into the market; they are divided into *healthy* and *sick* on the basis of their prospects. *Losers* are self-explanatory.

The volatility of information technology, and thus, supposedly, its standards, may call such judgements into question, yet the stability of the fate of these standards over the two years since initial assessments were made is remarkable. The few shifts worth noting include:

- De facto microcomputer standards may put winners from the UNIX cluster at risk

- Two CALS standards, CGM and SGML, are becoming popular more quickly than seemed likely earlier

- Official compression standards are facing a tougher fight from software-based methodologies and new technologies

- ATM may eclipse the emergence of frame relay and SMDS.

Table 6.3 sorts standards by origin and spread. Of the 41 listed, 24 originated in the U.S. (broadly defined to include U.S.-based multinationals, imports such as Ada in response to U.S.-generated requirements, foreign nationals based in the U.S., and the now global Internet community). Although many of these 41 are used overseas, 10 are confined mainly to North America. Another 12 (8 from ITU) are considered global in origin, with strong U.S. input. Of the five distinctly Japanese in origin, two are unlikely to see much use outside Japan. As a rough generalization, the U.S. originates perhaps two-thirds of all software

Table 6.2 The status of specific standards

	Stable winners	Unstable winners	Chaotic winners	Niche	Comers	Healthy babies	Sick babies	Losers
Interoperability	SNMP, Group 3 Fax, SS7, Fanuc Controller	TCP/IP, X-Windows	802 LAN, Modem	CMIP, MUSE, Z39.50, X.400/500, ISDN	H.261	FCC-HDTV, ATM, Frame Relay	NGC, SMDS	OSI Organic
Portability	BIOS/DOS, SQL, VHDL	UNIX		Ada			PCTE	TRON
Data exchange	Postscript, TIFF	EDI X.12		Group 4 Fax, DES/DSS, EDIFACT	SGML, CGM, SDTS, JPEG/MPEG		STEP	IGES

Table 6.3 Source and spread of standards

	U.S. origin, not exported	U.S. origin, exported	Global	Japan
Interoperability	SNMP, NGC, TCP/IP, FCC-HDTV, Frame Relay	X-Windows, Modem, Z39.50, 802 LAN, SMDS	CMIP, SS&, H.261, OSI Organic, X.400/500, ATM, ISDN	Group 3 Fax, Fanuc controller, MUSE
Portability		BIOS/DOS, UNIX, Ada, SQL, VHDL, CORBA	PCTE	TRON
Data exchange	EDI X.12, HyTime, IGES, DES/DSS, SDTS	SGML, Postscript, TIFF	STEP, CGM, EDIFACT, JPEG/MPEG	Group 4 Fax

and the same share of its standards. The U.S. chairs only one-fifth of the ISO's computer subcommittees, however, and has only one vote in the ITU.

The search for the one true standard and the process of formal standardization are not the same (see figure 6.13). Consensus standards may be unnecessary in some situations; where they are needed, informal arrangements may suffice. The Internet and X/Open produce workable and robust standards, and vendor consortia (such as the ATM Forum) have proved capable of filling gaps and tightening loose ends left by more formal efforts. Conversely, some formal efforts result in competing standards (e.g., SGML versus ODIF) or standards that need considerable refinement to be useful.

To supply a de facto standard, a vendor does not need to be the industry gorilla. The influence of IBM on some standards has varied greatly: from positive (SQL, DOS/BIOS PCs), to neutral (its Extended Binary Coded Decimal Inter-Change [EBCDIC] alternative to ASCII, its Distributed RDA), to counter-positive (OSI and UNIX were favored to limit IBM's dominance). Will Microsoft, often viewed as IBM's successor, be more successful? User-written standards (e.g., Ada, MAP) are not necessarily winners either.

Table 6.4 presents standards in five categories according to the importance of formalization to their spread. *Nil* means that formal standards bodies have yet to play: personal computer standards, Internet-based standards, and those where government efforts are ongoing. For five standards, formalization came *after the fact*, that is, after development, and affected spread only modestly. Five were developed outside standards bodies and taken inside for *imprimatur*, which then became critical to their credibility. The rest, labelled *critical*, were

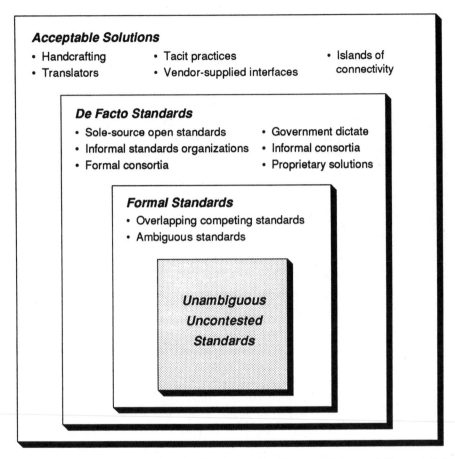

Figure 6.13 Standards and Standardization. © President and Fellows of Harvard College, Program on Information Resources Policy.

deliberately and specifically developed in standards bodies and are mostly interoperability standards. The U.S. government has played a major role in almost half of the forty-one standards. Nine were created by government policy or program. Three others were strongly supported by GOSIP, another three by CALS.

In spite of so much government activity, public policy does not merit high marks. NIST's emphasis on open systems, software portability, and vendor independence accurately and wisely presaged the market, but execution has been less stellar: GOSIP did little good, POSIX was a poor vehicle for UNIX

Table 6.4   The role of standards organizations

	Nil	After-the-fact	Imprimatur	Essential
Interoperability	SNMP, NGC*, X-Windows, TCP/IP*, FCC-HDTV*, SMDS, Fanuc Controller		Group 3 Fax, Z39.50*, 802 LAN, MUSE	CMIP†, SS7, Modem, H.261, X.400/500†, ATM, Frame Relay, ISDN, OSI Organic†
Portability	BIOS/DOS, TRON†, CORBA	UNIX†, Ada*, SQL, VHDL*		PCTE†
Data exchange	DES/DSS*, Postscript, TIFF, SDTS*	SGML†	IGES*, Group 4 Fax	EDI X.12, HyTime, STEP†, CGM†, EDIFACT, JPEG/MPEG

* Sponsored by U.S. Government.
† Other U.S. Government involvement.
© 1994 President and Fellows of Harvard College. Program on Information Resources Policy.

standardization, and NIST lost credibility in cryptology controversies. The emphasis of the DOD on the portability of software and documentation was wise, although the uniqueness of the Department's problems are often unrecognized. The DOD to its credit has promoted TCP/IP, SGML, and CGM, but IGES is universally disparaged and the failure of Ada to win support outside aerospace (while otherwise a good language) has left its users out on a technological limb. The free market shibboleths of the FCC prevented the emergence of AM stereo and left ISDN without support, but its mandate that HDTV must fit into existing bandwidths spurred image compression. The government, lacking the heavy-handedness of its European counterparts, has at least let the native U.S. genius at software proceed unimpeded.

So why has public policy not been better? First, because government is ponderous; it gets under way slowly and once a course is set plods on, well after everyone else may have taken a different path. Second, because federal policy has an inordinate respect for international standards bodies, even though the U.S. is underrepresented in them. Third, because public policy often responds to the peculiar needs of users in the government in general (such as vendor neutrality) or in the DOD in particular (such as the need to support large, centralized projects). Federal standards policy is inescapably an aspect of economic strategy: Deliberate choices are made (passing the buck to an international organization is still a choice) whose success would create winners and losers and has ramifications for the entire economy (as proponents might wish, even though such efforts are technically oriented to government users only.

If the rough road to the common byte teaches anything, it is that successful standards start small and grow with consensus on the core. The linked standards of UNIX, the C programming language, and TCP/IP all started as simple, elegant solutions to problems that grew to meet increasingly complex needs; SQL or X12 started life much smaller than they stand today.

The OSI edifice, in contrast, is large, complex, and notoriously unsuccessful in North America; the parts that did well—X.25 and X.400—were not written by the ISO. ISDN has been similarly retarded by its bulk. Technologies that become standards without being tested in working products that are accepted by the market are risky. Ada is a prime example of specifications preceding realization.

Although any specific approach to standards must be sensitive to particulars of the relevant technology, applications, and markets, the one emerging from the standards community reflects these lessons: Collect a small group of vendors, write a small, simple specification that covers the important functions, omit nonessentials, leave room for both new technologies and possible backtracking, identify real-world test-beds for the standard, and get it out the door as soon as possible. This approach suggests government standards policy concentrate on the following questions:

- What problem is standardization needed to solve?
- Must the problem be solved through collective means; must it be solved internationally?
- What is the smallest solution, and can it be broken into manageable chunks?
- What are the best tools (e.g., imprimatur, research and development, targeted purchases, regulation) to promote convergence that also permit backing off if they fail?
- Should a domestic solution be exported?

Are standards ultimately irrelevant? Given enough time, faster hardware and smarter software will, if not end the standards problem, reduce it to very low levels of discomfort. Yet the architecture of information that today's standards permit will persist, because the social relationships they create reinforce themselves. Decisions on who can say what to whom about what have both explicit and implicit dimensions, and standards play a powerful role in the implicit ones. Getting the architecture right is what matters; standards policy then accommodates it, not the other way around. The vision of the international information infrastructure should persist; the communion of bytes should follow.

Acronyms

ABI	applications binary interface
ADSL	asymmetric digital subscriber line
AI	artificial intelligence
ANDF	architecturally neutral distribution format
ANSI	American National Standards Institute
API	applications portability interface
ARPA	Advanced Research Projects Agency (under the DOD)
ASCII	American Standard Code for Information Interchange
ATM	asynchronous transfer mode
BIOS	basic input-output system
BPS	bits per second
CAD	computer-aided design
CALS	Continuous Acquisition and Life-Cycle Support
CAM	computer-aided manufacturing
CASE	computer-aided systems engineering
CGM	computer graphics metafile
CMIP	Common Management Information Protocol
CO	central office
COBOL	COmmon Business-Oriented Language
CODEC	encoder-decoder
CORBA	common object-request broker architecture
COSE	common open systems environment
DOD	Department of Defense
DOS	disk operating system
DXF	Digital Exchange Format
EBCDIC	Extended Binary Coded Decimal Inter-Change
EDI	electronic data interchange
EDIFACT	EDI for Administration, Commerce, and Transport

FAA	Federal Aviation Administration
FCC	Federal Communications Commission
FIPS	federal information-processing standards
FORTRAN	Formula Translator
GOSIP	Government Open Systems Interconnection Protocol
HDTV	high-definition television
IGES	Initial Geometric Exchange Specification
IOC	initial operational capability
IS-IS	intermediate system–intermediate system
ISDN	integrated systems digital network
ISO	International Organization for Standards
ITU	International Telecommunications Union
ITU-R	ITU, radio standards subcommittee
ITU-T	ITU, telecommunications standards subcommittee
JOVIAL	Jules' Own Version of International Algebraic Language
JPEG	Joint Photographics Experts Group
LAN	local area network
MAP	Manufacturing Applications Protocol
MPEG	Motion Picture Experts Group
MUMPS	Massachusetts's General Hospital Utility Multi-Programming System
MUSE	MUltiple Sub-Nyquist Encoding
NASA	National Aeronautics and Space Administration
NATO	North Atlantic Treaty Organization
NII	National Information Infrastructure
NIST	National Institute of Standards and Technology
ODIF	Open Document Interchange
OMG	Object Management Group
OSF	Open Software Foundation
OSPF	Open Shortest Path First
PBX	private branch exchange

PCTE	portable common tools environment
POSIX	Portable Open Systems Interface for computer environments
PRI	primary rate interface
RDA	remote database access
RFP	request for proposals
SDTS	spatial data transfer standard
SGML	Standard General Markup Language
SMDS	switched multimegabit data services
SNA	Systems Network Architecture
SNMP	Simple Network Management Protocol
SQL	Structured Query Language
STEP	Standard for the Exchange of Product
TCP/IP	transmission control protocol/Internet protocol
TRON	The Real-time Operating Nucleus
VHDL	VHSIC hardware description language
VHSIC	very high-speed integrated circuit
WAN	wide area network
XPG	X/Open Portability Guide

III Information as a Resource

7   Building Blocks and Bursting Bundles

Anthony G. Oettinger

Familiar words evoke ideas and things whose time may have gone. Tying thought to the past, they favor the *status quo*. The new words in someone's visions are unfamiliar at best. Often they are empty; often, the hype of promoters. In times of change, the right concepts, the right building blocks for those who wish, as Henri Bergson put it, to think as men of action and to act as men of thought must be stable, rich, intelligible, and impartial enough to serve many in more venues than the here and the now.

This chapter sets forth building blocks evolved by me and my colleagues at the Harvard Program on Information Resources Policy and used by our affiliates in business, government, and academe.[1]

The first building block is a concept of information resources akin to the familiar concepts of energy and of materials and complementary to these concepts. Information, energy, and materials make up the world.

Information resources in turn are made up of information products or services. These products and services are bundles of substance, format, and process. Substance, format, and process can be used alone or in an infinite number of combinations. They can be taken apart and put together again. The way they are combined or used depends on convention, namely on the fairy tales dominant at the moment. Thinking in terms of these building blocks helps avoid entrapment by conventions that were appropriate to some moment in history but whose time has long since gone. When needed, untying the basic building blocks sets free once again the creative and discretionary possibilities in their multiple potential combinations.

Information *substance* comes in many familiar varieties, among them wisdom, knowledge, data, news, and intelligence.

Information *formats* include concrete tokens (like ink on paper) for abstract patterns (like the roman, italic, Morse, or Braille alphabets) that express still more abstract symbols (like words). Vocabularies vary from person to person and from nation to nation. Different patterns satisfy different practical or aesthetic needs. New technology makes some tokens cheaper, easier to use, or prettier than others.

Information *processes* change as technologies and societies change. The contemporary information evolution is the story of new electro-optical digital compunications (computer-and-communications) technologies competing in late 20th-century societies with printing-press technologies born of the steam technology and of the industrial revolution of the 19th century.

Building Blocks and Bundles

As needs and tastes for substance change and as new formats and processes come to hand, bundles of an earlier time come undone. Familiar products and services come apart. New ones come and go through trial, error, more trials, and more errors until stabler mixes settle in once again.

In *From Memory to Written Record*, M. T. Clanchy gives the following vivid account of changes in the way people thought about the role of substance, process, and format in England between 1066 and 1307:

Numerous [parchment] charters of the twelfth century are addressed to "all those seeing and hearing these letters, in the future as in the present" or to "all who shall hear and see this charter"; these two examples come from the charters of Roger de Mowbray who died in 1188. The grantor of another charter, Richard de Rollos, actually harangues his audience, "Oh! all ye who shall have heard this and have seen!" Early charters likewise quite often conclude with "Goodbye" (*Valete*), as if the donor had just finished speaking with his audience. Documents made it possible for the grantor to address posterity ("all who shall hear and see") as well as his contemporaries. In the opening words of the Winchcombe abbey cartulary, "when the voice has perished with the man, writing still enlightens posterity." Writing shifted the spotlight away from the transitory actors witnessing a conveyance and on to the perpetual parchment recording it. By the thirteenth century, when charters had become more familiar to landowners, donors cease addressing their readers, as Richard de Rollos did, and likewise they no longer conclude with *Valete*. Once it was understood that charters were directed to posterity, it must have seemed foolish to say "Goodbye" to people who had not yet been born. In place of such conversational expressions, thirteenth-century charters are more stereotyped; they are often impersonally addressed in some such form as "Let all persons, present and future, know that I, A of B, have given X with its appurtenances to C of D."[2]

What we now call snapshots and movies are pictorial substance and photographic processes combined with the celluloid format described by Daniel

Boorstin:

In 1873 Hyatt invented and registered the name "celluloid." What he had invented was actually not a new combination of chemicals but a new way of molding the plastic and making it stay hard. For some years Hyatt used celluloid only for making solid objects. . . .

The opportunity for Hyatt's celluloid to help transform the American consciousness came from the collaborating talents of another upstate New Yorker who combined a bent for invention with a talent for organization and for marketing. . . . George Eastman . . . saw that the perfection of dry-plate photography would be more than merely a convenience for professional photographers, because now, for the first time, the taking of a picture could be separated from the making and the developing of the plate. But he also saw that a popular market for photography would have to await a substitute for the heavy, breakable, hard-to-ship glass plates. Until the 1880's, of course (because photographs were commonly made on emulsion-coated glass), photography was not especially associated with the word "film." What Eastman needed was some flexible, light, and unbreakable substance that could be coated with the photographic emulsion. In 1884 Eastman patented a way of coating strips of paper so that they would work in a camera, and from this starting point he initiated the popular revolution in photography. . . .

With his new celluloid roll film, easily loaded and easily developed (no need any more for the delicate stripping operation), Eastman opened up the world of amateur photography. The novel features of the Kodak, as an English historian observed, "enabled the camera, like the bicycle, to enrich the leisure hours of the many." . . .

Now cut to Thomas Edison:

Edison very early sensed the importance of celluloid. The perfection of a feasible camera and projector that would show moving pictures of considerable duration depended on finding a suitably flexible substance for the film. It is hard to imagine how Edison could have made his movie camera without celluloid, or something like it. . . .

When he heard of Eastman's improved roll film, he urged Eastman to help him make a motion-picture camera by producing the flexible film in long strips.

Could a series of photographs that had been taken on a single film somehow provide the pictures to be viewed in motion? For a feasible motion-picture system this idea was as crucial as Eastman's idea of separating picture taking from picture developing had been in popularizing still photography.[3]

In paragraphs that shine with hindsight, the historian sums up what is, while it happens, a dark maze of complicated actions and reactions—like those of the established information sector bouncing off newcomers stumbling across its paths or old competitors lurching along new paths, running into roadblocks or sinkholes sometimes visible, sometimes not, set up by government or opened up by the fickle finger of fate.

But what kinds of bundles for what ends? In the Information Business Map (described in the Preface and more completely in chapter 10), the familiar concepts of products and services cross with form and substance to make the compass rose of an Information Business Map with which to chart these actions and reactions.

Examples drawn from the mass media illustrate how such a tool can help businessmen, voters, public officials, or just plain interested persons trying to steer themselves through the dawn of the Information Age. In this transitional period, snapping that "a newspaper company is in the newspaper business, of course" is not a curt and well-deserved put down of a stupid question. It is mostly wrong. Like *television* or *radio*, *newspaper* is a term for a particular bundle of means, not for general ends.

Yet the means—the formats and the processes—nowadays are precisely the least stable elements in information business bundles. Indeed, describing the ends of information businesses in substance-format-process terms begs the question at the very heart of change, namely: What kinds of bundles are best for what kinds of ends? Instead, four distinct needs that information meets—escape, social connection, surveillance, and opinion formation/decision making—serve as examples of concepts with which to describe ends. This paper defines and illustrates these concepts in terms of the mass media and from the perspective of evolving information purveyors. The same concepts are also applied to the perspective of evolving information consumers, specifically those who exercise responsibility and authority.

Information resources differ from energy and material resources in that information is the organizing resource that allows people to integrate energy, material, and information resources to achieve their personal ends or, as leaders and managers, those of their organizations. For the fourth concept, opinion formation/decision making, this study therefore details how information users' needs might best be matched with alternative substance, format, and process bundles, concentrating on information required for exercising responsibility and authority.

Information as a Resource

Information is a basic resource, like energy and materials (figure 7.1). Without materials there is nothing; without energy nothing happens; without information nothing makes sense.

Looking at information as a basic resource points up what information has in common with energy and materials, not how it differs from them. In particular,

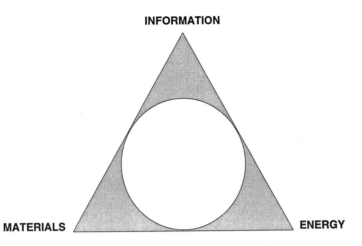

- *Without materials, nothing exists*
- *Without energy, nothing happens*
- *Without information, nothing makes sense*

Figure 7.1   The basic resources

all the key questions about the stakes in any resource go for information resources as well: Who has the resources, who wants them, how can you get them, what are the terms of trade, and how are these terms set? The stakes and these questions are timeless; new generations of stakeholders, changing information technologies, and changing social institutions and other conventions change only the answers.

There is no magic in the information, energy, materials trio, no mystical meaning of three. Einstein once speculated that material is energy and vice versa. Since Hiroshima, everyone knows that material can turn into energy. Astronomers believe that far out in the universe, energy turns into material. For peaceful and earthly affairs, though, it is still convenient and common to set materials apart from energy and to set both apart from information as the three basic resources that people rely on.

Distinguished from matter, energy looks like patterned matter. Energy is high when a loose rock is poised high on a cliff; energy is low when the rock rests at the bottom. Energy is high when a home run hit streaks off the bat; energy is low when the baseball is still cradled in the waiting pitcher's hand. That's the only way it is in the only universe we know.

Information likewise looks like patterned matter. An arrow made with three branches on a path conveys a large amount of information. Three branches just lying there convey a small amount of information. Ink lines laid out as an *A* convey more information than ink lines from a spill.[4]

The patterned relations between energy and materials belong to the innate order of our universe. The patterned relations between information and materials are ordained only by human conventions that quite arbitrarily link symbols to patterns to tokens in the ways that are told in the following section. Moreover, the energy it takes to arrange materials into information-carrying patterns like an arrow or an *A* is minuscule compared to the energy it takes to hit a baseball or to move a rock from the bottom to the top of a cliff.[5] As David taught Goliath, brains can overpower brawn. The modern military call this a force multiplier. There is often a gain in effectiveness, or at least a more efficient use of energy and materials, when information resources organize a smaller amount of energy or materials or both to displace larger amounts.

Materials, energy, and information are necessary resources. They are not sufficient. Without information nothing makes sense, but that's not to say that things *must* make sense even with information. This paper is not about how to make sense. It is about tools with which to make sense when one can. Nor does it claim a greater or lesser worth for different kinds of information. The worth of information is in the mind of the beholder, just as the worth of a loaf of bread is set by the beholder's stomach. As economic goods, information resources are just like other economic products or services. The differences between information and bread are of neither lesser nor greater importance than the differences between either of them and scrap metal or real estate.

The materials, energy, information trio is not an exclusive resource classification. Every person plays two distinct roles on the information stage. In one capacity, for instance as subordinate or as pollee, we *are* information resources. In another capacity, for example as superior or as pollster, we *consume* information along with material and energy resources. Another convention carves up resources into labor and capital. That partition is no sharper and no holier than the partition into materials, energy, and information. Seen as labor or as capital, people are mostly information and energy resources. People used to be material resources only for cannibals, for concentration camp keepers digging dental gold, or as medical school cadavers. Only in recent times have organ transplants lent a positive cast to using people as material resources.

The boundary between labor and capital is fuzzy and socially, industrially, or historically conditioned. But no one doubts that changes in the relative abundance and prices of labor and capital are a major aspect of economic change. Another major aspect of economic change is change in the relative abundance and prices of materials, energy, and information. The story of changing proportions of labor and capital is neither much clearer nor much murkier for information resources than for the same story for materials or for energy. It just has not yet been told, having barely begun to unfold. The invention of practical steam engines in the 19th century opened an era of hitherto unheard-of massive abundance of energy resources with equally unheard-of massive power. The ensuing shifts in the relative use of material, energy, and information resources are already the stuff of history. So are related shifts in proportions of labor and capital.[6]

The electronic compunications way with information resources is powerful, versatile, and abundant on a massive scale unheard of prior to the 20th century. The phenomenon is barely adolescent and still far from mature. By providing entirely new formats and processes with the evolution toward digitization, it upsets the stability of the traditional substance-format-process bundles. It calls into question labor/capital proportions within information resources and also the proportions of information resources to energy and material resources.

The Substance, Format, and Process Sides of Information Resources

In stabler times, chopping up more or less innocent and useful information goods like newspapers or TV into such seeming fluff as substance, format, and process deservedly might have seemed metaphysical in the most insulting sense. But when the stuff of the real world is coming unglued, *not* going for these stable building blocks quickly gets impractical to the point of dereliction of duty. When traditional ties which have lingered too long continue to bundle substance of specific kinds or purposes with specific means for dealing with that substance, the arrangement gets in the way of grasping and grappling with essentials of change.

Stereotypically, for example, news went with ink on paper and massive presses, and with rewrite men, heroic editors with green eyeshades, and little merchants staggering around the block under a Sunday's load. Mass entertainment was live hoofers on sawdust stages in the 1920s, silver grains on celluloid film projecting motion onto the screens of movie palaces in the 1930s and 1940s, and phosphorescent images with commercials on the tubes of home entertainment centers since the 1950s.

Personal communication for many still means ink, paper, envelopes, licking stamps, and the ring of the postman; for others, it is now mainly a finger in the dial or on the beeping buttons, the ring or peep of the telephone and a voice at the other end; for still others it is the electronic mail boxes in some network of personal or business computers. Dickens' Bob Cratchit and Uriah Heep are ancestors both of the keypunchers of yesteryear's clerical warrens in banks and insurance companies and of the data entry clerks sought in the want ads of the 1980s.

Electronic digital compunications technologies are already powerful, versatile, and abundant enough to take on all of the above functions, certainly in part if not as a whole. In brief, *all* kinds of substance can be put in electronic digital formats, processed by computers in huge quantities at great speed, and sent around the universe riding on electrons or photons at per-unit costs that keep going down compared to the costs of one of nearly everything else. Economic factors alone call into question the bundles based on other formats and processes. How rapidly do bundles actually come apart? When do new ones get formed? These questions are beyond the scope of this paper, but are addressed elsewhere for electronic-print competition.[7]

Substance

From many conventional standpoints, the term "substance" as used here lumps together too much that seems distinctive: knowledge, data, information (in the narrow sense that some treat as synonymous with data), news, intelligence, and numerous other colloquial and specialized denotations and connotations. For instance, some intelligence professionals adhere to Ray Cline's distinction between raw and finished intelligence:

In its narrowest context, intelligence is simply information. It may be collected in some clandestine manner, that is, secretly and often at some personal risk because the facts sought are being deliberately withheld. In a broader sense, intelligence on foreign affairs includes such additional categories as press reports, foreign radio broadcasts, foreign publications, and—in the government—reports from our Foreign Service officers and military attachés.

In the world of international affairs, intelligence is only useful if it is subjected to evaluation and analysis to put it into the context of ongoing U.S. national security and foreign policy concerns. It must be evaluated for accuracy and credibility in the light of its source or its collection method, for the validity and significance of the content, after being collated with other available data, and for its impact on U.S. interests, operations, or objectives. The result of this total intelligence process is a report intended to assist policy and operational officers in making decisions.[8]

Scientists often distinguish observed fact from theory, what Thomas Kuhn describes as the system of "intertwined theoretical and methodological belief that permits selection, evaluation, and criticism." As he explains:

If that body of belief is not already implicit in the collection of facts—in which case more than "mere facts" are at hand—it must be externally supplied, perhaps by a current metaphysic, by another science, or by personal and historical accident. No wonder, then, that in the early stages of the development of any science different men confronting the same range of phenomena, but not usually all the same particular phenomena, describe and interpret them in different ways. What is surprising, and perhaps also unique in its degree to the fields we call science, is that such initial divergences should ever largely disappear.[9]

Some business people draw a line between financial accounting and managerial accounting. As one textbook puts it:

Financial accounting reports on the overall activities of the organization and is always restricted to past events. These include any financial transactions, such as a sale, a payment, or a change in value of something. Financial accounting is based in the past. It is a history of the organization.... managerial accounting often moves into the realms of speculation and future events. It deals with concepts such as incremental costs, marginal revenue, sunk costs and potential break-evens. For managers the use of managerial accounting information is a very important part of the decision-making process.[10]

But distinctions between raw and finished intelligence, facts and theories, financial and managerial accounting, information and knowledge, or our facts, their facts, and true facts are incidental, not basic, in sorting out information resources. Rather, such distinctions reflect always relative and mostly subjective judgments. For instance, one person's knowledge is often another person's raw data. What a vice president for marketing, production, or finance thinks he or she knows is just data to the chief executive officer's staff. What a scientist thinks he or she knows about the merits of a flu vaccine or the safety of a nuclear reactor is just data for presidential politics and policy.

Data, knowledge, and the rest are kinds of information substance—of greater or lesser value, of greater or lesser cost. Out of the broader notion of information resources, the concept of substance brings out the essence of information, the thing that either a picture or a thousand words conveys, the thing evoked when speaking of matters that are substantive rather than formal or procedural. What happens if we pay more attention to generic traits that are common to all varieties of substance than to the differences among particular species of substance and their particular purposes or values? This is a starting point in this paper.

Format: Discretion and Pattern

Information substance infuses into a wide variety of more or less readily inter-changeable forms. Pictures and words are the most common substance-bearing forms. Words come as speech and words come as writing. Written words alone have many incarnations: toe marks in sand, gouges in stone, ink marks on paper, glowing phosphor patterns on television screens, electrical currents in communications facilities, electromagnetic waves from earth stations to satel-lites and back, quantum states in computer memories, laser beams in glass fibers. The concept of information formats brings these diverse ways of embodying information substance out from the idea of information resources.

Setting substance apart from format makes it plain how discretionary the ties are between specific kinds of substance and specific kinds of formats. News substance, for example, is not inexorably tied to paper format. The anomalous English word "newspaper" suggests such a tie but, by contrast, French "jour-nal," German "Zeitung," and Russian "gazeta" do not confound substance with format. Of course news can also be gleaned from radio or television, heard over the phone or, today as in olden times, passed on by word of mouth.

Telling substance apart from format lets creative thinking about the endless possibilities in combining and recombining substance and format off the leash of traditional combinations. Analogies with more familiar resources show why.

Energy and substance are both patterned matter. More explicitly, energy is to materials-in-general as substance is to materials-as-format. Both energy and information substance are abstractions. This very abstractness frees them from bondage to arbitrary incarnations in particular materials. What is gained by speaking of energy in the abstract is the ability to ask intensely practical and concrete questions, such as "Is energy cheaper as coal, as hydro, as solar, as nuclear, or as some other mode? or safer? or more convenient? or whatever?" If energy is coal and coal is energy, how can energy be something other than coal? When energy and coal are one lump, the very question seems absurd. But when something distinct and abstract—energy—stays put as its embodiments shift from concrete mode to concrete mode, it gets easier to juggle desirable traits— price, environmental impact, convenience, or whatever, secure in the under-standing that the essential good, the energy, is unscathed.

That is exactly like being able to talk of the relative cost and effectiveness of getting a political message—a bit of substance—to some intended audience by such different format-process combinations (modes) as newspapers, broadcasts, or phone calls. What is gained by speaking of substance is the ability to pose intensely practical and concrete questions such as "Will this story make more money as a book? a movie? or a TV mini-series?" Or "How much campaign money do I put into TV ads, direct mail, or a phone campaign?" Or "How much should we budget for flesh-and-blood spies and how much for National Technical Means of Verification, as the treaties put it, to promote arms control?"

Abstracting generic information substance from its embodiments in specific format-and-process modes is necessary for avoiding marketing myopia as described by Theodore Levitt in an article so titled. "The railroads are in trouble," wrote Levitt in 1960, "because they assumed themselves to be in the railroad business rather than in the transportation business":

Even after the advent of automobiles, trucks, and airplanes, the railroad tycoons remained imperturbably self-confident. If you had told them 60 years ago that in 30 years they would be flat on their backs, broke, and pleading for government subsidies, they would have thought you totally demented. Such a future was simply not considered possible. It was not even a discussable subject, or an askable question, or a matter which any sane person would consider worth speculating about. The very thought was insane. Yet a lot of insane notions now have matter-of-fact acceptance—for example, the idea of 100-ton tubes of metal moving smoothly through the air 20,000 feet above the earth, loaded with 100 sane and solid clients casually drinking martinis—and they have dealt cruel blows to the railroads.[11]

Abstraction is not sufficient. Rather, Alvin von Auw, who was close to several of AT&T's board chairmen in the years just before the 1984 breakup of the Bell System, testifies that AT&T management noted the necessity of this rethinking:

Whatever for good or ill marketing dogma may have contributed to the economy at large, can there at this juncture be any serious quarrel with the conclusion that two at least of Levitt's three basic formulations have contributed significantly and perhaps crucially to the revitalization of AT&T? It is difficult to conceive how AT&T might prosper—or for that matter survive—in the changed and still changing world it confronts in the absence of the redefinition of its business mission that its own marketing prophets urged upon it: "No longer do we perceive that our business will be limited to telephony or—for that matter, telecommunications. Ours is the business of information-handling, the knowledge business. And the market we seek to serve is global."[12]

Von Auw also testifies that abstraction from modes is not sufficient. Marketing that "focuses on the customer's needs and shapes the organization to meeting them" is, von Auw agrees with Levitt, another ingredient of success although catering to every customer whim can also be just another good intention that paves the road to hell.[13] Von Auw recollects "the tardiness of

AT&T's recognition of the growing diversity of its customers' requirements in the late '60s and early '70s," and adds:

Still vivid in the memory of at least one of the participants is a 1969 conference of Bell operating vice presidents and the pungently expressed frustrations of some of its veteran members at the cautiously proffered suggestion that meeting the needs of data communications users might require specialized operating organizations, specialized test centers, even special service measurements. Certainly the recollection confirms Levitt's observation that "executives with such backgrounds"—that is, in the operating end of capital intensive industries—"have an almost trained incapacity to see that getting 'volume' may require understanding and serving many discrete and sometimes small market segments, rather than going after a perhaps mythical batch of big or homogeneous customers."[14]

Formats are ultimately material. Ink on paper is material. So is the metallic or plastic lettering that spells out the brand name on the rear of a car. The pattern of a metallic *A* differs from the pattern of a metallic car body: same material, different function, and different pattern. That is why formats are only ultimately material. To be really useful, the idea of format needs the idea of pattern, just as builders need abstract pattern to speak of arches, flying buttresses, or I-beams.

Arches can be made of stone or brick or concrete or plywood or steel. Steel can make arches or I-beams or L-beams or rails or fenders. This flexibility of choice, this broad discretion, is explicit only when pattern is abstracted from material. Dissecting format into a hierarchy of symbols, patterns, and tokens (figure 7.2) gives a similarly valuable freedom of choice.

Suppose the substance to be formatted is the idea of a cat. One discretionary choice is whether to express this idea in French, in English, or in some other language. By this decision one chooses a symbol for the idea of a cat.

Choosing the symbol leaves other useful choices wide open. The symbol can be patterned in lower case or in capital roman type, in Morse code or in Braille. The respective practical or aesthetic advantages of the different patterns are plain. The same choice among patterns is open whether the French word or the English word has been picked as the symbol. That all these combinations are possible, and more, is inexpressible if symbol and pattern are not told apart one from another and both told apart from substance.

A symbol and a pattern are both abstract, like an arch-shape or an I-shape or an L-shape or a rail-shape. A token concretely embodies the abstract pattern for the abstract symbol for that abstract chunk of substance which is the idea of a cat. We sidestep the truly metaphysical questions about how the idea of a cat relates to either one warm purring critter or else to all catdom. An open choice

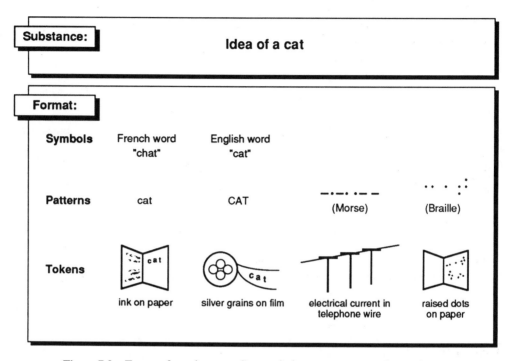

Figure 7.2   Format for substance: Cat symbols, cat patterns, and cat tokens

of tokens helps even when the symbol and its pattern are already fixed. The aesthetic and commercial differences between ink-on-paper and silver-grains-on-film as tokens for "cat" are evident. The Morse and Braille patterns show off best when linked with electrical and embossed tokens, respectively. But both the Morse and the Braille patterns had to be infused into ink-on-paper tokens to make the token for figure 7.2, namely this paper's palpable page.

Process

Manipulating real-world information substance means applying a process, not abstractly to disembodied substance but concretely to material tokens. The process idea is the third and last element of the dissection of information resources into their substance, format, and process building blocks. Figure 7.3 shows how such real information processors as human brains, hands-with-pen-and-paper, and printing presses together mediate the processes of gathering,

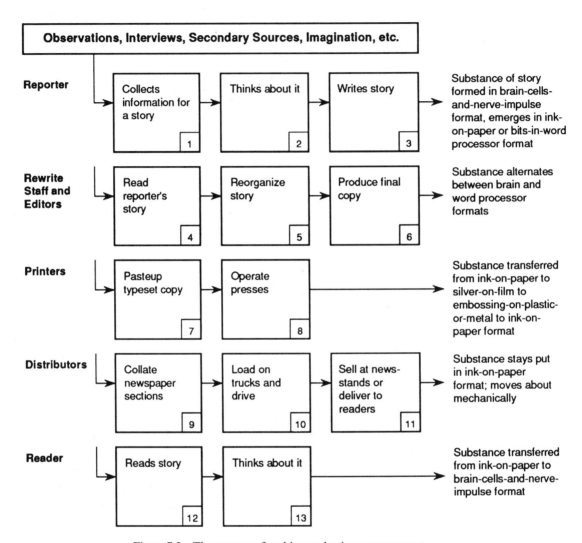

Figure 7.3   The process of making and using a newspaper

storing, manipulating, transmitting, evaluating, and using substance in various formats.

Because abstract substance is, in the real world, always embodied in concrete tokens, modifying substance involves applying energy to some substance's token to change that token into a token for the modified substance. In some ways that's just like applying energy to a steel ingot to roll it into an I-beam for a skyscraper or like applying energy to sheet metal to stamp it into a fender for a car. A key difference is that working over material-as-information-token normally takes minuscule amounts of energy compared to working over material-as-piece-of-a-building-or-car. How much muscle it takes to erase an *A* typed by mistake and how much muscle it takes to wreck an A-frame house give a sense of the relative scales of energy consumption.

In the industrial revolution the search was on for new ways to apply new steam technology across the range of energy-consuming human endeavors. The Information Evolution is the search for new ways to bundle substance with new electronic digital formats and processes, displacing, wherever possible, the energy- and material-intensive modes of an earlier era.

These ideas are not new. The myth of wily Odysseus, like the myth of David and Goliath, is the story of brain over brawn, of the clever use of information as a force multiplier. Using their radar better than either the Germans or the British Bomber Command, the British Fighter Command flew their few planes so well in World War II's Battle of Britain that the Germans thought they faced many more. The radar force multiplier ushered in the contemporary electronic manifestations of brain over brawn. Formatting and processing techniques born of wartime intelligence, command, and control needs became available for use in other bundles of substance, format, and process.

Information Goods and their Purveyors: Bundles and Bundlers

Every information product or service is a bundle of substance, format, and process. Newspapers, for instance, bring the substance of national news, local news, ads, crossword puzzles, horoscopes, and so on to their readers in an ink-on-paper format through the process in figure 7. 3.

Figure 7.4 provides a basis for visualizing information products and services as bundles of substance, format, and process. The axes of figure 7.4 are substance, format, and process. The planes made by the three pairs of axes in turn portray conventional functions within information businesses. Tying substance

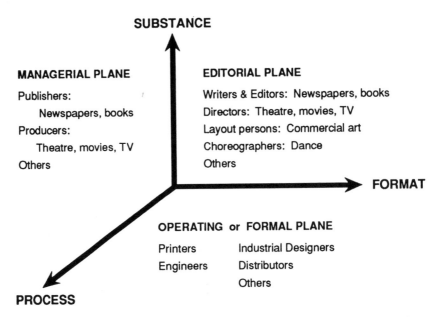

SUBSTANCE

MANAGERIAL PLANE

Publishers:
    Newspapers, books
Producers:
    Theatre, movies, TV
Others

EDITORIAL PLANE

Writers & Editors: Newspapers, books
Directors: Theatre, movies, TV
Layout persons: Commercial art
Choreographers: Dance
Others

FORMAT

OPERATING or FORMAL PLANE

Printers   Industrial Designers
Engineers   Distributors
                  Others

PROCESS

Figure 7.4 Information businesses: Substance, format, process, and their bundles

to process defines a *managerial* plane; infusing substance into format defines an *editorial* plane, and subjecting concrete formats, as materials, to concrete energy-consuming processes defines a formal or *operating* plane devoid of substance. One person or one organization might, of course, do all three bundlings, as in the romantic idealization of the small-town editor/publisher with a green eyeshade on his head, black ink on his hands, and a bicycle seat under his rump. In other information businesses, people with other titles do the managerial, editorial, and operating functions.[15]

The presence or absence of substance is relative, depending on who's doing what, by what conventions, under what circumstances. A sublime haiku is Greek to one who knows no Japanese even though nothing has changed in the ink or the rice paper. To Shakespeare, a tale told by an idiot was purely formal, "full of sound and fury, signifying nothing." There is no record of what it meant to the idiot.

I once asked a friend, a violinist in the Boston Symphony Orchestra, what he thought of a performance I had just left enthralled. Said he, "We get paid to play, not to think," much as last night's printer might reply about this morning's news stories.

Arguments so convoluted that they would confound Talmudists, Jesuits, and Immanuel Kant combined take place in Washington's administrative, legislative, and judicial hearing rooms over whether certain telephone company operations are purely formal or shade over into the substantive. Likewise in Brasilia, New Delhi, Rome, and Tokyo, and in innumerable board rooms. At stake is not abstruse theology or the hereafter but who may do what kind of business with or without government regulation right down here and now: Does this or that piece of market turf belong to local phone companies, AT&T, IBM or Crazy Eddie? To Americans, Europeans or Japanese?[16] For this paper, something is pure form, innocent of substance and found in the formal or operating plane, whenever the point being made is about a material format undergoing an energy-consuming process, like a violin string being vibrated by the bow, whether the format actually incarnates substance for someone or not. It costs energy either way.

What various media have in common and how they differ can be sorted out by using the ideas summed up in figure 7.4.

News can be delivered in print or news can be delivered by radio, as shown in figures 7.5 and 7.6. The bundle in figure 7.5 is usually called a newspaper section, that in figure 7.6 a radio broadcast segment. The two figures show the same substance delivered in two distinct substance-format-process bundles made by distinct bundlers. As always, what you make of such a thing depends on who you are and what you might want to prove.

Some will think it plain that there is no difference between the two media: Both convey roughly the same news—say, the announcement of the election of a president of the United States—only one does it orally, the other in writing. In fact, both newspaper and radio get some of their information from the same wire service. From this standpoint the identical placement along the substance axis in figures 7.5 and 7.6 and the overlap at the Associated Press feed on the process axis overwhelm the differences on the format axis and the differences in delivery processes.

Others will think it just as obvious that the medium is the message. That fairly leaps to the eyes through the different positions of the cubes in figure 7.5 and figure 7.6 that denote the entire bundles, and likewise through the different positions of the squares that denote the editorial, managerial, and operating contributions to these bundles. Besides, one can point out that the wire feeds to radio and to newspapers are separate. A.P. writes stories for radio that are shorter than the stories it feeds to newspapers. Where a newspaper article might run 800 words, the radio announcement runs only 50. The bare facts may be the

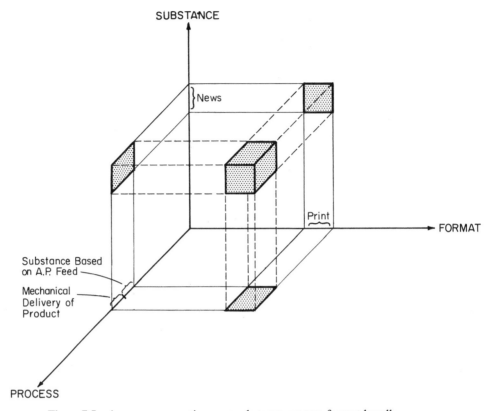

Figure 7.5 A newspaper section as a substance-process-format bundle

same, but the treatment and the impact are something else again. Perhaps that is what Marshall McLuhan meant by his delphic coinage of the "medium is the message" phrase:

In a culture like ours, long accustomed to splitting and dividing all things as a means of control, it is sometimes a bit of a shock to be reminded that, in operational and practical fact, the medium is the message. This is merely to say that the personal and social consequences of any medium—that is, of any extension of ourselves—result from the new scale that is introduced into our affairs by each extension of ourselves, or by any new technology.[17]

What stays put and what changes in shifts from one medium to another lends itself to differing interpretations. Figures 7.5 and 7.6 illustrate the extreme but

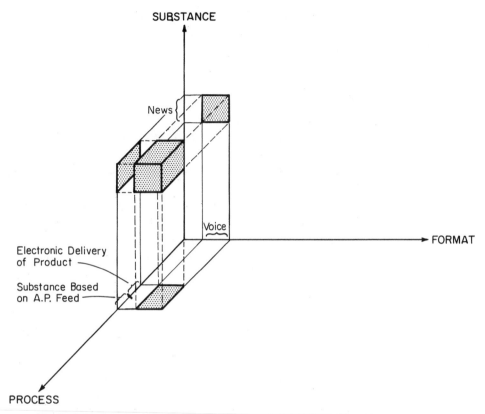

Figure 7.6   A radio broadcast as a substance-process-format bundle

useful idea that there is something invariant—an abstract and inviolate under-lying message or substance—common to both the oral and the written state-ments that someone has been elected president. The same figures capture another useful idea not at all antithetical to the first, namely that the flavor of a format-process combination or its temperature—as in McLuhan's controversial hot media, cool media distinction—is somehow substantive and not purely formal.[18] At this extreme, the medium *is* the message. Anything is always at least a symbol for itself, whatever other conventional or unconventional per-ceptions it might evoke. Arcane arguments in between—say, over whether the smell of the leather and the sight of the gold in a rich binding are or are not part of the message of a book—can at least be expressed by the visual metaphor for substance-format-process bundles.

Of course that does nothing to settle the arguments. At least in one real world, such distinctions are mostly axe-grinding. For instance, the concept of the movie rights to a book is a respectable, even a legal truth, even an enforceable right, if one believes or at least gets a judge or a legislature to say that there is something—reasonably approximating what is meant here by the disembodied substance of a story—which might be incarnated in both a book format and a movie format and manufactured and distributed through the processes of both Madison Avenue and Hollywood for greater profit than through either alone. This extreme might be tagged as the *alias* view of a story (figure 7.7a), wherein one and the same story does business as and reaps rewards for its author as both book and movie, for instance *Gone with the Wind*–story d.b.a. *Gone with the Wind*–book and also d.b.a. *Gone with the Wind*–movie. If litigation is war, as some lawyers believe, then controlling presumptions like this is what controlling the high ground is to an embattled Marine.

Under critical pressure, however, either the book's author or the screenwriter might take refuge in an *alibi* view of a story (figure 7.7c). The author's alibi, if the movie bombs, is that he and his story weren't there at all. It was altogether another story, by that scribbler the screenwriter, that masqueraded under the book's name. Figure 7.7b suggests the more common "my story, but butchered" that lies between the aliases "my story, the book and my story, the movie" and the alibi "not my story at all."

After-the-fact justifications of *realpolitik* by such fairy tales and by their reification into law are the rule in public and private decision making, not the exception.[19] In part this is because even now what defines a real-world medium bundle and its bundler's turf is less self-evident and less solid than it seems or than might be sworn to in court.

Evolving Information Purveyors: Media Come, Media Go

Many real-world people and organizations tie many real-world substance-format-process bundles. Among them are the businesses lumped under the "mass media" rubric. Newspapers are among the many familiar products and services that these businesses turn out. Like every other medium, the newspaper is a substance-format-process bundle that came out of its own particular sequence of historical events.

Some bundles are more ephemeral than others; none is a prime mover unmoved or even virgin-born. The dominant newspaper format, for example,

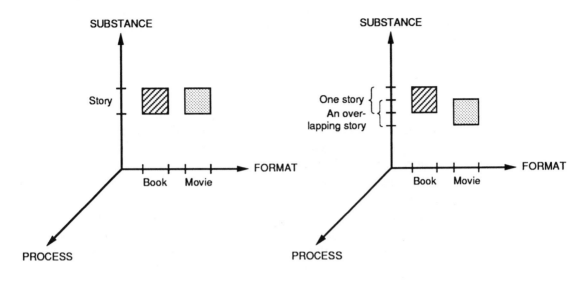

A. Alias

B. In between

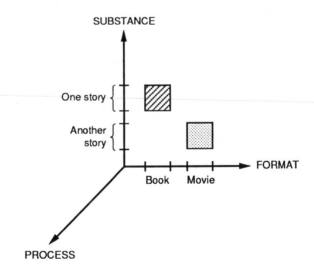

C. Alibi

Figure 7.7 Alias and alibi: The story as book and the story as movie

issues from an accidental coupling of technology and policy. Many newspaper people express an almost mystical reverence for the size of the standard newspaper exemplified by the *New York Times* or the *Wall Street Journal*. They commonly affect a sneer at tabloids, newspapers sized like the *New York Daily News* or the *National Enquirer*. Indeed, rival papers often hint that the tabloid format connotes pandering to popular if not altogether depraved tastes, while the larger standard format brims over with the truths of responsible journalism.

Few in the trade question all this mysticism. Most act as if the high-class format came with Adam and Eve. The reality is rather prosaic.

When steam-driven presses came out around 1814, they could handle at most a certain size of paper. Until 1855 the British taxed newspapers by the number of pages. It was only natural for newspaper businesses to adopt the largest practicable page size in order to minimize the tax bite. All the rest is snobbery, fueled by the fact that tabloid publishers do aim their substance at the lower income mass market.

Essentially unchanged since those days is the *presentation* format that newspaper readers see and feel (figure 7.3, box 12) and which annoyingly rubs black ink off on their hands. "Essentially" here means that the casual observer might hardly notice differences that are gargantuan to the cognoscenti of the trade.[20]

The formats used in manufacturing newspapers (figure 7.3, boxes 1–8) are largely invisible to the reader. They also have changed but little. Prior to the early 1970s, a 19th-century newspaper owner would have recognized almost everything that happened at the paper from the time a reporter set his story on paper to the time when that story rolled off the presses. During the 1970s, however, the internal processes of newspapers shifted from hot metal technology to computer-based photocomposition technology, from mainly mechanical to mainly electronic processes, from internal formats based on ink and paper to beeps and bleeps in wires (figure 7.3, boxes 7–8 and even boxes 3–8). Although unnoticed by the ordinary newspaper reader who, from outside the business, sees only the conventional presentation format (figure 7.3, box 11), this change in internal formats and processes typifies how diffusing compunications technologies are transforming not only the mass media but the information industries in general.

Mass Media: Landmarks

One thing is sure about the future. It begins now. And it is certain that when you don't know where you are it is hard to figure out where you are going. A brief snapshot of mass media during the early 1980s will serve as a sample of landmarks with which to gauge what change has taken place since then and with which to navigate the course of still-evolving change.

At the turn of the '80s, the U.S. mass media industry included:

Newspapers

Editor & Publisher tabulated some 1700 products listed as English-language daily newspapers. Most were of general interest in a particular geographical area. They depended on advertising for about 70% of their revenues and on their readers for the remaining 30%. There were also foreign-language dailies and special-interest dailies, ranging from the *Wall Street Journal* to *Woman's Wear Daily*. Besides these, the *Ayer Directory of Publications* listed approximately 9000 less-than-daily newspapers, many of them weekly publications in towns too small to support a daily. Usually included under the newspaper rubric, though subject to varying perceptions, were the many "shoppers." Shoppers were usually distributed free and carried some editorial material, but they were primarily if not totally devoted to display advertising and classified or even jumbled advertising. Most newspapers were owned by firms that publish more than one publication.

Magazines

The annual *Ayer Directory* classified more than 10,000 bundles as periodicals. These included some 1200 consumer magazines, as well as business, trade, and professional publications; scholarly journals; and association, alumni, and similar periodicals. Although many such bundles accepted and depended on advertising, others were supported exclusively by circulation revenues, dues, or other subsidies. As with newspapers, most consumer and business magazines were part of multi-publication groups.

Broadcast Television

Three major commercial television networks fed the bulk of the programming of 800 VHF and UHF stations. In addition, there were educational or public stations and a loose network to serve them, financed by government appropriations plus private and corporate donations. The networks themselves each owned five VHF stations scattered among the major markets, while other firms also owned chains of local stations. Most programming was purchased by networks from independent film producers and studios. On occasion, *ad hoc* networks came into being for some particular purpose or series.

Broadcast Radio

The rise of television had already changed the nature of radio from a national- and network-programmed medium to a largely local and independently programmed medium. There were seven radio networks and 8000 commercial AM and FM stations. The latter were the fastest-growing segment of the industry. In addition, there was a relatively small cadre of public/educational stations.

Cable Television (CATV)

Unlike the more established media, cable then functioned mostly as a distributor rather than as a creator of substance. Cable began as a provider of stronger reception of conventional broadcast signals in remote areas. In 1983, 5000 cable systems relied on broadcast television signals from the network affiliates, retransmission of some independent stations, and a growing number of cable programming networks for their fare. In most cases, there were also one or more premium pay-TV services that provided theatrical films and some productions specially produced for this form of distribution. There was little cable-operator-originated programming, other than news headlines, weather, and sports scores, often by means of automated displays rather than live announcers.

Books

The U.S. Commerce Department enumerated 2000 book publishers, but this statistic may have understated the true number of small but active publishers. R.R. Bowker Co. identifies more than 500,000 titles in print, with as many as 50,000 new titles appearing each year. Books included such diverse segments as trade, college and elementary-high school textbook, religious, professional, and university press and mass market paperbacks. Channels of distribution varied significantly for different types of books and required the participation of wholesalers, jobbers,retailers, and postal services.

Motion Pictures

There were an estimated 4900 producers and distributors of films, most of them in the non-theatrical end of the business. Theatrical movies were shown on 17,000-plus theater screens, many of which were part of "circuits" or chains. Most theatrical films were distributed by nine major firms and, more than any other segment of the media, depended on foreign sales for a major portion of revenue and profit. Non-theatrical films included educational, promotional, and other business films. The federal government was particularly active here, either through its own production or in contracts to independents.

Non-Broadcast Video

The role of video had just begun to grow in both homes and business/government/educational organizations. Business and government spent an estimated $1.1 billion on non-broadcast television hardware and programming in 1980. Many large firms had their own "networks" that served television outlets in their scattered corporate and divisional offices, using copies of videocassettes prepared in-house or standardized purchased programming. Schools and colleges used closed-circuit and taped programs for instruction. The home market in 1983 consisted largely of recycled theatrical films and a few specially made special interest programs for the 6.3 million home videocassette units. At least 18 firms were marketing one-half inch cassette units for the home market, while a handful of firms had entered the licensing and production of programming area. Albeit small, non-broadcast use of the television set was the fastest growing segment of the mass media. By the end of the decade it had grown enough to justify the re-release of the popular film *E.T.* in the videocassette format for the Christmas trade. RCA was no more and the NBC network had been sold to GE.

Newsletters

These were distinctive bundles generally regarded as being neither magazines nor newspapers. They were periodicals, usually devoted to a specialized topic and hence a specialized audience. Most often they were sold on a subscription basis at a relatively high price, with little or no advertising. Although some had a circulation of 100 copies or less, they sometimes were highly influential among their readership.

Databases

The rapid and continuing reduction in the cost of computer storage and processing had stimulated a new form of database storage and retrieval. Vast quantities of data on a broad list of subjects had become accessible from remote terminals, mostly to business, government, and other institutional users who were willing to pay to get timely information. A sub-industry of database utilities had also been created to facilitate the dissemination of this information.

Advertisers

Most of the media were supported totally or predominantly by income from advertising. Users consequently received the substance for free (in the case of broadcasts or "shoppers") or for less than the full cost of production (daily newspapers, most magazines). Trade books and theatrical films were the two major media that were user supported, although some question whether or not low prices for fourth-class mail were subsidizing mail-order book publishers. In 1982, U.S. organizations as varied as the U.S. Army and Frank Perdue's chicken business spent about $67 billion on advertising, most of that through the mass media. The largest share went to newspapers, followed by television. Advertising expenditures had stayed at a nearly constant 2% of the gross national product since 1940.

U.S. government

The U.S. government was in the media business through films and publications for sale. As the State, it supervised media businesses as it does other businesses, subject to provisions, like the First Amendment to the Constitution, that are specific to information businesses. It also consumed media.[21]

Consumers

As just noted, users of the media got most of them for direct expenses on their part less than full cost of production. The major direct expense to receive broadcasts was the one-time investment in a television or radio receiver. Massive investment in VCRs occurred throughout the 1980s. The price of a daily newspaper covered about 30% of its cost (including profit margin), while consumer magazines charge readers about 40%–50% of cost. Many trade magazines were also provided free of direct cost. Consumers directly covered the total costs of trade books and theatrical films. Many films in the non-theatrical category were sponsored. Cable and premium channel use was supported mostly by users, but cable operators did get some sponsored films and were looking for greater support from advertisers. Nonetheless, at the $44 million level of 1981, consumers were spending less than advertisers on mass media. What consumers paid indirectly in attention to advertising or through the prices they paid for advertised products is not examined here.[22]

In absolute size, the revenues of the traditional segments of the media, as reported by various trade associations and the U.S. Department of Commerce, were about $58 billion in 1981, or 2.3% of gross national product (figure 7.8).

	Value of product shipments or revenue, 1981 ($ billions)	Percent of total
Newspapers	$19.5	28.4%
Broadcasting	13.5	19.7
Magazines	9.9	14.4
Cable TV	2.1	3.1
Books	6.9	10.0
Theatrical film	4.4	6.4
Newsletters, databases, spoken word, videocassettes, etc.	1.4	2.0
	$57.7	84.0%
Consumer electronics (television radio receivers, home video recorders, phonograph and hi-fi equipment)	11.0	16.0
	$68.7	100.0%

Figure 7.8   Major mass media benchmark: 1981 revenues

By way of comparison, General Motors (GM) had sales of $60 billion, Exxon $97 billion, and IBM $34 billion. Media firms employed a total of about 1.2 million people, compared to 1.1 million people for the Big Three automakers alone. Even adding the value of consumer electronics shipments (including imports) did not materially change the standing of the overall media industry.

This media industry rested on an infrastructure with a variety of indirect participants (figure 7.9). For instance, the print media depended on manufacturers of newsprint and of the number 5 coated groundwoods paper used by newspapers and magazines, respectively. About 90% of all newsprint produced in the United States and Canada went to newspapers, while number 5 coated stock was periodically in such short supply that magazines had to import some from West Germany and from Finland. Manufacturers of these grades of papers had their fortunes closely allied with the publishing industry. Ink, a petroleum-based product, was an increasingly large expense for publishers, especially of newspapers at a time when oil prices had peaked.

Print media also relied on various transportation modes, especially trucks and trains, for both the delivery of their raw materials and the distribution of their products. The magazine industry depended heavily on the U.S. Postal Service—a relationship that many publishers then questioned in light of greatly increased second-class mailing tariffs.

All the media, but print especially, were affected by the cost and the availability of energy. The paper-manufacturing industry was the fourth largest user of purchased energy, while big-city newspaper presses used much electricity. Television and radio broadcasters needed electricity to send out their signals and television sets needed electricity to receive them. Broadcasters also needed hardware such as cameras, editors, and transmitters. Finally, all the media relied heavily on the telecommunications system of wires, microwave, light-guides, and satellites that AT&T and emerging competing telecommunications companies supplied. Relative to the print and film media, the electronic media were less sensitive to the cost of electricity, but they depended more on its uninterrupted availability.

As they went into the 1980s, newspaper publishers faced skyrocketing newsprint costs, while the cost of computer storage plunged even faster. Magazine publishers, like their newspaper counterparts, had been reaping healthy profits, yet they worried about postal rates and paper costs. Many in the print media businesses were looking at the newer formats and processes. They saw videotext and teletext technologies, video disks, electronic databases for business, electronic games, and personal computers, but were unsure of what it all meant to them.

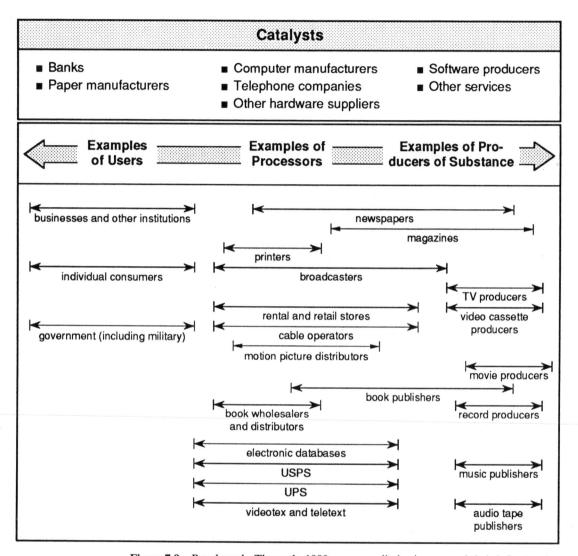

Figure 7.9   Benchmark: The early 1980s mass media businesses and their infrastructure

Their brethren in the electronic media faced the bursting of their own distinctive bundles. For instance, the home television set was being used for private showings of theatrical films or to display computer output; homes with cable service could look at programs unavailable on the old-line networks or, for that matter, anywhere off the air. There was talk of "narrowcasting," i.e., special interest programming for identifiable market segments rather than the broadcasting, which tried to appeal to the greatest mass of viewers.

Blurring Boundaries

Government agencies were having to figure out how regulations and statutes should or could apply to media and technologies which did not exist when these rules were made. The very concepts used to speak of the media world had grown blurry.

Mass communications had often been defined as delivering one message at one time to all of a large, heterogeneous, and unseen audience in different places. The bundlers that purveyed substance that way were termed *mass* media. This tag reflected a traditional distinction between mass communication and media and other types of communication and media, such as point-to-point communication by telephone and telegraph or by individually addressed letters by mail.

Whatever sharpness this distinction once had got lost when a wider variety of formats and processes came on the scene. Personal computers and so-called "dumb terminals" at the office or at home enabled people to pick the substance they wished to get, although they might be drawing on a large common database to do so. Devices had become available for dialing up thousands of phone numbers in order to play more or less identical recorded messages to the recipients. Video and audio cassette recorders enabled people to record broadcasts in order to play them back whenever and how often they wished. Mass mailings often addressed only to "occupant" were not new, and there was speculation that electronic mail might further accent the mass flavor of the once point-to-point mail medium.

In earlier times one could usefully look upon newspapers, magazines, books, movies, radio, and television as the mass media. By 1980 one had to think through again the meaning of "mass" and, even more crucial, one had to confront a blurring of the boundaries among the media, a loss of the stability and the distinctiveness of their product or service bundles. "Television," for example, had begun to mean something that no longer exclusively displayed broadcast TV signals, but that also displayed signals retransmitted by CATV or originated for CATV, signals from videocassettes or disks played right on premises, or even news and other substance sent by telephone lines from a computer.

But the older media descriptions never were, in fact, as clear cut as it seemed. What is a magazine? It usually has a paper cover, but not always. *Horizon*, like many books, had a hard cover for a time. A magazine is usually printed on glossy coated paper, but some, like *Rolling Stone*, were printed on newsprint. Most magazines carry advertising, but they need not do so to qualify for the label. *Reader's Digest* did not accept advertising until 1955. Magazines are usually thought of as published regularly during the year, but there are many publications that look like magazines but only appear annually or even just once. At what point does a newsletter become a magazine? Why is the tabloid weekly *National Enquirer* treated as a magazine in most compilations of periodicals and by advertisers, although its format is that of many newspapers?

When asked to classify a particular medium, many people ultimately resort to "show me and I'll tell you what it is." But even that can fail. When you have bought a pre-recorded videocassette of *Rocky III* and play it on a television set, is the medium film or television? Someone watching the show on a TV set may not even know and likely will not even care whether he or she is watching a broadcast, a cablecast, a cassette, or a disc. Where the bundler sees a distinctive bundle, the consumer sees a commodity perhaps as fungible as any dollar bill is with any other. And with the bundles themselves having grown unstable as new formats and new processes have come on the scene, it's "media come, media go."

A Language for Change: Basic Building Blocks Stay

Media may come and media may go, but the basic substance, format, and process building blocks stay on as the tools of choice for expressing change. Thinking explicitly in terms of these building blocks helps avoid entrapment in bundles tied by the exercise of discretion appropriate to a moment in history but whose time has long since gone. Loosening up the basic building blocks releases yet again all the creative possibilities in their discretionary potential combinations.

"Television" is one word for what two distinct bundlers, the broadcasters and the CATV operators, deliver to a home set with its tube, generically called a video display terminal (VDT). In the late '60s and early '70s, the products of these two distinct businesses spoke roughly the same thing. More precisely, the broadcasting and the cable industries of that time were both in the business of sending the very same substance to be consumed in the very same presentation format. Even their processes were set apart only by differing transmission techniques. The cable business promised better reception by packaging over-the-air reception of the broadcasting bundle by a big antenna on a hilltop with cable retransmission of that bundle.

This commonality, hence the potential for competition between them, was lost on neither the television nor the cable industry. But at the start neither of the two paid much attention to the possibility that both would eventually revert to old conflicts with the telephone industry, by virtue of the latter's latent capability for selling more or less equivalent processes. For example, WNBC, which was NBC's New York City AM-radio flagship until it was sold by GE in 1988, was born WEAF in 1922 at AT&T's headquarters at 195 Broadway. American broadcasting and telephony were made to divorce by an agreement reached in 1926 whereby "AT&T was to sell its broadcasting station in New York to RCA with RCA committing itself to utilizing AT&T's lines instead of Western Union's for the purpose of interconnecting the broadcasting stations."[23]

A magazine printed on newsprint and a newspaper are bundles of different substance delivered in similar but not identical formats through similar but not identical processes. Their layouts differ and so do their delivery schedules.

In terms of the substance, format, and process building blocks, a substance creator—a storyteller for example—can think about and cut a deal with all the alternative operating (format and process) institutions for making and marketing his or her product and not be locked into the formats and processes of only one among the movie business, the broadcast business, the cable business, or the disc or cassette business. Customers for the substance can shop for the cheapest distribution process and the most satisfying presentation format available.

In the traditional media, the presentation format from which customers ultimately got their substance was mostly the same as the formats used in production. Except for what took place inside the reporter's head or the typesetter's, all the processes in figure 7.3 used to rely solely on ink-on-paper formats visible and intelligible to any literate person. Hence the distinctions, so common in the manufacturing industries, between intermediate and finished products, or between production for the final consumption trade and production for the OEM (original or outside equipment manufacturer) trade have been less important in the traditional media businesses. A tomato processor might sell whole, peeled, puréed, sauced, or ketchuped tomatoes directly under his own label, or indirectly under a national brand's, or under a supermarket's label, or in a club's or a restaurant's dish. The same can hold for washing machines and their parts. An information business equivalent is the Associated Press, which cans and distributes print and radio stories for local newspapers and broadcasters to sell or to serve up.

When intermediate electronic processes came into the traditional information industries, they gave more flexibility even to making the same old product. This flexibility makes intermediate formats—and commercial practices analogous to the industrial OEM trade—a possibility starting to be more widely exploited by the media and, indeed, by the information industries in general. By the late 1980s Dow Jones repackaged *Wall Street Journal* substance for its Dow Jones News Retrieval electronic database service. The *Washington Post* was among several newspapers that fed substance, after a brief delay, into Mead Data Central's NEXIS electronic database service.

Processes as they were defined previously encompass all the functions of gathering, creating, storing, manipulating, distributing, and otherwise handling substance. This includes a reporter's researching and writing a newspaper article, then storing it in computer memory for editing. It includes a computer's hyphenating and justifying the text for typesetting and makeup. It covers the mechanical printing of the text on a rotary press, workers' loading the papers on a truck, someone's driving around town dropping off bundles, and boys' or girls' delivering the papers to neighborhood doorsteps. It encompasses eyeballing the page in a comfortable armchair. Finally, it even encompasses authorized or pirated copying of an article for further processing of all kinds.

The traditional media happened to sort and to name themselves by traditional format or process concepts and labels. The newspaper, book, and magazine businesses are typed and tagged by the presentation format that they sell. More recently, intermediate process names, "radio," "cable," "videocassette," "home computer," and so on, have been used to denote a medium. This gets confusing. Both cable and videocassette, for example, are merely alternative means of delivering substance in a VDT's video-and-aural presentation format. To a viewer they are still television, so a producer of feature films for theatrical release can, for instance, look to the video presentation format for an increasing share of the market. The universal-optical-fiber-to-the-home world that telephone companies were praying for in the late 1980s is another alternative distribution channel.

Whether the product is delivered by cassette, disc, coaxial cable, optical fiber or broadcast can be vital to form and efficiency but does not of itself necessarily affect substance and effectiveness. As was suggested above this is a matter of emphasis. Arguments over the effect of form (that is, format-and-process) on substance, as contrasted to the effect of form on practical economics, often have the flavor of philosophical arguments over when a quantitative change becomes a qualitative one. The outcomes of such arguments can make or break advertising agencies or conglomerates or presidential image makers.

Just as picture and sound bundlers began to try out new forms, so newspaper publishers began to experiment in the early '80s with the idea that some of what they tied into a bundle on paper, like classified ads or stock prices, might be more efficiently delivered to the VDTs of only those subscribers who requested specific substance from the publisher's or someone else's computer. The newspaper business might therefore turn into a service industry relying in part on ink-on-paper presentation formats and in part on video presentation formats. Increasingly, database publishers have found that computer processing and video presentation of their substance is an efficient and profitable way to offer services—although the substance may be the same as before.

Using the substance, format, process building blocks to describe media can forestall dying asleep in old harnesses. The concept of a magazine, for instance, hitches traditional bundles of substance to a traditional ink-on-glossy-paper form which is but one of the many forms available to the creators of these substantive bundles. Yet traditional magazine publishers rarely see themselves as video producers. But, by understanding that a special substantive expertise is the basis of the printed magazine form, they may come to a generalized view of the business that leads naturally to productions in video form congruent with available editorial substance.

This reasoning also goes for newspaper publishers, broadcasters, book publishers, record producers, and others. The blurring of artificial, formal distinctions traditionally made between substantively similar bundles was evident once CBS' "60 Minutes" referred to itself as a "video magazine" and Westinghouse Broadcasting called its prime-time access program "Evening Magazine." Time, Inc., tried to translate the fast pace and airy substance of its print *People* weekly directly to a video presentation using the same concept.

Before the substance, format, and process building blocks were made explicit by the Harvard Program on Information Resources Policy, they were implicit in strategic planning in and around the media industry. In the early '80s some newspaper companies were trying out news services for cable channels or video-text systems. At least one broadcaster was starting to repackage existing news reports for videocassette or video tape sales, and movie distributors had already become accustomed to expanded distribution channels for their theatrical productions via broadcast, pay cable, cassettes, and disks.

These are just a few samples of possible creative outcomes of recombining substance, format, and process building blocks to create or enlarge markets, to reduce costs, to increase profit margins, and so on. Exploiting the new media menu provided by new formats and processes poses both challenges and opportunities to those in the media businesses.

A Means to What End?

Setting substance apart from process and format allows considering its traits and its uses free from the accident of any particular historical bundling of substance with formats and processes. But substance even without form remains a means, not an end. A fact may be a fact, a theory may be deeply true, and a work of art may be exquisitely beautiful. But if not suited to the needs of the moment they all are tools searching for work, solutions searching for problems, products searching for customers. The ends, the purposes, that substance might serve whatever its form must be described by building blocks other than substance, format, and process, and other than the bundles these building blocks make up. To do otherwise courts the circularity of describing news as what is in a newspaper and begs the question at the very heart of the search for appropriate responses to change: What mix of bundles by what mix of bundlers is best for what ends?

Findings have suggested that consumers use the mass media to satisfy four types of information needs: escape, social connection, surveillance, and opinion formation or decision making.[24] Different substance, process, and format bundles can be expected to satisfy different needs in different ways. And consumers use the media differently, depending on what mix of needs they want to satisfy.

- Escape is the need for social and psychological retreat or entertainment. Reading the comics, doing the crossword puzzle in the newspaper, or going to a movie theater are among the media uses that meet this need.

- Social connection needs go along with perceptions of one's social role. The sought substance is apt to be defined by "I know it when I see it." Thus, someone who feels part of the jet set may read newspaper stories about the goings on among the beautiful people or buy *Town and Country* magazine. At other times, a person may think it more important to be up-to-date on a sports star's free-agent status.

- Surveillance needs trigger questions more specific than for social connection, such as "Did the space shuttle get launched this morning?" "Are there any houses for sale in that neighborhood?" "What time do buses leave for New York Saturday morning?" or "Did the Phillies beat the Mets last night?"

- Opinion formation/decision-making needs are expressed by questions ranging from "How should I vote on the bond issue question?" to "What are the features of today's refrigerators that I should be looking for, now that I need a new one?" As with surveillance, the substantive need may be relatively well articulated. But the sources for the information may be less sharply defined, requiring a different approach to the search for substance.

These four functional building blocks for articulating user needs, or others like them, are preferable to the traditional substantive and therefore circular categories—news, sports, or advertising, for example—as specifications to be matched against alternative substance, format, and process bundles. Surveillance needs, for instance, might effectively and cheaply be met by random access of an electronic database, but social connection needs would be less readily satisfied by that form. In this light, a baseball box score and a bus schedule—both of them substance for surveillance—are seen to have more in common with each other than the box score has with the play-by-play of the same baseball game. Seen in the traditional light, both the box score and the play-by-play are sports substance, but seeking out the box score is surveillance behavior, while reading about the color of the game has more to do with social connection.

Information resources differ from energy and material resources in one truly distinctive way. Substance is the organizing principle with which people integrate energy, material, and information resources to attain their personal ends or, as leaders and managers, the objectives of their organizations. The exploration that follows—of how the needs or wants of information users might best be matched with alternative substance, format, and process bundles—therefore concentrates on substance that is useful in exercising responsibility and authority.[25]

Evolving Information Consumers: Information for Responsibility and Authority

People in organizations create and use the substance of information resources for all four of the building block needs set forth in the preceding section: escape, social connection, surveillance, and opinion formation/decision making.

The *form* of information resources, namely format undergoing process, is the very essence of organization. It shapes and, in its pattern aspect, *is* the structure that makes organisms or organizations out of energy and materials.

The concrete information formats and processes of an organism or an organization make up its nervous system. Organisms don't have much say over the makeup of their own nervous systems, although genetic engineering may some day change that. But the nervous systems of organizations are artifacts, bundles of formats and processes that can be consciously molded, to the extent we know how, for better or worse performance.[26]

The organizational nervous system of the moment expresses the organization's needs for substance, assimilates that substance, and, among other functions, mediates the exercise of responsibility and authority within the organization and by the organization in the world outside it.

The nervous system or format-and-process bundle that an organization evolves and the substance which that nervous system makes or picks day by day, make up a substance, format, and process bundle vital to the organization. This bundle differs from the media bundles not in kind but only in aspect. From a producer's vantage point, we looked at media bundles as products or services. Here we see the organizational bundle from its user's perspective. A consulting or software firm might conceive of a management information system, for example, as a product or service. Installed and in use, it is a piece of its buyer's organizational nervous system.

Evolving the nervous system of an organization and the ongoing choices of information substance that this nervous system makes are both vital functions, the one strategic and the other operational. How well does an organization do its daily routine? How deftly does it meet its crises? And, ultimately, will it live or die? That all depends on how well the organization's nervous system works, on how well its people's brains and their words and their pictures and their numbers do their job. It all depends on brain at least as much as it depends on how well the organization's brawn works, on how well its people's muscles and their plowshares and their swords do their job.

Any innovation or any obsolescence in formats and processes, any coming apart and together of substance, format, and process bundles, directly affects all information resource markets, not just the media's. The markets for non-information businesses, airlines or hairlines, candy stores or department stores, pin makers or auto makers, are impacted only indirectly. But the nervous systems of all businesses, information businesses among them, are all directly affected.

The information businesses get a double dose as *information* businesses and as information *businesses*, but no business is immune from any opportunity or any threat that change, internal or external, presents to its nervous system, to its means for exercising responsibility and authority. What goes for business goes for any organization including government in all its functions from garbage collection to national security.

What Process Does

The workings of the U.S. national nervous system in the first moments of a crisis come alive in the following reminiscences of the 1965 Northeast power failure and blackout. In this 1983 interview, D.H. is Donald F. Hornig, formerly Special Assistant to President Lyndon B. Johnson for Science and Technology. F.A., the interviewer, is LTC Francis W. A'Hearn:

D.H.   The power failure occurred about five minutes of six. At that time the President was driving on his ranch in Texas on an inspection tour, so he heard the announcement on his car radio. That was the first thing he heard. What he did immediately was to call the Secretary of Defense. At that point Bob McNamara had not yet heard about the blackout.

Before I continue this story I must tell you the other half. I had a daughter in Cambridge. When everything went down her reaction was, "My God, there has been a nuclear attack." If so, the family in Washington had presumably been vaporized or something, so she immediately got on the telephone and called my wife. Surprisingly, the call got through immediately. She told my wife that all the power was out and, as far as she knew, everything was out all over the Northeast. My wife fortunately said to herself, "I'd better get hold of Don right away," so they didn't chat. Instead, she called me at my office in the old Executive Office Building. I thanked her and immediately switched on a TV beside my desk.

On the TV they announced that New York had just gone down and that there was no power as far west as Buffalo. It seemed quite clear that it was accidental, but nobody really knew just what was going on.

Just at that moment my phone rang, and Bob McNamara said "Don, I just had a call from the boss, who said that the whole Northeast is blacked out. Do you know anything about it?" I said yes and told him everything I'd just seen and heard on TV!

F.A.   At that point your only source of information was what you had seen on TV following your daughter's phone call?

D.H.   The only reason I happened to learn it was that my panicky daughter called my wife, who called me and I turned on the TV and got it from there. At that point McNamara—given all his communications—hadn't been informed other than by the President.

F.A.   And the President heard it on the radio.

D.H.   A funny post script to that whole episode came later. I called the Federal Power Commission to tell Chairman Swidler they had better get on top of this, to which they replied, "We are a regulatory agency, not a technical agency." I reminded them that I figured that by the time the President wanted definitive information from them as to what was happening, the Power Commission had better have some information.

About ten minutes later they called me back and said, "Dr. Hornig, it's all under control; we now have an open line to the *Wall Street Journal*."

F.A.   Their source of information was commercial, too, then?

D.H.   Presumably the *Journal* was on the regular A.P. wire.

F.A.   It's interesting to me that President Johnson called his Secretary of Defense, McNamara. Was there any hint, do you suppose, at the time that something other than a natural domestic problem had caused that?

D.H.   Not really, but it's the first thing everyone worries about. Is it sabotage? Is it a prelude to something else? Is this Act I in an unfolding drama? There was no hint that there had been any kind of attack, but there was nothing to suggest that it might not have been sabotage. It happened dramatically and quickly, you know.

F.A.   I recall it. I guess I was in college at the time. That happened in 1965.

Was there any suggestion that President Johnson or McNamara were upset or concerned by the way they learned about it through other than official sources?

D.H.   I don't think so. In fact there wasn't much time delay. The whole thing unfolded in about five minutes from when the first breakdown occurred near Buffalo to the time when New York lost power. That places a real strain on communications.

One of the communications failures was to the poor controller in New York who watched his voltage go down and his frequency go down and knew something was desperately wrong. But you know, voluntarily cutting out New York City from the power net is serious business. At that stage, at 6:00 at night when it was dark—remember this was winter—they were borrowing so much power from the outside that anything he did to isolate the city would have blacked it out. That's a great big decision to take. So he tried desperately to call Niagara Falls, at the other end of the big power trunk, where the power was coming from and where the trouble was coming from. He was trying to get the guy in Buffalo on the telephone and all he could get was a busy signal. So, while he was trying to get a phone call through, the whole system collapsed.

This all took minutes, so by the time the President heard it, the news couldn't have been more than a few minutes old. By the time it got through the whole sequence I have described I suppose another five or ten minutes elapsed, so it wasn't as if terrible things had been going on in the country without his being aware.

F.A.   It is an interesting story . . . that the President was first alerted by his own car radio while he was down at his ranch in Texas.

D.H.   Right.

F.A.   Is your sense that today, for instance, if things went wrong like that, whether by natural causes or . . .

D.H.   My sense is that it would work exactly the same way again because even in military situations it works that way. Once upon a time we looked into the way in which information got back from Vietnam in crisis situations. We looked for an episode which wasn't so big that it just had to get through quickly, and not so small that if you found that things didn't work, you'd say it's probably good judgment on somebody's part not to bother the White House. So, we picked the attack on the consulate in Hue, a middle range episode, and then looked to see how the news got to the White House.

Well, without going through the details, the first message in was a CIA intercept of a Reuters news dispatch which went directly from Hue over commercial cables to London, rather than our transmissions from Saigon which came in something like half an hour later.

Now, again, you couldn't say anything was grossly wrong. There was no national action that had to be taken, but again it illustrates that anytime anything happens in the world, lots of things start happening. In this case a semi-military channel functioned as it might be expected to function.

F.A.   That's fascinating. I guess my sense is also that today things pretty much work along those kinds of lines.

D.H.   That's all right! I think that's one of the strengths of the system.

I'm on a National Academy Committee which is looking at post-attack situations, and it's called Committee on a Survivable National Communications System. If you ask what the real hope for survivability is, it's probably not in hardness, but it probably is in redundancy, although you still have to make plans to put the remaining pieces together.

F.A.   That's an interesting thought. Perhaps having these commercial nets strung out all over is really one of our strengths.[27]

It is plain that the U.S. national nervous system is a rich blend of the public and the private, of flesh-and-blood and artifact. Formats and processes come in people, and they come in things. But the technicalities of format and process, glamorous to some, pedestrian to others, often get blown out of proportion, absent perspective on what substance it is that the formats and processes can really deliver.

Jane, in Donald Barthelme's *Snow White*, writes to a Mr. Quistgaard whose name she has seized from the telephone book: "It may never have crossed your mind to think that other universes of discourse distinct from your own existed, with people in them, discoursing."[28]

Imagine a Universe of All Possible Discourse (UAPD, pronounced "whopped") that takes in Jane's, Mr. Quistgaard's, Fido's, Socrates', Attila the Hun's, Einstein's, and so on, now, then, and forever. The universe of an organization's decision-making discourse (uodd, pronounced "would") lies within the UAPD, and exchanges new and old substance with it. In changing times, both the UAPD and the uodd are in flux.

The substance that a decision maker has in mind comes from the UAPD in three main ways: through inside the organization, through outside the organization, and through his or her personal knowledge. All three types of process may be either formal or informal. Figure 7.10 gives concrete examples of processes under the six heading combinations. The processes may go on regularly or sporadically, they may have short-term tactical or long-term strategic

	From Inside Sources	**From Outside Sources**	**From Personal Knowledge**
Formal Processes	• Management information systems • Scanning • Special studies	• Media • National Association of Manufacturers, Committee for Economic Development, Harvard Program on Information Resources Policy, and so on. • Consultants • Market research firms	• Schooling • Training
Informal Processes	• "What do you think, Joe?" • "Pssst...do you know that...?"	• Golf course • Cocktail parties	• Experience

Figure 7.10   Decision maker's information-seeking process

objectives, and they may produce new substance or confirm old. They occur in neither fixed nor universal mixes or sequences.

The formal processes inside an organization include its new-fangled computerized or its old-fashioned paper-driven management information systems or decision support systems (MIS or DSS—jargon and concomitant hype go in and out of fashion), the scanning activities of a corporate planning staff, or special studies made by *ad hoc* task forces set up to respond to some crisis. Informal processes include casual encounters at the water cooler or in the elevator where you ask Joe and Jane what they think or else they tell you without being invited.

Formal processes outside an organization include the mass media's processes. They also include the doings of consultants, of market research firms, and of organizations like the National Association of Manufacturers, the Committee for Economic Development, Harvard's Program on Information Resources Policy, all the think tanks of various kinds that businessmen, professionals, and others set up as formal sources for the development of ideas, plus national or industrial espionage nets. Informal outside processes include meeting people on the golf course, over cocktails, or wherever Deep Throat lurks.

Finally, every decision maker pulls more or less substance out of his or her head. Some of this originally came from formal schooling or training of varied kinds. Other bits and pieces came in less formally through more or less deliberate personal experiences.

Formal or informal, these processes are mediated by what General John Cushman portrays as "living webs of systems, . . . mixes of man-made systems and of man himself, going through a swift, tumultuous, and challenging technological evolution which man must harness for maximum effectiveness in war and in its deterrence."[29] Both the large scope and the occasional informality of the processes are illustrated by Hornig's explicit references to the media and the telephone and by the implied role of other webs.

However pristine and pellucid one might imagine substance to be in the pure precincts of the UAPD, the web of systems through which the decision maker sees that substance obscures it with the fog of war. Quite literally, as Karl von Clausewitz has observed, "Fog prevents the enemy from being discovered in time." Figuratively, there is fog because "a great part of the information obtained in war is contradictory, a still greater part is false, and by far the greatest part is somewhat doubtful."[30] Or, as Donald Hornig's account has Defense Secretary McNamara putting it as he peered through the fog of peace: "Don, I just had a call from the boss, who said that the whole Northeast is blacked out. Do you know anything about it?"[31] Or, in what mercifully was only an exercise during the Jimmy Carter administration:

Dr. Brzezinski got on the telephone and called the man you all have heard about who carries the little briefcase with all the codes inside, and said, "This is an exercise. I am the President of the United States. We have just gotten warning that a raid of nuclear warheads is en route to the United States. Get me out of here. This is an emergency exercise. We are going to war." The helicopter that is supposed to be on alert at all times, to land on the White House lawn and whisk away the National Command Authority, almost got shot down by the Secret Service. (By the way, this was kept secret for quite some time until it got blown in the newspapers, which is the only reason I am able to tell this story. I think we were ashamed of the horrible state of readiness we were in.) The sum and substance is that the exercise of trying to evacuate the National Command Authority was a nightmare, just a complete disaster.[32]

Beyond the thinkable or the unthinkable seen through a fog of war, of shooting war or of cold, in battlefield or office, marketplace or courtroom, beyond what is known like the fingers of one's hand and beyond even what is known to be unknown, like the number of jelly beans in a jar to be guessed at a fair, there looms much worse. How worse that might be is made plain by the following exchange that took place in a 1975 U.S. Senate hearing on Electronic Funds Transfer Systems (EFTS), specifically on the then new-fangled and controversial automated teller machines of banks:

Senator McIntyre: You referred in your statement that the plan to have technology that is being embraced here goes 5 years back—no, did you say 20 years?

Dr. Oettinger: I said the ideas for EFTS have been around for 20 years, the technology perhaps for 10.

Senator McIntyre: ·Do you know what an Unk Unk is?

Dr. Oettinger: Excuse me?

Senator McIntyre: Do you know what an Unk Unk is?

Dr. Oettinger: No, sir.

Mr. Cox: Are you going to tell us?

Dr. Oettinger: You have us in suspense now.

Senator McIntyre: I am on the Subcommittee on Military R & D. That is known as "unknown unknown." Every time we start off on a research technology, we know there are certain unknowns, but the Unk Unk is the unknown unknown. I think sometimes people worry about the unknown unknown.[33]

A Perfect Omniscience might have a totally clear and coherent overview of the boundless UAPD, as shown in figure 7.11. Mere mortal decision makers, however, see only pieces of the UAPD and those only through a fog, dimly. Although capable of surmising the existence of Unk Unks, a mortal can't act directly on that surmise, since one surely cannot ask a pointed question about what one doesn't know one doesn't know.

One person's piece of the UAPD may not even overlap with another's—"it may never have crossed your mind to think that other universes of discourse distinct from your own existed, with people in them, discoursing."[34] Yet so long as there is active and intelligent life, each decision alters perceptions of the UAPD, and influences the next decision, in a continuing cycle.

Process and Organizational Survival

Making decisions, setting directions, laying down policy, exercising leadership is just one of the functions, the command function, of organizational nervous systems. Another is the function of intelligence gathering, probing the surroundings to see, to understand, and to evaluate threats and opportunities, in short, to inform before decisions are made. Once intelligence has informed, command ordains autocratically, democratically, collectively, or however. The

SUBSTANCE KNOWN TO PERFECT OMNISCIENCE

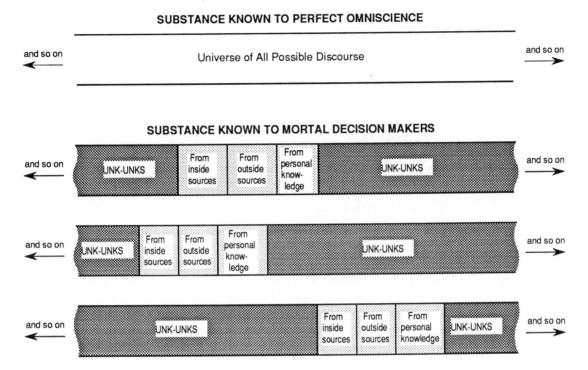

Figure 7.11   Unk-unks and the fog of war

control function then monitors what is done, tries to figure out what has happened and adjusts future actions accordingly. Intelligence, command, and control (I-C-C) functions are essential for any organism or organization, a paramecium or the Pentagon.

This way of tagging the needs at different stages of decision-making cycles and of tagging the nervous system functions that meet these needs is far from a universal language. Business people and business schools might, for instance, put scanning for intelligence, strategic planning for command, and reporting for control. Media-oriented folk see in the intelligence need the finer grain of substance needed for escape, social connection, surveillance, and opinion formation/decision making. Professional intelligence people see intelligence as still much finer grained.[35]

Reality defies these attempts to lay a veneer of order on it. Nonetheless, any organization that wants to survive must keep on getting the "right" information to the "right" people at the "right" time by whatever means are at hand, especially so while its ends are changing. All those "right's" signify the almost total lack of agreement about what right information might be, who the right people are, and what the right time is.[36] What consensus there is tends to prevail retroactively. For mortals what matters is an edge over nature, competitors, or the enemy, not perfection. Armies, it is said, win wars not because they are perfect, but because they fight other armies. In business, likewise, it is not perfection that succeeds, but an edge over the competition. And knowing how to make fire gave mankind an edge long before the beginnings of scientific understanding of combustion processes.

There is some consensus as to what the right stuff might be; accurate, selective substance is one element of rightness. Here "selective" means germane to the strategic goals of an organization, and not merely selected according to some whim or by some criterion unrelated to what matters to the particular organization at the particular time. Right also means a process fast enough to allow timely reaction to good news or bad. And, finally, if substance does not come to decision makers in an effective format, it is of no value even if accurate, selective, and timely.

As with the media, new formats and processes call into question the substance, format, and process bundles to which decision makers have grown accustomed, their organizational nervous systems. The informal bundles are affected as much as the formal when the whole world can gather round the water cooler by phone while remote terminals make the home office's formal database accessible from remote branches or outposts. The exercise of responsibility and authority in turn influences what substance, format, and process bundles will be in hand at the next turn of the wheel, if for no other reason than that the nervous system of any organization is always homemade.

Notes

1. See, for example: Rubin, Jerome S. and Janet Wikler, *Publishing as a Creature of Technology*. Cambridge, MA: Program on Information Resources Policy, Harvard Univ., 1989.

2. Clanchy, M. T., *From Memory to Written Record: England 1066–1307*. Cambridge, MA: Harvard Univ. Press, 1979, pp. 202–203.

3. Boorstin, Daniel J., *The Americans*, Vol. 2: *The Democratic Experience*. New York: Random House, 1973, pp. 373–378.

4. For an elaboration of these ideas, see Odom, Howard T., "Self-Organization, Transformity, and Information," *Science*, Vol. 242, Nov. 25, 1988, pp. 1132–1139.

5. Brillouin, Leon, *Science and Information Theory*. New York: Academic Press, Inc., 1956.

6. For details, see Beniger, James R., *The Control Revolution: Technological and Economic Origins of the Information Society*. Cambridge, MA: Harvard Univ. Press, 1986.

7. See Ernst, Martin L., *Electronic–Print Competition: Determinants of the Potential for Major Change*. Cambridge, MA: Program on Information Resources Policy, Harvard Univ., 1989; McLaughlin, John F., "Marketing Megalomania: The Lure of the Information Business," *PIRP Perspectives*, Harvard Program on Information Resources Policy, February 1989.

8. Cline, Ray, *Secrets, Spies and Scholars*. Washington, D.C.: Acropolis Books, 1976, p. 7.

9. Kuhn, Thomas, "The Structure of Scientific Revolutions," in *International Encyclopedia of Unified Science*. Chicago: The Univ. of Chicago Press, 1970, p. 17.

10. Compaine, Benjamin M. and Robert F. Litro, *Instructor's Manual for Business: An Introduction*. Chicago: The Dryden Press, 1984, p. 372.

11. Levitt, Theodore, "Marketing Myopia," in *Harvard Business Review*, September–October 1975, pp. 26, 176. (Reprinted from the original 1960 publication).

12. von Auw, Alvin, *Heritage and Destiny: Reflections on the Bell System in Transition*. New York: Praeger Publ., 1983, p. 169.

13. McLaughlin, John F., "Marketing Megalomania."

14. von Auw, p. 170.

15. I am indebted to many colleagues and friends for their contributions to the development of both the substance-format-process framework and its graphical representations. Larry Mancini suggested the managerial, editorial, and operating interpretations during a discussion in Kansas City in September of 1981 that also involved several of his colleagues at United Telecommunications and several of my colleagues from the Program. Earlier versions are on record in the following works: Compaine, Benjamin M., *A New Framework for the Media Arena: Content, Process and Format*. Cambridge, MA: Program on Information Resources Policy, Harvard Univ., 1980, pp. 10–11; Ongstad, Per, *Information Resources Policy Viewed by an Outskirter*. Cambridge, MA: Program on Information Resources Policy, Harvard Univ., 1981, pp. 35–37.

16. These arguments and stakes are exemplified in the U.S. by decades of proceedings before the Federal Communications Commission in Computer Inquiries I, II, III, before the courts in the U.S. government's antitrust suit against the Bell System that dismembered it into AT&T and the seven regional holding companies, and in attempts to get the Congress to define concepts like information services, electronic

publishing, and protocol conversion. For administrative, judicial, and legislative details, see United States District Court for the District of Columbia, *United States of America v. AT&T, Western Electric, and Bell Labs.: Modified Final Judgement*, Washington, DC, 08/24/82, Civil Action No. 74–1698; Federal Communications Commission, *Memorandum Opinion and Order on Further Reconsideration, Phase I: Third Computer Inquiry or Computer Inquiry III*, Federal Communications Commission, Washington, DC, 02/88, CC Docket No. 85–229; United States Congress, House of Representatives, 101st Congress, 1st Session, *Consumer Telecommunications Services Act of 1989: H.R. 2140*, U.S. Congress, House of Representatives, Washington, DC, 04/27/89, H.R. 2140.

17. McLuhan, Marshall, *Understanding Media*. New York: McGraw-Hill Book Co., 1964, p. 7.

18. Finkelstein, Sidney, *Sense and Nonsense of McLuhan*. New York: International Publ., 1968, pp. 79–84; and Theall, Donald, *The Medium Is the Rear View Mirror*. Montreal: McGill-Queens Univ. Press, 1971, p. 13.

19. For details, see Oettinger, Anthony G., "Political, Scientific and Other Truths in the Information World." University of Pittsburgh School of Library and Information Science, Samuel Lazerow Memorial Lecture, November 10, 1988; and Oettinger, Anthony G., *The Formula Is Everything: Costing and Pricing in the Telecommunications Industry*. Cambridge, MA: Program on Information Resources Policy, Harvard Univ., 1989.

20. Details of newspaper evolution are available in, for example, *Editor & Publisher*, a weekly independent trade journal for the newspaper industry. See also Benjamin M. Compaine's *The Newspaper Industry in the 1980s*. White Plains, NY: Knowledge Industry Publ., Inc., 1980; and Anthony Smith's *Goodbye Gutenberg*. New York: Oxford Univ. Press, 1980.

21. For examples, see Office of Technology Assessment, U.S. Congress, *Federal Government Information Technology: Management, Security and Congressional Oversight*, GPO, Washington, D.C., 1986, OTA-CIT-297; OTA, U.S. Congress, *Defending Secrets, Sharing Data: New Locks and Keys for Electronic Information*, U.S. Government Printing Office, Washington, D.C., 10/87, OTA-CIT-310, GPO#: 052-003-01083-6, $8.50; OTA, U.S. Congress, *Power On!: New Tools for Teaching and Learning*, U.S. Government Printing Office, Washington, DC, 09/88, OTA-SET-379, GPO #052-003-01125-5. OTA, U.S. Congress, *Medlars and Health Information Policy: A Technical Memorandum*, U.S. Government Printing Office, Washington, DC, 09/82, OTA-TM-H-11, NTIS#: PB-83-168-658; OTA, U.S. Congress, *Federal Government Information Technology: Electronic Surveillance and Civil Liberties*, U.S. Government Printing Office, Washington, DC, 10/85, OTA-CIT-293, 2 copies, GPO#: 052-003-01015-1, $3.00, NTIS#: PB 86-123 239/AS; OTA, U.S. Congress, *Informing the Nation: Federal Information Dissemination in an Electronic Age*, U.S. Government Printing Office, Washington, DC, 10/88, OTA-CIT-396, GPO#: 052-

003-01130-1, $14.00; OTA, U.S. Congress, *The Electronic Supervisor: New Technology, New Tensions*, U.S. Government Printing Office, Washington, DC, 09/87, OTA-CIT-333.

22. This material on mass media was adapted from Compaine, Benjamin M., *A New Framework for the Media Arena*, p. 22 ff.

23. Borchardt, Kurt, *Structure and Performance of the U.S. Communications Industry: Government Regulation and Company Planning*. Boston: Harvard Business School, Division of Research, 1970, p. 60. See also: Barnouw, Erik, *Tube of Plenty*. New York: Oxford Univ. Press, 1975, pp. 44–45.

24. Christine Urban, "Factors Influencing Media Consumption," in Compaine, Benjamin M., ed., *Understanding New Media*. Cambridge, MA: Ballinger Publishing Co., 1984.

25. Martin Ernst has analyzed user needs for information and the relationships between these needs and presentation mode choices in Ernst, *Electronic–Print Competition*, 1989.

26. Generic problems of designing organizational nervous systems are described in Arrow, Kenneth J., *The Limits of Organization*. New York: W.W. Norton, 1974, pp. 53–56; Simon, Herbert A., "Designing Organizations for an Information-Rich World," in Greenberger, Martin, ed., *Computers, Communications, and the Public Interest*. Baltimore: The Johns Hopkins Univ. Press, 1971, pp. 42–44; Oettinger, Anthony G., "Compunications in the National Decision-Making Process," in *Computers, Communications, and the Public Interest*, pp. 74–76; Snyder, Frank M., *Command and Control: Command and Control: The Literature and Commentaries*. Washington, D.C.: National Defense University Press, 1993.

27. A'Hearn, Francis W., *Northeast Power Failure and Lyndon B. Johnson*: Interview with Donald Hornig. Cambridge, MA: Program on Information Resources Policy, Harvard Univ., 1983.

28. Barthelme, Donald, *Snow White*. New York: Atheneum, 1967, p. 44.

29. Cushman, John H., *Command and Control of Theater Forces: Adequacy*. Washington, D.C.: AFCEA International Press, 1985, pp. 13–18. See also A'Hearn, Francis W., *The Information Arsenal: A C3I Profile*. Cambridge, MA: Program on Information Resources Policy, Harvard Univ., 1983, pp. 84–87; Oettinger, Anthony G., "A Bull's Eye View of Management and Engineering Information Systems," *Proceedings of the 19th National ACM Conference*, ACM Publication P 64. New York, 1964. (Reprinted in Alan F. Westin, *Information Technology in a Democracy*. Cambridge, MA: Harvard Univ. Press, 1971, p. 250 ff.); Perry, William G., "Examsmanship in the Liberal Arts: A Study in Educational Epistemology," Harvard College, 1963. Reprinted in Zeender, Karl and Linda Morris, eds., *Persuasive Writing: A College Reader*. New York: Harcourt Brace Jovanovich, 1981.

30. von Clausewitz, Karl, *On War*. Washington: Infantry Journal Press, 1950, pp. 51–55.

31. A'Hearn, *Northeast Power Failure and Lyndon B. Johnson*, p. 1.

32. Rosenberg, Robert, "The Influence of Policy Making on C^{3}I," *Seminar on Command, Control, Communications and Intelligence*, Spring 1980. Cambridge, MA: Program on Information Resources Policy, Harvard Univ., 1980, p. 60.

33. U.S. Congress. Senate Committee on Banking, Housing and Urban Affairs. *Electronic Funds Transfer Moratorium Act of 1975: Hearings Before the Subcommittee on Financial Institutions*. 94th Cong., 1st sess., March 14, 1975. Washington, D.C.: GPO, 1975, p. 176.

34. Barthelme, *Snow White*.

35. Cline, *Secrets, Spies and Scholars*. See also Graham, Daniel O., "Quality in U.S. Intelligence," in Roy Godson, ed., *Intelligence Requirements for the 1980's: Elements of Intelligence*. Washington, D.C.: National Strategic Information Center, 1983, pp. 21–23.

36. For a classic description of these dilemmas see Wohlstetter, Roberta, *Pearl Harbor: Warning and Decision*. Stanford, Calif.: Stanford Univ. Press, 1962.

8 Publishing as a Creature of Technology

Jerome S. Rubin and Janet Wikler

We were asked to cast our thoughts toward the year 2000 and beyond—the end of the second millennium as the Christian world reckons time.

Historians formerly believed that as the year 1000 approached, mankind prepared for the Last Judgment, waiting in terror for the fatal dawn. In the words of Michelet,

C'était une croyance universelle au Moyen Age, que le monde devait finir avec l'an 1000 de l'incarnation. Avant le christianisme, les Étrusques aussi avaient fixé leur terme à dix siècles, et la prédiction s'était accomplie.[1]

Given man's appalling capacities for self-destruction today—nuclear weapons and irreversible environmental damage—the end of the world seems a more likely threat as the year 2000 approaches than it did as the Christian world prayed its way toward the year 1000. It is, however, an underlying assumption of this symposium that the world will in fact survive until the year 2000 and that the dissemination of information—publishing—will continue to be an important human activity.

The technologies used to disseminate information have changed considerably over time and are changing with extraordinary rapidity today. To put today's and tomorrow's changes in perspective, it may help to examine their antecedents.

Since the earliest cave drawings, human beings have tried to communicate across the bounds of time by making permanent representations in symbolic form. The earliest known system of writing as a device for recording language was developed over 5,000 years ago in Mesopotamia by the Sumerians, and the Egyptians, probably under Mesopotamian influence, evolved their system very shortly thereafter. More than two millennia later the Greeks created a full alphabetic system of writing, and since then the principles of writing have not undergone any fundamental change.

Writing, the greatest technology devised by man, spawned ancillary technologies—including, of course, the preparation of surfaces on which to write. As early as 3500 B.C., the Egyptians were recording their hieroglyphics on papyrus. The most important writing material of the ancient world, papyrus was made from the fibrous stem of the papyrus reed (*byblos*), which grew profusely in the Nile Delta. Not only Egypt, but Greece and Rome, relied on papyrus.

Parchment, the other great ancient writing material, is the specially prepared skin of animals, mostly sheep, lambs, goats, and calves. The word *parchment* derives from Pergamum, an important center of Hellenistic culture near modern-day Izmir, which was also the center of parchment manufacture beginning in the third century B.C. Although the terms *parchment* and *vellum* are often used interchangeably, the word *vellum* is usually applied to the finest parchment, made from the skin of a calf. (The etymology is clear.)

The technology of making paper, the basic writing material of the modern world, was invented by an official of the Imperial court of Han China in 105 A.D., and spread westward very slowly. It reached Samarkand in 751 and Baghdad in 793, during the golden age of Islamic culture. Although paper was extensively employed in the Arab world shortly thereafter, it was not in common use in Europe until the fourteenth century—and it came to Europe via Islam's domination of Spain. Paper, a plant-based writing material like papyrus, assumed the name of its ancient, half-forgotten predecessor.

Through most of classical antiquity, the standard form of book was the papyrus roll or scroll, consisting of papyrus sheets glued together. Taking its name from *byblos*, it was commonly called *biblion*—which in turn gave its name to The Book, the Bible.

But the unrolling and rewinding of a long book was inconvenient and time-consuming. The development of parchment made possible the codex, or book in the form we know today. Papyrus, unlike parchment, cracks when folded; in addition, parchment could be sewn easily and scribes could write on both sides of it. The new technology, which became popular in the early days of the Christian era, involved cutting parchment into rectangular sheets, folded once into a *folio*, or twice into a *quarto*, or thrice into an *octavo*, and so on. Despite the great technological advantages of the codex, it was at first used primarily for account books; the resistance to change of both readers and booksellers permitted the literary roll to survive for centuries. The sacred Torah is still a scroll, and many legal documents continued to be written in scroll form until the twentieth century in several countries, including Britain, where the Master of the Rolls remains the title of one of the highest judicial officers. (But the conservatism of lawyers is to be expected; the law, after all, is the second-oldest profession.)

The other important writing technologies are those of inks and writing implements. The ancient inks of Egypt and China consisted of lamp-black mixed with gum or glue and formed into sticks which were mixed with water when used by the scribe. The colored juices or extracts of various plant and animal substances also served as inks in ancient times—including the black discharges of cephalopods such as octopus, squid, and cuttlefish. In later antiquity and throughout the Middle Ages, ink was also made from oak-galls steeped in a solution of vitriol (ferrous sulphate). By Gutenberg's time and until the late eighteenth century, inks were typically made by mixing varnish or boiled linseed oil with lamp-black.

The principal writing instruments of the ancient Western world were reeds. But in northern Europe, where reeds suitable for writing purposes do not grow, the quill of the feather became the principal writing instrument. A Latin word for feather, *penna*, has given us our pen, just as another Latin word for feather, *pluma*, gave *plume* to the French.

The technologies of writing were necessary but not sufficient; little written material was produced in the early Middle Ages, since, in the Christian world, writing and reading were skills centered in the monastery. The great majority of people relied on memory and oral tradition to spread information and preserve knowledge.

William the Conqueror was largely responsible for initiating the transition from oral tradition to written record in medieval England. His famous Domesday Book was a written survey of the conquered land. But the Domesday Book was never updated; its contents remained frozen in time and thus had little practical value.

As foreigners ruling in a tradition of conquest, William's successors bombarded the English with written demands for information and money. Land charters were put in writing, government bureaucracy flourished, and the number of documents grew. People needed to read and write to cope with government demands, and literacy became widespread. Yet it was centuries before the value of written records was fully understood. Making documents, keeping them in archives, and subsequently using them again for reference were three distinct stages of development. While the peoples of classical antiquity had developed and used indexing techniques, many medieval documents, especially government records, were not indexed. The medieval archivist seeking specific information had no way of knowing which page or roll to search.

Despite the proliferation of documents in the Middle Ages, writing was labor-intensive, and books expensive and rare. Although movable type for printing had been invented as early as the eleventh century A.D. in China, it had not spread beyond that country's borders. Gutenberg's re-invention of the technology in the mid-fifteenth century opened up for the first time in the Western world the ability to mass-produce written material, permitting man to communicate easily across space as well as time, and giving rise to the modern publishing industry.

The revolutionary technology of printing with movable type spread quickly throughout Europe. For the first time, written works could be replicated quickly and disseminated widely; among other things, the resulting standardization led to broader use of such retrieval techniques as indexing.

To "publish" a book was to print it; as the dangerous technology of printing came into general use, governments sought to control it through censorship; printers in Europe were granted exclusive rights to print and sell works, both new and old, that the official censors had approved for publication. These rights, which treated the printed book as an object and had no concern for authorship, were nonetheless the precursors of copyright. The author's right to protection was recognized for the first time in the Statute of Anne, the British copyright law of 1710. The infant French Republic provided a similar right in 1793, and other European countries followed suit during the nineteenth century. The first federal copyright act in the United States was adopted in 1790.

For many years after Gutenberg, the prices of printed materials remained artificially high despite the ease and relatively low cost with which they could be produced. In England, for example, as the feudal system declined and the mercantile middle class emerged, the upper classes sought to ensure their privileged status by preventing the masses from learning to read and by keeping books expensive. In the long run, however, their efforts proved futile. Printing, binding, and paper-making techniques continued to improve; the ability to read became increasingly essential to an individual's functioning in society; more and more people became literate; and libraries, coffee-shops, and publishing "pirates" made reading matter widely available. The Industrial Revolution not only provided the new technologies of the steam-driven press and mechanically produced wood-pulp paper, but also a changed political and economic climate that imposed demands for widespread literacy. In that environment, there was no stopping the rapid dissemination of ideas and information that printing had made possible.

While print was revolutionizing society, other new technologies were being developed to speed the dissemination of information. The nineteenth century and the early part of this century brought major advances in the means of information transmission, with telegraph, telephone, and radio. Although the nineteenth century saw the development of photography and the phonograph, technologies that permitted the storage and replication of images and sound, the audiovisual era did not really begin until the 1920s, when motion pictures and radio came into widespread use. By that time, wires and radio waves were routinely used to carry coded signals, and experiments in television were underway.

The nineteenth-century British mathematician Charles Babbage hailed the printing press as the great accelerator of progress. "Until printing was very generally spread," he wrote, "civilization scarcely advanced by slow and languid steps; since that art has become cheap, its advances have been unparalleled, and its rate of progress vastly accelerated."[2] Paradoxically, in developing his "analytical engine," Babbage himself helped lay the foundation for the computer revolution transforming publishing—and our entire civilization—today.

The impact of the computer may be even more profound than that of the printing press. Today, text, sound, and images are stored in computer memories as combinations of on-off signals. These digital combinations, or codes, are transmitted through wires, cables, and optical fibers, and over the air, and are decoded by receivers that transform them once again into images, sound, and text.

The computer and other electronic technologies have led to what the late Ithiel de Sola Pool of MIT called "the convergence of modes."[3] This phenomenon, Pool pointed out, "is blurring the lines between media, even between point-to-point communications, such as the post, telephone, and telegraph, and mass communications, such as the press, radio, and television."[4] Services that in the past were provided in separate ways now share wires, cables, and radio waves. And services that once depended on a single medium, such as print, can be provided in a number of different ways.

Pool illustrated this point with examples:

The telephone network, which was once used almost entirely for person-to-person conversation, now transmits data among computers, distributes printed matter via facsimile machines, and carries sports and weather bulletins on recorded messages. A news story that used to be distributed through newsprint and in no other way nowadays may also be broadcast on television or radio, put out on a telecommunication line for printing by a teletype or for display on the screen of a cathode ray tube (CRT), and placed in an electronic morgue for later retrieval.[5]

In an attempt to deal with all this, we have created hybrid terms. We speak of "video magazines," "database publishing," "electronic newsletters," and so forth. The term "electronic publishing" typifies the confusion. By "electronic publishing" do we mean using electronic processes, like word processing and computerized typesetting, to make our traditional printed products? Do we mean taking information that we have traditionally provided in printed form and delivering it on floppy disc or CD-ROM or on-line? Do we mean taking ideas originally presented in book form and "translating" them for videotape or videodisc? Do we mean all of this, and more?

Even the word "information" itself has become so over-used that its use threatens to obscure rather than illuminate our thinking. Is a stream of digital computer code "information"? Are scholarly theories "information"? Is the text of Joyce's *Ulysses* "information"? Is a graphic representation of a molecule that can be rotated on a video screen "information"? Is a crossword puzzle "information"? Is the sound of Beethoven's Ninth Symphony "information"? Does a book that describes how the heart valves work provide the same "information" as an interactive videodisc that permits an individual to touch an image of the heart valves and see them in action? Where are the boundaries between data and information, on the one hand, and information and knowledge, on the other?

We may be able to minimize confusion by adopting the use of a neutral term like *substance* to mean the invariant substantive content of whatever we provide.[6] Substance can be embodied in any of a number of *formats*, and the same substance can be embodied in more than one format. In the heart valve example, the substance would be the same in the book and the videodisc, but the format would vary. Similarly, a written score of Beethoven's Ninth Symphony would provide the same substance as a recording of the music, but in a different format.

Process acts on substance to produce one or more formats; process may also change substance itself. The traditional book publisher adds value to substance by applying a series of processes. First, the publisher *obtains substance*, either from an outside source, such as an author, or by using in-house researchers and writers. The substance is put through an *editorial process*, during which it is refined. Another process, usually involving a combined editorial and graphic-design effort, *specifies a format* in which the substance will be embodied. The next process, *manufacturing*, includes typesetting, platemaking, printing, and binding. Finally, the publisher puts the finished products through a *distribution process*, which includes making readers aware of the product's availability through marketing and sales, and getting the product physically into their hands, either through intermediaries like wholesalers and booksellers or by shipping to them directly.

This terminology of substance, format, and process was developed by the Harvard Program on Information Resources Policy (with some help from me [Rubin]). As Harvard's Tony Oettinger puts it, "Every information product or service is a bundle of substance, format and process."[7] Oettinger points out that "infusing substance into format defines an *editorial* [function], and subjecting concrete formats, as materials, to concrete energy-consuming processes defines a formal or *operating* [function] devoid of substance" (e.g., printing and distribution).[8]

The potential of a new technology is rarely understood by the first generation of its users. It took centuries before people realized the value of updating written records, storing them in archives, and indexing them for future use. Not until television began to bring the battlefields of distant wars, the eerie landscape of the moon, and the outer reaches of the solar system into our living rooms did we begin to comprehend its power. Xerography was originally viewed as a substitute for carbon paper rather than a cheap and easy way of copying images; and the computer at its inception was seen as a calculator, replacing the slide rule and the abacus.

In the same vein, the typical publisher's initial response to computer technology was to see it as a facilitator of the traditional manufacturing processes. Next, the publisher began to suspect that the computer might provide opportunities for creating products in new formats, and the term "database publishing" came into vogue. Continuing to focus on substance as their critical asset, publishers sought opportunities to create electronic by-products of their traditional printed wares. From a single initial effort, it appeared, two revenue streams might flow. Giving little thought to the differences among computer programs, publishers further tried to expand their businesses by buying the rights to publish "software" brought to them by outside "authors." If the substance was good, the publishers reasoned, the customer would value it all the more because it resided on a floppy disc.

For the most part, publishers' efforts in "electronic publishing" have been financial failures. But a handful of ventures have been successful. One that was very successful was LEXIS, a computer-assisted legal-research service that I [Rubin] launched in 1973 with a few colleagues. It is almost certainly no accident that LEXIS was not created by a publisher. When LEXIS was developed, legal publishers saw their role as providing substance to their readers in fixed and pre-determined formats. By contrast, in building LEXIS, we put process in the hands of the users, so that they could control both substance and format at will.

The LEXIS software permitted a user to search the full text of primary-source material without the intermediation of a human indexer or editor, and to retrieve only those portions relevant to his or her needs. After employing the process provided by the software to select relevant material, the user could apply another process to specify a format in which the material would then be displayed—on the screen or in print, in full or in windows of context.

The substance that went into LEXIS was almost entirely in the public domain. Our proprietary added value was the process we provided to the user —a process that proved to be sufficiently valuable that we were able both to take significant market share from traditional publishers and to increase substantially the total number of dollars spent for legal information.

The ability to put process and format, independent of substance, into the hands of the user has spawned a new kind of "publishing" industry today. Companies like Microsoft, Lotus, Ashton-Tate, and others, in offering word-processing, spreadsheet, and database-management software, provide only the minimum substance needed for users to process their own substance and put it into varied and useful formats.

Acknowledging the migration of process and format from the publisher to the user is essential to our recognizing and evaluating new business opportunities as we approach the year 2000. We perpetuate a false dichotomy when couching the debate simply in terms of whether to deliver substance in print or electronic form. We should, rather, find ways to enable our customers to engage in the processes of selecting substance at will, manipulating it in a number of ways, and specifying a variety of formats.

The new technologies present serious threats as well as significant opportunities—especially to our traditional asset, the intellectual property, or substance, that has been our stock in trade. University professors take portions of our textbooks and have them photocopied, along with portions of other publishers' textbooks, to make anthologies for their students. Optical scanners digitize the text of our printed material and make it endlessly available. Video and audio cassettes are duplicated on inexpensive home equipment. Substance sent by telephone lines to remote terminals is routinely printed by users or downloaded onto floppy discs. If we add value to substance by coupling it with processing programs and provide both on floppy discs, the entire work can be copied—easily, cheaply, and quickly. Even the CD-ROM, originally viewed as a non-writable, piracy-proof medium, can now be duplicated with relative ease.

Anne Branscomb, of the Harvard Program on Information Resources Policy, highlights the difficulties of defining "permissible use" of copyrighted material in a new-technology era:

Can you print out the entire twenty volumes [of an encyclopedia on a CD-ROM]; if not, how much can you reprint before you have infringed the copyright? Can you down load portions or is this making a copy? Can you display portions in the classroom, or is this a public display, a "performance" or perhaps a "retransmission"? May you network the contents to many locations, as in a university environment to many classrooms or campuses? Isn't this making multiple copies much in the same way as on a Xerox machine? If royalties are not to be paid to the many creative and talented people who contributed to the twenty volumes is there some other way to provide the infrastructure for intellectual productivity? How can the system detect such "uses" or copying if the record is not preserved for posterity? If the record is preserved does it create costs which inhibit meaningful use? Current copyright law protects the originator's value only on the "first sale" of a copy. There is no royalty on the "use" or rental thereof. However, if only a few copies are needed to provide access to masses of users, then the original charge must cover all of the development and marketing costs.[9]

And the problem is deeper than defining "permissible use." The fundamental concept of copyright as we know it is called into question by electronic technologies. Gutenberg provided a means of creating identical multiple copies. Electronic technologies, on the other hand, provide a means of creating infinite *variations* of the same material. A small subculture of computer scientists who write and edit on data networks illustrates this phenomenon, which we can expect to spread. Someone types comments on a computer terminal. Colleagues gain access to these comments on the network and modify, expand, or change them. Different versions are thus created continually, and each one can be stored on the computer. There is no one "author," nor is there any "definitive version" of the material. We are returning in spirit to Plato's Academy and the pre-copyright world of oral dialogue.

Pool speculated that, in the not-too-distant future,

Computer-based textbooks may exist in as many variants as there are teachers. All teachers on occasion desire to correct or modify the textbooks they use; if the texts are in a computer, they can and will do that. Each teacher will create a preferred version, which will be changed repeatedly over the years. Or in a literature or drama course one exercise might be to take a text and try to improve it. Reading thus becomes active and interactive. Penciled scribbles in the margin become part of the text and perhaps even part of a growing dialogue as others agree or disagree.[10]

Substance may even be generated with no human author at all. Computers can be programmed to generate indices, and by the year 2000 programs may be written that will enable the computer to generate worthwhile abstracts of text. The computer programs are copyrightable under current law. But what about the indices and abstracts that the programs generate?

As Branscomb puts it,

Information technology is turning our legal concepts as well as the philosophical roots of intellectual property topsy turvy, and stakeholders are going to have to learn to live with the new world which information technology is in the process of creating.

The real challenge is how to preserve an environment which encourages creativity but does not permit "rip offs" which discourage investment capital and inhibit the allocation of R&D funds.[11]

As if piracy and the other threats to copyright were not problems enough, new competitors are entering our markets as the lines blur between formerly separate industries. Cable television systems provide programs that compete with our educational and professional offerings. Television news and feature programs compete with newspapers and magazines. On-line vendors provide databases with retrieval systems that may undermine the sales of printed works. Many trade books generate more income from movie and television rights than from their sales in the original printed form. In some countries, telecommunications providers compete with publishers in offering substance as well as the processes of sending, storing, organizing, and manipulating it. Even our own customers, armed with personal computers, laser printers, and computer-generated mailing lists, are getting into the competitive act.

In response to the convergence of media, communications conglomerates have emerged. Our company, Times Mirror, owns book- and magazine-publishing ventures, cable television systems, and broadcast television stations as well as newspaper companies. Gulf & Western, Dow Jones, Time, Inc., McGraw-Hill, International Thomson, News International, Maxwell Communications, and many others are variations on the same theme. But for the most part, the boundaries between media still exist within these conglomerates.

Paradoxically, the barriers to entry into publishing are both lower and higher than they have been. While tiny startups armed with Macintosh computers and laser printers are making serious inroads into many of our market niches, the costs of developing significant multi-media businesses can be staggeringly high. And the costs of maintaining these businesses through continued enhancement can be higher still—a point frequently overlooked. It takes considerable time and money to develop and continually enhance powerful systems that are easy to use, reliable, and fast. New, difficult-to-find skills are needed, skills of managing process as well as substance and format. Moreover, in business and professional markets, customers seek the convenience of "one-stop shopping" in databases carried over telecommunications lines or residing on CD-ROMs. Few publishers by themselves can offer the critical mass of substance that our markets are beginning to demand.

The highly leveraged nature of the new publishing businesses and the need for critical mass in many major markets will add fuel to the consolidation and concentration that have already begun. In addition to joining through merger and acquisition, publishers will need to unite with one another—and with companies in other industries—in joint ventures, licensing agreements, and other strategic alliances to continue to meet the needs of their markets and to compete effectively. Global networks will be the norm, rather than the exception.

Traditionally, the publisher has acted as intermediary between author and user, selecting and refining those portions of substance it deems most likely to be useful, and embodying that substance in fixed formats of various kinds. In the future, intermediation by the publisher may be even more critical; but increasingly it will be intermediation of a new and different kind. In a service like LEXIS, human intermediation is largely replaced by an electronic process. Yet some human intermediation is still required; someone must determine not only what substance to include in the database but also how the user will gain access to various portions of the substance, what processes will be provided to enable the user to select substance and format, and so forth. As artificial-intelligence techniques improve, the human effort that determines the electronic intermediating capabilities may become even more important. Knowledge engineers, designers, and programmers will be needed to debrief experts and create complex systems that will make substance, process, and format optimally available.

The fragmention of markets spawned by electronic technologies creates further complexity. Today's real world is characterized by small or incompatible installed bases of hardware, formidable development costs, and users at widely varying levels of readiness to accept new technologies. Our opportunities are limited not by what technology and imagination permit us to make, but by what our customers will pay for. Nonetheless, as we move toward the year 2000, it will help to approach our businesses along the three dimensions we have discussed. In obtaining and refining substance, we must consider the multiple ways in which people may want to select, process, and retain it. Selling multiple copies of the same substance in an identical format to large numbers of users will be an increasingly difficult way to turn a profit.

It is easy to see that inherently dynamic substance, such as financial or even scientific or legal material, must be updated constantly. Perhaps less obvious is the need continually to improve the processing technologies and the formatting possibilities as well. With changing technology, there is a complicated "tail-chasing" relationship between skills and tools. People design new tools to take advantage of skills already in existence. But as people use the tools, they develop new skills, and the old tools become less satisfactory. By failing to anticipate and respond to new needs that developed as people learned to use Visicalc, a company that could have become a giant faded away. Lotus Development Corporation saw and seized the opportunity; ironically, Lotus itself is today being threatened by aggressive, innovative competitors.

We must, therefore, be always on the move—updating substance, improving process, and creating new possibilities for format. To ensure its revenue flow, even a publisher of substance that does not lend itself to updating, such as fiction, may need to provide multiple formats and processing and formatting options to the user. Today's paperback novel reader may, before the year 2000, insert a credit-card-size piece of plastic into a high-resolution, flat-screen holder the size of a mass-market paperback; select the size, face, and color of the type; and push buttons to turn the pages, or have the pages turned automatically at his or her own reading pace. It is conceivable that the reader may dispense with text altogether, electing instead to view pictures while listening as the words are read aloud. The reader may make choices that determine the outcome of the plot; may choose to receive critical reviews or descriptions of related material; and, by inserting a blank card into the machine and plugging it into a telephone, may order, pay for, and obtain additional works.

A textbook publisher might use a similar technology to even greater advantage, enabling students to rotate molecules, "see" the results of physics experiments, and so forth. The technical possibilities in all our markets are endless; the challenge will be to capitalize on these possibilities for economic advantage.

The era of the printed word is but a short chapter in the history of human communication. From the development of true writing it took almost five millennia for the modern publishing industry to be spawned by the technology of printing with movable type. Although for publishers print is still the dominant medium, it has been around for only about half a millennium and its era of overwhelming supremacy—before the audiovisual revolution after World War I—lasted only about three-quarters of a century. As we move toward the year

2000, text will appear increasingly in a number of other formats, and substance will be conveyed in many non-textual modes as well.

Just as the literary roll survived for centuries after the invention of the codex, literature may be the last survivor of the printed book. But, as George Steiner has pointed out, "The relationship between books and literature, as we have known it in the European-American communities, arose from an exceedingly complex and inherently unstable concatenation of technical, economic and social circumstance. It may well be that the 'age of the book' in its classical sense is now coming to a very gradual end."[12]

We believe that print is likely to withstand the avalanche of competing media for quite some time—albeit circumscribed in application and diminished in importance. But growth in publishing—and, in some cases, survival—will lie in our ability to work creatively in multiple dimensions. The successful publisher will learn to use each medium to its best advantage, providing an ever-changing variety of substance-process-format bundles.

We may find instructive the old story about a drunkard who was looking under a street lamp for a lost key. "Is this where you dropped it?" asked a passer-by. "No," replied the drunk. "I dropped it over there, but the light is better here." As we move beyond the year 2000, we must seek the key to success not in the clear, familiar light of the printed word, but on the dark and shifting landscape of substance, process, and format.

Notes

1. "It was a universal belief in the Middle Ages that the world would end by 1000 A.D. Before Christianity, the Etruscans also had set their time span at ten centuries, and the prediction came true." Michelet. *L'Histoire de France*. Paris, 1869, Livre IV, Chapitre Premier; reprinted as Michelet. *Le Moyen Age*. Paris, Editions Robert Laffont, S.A., 1981, page 229.

2. Altick, Richard D. *The English Common Reader: A Social History of the Mass Reading Public 1800–1900*. Chicago and London, The University of Chicago Press, 1957, pages 129–130, quoting from Timperley, *Encyclopaedia of Literary and Typographical Anecdote*, page 808.

3. Pool, Ithiel de Sola. *Technologies of Freedom*. Cambridge and London, The Belknap Press of Harvard University Press, 1983, page 23.

4. Ibid.

5. Ibid.

6. See Chapter 7 for an expanded introduction to the subsance-process-format model.

7. Oettinger, Anthony G. *The Information Evolution: Building Blocks and Bursting Bundles.* Cambridge, Mass.: Program on Information Resources Policy, Harvard University, 1989, page 21.

8. Ibid., pages 21–22.

9. Branscomb, Anne W. *Nurturing Creativity in a Competitive Global Economy: Intellectual Property and New Technologies.* Cambridge, Mass.: Program on Information Resources Policy, Harvard University, May 1988, page 38.

10. Pool, Op. cit., pages 213–214.

11. Branscomb, Op. cit., page 49.

12. Steiner, George. "Literature Today," in *Books in the 1990s.* London: International Publishers Association and Butterworth & Co. (Publishers) Ltd., 1988, page 41.

9   Communications—For Better or for Worse

Daniel Bell

Human societies have seen four distinct revolutions in the character of social interchange: in speech, in writing, in printing, and, now, in telecommunications. Each revolution is associated with a distinctive, technologically based way of life.

Speech was central to the hunting and gathering bands—the signals that allowed men to act together in common pursuits. Writing was the foundation of the first urban settlements in agricultural society—the basis of record keeping and the codified transmission of knowledge and skills. Printing was the thread of industrial society—the basis of widespread literacy and the foundation of mass education.

Telecommunications (from the Greek *tele*, or "over a distance")—the ties of cable, radio telegraph, telephone, television, and, now, newer technologies—are the basis of an "information society."

Human societies exist because they can purposefully coordinate the activities of their members. (What is a corporation if not a social invention for the coordination of men, material, and markets for the mass production of goods?) Human societies prosper when, through peaceful transactions, goods and services can be exchanged in accordance with the needs of individuals.

Central to all this is information. Information comprises everything from news of events to price signals in a market. The success of an enterprise depends in part on the rapid transmission of accurate information.

The foundation of the Rothschild fortune was advance information by carrier pigeon of the defeat of Napoleon at Waterloo, so that the Rothschilds could make quicker stock market decisions. (The rapidity of transmission of information on companies today is responsible for the random walk theory of stock market prices, since such rapidity minimizes the time advantage of inside information.)

General equilibrium theory in economics is dependent on "perfect information," so that buyers and sellers know the full range of available prices on different goods and services, and the markets are cleared on the basis of relative prices and ordinal utilities.

What was once possible by walking around a local market now has to be done through complex transmission of news, which flashes such information to clients in "real time."

A New Communications System

Today, more than a century after the creation of the first effective telecommunication device, telegraphy, we are on the threshold of a new development that, by consolidating all such devices and linking them to computers, earns the name of a "revolution" because of the various possibilities of communication that are now unfolding. This is what Simon Nora and Alain Minc, in an extraordinary report to the president of the French Republic, call *télématique*, or what my Harvard colleague Anthony Oettinger calls *compunications*.[1]

Télématique, or compunications, is the merging of telephone, computers, and television into a single yet differentiated system that allows for transmission of data and interaction between persons or between computers through cables, macrowave relays, or satellites. Thus communications become faster, but they also are organized in totally new ways. It would be far beyond the scope of this article to specify these ways in detail, but it is possible to suggest some of the basic new modes and illustrate the consequences:

Data Processing Networks

These would register purchases made in stores automatically through computer terminals as bank transfers. Orders for goods, such as automobiles, can be sent through computer networks and transformed into a programming and scheduling series to provide for individual specifications of the items ordered. In a broad sense, this could be a replacement of much of the "paper economy" by an electronic transfer system.

Information Banks and Retrieval Systems

These would recall or search for information through computer systems and would print out a legal citation, a chemical abstract, census data, market research material, and the like.

Teletext System

In these systems, such as the British Post Office Prestel system (formerly called View Data), or the French Tic-tac and Antiope systems, news, weather, financial information, classified advertisements, catalog displays, and research material are displayed on home television consoles, representing a combination of the yellow pages of telephone books, the classified advertisements of newspapers, standard reference material, and news.

Facsimile Systems

Here, documents and other material (invoices, orders, mail) can be sent electronically rather than by postal systems.

Interactive On-Line Computer Networks

These allow research teams or office managers or government agencies to maintain communication so as to translate new research results, orders, or, perhaps, financial information into further action.[2]

These are not speculations or science fiction fantasies; they are developed technologies. The rate of introduction and diffusion will vary, of course, on the basis of cost and competition of rival modes, and on government policies that will either facilitate or inhibit some of these developments.

The rate of diffusion is further compounded by capital problems: The need for a large-scale shift to new, independent sources of energy requires a large, disproportionate allocation of capital to purposes that are, inherently, "capital-using" rather than "capital-saving." Thus the marginal efficiency of capital (as reflected in social capital-output ratios) tends to fall. The uncertainty of inflation leads, sometimes, to the postponement of capital investment or the short-term substitution of labor inputs rather than capital inputs, thus dragging down further a society's total productivity. These are economic and political questions which, again, are outside the scope of this article.

If we assume, however, that many of these new technologies and modes will eventually be introduced, what can we say of their consequences? It is hazardous, if not impossible, to predict specific social changes and outcomes. What one can do, however, is to sketch broad social changes that are likely to occur when these new modes are all in use. And that is the purpose of the following two sections.

Societal Infrastructure

Every society is tied together by three different kinds of infrastructure—transportation, energy grids, and communications:

Modes of Transportation

The oldest of these infrastructures is transportation, which first took place by trails, roads, and rivers, and, later, by canals. Trade was the means of breaking down the isolation of villages and served as a means of communication between distant areas. Transport thus has been the major linkage between settled areas.

Because of transport requirements, all the major cities of the world have been built near water. The industrial heartland of the United States, for example, was created by the interplay of resources and water transport.

Thus the iron ore from the Mesabi Range could move on Lake Superior, and coal in southern Illinois and western Pennsylvania could be tied to the Great Lakes by a river system. Such a network allowed the development of a steel and then an automobile industry. The water transport system served to thread together the industrial cities of Chicago, Detroit, Cleveland, Buffalo, and Pittsburgh.

In Germany, in the early eighteenth and nineteenth centuries, most commerce flowed from north and south because of the course of the major rivers such as the Rhine, the Elbe, the Oder, and the Weser. The coming of the railroad, linking east and west, greatly facilitated the unification of Germany by 1870 and its development as an industrial and military power.

Power Sources

The second infrastructure has been energy. At first waterwheels on rivers were used for power, followed by hydroelectricity, then oil, gas, and electricity.

The interaction of the energy and transport systems allowed for the spread of industries and towns, since electricity grids could transmit power over hundreds of miles. The result was the development of large industrial complexes, occupying vast spaces, through the long-distance transmission of energy.

Communications Systems

The oldest communications infrastructure is the postal service. Much later came the development of the various telecommunications systems.

The revolution in communications now makes it likely that there will be a major shift in the relative importance of the infrastructures: communications will be the central infrastructure tying together a society. Such a network increases personal interaction and drastically reduces the costs of distance. It affects the location of cities, since the "external economies"—gains because of proximity, such as in advertising, printing, and legal services for banks—once possible only in central city districts are now replaced by communication devices.

Most important, the new communications enlarge the arenas in which social action takes place. It is only in the past 30 years or so that many countries, because of revolutions in air transport and communications, have become national societies, in which impacts in any one part of the national society are immediately felt in any other part.

In the broadest sense, we have for the first time a genuine international economy in which prices and money values are known in real time in every part of the globe. Thus, for example, treasurers of banks or controllers of corporations can subscribe to a Reuters international money market service and obtain, in real time, quotations on different currencies in 25 different money markets from Frankfurt to London to New York to Tokyo to Singapore to Hong Kong, so that they can take advantage of the different rates and move their holdings about.

By satellite communication, through television, every part of the world is immediately visible to every other part. The multiplication of interactions and the widening of the social arenas are the major consequences of a shift in the modalities of the infrastructure. This is a problem we shall return to later.

Postindustrial Society

The revolution in communications, the creation of an information society, also speeds the development of what I have called a postindustrial society.[3] Table 9.1 schematically compares preindustrial, industrial, and postindustrial types of developments.

Most of the world today—that is, principally the countries in Asia, Africa, and Latin America—is preindustrial in that at least 60% or more of its labor force is engaged in extractive industries. The life of these countries is a "game against nature," in which national wealth depends on the quality of the natural resources and vicissitudes of world commodity prices.

A smaller section of the world, the countries around the North Atlantic littoral plus the Soviet Union and Japan, is made up of industrial countries where the fabrication of goods, by the application of machine technology with energy, is the basis of wealth and economic growth.

Some of these latter countries are now moving into the postindustrial world. In the postindustrial state, first there is a shift from the production of goods to the selling of services.

Services exist in all societies but, in preindustrial societies, these are primarily domestic services. In industrial societies, these are ancillary to the production of goods, such as transportation, utilities, and financial services. In postindustrial societies, the emphasis is on human services (education, health, social services) and on professional services (computing, systems analysis, and scientific research and development).

The second dimension of postindustrial society is more important: the fact that, for the first time, innovation and change derive from the codification of theoretical knowledge. Every society has its base, to some extent, in knowledge. But only recently has technical change become so dependent on the codification of theoretical knowledge. We can see this easily by examining the relation of technology to science.

Steel, automotive, utilities, and aviation industries are primarily of the nineteenth century in that they were created largely by inventors—"talented tinkerers"—who knew little about the basic laws or findings of science.

This was true of such a genius as Edison, who invented, among other things, the electric lamp, the gramophone or record player, and the motion picture. Yet he knew little of the work of Maxwell or Faraday on electromagnetism, the union of whose two fields was the basis of almost all subsequent work in modern physics. This was equally true of Siemens with his invention of the dynamo, and Bell with the telephone, or Marconi with the radio wireless.

The first "modern" industry is chemistry, in that the scientist must have a knowledge of the theoretical properties of the macromolecules that he is manipulating in order to know where he is going. What is true of all the science-based industries of the last half of the twentieth century, and the products that come from them—electronics equipment, polymers, computers, lasers, holograms—is that they derive from work in theoretical science, and it is theory that focuses the direction of future research and the development of products.

The crucial point about a postindustrial society is that knowledge and information become the strategic and transforming resources of the society, just as capital and labor have been the strategic and transforming resources of industrial society. The crucial "variable" for any society, therefore, is the strength of its basic research and science and technological resources—in its universities, in its research laboratories, and in its capacity for scientific and technological development.

In these respects, the new information technology becomes the basis of a new intellectual technology, in which theoretical knowledge and its new techniques (such as systems analysis, linear programming, and probability theory), hitched to the computer, become decisive for industrial and military innovation.

Corollary Problem

Two important consequences of the revolution in communications round out the picture of social change. One is that, because of a combination of market and political forces, a new international division of labor is taking place in the world economy; the other involves a widening scale of political effects across the world.

Economic Changes

The developing countries, in proclaiming a new international economic order at Lima in 1975, have demanded that 25% of the world's manufacturing capacity be in the hands of the Third World by the year 2000. This is a highly unrealistic target. Yet some tidal changes are already taking place.

Table 9.1   The postindustrial society: A comparative scheme

Modes	Preindustrial	Industrial	Postindustrial
Mode of production	Extractive	Fabrication	Processing & recycling services
Economic sector	Primary	Secondary	Tertiary
	Agriculture	Goods producing	Transportation
	Mining	Durables	Utilities
	Fishing	Nondurables	
	Timber	Heavy construction	Quaternary
	Oil & gas		Trade
			Finance
			Insurance
			Real Estate
			Quinary
			Health
			Research
			Recreation
			Education
			Government
Transforming resource	Natural power—wind, water, draft animal-human muscle	Created energy—electricity, oil gas, coal, nuclear power	Information*—computer and data transmission systems
Strategic resource	Raw materials	financial capital	Knowledge**
Technology	Craft	Machine technology	Intellectual technology
Skill base	Artisan, framer, manual worker	Engineer, semiskilled worker	Scientist, technical & professional occupations

Table 9.1 (continued)

Modes	Preindustrial	Industrial	Postindustrial
Methodology	Common sense, trial and error, experience	Empiricism, experimentation	Abstract theory: models, simulations, decision theory, systems analysis
Time perspective	Orientation to the past	Ad hoc adaptiveness, experimentation	Future orientation: forecasting and planning
Design	Game against nature	Games against fabricated nature	Game between persons
Axial principal	Traditionalism	Economic growth	Codification of theoretical knowledge

* Broadly, data processing. The storing, retrieval, and processing of the data become the essential resource for all economic and social exchanges

** An organized set of statements of facts or ideas, presenting a reasoned judgment or experimental result, that is transmitted to other through some communication medium in some systematic form.

There is one group of developing countries—among them Brazil, Mexico, South Korea, Taiwan, Singapore, Algeria, Nigeria—that is beginning to industrialize rapidly. It is likely that, in the next decades, traditional, routinized manufacturing, such as the textile, shipbuilding, steel, shoe, and small-consumer appliances industries, will be "drawn out" of the advanced industrial countries and become centered in this new tier.

The response of the advanced industrial countries will be either protectionism and the disruption of the world economy or the development of a "comparative advantage" in, essentially, the electronic and advanced technological and science-based industries that are the feature of a postindustrial society. How this development takes place will be a major issue of economic and social policy for the nations of the world in the next decade.

Expanded Political Arena

The second, more subtle, yet perhaps more important, problem is that the revolution in communications necessarily means a change in scale—an expansion in the political arenas of the world, the drawing in of new claimants, and the multiplication of actors or of constituencies.

In the last decade or more we have heard much of the acceleration of the pace of change. It is a seductive yet, in the end, a meaningless idea other than as a metaphor. For one has to ask, "Change of what?" and "How does one measure the pace?" There is no metric that applies in general, and the word *change* is ambiguous.

As Mervyn Jones, the English author, once pointed out, a man who was born in 1800 and who died in 1860 would have seen the coming of the railway, the steamship, the telegraph, gas lighting, factory-made objects, and the expansion of the large urban centers. A man who was born in 1860 and who died in 1920 would have seen the telephone, electric light, automobile, and motion pictures. He might be familiar with the ideas of Darwin, Marx, and Freud. He would have seen the final destruction of most monarchies, the expansion of the ideas of equality, and the rise and breakup of imperialism.

How does one measure the events of the past 40 years in order to say that the pace of change has increased? If anything, one might say that, since growth is never exponential in a linear way but follows an S-shaped or logistic curve, we are close to "leveling off" many of the so-called changes that have transformed our lives (e.g., transport and communications will not increase appreciably in speed). And in the world increase in population, we seem to have now passed the "point of inflection," that midway point where the S-curve of change is now slowing down.

But what is definite is that the scale on which changes have taken place has widened. And a change in scale, as physicists and organization theorists have long known, requires essentially a change in form. The growth of an enterprise, for example, requires specialization and differentiation and very different kinds of control and management systems when the scales move from, say, $10 million to $100 million to $1 billion.

The problem becomes politically acute for political systems. Rousseau, in *The Social Contract*, set forth a "natural law" that the larger a state becomes, the more its government will be concentrated, so that the number of rulers decreases as the population increases. Rousseau was seeking to show that a regime necessarily changes its form as the population increases, as the interactions between people multiply, and as interests become more complicated and diverse.

The problem for modern political societies—especially those that wish to maintain democratic institutions, the control of government by the consent of the people, and an expanding degree of participation—is to match the scales between political and economic institutions and activities. The fact that government has increasingly become more distant from and yet more powerful in the lives of persons has led increasingly, as well, to separatism, localism, and breakaway movements in society.

At the same time, the scale of economic activities on a worldwide canvas has indicated that we lack the governing mechanisms to deal with, for example, monetary problems, commodity prices, and industrial relocation on the new scales on which these actions take place. As I remarked in an earlier article, what is happening today is that, for many countries, the national state is becoming too big for the small problems of life and too small for the big problems of life.[4]

Implications for Personal Liberty

All of these structural changes lead to the pointed question of the fate of individual and personal liberties in this "brave new world." We have had, from Aldous Huxley to George Orwell, dire predictions of the kinds of controls—the expansion of Big Brother totalitarianism—that may be coming as a result of such technological changes. Indeed, an old Russian joke asks: Who is Stalin? Answer: Genghis Khan with a telephone. And there are many humorous examples of how the new technologies permit the growth of scrutiny mechanisms and intrusions in personal life.

A story in the *London Times* on the growth of security procedures in Germany reports that the movements of a German business consultant who has to cross the border into Switzerland several times a day were reported to a computer center so that he suddenly found himself on a list of persons to be watched. But the moral of the story is not that the computerization of the border crossings increases the power of the police, but that because of the political threats of terrorism such procedures had to be adopted.

The issue of social control can be put under three headings:

1. Expansion of the techniques of surveillance.

2. Concentration of the technology of record keeping.

3. Control of access to strategic information by monopoly or government imposition of secrecy.

In all three areas there has been an enormous growth of threatening powers and, in a free society such as ours, a growing apprehension about their misuse.

The techniques of surveillance, since they are the most dramatic, have received the most attention. In George Orwell's *1984*, the government of Oceana monitors party members by a remote sensor of human heartbeats. The sensors are located in the two-way television screens in all homes, government offices, and public squares. By tuning in on individuals and measuring their heartbeats, Big Brother can discover whether an individual is engaged in unusual activities.

Recently, a young physiologist discovered, to his dismay, that he had invented such a device himself. Seeking to measure the physiological activities of salamanders less painfully than by plugging painful electrodes into the animals' bodies, he created a delicate voltage sensor that measures the extremely minute electrical field that surrounds the bodies of all living organisms, so that one can now detect, and record from a distance, an animal's heartbeat, respiration, muscle tension, and body movements.

Told that he had invented the device that Orwell had imagined, he made a study of the predictions Orwell made in *1984* and found that, of the 137 devices Orwell had described, some 100 are now practical, 30 years after the publication of the book.[5] Also, in Solzhenitsyn's *First Circle*, it may be recalled, the prisoner-scientists in the secret police laboratory were working on devices to identify telephone callers by voiceprints and also to unscramble coded telephone conversations—devices which are in use today.

The computerization of records, which intelligence agencies, police, and credit agencies use, is by now quite far advanced, and so much so that individuals are constantly being warned to check to see that their credit ratings are accurately recorded in computer memories, lest they be cut off, especially in cashless and checkless transactions, from the purchase of goods that they need.

The problem of secrecy is old and persistent. Recently, *Science* magazine reported that, at the request of the National Security Agency (NSA), the Department of Commerce had imposed a secrecy order that inhibited commercial development of a communications device, invented by a group in Seattle, for which a patent had been applied. The technique involved in the patent application goes beyond the voice-scrambler technology used in police and military communications and takes advantage of the spread-spectrum communication band to expand the range of citizens' band and maritime radios. *Science* reports:

The inventors are fighting to have the order overturned so that they can market their device commercially. They regard their struggle as a test of whether the government will allow the burgeoning of cheap, secure communications technology to continue in the private sector or whether it will keep a veil of secrecy over the work—effectively reserving it exclusively for military and intelligence applications.[6]

Real as these issues are for liberty in the personal and economic sense, they are not the true locus of the problem. It is not in the technology per se but in the social and political system in which that technology is embedded.

The most comprehensive system of surveillance was first invented by that malign individual Joseph Fouché, who served as police chief for Napoleon I. A former Catholic priest, he became a militant leader of the French Revolution, having directed the massacre at Lyons; and after Napoleon he continued as police chief during the Bourbon restoration of Louis XVIII. Fouché was the first to organize every concierge in Paris as an agent of the police and to report to local headquarters the movements each day of every resident of the buildings. The scale of operations has expanded since Fouché's day. Technology is an instrument for keeping abreast of the management of scale. The point can be made more abstractly, yet simply. Technology does not determine social structure; it simply widens all kinds of possibilities. Technology is embedded in a social support system, and each social structure has a choice as to how it will be used. Both the Soviet Union and the United States are industrial societies, using much the same kind of technology in their production systems. Yet the organization of industry, and the rights of individuals, vary greatly in the two societies.

One can take the same technology and show how different social support systems use them in very different ways. For the automobile, one can show very different patterns of use, and consequent social costs, without changing a single aspect of the automobile itself. Thus, in one kind of society, one can have a system of complete private ownership of the automobile where the individual can come and go largely at his own pleasure.

But such a pattern involves a high cost to the individual for the purchase of the car, the insurance, gasoline, and depreciation, as well as a cost to the community for more roads, parking garages, and the like.

Yet one can envisage a very different pattern, which some cities have tried, where automobiles are barred from a large area and in their place is a "public utility" system in which an individual subscribes to a car service. He goes a short distance—no farther, say, than a usual bus stop—to a parking lot; takes a car, using a magnetic-coded key; drives off in that car to his destination; and simply leaves the car in that other lot, again no farther than a bus-stop distance from where he wants to go.

The user has a great degree of mobility (as with a taxi service, yet without the cost of a driver), but fewer cars are needed in this kind of distributive system. The cost to the individual is the walk to and from the parking lot and the brief wait for a car that may be necessary if there are shortages.

Such a system represents an expansion of the car-hire service that is available at airports and throughout a city in many countries today. The illustration is trivial (and I am not arguing for one or another of the patterns to be imposed on a society); yet the import of the example is not so trivial: namely, a single technology is compatible with a wide variety of social patterns, and the decision about the use of the technology is, primarily, a function of the social pattern a society chooses.

To expand this proposition, the following theorem holds: The new revolution in communications makes possible both an intense degree of centralization of power, if the society decides to use it in that way, and large decentralization because of the multiplicity, diversity, and cheapness of the modes of communication.

It is quite clear that an elaborate compunications system allows for intensification of what in military parlance is called command and control systems.

Through such systems, the U.S. Air Force was able, a dozen years ago, to set up a watch pattern that kept track of all aircraft or unidentified flying objects over the North American air space, and relayed that information, in real time, to a centralized control station that in turn monitored the information.

Without such a system, one could not have basic security against an enemy attack. Yet, in the Vietnam War, the development of the command and control system meant that tactical decisions, which in the past were made by field commanders, were often made on the basis of political decisions in Washington. The Vietnam War was an extraordinary instance of the centralization of military decisions on a scale rarely seen before.

In Chile, from 1971 to 1973, the British organization theorist, Stafford Beer, set up an effort to prepare a single computer program to model—and eventually control—every level of the Chilean economy. Under his direction, with the cooperation of the Allende government, an operations room was created to plan for centralized control of Chilean industry.

This was not a simulations model, as used by Jay Forrester and his associates to demonstrate what might be if certain assumptions held, but an operational recursive model (i.e., a set of "nestings" or minisystems built into a pattern of larger systems) to direct the course of the economy from a single center. Whether this would have been possible is moot; the effort was cut short by the overthrow of the Allende government in September 1973.

And yet, by the very same technology, one can go in wholly different directions. Through the expansion of two-way communication, as in various cable television systems, one could have a complete "plebiscitarian" system whereby referenda on a large variety of issues could be taken through responses back from computer terminals in each house. For some persons this would be "complete" democracy; for others it might mean a more manipulative society, or even the tyranny of the majority, or an increase in the volatility of political discussion and conflict in society.

Without going to either extreme (and, at times, the extremes meet), what is clear is that the revolution in communications allows for a large diversity of cultural expressions and the enhancement of different lifestyles simply because of the increase in the number of channels available to people. This is happening already in radio, for example, where stations cater to very different tastes, from rock to classical music, from serious talk shows to news and game shows. With the multiplication of television channels and of video cassettes, the variety of choice becomes staggering.

Under free conditions, individuals can create their own modes of communication and their own new communities. No one, for example, foresaw the mushrooming of citizens' band radios, and the ways in which they came to be used. These allow strangers to communicate readily with one another. The first, fascinating, social pattern was the development of an informal communications and warning system by truckers on the major roadways, warning one another of traps by law enforcement agents or of road conditions ahead. Sometimes truckers simply used the CB radio to enlarge social ties in what is an essentially lonely occupation.

The CB radio has become a major means of communication in isolated village areas, as in Nova Scotia—a form of community telephone line. And, with two-way video cable television, community interchange may become possible between the elderly or hobby enthusiasts or others with special interests and needs.

In a larger political sense, the extension of networks because of metaphoric face-to-face contact will mean that political units can be reorganized more readily to match, and be responsive to, the scales of the appropriate social unit, from neighborhood to region.

In the end, the question of the relation of technology to liberty is both prosaic and profound. It is prosaic because the technology is primarily a facilitator or a constraint, available to intensify or to enhance whichever direction a political system chooses to go. It is profound because as I said, man is a creature capable both of compassion and of murder. Which path is chosen goes back to the long, agonized efforts of civilized communities to find institutional arrangements that can allow individuals to realize their potentials and that respect the integrity of the person.

In short, the question of liberty is, as always, a political consideration. Even speaking of threats to liberty because of the powerful nature of the new surveillance technologies is a misstatement; such a view focuses on technological gadgetry rather than on organizational realities.

Orwell, with his powerful imagination, could conjure up a Big Brother watching all others. But there is not, and cannot be, a single giant brain that absorbs all information. In most instances, the centralization of such controls simply multiplies bureaucracies, each so cumbersome and jealous of its prerogatives (look at the wars between intelligence agencies in the United States!) as to inhibit, often, the effective use of information.

If anything, the real threat of such technological megalomania lies in the expansion of regulatory agencies whose rising costs and bureaucratic regulations and delays inhibit innovation and change in a society. In the United States, at least, it is not Big Brother, but Slothful Brother, that becomes the problem.

I do not mean to minimize the potential for abuse. It exists. But there are also agencies of concern, such as the press. Justice William Douglas wrote in 1972: "The press has a privileged position in our constitutional system, not to enable it to make money, not to set newsmen apart as a favored class, but to bring fulfillment to the people's right to know."

The crucial issues are access to information and the restriction of any monopoly on information, subject, under stringent review, to genuine concerns of national security. The Freedom of Information Act was the fruit of a long campaign in the 1960s to open up the records of government agencies so that individuals would have access to information about themselves or information about government agency activities involving public matters.

In a somewhat different context, when the first large computers were created, technologists compared them to large generators distributing energy and assumed that the most efficient model of computer use would be regulated computer utilities, which would sell computer time or data services to users. The rapidity of technological change, resulting in the multiplication of mini- and microcomputers, as well as some second thoughts about the diverse markets for computer usage, led to complete abandonment of the ideas of computer utilities and recognition of the competitive market as the best framework for computer development.

The possible growth of the teletext systems described earlier, of cable television, and of video cassettes may lead to the upheaval of the major television network systems and to new modes of news presentation, similar to the new competition AT&T faces today in transmission systems.

In sum, from all this arises a moral different from what we might expect. While technology is instrumental, the free and competitive use of various technologies is one of the best means of breaking up monopolies, public and private. And that, too, is a guarantee of freedom.

Notes

1. See Simon Nora and Alain Minc, *L'Informatisation de la société* (La Documentation Francaise, January 1978); and the annual reports of the Harvard University Program on Information Technology, 1976 and 1977.

2. I have expanded on some of these in "Teletext and Technology," *Encounter* (London), June 1977; and "The Social Framework of the Information Society," in *Computer Age: A Twenty Year View*, ed. by Michael Dertouzos and Joel Moses (Cambridge, Mass.: MIT Press, 1980).

3. For an elaboration of this concept see my book, *The Coming of Post-Industrial Society* (New York: Basic Books, 1973).

4. See my essay, "The Future World Disorders: The Structural Context of Crises" in *Foreign Policy*, (U.S.), Summer 1977. For an acute discussion of Rousseau and the problems of size and representation in society, see Bertrand De Jouvenel, *The Art of Conjecture* (New York: Basic Books, 1967).

5. See David Goodman, "Countdown to 1984," *The Futurist*, December 1978.

6. *Science*, 8 November 1978.

IV   The Information Business

10 Charting Change: The Harvard Information Business Map

*Anthony G. Oettinger and John F. McLaughlin, with
Anne E. Birinyi*

The fundamental question for all information businesses is how best to match substance for which there is a demand, market demand or administered demand, with formats and with processes that can meet that demand in the most advantageous way.

Every organization faces essentially that very same fundamental question, but asked about the organization's nervous system. Some organizations themselves make most of their own nervous system. They run a little inside information business. Other organizations mostly buy outside, both substance and form. But whatever the mix of make or buy, no organization can escape, if not the responsibility for, then at least the effects of, the structure and the performance of their own nervous system.

The Harvard Information Business Map is a tool that was developed primarily by John McLaughlin to help address that fundamental question from either the purveyor's or the user's standpoint. Translated into Dutch, French, German, Italian, Japanese, and Swedish (at last count), and used on paper and diskette media, the Map has been widely used to chart business plans in information businesses and plans for the internal nervous systems in all kinds of organizations.[1]

The Map helps to chart both the past and the future by laying out relationships among basic building blocks in a way that helps to fend off being trapped in the past or taken in by the future. It does this by blending abstract but conventional economic building blocks with the substance, format, and process components of information resources. It does it also by displaying labels for entities that live and breathe in the here and now and do not just sigh for the past or pant for the future.

The Map's vertical axis (figure 10.1) ranges from products in the south to services in the north. The polar product–service distinction is common to both

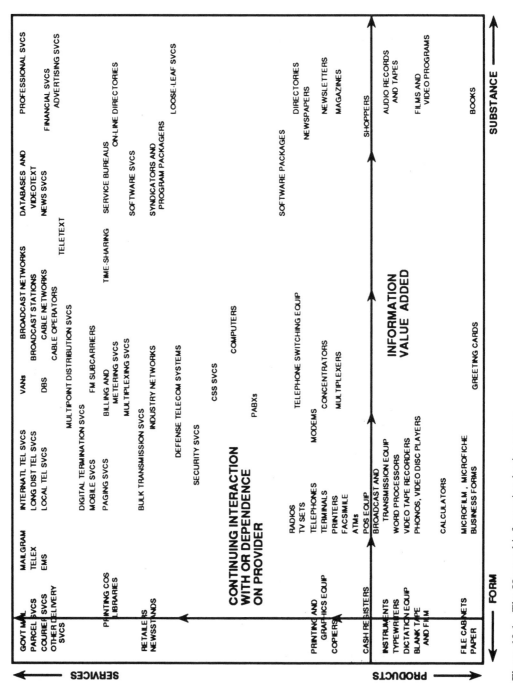

Figure 10.1 The Harvard information business map

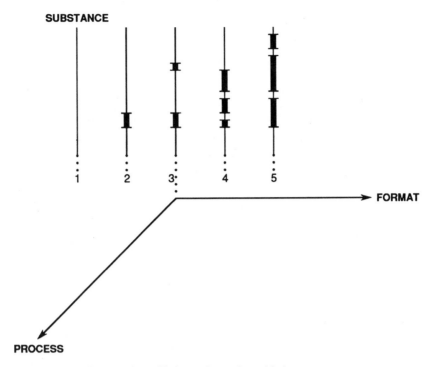

Figure 10.2   The meaning of information value added

business practice and academic economics. At one pole, the idea of service connotes the consumer's continuing interaction with or dependence on the provider of the service. At the other extreme, a product in its purest form implies no interaction—at least no necessary interaction—between supplier and consumer once something has been bought. Interaction is a matter of degree. The sale of products and the sale of services can be combined into mixed strategies—hence a continuum of possibilities between the poles.

The horizontal axis draws on the ideas of substance, format, and process. Format-and-process combined as form define the west end of the horizontal axis. The east end is pure substance. Figure 10.2 suggests a meaning for the east-west continuum. The five sample substance axes show increasing information value added in visual metaphors.

Books, at the southeast corner of the Map, are substantive products as quintessential as they come. The corporeal forms, the tokens, for items at the east end are of far less consequence than the substantive aspects of these items.

Even the pattern of their formats matters not in comparison to their substance. A book is bought mainly for what it says, not for the paper it's printed on.

Of course, real-world books are never disembodied. That means that some can find expensive leather bindings beautiful, they can thrill to the touch of particularly fine rag paper, they may glory in the magnificence of gilt illustrations or, with French-produced books of the old style, they can derive perverse joy from slicing through virgin signatures that no one else has read before. But those aesthetic considerations are, in most instances and for most people, but a small element of what a book is prized for.[2] Likewise, book burning is usually seen as an aberration, a brutish political act, although better the warmth from burning books than death by freezing. These exceptions merely prove the rule. When most of us casually think of a book, we think of what it says, not of how it is made and surely not of the fact that it is an ink-on-paper token. If anything, we are more likely to notice whether the book is hard cover or paperback, which alters the price of a book but not its substance.

Like the word "book," the other entries inside the Map frame are words that are current as of the Map's date. This means that there is hard evidence of some active business or group of businesses which actually and publicly calls itself by the entry. No entry denotes some configuration that existed in the past or else might be envisaged for the future, but without known instance here and now.

Evidence for the existence of the bundle denoted by a word is its widespread usage in transactions or, at the very least, the existence of a trade association, a newsletter, or some other substantial evidence of a self-conscious and active business group actually selling something, even pie in the sky; for example, a videotext newsletter, an electronic mail newsletter, and so on.

This stress on explicit evidence for active existence accounts for the absence of organizational nervous system names from the Map despite the claims made about the usefulness of organizational nervous systems to every organization and not just to information businesses. What names are used for information resources within organizations are often idiosyncratic, not generic. And insofar as an organization takes its nervous system for granted, it may not even have words for the system or for the system's private parts.

Compared to information suppliers, information consumers are under little pressure to seek common and widely recognized terms. The burden is thus unavoidable for information consumer readers to identify from the supplier labels inside the Map what things they do for themselves, what things they get done for them by outsiders, and what things they don't do at all.

The entries in the Map are names of products or services or lines of business and not of companies. One company might encompass only one of these products or services among its lines of business or it might include several. The fact that some of the names coincide with common names of certain types of corporate entities is coincidental. This is the case for "newspapers," which means that traditional product and not the corporate entity that produces it. Figure 10.5 shows why this matters.

"Paper," in the southwest corner, epitomizes purely formal products. An empty piece of paper conveys no substance whatever, at least within the convention that substance is only what writing, printing, or drawing denote. A piece of blank paper left as a book mark clearly says "here is where you were," but, like the smelling or the burning of a book, this iconic use of a blank piece of paper is a practice that is noted but not given great significance here.

"Business"—or government—"Forms" are mapped to the right of blank "Paper" but way to the left of "Books." This reflects the judgment that forms embody slightly more substance than a blank piece of paper but far less than a book. The headings of a form like IRS 1040 themselves convey some substance. The headings, rulings, and other elements of the form constrain what additional substance might be entered on the form. Here again, we cast aside such common perversions as scribbling on the back of a form or making a paper airplane of it. The Map is a tool for rough and ready reckoning, not for picking a way through the shoals of recondite conundrums.

Up in the northwest corner of the Map, "Government Mail" epitomizes formal services. Government mail is a service. One cannot use it without continuing to interact with and to depend on its provider. It is a formal service in that control over substance rests with the consumer of the service, not with its provider. Aberrations such as wartime censorship by the military or peacetime steaming open of mail by intelligence agencies are ignored here. So is the minimal amount of substantive interaction implied by postal use of the address to route the mail. The positioning of "Mailgram" and "Telephone Services" somewhat to the right of "Government Mail" reflects the greater economic possibilities for substantive manipulation of information in those businesses. These possibilities touch off much controversy about the evolving roles of the telecommunications and the mail industries, specifically, over how much their activities might or might not be permitted to spill over into the activities of the data processing and the media industries, and vice versa.

Last of the extremes of the Map, "Professional Services" lie in the northeast corner. A doctor in his or her diagnostic or prescription-writing capacity, but not in the meat-cutting capacity, epitomizes purely substantive professional information services. What value there is in the service attaches to the substance gathered or conveyed. Surgeons, by contrast, are valued for combining the know-what-to-do that distinguishes them from the barbers of old with the finely tuned know-how-to-do-it that sets them apart from butchers.

The Map has its limitations. Positioning an entry along either axis is somewhat subjective. As a general rule, items are set in the Map as seen by a customer. But different customers could place the same item differently along either axis. To some degree, providers might place things differently from customers. This may be less a shortcoming of the mapping technique than an accurate rendering of the structural ambiguities of the information business.

Like geographical maps, the Information Business Map is limited by two dimensions. Some items that overlap conceptually show up above, below, or next to one another for visual clarity. The information conveyed is selective and limited, although one might display terms such as "Computers," "Mail," or "Telephone" in large, heavy type and "FM Sub-carriers" or "Newsletters" in small type to differentiate their relative annual sales. The differentiations made in figure 10.3 are finer grained than those on the Map; that is, figure 10.3's entries indicate many more properties (qualities) of a good than where it lies on the product–service axis or the form–substance axis.

These mapping rules do not show numerous components that are integral parts of the information business. Semiconductors, optical character recognition devices, and electric power, for example, are integral to many of the entries. These items are excluded from the Map, but "Paper" and "Telephone Switches" are in. It is often difficult to tell whether something is a component worthless in isolation, a generic technology, or an end product that belongs on the Map.

Whether a particular item is included and where it is put also depends on the chosen level of aggregation. For simplicity, for example, "Financial Services" is one entry in the basic Map of figure 10.1. Figure 10.4 shows how further disaggregation of financial services into specific products or services might cause substantial relocations in every direction. "Newspapers" is a single item toward the southeast of the Map. This placement reflects the whole of the traditional newspaper bundle. If the newspaper were unbundled into news, classified ads, horoscopes, comics, crossword puzzles, stock quotations, and so on, some of these pieces would go closer to books, some closer to professional services, and so on.

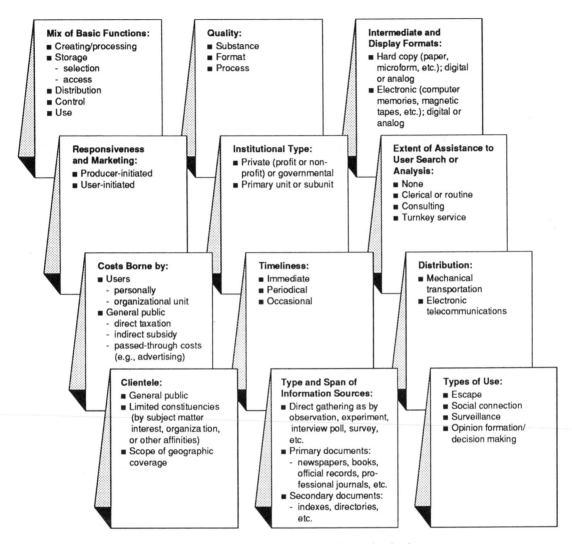

Figure 10.3 Differentiating traits of the information business

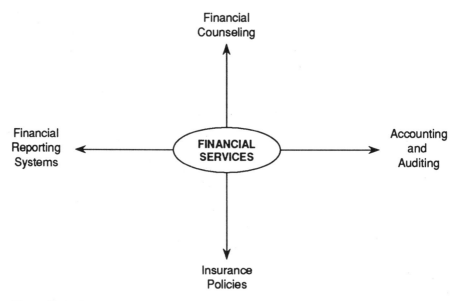

Figure 10.4   Map entry location depends on aggregation level

"Computers" go squarely in the middle because disaggregated they would literally be all over the Map. Computers are marketed as products or as services with all possible mixes in between. A computer bereft of its operating system, not to speak of its application software, is as emptily formal, not to say inert, as a blank piece of paper. Like the empty paper, it too has limitless substantive potential. A one-purpose computer, like some of the early game-playing or educational devices trotted out before Christmas, is as set in its substantive repertoire as one book is. The nature and scope of its programming determine where any particular computer falls between east and west.

How a newspaper and a newspaper company differ leaps out of figure 10.5. Dow Jones & Company, Gannett Company, Harte-Hanks Communications, Lee Enterprises, New York Times, The Times Mirror Company, and the Washington Post Company are plotted on this Map. Each company is generally classified as a newspaper publisher. Each indeed publishes at least one newspaper, as denoted by the heavy oval around the newspaper entry. Each company is also in the lines of business marked by the other ovals. As many lines link the newspaper entry with the other entries as there were companies in each of the other lines of business as of 1983–84. Newspaper companies, far

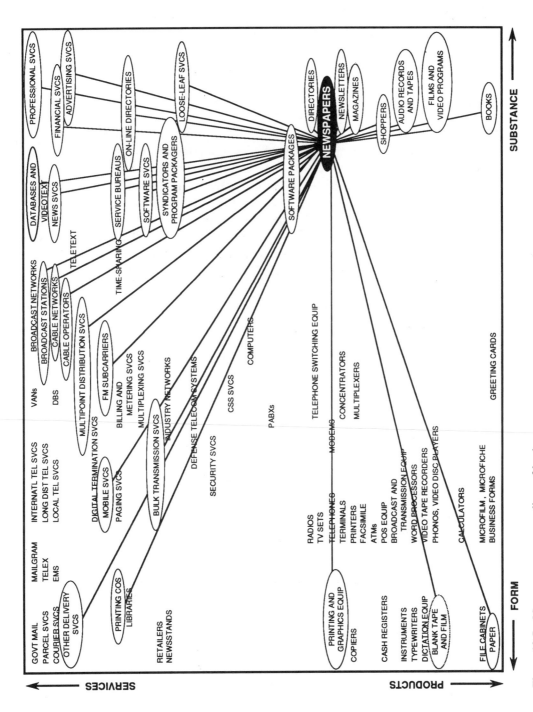

Figure 10.5   Newspaper company lines of business

from confined to producing newspapers, are literally all over the Map. So, as it happens, are telephone companies.

AT&T's activities before its 1984 divestiture are depicted in figure 10.6. Under the terms of the settlement of an antitrust suit brought by the United States, the new AT&T company, smaller because divested of its local operating companies, was freed to enter essentially all lines of business shown as entries on the Map.

With both newspaper companies and telephone companies all over the map, the possibility of competition, conflict, and compromise among these institutions became actuality in bitter legislative and regulatory debates beginning around 1980. The debates got all-the-more acrimonious since the newspaper companies perceived that because they increasingly depended on the telephone companies to supply their vital telecommunications, they are singularly vulnerable to any anti-competitive actions by telephone companies in those arenas where the two might compete. The Map helps to make this evolutionary ferment visible and immediate.

Ever since the printing press came into widespread use, the publishing business encompassed stable bundles from the corners of the Map. Figure 10.7 shows the publishing industry through the 1970s and, quite likely, the way much of it will stay for the foreseeable future. This picture differs little from when Benjamin Franklin was publishing the *Pennsylvania Gazette* out of his printing office while serving, perhaps not just coincidentally, first as postmaster at Philadelphia and later as deputy postmaster-general for America.

The traditional publishing process begins with professional services that create or gather substance. Production then uses printing and graphics equipment in a process that relies throughout on photographic and ink-and-paper technologies. The products are traditional paper-based books, newspapers, shoppers, magazines, newsletters, directories, and the like. Finally, these are distributed through traditional mechanical modes (figure 10.7).

The advent of relatively cheap communications technologies (figure 10.8) brought the opportunity to alter the traditional process. At the start of the '80s, electronic publishing was still an infant business. It used elements of traditional publishing combined with more recently developed and bundled elements. The first stage of modification was wholly internal, affecting the formats and the processes of production and their internal formats, but not the presentation format of products. By 1980, most daily newspaper operations and many magazine and book publishing operations had text entered into computers via terminals with video display. Editors retrieved the text from the computer onto

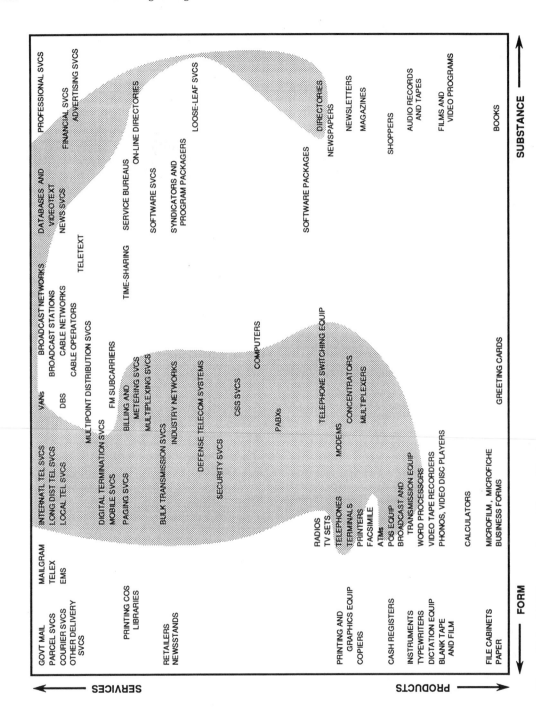

Figure 10.6 AT&T pre-settlement lines of business

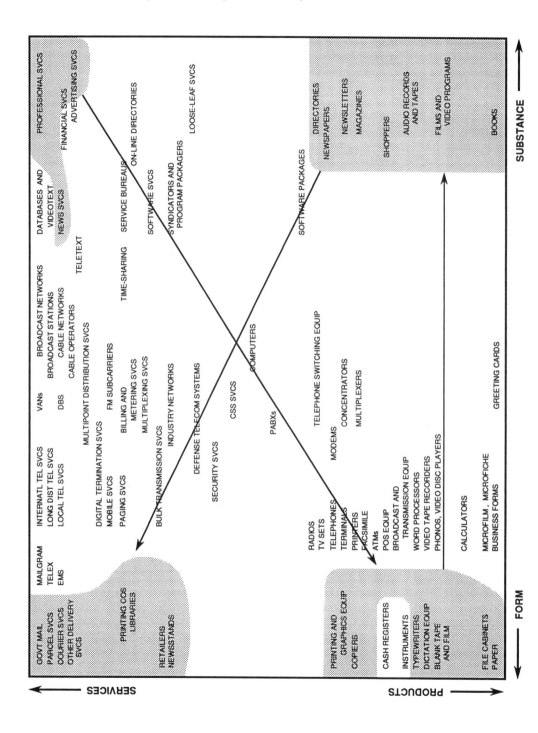

Figure 10.7 The traditional publishing process

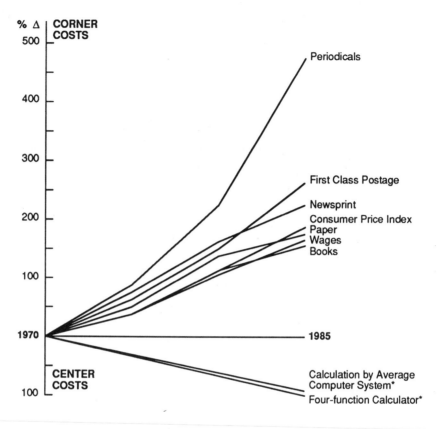

% Δ | **CORNER COSTS**

*Program on Information Resources Policy data.

Figure 10.8   Widening cost spread favoring compunctions technologies over traditional information technologies

their own video displays for editing. Internally, therefore, many publishing operations were already electronic instead of paper based. Only at the last stage of production was editorial substance transferred from electronic to paper format for mechanical distribution and traditional consumption.

The second stage, emerging in the early '80s, was making such computer-stored text—and some graphics—available to the end user without either printing or mechanical distribution by the supplier. Substance, stored by computer in electronic digital formats, is sent through the facilities of broadcasters, of CATV companies, of telephone companies, or of the United States Mail, the

United Parcel Service, and others, to a terminal at the consumer site, either in an institutional setting or, less frequently in the early '80s than by the late '80s, in a home. The effect is a migration from the higher-cost corners of the Map toward the lower-cost center (figure 10.9).

The transmission might be a continuous offering of a whole database, as in a teletext service that gives the end user at most the ability to grab on the fly one or more frames or pages of substance as it goes by. This is like selling a conventional printed database limited in size mainly by the existing technology and the economics of the production and delivery. From such a product, the reader picks and reads only what interests him or her. For example, a newspaper is theoretically expandable to include everything that has been written by local writers, plus all of the wire service and syndicated service copy that has come in since the last edition. The constraints on the size and speed of the presses, the capacity and cost of trucks and of labor, the cost of newsprint, and the like, are what require a more limited product to be made. A teletext service is constrained by acceptable response times for finding a requested frame.

The size of the effective database can be substantially increased by limiting transmission to only what a user actually requests. This mode of operation is an interactive service. In this case, the primary constraint is on the size of the computer needed to store the substance and to handle multiple users simultaneously. Transmission is more elaborate than in a service of the teletext type, since a selection and ordering signal from the user to the supplier is needed in addition to the substantive transmission from the supplier to the user. Moreover, the substance sent from the publisher's computer must be addressed to the specific individual who requested it—a more complex and expensive task than making frames or pages available to all grabbers.

A new set of players started to come into the publishing industry. They included electronic goods distributors such as Tandy Corporation; data processing specialists, such as H&R Block's CompuServe; banks, such as Citibank and Bank One (Ohio); enhanced-service telecommunications firms, like GTE's Telenet and of course AT&T. In addition, many firms already in the publishing industry were experimenting with or deploying ventures ranging from pieces of electronic publishing enterprises to full systems. Among these were Times Mirror Company, Dow Jones, CBS, Reader's Digest, Time Incorporated, Knight-Ridder, and Cox Communications.

None of the foregoing implies that traditional hard-copy publishing and distribution were in immediate danger of becoming obsolete. However, the Map of the electronic publishing process (figure 10.10) shows the blurring of bound-

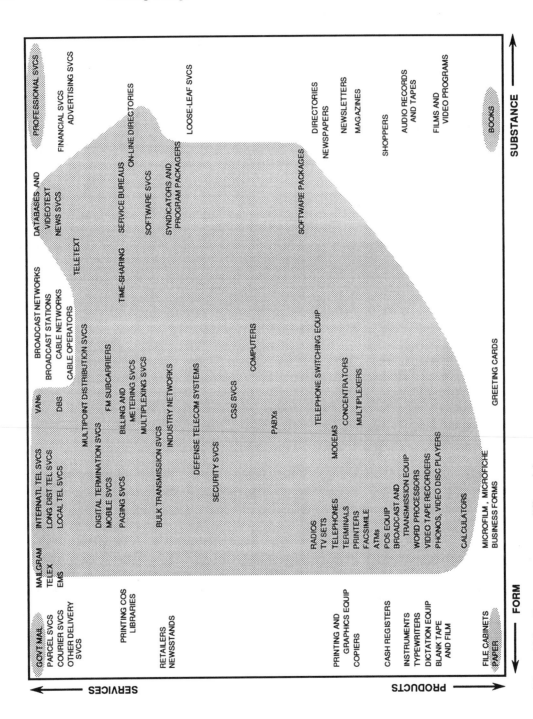

Figure 10.9 Corner–center cost differentials

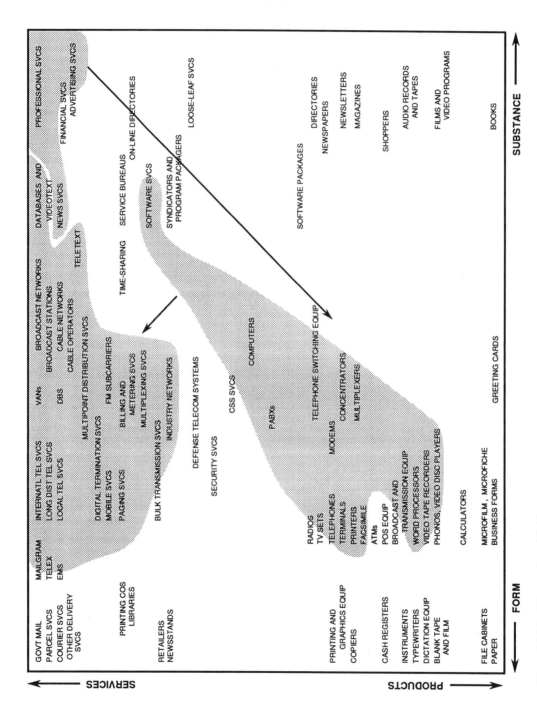

Figure 10.10 Electronic publishing

aries and the movement toward the center of the map characteristic of the information business since the 1930s.

Figure 10.10 shows electronic publishing processors still firmly anchored in human professional services, much as they were in Benjamin Franklin's time. Despite recurrent predictions of revolution, this has stayed the stablest of all factors in publishing. The production tools, however, are increasingly compunications-based in combinations determined at least as much by political and policy factors as by technology.

It is not only that processes for creating or gathering substance are changing slowly. The processes of information manipulation, storage, and transmission have been subject to rapid change, along with the formats for both internal production and ultimate presentation to the user. The substance being delivered has not itself changed as rapidly. Consequently, the editorial front end remains relatively unaffected by changes in process and format. Reporters still have to get a story, write it, and have it edited. Photographers, graphic designers, advertising salespeople, filmmakers, and others will continue to perform tasks similar to today's, though perhaps with different equipment and priorities.

Appendix: A Brief History of the Information Business Map

John F. McLaughlin with Anne E. Birinyi

The Program on Information Resources Policy first published the mapping scheme in December 1979.[3]

The original map (figure 10.A-1) was the result of many efforts to depict graphically the interrelationships among various industries and technologies for which "information" was a common denominator. Earlier attempts included efforts to portray telecommunications services, computer hardware, time-sharing, and publishing activities on a single spectrum using some of the terminology such as "data transmission" and "data processing" that arose from the FCC's Computer Inquiry I. This background helps to explain the initial use of "conduit" and "content" as the horizontal axis of the map.

The addition of a second dimension using the "products" and "services" axis facilitated the portrayal of competing means of satisfying customer needs, and reflected a division of the world recognized by both economists and marketing people.

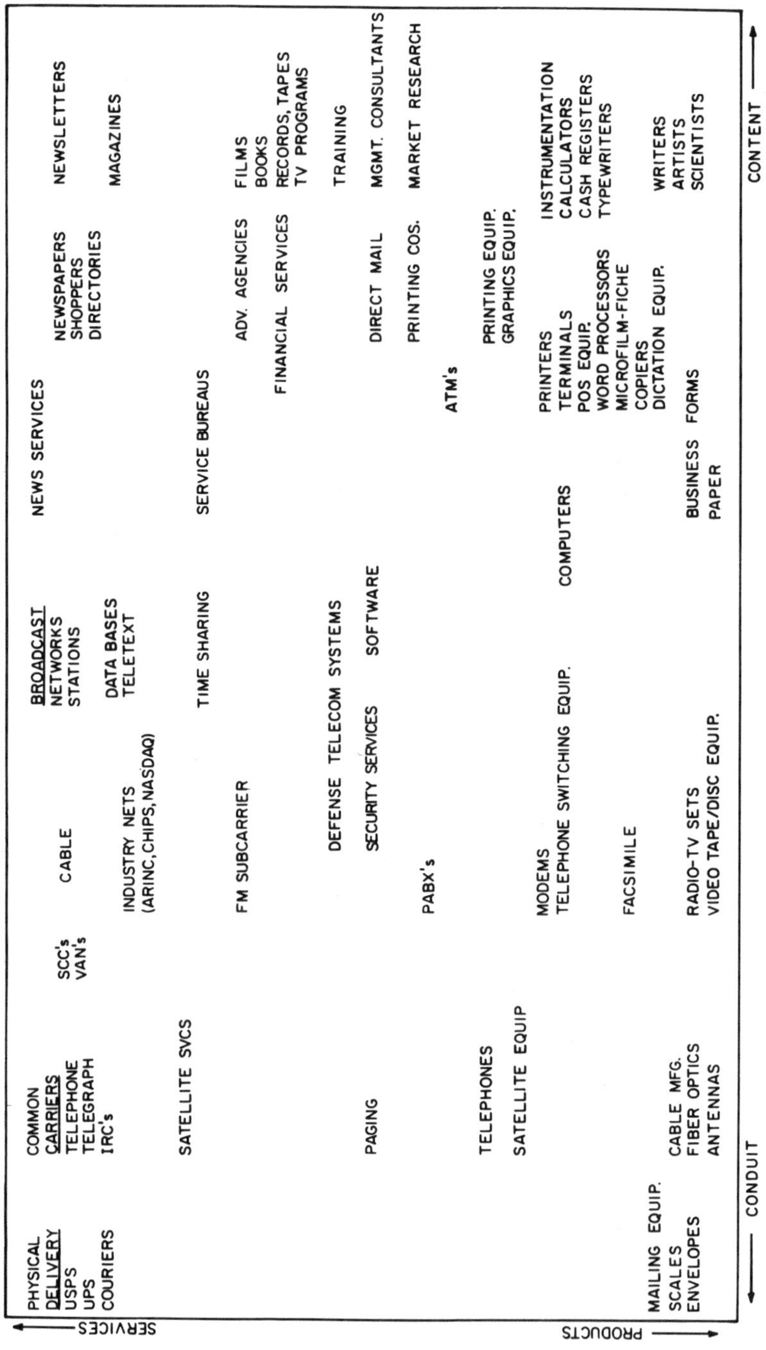

PHYSICAL DELIVERY
USPS
UPS
COURIERS

COMMON CARRIERS
TELEPHONE
TELEGRAPH
IRC's

SCC's
VAN's

CABLE

INDUSTRY NETS (ARINC, CHIPS, NASDAQ)

SATELLITE SVCS

FM SUBCARRIER

DEFENSE TELECOM SYSTEMS

SECURITY SERVICES

SOFTWARE

PAGING

PABX's

TELEPHONES

SATELLITE EQUIP

MODEMS
TELEPHONE SWITCHING EQUIP.

FACSIMILE

RADIO-TV SETS
VIDEO TAPE/DISC EQUIP.

MAILING EQUIP.
SCALES
ENVELOPES

CABLE MFG.
FIBER OPTICS
ANTENNAS

BROADCAST
NETWORKS
STATIONS

DATA BASES
TELETEXT

TIME SHARING

NEWS SERVICES

SERVICE BUREAUS

NEWSPAPERS
SHOPPERS
DIRECTORIES

NEWSLETTERS

MAGAZINES

ADV. AGENCIES

FINANCIAL SERVICES

FILMS
BOOKS
RECORDS, TAPES
TV PROGRAMS

TRAINING

MGMT. CONSULTANTS

MARKET RESEARCH

DIRECT MAIL

PRINTING COS.

ATM's

PRINTING EQUIP.
GRAPHICS EQUIP.

PRINTERS
TERMINALS
POS EQUIP.
WORD PROCESSORS
MICROFILM-FICHE
COPIERS
DICTATION EQUIP.

COMPUTERS

INSTRUMENTATION
CALCULATORS
CASH REGISTERS
TYPEWRITERS

BUSINESS FORMS
PAPER

WRITERS
ARTISTS
SCIENTISTS

SERVICES

PRODUCTS

CONDUIT

CONTENT

Figure 10.A-1   The 1979 information business map. © 1980, by President and Fellows of Harvard College.

The second version of the map (figure 10.A-2) was published in July 1980.[4] The 1980 map represented a considerable change from the 1979 version. The alterations in map entries and their placement stemmed from critical reviews by many of our associates and reflected extensive discussions with dozens of participants in the information business.

Some of the major changes between the 1979 and 1980 versions included:

1. Moving a group of items that were obviously products, such as newspapers and magazines, from the upper right quadrant to the lower right quadrant.

2. Moving writers, artists, scientists, and management consultants from the lower right to the upper right and regrouping them as professional services.

3. Moving items such as typewriters, terminals, printing equipment, and paper from the lower right to the lower left.

4. Moving computers, not surprisingly in retrospect, into the central spot on the map, as a reflection of their growing centrality in both the products–services dimension and the conduit–content plane.

Although these shifts appear remarkable now for the very fact that they were ever necessary, they indicate the importance of two fundamental and related principles: preserving a consumer orientation in the map and choosing the proper labels for the axes.

While the first map expanded the original spectrum into two dimensions, it did so in a fairly rudimentary way that conveyed a producer's orientation rather than a consumer's. The reason lay in our failure to define more completely the labels "products" and "services." On the 1979 map, "services" seemed to consist primarily of distribution mechanisms for information ouputs—particularly discrete, packaged outputs—while "products" were regarded as inputs or tools, whether human or machine. These interpretations caused substantial distortions in the 1979 map, particularly on the right-hand side. Writers and scientists showed up alongside typewriters and calculators as inputs into a production process rather than as free-standing suppliers of information in their own right. Meanwhile, the books/films/tapes block floated in the middle, midway between product and service; they were the final outputs of a production process, but they lacked the frequency of distribution implicit in a subscription-based "service" in the 1979 sense, such as a newspaper or magazine.

The choice of labels for the other axis compounded the problem. "Conduit" and "content" perpetuated the conceptual bounds of the original spectrum. "Conduit" remained exclusively a matter of transparent distribution, shunting

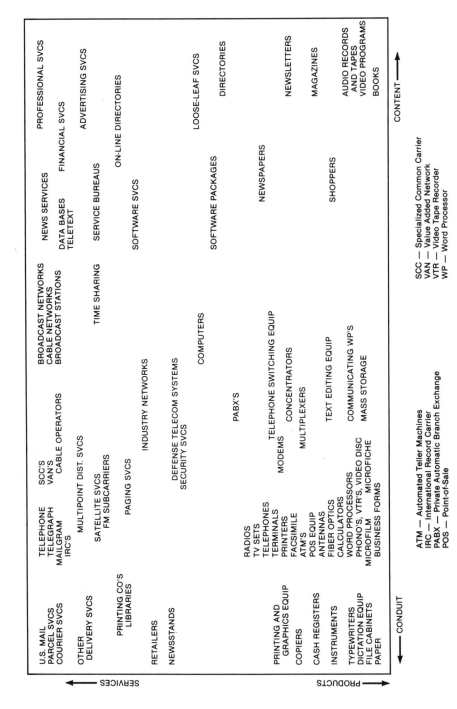

Figure 10.A-2   The 1980 information business map. © 1980, by President and Fellows of Harvard College.

all production-related entries over to the right. "Content," meanwhile, implied containing something and therefore placed undue emphasis on packaging information in some form; hence the clustering of all publishing-related entries on the right. This orientation particularly accounts for how newspapers and magazines were placed in the upper right corner: They were visible outputs of not merely a distribution mechanism but a containment process as well. The inconsistency of the original map can be seen in the fact that the middle of the content realm contained two unrelated groups, from opposite ends of the axis, put there for two different reasons—books because they were containment-based products without inherent distribution mechanisms, and consultants because they were (loosely) distribution-based services without inherent containment processes. Absent from this arrangement was any sense of what constituted an information product as opposed to an information service in the consumer's view.

While the rearrangement of the map from 1979 to 1980 perhaps foreshadowed it, the relabeling of the horizontal axis from "conduit" and "content" to "form" and "substance" ultimately came as a reaction to our growing discontent with the political baggage that "conduit" had acquired over the years.

Subsequent revisions in the map entries have been less dramatic than the initial reordering. Figure 10.A-3 is the basic map used in 1984 while figure 10.A-4 is the 1985 version. Other changes during this period reflect developments in both technology and the U.S. regulatory regime. On the technology front, for example, text-editing equipment and communicating word processors seemed to be discrete technologies in 1980. By 1984 these entries appeared to have been superseded or subsumed by word processors, modems, and computers. Conceptually, we had little problem in keeping a single entry for telephone (or perhaps voice telephony), but as the regulatory world has shifted to a division of telecommunications services along geographical rather than functional lines, we have changed the map to show local, long distance, and international telecommunications services.

Between 1985 and the latest version of the map we have made only one change, the addition of CSS SVCS (Carrier Smart Switch Services) (Carrier Smart Switch) services. We would expect, however, that the map will continue to change. Some candidates for repositioning include:

1. "Networks," in a generic sense, might begin to replace computers as the central portion of the map. The current clustering of PABXs, telephone

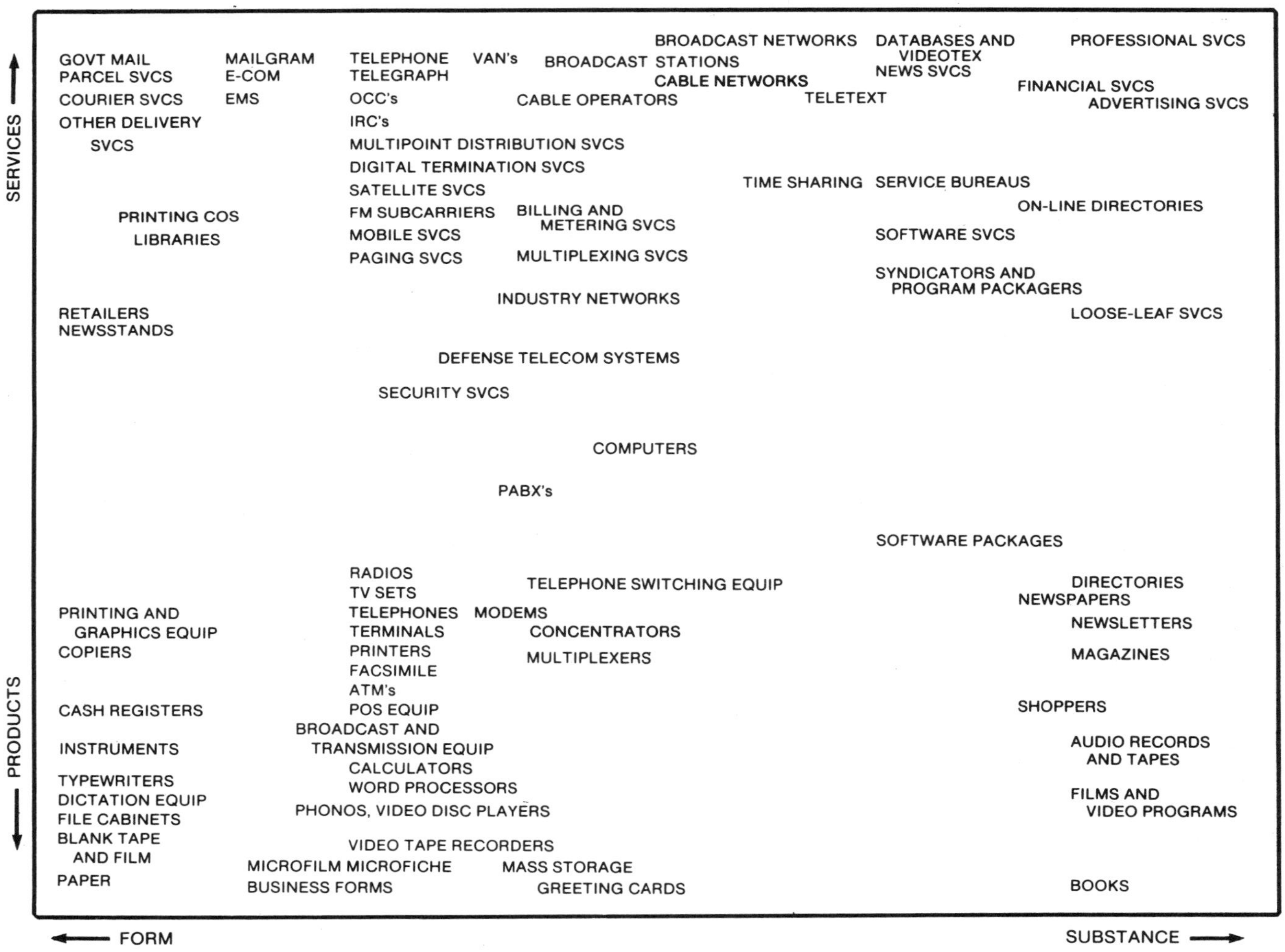

SERVICES

PRODUCTS

FORM →

← SUBSTANCE →

GOVT MAIL
PARCEL SVCS
COURIER SVCS
OTHER DELIVERY SVCS

PRINTING COS
LIBRARIES

RETAILERS
NEWSSTANDS

MAILGRAM
E-COM
EMS

TELEPHONE
TELEGRAPH
OCC's
IRC's
MULTIPOINT DISTRIBUTION SVCS
DIGITAL TERMINATION SVCS
SATELLITE SVCS
FM SUBCARRIERS
MOBILE SVCS
PAGING SVCS

INDUSTRY NETWORKS
DEFENSE TELECOM SYSTEMS
SECURITY SVCS

VAN's
CABLE OPERATORS
BILLING AND METERING SVCS
MULTIPLEXING SVCS

BROADCAST NETWORKS
BROADCAST STATIONS
CABLE NETWORKS
TELETEXT
TIME SHARING
SERVICE BUREAUS

DATABASES AND VIDEOTEX
NEWS SVCS
SOFTWARE SVCS
SYNDICATORS AND PROGRAM PACKAGERS
ON-LINE DIRECTORIES

PROFESSIONAL SVCS
FINANCIAL SVCS
ADVERTISING SVCS
LOOSE-LEAF SVCS

PRINTING AND GRAPHICS EQUIP
COPIERS

CASH REGISTERS
INSTRUMENTS
TYPEWRITERS
DICTATION EQUIP
FILE CABINETS
BLANK TAPE AND FILM
PAPER

RADIOS
TV SETS
TELEPHONES
TERMINALS
PRINTERS
FACSIMILE
ATM's
POS EQUIP
BROADCAST AND TRANSMISSION EQUIP
CALCULATORS
WORD PROCESSORS
PHONOS, VIDEO DISC PLAYERS
VIDEO TAPE RECORDERS
MICROFILM MICROFICHE
BUSINESS FORMS

TELEPHONE SWITCHING EQUIP
MODEMS
CONCENTRATORS
MULTIPLEXERS

COMPUTERS
PABX's

MASS STORAGE
GREETING CARDS

SOFTWARE PACKAGES
DIRECTORIES
NEWSPAPERS
NEWSLETTERS
MAGAZINES
SHOPPERS
AUDIO RECORDS AND TAPES
FILMS AND VIDEO PROGRAMS
BOOKS

Figure 10.A-3   The 1984 information business map. © 1984 Program on Information Resources Policy, Harvard University.

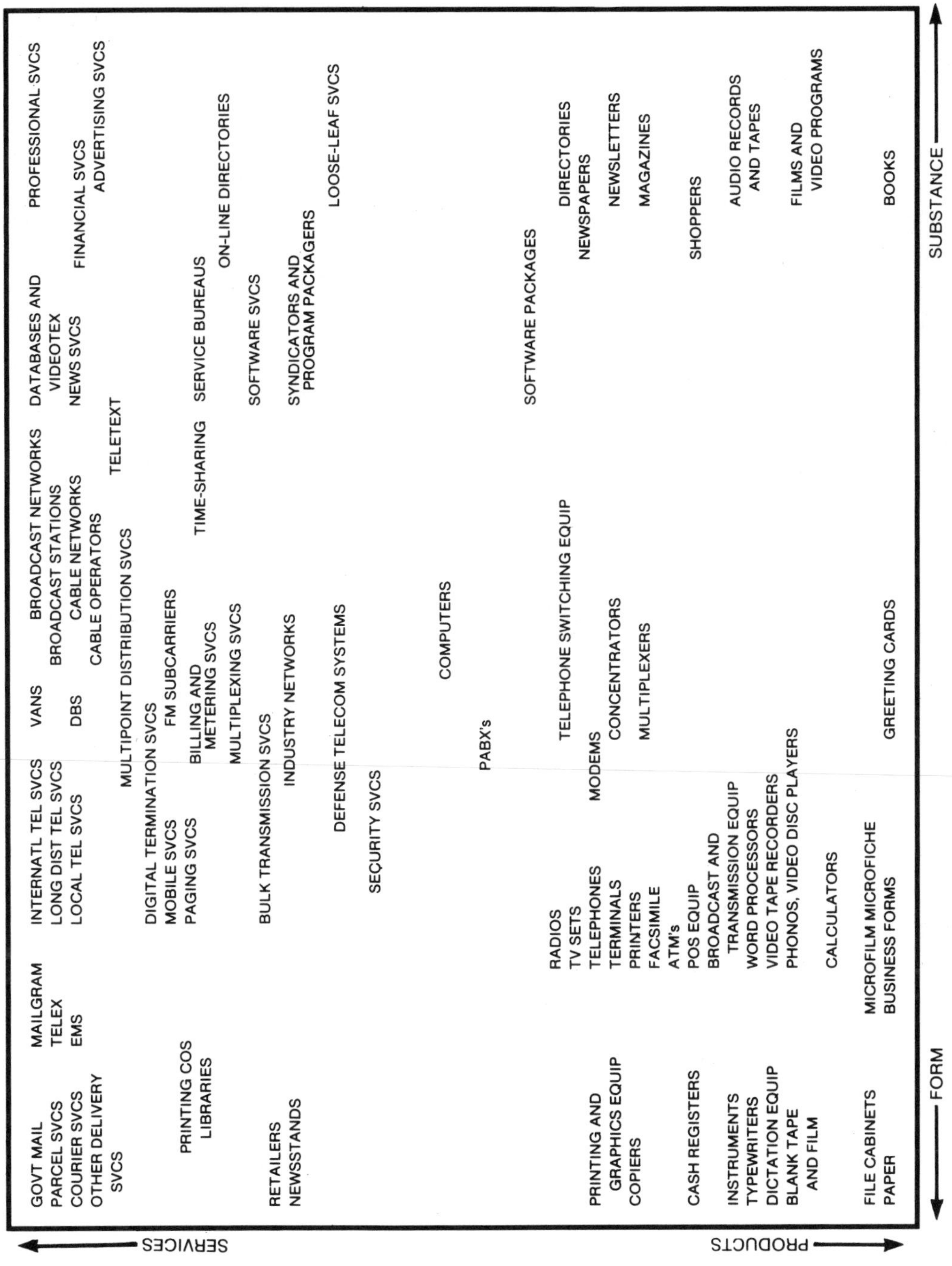

PROFESSIONAL SVCS
FINANCIAL SVCS
ADVERTISING SVCS

ON-LINE DIRECTORIES

LOOSE-LEAF SVCS

DIRECTORIES
NEWSPAPERS
NEWSLETTERS
MAGAZINES

SHOPPERS

AUDIO RECORDS
AND TAPES

FILMS AND
VIDEO PROGRAMS

BOOKS

DATABASES AND
VIDEOTEX
NEWS SVCS

SERVICE BUREAUS

SOFTWARE SVCS

SYNDICATORS AND
PROGRAM PACKAGERS

SOFTWARE PACKAGES

TELETEXT

TIME-SHARING

BROADCAST NETWORKS
BROADCAST STATIONS
CABLE NETWORKS
CABLE OPERATORS

MULTIPOINT DISTRIBUTION SVCS

FM SUBCARRIERS

BILLING AND
METERING SVCS

MULTIPLEXING SVCS

INDUSTRY NETWORKS

COMPUTERS

PABX's

TELEPHONE SWITCHING EQUIP

CONCENTRATORS

MULTIPLEXERS

MODEMS

VANS
DBS

DIGITAL TERMINATION SVCS
MOBILE SVCS
PAGING SVCS

BULK TRANSMISSION SVCS

DEFENSE TELECOM SYSTEMS

SECURITY SVCS

RADIOS
TV SETS
TELEPHONES
TERMINALS
PRINTERS
FACSIMILE
ATM's
POS EQUIP
BROADCAST AND
TRANSMISSION EQUIP
WORD PROCESSORS
VIDEO TAPE RECORDERS
PHONOS, VIDEO DISC PLAYERS

CALCULATORS

GREETING CARDS

INTERNATL TEL SVCS
LONG DIST TEL SVCS
LOCAL TEL SVCS

PRINTING COS
LIBRARIES

RETAILERS
NEWSSTANDS

MAILGRAM
TELEX
EMS

GOVT MAIL
PARCEL SVCS
COURIER SVCS
OTHER DELIVERY
SVCS

PRINTING AND
GRAPHICS EQUIP
COPIERS

CASH REGISTERS

INSTRUMENTS
TYPEWRITERS
DICTATION EQUIP
BLANK TAPE
AND FILM

FILE CABINETS
PAPER

MICROFILM MICROFICHE
BUSINESS FORMS

SERVICES

PRODUCTS

SUBSTANCE

FORM

Figure 10.A-4   The 1985 information business map. © 1985 Program on Information Resources Policy, Harvard University.

switching equipment, industry networks, and CSS services probably reflects the continuing convergence of the technologies.

2. The 1986 map shows databases and videotext as being somewhat to the left of the pure substance side of the map. This positioning is accurate within the context of the early 1980s when substance and delivery mechanisms for such services tended to be packaged together. Until recently, for example, a subscriber to Lexis/Nexis or many other database services needed a dedicated, system-specific terminal device to access the particular service. In the past few years, however, many database vendors have expanded their potential market by facilitating the use of personal computers as terminals. This trend may well argue for moving databases further to the right as more substance- and less form-oriented.

Notes

1. John F. McLaughlin with Anne Louise Antonoff, *Mapping the Information Business.* (Cambridge, MA: Program on Information Resources Policy, Harvard University, 1986.)

2. Martin Ernst has noted the "ergonomic" advantages of print over electronic presentations of information, especially for users in certain situations. See Ernst, *Electronic–Print Competition.*

3. John F. McLaughlin with Anne E. Birinyi, *Mapping the Information Business*, Working Paper W-79-8 (Cambridge, MA: Program on Information Resources Policy, Havard University, 1979).

4. John F. McLaughlin with Anne E. Birinyi, *Mapping the Information Business* (Cambridge, MA: Program on Information Resources Policy, Harvard University, 1980).

11   Size, Growth, and Trends of the Information Industries, 1987–1996

Derrick C. Huang

Size and Growth

In 1995, the total output of the "information industries," as measured by revenues, was $869 billion, up from $622 billion in 1990, a 40% increase.[1] Figure 11.1 shows the growth of each major sector of the information industry and the contribution of each sector to the total. As seen in table 11.1, along with its rise in absolute dollar terms, this group's contribution to the U.S. economy has been consistently increasing: The information industries' share of the total gross domestic product (GDP) rose from 10.8% in 1990, to 11.0% in 1992, to 12.0% in 1995.[2] From 1990 to 1995, this group has maintained a compound annual growth rate (CAGR) of 6.2%, compared with the 4.8% CAGR of the GDP.

Trends and Observations

One noticeable trend is the maturing of the overall information industries. With the exception of a few new segments, most information businesses no longer post explosive growth, but expand at steady and predictable rates, most of which are several percentage points faster than the GDP. Some older, more mature businesses, such as local telephony and publishing, even lagged the economy as a whole.

Figure 11.2 plots the size of several industries against their 1990–1995 growth rate. Not only does the large local telephony business show a modest growth rate, but the smaller though also mature media industries—newspapers;

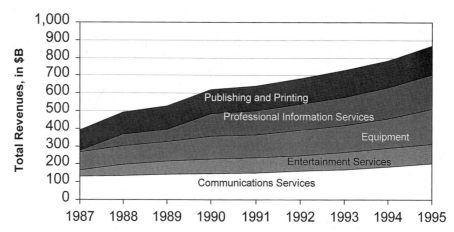

Figure 11.1   Information industries revenues, 1987–1995

broadcasting in particular—are among the slowest growing. Computer and computer services revenues are gaining on telephony as they grow at about three times the rate. Among the selected industries, cellular telephony is by far the fastest growing, having achieved the size of the cable television industry despite being a much newer business.

Despite maturing, overall it seems that the growth of information businesses has accelerated slightly from the steady pace of the 1980s and early 1990s: The total information businesses showed higher 1992-to-1995 CAGR, 8.5%, than that from 1990 to 1995 at 6.2%. Possible drivers for such increase may include growing networking requirements in restructured corporations, increasing availability and complexity of information content and means, and popularity of the Internet as a mainstream communication channel.

Two businesses—cellular/wireless telephony and satellite communications—exhibited growth rates higher than 20%, as seen in table 11.2. They share several common traits. First, their penetration has not reached a stable state. Cellular, a relatively new service, is still in its "infant" stage. Satellite communications, on the other hand, has been in existence for some time, but new applications (such as very-small-aperture-transponder [VSAT] service to private enterprises and low-earth-orbit [LEO] mobile service to global travelers) have kept the satellite growth high. Second, the functionality—mobility and remote accessibility—that they add to the traditional landline voice telephony are highly demanded and not easily replaceable by other means. And third, due

Table 11.1 Summary: Information industries, GDP, and major users (billion $)

	1987	1988	1989	1990	1991	1992	1993	1994	1995	CAGR '90–'95	CAGR '92–'95
Communications services	130.88	135.50	142.84	147.04	153.08	161.04	171.13	186.76	205.08	6.9%	8.4%
Visual, audio entertainment svc	37.32	64.08	75.10	81.37	82.64	88.73	94.46	103.43	109.60	6.1%	7.3%
Equipment—hardware/software	97.72	103.09	106.38	128.67	128.99	140.98	152.56	167.63	196.07	8.8%	11.6%
Professional information services	9.34	64.78	69.30	128.40	136.66	147.16	158.28	172.15	193.91	8.6%	9.6%
Publishing and printing	117.65	124.29	131.87	136.27	137.59	144.40	150.71	154.81	164.75	3.9%	4.5%
TOTAL information industries	392.91	491.74	525.48	621.74	638.97	682.32	727.14	784.77	869.40	6.9%	8.4%
GDP	4692.3	5049.6	5438.7	5743.8	5916.7	6224.4	6553.0	6935.7	7253.8	4.8%	5.2%
Information industries %	8.4%	9.7%	9.7%	10.8%	10.8%	11.0%	11.1%	11.3%	12.0%		
Professional services: main users	N/A	224.28	250.56	257.92	278.39	308.71	336.33	351.56	402.93	9.3%	9.3%

© 1998, Program on Information Resources Policy, Harvard University, Cambridge, Mass., U.S.A.

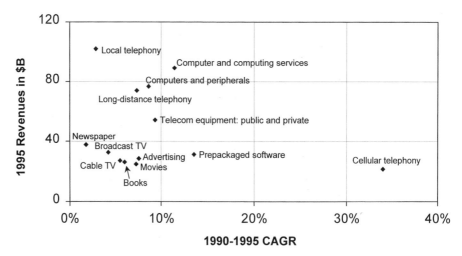

Figure 11.2 Compound annual growth rate of selected information industries

to newly available services—personal communications service (PSC) and local multipoint distribution service (LMDS) in the cellular case, and low-earth-orbit (LEO) satellite service in the satellite case—are likely to keep prices dropping and, consequently, demand growing. Together, these factors provide momentum for these two businesses to continue to grow at a faster pace than the rest of the group in the foreseeable future.

Several well-established sectors show persistent vigor with double-digit growth rates: communications equipment (table 11.3), and professional services for computer and communications (table 11.4). This trend manifests the fact that the more extensive and diverse computing and communications become, the more complex and specialized are the underlying systems that provide the services. With increasing diversity of offerings, complexity of technologies, and competition in the marketplace, the high growth rate of professional services (table 11.5) and (advanced) equipment is likely to continue.

On the other hand, some mature, traditional information sectors showed growth rates well below the rest of the industry and slower than the economy in general. Publishing and printing (table 11.6) grew 3.9% between 1995 and 1995, compared to 4.8% for GDP. The newspaper industry eked out a 1.7% annual increase. Visual and audio entertainment (table 11.7) did somewhat better, but only recorded music showed a double-digit annual growth rate.

Table 11.2　Communications services (in billion $)

	1987	1988	1989	1990	1991	1992	1993	1994	1995	1996	CAGR	
											'90–'95	'92–'95
Local telephony	84.90	85.91	87.92	89.13	91.03	92.41	95.50	98.44	102.24	108.28	2.8%	3.4%
RBOCs	64.98	65.18	66.18	67.01	67.90	68.94	71.33	73.37	74.86	78.68	2.2%	2.8%
IOCs	19.92	20.73	21.74	22.12	23.12	23.46	24.17	25.07	26.22	27.53	3.5%	3.8%
CLECs	N/A	N/A	N/A	N/A	N/A	N/A	N/A	N/A	1.16	2.06	N/M	N/M
Long distance												
Telephony	44.78	47.49	51.18	52.10	54.44	58.37	61.53	67.35	74.14	82.03	7.3%	8.3%
Cellular/wireless												
Telephony	1.20	2.10	3.73	5.00	6.41	8.77	12.25	16.06	21.62	26.42	34.0%	35.1%
Wireless messaging	N/A	N/A	N/A	N/A	N/A	N/A	N/A	1.34	1.89	2.37	N/M	N/M
Internet access	N/A	N/A	N/A	N/A	N/A	N/A	N/A	1.30	2.30	3.40	N/M	N/M
Satellite												
Communications	N/A	N/A	N/A	0.80	1.20	1.50	1.85	2.27	2.89	3.31	29.3%	24.4%
Total	130.88	135.50	142.84	147.04	153.08	161.04	171.13	186.76	205.08	225.81	6.9%	8.4%

© 1998, Program on Information Resources Policy, Harvard University, Cambridge, Mass., U.S.A.

Table 11.3 Equipment—hardware and software

	1987	1988	1989	1990	1991	1992	1993	1994	1995	CAGR '90–'95	CAGR '92–'95
Telephony CPE	1.77	2.31	2.85	3.44	3.69	3.75	3.95	4.14	4.21	4.1%	3.9%
Network-based telephony equipment	16.62	16.70	15.40	16.52	16.92	19.86	21.70	23.27	26.89	10.2%	10.6%
Broadcast, cable TV, and studio equipment	1.56	1.76	1.80	1.84	1.82	1.95	2.08	2.47	2.70	8.0%	11.5%
Miscellaneous private telecom equipment	11.40	12.21	14.02	14.73	13.07	15.16	16.20	20.08	23.12	9.4%	15.1%
Computer and peripherals	48.28	49.80	51.34	50.79	50.12	51.93	54.82	59.25	76.60	8.6%	13.8%
Prepackaged software	N/A	N/A	N/A	16.52	18.31	21.24	24.65	27.60	31.09	13.5%	13.5%
Household video equipment and media	13.08	14.95	15.55	15.86	15.93	17.37	18.94	19.77	20.24	5.0%	5.2%
Household audio equipment and media	5.02	5.36	5.43	5.59	5.53	5.75	5.96	6.54	6.71	3.7%	5.3%
Electronic gaming	N/A	N/A	N/A	3.38	3.60	3.97	4.28	4.50	4.50	5.9%	4.2%
Total	97.70	103.09	106.38	128.67	128.99	140.98	152.56	167.63	196.07	8.8%	11.6%

© 1998, Program on Information Resources Policy, Harvard University, Cambridge, Mass., U.S.A.

Table 11.4 Professional information services

	1987	1988	1989	1990	1991	1992	1993	1994	1995	CAGR '90–'95	CAGR '92–'95
Computer programming services	N/A	N/A	N/A	21.32	23.38	24.65	27.96	32.43	37.45	11.9%	15.0%
Computer systems integration	N/A	N/A	N/A	12.92	13.75	15.18	17.08	18.95	20.59	9.8%	10.7%
Computer and data processing	N/A	N/A	N/A	17.82	18.82	20.45	22.60	26.64	31.14	11.8%	15.1%
Information retrieval service	N/A	N/A	N/A	3.55	3.69	3.93	4.32	4.64	5.49	9.1%	11.8%
Credit reporting and collection	4.69	4.88	5.38	5.83	6.02	6.38	6.94	7.04	7.66	5.6%	6.3%
Direct mail service	4.66	5.62	5.98	6.96	6.55	6.80	7.61	7.90	8.47	4.0%	7.6%
Advertising	N/A	18.34	19.02	19.94	20.25	22.67	23.78	24.96	28.60	7.5%	8.0%
Postal service	N/A	35.94	38.92	40.07	44.20	47.10	47.99	49.58	54.51	6.3%	5.0%
Total	9.34	64.78	69.30	128.40	136.66	147.16	158.28	172.15	193.91	8.6%	9.6%

© 1998, Program on Information Resources Policy, Harvard University, Cambridge, Mass., U.S.A.

Table 11.5 Professional services (users of information) (in billion $)

	1988	1989	1990	1991	1992	1993	1994	1995	1996	CAGR '90–'95	'92–'95
Securities brokerage	66.10	76.86	71.36	84.89	90.58	108.84	112.76	143.41	N/A	15.0%	16.6%
Accounting, auditing, bookkeeping	29.70	33.30	34.24	35.00	37.19	40.00	43.06	49.70	56.00	7.7%	10.1%
Management consult, public relations	52.53	57.32	61.20	63.50	72.49	75.74	81.94	95.46	110.00	9.3%	9.6%
Legal services	75.95	83.07	91.12	95.00	108.44	111.75	113.80	114.36	117.00	4.6%	1.8%
Total	224.28	250.56	257.92	278.39	308.71	336.33	351.56	402.93	283.00	9.3%	9.3%

© 1998, Program on Information Resources Policy, Harvard University, Cambridge, Mass., U.S.A.

Table 11.6　Publishing and printing (in billion $)

	1987	1988	1989	1990	1991	1992	1993	1994	1995	1996	CAGR '90–'95	'92–'95
Newspaper	31.85	32.93	34.59	34.64	33.40	33.78	34.65	36.09	37.73	39.54	1.7%	3.8%
Periodicals	17.33	18.61	20.04	20.40	20.25	22.10	22.65	21.89	23.91	25.01	3.2%	2.6%
Book printing and publishing	15.88	17.14	18.15	19.45	20.46	21.38	23.43	24.44	26.03	27.53	6.0%	6.8%
Commercial printing	44.79	47.46	50.96	52.90	53.95	56.23	58.17	60.41	65.09	69.19	4.2%	5.0%
Miscellaneous publishing	7.81	8.15	8.13	8.88	9.54	10.91	11.81	11.98	11.99	12.78	6.2%	3.2%
Total	117.65	124.29	131.87	136.27	137.59	144.40	150.71	154.81	164.75	174.05	3.9%	4.5%

© 1998, Program on Information Resources Policy, Harvard University, Cambridge, Mass., U.S.A.

Table 11.7 Visual and audio entertainment services (in billion $)

	1987	1988	1989	1990	1991	1992	1993	1994	1995	1996	CAGR '90–'95	CAGR '92–'95
Movie	7.17	18.19	19.48	20.83	21.34	22.57	23.92	26.16	27.20	22.41	5.5%	6.4%
Box Office	*4.25*	*4.46*	*5.03*	*5.02*	*4.80*	*4.87*	*5.15*	*5.40*	*5.49*	*5.91*	*1.8%*	*4.1%*
Home Video Sales	*N/A*	*10.00*	*10.10*	*10.80*	*11.50*	*12.20*	*12.80*	*14.20*	*15.00*	*16.50*	*6.8%*	*7.1%*
Home Video Rentals	*2.92*	*3.74*	*4.35*	*5.01*	*5.04*	*5.50*	*5.97*	*6.56*	*6.71*	*N/A*	*6.0%*	*6.9%*
Broadcast TV	22.94	24.49	25.36	26.62	25.46	27.25	28.02	31.13	32.72	35.96	4.2%	6.3%
Cable TV	N/A	13.60	15.68	17.66	19.53	21.24	23.02	23.24	25.01	27.64	7.2%	5.6%
DBS	N/A	N/A	N/A	N/A	N/A	N/A	N/A	0.30	1.00	2.80	N/M	N/M
Broadcast radio	7.21	7.80	8.32	8.73	8.48	8.65	9.46	10.53	11.34	12.10	5.4%	9.4%
Music	N/A	N/A	6.26	7.54	7.83	9.02	10.05	12.07	12.32	12.53	10.3%	10.9%
Total	37.32	64.08	75.10	81.37	82.64	88.73	94.46	103.43	109.60	113.46	6.1%	7.3%

The Information Industries

This chapter organizes information businesses into five categories, based on the common nature of their outputs. The following is a description of all the industries included in this chapter.

1. *Communications services* facilitate communications between two or more parties, with no consideration of content:
   - local telephony, made up of revenues from regional Bell operating companies (RBOCs), independent operating companies (IOCs) in the suburban and rural areas, and the emerging competitive local exchange carriers (CLECs) that only recently started their services competing with incumbent local telephone carriers;[3,4]
   - long distance telephony, including both domestic and international long-haul services;[5]
   - cellular/wireless telephony, including cellular service, special mobile radio (SMR) service, and the newly created personal communications service (PCS);[6]
   - wireless messaging, or paging;[7]
   - Internet access, surfaced only in very recent years, offering connection to the Internet for end users;[8]
   - satellite communications, including fixed services, such as satellite links that deliver television programs from studios to affiliated stations, and mobile services, such as commercial air flight telephone service.[9]

2. *Visual and audio entertainment services* deliver visual and audio content to end users:
   - broadcast television, based on advertising revenues of networks and local stations;[10]
   - broadcast radio, based on advertising revenues;[11]
   - cable television, including basic subscription, premium channels, pay-per-view, and advertising revenues;[12]
   - direct broadcast satellite (DBS), emerged in 1994 to challenge cable television; includes basic subscription, premium channels and pay-per-view revenues;[13]

- movies, including revenues from box office and home video versions;[14]
- music.[15]

3. *Equipment—hardware and software*, are essentially the physical things that make the above services work:

   - telephony customer premise equipment (CPE), including home telephones, cellular handsets, answering devices, and fax machines;[16]
   - network-based telephony equipment, including private branch exchange (PBX), central-office switching, transport and access systems, fibers and cabling, data communications equipment, messaging systems, and so on;[17]
   - broadcast, cable TV, and studio equipment, including production and distribution equipment, both digital and analog;[18]
   - miscellaneous private telecommunications equipment, for telemetering, monitoring, navigation, and communications used by commercial, industrial, and military users;[19]
   - computer and peripherals, including all sizes of computers such as personal computers, work stations, mainframes; and computer peripherals such as disk drives, monitors, CD-ROM readers, printers, and so on;[20]
   - prepackaged software, also known as "shrink-wrap," off-the-shelf, or noncustomized software;[21]
   - household video equipment and media, including television sets, video cassette recorders (VCRs) and tapes, laser disc players and discs, camcorders, home satellites, and so on;[22]
   - household audio equipment and media, including audio systems, tape recorders, players and tapes, radios, compact disks (CDs) players and CDs, and so on;[23]
   - electronic gaming equipment and software, including the consoles and game disks, CDs, and cartridges.[24]

4. *Professional information services* create and deliver information to users, or add values to other information and communications equipment and services:

   - computer programming services;[25]
   - computer systems integration;[26]
   - networking and data processing, including such services as electronic data interchange (EDI), electronic fund transfer, electronic mail delivery, and data processing;[27]

- information retrieval services, providing information via electronic or optical means, such as tapes, disks, CDs, and Internet;[28]
- credit reporting and collection;[29]
- direct mail services;[30]
- advertising, receipts of advertising agencies;[31]
- postal services, revenues of the United States Postal Services.[32]

5. *Publishing and printing*:

- newspapers, including daily, weekly, specialized, and foreign language;[33]
- periodicals, including consumer, trade, and professional;[34]
- books, including printing and publishing;[35]
- commercial printing;[36]
- miscellaneous publishing.[37]

In addition, this chapter also includes data of industries that represent the largest users of information and communications:

- securities brokerage;[38]
- accounting, auditing, and bookkeeping;[39]
- management consulting and public relations;[40]
- legal services.[41]

Notes

1. Throughout this report, the author chose to measure the size of the information industries based on economic activities, or "monetary output." Despite the fact that this measurement captures the majority of the activities, it does miss out on certain areas. For instance, nonprofit organizations such as public television do not report revenues in the same way as for-profit, public-held companies do. Also, there are activities whose impact cannot be measured by dollar output—library service is a prime example.

   All the revenue numbers cited in this report, including the GDP, are in current dollars, not in constant (or inflation-adjusted) dollars.

2. Caution should be exercised in calculating the percentage contribution to the GDP from any industries or businesses. The GDP measures "value added," or output created net of all inputs, of each domestic industry. On the other hand, this report counts the revenues, or the gross outputs, of different businesses. As a result, summing up all information industries poses considerable "double counting" of outputs.

3. The United States Telephone Association, *Statistics of Local Exchange Carriers* (annual).

4. The New Paradigm Research Group and Connecticut Research, *1997 Annual Report on Local Telecommunications Competition*, p. 28.

5. The Federal Communications Commission, *Statistics of Common Carriers* (annual) and *Statistical Trends in Thelephony* (annual).

6. U.S. Department of Commerce, *Statistical Abstract of the United States 1997*, table 894. Data come from Cellular Telephone Industry Association.

7. Summation of the service revenues of the largest paging and wireless data firms, including American Paging, Arch Communications, Metrocall, MobilMedia, Mobil Telecom, PageMart Wireless, Paging Networks, and Pronet. Data come from Bear Stearns, *Wireless Messaging* (1998).

8. Yankee Group (Boston, MA) estimates.

9. U.S. Department of Commerce, *U.S. Industry and Trade Outlook '98*, pp. 30–31, and U.S. Department of Commerce, *U.S. Industrial Outlook '93*, pp. 28–29.

10. *Statistical Abstract 1997*, table 916, and U.S. Department of Commerce, *Statistical Abstract of the United States 1995*, table 929. Data come from McCann-Erickson in *Advertising Age*.

11. *Statistical Abstract 1997*, table 916, and *Statistical Abstract 1995*, table 929. Data come from McCann-Erickson in *Advertising Age*.

12. *Statistical Abstract 1997*, table 901, and *Statistical Abstract 1995*, table 912. Data come from Paul Kagan Associates, *The Cable TV Financial Databook*, annual.

13. *U.S. Industry and Trade Outlook '98*, p. 32, and *U.S. Industrial Outlook '93*, pp. 30–37.

14. Motion Picture Association of America, *MPAA 1996 US Economic Review: Theatric Data*, from MPAA website at www.mpaa.org. Home video sales are from *U.S. Industry and Trade Outlook '98*, p. 32, and *U.S. Industrial Outlook '93*, pp. 30–37. Home video rental data are from U.S. Bureau of the Census, *Service Annual Survey 1995*, pp. 63–64.

15. Data come from a 1997 report on the Recording Industry Association of America website at www.riaa.org.

16. Electronic Industry Association, *Electronic Market Data Book 1997*, p. 8.

17. Ibid., p. 32. Data come from U.S. Department of Commerce, by adding up telephone and telegraph equipment and fiber optic cable numbers.

18. Ibid., p. 32. Data come from U.S. Department of Commerce.

19. Ibid., p. 32. Data come from U.S. Department of Commerce.

20. Ibid., p. 66. Data come from U.S. Department of Commerce.

21. *Service Annual Survey 1995*, pp. 39–40.

22. *Electronic Market Data Book 1997*, pp. 10–12, 20, by adding up data for TV, VCR, camcorder, home satellite, and video tapes.

23. *Electronic Market Data Book 1997*, p. 8, by adding up data for home audio systems, portable audio systems, radios, and tapes.

24. *Electronic Market Data Book 1997*, p. 8.

25. *Service Annual Survey 1995*, pp. 39–40.

26. Ibid.

27. Ibid.

28. Ibid.

29. Ibid.

30. Ibid.

31. *U.S. Industry and Trade Outlook '98*, pp. 47–49, and *U.S. Industrial Outlook '93*, pp. 52–54.

32. *Statistical Abstract 1997*, table 913, and *Statistical Abstract 1995*, table 924. Data come from *Annual Reports of the Postmaster General*, annual.

33. *U.S. Industry and Trade Outlook '98*, pp. 22–25, and *U.S. Industrial Outlook '93*, pp. 21–24.

34. Ibid.

35. Ibid., for both book printing and book publishing.

36. Ibid.

37. Ibid.

38. *Statistical Abstract 1997*, table 826. Data come from Securities and Exchange Commission annual reports.

39. *U.S. Industry and Trade Outlook '98*, pp. 3–49, and *U.S. Industrial Outlook '93*, pp. 52–54.

40. *U.S. Industry and Trade Outlook '98*, pp. 4–49, and *U.S. Industrial Outlook '93*, pp. 54–54.

41. *U.S. Industry and Trade Outlook '98*, pp. 46–49, and *U.S. Industrial Outlook '93*, pp. 53–54.

12   Managing Information: Back to Basics

Benjamin M. Compaine and John F. McLaughlin

Progress in electronics has made the collecting, storing, manipulating, analyzing, and distribution of information faster, cheaper, and easier than ever. And every organization seems to be taking advantage of this progress. Given the rapid change, this may be a good time to take stock of where we are and how we are coping with management information. If managers are not to be overwhelmed by the torrent of information coming their way, they must be more attuned than ever to making sure that the information they have is the information they need, from whatever source makes sense.

Take as a start these two hypothetical examples.

The chief executive officer of a Midwestern manufacturer was perplexed. "Our management information system is terrific. I know what it cost me for every nut and bolt assembled on any shift. Not one of my competitors, here or abroad, can have a better handle on costs. But I'm getting clobbered. My market share is declining monthly."

Eight hundred miles away in New England, two friends and business associates, neither quite 30 years old, at that moment could have been toasting a recently completed successful public stock offering. In storybook fashion, they started their electronics business in the basement. "I just knew this was gonna be a success," gushed Founder One. "Everyone I ran into at the computer users group was complaining that no one could help them with this problem. Well, we did."

Such vignettes have become almost cliches today: the depression of the old manufacturing industries and the proliferation of successful high-technology firms. But these specific stories were conceived to focus on a poorly understood piece of the industrial story. For while the old, established businesses were busy installing and perfecting exquisite formal management information systems (MIS), the new wave of entrepreneurs has been successful by vacuuming up intelligence from the world outside their organization and turning the insights gained thereby into new products and services. To be sure, these entrepreneurs will soon find that they have to add a formal management information system to stay competitive. But it does not necessarily follow that they will abandon the informal intelligence-gathering function that got them their first $100 million. The older businesses would do well to pay attention to the ways of many of these upstarts.

Today, the stakes for having the right information in a timely fashion are higher than ever. Information available via compunications (computers tied together through telecommunications) is not only a cost-savings or reporting mechanism. It has been recast as the output of a "decision-support system" or the raw material for providing new opportunities for mature businesses. There appears to be a new level of consciousness of the role of information in organizations. Nonetheless, there is a missing link in the themes in the current body of advice. They tend to focus on formal systems at the expense of an examination of how individual decision makers actually get and use information in their daily rounds.

This analysis describes why we believe that decision makers in organizations of all sizes and classifications should consider their priorities and their approaches to the information-gathering function. It explicitly identifies and describes the roles of "unk-unks" and the "fog of war" as factors that cloud the decision-making process even in the face of the tidal wave of information that seems to be flowing into the workplace. Finally, we suggest some general strategies for understanding and coping with the expanded role of information in modern organizations.

Information as a Resource—the 5% Edge

Today's managers hear repeatedly that they have been moving into an information society or information economy. It is perhaps more accurate—and consistent with past formulations to refer instead to an information-*intensive* society. That is, the Industrial Revolution was largely a case of substituting energy from minerals for that of people and animals—a shift from labor to capital-intensive production. For the past 30 years or so, society has been in the midst of an evolution (in the grand sweep of history it may some day qualify as its own revolution) in which information is being substituted for both energy/labor and material/capital with greater intensity than ever. Anyone can see this in the information-processing power of computers that are able to be far more accurate and comprehensive than the clerks they replaced in billing functions. Similarly, the information processed by microprocessor-controlled automobile engines increases their efficiency, thereby reducing energy needs. And computer-aided-design programs that run on desk-top computers not only replace a room full of drafting tables and draftsmen, but change the traditional relationship between draftsman and engineer.

Information has always been a resource, but in earlier eras, for the most part, it has been a poorly understood component compared to other, more tangible resources. Today, information is easier to conceptualize on an equal footing with other resources. That is, we intuitively know that without energy, nothing would happen, or without material, there is nothing. Similarly, but perhaps less obviously, without information, all is chaos. A few of today's decision makers are beginning to understand and internalize this notion. To work smartly and competitively, managers will have to institutionalize the concept of information as a resource.

For in today's highly competitive, often fast-moving global economy, having only a small edge in the timing or reliability of information may be the difference between an organization's surviving and thriving. Traders in many commodities have known the advantage of having just a few minutes—or even seconds—lead time in a market swing to buy in or bail out. Such an advantage—in strategic as well as practical information—is becoming a leading factor for a broader range of industries.

Keeping ahead of the competition does not necessarily require one to be very much better than the rest. In business, it may mean being 5% better over time. There is the story of the two hikers who spot a grizzly bear stalking them. One hiker sits down and takes off his hiking boots, replacing them with his running shoes. "What good will that do?" asks his companion. "You can't outrun a bear." Lacing up his Nikes, the friend responds, "I don't have to outrun the bear. I just have to outdistance you."

A broadened view of information as a resource is the similar edge for the manager.

The current era is not the first in which changing information technology has had a widespread impact on organizations and their managers. Alfred Chandler points out this idea in his book *The Visible Hand* in referring to the growth in the complexity of organizations in the 19th century.

Metalworking and textile factories were the two most complex industrial organizations in the United States in the first half of the 19th century. They were viewed as the prototypes for the increasing sophistication of factory management and organization. But by today's standards they were small, relatively simple organizations. The largest metalworking plant in the United States in 1815 was the Springfield Armory, with 250 employees.[1] The largest woolen manufacturers in the world in 1850, Bay State Mills in Lawrence, Mass., had only 2200 employees.[2] But accelerating industrialization and national markets required larger, far more complex organizations. Thus, by 1891, the Pennsylvania Railroad, for example, grew into an organization with more than 110,000 employees.[3]

Many changes had to occur to allow managers to operate organizations of that size and to function reasonably effectively. Among the information-related developments were the invention and spread of the telegraph, the expansion of the postal service, and the development of the telephone. Other less-heralded but equally important changes occurred to permit the needed growth of internal correspondence, such as typewriters, mimeographs, and the vertical filing system.[4] Thus, developments in information technology created the conditions that allowed organizational structures to respond to the production economies made possible by the Industrial Revolution.

Role of Intelligence

At its most theoretical level, intelligence refers to all the information about what's happening in the universe, including developments in politics, technology, sociology, economics, and so on. In effect, we are talking about a rather mind-boggling Universe of All Possible Discourse, which, for convenience, will be referred to from here on as UAPD (figure 12.1). Fortunately for their effectiveness, if not their sanity, decision makers in an organization have a much smaller universe of decision making, that which is bounded largely by the decision maker's institution.

Both of these worlds are in flux, especially the UAPD, which is constantly expanding as more information comes on the scene all the time. Decision makers have to keep an eye not only on their own small universes but on the UAPD as well, looking for information useful in managing the organization while bringing it into consonance with the threats and opportunities presented by the UAPD.

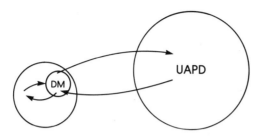

Figure 12.1   Intelligence for decision making. © 1986 President and Fellows of Harvard College, Program on Information Resources Policy.

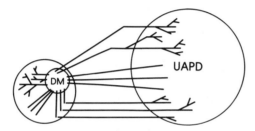

Figure 12.2   Complex webs of systems. © 1986 President and Fellows of Harvard College, Program on Information Resources Policy.

A few managers work in organizations that are large enough to affect the universe of discourse. An IBM may be able to establish a *de facto* technical standard, for example. But most managers, most of the time, are successful if they can keep out of the way of threats or even leverage a minor opportunity. Part of what managers must do is find out what is going on in their own organizations and in the world outside, and try to bring the former into some sort of equilibrium with the latter to achieve some desired end.

What successful managers end up with is a complex web of systems for intelligence gathering, illustrated by figure 12.2. This network encompasses those in the organization charged with gathering and reporting information on what is happening within the organization. Some people may be charged with looking at the broader universe of discourse and feeding back to decision makers their views of that world. At the same time, decision makers are observing both the organization and the outside world themselves to make their own evaluation of what is going on.

Sources of Decision-Making Information

Decision makers utilize this complex web of systems as an information network, sometimes consciously, generally reflexively. Often however, this web is an underutilized tool. Managers have contact with 10 to 20 superiors, including the chief executive officer, who in turn has a board of directors to contend with. They have dozens of peers inside and outside the organization as well as within and without the industry. These are people they have grown up with and have been associated with, all of whom serve as sources of information. Managers talk with their immediate subordinates, typically 5 to 15 of these, as well as 50 to 500 of their subordinates farther down the line.[5] Many of these contacts are continuing sources of information.

General managers also have a myriad of contacts outside the organization and industry: bankers, brokers, and analysts—all possible sources of financial information. There may be hundreds of suppliers and customers, competitors, the press, government regulators or other officials, and the general public as well.

Effective decision makers constantly exercise this network of contacts. In a five-minute conversation on the telephone with just one of these sources, a manager can cover a dozen topics. In other cases, a manager can be very successful in soaking up intelligence in the process of walking down the hallway and taking the elevator, asking questions of people on the run.

Sources of information fall into three categories of intelligence sources: those *inside* the organization, those *outside* the organization, and the *decision maker's own knowledge*—those things he already knows or is convinced he knows. Much of the decision maker's knowledge probably came from inside or outside information sources at some earlier time, but it becomes part of the storehouse of knowledge—not always accurate—that managers accumulate over the years.

These sources may come via either formal or informal processes. Figure 12.3 summarizes the types of sources in each cell of the model. The formal processes are those that generally form part of the consciously designed organizational nervous system. The formal inside sources in particular have been the subject of most study and theory. The informal side of organizations has been researched, but typically from the viewpoint of understanding patterns of authority, responsibility, motivation, or power. Information sources have been at best an incidental sidelight.

	Inside Sources	Outside Sources	Decision Maker's Knowledge
Formal Processes	Management Information Systems Scanning Special Studies	Media Trade Associations Consultants	Education Training
Informal Processes	Water-Cooler: "What Do You Think, Joe?"	Golf Course Cocktail Parties	Experience

Figure 12.3 Sources of decision making information. © President and Fellows of Harvard College, Program on Information Resources Policy.

The informal side of intelligence gathering, however, although not as easily described as the formal MIS, seems to play a far more crucial role than has been appreciated up to now. Many of the people who traditionally worry about designing management information systems seem to believe that the chief executive officer should not really get information other than what is filtered through the formal system—or at least should not base any decisions on such spurious information. If this assertion does accurately characterize actual attitudes on the part of users or suppliers of intelligence, then it betrays a gross misunderstanding of the validity or legitimacy of other intelligence sources. The outcome for decision makers could be—or has been—disastrous.

Perhaps the clearest example of the consequences of focusing on the top left-hand box of the matrix at the expense of the informal processes can be seen in the U.S. domestic automobile industry. By the 1960s, Detroit had developed a legendary expertise in cost accounting. With the help of MIS, the auto makers knew what it cost to put a nut on the wheel of any model made in any plant on any shift on any day. Such attention to detail was perhaps an obsession. Meanwhile, imports had passed 10% of the U.S. market as early as 1968 and hit 15% in 1970.[6] Auto industry executives cannot hide behind excuses of being suddenly blind-sided by the quadrupling of gasoline prices after the Arab oil embargoes in 1973 and 1979.

During this time, U.S. auto executives would most likely have gotten a better payback if they had spent more time going to cocktail parties in San Diego or

Atlanta and heard why people loved their Toyotas or were willing to pay a premium price for a BMW. Less time spent on cost accounting and more time spent chatting with peers and customers outside their industry would have been a great improvement for managers at Ford, GM, and Chrysler. To be sure, too many businesses have folded because the chairman spent too much time with clients at the golf course believing that he was getting important information, while not paying attention to his cash flow situation. Nevertheless, managers err too often toward the other extreme, not recognizing the legitimacy of all sources of information.

Inside vs. Outside: Comparing Managers to Entrepreneurs

Managers in large, bureaucratic organizations have access to all sorts of inside information, both formal and informal. Entrepreneurs, by definition, start without an organization. Thus they depend almost exclusively on outside information as well as on their own knowledge. As the entrepreneur's successful venture grows, he risks becoming a captive of the organization's newly generated inside information.

This is a phenomenon seen in the magazine publishing business, among others. Before a publisher such as Time Inc. launches a new magazine, for example, an idea works its way through a magazine development group. It goes through an analysis of likely revenue streams based on advertising and circulation projections. It appears in mocked-up versions. All along, Time's managers are drawing on their inside information sources as well as on their decision-makers' knowledge. And they may spend millions of dollars before an issue is published.

The magazine publishing entrepreneur, on the other hand, must beguided more from the outside: from consultants who are working with greater abstractions in their formulas than the Time Inc. insiders. They face more direct pressure from bankers or investors than an internally financed venture (only remotely mindful of stockholders). In general, with fewer financial resources, the entrepreneur must act heavily on hunches, insights, or personal knowledge (which is why video magazines tend to be founded by video buffs or computer magazines by hackers). In the end, the literature on magazine start-ups shows that relatively low-budget entrepreneurial ventures can succeed (e.g., *Byte*), while well-funded corporate start-ups often fail (e.g., Gruner & Jahr's *Geo*).

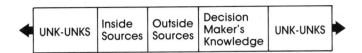

Figure 12.4 But every decision is made within a context of "unknown-unknowns." © 1986 President and Fellows of Harvard College, Program on Information Resources Policy.

Added Complications: Unk-Unks and the Fog of War

Inside, outside, and decision-makers' knowledge as categories are a necessary but simplified approach to the intelligence problem. They represent set points in that Universe of All Possible Discourse. Figure 12.4 adds to these observable categories another set of unilluminated points—the "unknown-unknowns," or the things you don't know you don't know. These are the factors that decision makers did not even realize existed, let alone perceive as having bearing on their decision.

Unknown-unknowns sometimes have more bearing on a problem than the factors that decision makers already know about or know they need to know about. This phenomenon was discovered a few years ago by the newspaper industry managers when they learned—almost too late—that the movement in Congress and the Federal Communications Commission to permit AT&T to enter competitive, non-telephone businesses exposed publishers to potential competition for their profitable classified advertising from an electronic Yellow Pages. Similarly, commercial banks took it on the chin when money-market mutual funds came along, and bankers are still reeling from various unforeseen international events (such as the precipitous drop in oil prices) that affect their own portfolios in ways they never anticipated.

"The fog of war" is a concept that, despite its military origins, applies as neatly to all sorts of decision making. Military strategist Karl von Clausewitz said, "A great part of the information in war is contradictory, a still greater part is false, and by far the greatest part is somewhat doubtful."[7] Thus, in any given decision there are relative degrees of what decision makers actually know, whether it's from inside or outside sources or from what decision makers know or think they know.

Managers know that they must make decisions based on incomplete or imperfect information. If the decision is important enough and if the time horizon is such that the manager can devote appropriate resources to it, the unk-unks and fog of war can be reduced. The value of the concepts of unk-unks and the fog of war is that they suggest how much—or how little—knowledge can actually be encompassed in any given decision.

Managers who have longevity in a particular job or area of their organization would therefore have an advantage over those who are rotated to positions in different functions on a regular basis. The former have reduced the unk-unk territory over the years while expanding the decision-makers' knowledge. The latter are constantly moving up the learning curve in a new functional job. It may be argued that these less-experienced managers are less able to cope with the fog of the competitive wars and therefore liable to make more mistakes.

Although there are strong arguments for creating generalists by moving fast-track managers from finance to operations to marketing and so on, there may be a substantial cost in efficiency. Among the most prominent organizations that have taken the rotation concept the furthest were AT&T and the U.S. military. From the viewpoint of managers, AT&T was an attractive place to work because of this policy, including stints with its old operating companies, then back to the parent. Today, having been thrust into the competitive environment, AT&T has found itself able to cut tens of thousands from its managerial ranks. It is not coincidental that free-wheeling job rotation has been drastically reduced.

The military, like the old AT&T, has a similar monopoly organization approach. Its officers at all levels spend two or three years in each assignment. In the game of getting their ticket punched in the proper areas, officers move among diverse commands. Even as they play the game, many complain that they are moved out just about the time they learn their jobs. Anyone familiar with the Pentagon knows the frustration of dealing with a new officer just when his predecessor had been educated. Meanwhile, the people above and below are being moved around as well, so there are few sources of reliable informal information.

Changing Mixes and Information Mismatches

For any decision, there is a unique bundle of inside information, outside information, decision-maker's knowledge, and unk-unks. The specific mix will vary with one's place in the hierarchy, as well as with the nature of the decision itself.

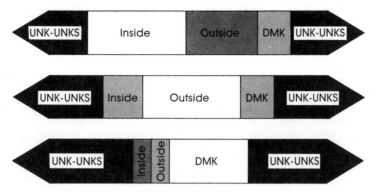

Figure 12.5 The mix changes for each decision in each organization. © President and Fellows of Harvard College, Program on Information Resources Policy.

Unfortunately, many formal information systems do not recognize this. It is not easy, or perhaps even possible, to design a system to cover all events for all possible situations. The typical decision in the typical organization—illustrated by the bottom bar in figure 12.5—is made without a great deal of reliance on anything but the decision-maker's knowledge.

Managers don't give most of the relatively routine decisions much thought. It is the exceptional problem for which the decision maker recognizes that lack of sufficient intelligence and the importance of the decision require spending some resources to gather specific information.

However, the most difficult type of decision from an intelligence perspective is one in which more than one person is involved. In such cases, it is not unusual to have mismatches among each person's mix of inside, outside, decision-maker's knowledge, and unk-unks, as illustrated in figure 12.6.

For example, in a new product introduction, the three decision makers may include marketing, production, and financial managers. The first may want to maximize the number of styles, sizes, or whatever. Marketers are conscious of customers and would tend to be high on outside information. The production manager, on the other hand, wants to keep the number of machine set-ups as low as possible and has to contend with work flows and scheduling. There is a high degree of reliance on inside information. The financial manager wants to know the timing of expenditures for equipment, inventory build-up, promotion outlays, and cash flow. He has to coordinate all of this activity with other cash demands, lines of credit from bankers, and so on.

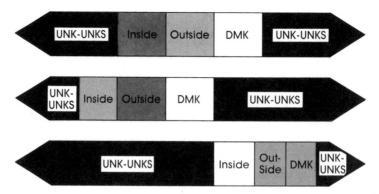

Figure 12.6   And complex decisions in large organizations may entail complete information mismatches. © 1986 President and Fellows of Harvard College, Program on Information Resources Policy.

These three decision makers also have different ranges of unknown-unknowns. The production manager's own knowledge—about, say, the difficulty of using a particular dye to produce a particular shade that the market manager decides is essential—may be a complete unknown to the marketer, who never even thought of this step as a problem. Neither of these managers may have been aware that the demands of the company's seasonal line of credit make it unlikely that the funds will be available for a Spring start-up. Hence, there are three (or more) decision makers optimizing on totally different factors in the decision, and each dealing with totally different sources of information.

This scenario describes a common type of situation in organizations, one that is usually handled by having committees or task forces drawing on representatives of the departments involved. Nevertheless, two points need be made. First, the greater the mismatches in the information base of those involved in the decision, the more cumbersome is the communication among them and hence the longer it will take to get to the point where all parties understand one another. What is one manager's own knowledge and thus does not seem to need any elaboration is another manager's unknown-unknown. Neither will therefore raise the issue, even though it may constitute an essential assumption somewhere down the line. One can readily foresee serious consequences for the decision and any action it promotes. The flip side of this dilemma is that organizations that try to minimize mismatches by involving in a decision a homogeneous group of managers who all "speak the same language" may risk missing some important questions that would be raised by someone with a different set of information and unknown-unknowns.

For example, a publishing company that offers an electronic on-line information service was deciding on adding a new database. The initial meetings involved the editorial and the business development managers. These two shared similar information sources and language. At the last minute, they included the director of computer hardware in their decision. After they brought him up to speed on what they were about to do, he presented them with some technical questions that made them rethink their decision. The editorial and business development managers had assumed that the new database would fit into the existing structure. The technical manager knew it would not be so simple.

The second point of the information mismatch is that information systems need to be changed to fit the need of the incumbent managers. An analogy is climbing into a rental car that was last driven by someone six inches taller or shorter than you. Keeping the seat in the old position would be not only uncomfortable but perhaps dangerous as well.

This is most obvious at the level of the chief executive. A particular information system may have been designed for good reason for a chief executive who came from a financial background. The formal reports generated by the management information system, the outside newsletters, and subscription services, etc., that got fed to the CEO were weighted with financial data, analysis, interpretation. When a succeeding CEO from a different background inherits this information system, no one remembers why it was structured the way it was, and it continues to spew forth information that may be inappropriate or ill suited to the new decision maker. It may be only after months or, even worse, after a crisis that the new manager recognizes the need for new sources of information.

Indeed, the problem of information mismatches is often most critical in crisis situations. In the most extreme crises, those involving national security and the president of the United States, the people whom a president will most likely want around him in the Situation Room are not an assortment of experts whom he has never met before and who all speak different "languages." The president is apt to surround himself with the cronies who share his information sources and with whom he can speak without having to explain himself or risk being misunderstood. The danger lies in missing some unknown-unknowns, but that may be the lesser of the risks in a fast-breaking crisis.

Few other organizations would face crises of national security magnitude. But the principle of the trade-offs between shared information sources with efficiency in decision making, on the one hand, and overlapping information sources with reduction of unknown-unknowns on the other hand is a reality, if largely unrecognized, for all decision makers.

Optimizing Information for Decision Makers

An old tenet deserves a fresh look here: the assumption that as soon as an organization starts to design a formal institutional information system, it should begin by *eliminating* information sources. There are good reasons for doing so. The formal system does not need to reinvent many of the things that the system handles every day. These are the routine items for which computers and the formal institutional information systems were set up in the first place. The goal is to leave time available to decision makers to select *ad hoc* from that information which is most needed for the less routine decisions. The combination of the formal/routine with the informal/*ad hoc* process aims to minimize nasty surprises after decisions have been made, or to recognize that some action should have been taken in the first place.

But decision makers in large, structured organizations need to know when to supplement or even bypass their formal MIS with intelligence gathered via informal channels. There remains the question of whether one can "institutionalize" an informal information process without thereby encasing it in the formal management information system, and indeed whether "institutionalizing" would be a step forward in any event. How can managers navigate through the thicket just described? Unfortunately, in the area of information for decision making, management remains every bit as much an art as a science. We have no stone tablets with the six points that will improve the reader's success. There is no single system that fits all circumstances.

Having said this, we believe that several generalizations can provide some help to managers who want to enhance the decision-making process in their organizations.

1. The highest-order generalization is, above all, be flexible. Individual managers must be not only permitted but encouraged to modify the information flow that comes to them when they move into a new position. They must be allowed to adjust the driver's seat to their own measurements.

2. Specifically, individual managers should consciously make part of their current job, and part of any future position, an early evaluation of what mix of information sources they have available, they now use, and they might use. Managers should know something about the background, strengths, and weaknesses of the person they replaced as a starting point for having some understanding of what information sources their predecessor might have been partial to or tended to ignore. Managers should then rearrange their own mix of sources based on their own set of decision-maker's knowledge. This might involve ordering up different reports from the MIS, stopping others, changing the flow of newsletters, even seeking out a new opponent for racquetball to fill in a gap in the informal outside information.

3. Decision makers should seek to identify as many unk-unks as feasible given the gravity of a decision. In most daily decisions this process is irrelevant. But for those decisions involving commitment of substantial resources, managers might want to take some extra steps to seek out information not only from consultants, but from friends, associates in other parts of the firm, and so on.

4. When there is time, decision makers should spend a few extra minutes thinking about the mix of managers involved in a major decision. Do they come from diverse backgrounds in the organization? Has the decision maker bought a quick consensus at the expense of involving others in the process who might ask the critical question that no one else thought to ask?

5. Re-evaluate any organizational policies of playing musical chairs with executives. Producing generalists is wonderful if the organization can afford it. But there is great economy and efficiency in having a cadre of managers who know their jobs well and know intuitively where to go to get the information they need for a decision.

6. Nothing in the foregoing should be viewed as being particularly critical of the formal management information system itself. Knocking traditional MIS approaches was not our objective—and such criticism occurs so often it has become almost a cliche. Rather, managers need to recognize that such systems fill one square in the matrix. Formal systems are useful so long as managers understand they don't cover the entire area of decision-relevant information.

Coincidentally, in the course of this work we have also been impressed by the robustness of the common telephone as an important management tool for informed intelligence as well as for command and control. Evidence keeps mounting that successful managers use the telephone with great effectiveness in scooping up timely information, where and when it is needed, with relatively little wasted motion. In a telephone conversation with someone he or she knows, a manager may glean more information than from pages of memos. A manager can pick up the telephone and reach practically any place on earth without concern for whether it's part of the organization's predetermined information system.

Work on information as a resource is still in a developmental stage. At this point its primary value is in raising this notion of the range of sources of legitimate information and in making managers more aware of the information process in their organizations, beyond the use of formal institutional sources. The overwhelming tendency of most managers and academics in the past 30 years has been to concentrate on the inside, formal sources of information.

Notes

1. Alfred D. Chandler, Jr., *The Visible Hand: The Managerial Revolution in American Business* (Cambridge, Mass: The Belknap Press of Harvard University Press, 1977), p. 72.

2. U.S. Bureau of the Census, *The 8th Census of the United States Manufactures* (Washington, D.C., 1865), p. xxxii.

3. Chandler, p. 204.

4. See JoAnne Yates, "From Press Book and Pigeonhole to Vertical Filing: Revolution in Storage and Access Systems for Correspondence," *The Journal of Business Communication*, 19:3, pp. 5–26.

5. John P. Kotter describes these relationships in *The General Managers* (New York: The Free Press, 1982).

6. *Statistical Abstracts of the United States: 1984*, 104th Edition (Washington, D.C.: 1984), p. 575.

7. Karl von Clausewitz, *War, Politics, and Power*, ed. Edward N. Collins (Chicago: Henry Regnery Company, 1962), p. 128.

13   Knowledge As a Strategic Business Resource

William H. Read

Knowledge and business have long been linked with each other. Benjamin Franklin once said: "An investment in knowledge pays the best interest." Fundamentally, general managers of business enterprises strive to successfully integrate three basic resources. They combine knowledge with materials and energy to produce goods and services.

Achieving the right mix of these resources depends in part on the price and performance of each of these resources at a particular time and in a particular market. Relatively inexpensive and abundant sources of energy, for example, have enabled industrial-age managers to produce goods on a mass basis that had not previously been possible.

In the Information Age, energy, as well as materials, remains vitally important, but knowledge is the basic resource that has been gaining renewed attention. During the 1990s, major management consulting firms have created knowledge practices, a number of large business organizations have appointed Chief Knowledge or Chief Learning Officers, knowledge conferences were popular, and business journals regularly published articles on various aspects of the topic.

The goals of this chapter are to present an overview of knowledge as a strategic business resource, and then, drawing on a survey of contemporary scholarly writings, to present five categories of knowledge resources that are common to all firms and to suggest how each of these resources can be effectively managed.

A disclaimer is offered at the outset. This paper does not attempt to distinguish between information and knowledge. What a front-line worker may "know" is often "information" or even just "data" to corporate staff, yet the substance is the same. Philosophers, dating back to Aristotle and Plato, have engaged the definition question and no lasting consensus has emerged. What may be said is that every firm has a set of intangible, intellectual assets that comprise a basic resource that this paper refers to as knowledge resources.

Knowledge Resources

Daniel Bell identified knowledge-based organizations as the leading type of enterprise in postindustrial societies.[1] They are distinctive from industrial-age organizations, Bell said, in that they rely principally on the intangible intellectual capital of their employees, not on the manual efforts of semi-skilled workers. They rely as well on advanced information technologies to modernize their business processes. And their orientation is to the future, with emphasis on models, simulations, and system analysis. The modern firm, Bell said, no longer is the product of a "talented tinkerer" like Thomas Edison, but is an enterprise in which *"knowledge and information become the strategic and transforming resources."*[2] (Emphasis added)

It is obvious that knowledge is a strategic resource for industries like software engineering that rely on intellectual property for their prosperity. But as Walter B. Wriston has observed, even a traditional industry, like steel, can benefit by improved management of its intangible resources: "A piece of steel, whether raw or as part of a new automobile or skyscraper, is very different today from what it was a generation ago. It still contains a lot of iron mixed with other metals, but it contains a great deal more information."[3]

Has knowledge become what management expert Peter F. Drucker terms "the basic economic resource"?[4] Favorable results flowing from total quality management, reengineering, self-directed teams, and the creation of learning organizations provide anecdotal evidence in support of Drucker's thesis.

However, economic theories are few.

Among those pursuing an economic theory is Paul Romer. A proponent of "New Growth Theory," he contends that the emerging economy is based on ideas more than objects and that "Ideas and knowledge are abundant and that they build on each other and can be reproduced cheaply or at no cost at all."[5] If enterprises keep finding new ideas, keep innovating, keep discovering, then there are no limits to growth. New Growth Theory holds that the process of creating ideas and innovative techniques will fuel long-run improvements and sustain an ever-improving standard of firm competitiveness.

The idea deviates from classic economic theory in which wealth-creation is the result of the efficient allocation of scarce resources—financial capital, land, and labor. Moreover, it contradicts *The Principles of Scientific Management*, the treatise published in 1911 by Frederick Winslow Taylor.[6] Efficient industrial organization, Taylor argued, came with the "substitution of a science for the individual judgment of the workman." By separating the planning of work from the actual work itself, Taylor believed that managers could analyze all the parts of the process and then decide on the "one best method" that workers should employ in order to maximize efficiency.

Romer offers an illustration that challenges Taylor's central concept of "one best method." He cites the "simple manufacturing process that requires you to attach 20 different parts to a frame."[7] When added together, he calculates, there are a near-infinite number of different possible sequences. Where U.S. car manufacturers once thought they had figured out just about all you needed to know about assembly line production, Japanese competitors achieved advantages by empowering their workers to experiment—after all, the possibilities were near-limitless.[8]

If "Taylorism" has informed earlier generations of managers, what are the principles that are to inform today's generation? One commentator writes that "[T]he majority of new managerial ideas—like cross-functional teams, self-managed work groups, and the networked organization—are either direct or indirect responses to the inadequacies of Taylor's original model. Yet," this commentator finds, "for all the proliferation of specific techniques, the fundamental principles of a new managerial paradigm are far from clear."[9]

What is clear, however, is that a new balance is increasingly possible; a balance between the efficient use of physical resources and the effective use of intangible resources. To the extent that land, labor, and capital resources are scarce, managers should strive to efficiently allocate those resources. To the extent that knowledge and information resources are unlimited, managers should strive to effectively create and apply those resources.

In practice, the efficient management of physical resources and the effective management of intangible resources are not exclusive; rather, they differ in degree and are proportionate to each other depending on the business situation. The trick for managers is to decide which is strategic under what circumstances and then to apply good management practices.

Bell argued that knowledge resources have been on the rise. Drucker suggested that in the United States this rise began after World War II with enactment of the GI Bill, which opened higher education to millions of Americans.

Whatever the cause, the increase in knowledge and information resources has led to significant consequences. Entry barriers are broken down. Costs go down. New things become possible. The priesthood of suppliers and experts is undermined. Power moves to customers, consumers, and users. The perception of uncertainty grows, and a sense takes hold of being on the threshold of an unpredictable future.[10]

In these conditions, the effective management of knowledge resources becomes essential. The purpose of this paper is two fold: One is to identify a set of knowledge resources that are common to business enterprises; the other is to suggest how these resources can more effectively be managed. Knowledge resources that are common to all enterprises can be categorized as:

- Business concept(s)
- Enterprise know-how
- Organizational design
- Knowledge workers
- Knowledge mediated with information technology (IT)

Because knowledge resources can be key wealth-creating assets, and because high-value knowledge is hard to accumulate in organizations—and even harder to organize and effectively deploy—managers will want to learn how to master a process of knowledge management. They will want to become innovators in knowledge resources in order to achieve competitive advantage.

Typically, managers begin this process by trying to better understand new information and communications technologies. That is, they start with the "tools." Information technology tools should continue to experience soaring performance and plunging cost as IT improves by about an order of magnitude every five years.

But IT tools are just a part of the story.

Alan M. Webber, whose magazine *Fast Company* focuses on the new economy, explains it this way:

The revolution in information and communications technologies makes knowledge the new competitive resource. But knowledge only flows through the technology; it actually resides in people—in knowledge workers and the organizations they inhabit.[11]

All this suggests that managers need a new set of guideposts; a framework for thinking and acting with regard to knowledge resources (see table 13.1, Growth models for managers).

Table 13.1   Growth models for managers

	Industrial	Post industrial
Wealth creation	Primary managerial activity is to efficiently allocate scarce resources (land, labor, financial capital)	Primary managerial activity is to effectively create and apply knowledge (ideas, discovery, inventiveness, innovation)
Firm structure	Hierarchical organization with command and control	Flat organization around the flow of information
Workforce	Supervised subordinates	Teams of knowledge workers
Nature of work	Tasks are planned and executed separately for mass production	Projects are integrated and outputs customized

Business Concept(s)

In the industrial age, business progress was born of experimentation. The results shaped an organization's behavior, informed decisions about what to do and what not to do, and produced a set of assumptions about what worked and what didn't. What evolved was what Drucker has termed a company's *theory of the business*.[12] Often it took years for such a theory to emerge, but when it did it could produce wondrous results.

General Motors' 70 years of prosperity and a near-equal number of years for AT&T attest to this. GM's knowledge of the car-buying market and efficient manufacturing process, and AT&T's monopoly on network-building capability were powerful and long-lasting formulas for success. But eventually they, like other business theories, became obsolete. And when that occurs, there can be a costly mismatch between what a company knows how to do, and what it should do. While "how to" tools abound, the "what to do" issue can be devilishly difficult to address. And, if anything, the longevity of any *theory of the business* seems to be lessening. Arguably, the proliferation of all the many new major management techniques, of all the "how to" tools, is a response to the quest for winning theories on "what to do."

In the 1980s and '90s this divide between "how" and "what" has been dramatized in corporate battles between such firms as General Motors and Toyota, CBS and CNN, Pan Am and British Airways, RCA and Sony. As Gary Hamel and C. K. Prahalad point out, "Competitiveness is born in the gap between a company's resources and its manager's goals."[13] GM, CBS, Pan Am, and RCA all had greater tangible resources for their managers to efficiently allocate, but Toyota, CNN, British Airways, and Sony all had superior strength in effectively using their intangible, intellectual resources of being able to conceptualize the future of their respective businesses.

Hamel and Prahalad believe that managers must acquire "frames of reference"—the assumptions, premises, and accepted wisdom that bound or "frame" a company's understanding of itself and its industry.[14]

They must, in short, conceptualize the business. And they must conceptualize it in a way that leads to initiative and trust among their employees. In head-to-head competition, Hamel and Prahalad write, "Competition is not just product versus product, company versus company, or trading block versus trading block. It is mind-set versus mind-set, managerial frame versus managerial frame."[15] In this sphere of competition, individual initiative is critical, and trust is crucial to achieving the participation of every individual in the organization. President Kennedy embraced these requirements when he declared that America would "put a man on the moon by the end of the decade," and thereby accelerated a technology and knowledge race, with immense implications. Komatsu's goal of "encircling Caterpillar" triggered a similar competition, as did Ted Turner's launching of CNN.

Because concepts count, managers are faced with the challenging job of thinking ahead. Intellectual energy is needed to provide *conceptual answers* to questions like, What new products or services should we pioneer? How should we shape the future of our industry? What competencies must we build or acquire?

For every business, there are particular individuals who strive to answer such questions. In startups, the answers usually come from an entrepreneur, often using intuition and a personal sense of commitment. In large organizations, the CEO, with the help of a planning staff, holds the responsibility. In times of crisis, or chaos, a "czar" sometimes arrives to take command. In each case, a "point of view" gets expressed, and the organization operates on this premise.

In the knowledge-based organization, a different model is recommended, in part because the organization's strength relies on its intangible assets, and in part because people of intellect tend to do their best work when they are intellectually motivated—and involved. This does not mean that top management should avoid a unilateral conceptual statement. When Jack Welch, the CEO of General Electric, said that every GE division should be number one or two in its industry, he clearly conceptualized the performance he expected. At the same time, he signaled his managers that he believed they were smart enough to achieve that goal and now had the mandate to sustain or achieve it.

One of the best illustrations of conceptualizing the business comes from Electronic Data Systems, which revisited its assumptions and direction by involving 150 key managers who, through an enormous and thoughtful effort, restated EDS's strategy in these words: globalize, informationalize, and individualize.

The EDS experience is reminiscent of efforts by successful Japanese companies. NEC's concept of "Computers and Communications" seeks synergy between industries, while "Optoelectronics" helps Sharp define new technologies and markets.

In his study of "The Knowledge-Creating Company," Ikujiro Nonaka argues that "the best Japanese companies offer a guide to organizational roles, structures, and practices that produce continuous innovation" by successfully managing the creation of new knowledge.[16]

At the top, he found that management provides a framework. The framework may address one or more critical questions: What are we trying to learn? What do we need to know? Where should we be going? Who are we? Answers provide conceptual umbrellas ("Computers and Communications" and "Optoelectronics") or perhaps a more equivocal statement to give employees freedom of opportunity (Honda executives launched a new car initiative with the phrase "Let's gamble").

Front-line workers, Nonaka reports, are full of tacit knowledge—expertise at the fingertips. And they are constantly encouraged to share that knowledge by making it explicit to others in the company. The role of the middle manager is to facilitate or mediate between a company's grand concept, like Matsushita's "Human Electronics," and the efforts of front-line workers. These managers frequently use figurative language to bridge the worlds of "what should be" and "what is." When senior Honda management said, "Let's gamble," the project team leader responded with the "Theory of Automobile Evolution," thus challenging his colleagues to ask, If a car were an organism, how would it evolve? Sometime later, this concept gave birth to the term "Tall Boy" which in turn eventually led to the Honda City, a distinctive new urban car.

There is a risk here that "Let's gamble," "Tall Boy," and "Theory of Automobile Evolution" will ring of "sound bite" solutions to the challenge of managerial responsibility. Clearly, more is involved. But no firm can long be successful without having a successful concept, or theory of its business. And that concept will have to be communicated in a way that its workforce of knowledge employees can respond with initiative—and respond positively because they trust that management has done its homework in this critical realm. A lack of trust can incur a negative response if employees perceive it as a phony, even destabilizing initiative.

Drucker instructs senior management to periodically "abandon" every organizational assumption, to study noncustomers for early signs of problems, to recognize when a firm has outgrown its theory, and to change theories before there is a crisis.[17] Drucker says: "To establish, maintain, and restore a theory does not require a Genghis Khan in the executive suite. It requires hard work."[18]

The effort at conceptualizing the business looks first at the industry and the environment in which it does—and will—operate. It looks next at what the firm is attempting, or should be attempting to do. And finally, it examines the issue of firm know-how. All must fit together, and all must pass a "reality" test; that is, all must yield what Drucker terms "a *valid* theory of the business."[19]

Of equal importance, concepts about how to run the business must be constantly evaluated so that the business has the ability to change itself. When conceptual change is lacking, corporate culture—"the way we do things around here"—turns from being a strength to an impediment to acquiring those new competencies needed to reinvent a firm that has outlived its original concept of the business. Symptoms of having outlived an original, and successful, concept appear in the form of arrogance and excessive bureaucracy, and too often the treatment is a combination of defensive action and "fixes." These seldom work for long, as General Motors, among others, has learned so painfully.

Conceptualizing is akin to the work of inventors: Great inventors, it is said, achieve their greatness with 10 per cent inspiration and 90 per cent perspiration. Business theories for great knowledge-based organizations require similar efforts of conceptualization and articulation.

Enterprise Know-How

"In a world of increasingly global competition ... the basis of competition has shifted more and more to the creation and assimilation of knowledge," according to Michael E. Porter, a leading theorist on business competition.[20] "Companies achieve competitive advantage," says Porter, "through acts of innovation [that] always involve investments in skill and knowledge, as well as in physical assets and brand reputation."

When firms view their knowledge investments narrowly, focusing mainly on proprietary intellectual assets for which they can obtain governmental protection through patents, copyrights, and trade marks, they may either miss other opportunities or incur unforeseen risks. This is not to imply that intellectual property is unimportant; to the contrary, it can be commercially valuable. And the task of mangers is to use these assets wisely, deciding, for instance, when to engage in licensing agreements and under what terms.

Intellectual property is a form of what may be called "migratory knowledge"—knowledge that can be packaged, and distributed.[21] Unless protected, this type of knowledge cannot be relied upon for sustainable competitive advantage. Competitors can engage in intelligence-gathering practices, reverse-engineering exercises, and hiring away key personnel in order to access this type of knowledge.

When innovation rests on this kind of knowledge, a firm must constantly strive to upgrade it, lest competitors first catch up and then bypass it. When knowledge can be packaged and distributed, it is easily transferable and can diffuse rapidly, thus yielding only temporal advantage. Relentless upgrading is the only remedy to this challenge.

There is, however, another form of knowledge that can diminish risk and enhance competitive advantage: I call it high-value enterprise know-how. High-value enterprise know-how should be a principal knowledge resource of every organization.

When a firm has high-value know-how, it has capabilities and competencies that are longer lasting and not easily replicated. Through investment and experience, Boeing has acquired high-value enterprise know-how about commercial jet aircraft; Toyota about the production of automobiles; Microsoft about the writing of software.

High-value know-how can reside in individuals (a master violin maker), in groups of individuals, or teams (the scientists of the Manhattan project), and in companies. A company, in fact, is usually a large team or collection of teams in which skills and knowledge are embedded in the minds of managers and workers. Through formal and informal relationships they come together to achieve the goals of the firm.

High-value enterprise know-how goes hand-in-hand with a good business concept. How does a firm, having a winning concept, acquire high-value know-how? Three possibilities can be considered: contracting with another organization, merging with or acquiring another organization, and building know-how internally.

Contracting is the least feasible method. To begin with, this kind of knowledge is not easily packaged and distributed. Moreover, the idea of even trying to write a contact for a capability-creating relationship, with all its uncertainties and contingencies, would be exceedingly challenging, even to the most gifted attorney. Hiring a consultant might help, but in the end consultants can only advise or recommend courses of action. Put differently, you can contract for teaching, but not for learning.

Mergers and acquisitions seem more promising, although the record of such transactions presents a sobering picture.[22] Alliances—something less permanent, and more focused—were fashionable in the 1990s, especially when the firms involved were seeking know-how about supporting capabilities. As one executive advocate of alliances commented: "It's a dangerous thing to think we know everything."[23]

The third option is to build high-value know-how internally, that is, within the enterprise. Intuitively, every manager probably embraces this option. It would be reckless to think and act otherwise. But the basic problem with autonomous efforts is that they are often too slow in a world that is too fast. This is particularly true for an established firm whose internal know-how is experiencing eroding value.

A number of techniques have been proposed and are in use to address this problem. They include "benchmarking," sharing of "best practices," and the use of new technologies like "groupware." Xerox, Philip Morris, and Hughes are among the companies who have used such techniques and report favorable results.[24]

As good as these new techniques may be, one wonders whether they will have long-lasting effects, that is, whether they will yield sustainable competitive advantages. My guess is that they will not, because most of the knowledge gained is migratory in nature and therefore is, or will quickly become, available to competitor companies.

In searching the literature for evidence of competitively sustainable high-value know-how that resides within an enterprise, I came across the research on the pharmaceutical industry by Rebecca Henderson and Iain Cockburn in which they report:

... The longevity of pharmaceutical companies attests to a unique managerial competency: the ability to foster a high level of specialized knowledge within an organization, while preventing that information from becoming embedded in such a way that it permanently fixes the organization in the past, unable to respond to an ever-changing competitive environment.[25]

Henderson and Cockburn found that pharmaceutical companies both understand how to create high-value know-how and, equally important, how to avoid becoming prisoners of eroding know-how.

"The managers of these companies," Henderson and Cockburn report, "did all the things that business pundits recommend: they used sophisticated resource-allocation procedures, hired the best people, and encouraged cross-functional and cross-disciplinary communications. [Moreover] ... they focused on continuously refurbishing the innovative capabilities of the organization. They actively managed their companies' knowledge and resources."[26]

What was their paradigm?

First they "kept connected" to external knowledge sources including their peers, since no one company can hope to master all of its knowledge environment. Second, they allocated financial resources in a contentious, intellectual process, foregoing last-year-plus-five-percent-thinking, and substituted stimulating debates that in turn stimulated the rapid transfer of information across the company. Finally, they actively managed the tension in choosing organizational design, with the most successful companies never being satisfied with any single answer. One senior manager is quoted as saying, "Having tried every organizational model we know, nothing works as well as being continually aware of the need to be both at the leading edge ... and in total command of the important developments in other areas."[27]

High-value enterprise know-how means "how we do things in this company and achieve success." To constantly maintain high-value know-how, to be in a position that enables the manager to say, "Yes, the way we do things around here gives use a competitive advantage!" requires a special managerial competency. One, management must reach out for knowledge, internally and externally. Two, management should sponsor intellectual exercises, in which ideas are debated and constructive confrontation produces both a flow of new information and support for projects based on that information flow. And, three, management should never accept an organizational design as perfect (more will be said on this topic in the next section).

In combination, these steps can yield high-value enterprise know-how. They can produce a winning how-to formula, while lowering the risk that the formula becomes static and outmoded. With such a formula in place, a firm becomes a learning organization—"an organization skilled at creating, acquiring, and transferring knowledge, and at modifying its behavior to reflect new knowledge and insights."[28]

This definition, offered by David A. Garvin of the Harvard Business School, brings to mind companies like Corning, General Electric, and Honda—each of which has learned how to translate new knowledge into new ways of behaving, which is to say, into acquiring high-value enterprise know-how that yields competitive advantage.

Garvin recommends a few simple steps a company can take to change itself.[29] One is to "foster an environment that is conducive to learning"—the intellectually driven budget planning of the pharmaceutical companies being an example. Another is to "open up boundaries and stimulate the exchange of ideas," because, he says, boundaries not only inhibit the flow of information, they isolate individuals and reinforce old assumptions (see the following dicussion on "Organizational Design"). He also suggests creating "learning forums" —programs or events designed with explicit learning goals in mind. Again, these are ideas long embraced by the successful pharmaceutical companies and championed by GE's Welch, among others.

Garvin's principal point, which is embraced here, is that "high philosophy and grand themes" are—by themselves—inadequate to the challenge. Managers must engage "the gritty details of practice." Until they do, their organizations will muddle along in their "how we do it" world of yesterday, and not acquire the ability to create for themselves the unique know-how for competitive success they will need tomorrow.

Organizational Design

In *Through the Organizational Looking Glass*, Charles Handy argued that "You can't plan tomorrow's organization with today's assumptions." Writing in 1980, he foresaw a period of discontinuous change where the assumptions we had been working with as a society and in organizations would no longer necessarily be true.[30]

Handy predicted that a new set of assumptions would take hold in which management viewed contractual organizations as the most efficient, labor would be considered an asset, and organizations would evolve into communities.

The 1990s interest in *outsourcing* and *fees-for-work-done*, instead of *wages-for-time-spent*, were signs that some managers do view contractual organizations as efficient. Although other managers still believe that their employees need them more than they need their employees, that style of thinking may in fact be yielding to the perception that knowledge workers are a firm's most valuable resource—and retaining those resources is critical for success. In financial service firms, for instance, "star" money managers can be compensated more handsomely than top management. Perhaps the most important shift is to the concept of an organization as a community, which implies unit or team sizes in which everyone knows everyone else, and all participants share a sense of ownership (whether financial or psychological), and where authority stems from consent, not command-and-control.

Max Weber, the German social scientist and father of organizational theory, might not approve. At the turn of the century, Weber outlined and described the features of bureaucracy as the ideal form of organization. Drawing on the structures of the military and the church, Weber sought to make organizations rational and efficient using four prescriptions: (i) differentiation of tasks, (ii) coordination by a hierarchy of authority, (iii) separation of planning and execution, and (iv) the use of technical criteria for recruitment and promotion.[31]

Weber's influence is still felt today, but it has come under attack as the need for organizational learning and faster decision making have become competitive imperatives. As a consequence, decentralization has gained greater acceptance as a means to promote continuous self-improvement and innovation. All this has led to the evolution of teams who are assigned projects. Hence the requirement to organize, and reorganize, around information.

In determining what projects need to be undertaken, management needs to address the issue of information flow and decision making. The issue is critical since decision making improves with the quality of information. "We are rebuilding organizations around information," according to Drucker, "and that means information becomes a structural element."[32] One fallacy, he warns, is to rely on the Chief Information Officer to determine what information is required. To Drucker, CIOs are mere toolmakers.

In knowledge-based organizations, "Everyone takes[s] information responsibility ... everyone asks [or should ask, in Drucker's opinion], 'Who in this organization depends on me for what information? And on whom, in turn, do I depend?'"[33] It should be the responsibility of every knowledge worker to do a personal information audit. And it should be the responsibility of every manager to act on the results of such audits.

Personal information audits can open an organization's eyes to the need to abandon the Weberian bureaucracy that has served as the foundation for traditional organizational structures (functional, divisional, and matrix). The concept of the knowledge-based organization, some say "networked" organization, differs from the traditional models in that workers with specialized know-how provide the building blocks of the organization. Cross-functional teams are assembled to address specific problems, opportunities, or needs. Autonomous work groups on assembly lines are relatively permanent. A Hollywood film production is a one-time project. Yet each is discrete with its own organizational mission. The role of top management primarily is that of strategic direction and oversight.

In this new type of organization, boundaries get blurred, both inside and outside boundaries. Everyone is expected to deal with the environment, for there is no core to seal off the external world and thereby attempt to lessen uncertainty. Informality flourishes, and expertise is valued. The main advantage of this organizational model is adaptability. And adaptability is essential in an economy that places heightened value on innovation and entrepreneurship. In the knowledge-based organization, the individual who holds tactic and specialized knowledge will have to exercise a high degree of self-discipline, as hierarchical authority, and therefore managerial accountability, is diminished. Moreover, the knowledge worker becomes responsible for communications and relationships within the context of projects, not traditional departments, since much of the firm's work will not done there anymore.

Expected benefits of this new type of organization include: time efficiency goes up, responsiveness improves, adaptability becomes a competency, and innovation flourishes.[34] But to achieve these benefits, management must recognize that the division of labor is no longer measured by inputs and outputs, but rather by knowledge; that coordination is a team responsibility, not one of hierarchical supervision; that decision making is highly decentralized; that boundaries are porous and changing; that the organizational structure is highly informal; and that the basis of authority is knowledge, both knowledge of ends and knowledge of means.

Because all organizations exist to enable a group of people to coordinate their efforts and get things gone, the shaping of a knowledge-based organization is a top priority of management. Executives need to focus on identifying what the informational requirements will be to achieve the objectives of the projects at hand. And then to organize around those requirements. In Hollywood and on Wall Street, in Japanese factories and in research universities, in consulting firms and in many entrepreneurial firms, the concept of the knowledge-based organization, with its unifying flow of information, is the norm. Yet it is far from being widely accepted. There is some peril in this, for as Handy concluded, when he peered through the "organizational looking glass" more than a decade and a half ago, "Many traditional operators will wake up one morning to find themselves obsolete."[35] That need not necessarily occur, however, once managers act to achieve a new balance between efficiency and effectiveness and then implement that balance with a redesigned organization.

Knowledge Workers

The fact is, more and more jobs—no matter what the title—are taking on the contours of knowledge work. People at all levels of the organization must combine the mastery of some highly specialized technical expertise with the ability to work effectively in teams, form productive relationships with clients and customers, and critically reflect on and then change their own organizational practices. And the nuts and bolts of management —whether of high-powered consultants or service representatives, senior managers or factory technicians—increasingly consists of guiding and integrating the autonomous but interconnected work of highly skilled people.[36]

How far different is today's managerial challenge than in the era of Frederick Winslow Taylor, the turn-of-the-century expert on work, who considered workers as nothing more than "dumb oxen."

Of course, Taylor's harsh judgment has been considerably modified over the years, first in the classic Hawthorne Experiments of Elton Mayo, who concluded that worker output was affected not only by a job's scientific design, but also by social norms, and later by Frederick Herzberg's pioneering research on motivation and job satisfaction.[37]

If Mayo and Herzberg's findings weakened the influence of the classic school, the sociotechnical systems theory that originated with a group of British researchers at the Tavistock Institute of Human Relations provided the breakthrough to new thinking about involving employees in the planning, as well as the execution of work.[38] Early experiments of this theory were successfully conducted in the United States at plants in Topeka, Kansas, by General Foods; in Jamestown, New York, by Cummins Engine; and in Lima, Ohio, by Procter & Gamble.

As the "contours of *knowledge work*" was spreading to the factory floor, another phenomenon was also becoming evident: the professional worker was growing in numbers and occupations. What historically had been known as the "learned professions" (clergy, educators, lawyers, and physicians) now included proliferating numbers of accountants, brokers, consultants, data processors, engineers, financial analysts, and so on.

Workers who make and move things have been declining as a percentage of the workforce, while workers who talk on the phone, use computers, write reports, and attend meetings have been on the rise. A new balance was being struck in the workplace. For both industrial and knowledge workers, new and difficult questions are at hand. Both may agree that increased productivity would be beneficial, but measuring the productivity of a knowledge worker can be especially difficult. Is a surgeon to be judged on how many operations she performs in a month, or how many patients recover to live long, useful lives? Quality of performance can be viewed as more important than quantity; effectiveness more important than efficiency.

Even more challenging is the fact that knowledge workers cannot easily be supervised, for by definition they possess specialized knowledge, that is, they know better than their "superiors" how to do what they are most qualified to do—write a software program, trade futures, prepare a tax filing, create advertising copy, or repair a nuclear reactor. This undermines traditions of hierarchical authority and managerial control. Studies have shown that knowledge workers do not perceive themselves as "subordinates." To the contrary, they highly value operational autonomy, their preferred option being to have freedom to work within a set of rules.[39]

How then is a manager to go about guiding and integrating the work of knowledge workers in ways that are beneficial to the firm's successful performance? A set of recommendations is offered.

Focus the knowledge worker on doing what she or he does best—and eliminate the rest. Engineers who spend more time doing paperwork than at their workstations will underperform, and probably be less happy.

One technique to achieve *focus* is to use the "best work" method, in which the knowledge worker provides a periodic letter to management.[40] The employee answers four questions: What was your best work of the last period? What was its objective? Why was this your best work? How could you have done better? The "best work" method is simply a technique to help insure that the knowledge worker stays focused.

Establish a partnership between managers and knowledge workers, so that both parties have clear responsibilities. Ask knowledge workers, for example, to take responsibility for results, and managers in turn to take responsibility for providing the knowledge worker with the information and tools she or he will need to do the job.

Having the right information is particularly important, as Benjamin M. Compaine and John F. McLaughlin describe in chapter 12. In a new job, they write, "[You] should recognize the need to adjust the sources of information [you] are receiving from that which had been flowing to the previous holder of the job. The individual's personal information system is determined in large measure by that person's own knowledge, which is probably different from his predecessor's."

Team knowledge workers with colleagues that fit each particular project. This is important for two reasons. First, management's job is to provide strategic direction. It has to say what needs to be done. And what it needs its workers to accomplish. And why. When these questions are answered, the right kind of knowledge team can be assembled. Second, highly skilled knowledge workers value achievement and are more likely to remain committed to a firm where that value is fulfilled.

In building a team, management should be good at both managing individuals and at being able to combine different kinds of knowledge. The latter is important to create effective cross-functional teams; the former requires individual placement based on an individual's unique competencies, as opposed to just credentials. There can be a major difference in deciding a team placement between, say, two senior engineers with identical credentials, but with different competencies (viz., one is decisive under pressure while the other tends to procrastinate).

Studies of team performance stress urgency and direction, skills over personalities, setting clear rules of behavior, paying particular attention to the kick-off phase, getting some early results, getting good feedback, and challenging the team with new information and fresh facts. When managed well, teams of knowledge workers can and do achieve high performance.[41]

Provide training and educational opportunities so that every knowledge worker can maintain and improve her or his skills and competencies. Michael Hammer, co-author of *Re-Engineering the Corporation*, advises companies to "quintuple their investment in education ... [because] everybody who works in a company needs to understand the business."[42]

Workers themselves understand the need for training and education; indeed, one study found that personal growth was the highest motivation among knowledge workers. In recognition of this, companies like Motorola and Intel operate their own "universities" where employee knowledge workers often serve as instructors. Asking knowledge workers to teach others is an excellent idea, for teachers reap many rewards, not the least of which is that they are compelled to deepen their own expertise.

Understand that knowledge work is different than the work of management. When firms fail to recognize the difference and make the mistake of promoting a good knowledge worker into the ranks of management, they sometimes find that he or she is not cut out for it. Knowledge workers have specialized expertise, which usually is very different than the skills required of a good manager. Of course, some individuals possess both—but not all.

The problem arises with the traditional promotion system, when climbing the corporate ladder is the only means to get ahead. The risk is real that a knowledge worker will be promoted beyond his or her competence. To deal with this issue, firms should adopt pay policies based on knowledge or skill, not just on the number of people supervised or level of corporate responsibility.[43]

For their part, knowledge workers will have to understand that "a successful career will no longer be about promotion." Says Hammer: "It will be about mastery."[44]

Each of these techniques—focus the knowledge worker on what she or he does best, establish partnerships in which each party accepts responsibility, form teams that fit the task, provide learning opportunities, and understand that knowledge workers do not necessarily have managerial skills—will enable the knowledge worker and the firm to collectively work smarter and thereby enhance the value of the firm through strategic management of knowledge resources.

Knowledge Mediated with Information Technology

Over the past 30 years, the design and management of IT resources concentrated on the 'T'—technology—and largely ignored the 'I'—information. This approach reflects the roots of IT architecture and management in the mainframe era, when technology processed "data" and people processed "information" and "knowledge."[45]

As information technology has evolved—and continues to evolve—it has two significant implications for management of knowledge resources. One, IT can be used as a resource to transform the nature of work. Two, IT can be used to create value through the effective management of organizational knowledge. Work transformation and organizational knowledge can come together, as illustrated by the following excerpt from the *New York Times*:

Workers like John A. Cruz are the great hope for old corporate center cities like Hartford, and perhaps their greatest threat as well: He's been liberated from his office.

Rootless, mobile, armed with 120 megabytes in his briefcase, Mr. Cruz—a 32-year-old account executive at Travelers Insurance—is one of the new breed of high-tech nomads who are changing the face and the culture of many companies.... They specialize in being anywhere and nowhere. Mr. Cruz has done computer insurance audits in parking lots and at restaurant counters. His laptop computer is actually used on his lap.... Under fierce pressure to cut costs, insurance executives say that two important insights make the mobile workforce irresistible. First, insurance is essentially a disembodied product anyway, ideally suited to being electronically blipped, faxed and phoned from one place to another, without regard to place. The second is that all the apparatus of modern telecommunications—laptops, modems, cellular phones, voice mail, electronic mail and beepers—keeps everyone in touch all the time and lets managers track non-office workers and their performance even more closely than people sitting just down the hall.[46]

A lesson here is that every organization has storehouses of knowledge resources, the kind of stuff that lets John Cruz do insurance audits by tapping into a remote company database. Besides financial data, a typical database might hold valuable information on a firm's best customers and their buying habits. Employees themselves can be valuable storehouses of knowledge on what works and what doesn't. Information technology can help "mine" the first, and facilitate the timely transfer of the second.

One illustration is the American Express program to build customer loyalty. The company "mines" its "data warehouses" and learns that one of its best customers, Joe Smith, regularly dines at fine French restaurants. In Joe's next bill, he receives a "thank you" coupon from American Express good for a complimentary dinner at one of his favorite French bistros.

Another example can be found at McKinsey & Company, which has over 12,000 documents in its computerized Practice Development Network, PDNet. When a McKinsey director in Sydney needed to quickly start up an engagement for an important new consulting client, PDNet yielded 179 relevant documents that put at his fingertips valuable knowledge and information from more than 60 of the firm's consulting professionals worldwide.

In 1958, a year when large companies were installing their first computers to automate routine tasks, Harold J. Leavitt and Thomas L. Whisler made some predictions about what corporate life with the computer would be like in the future. Their article, "Management in the 1980s," foresaw that the role and scope of middle managers would change and that top management would take on more responsibility for innovating, planning, and creating.[47] Leavitt and Whisler, in retrospect, were pretty good at predictions.

Looking ahead, what can be expected about corporate life and information technologies in the 21st Century? Based on what we know about the previously discussed dimensions of the knowledge-based organization, we can expect that IT will serve to focus corporate energies on projects, not tasks, on processes, not procedures. We can expect that IT will contribute to innovation and to the redefinition of how work is done.

One group of experts expects that "companies of the future will closely resemble professional service firms today. The most successful firms attract and retain employees by providing an environment that is intellectually engaging. The work is challenging, the projects diverse, and the relationships with clients fairly independent."[48]

In the course I teach at Georgia Tech on knowledge management, one of the first cases my students read is Mutual Benefit Life, the country's 18th-largest life insurance company, which abandoned its rigid, sequential applications process and substituted a case manager system. Instead of the old multistep process involving credit checking, quoting, rating, underwriting, and so on, Mutual Benefit created a new position, a single individual to handle all these matters, with the support of powerful PC-based workstations that run an expert system and connect to a range of automated systems on a mainframe.

The result: These knowledge workers, called case managers at Mutual Benefit, can complete an application in hours, not weeks; they handle twice the volume of new applications the company previously could process; and the company was able to eliminate 100 field office positions.

Mutual Benefit Life is an example of how work can be transformed using information technology. But it is also clear from this case, as well as others, that technology is only a tool—a piece of infrastructure that enables (some prefer "empowers") knowledge workers to attain high performance results.

Michael Hammer, a theorist and advisor on reengineering work, recognizes the value of information technology as a tool. His reengineering principles include having the organization that produces information also process it; having the classic conflict between centralization and decentralization reconciled using on-line databases, telecommunications networks, and standardized processing systems to get the benefits of scale and coordination while maintaining the benefits of flexibility and service; and by having workers become self-managing and self-controlling by using IT that has built-in monitors and controls.[49]

All this suggests the potency of IT in the knowledge-based organization, but it should not suggest that *technology* alone will become the 21st-century "silver bullet" of competitive advantage. Indeed, the paradox of information technology is that, while technology becomes ever more important, it cannot become, as one observer concludes, "management's primary solution."[50] The reason is straightforward: Technology is "every competitor's potential solution" as well. This is especially true as the technology rapidly diffuses as a consequence of continuous scientific advancement.

On the other hand, knowledge resources that are associated with technology can create significant value for the postindustrial firm, even competitive advantage. Examples include information-based products and services, such as financial derivatives and database publishing.

In their research on "Managing in the Marketspace," J. F. Rayport and J. J. Sviokla offer the example of "news*papers*" not printed on paper but delivered as an electronic service.[51] The disaggregated content of the "newspaper"—the newspaper's knowledge resources—when distributed by an intermediary like America Online presents a different value proposition, because information technology has changed the way in which the "news*paper*" is processed and formatted.

Clearly, managing in marketspace will require new thinking and a better understanding for what is possible by managers. Oettinger, in Chapter 7 of this book, finds that changing technology offers new possibilities in business for different "bundles" of information (e.g., printed versus electronic news delivery) and that decision makers will need to focus carefully on the basic information "building blocks" of substance, process, and format as they seek to create new conventions that provide information value.

In sum, information technology and knowledge resources are vital to modern business organizations, and the two are more and more closely associated. From a technological perspective, opportunities are at hand to transform the way individual and organizational work can be more effectively and efficiently accomplished. From the perspective of knowledge resources, the challenge for managers is to increase firm value through effective management of their intangible, intellectual resources using information technology.

A Final Word

For traditional industrial organizations there exists a set of well-defined metrics to measure firm performance. Accounting and financial measures have been

Table 13.2 Manager's checklist: Knowledge resources

	Ask	Act
Business concept	Is my part of the business conceptually sound?	Form an "A Team" to evaluate the current business concept; form a "B Team" to propose alternate business concept(s)
Know-how	Does my part of the business have know-how that is competitively sustainable?	Have "A Team" evaluate; have "B Team" propose alternatives.
Organizational design	Does the flow of information in my part of the business foster or hinder innovation?	Make two lists. List the innovations in your organization during the last year. Make a second list of innovations you wish your organization had achieved during the year. Now, ask again the question about the flow of information.
Knowledge workers	Do I supervise, or do I manage a team of individuals who have specialized knowledge?	If you "supervise," learn how to manage subordinates. As a manager, focus both on the team and on the personal growth of each team member.
Information technology	Is our IT used to only process data? Or is it used to manage knowledge, too?	Commit in the next IT budget to fund knowledge management IT application(s).

developed in considerable detail, are well understood, and are widely applied. For knowledge resources, metrics are at best emerging.

Important work in this regard has been underway at Georgia Tech by Dr. Gary Tjaden. Elsewhere, an interim approach, called the "balanced scorecard," has been developed by Robert S. Kaplan and David P. Norton.[52]

The "scorecard" recognizes that, while financial measures worked well in the industrial era, by themselves they are insufficient tools for providing effectiveness feedback in the postindustrial era. "They are out of step," Kaplan and Norton say, "with the skills and competencies companies are trying to master today."

Their solution is to marry financial measures with operational data on customer satisfaction, on internal processes, and on the firm's innovative and improvement activities. This kind of scorecard, they find, "tracks the key elements of a company's strategy—from continuous improvement and partnerships to teamwork and global scale."[54]

Without fully developed new measuring tools, those who prefer to manage by the numbers ("If you can't count it, you can't manage it!") may be frustrated.

Still, new-found commitments to innovation, creativity and entrepreneurship were underpinning a quiet revolution that in the 1990s was taking place in many firms. Quietly the command-and-control organization is giving way to the knowledge-based organization. Managers have been rebalancing their resource portfolios to increase the effective use of intangible knowledge while still keeping an eye on the efficient use of scarce, tangible resources.

For those who wish to become more active managers of knowledge resources, a "Manager's Checklist" is presented in table 13.2.

Notes

1. See Bell, Daniel, *The Coming of the Post-Industrial Society*, New York, Basic Books, 1968.

2. Chapter 9, p. 338.

3. Wriston, Walter B., *The Twilight of Sovereignty: How the Information Revolution Is Transforming Our World*, New York, Charles Scribner's Sons, 1992.

4. Drucker, Peter F., *The Post-Capitalist Society*, New York, HarperCollins, 1993.

5. Bernard Wysocki, Jr. "For Economist Paul Romer, Prosperity Depends on Ideas," *The Wall Street Journal*, January 21, 1997, p. 1.

6. Taylor, Frederick Winslow, *The Principles of Scientific Management*, New York: Harper, 1911.

7. Ibid.

8. "If you calculate all the possible different sequences for attaching those 20 parts, you get 10(18)," according to Romer. "That number is about the same as the number of seconds since the big bang. So you get these amazingly large number of possibilities out of even extremely simple systems." *Forbes ASAP*.

9. Freedman, David H., "Is Management Still a Science?" *Harvard Business Review,* November–December 1992.

10. See, e.g., LeGates, John C. B., *The Sound, the Fury, and the Significance*, incidental paper, Harvard Program on Information Resources Policy, January 1995.

11. Webber, Alan M., "What's So New About the New Economy?" *Harvard Business Review*, January–February 1993.

12. Drucker, Peter F., "Theory of the Business," *Harvard Business Review*, September–October 1994.

13. Hamel, Gary, C. K. Prahalad, "Strategy as Stretch and Leverage," *Harvard Business Review*, March–April 1993.

14. Ibid.

15. Ibid.

16. Nonaka, Ikujiro, "The Knowledge-Creating Company," *The Harvard Business Review*, November–December 1991.

17. Drucker, op. cit. 16.

18. Ibid.

19. Ibid.

20. Porter, Michael E., "The Competitive Advantage of Nations," *Harvard Business Review*, March–April 1991.

21. For a discussion of "migratory knowledge," see Badaracco, Joseph L. Jr., *The Knowledge Link*, Harvard Business School, Boston, 1991, ch. 2.

22. See, e.g., Porter, Michael E., "From Competitive Advantage to Corporate Strategy," *Harvard Business Review*, May–June 1987, in which a select record of corporate diversification is examined.

23. Jack Kuehler, President of IBM, quoted in Badaracco, op cit., at p. 107.

24. Prepared presentations, "The Knowledge Imperative Symposium," organized by Arthur Anderson and The American Productivity & Quality Center, Houston, September 1995.

25. Henderson, Rebecca, "Managing Innovation in the Information Age," *Harvard Business Review*, January–February 1994.

26. Ibid.

27. Ibid.

28. Garvin, David A., "Building a Learning Organization," *Harvard Business Review*, July–August 1993.

29. Ibid.

30. Handy, Charles, "Through the Organizational Looking Glass," *Harvard Business Review*, January–February 1980.

31. Weber, Max, *The Theory of Social and Economic Organization*, ed. Henderson, A. D., Talcott Parsons, Free Press, 1946 translation.

32. Drucker, Peter F., "The Coming of the New Organization," *Harvard Business Review*, January–February 1988.

33. Ibid.

34. See Nohria, Nitin, "Note on Organization Structure," *Harvard Business School Note*, 9-491-083, March 24, 1992, Exhibit 7, p. 19.

35. Handy, op. cit.

36. Argyris, Chris, "Teaching Smart People How to Learn," *Harvard Business Review,* May–June 1991.

37. Mayo, Elton, *The Human Problems of an Industrial Civilization,* New York, Viking, 1933; Herzberg, Frederick, Bernard Mausner, Barbara Bloch Snyderman, *The Motivation to Work*, New York, John Wiley and Sons, 1959.

38. Trist, Eric L., "The Sociotechnical Perspective," in Van de Ven, Andrew H., and William F. Joyce, eds., *Perspectives on Organization Design and Behavior*, New York, John Wiley & Sons, 1981, ch. 2.

39. See, e.g., Tampoe, Mahen, "Motivating Knowledge Workers—The Challenge for the 1990s," *Long Range Planning*, Vol. 26, No. 3., 1993.

40. Helton, B. Ray, "The 'Best Work' Method of Knowledge Worker Assessment," *IM*, September–October 1988.

41. Katzenbach, Jon R., Douglas K. Smith, *The Wisdom of Teams*, Harvard Business School Press, Boston, 1993.

42. *Wall Street Journal*, January 24, 1995, p. B1.

43. See, e.g., Ingram, Earl, "The Advantage of Knowledge-Based Pay," *Personnel Journal*, April 1990; White, Michael, "Linking Compensation to Knowledge Will Pay Off in the 1990s," *Planning Review*, November–December 1991.

44. *Wall Street Journal*, op. cit. 47.

45. Applegate, Lynda M., "Designing and Managing the Information Age IT Architecture," *Harvard Business School Note*, 9-196-005, September 26, 1995.

46. "High-Tech Mobile Workers Transform Face of the Culture of Companies," *The New York Times*, February 8, 1994, C19.

47. Leavitt, Harold J., Thomas L. Whisler, "Management in the 1980s," *Harvard Business Review*, November–December 1958.

48. Applegate, Lynda M., James I. Cash, Jr., D. Quinn Mills, "Information Technology and Tomorrow's Manager," *Harvard Business Review*, November–December 1988.

49. Hammer, Michael, "Reengineering Work: Don't Automate, Obliterate," *Harvard Business Review*, July–August 1990.

50. Clark, Kim B., "What Strategy Can do for Technology," *Harvard Business Review*, November–December 1989.

51. Rayport, J. F., J. J. Sviokla, "Managing in the Marketspace," *Harvard Business Review*, November–December 1994.

52. Kaplan, Robert S., David P. Norton, "The Balanced Scorecard—Measures that Drive Performance," *Harvard Business Review*, January–February 1992.

53. Ibid.

14　New Competition and New Media

Benjamin M. Compaine

Since the first drawings on the walls of caves, there has been a regular infusion of "new" competition in the realm of the media. Often, some new technology or technologies applied to the task have fostered this new competition. The development of an alphabet in Greece in the seventh century B.C.; improvements in the implements of writing over succeeding centuries; and the familiar litany of printing press, steam engine, and electronics quickly bring us to contemporary media processes.

Each development in some way expanded competition, in that new media processes generally have added to rather than replaced older media processes. Whereas the laboriously handwritten manuscript was once the only form for text—and therefore the scriptorium maintained control over its reproduction, price, and distribution—today we have mass-printed books and even electronically transmitted text for viewing on a video screen.

This latter is therefore simply the latest in the historical lineage of new technology creating new competition for the old. With perhaps the exception of cave drawings, just about all previous technologies have survived in parallel as means for mass communication.

Still, life has become more complicated for anyone interested in the subject of competition in media. In part, this is because competition in media has at least one dimension more than does competition in, say, toothpaste or virtually any other commodity. The media—newspapers, magazines, books, television, radio, records, films, electronically accessible data bases—have a special place in virtually all literate societies as they are charged with conveying messages. In democratic societies, we are usually interested in maximizing a diversity of ideas, opinions, and information of all sorts. In closed societies, the media are as important, but usually with the goal of providing a uniform "party line," and hence with limited diversity. This chapter focuses on competition in pluralistic societies that hold dearly diversity of information sources.

Quantifying the Media Industry

There are economists who specialize in measuring the extent of competition—or its obverse, concentration—in an industry. Economists are good for quantifying things and then measuring them. In the media business, that itself presents two problems. The media can be treated by economists as any other industry for purposes of measurement. They can count up who owns what, calculate percentages, devise indices of pricing power.

Problem One: What Is the Relevant Market?

Although this may seem rather straightforward, the first problem is that the technology of recent years has made the definition of the appropriate divisor for concentration indices debatable. That is, what is the appropriate market? Figure 15.1 outlines the boundaries of the traditional media business.[1] But to study media competition, should one look at the market for newspapers isolated from that for magazines? To what extent are broadcast television and even radio fungible for the substance of the print media? Traditionally, economists and their usual employers—private and government lawyers—have looked at a specific medium, such as newspapers. It can be legitimately argued that that approach, if it ever was valid, is becoming less so as the technology of the alternative media forms merge into one another.[2]

Still on this first problem of market definition, there is a question of who is the user of the media. Some media, such as newspapers and magazines, and, in the United States to a degree more than almost anywhere else, broadcast television and radio, are paid for in total or large measure by advertisers. Thus, an appropriate measure of economic concentration for these media may not be in how much consumers pay to receive them but to what extent there is market power in the pricing of advertisements. On the other hand, media forms such as books, records, and theatrical films are funded mostly or totally by their users, in which case the economic consideration is the ability of suppliers to charge nonmarket prices to consumers.

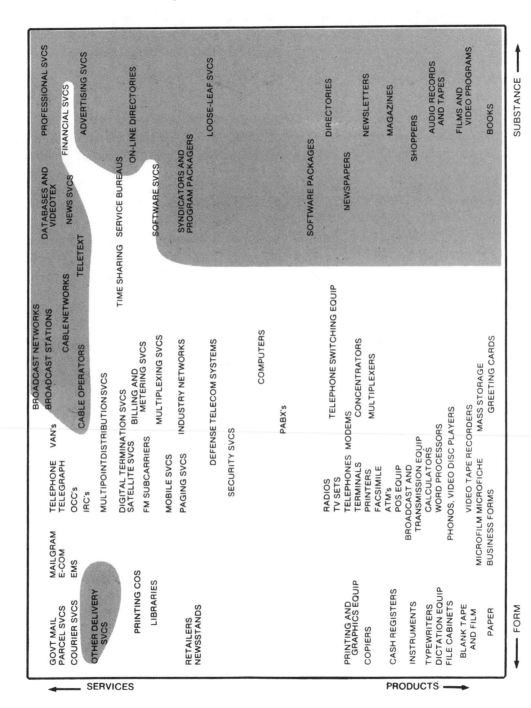

Figure 14.1 The mass media space on the information business map. © 1984 President and Fellows of Harvard College, Program on Information Resources Policy

In addition to competition within a particular media segment and competition among media industries, geographical competition is a factor. Newspapers in the United States and Canada, and to lesser degrees elsewhere, are largely local media. Although the United States has about 1700 daily papers and no more than about seven percent of total daily circulation is controlled by any one firm, only about 30 central cities have fully competitive newspapers; and only one, New York, has three alternatives.[3] By comparison, residents of metropolitan Phoenix, Arizona had access to 10 television broadcast stations in 1996, while even in a small city like Yakima, Washington, there were four stations, all with separate ownerships. They compete with dozens of cable networks available to the 70 percent of households that subscribe to cable.[4] Thus, most people have more choice in the number of television signals they receive, even though there are fewer television stations nationally than there are newspapers. Book and magazine publishers, relying as they do on large regional and national markets, compete in a larger geographical context. Cable operators, while providing a dizzying array of channels, for the most part are monopoly providers within their highly restricted franchise territories and are subject to a decreasing amount of government control over their pricing. Finally, there is a new factor of potential global competition, as video cassette player/recorders proliferate and as direct broadcast satellite systems, perhaps out of the control of the nation to which their programming is receivable, start beaming signals in competition with land-based—and often government-controlled—television. In effect, we are seeing receding toward the horizon the traditional market boundaries with which so many were so comfortable.

Problem Two: How Much Is Enough?

The second problem for a discussion of competition is anchored to the lessening of the distinction among what had been well-understood media formats.[5] Today, "television" can be delivered not only over-the-air, but via cable, cassettes, discs, or directly from a satellite. The picture on the screen can be the type of text and graphics typically associated with magazines, books and newspapers. Thus, the conventional labels are less useful than ever. "Print" and "video" are essentially examples of *formats* in which the same content or substance can be displayed or otherwise manipulated by users. Words can come as speech or as writing. And that writing can be gouges carved in rock, toe marks in the sand, ink on paper, or glowing phosphors on a screen.

These are among a multitude of ways in which we can express information *substance*. Substance may be data, knowledge, news, intelligence, or any number of other colloquial and specialized denotations and connotations that can be lumped under the general rubric of "information."

Process is the application of instruments, such as typewriters, computers, printing presses, the human brain, telephone wires, or delivery trucks, to the creation, manipulation, storage, and transmission/distribution of substance in some intermediate or final format. For example, a traditional newspaper, an ink-on-newsprint format, relies on processes including entering thoughts of a reporter into a computer by manipulating a keyboard of a video display terminal with storage in the computer, and the eventual creation of a printing plate and distribution to consumers via trucks. Part of that process may be different should the same article be distributed to some consumers via a telephone link to a video display terminal. In that case, some of the process is the same (the entering and storing of information), the formats are different for the end user (text on screen vs. ink on paper), but the substance may remain constant.

How then does one measure how much diversity of sources is "enough"? If 20 firms account for 50 percent of newspaper circulation in the U.S., is that too few, enough, or can this be a sign of too many firms creating too much fragmentation in society? If not this number, then what? An even stickier question is, what are the adequate ground rules for assuring that any person's or institution's ideas—political, social, commercial, or whatever—have some opportunity for access to the media? And more difficult still, how does one measure which formats should have what conditions for access? That is, it may be relatively easy to provide access to a print newspaper for messages, as these have the most space flexibility. And as authoritarian societies know, the photocopying machine has become Everyman's printing press.

On the other hand, what about access to prime-time broadcast television? We know that up to now there has been limited spectrum available, particularly in the major metropolitan areas, and that prime time cannot be expanded by more minutes than nature has provided for us. Cable television, a newer process for a familiar format, alleviates the spectrum problem, but it can never eliminate the fact that a handful of channels will likely get the bulk of the viewing audience at any given time. Thus, even as technology provides us with more conduits for distributing information, there is no guarantee that the mass audience will want to receive much more than what has traditionally been mass entertainment. Indeed, in the United States, dozens of cable networks have been struggling to achieve even a one or two percent market share, as the bulk of the audience with access to dozens of stations persists in viewing the four traditional broadcast networks, plus three or four of the newer offerings, the most successful of which—the pay television networks—are showing other forms of mass audience fare.

The extent of competition in the media, as in other industrial sectors, is in large measure a function of the national policies that encourage or limit market forces. Societal norms set the boundaries for these policies, and politics then establishes the rules. In England, the spread of the printing press in the 16th century led to the establishment of the Royal Stationer, created by the Crown, through which all printing was controlled in the 17th and 18th centuries. In France, a government edict in 1686 fixed the allowable number of printing masters. Backed by government, an oligopoly gained control of the printing business. Thus, in 1644, Paris had 75 print shops with 180 presses. By 1701, the number of presses had grown to 195, but these had consolidated into 51 shops.[6] This early tradition of government's being involved in the structure of the information business was in large measure the motivation for the strong prohibition against such intervention written into the U.S. Constitution. Thus, whereas European governments have to varying degrees extended early intervention into newer media processes, such as telephone and broadcasting, the U.S. has maintained a relatively hands-off attitude.

This image of laissez-faire in the U.S. should not be exaggerated. It was the U.S. Congress that early in this century established the conditions for the assembling of a privately owned but highly regulated telephone system. And while broadcasters have had far more latitude in operating than virtually anywhere else in the world, their programming decisions have been shaped to some degree by regulatory requirements such as the fairness doctrine.

Competition and Concentration in the United States

By any standard other than the most narrow, there is little evidence to substantiate a conclusion that there is unhealthy concentration of ownership of the traditional media in the United States. By some measures, that ownership is substantially less concentrated than it was 30 or 40 years ago.[7] For the first time, local newspapers are competing for reader attention (if not yet for advertisers) with a national paper (*USA Today*) and national editions of the *New*

York Times and the *Wall Street Journal*. Direct mailers, 9000 weekly news-papers, and thousands of "shopper" newspapers are providing strong competition for local advertising support for the daily papers. The national television networks are losing audience share to independent television stations and to cable-delivered networks. The broadcast chain with access to the largest television audience through its own stations is not one of the networks but Metro-media. The number of magazine and book titles proliferates, and the number of new publishers has kept pace with the acquisition of established ones.

The number of firms with a major stake in some segment of the traditional media continues to grow. By one count, 64 organizations are major players in at least one media segment and few are dominant in even two segments.[8] In 1982, only five firms were true media conglomerates, having major holdings in at least three of the six industries measured: newspapers, magazines, broad-casting, book publishing, cable television, and theatrical film production.

With the dispersion of substance available via satellite and telephone, access *by* more sources *to* more sources is likely to increase further, not diminish. Some commentators are in fact concerned now about fragmentation of society and information overload as the result of the overwhelming variety of formats for substance.

The proliferation of new communication processes over the years has made it increasingly difficult for any single entity, even governments that have the will and power, to have total control over the mass media. The Shah of Iran learned that lesson the hard way. Although his government controlled the broadcast and major-press spigot, it was not able to stop the inflow of messages from the Khomeini forces in Paris, which used small, cheap audio cassettes to smuggle in instructions and inspiration for low-tech duplication and distribution. By putting in a sophisticated telephone system, the Shah gave his enemies direct-dial international phone calls, much harder to monitor than those going through an old-fashioned switchboard. And the Xerox machine became the printing press of choice—cheap and harder to control than a large roll-fed offset press.

Over the years the Soviet Union has engaged, with varying degrees of intensity, in jamming broadcasts aimed into its territory from the West. The Soviets no doubt view such broadcasts as a far more pervasive factor in challenging their control than the few books that can be physically smuggled in, or locally written underground tracts that are limited in quantity to the number of copies that can be made with carbon paper. (Unlike the Shah, the Soviets go to great lengths to restrict availability of and access to the relatively small number of photocopying machines—a factor for which they may pay an economic price as well). In Western Europe, broadcasting authorities have had periodic skirmishes with offshore "pirate" radio broadcasters. Today there is great handwringing over potential violation of national borders by the footprint of direct broadcast satellites for television and for data flows from computer to computer via telephone switches that do not respect the customs inspectors at the frontier.

It has been reported that bootlegged copies of the controversial movie *Death of a Princess* were being shown in living rooms in Saudia Arabia at the same time it was being broadcast—over that government's protests—in Great Britain and the United States.[9] In the Philippines, where there are seven networks and only a two percent penetration of VCRs, one of the most popular tapes has been of the videotape footage of the murder of Benigno Aquino that has not been shown over the air. (To escape detection, the material was smuggled into the country on tapes that were labeled as pornography. The first ten minutes or so were indeed what they were labeled, so the customs agents wouldn't readily find the contraband footage.)

One of the most dramatic pieces of evidence that technology is moving faster than the ability of governments to control the media is the competition that video cassette recordings are providing for broadcasters and movie-house operators. As might be expected, the penetration of VCRs has been greatest in those countries that already had the largest number of television sets. But as table 14.1 indicates, the United States and Canada lag well behind Western Europe in their use. Moreover, these figures likely understate penetration in Europe in that they express only machines exported by Japan. Although these account for almost all sales in the United States and Canada, the tabulation does not count the sizable number of the machines manufactured and sold in Europe. But even with those counted, leading the world in VCR ownership are the oil-rich Middle Eastern nations, where there are as many as five VCRs for every known television set.

What determines the penetration of VCRs? It appears that where there are not significant government-imposed barriers, a substantial factor is competition from other forms of television. In Western European nations, where there are typically two government-controlled or highly regulated television networks, VCRs gave viewers their first opportunity to become their own programmers, through renting or buying tapes. In England, where the tradition of renting televisions has carried over to VCRs, there is a booming tape rental market, with prices as low as 50p per night. A cynic might conclude that, when it has the chance, the mass audience demonstrates that it is not being fulfilled by the fare that the broadcasters are providing—at least not enough of the time. (The

Table 14.1   Videocassette recorder penetration in selected regions, 1983[a]

	TV sets in use (000)	VCRs exported to (000)	VCRs as % of TV sets	Median # of broadcast nets
W. Europe[b]	119,222	16,844	14.1%	2
U.S. and Canada	189,280	14,426	7.6	5
Middle East[c]	2,470	1,938	78.5	2
Australia and New Zealand	6,422	1,561	24.3	2

a. Videocassette recorders exported from Japan to indicated destination, 1976–1983. Does not take into account transhipments once in destination country or non-Japanese-made VCRs, primarily those made by Thomson in Europe.
b. Belgium, Denmark, Finland, France, Greece, Iceland, Ireland, Italy, Luxembourg, Malta, Monaco, Netherlands, Norway, Portugal, Spain, Sweden, Switzerland, United Kingdom, W. Germany.
c. Major oil producing or supported countries: Bahrain, Iran, Kuwait, Qatar, Saudi Arabia, United Arab Emirates.
Source: Calculated from compilation by CBS Inc. from *Table and Television Factbook*, 1984; Japan Tariff Association, *Japan Exports and Imports*, 1976–1983 editions.

other side of this coin is that viewers may find the quality of programming so compelling that they find it desirable to record one for later viewing while watching the other in real time.) In the United States, which has four over-the-air-networks and a growing number of cable-supplied networks, VCRs have seen healthy growth only in the past two years, and overall penetration is still relatively low.

Substitutability Among Video Options

If the need to foster diversity is a policy objective in democracies, then the degree to which various media processes are fungible is of import. The manufacturers of steel cans learned quite a while ago that their ability to set prices and gain market share was determined not only by their relatively few steel can competitors, but by others who made aluminum, glass, and even cardboard containers. Similarly, broadcasters, whether private or government-controlled, must recognize that they are not the only rooster in the video barnyard anymore, and that it will likely get more competitive rather than less so.

A statistical study by two economists at the Federal Communications Commission (FCC) has found "strong support [for] the proposition that VCRs and cable [television] are substitutes."[10] It also reported "some support to the conclusion that VCRs and broadcast television are complements."[11] While noting some paradoxes and data problems, the authors believe that their statistical evidence "tends to support the proposition that the video product market should be broadly defined—to include (at least) broadcast television, cable and VCRs."[12]

It is much too early to make any judgments about the impact of DBS. For all practical purposes, it does not exist as a mass-market service anywhere in the world, although bits and pieces are starting to become available. Probably ranchers in remote areas of the United States are the largest identifiable market for DBS to date, having purchased large antenna dishes to capture the signals intended as raw feeds to cable headends and broadcasters. For this constituency, DBS is a substitute for a lack of broadcast television.

Substitutability Among Print Options

Print publishers have felt the heat of competition longer than their newer electronic brethren. Before radio made its way into the mass-media mix in the 1930s, the newspaper industry in the United States held 45 percent of media advertising, and consumer magazines about 8 percent (figure 14.2). While magazines held their share through the 1950s, radio and, to a lesser extent, television, eroded newspaper share to 31 percent by 1960. Newspapers have lost a small amount of market share to television in the past 25 years, with newspapers' share now down to about 27 percent, and magazines' near 6 percent. In large measure, this erosion accounts for the inability of cities to support the competing newspapers that existed before there was electronic media competition for consumer attention and advertiser expenditures.

Newspaper-publishing companies in the United States did not sit around idly while their franchises deteriorated. In 1983, one-third of the 447 television stations in the 100 largest markets were owned by firms that also published newspapers. However, as the result of an FCC policy discouraging newspaper–television affiliations in the same market, by 1983 only 8 percent of the stations in the 100 largest markets were owned by the local newspaper.[13] They also owned about 600 out of about 9500 radio stations. Companies that own news-

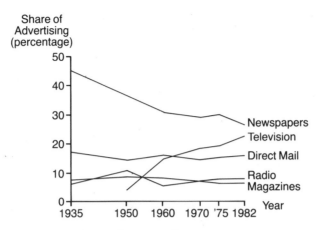

Figure 14.2   Share of ad expenditures

papers have been a diversified group, as the holdings of seven companies on figure 14.3 indicate.

Today, publishers of newspapers face two forms of real and potential competition. As far as most publishers are concerned, the real competition they face is from the U.S. Postal Service and the highly computerized firms that have grown to take advantage of postal rates for mailing printed circulars that the publishers themselves compete to deliver as part of the newspaper. The direct-mail business has thrived through the years. Before television, direct mail accounted for about 14 percent of advertising expenditures. With no dramatic shifts over the years, it now has about a 16 percent share. The ability of direct mailers to compete with newspapers is purely a function of price, which in turn is determined by several layers of postal agencies. The mailing companies (as have publishers themselves) have taken full advantage of computer technology to improve their product, but still depend on physical handling and delivery for reaching the consumer.

The potential competitor for newspapers goes under the name of electronic publishing. It is much too soon to know when, if at all, these computer- and telecommunications-based services will have an effect on local newspapers. This is because such services still require hardware in the home that costs hundreds of dollars at a minimum and ongoing telecommunications costs that alone could be greater than the current price of a printed newspaper. Advertisers, who provide about 80 percent of the revenue for daily newspapers in the United States, are far from certain as to how they could use the electronic systems.

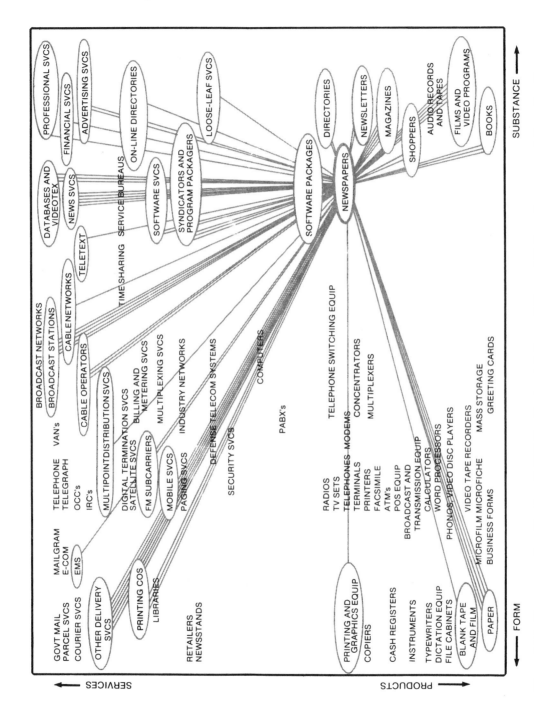

Figure 14.3 Newspaper diversification. © 1984 President and Fellows of Harvard College, Program on Information Resources Policy.

Implications

What does all this say about concentration or competition? Where does it leave the small player who wants to get a piece of the action, including those who want to make sure they have access to be "speakers" or providers of substance? And what, if anything, are the implications of the U.S. experience for Europe and the rest of the world?

Clearly, many of the players involved with the newer media services are the same ones we know in the traditional media. But many of the newer players are from territory that seemed light-years from the media. In that sense, the number of competitors is increasing as the interests of the players blur and merge. This may add to the already growing confusion over the appropriate boundaries for identifying the relevant industry to investigate or regulate.

We might look to the old print business for some hint of the future of the electronic one. One reason that the print business has had more freedom to operate is that it was not constrained by the limits of the technology, as was broadcasting. Printing presses might be expensive, but there was no technological limit to the number that could be made available, unlike 6-MHz frequencies, for example. Moreover, publishers rarely had to depend on owning their network for distribution. The existence of a government-supported, common carrier postal system, that reached every household and business, from the top of Rockies to the bottom of the Grand Canyon, assured publishers access to customers.

The parallel institutions in electronics have been the telegraph and telephone networks. Until recently, however, these were largely restricted to point-to-point carriage of voice or low-volume analog signals. Today, the harnessing of computers to the telecommunications networks makes possible the economic transmission of a vast volume of data. The twisted copper wire pair goes nearly every place the postman goes. So long as the telephone system is a common carrier, virtually anyone will be able to become an electronic publisher with a far lower capital investment than was necessary when one also had to own—or pay for the use of—a printing press.

The viability of this approach—and its time frame—will depend on public policy, which will directly or indirectly determine the speed at which the public-switched telephone systems implement digital electronic switching, upgrade current systems to provide for faster transmission of data throughout the system, install a widely available multiplexed capability, and otherwise configure end-to-end systems that handle data as facilely as they have handled voice. In the absence of concerted efforts on behalf of the public network (whether through market forces or government-induced policy), we are likely to see systems that large-volume users will install to bypass the public network, to the extent they are legally permitted, thus gaining advantages not available to the low-volume users.

Summary

The issues are the same for the United States, Canada, Europe, Japan, Australia, and elsewhere in the industrialized countries. Among them are:

- the uncertainty of new opportunities and perceived threats for existing media players;
- a widening universe of players who will want to compete with the traditional ones vs. regulatory or other restrictions on their doing so;
- the role of government in pushing, restraining or merely establishing the playing field for one technology or industry sector competing with another;
- the stakes for control over the nature and distribution of substance for commercial, cultural, or political ends by private and public players.

As there is neither a right nor wrong policy in addressing these and other issues, it is rather safe to predict that no two nations will adopt identical strategies. What is appropriate in the vast heterogeneous expanse of the United States may not be appropriate for a more homogeneous European nation. Still, policymakers will have to think through some of their decisions' less obvious possible consequences to the various players. A decision to establish a national policy for a particular piece of technology may cut off the benefits that would be derived by waiting for other technologies to come together, to gestate and take hold spontaneously.

On the other hand, leaving nature to take its course may result in a certain amount of wheel-spinning, waste, and confusion. In general, however, as time goes on, any entity or small group of entities will likely have more difficulty attempting to control the substance or process of delivery of that substance, short of implementing a totalitarian regime. And even those societies will find their job of control more challenging. Over the centuries, technology has helped expand competition for the creation and distribution of ideas, information, and entertainment. We are not at the beginning of an era, but in the midst of that long-term trend.

Notes

1. For a complete discussion of the construction and application of the information business map, see John F. McLaughlin, "Mapping the Information Business," in Benjamin M. Compaine, ed., *Understanding New Media* (Cambridge, Mass.: Ballinger Publishing Co., 1984); or Chapter 10 of this volume.

2. Similar technology is being used to produce media that are called by different names. National newspapers such as *USA Today* and the *Wall Street Journal* are sending facsimiles of their composed pages to remote printing sites using data transmission and satellites similar to the way that programmers send their materials to cable operators. Internally, the electronic newspaper is for real, as computers and video displays have replaced typewriters and copy paper. Videotext and teletext use broadcast, cable, or telephone transmission to video displays for text and graphics that otherwise would look at home printed on paper. [And the World Wide Web has further blurred the distinction of what is a news*paper*. Ed.]

3. This tendency to one-newspaper cities is not quite as bleak as it may sound. Accompanying the demise of competition in central cities has been the development of newspapers in suburban areas that have grown up around the central cities in the past 35 years. Thus, many people and advertisers still do have a choice of newspapers—the metropolitan daily or the local daily. (By the mid-1990s, there were slightly over 1500 daily newspapers. The largest chain, Gannett, held just under 10% of national circulation.)

4. Benjamin M. Compaine, "Reassessing Video Competition: Has Technology Regulation Made a Difference? Paper presented at the Telecommunications Policy Research Conference, Sept. 28, 1997. Available at http://www.shore.net/~bcompain.

5. The model of content, process, format is an early version of that described in Chapter 7.

6. Robert Darnton, *The Great Cat Massacre and Other Episodes of French Cultural History* (New York: Basic Books, Inc., Publishers, 1984), p. 79.

7. See Benjamin M. Compaine et al., *Who Owns the Media? Concentration of Ownership in the Mass Communications Industry* (White Plains, N.Y.: Knowledge Industry Publications, Inc., 1982). A contrary view is present in Ben H. Bagdikian, *The Media Monopoly* (Boston: Beacon Press, 1983). A response to Bagdikian can be found in a review of this book by Benjamin Compaine, "Winner Take (Nearly) All," *Nieman Reports*, Autumn 1983, pp. 39–41. In research being completed by this author in 1998 for a new edition of *Who Owns the Media?* preliminary data seem to

support a similar finding. That is, while mergers and acquisitions garner headlines, the expansion of the media in general and the rise of newer firms (News Corp. was not a major player in 1982 nor Hollinger International, a major newspaper publisher) has provided the media arena with many players, very few of whom are a major presence across more than two media segments.

8. Compaine, *Who Owns the Media?* pp. 452–455.

9. Thomas White and Gladys Ganley, *The "Death of a Princess" Controversy* (Cambridge, Mass: Program on Information Resources Policy, Harvard University, 1983), P-83-9, p. 39.

10. Jonathan D. Levy and Peter K. Pitsch, "Statistical Evidence of Substitutability Among Video Delivery Systems," Federal Communications Commission, Washington, D.C., April 1984, p. 27.

11. Ibid.

12. Ibid, p. 31.

13. Herbert H. Howard, "Group and Cross-Media Ownership of Television Stations, 1984," National Association of Broadcasters, June 1984, p. 3.

V Information Policy

15 Information and Communications Policy Research—More Important, More Neglected

Eli M. Noam

The first U.S. telegraph message, sent from Baltimore to Washington in 1844, was "What hath God wrought?" The same question could be asked one and a half centuries later when American communications were being transformed by technology, policy, and entrepreneurialism.

The American communications policy experience followed the path from a relatively short-lived unbridled laissez-faire capitalism to a regulatory system that kept steadily expanding in the decades following the Great Depression and World War II. But in the 1970s, communications policy in the U.S. began to shift in the opposite direction, towards a lessening of restrictions.

These policy changes were partly due to a general political and economic climate favoring a philosophy of limiting the role of the state, which made the public more receptive to allowing new entrants as an offset to corporate power, and as a substitute to direct governmental intervention. Additionally, in the case of major communications, advances in electronic technology destabilized the long-standing market structure. Meanwhile, the importance of information as an input for all economic activities grew, and with it the pressure by large users for low-cost telecommunications. On the consumer level, increases in leisure time, education, and diversity raised the demand for differentiated entertainment products.

As a result, during the past two decades, individualized and mass electronic media were changed from national monopolies and oligopolies to new and increasingly open structures. As these historic changes unfolded, where was academic policy research? With a few notable exceptions—the Program on Information Resources Policy being most prominent—there was an absence of traditional academic disciplines in this transformation.[1]

Technologists in electrical engineering and computer science departments provided the tools that enabled change. They (and business-school strategy researchers) often played a booster role that looked, often overoptimistically, at the potential of technical progress. But their role in policy research was fairly small. Political scientists and historians have had an astonishingly low profile considering the magnitude of change and its long-term implications on the political and social system. Legal academics have played some role by investigative research on monopoly issues, analyzing free-speech principles as applied to electronic media, researching intellectual property and privacy issues, and dissecting new communications statutes. Among other social scientists, *economists* have probably been the most influential, providing the general free-market case which helped to destabilize the "natural" monopoly system. Economists were also active—often in the employ of interest groups—in the implementation process of policy change. But once the argument of removing entry barriers had been accepted, they contributed little to a vision of the future.

Thus, as society entered the information age and the information economy, and as its political institutions wrestled with the revolutionary consequences of transition, academic policy research was strangely marginal. Part of the reason was that academic institutions were poorly organized for themes that were not part of traditional research agendas of traditional academic disciplines, organized around traditional departments.

A second problem was, ironically, that because of the great importance of the subject to the world at large, those academic researchers with strength in the field were in great demand as consultants, expert witnesses, etc., thus reducing their academic role as well as their neutrality.

To establish communications policy research therefore required individuals who could both create intellectual capital and institutional infrastructure, while preserving credibility. This requires not self-proclaimed statements of impartiality, but above all a funding mechansim that adds veracity to such proclamations.

As a result, mainstream communications departments have played only a minor role in the enormous changes in communications policy. At the time that the communications system was on the table of national policy, when new institutional arrangements were being established, the academic field of communications studies did not communicate well with the public policy process, whether in Washington, Brussels, or other capitals.

In consequence, mainstream scholarship in communications departments has been without a real-world role, in contrast to some other fields such as environmental studies, which successfully overcame the structural impediments that limit academia's influence and participation in the public arena. Policy makers often ignore social science research, but scholars also underestimate their own weight. Policy ideas may not win, but they matter. While convenient ideas may get amplified more than those that threaten, the policy process is also a voracious consumer of ideas.

There were many questions to address, but for a long time the answers were mostly conventional. The old policy arrangements had some undeniable social merit as well as power and benefits to disburse to their participants. In most countries communications were a public service oriented to the public welfare. But the reality was more complex. In point-to-point telecommunications, long-standing monopolies had become bloated and slow. Technological decisions tended to be captured by domestic supplier industries. Even so, the change to a more open network environment was accompanied by scholarly assertions of impending social doom, few of which were retracted when the predicted calamities failed to materialize.

In television, too, the reality of the traditional public monopoly broadcast system that existed in many countries fell far short of the idealized expectation of quality programming. The pervasive politicization of the powerful public institutions was not given much research attention. Nor was there much study of the negative impact on national and regional cultures and on artistic independence resulting from a system in which a single national public broadcast monopoly served as the gatekeeper and chief financier of the film and video creativity of an entire society. Despite a vast body of political science research, it was often assumed that such an institution would act for the public, without regard to its self-interest or that of its political patrons.

Part of the problem has been the frequent absence of an adequate and updated fact base. In the academic pecking order, theory is more prestigious than empiricism or policy. Yet theory must refer to a fast-changing reality, especially if it has political implications and if it is to guide applied research. With inadequate incentives inside academia, the empirical and policy base of communications research was further weakened by a brain-drain of those with the strongest fact base into private consulting and think tanks.

Beyond Regulation

Will the next generation of policy researchers prove to be different? This requires, the identification today of issues that will become more salient tomorrow.

The replacement of communications monopolies by a partly competing, partly collaborating, interconnected, and non-hierarchical *network of networks* fundamentally changes the face of the media industries. Specialized *integrators* such as Internet service providers become central institutions of communications, replacing many of the roles of today's telephone companies, broadcasters, and cable operators. Networks will move from public to private, and from private to individualized.

Such a structure will be radically different from the present media system, and it invites policy analysis. For example,

- Is there a role for public control?
- Could any overall equilibrium emerge out of decentralized sub-optimizing actions?
- Are issues of distribution and privacy resolved in such a system?
- Is standard-setting necessary or possible?
- How do partially regulated environments function?

Similarly, the interrelation of the various electronic communications networks must be thought through carefully. This is not just a technical and economic matter. Interconnection and access rules define the rights of various media and thereby the participatory rights of their users. They are nothing less than a constitutional framework for the communications infrastructure.

Beyond the Free Internet

One of the many questions about the future of the Internet is whether it will be free. A free Internet in the economic sense is not tenable, and questions about Internet prices and industry structures are important. A free Internet in the legal sense is even more intriguing. One question about future policy is whether the Internet will be regulated. Many Internet enthusiasts dismiss the question as irrelevant. They believe the myth that one cannot regulate the Internet. However, communication is not just a matter of signals but of people and institutions. Virtuality is an appealing notion. But one should not forget that physical reality is alive and well. Senders, recipients, and intermediaries are living, breathing people, or they are legally organized institutions with physical domiciles and physical hardware. The arm of the law can reach them. It may be possible to evade such a law, but the same is true when it comes to tax regulations. Just because a law cannot fully stop an activity does not prove that such law is ineffective or undesirable.

This does not mean that we should regulate cyberspace (whatever it is). But that is a normative question of values, not one of technological determinism. And that choice will not be materially different from those which societies generally apply to the panoply of activities. Why should computer communications and its applications be different? As the Internet moves from being in the main a nerd-preserve and an office park, and becomes a shopping mall and community center, it is sheer fantasy to expect that its uses and users will be beyond the law.

Today, for better or for worse, each society will apply its own accumulated wisdom, prejudices, self-interests, and misconceptions to the rules governing cyberspace. New situations where powerful traditional institutions are on the defensive lead to more rules, not less.

The techniques for control vary depending on the target. Transmission backbones can be set and controlled. Interconnection and traffic hand-off points can be regulated. ISPs can be held liable for content, and they could be licensed. Hardware can be required to have a screening chip. Content providers can have their servers traced and licensed. Organizations can be held liable for content on their computers, available to employees. Routing tables can be controlled. Taxes and tariffs can be levied. Anonymous remailers could be outlawed.

Such rules, or similar ones, are not desirable. But they are unavoidable in the dynamic that will unfold. For every revolution there is a counter-revolution. And because the revolution is farthest along in America, the counter-revolution is likely to emerge here, too.

Beyond Television

In the past, the scarcity of electromagnetic spectrum allocations accommodated only a tiny number of television channels, resulting in program content that averaged many viewing interests in order to aggregate large audiences. The outputs of a medium are defined by its structure. In what ways then will the change in the media structure alter production, news, programs, and distribution? These are areas that are under-researched. The broadening of transmission bandwidth beyond traditional limited television leads to a measurable widening of program options and viewer's differentiation, both in the high- and the low-culture ends of the program spectrum. This process will take several decades but it is on its way. Future cyber media based on electronically accessible video-libraries will further drastically affect program differentiation, viewer control, and program provision from alternative sources.

Beyond the Nation-State

Under the old information order, territorially organized electronic communications networks were based *technologically* on the need for a network architecture that minimized transmission distances; *politically*, on the desire of the state for control over communications; *economically*, on incumbent firms' desire for profitable protection; and *socially*, on the shared reference of national culture. But in the future, with the cost of transmission increasingly distance-insensitive, both telecommunications and mass media networks will become globally organized. This will have important effects. One is on the structure and operations of these networks themselves. A second is on the nature of policy and regulation which will increasingly migrate to regional or international arrangements. And the third is the nature of public communities. Communications media will not create a global village, but instead help organize the world as a series of electronic neighborhoods transcending national frontiers. In the process, the nature of politics will change, and with it policy.

Outlook

Mainstream academic communications disciplines have not kept pace with the concrete questions of public treatment of information, even though the subject of study, information, has achieved centrality in society and economy. For the field of communications policy studies to blossom it must expand.

A first broadening must be into adjoining media. In the past, communications studies have concentrated on mass media, paying little attention to point-to-point and computer communications. Yet the blurring of boundaries separating electronic media and the creation of multi-media technologies, group networks, and interactive personal communications render many distinctions obsolete.

A second broadening takes us beyond the bounds of pure academia. Communications scholars must both address and occasionally venture into a real world whether in production, government, media firms, or public interest advocacy, to name a few. While one must be alert to excessive closeness, research and teaching will benefit overall from such experience.

Third, even within the academic realm, communications studies must overcome insularity. The field of communications studies will hopefully maintain and strengthen its own disciplinary multiculturalism, be it by historians of communications, philosophers, sociologists, or interpreters of culture, to name a few. Yet, despite communications studies being broad in concept, there is an absence of strong links to some disciplines not at the center, such as technology, law, and economics.

And fourth, communications studies must re-establish a strong empirical and applied base within the field, so that theory, methodology, empiricism, and policy will reinforce each other again.

Without such efforts, communications studies will not be able to identify the future of communications or illuminate society's treatment of it, i.e., of policy. If the chasm between the academic field and its subject-matter of study becomes too wide, a self-correcting mechanism takes over. The rapidly moving world of communications media, technology, and infrastructure will force communications studies to change focus, directly or through the next generation of students and researchers.

Note

1. The editors wish to note that the Columbia Institute for Tele-Information, founded by Eli Noam, has also played an leading role in research that contributed to the policy process.

16   Policies for Freedom

Ithiel de Sola Pool

As computers become the printing presses of the twenty-first century, ink marks on paper will continue to be read, and broadcasts to be watched, but other new major media will evolve from what are now but the toys of computer hackers.[1] Videodisks, integrated memories, and data bases will serve functions that books and libraries now serve, while information retrieval systems will serve for what magazines and newspapers do now. Networks of satellites, optical fibers, and radio waves will serve the functions of the present-day postal system. Speech will not be free if these are not also free.

The danger is not of an electronic nightmare, but of human error. It is not computers but policy that threatens freedom. The censorship that followed the printing press was not entailed in Gutenberg's process; it was a reaction to it. The regulation of electronic communication is likewise not entailed in its technology but is a reaction to it. Computers, telephones, radio, and satellites are technologies of freedom, as much as was the printing press.

Communications Policy

In most countries the constitution sets the framework for communications policy.[2] America's basic communications policies are found in three clauses. Article 1, Section 8, gives Congress the power to establish post offices and post roads. The next clause gives Congress the power "To promote the Progress of Science and useful Arts, by securing for limited Times to Authors and Inventors the exclusive Right to their respective Writings and Discoveries." And the very first amendment prohibits Congress from passing any law abridging freedom of speech or of the press. This package of provisions provided publishers with the support they needed but barred the government from interfering with their free expression.

In the comparatively simple American society of the eighteenth century, when the media depended largely on the slowly changing technology of the printing press and when government consisted of the relatively spare mechanisms of the courts, Congress, and a tiny executive branch, communications policy issues were few. They arose most often from the ability of the government to use its fiscal powers both for and against the press. The American people did not oppose the government's use of its fiscal powers to support the press. The authorities did so through the postal system, official advertising, and sinecure appointments. The idea that government should stand at arm's length from the press developed later; the earliest federal policy was to foster the media. The other possibility that government might employ its coercive powers against the press was prohibited by the First Amendment.

As Congress, the executive branch, and the courts dealt with innovations in communications technologies and, during the two centuries following adoption of the First Amendment, sought to formulate policies appropriate to them, the Amendment's original principles were severely compromised. The three main decades of such change occurred at intervals a half-century apart. In the 1870s Congress and the courts extensively restructured postal policies, imposing censorious restrictions. Also in that decade, and shortly before it, the system of common carrier regulation of telegraphy evolved. Fifty years later, in the 1920s, radio broadcasting began. For that medium Congress required that broadcasters be chosen and licensed by the state. Then half a century later, in the 1970s, computer networks, satellites, and cable systems came into extensive use. Some of the regulatory responses to them seem quite unconstitutional.

Both the 1870s and the 1920s were decades of ambivalence about civil liberties. In the 1870s a rising reform movement about both morals and economics challenged the prevailing philosophy of laissez faire. Movements for temperance, prudery, voter registration, and labor protection clashed with ideas of minimal governance. Reformers pressed for acceptance of the regulation of mail as an instrument of censorship. The 1920s saw the Palmer raids, on the one hand, and the Brandeis–Holmes dissents and decisions, on the other.[3] The sensitivity of the Supreme Court to the First Amendment, starting in the 1920s and particularly after World War II, led it to blow the whistle and stem the trend toward postal censorship.

It was in the 1920s, however, that communications policy in the United States most seriously lost its way. Without adequate thought, a structure was introduced for radio which had neither the libertarian features of the common carrier system nor those of the free market. The assumption of the new system was that that spectrum was extremely limited and had to be allotted to chosen users. In Europe the chosen user was generally the government itself; in America it was private licensees. Since only a few would be privileged to broadcast, government felt it must influence the character of what they broadcast. The broadcasting organizations, unlike common carriers, selected and produced programs, but unlike print publishers, who also select what appears, there was no free entry for challengers. So government stepped in to regulate the radio forum and shape the broadcasters' choices.

By this process of evolution there came to be three main communications structures in the United States: the print model, free of regulation in general; the common carrier model, with government assuring nondiscriminatory access for all; and the broadcasting model, with government-licensed private owners as the publishers. The choice between them is likely to be a key policy issue in the coming decades. A convergence of modes is upsetting what was for a while a neatly trifurcated system. Each of the three models was used in its particular industries and for different types of communications. As long as this was the case, the practices in some industries might be less true to the First Amendment than the practices in others, but it did not much affect those media that remained in the domain of the First Amendment. What happened in one industry did not matter greatly for what happened in another.

If this situation were a stable one, there would not be much cause for worry, for if the nation retained a free printed press through which all viewpoints could be expressed, it would not lose its freedom even if broadcasting were totally government controlled. Having print as an island of freedom might be assurance enough against total conformity to authority. But the situation is not stable.

Very rapidly all the media are becoming electronic. Previously the print media were affected, but not themselves transformed, by the electronic media. The electronic media grew and enlarged their field of action but left the older media fundamentally what they had been before. This is no longer the case. With electronic publishing, the practices of the electronic media become practices of the print media too. No longer can one view electronic communications as a circumscribed special case whose monopolistic and regulated elements do not matter very much, because the larger realm of freedom of expression still encompasses all of print. Telecommunications policy is becoming communications policy as all communications come to use electronic forms of transmission.

Soon the courts will have to decide, for vast areas that have so far been quite free of regulation, which of the three traditions of communications practice they will apply. The facts that will face the courts will be a universally interconnected electronic communication system based on a variety of linkable electronic carriers, using radio, cable, microwave, optical fiber, and satellites, and delivering to every home and office a vast variety of different kinds of mail, print, sound, and video, through an electronic network of networks. The question is whether that system will be governed as are the regulated electronic media now, or whether there is some way of retaining the free press tradition of the First Amendment in that brave new world.

Resource Constraints

Historically, some media operate by different rules under the First Amendment from those applied to publications in print because of the existence of scarcities in the resources used in producing them. Abundance and scarcity of resources are the two ends of a continuum. At one end, communication is entirely unconstrained by resources; in the middle are situations in which there is constraint, but everyone can nonetheless have some ration of the means to communicate; and at the other end the constraints are such that only a privileged few can own those means.

Conversation illustrates the optimal situation in which communication is totally without resource constraints, the only limit is one's desire. There is also sidewalk enough in most places that anyone can picket a building without excluding others from passing by, though not when hundreds want to picket in the same place at once. In practice there is no resource bar to forming a congregation to worship together, as witnessed by storefront churches and congregations that meet in members' homes. Similarly, anyone can send a petition or write a letter of protest. The property required to carry out these acts is trivial.

Even in such domains, where normally anyone can communicate at will without noticeably reducing the opportunities for others, there are exceptional situations in which one person's wants do constrain others. Conversation may be abundant, but conversation with a particular partner is an imposition on that person. Assemblage as a congregation can be almost costless if in a member's home, but building a large church on a desirable lot is not. In each of these situations the cliche formula is that people have the right to do as they wish, so long as they do not interfere with the rights of others. But communication in such situations involves so few resource constraints that no special institutions are set up to deal with them.

The situation is more complex when the resources for communication, while not unlimited, are available enough that by reasonable sacrifice and effort a person can get hold of some. In this situation, allocation by the institutions of property and the market becomes a useful norm. An example is the printed magazine. Even the poor, by scrimping and cooperating, can produce periodicals, and some of them do. There are church bulletins for modest congregations, labor and protest papers, adolescent club and school papers. There are thousands of little magazines with stories and poems by unknown amateurs. To convert a publication into a success requires talent, capital, and energy; if the talent and energy are there, the capital may even be borrowed.

In such situations of moderate scarcity, however, not all people can have whatever means of communication they want. The means are rationed. The system of rationing may or may not be equitable or just.[4] There are an infinity of ways to partition a scarce resource. The method may be strictly egalitarian, as that which requires all legal candidates to be offered the same amount of air time under the same terms during an election campaign. The method may be meritocratic, as that which gives free education to those who score high in exams. The method may recognize privilege, as that which allows a descendant to inherit a communications medium or a seat in the House of Lords. The method may recognize cultural values, as that which occurs when a foundation makes grants to museums or symphonies. The method may reward skill and motivation, as that which allows communications institutions to earn profits that depend on their efficiency.

Each of these criteria for allocation has its value, and actual public policy represents different mixes of them. Equality may have both rhetorical appeal and a great deal of merit. Yet few people would opt for totally equal access to scarce means of communication, quite independent of considerations of talent, motivation, or social value in their use.

Property rights in the means of communication are a major method of allocation, but different property schemes produce different allocations. In some property schemes, if people who have radio frequencies do not use them, their right lapses and the frequencies revert to the allocating agency. This is like the small print which reads, "This ticket is nontransferable." In a market scheme, however, the owners may, within the limits of the law, pass on their resource to someone else as a gift or as part of a deal. A market scheme is predicated on a lack of faith in administered wisdom; it treats whatever allocations exist as a starting point only. It assumes that the distributed wisdom among the property holders is greater than that of a central planner.

The law creating a market defines the mix of deals that may be made and specifies some as illegal. A person moving may sell a house, but perhaps under zoning laws it may not be turned into a tavern. A shipowner with a radio license may sell a ship, including the radio facilities, but may not turn the ship's frequency to broadcasting. A cablecaster may sell a system to someone else but, under American rules, may not sell it to the owner of a television station in the same town.

Property is, in summary, simply a recognized partition of a resource that is somewhat scarce. A market is a device for distributing the use of that property. It measures the value people attach to different uses; it allows for shifts in the uses; and it depoliticizes decisions by decentralizing them. But a market is not a single device; it is a class of devices, and public policy defines the market structure.

Where some resource is either very scarce or not easily divisible, ordinary markets function badly. Spectrum, given the way it is now administered, is scarce enough that every small group cannot have its own television station. A telephone system is indivisible in that what is needed is a universal system. In such cases of monopoly or partial monopoly of the means of communication, there are problems for free societies. It was for such situations that the common carrier approach was developed in the nineteenth and early twentieth centuries. Common carriers are obligated to offer their resources to all of the public equally. In the American constitutional system this is an exceptional fallback solution. The basic American tradition of the First Amendment is either the free-for-all of free speech or the competitive market of the early press.

Since scarcity and indivisibility of resources compel a departure from the print model, it is important to estimate what major scarcities and indivisibilities will appear in the evolving electronic media. Despite the profusion of means of communication that are coming out of the technology of the late twentieth century, a number of truly scarce or indivisible elements will remain in the communications system. Despite the cliché of broadcast regulation that frequencies are exceptionally scarce, spectrum is not one of them. If spectrum were allotted by sale in a market, the prices would not be prohibitive, for there are now numerous alternatives, such as data compression or transmission by coaxial cables or optical fibers, which would become economic in the presence of relatively low costs for air rights. Spectrum is only of medium scarcity.

The orbit for satellites is today what spectrum was in 1927, something that at first glance seems inherently and physically scarce. If the technology of orbit usage remained that of the 1970s, orbital slots in the Western hemisphere would have run out by about the time this book got published, and in many other places shortly thereafter. However, techniques for orbit and spectrum saving are multiplying. The real problem is spectrum, not real estate on the orbit. There is abundant space for the satellites themselves. The difficulty is to find frequencies for communicating to and from the satellites without causing radio interference. Polarization, spot beams, time-division multiplexing, on-board switching, and direct satellite-to-satellite microwave or laser links are among the techniques that help. These require agreement to use technically efficient methods, which may not be the cheapest ones. The orbit problem turns out to be a special case of the familiar spectrum problem. To keep prices down requires agreement on and compliance with efficient standards and protocols. But at a price, as much of the resource as is wanted is likely to be available.

Though neither spectrum nor orbital slots are too scarce to be handled by normal market mechanisms, there are other more severe elements of monopoly in the system. One is the need that basic communications networks be universal in reach. If anyone is to be able to send a message or talk to anyone else, there must be universal connectivity, directory information, agreed-on standards, and a legal right to interconnect.

Another element of communications systems that makes for central control is the need to traverse or utilize the public's property. The social costs of not granting the right of eminent domain for transmission routes are very high. Also streets have to be dug to lay cables. These requirements affect many people who are not direct participants in the arrangements.

Finally, there are areas of natural monopoly where the larger the firm, the more efficient its operation, so in the end the smaller competitors are driven out of business. This has been the case for American newspapers. They depend heavily on advertising by merchants. Where there is more than one paper in a town, merchants find it more efficient to advertise in the larger one, and the smaller ones wilt.[5] The situation was similar when there was more than one phone company in a city; customers joined the larger system because there were more people whom they could then call. Customers would also pick the larger cable system if more than one served a neighborhood. The larger system that shared the fixed plant costs among more subscribers could charge less, and with more revenue it could offer more or better programs.

In communications, economies of scale are found especially in wire or cable transmission plants. The large investment in conduits reaching everywhere dominates the equation. There is no such strong economy of scale either in over-the-air transmission or ordinarily in programing or enhanced services. Where economies of scale and therefore natural monopolies do exist, some form of common carriage access is appropriate. It exists in phone service. Common carriage in some form may well come for cable as well.

Although there are elements of natural monopoly in both newspaper and electronic carrier markets, common carrier procedures have been applied in one and not the other. A newspaper may be the only one in its town, yet still it enjoys all the privileges of the ordinarily competitive printed media. Under the First Amendment, as interpreted in the Tornillo case, it cannot be forced to yield access to anyone.[6] The issue of whether, as a monopoly, it should be so compelled is not a trivial one. Barron's argument in Tornillo was not dismissible lightly, but the court did reject it and continued to give newspaper owners full autonomy of editorial decision.

The fact that the newspapers have maintained such freedom from a requirement that normally goes with monopoly distinguishes them from cablecasters, who are ordinarily required by their franchises to provide some access. Historical complexities, not simple logic, account for this paradox. In both cases, but especially for newspapers, the scope of the monopoly is incomplete. At least as important is the fact that newspapers, reared in the tradition of a free press, have behaved so as to discourage the issue from arising. Newspapers, as they moved into the status of monopolies, had the wisdom to defuse hostility by acting in many respects like a common carrier. Aware of their vulnerability, they voluntarily created something of an access system for themselves. Unlike their nineteenth-century ancestors, they see themselves as providing a forum for the whole community. They not only run columnists of opposite tendency and open their local news pages willingly to community groups, but also encourage letters to the editor. Most important of all, they accept advertising for pay from anyone. Only rarely does a newspaper refuse an ad on grounds of disagreement. If newspapers were as opinionated as they used to be in the days when they were competitive, public opinion would have long since acted against their unregulated monopoly.

Furthermore, newspapers are far from having a complete monopoly. Newspaper publishers, like cablecasters, argue that they are not a monopoly in an appropriately defined market. Even if there is only one newspaper in a town, there are many ways in which opinions get distributed in print. A handbill or periodical of opinion competes with a newspaper in the marketplace of ideas. News magazines and suburban papers also compete.

The Tornillo decision is not likely to be reconsidered. Newspapers are facing growing competition. Electronic information service and specialized national newspapers will erode still further their local monopoly. If such monopolies have not constrained open discussion in print up to now, they are even less likely to do so in the future.

Cablecasters claim that their situation is no different from that of the press, so they deserve exactly the same treatment. They argue that they too will maintain an open forum. Perhaps fifteen years hence one will be able to say that the cable industry saw the writing on the wall and behaved in a statesmanlike manner. Maybe it too will have voluntarily made channels available to all, even leasing channels to competitors. Maybe by then the newly emerging technology of a broadband ISDN on the telephone network will also have made it no longer sensible to talk of cable monopoly. But there is reason to doubt such expectations. The technical solution may come slowly, and the forecast of statesmanship is hardly supported by present behavior. Newspapermen come from a tradition of political combativeness and First Amendment principle; cablecasters come from the tradition of show business. Newspapers are an unregulated industry proud of their independence from the state; cable is a regulated franchised business. To look to the cable industry for such sensitivity to First Amendment considerations as to prevent the access issue from becoming intense is probably unrealistic.

There are economic reasons why radical surgery to separate carrier from content in cablecasting would not work in America. There is not now, nor will there be in the near future, the volume of carrier business needed for private cable businesses to expand in this way.[7] But given the temptation for a cable monopoly to stifle uses that do not interest it, and given the self-serving positions against requirements for channel leasing that the industry has taken, there is good reason for city governments, when franchising a cable monopoly, to require that at least leased access on a nondiscriminatory basis be provided. There are ways in which this can be done without destroying the economics of the systems. Nor does a leasing requirement in a franchise deny cablecasters their First Amendment rights.

Cable monopolies, owing to the physical problems of traversing the city's terrain, exist by grace of government franchise. Local newspapers are natural economic monopolies. This is a difference of a kind the courts have recognized.[8] The distinction can be stated in terms of resource constraint. Local newspaper monopolies arise from choices that consumers and suppliers make in the market, not from the existence of constraints that are so severe as to prevent the effective making of such market choices. Nonetheless, until the electronic media shake the present newspaper structure and bring readers into easy contact with competing news sources, local press monopolies will remain common. The paradox will continue of a monopolized print medium enjoying the freedom of the print tradition, while common carrier and regulated practices continue for electronic media, some of which operate under severe resource constraints and should therefore be obliged to provide access, and others of which do not.

The precise structure of common carrier regulation as embodied in the FCC's common carrier rules and the 1934 Communications Act is quite properly being questioned as burdensome. But the core of the common carrier concept, namely that a vendor with monopoly advantage in the market must provide access to customers without discrimination, remains often applicable to basic electronic carriers, as it was in the past to the mails.

The Policy Debate about Monopoly

Fear of monopoly has been at the core of most current communications policy debates and of most proposals to depart from the First Amendment tradition. "Monopoly" was the word used in 1927 by those attacking AT&T's attempt to set up a broadcasting common carrier. It is the word now being used by postal and telecommunications administrations in defense of their exclusive right to carry messages among the public. It is the word used to justify special restraints on AT&T.

Monopoly implies a single entity, but what is generally discussed is rather a matter of degree. A company of sufficient size to affect the market in which it operates is said in popular discourse to have some monopoly power. The television networks are frequently called monopolies, though there are three of them. The word "oligopoly" exists, but not in lay discussions. Furthermore, it describes only one of the ways in which partial monopoly power may exist. The very small publisher of a neighborhood shopping throwaway is most often a monopolist in the neighborhood but is in fierce competition for advertising with the city daily newspaper and thus has very little market power.

Market power is not identical with social or political power over communications, though they are closely related. The monopoly situations that are of concern for liberty are those where some resource needed to communicate is scarce enough that whoever owns it has considerable power over others who seek to use it. The economist's analysis focuses rather on power over other suppliers who compete in the market. A political analysis focuses instead on who gets to use the airwaves of a station that is licensed or who can send messages when a carrier controls the practical means for delivering them.

In rhetoric, the United States government favors diversity of voices and seeks to break up communications monopolies. The reality, however, is more ambiguous. Few monopolies exist from economic factors alone, and fewer still survive by private coercion alone. Mafiosos are not that strong. The force that preserves most monopoly privilege is the law. Some monopolies rest on patents, others on copyright, still others on franchises or licenses, some on property rights in unique locations, and many on regulatory policies that protect vested interests against assault. Most monopolies exist by grace of the police and the courts. From a social point of view some are desirable, others undesirable; but most would vanish in the absence of enforcement.

Antitrust policy, and thus most current debate over communications policy, has focused on the market-produced monopolies, for the monopolies that the government establishes by patents, copyrights, franchises, and laws are exceptions to the antitrust laws and so are perfectly legal. The government does not challenge them. When American government does grant a monopoly, its attitude is sometimes ambivalent. Monopoly grants are often designed to give a privilege and at the same time to limit it. Both copyrights and patents, for example, are for finite terms, require disclosure, and may not be used to keep a product off the market. They are monopolies intended in the end to promote rather than restrict access.

While the intent of regulation is often to provide some modest protection for the weak, the ultimate outcome is often more protection for the strong. American broadcasting regulation follows a policy of localism, that is, protecting local stations so a few superstations do not dominate the national air. This policy protects an oligopoly of broadcasters in every city. It gives them advantages not only in their own community but also against still bigger would-be national monopolists. Often regulation is thus used to give smaller companies some monopoly protection against larger ones. For decades neither AT&T nor Western Union were allowed to go into international telegraphy; it was reserved for four international record carriers which, it was believed, would be crushed if the domestic communication giants were allowed into the intercontinental business. For satellites too the policy of "open skies," by excluding AT&T, assured business in the formative years to a group of oligopolists.

The legal crutch that preserves weak companies is exculpated in the name of competition. If the crutch were removed, it is said, one more company would disappear, leaving fewer and larger contenders in control of the field. Thus in a normal communications environment there are little monopolies and big ones; each argues for the essentiality of its privilege, and each enjoys at most only a bit of monopoly.

Regulation, whatever its motives, tends to create these islands of segregated activity. Some firms are protected from others. Also, it is easier to control an activity when it is not mixed in with ones that are unregulated. A mix of competition and monopoly creates the possibility of cross-subsidization. Profits from a sheltered activity may be used to cut prices in competitive fields. The primary goal of antitrust policy in telecommunications has been to ensure that no one entity is simultaneously in both the naturally monopolistic portions of the phone business and in competitive markets.

At the same time, the goal of deregulation has been to free companies from the bonds of regulatory convenience and allow them to experiment in the market with the efficiencies of new technologies and joint products. In the United States this unleashing has been enjoyed by AT&T, but only AT&T without local operating companies. It has not been done for the postal service, nor is it likely to be done for such a tax-supported enterprise, though the same result may be achieved through private express carriers.

The postal system has an office in every neighborhood and delivery to every door. Historically, this made it seem a natural organization for also handling small parcels, which it now handles everywhere. It also appeared a natural organization for delivering telegrams. In countries where they are still delivered, this is done through the post office or else at enormous loss. Post offices also serve as convenient government field offices. In many countries a poor person's banking, plus the sale of money orders and sometimes insurance, is handled through the post office. The advantage of sharing joint costs among many functions of a distribution plant was perceived even at the birth of postal service, when monarchs got cheap mail service for themselves by allowing the recipients of their postal patent to carry the public's letters for a fee. Daily, to-the-door delivery could conceivably be made less of a fiscal burden if milk, eggs, newspapers, and mail were all handled together. It would be good economic policy for a postal service to get into other businesses in competition with haulers, telecommunications companies, banks, and dairies. Similarly telephone companies, which have a virtually universal billing system and a network for moving funds, may become billing services and, following that, credit organizations and financial intermediaries, or what are ordinarily called banks. By the same token banks may become communications carriers. Certainly computer and aerospace companies may find that they have the skills and facilities to offer transmission services.

Present American deregulatory policy encourages such competition. Any company can get into the game, except ones with a substantial monopoly position that could be used for anticompetitive practices. The popular cry now is to let the market determine which alternative vendors with their different joint costs, organization, and skills can efficiently provide each service.

At least as important as ideology in causing communications deregulation has been technological change. The use of coaxial cable and of ever higher frequencies has eroded spectrum shortage. The introduction of microwave transmission in the 1930s eliminated the problem of right of way. Microwave frequencies, though not unlimited, were abundant enough to allow a substantial number of competing carriers. Satellite communication has reinforced this trend, for nothing prevents there being several competing satellite transmission organizations.

Deregulation, however, is a pragmatic policy. The argument made against regulations has been that they are inefficient and unnecessary, not improper. It holds that with converging technologies, the removal of controls will produce competition. Where this does not turn out to be the case, the deregulators are ready to step back in and regulate. But in the arena of speech and press we need also to consider other guidelines that have been left in the outfield in recent policy controversies—ones that recognize the preferred position of freedom of discourse.

Guidelines for Freedom

Difficult problems of press freedom, as well as of economics, arise at the intersections of regulatory models. When resource constraints are small and circumstances neatly fit the historical pattern of publishing, or when resource constraints are severe and circumstances fit the historical situation of a common carrier, then norms exist. The difficulties arise in situations that have elements of each. This was the problem in deciding about the broadcasting system in the 1920s; it is also a problem in the regulation of electronic networks today.

Regulators find it convenient to segregate activities and to keep each organization on its own turf. Much of regulatory law consists of specifications as to who may engage in what activities. Frequency allocations are made for particular uses; CBers or amateurs may not broadcast entertainment; public broadcast stations may not carry ads.[9] In the United States, AT&T and Western Union have been largely partitioned, with AT&T kept out of telex and telegraph traffic and Western Union kept out of voice. Deregulation loosens such restrictions and allows companies to move onto each other's turf. But some segmentation persists.

A price is paid for this rigid delimitation of turf, not only in efficiency and innovation but also in freedom of speech. The notion that government may specify which communications entity is allowed to participate in particular parts of the information industry's vertical flow is hard to reconcile with the First Amendment. To research and write, to print or orate, to publish and distribute, is everyone's right. If government licensing of reporters, publishers, or printing presses is anathema, then so also should be the licensing of broadcasters and telecommunications carriers.

Yet the repeated argument has been made, which may be right or wrong in particular cases, that some degree of natural monopoly prevails in particular parts of the communications field. Whether because there were thought to be only 89 broadcasting frequencies, or because having more than one company digging up the streets was intolerable, or because the carrier that reached most persons was the one most worth joining, it seemed likely that a dominant organization would gain control of a communications resource that other citizens also needed. Under these circumstances the best solution seemed to be to define a monopoly's turf narrowly and to require those who had the monopoly to serve all comers without discrimination.

Since the institutions in such strategic positions are usually basic carriers of physical signals, one way to narrow their domain is to separate the carrier from content-related activities. But there are problems in doing this, in terms both of undercutting the economics of the business and, in America, of bending the Constitution. The unfortunate compromise that has often followed is to license and regulate the monopoly.

Such limited franchises have a way of being extended beyond their original rationale. Enfranchised monopolies that at one time are thought simply to reflect in an orderly fashion the natural realities of the market, and are indeed intended to restrict monopoly, get converted into matters of right. Stations and carriers that are licensed simply to ensure good service by carefully selected organizations when monopoly seems inevitable come to see themselves, and to be seen, as having a vested right in their franchise. Regulatory powers assumed by the government to cope with monopoly also acquire a life of their own.

This faces the communications field with a dilemma. Not all parts of the communications system fit well under the preferred print model. Bottlenecks do exist where there are severe resource constraints. And the regulations that in those situations seem to be required have an insidious bent. They acquire legitimacy; they outlive their need; they tend to spread. The camel's nose is under the tent.

Yet when there is severe scarcity, there is an unavoidable need to regulate access. Caught in the tension between the tradition of freedom and the need for some controls, the communications system then tends to become a mix of uncontrolled and common carrier elements—of anarchy, of property, and of enfranchised services. A set of principles must be understood if communications in the electronic era are to hold as fully as possible to the terms of the First Amendment. The technology does not make this hard. Confusion about principles may.

The first principle is that the First Amendment applies fully to all media. It applies to the function of communication, not just to the media that existed in the eighteenth century. It applies to the electronic media as much as to the print ones.

Second, anyone may publish at will. The core of the First Amendment is that government may not prohibit anyone from publishing. There may be no licensing, no scrutiny of who may produce or sell publications or information in any form.

Third, enforcement of the law must be after the fact, not by prior restraint. In the history of communications law this principle has been fundamental. Libel, obscenity, and eavesdropping are punishable, but prior review is anathema. In the electronic media this has not been so, but it should be. Traffic controls may be needed in cases where only one communicator can function at a particular place at a particular time, such as street meetings or use of radio frequencies, but this limited authority over time and place is not the same as power to choose or refuse to issue a license.

Fourth, regulation is a last recourse. In a free society, the burden of proof is for the least possible regulation of communication. If possible, treat a communications situation as free for all rather than as subject to property claims and a market. If resource constraints make this impossible, treat the situation as a free market rather than as a common carrier. But if resources for communication are truly monopolistic, use common carrier regulation rather than direct regulation or public ownership. Common carriage is a default solution when all must share a resource in order to speak or publish.

Under common law in the nineteenth century, vendors could not be made common carriers against their will.[10] If they offered a service to the general public, it had to be without discrimination, but if they chose to serve a limited clientele, that was their right. This philosophy applies well to publishing. One would not require the *Roman Catholic Pilot* to carry ads for birth control or a trade union magazine to carry ads against the closed shop. But these cases assume that diverse magazines exist. A dilemma arises when there is a monopoly medium, as when a monopoly newspaper in a town refuses ads to one party and carries them for another.

In the world of electronic communications, some but not all of the basic physical carriers, and only those, seem likely to continue to have significant monopoly power. It is hard to imagine a value-added network having the dominance in a community that a local newspaper has today. Even now the communications monopolies that exist without privileged enforcement by the state are rare. Even basic physical conduits become monopolies precisely because they cannot exist without public favors. They need permissions that only the state can grant. These favors, be they franchises to dig up the city streets or spectrum to transmit through the air, may properly be given to those who choose to serve as common carriers. This is not a new idea. In 1866 telegraph companies were given the right to string wires at will along post roads and across public lands, but only if they became common carriers. Where monopoly exists by public favor, public access is a reasonable condition.

Fifth, interconnection among common carriers may be required. The basic principle of common carriage, namely that all must be served without discrimination, implies that carriers accept interconnection from each other. This principle, established in the days of the telegraph, is incorporated in the 1982 AT&T consent decree. All long-distance carriers have a right to connect to all local phone companies. That is the 1980s outgrowth of the 1968 Carterphone decision which required AT&T to interconnect with an independent radio-telephone service.[11] Universal interconnection implies both adherence to technical standards, without which interconnection can be difficult, and a firm recognition of the right to interconnect.

Carriers may sometimes raise valid objections to interconnection. Some will wish to use novel technologies that are incompatible with generally accepted standards, claiming that they are thereby advancing the state of the art. Also, when they handle highly sensitive traffic, such as funds transfers or intra-company data, they may not wish to be common carriers and bear the risks of having outsiders on their system. Such arguments are often valid, though they may also be used to lock a group of customers out of using the carrier.

An argument in favor of general interconnectivity is that it facilitates market entry by new or small carriers. It also makes universal service easier. It may even be useful for national security, since a highly redundant system is less likely to be brought down. In short, there are conflicting considerations that must be balanced. As a policy, the requirement of interconnection is a reasonable part of a common carriage system.

Sixth, recipients of privilege may be subject to disclosure. The enforcement of nondiscrimination depends critically on information. Without control of accounting methods, regulatory commissions are lost in a swamp. I once asked the head of the Common Carrier Bureau of the FCC what he would ask for if he could rub Aladdin's lamp. "Revelatory books" was his reply.

Yet American lawmakers, who have imposed far more oppressive and dubious kinds of regulation, such as exit, entry, and tariff controls, have never pushed the mild requirement for visibility. Apart from requiring accounts, legislators have been highly considerate of proprietary information. A firm that enjoys the monopoly privileges which lead to being a common carrier should perhaps forgo, like government, some privileges of privacy. Unbundled rates for cable leasing, for example, help reveal who is being charged for what. Disclosure is not a new idea. Patents and copyrights are privileges won only by making their object public. The same principle might well apply to action under franchises too.

Seventh, privileges may have time limits. Patents and copyrights are for finite periods, and then the right expires. Radio and television licenses and cable franchises, though also for fixed periods, are typically renewable. Some monopoly privileges that broadcasters and cablecasters have in their licenses could expire after a fixed period. This is a way to favor infant industries but limit their privileges when they become giants.

Eighth, the government and common carriers should be blind to circuit use. What the facility is used for is not their concern. There may be some broad categories of use. Emergency communications often have priority. Special press rates for telegraph have been permitted, though their legality in the United States has been questioned.[12] But in general, control of the conduit may not become a means for controlling content. What customers transmit on the carrier is no affair of the carrier.

Ninth, bottlenecks should not be used to extend control. Rules on undeliverable mail have been used to control obscene content. Cablecasting, in which there is no spectrum shortage, has been regulated by the FCC as ancillary to broadcasting. Telegraph companies have sought to control news services, and cable franchisees have sought to control the programs on the cable. Under the First Amendment, no government imposition on a carrier should pass muster if it is motivated by concerns beyond common carriage, any more than the carrier should be allowed to use its service to control its customers.

Tenth, and finally, for electronic publishing, copyright enforcement must be adapted to the technology. This exceptional control on communication is specifically allowed by the Constitution as a means of aiding dissemination, not restricting it. Copyright is temporary and requires publication. It was designed for the specific technology of the printing press. It is in its present form ill adapted to the new technologies. The objective of copyright is beyond dispute. Intellectual effort needs compensation. Without it, effort will wither. But to apply a print scheme of compensation to the fluid dialogue of interactive electronic publishing will not succeed. Given modern technologies, there is no conceivable way that individual copies can be effectively protected from reproduction when they are already either on a sheet of paper or in a computer's memory. The task is to design new forms of market organization that will provide compensation and at the same time reflect the character of the new technology.

The question boils down to what users at a computer terminal will pay for. For one thing, they will pay for a continuing relationship, as they will continue to need maintenance. It may be easy to pirate a single program or some facts from a data base by copying from a friend of a friend of a friend who once bought it. But to get help in adapting it or to get add-on versions or current data, one might pay a fee as a tender for future relations. The magazine subscription model is closer to the kind of charging system that will work for electronic publishing than is the one-time book purchase with a royalty included.

A workable copyright system is never enacted by law alone. Rather it evolves as a social system, which may be bolstered by law. The book and music royalty systems that now exist are very different from each other, reflecting the different structures of the industries. What the law does is to put sanctions behind what the parties already consider right. So too with electronic publishing on computer networks, a normative system must grow out of actual patterns of work. The law may then lend support to those norms.

If language were as fluid as the facts it represents, one would talk in the electronic era of serviceright, not copyright. But as language is used, old words are kept regardless of their derivation, and their meanings are changed. In the seventeenth century, reproducing a text by printing was a complex operation that could be monitored. Once the text was printed on paper, however, it required no further servicing, and no one could keep track of it as it passed from reader to reader. In the electronic era, copying may become trivially easy at the work stations people use. But both the hardware and the software in which the text is embodied require updating and maintenance. In ways that cannot yet be precisely identified, the bottleneck for effective monitoring and charging is migrating from reproduction to the continuing service function.

Not only in copyright but in all other issues of communications policy, the courts and legislatures will have to respond to a new and puzzling technology. The experience of how the American courts have dealt with new nonprint media over the past hundred years is cause for alarm. Forty years ago Zechariah Chafee noted how differently the courts treated the print media from newer ones: "Newspapers, books, pamphlets, and large meetings were for many centuries the only means of public discussion, so that the need for their protection has long been generally realized. On the other hand, when additional methods for spreading facts and ideas were introduced or greatly improved by modern inventions, writers and judges had not got into the habit of being solicitous about guarding their freedom. And so we have tolerated censorship of the mails, the importation of foreign books, the stage, the motion picture, and the radio."[13] With the still newer electronic media the problem is compounded. A long series of precedents, each based on the last and treating clumsy new technologies in their early forms as specialized business machines, has led to a scholastic set of distinctions that no longer correspond to reality. As new technologies have acquired the functions of the press, they have not acquired the rights of the press. On print, no special excise taxes may be applied; yet every month people pay a special tax on their telephone bill, which would seem hardly different in principle from the old English taxes on newspapers. On print, the court continues to exercise special vigilance for the preferred position of the First Amendment; but other considerations of regulatory convenience and policy are given a preferred position in the common carrier and electronic domains. Since the lines between publishing, broadcasting, and the telephone network are now being broken, the question arises as to which of these three models will dominate public policy regarding the new media. There is bound to be debate, with sharp divisions between conflicting interests. Will public interest regulation, such as the FCC applies, begin to extend over the conduct of the print media as they increasingly use regulated electronic means of dissemination? Or will concern for the traditional notion of a free press lead to funding ways to free the broadcast media and carriers from the regulation and content-related requirements under which they now operate?

Electronic media, as they are coming to be, are dispersed in use and abundant in supply. They allow for more knowledge, easier access, and freer speech than were ever enjoyed before. They fit the free practices of print. The characteristics of media shape what is done with them, so one might anticipate that these technologies of freedom will overwhelm all attempts to control them. Technology, however, shapes the structure of the battle, but not every outcome. While the printing press was without doubt the foundation of modern democracy, the response to the flood of publishing that it brought forth has been censorship as often as press freedom. In some times and places the even more capacious new media will open wider the floodgates for discourse, but in other times and places, in fear of that flood, attempts will be made to shut the gates.

The easy access, low cost, and distributed intelligence of modern means of communication are a prime reason for hope. The democratic impulse to regulate evils, as Tocqueville warned, is ironically a reason for worry. Lack of technical grasp by policy makers and their propensity to solve problems of conflict, privacy, intellectual property, and monopoly by accustomed bureaucratic routines are the main reasons for concern. But as long as the First Amendment stands, backed by courts which take it seriously, the loss of liberty is not foreordained. The commitment of American culture to pluralism and individual rights is reason for optimism, as is the pliancy and profusion of electronic technology.

Notes

1. For the changing technologies of communication, see Hiroshi Inose and John R. Pierce, *Information Technology and Civilization* (San Francisco: W. H. Freeman; forthcoming), chs. 1–2.

2. After the Italian Supreme Court ruled unconstitutional a monopoly in local radio and television broadcasting, hundreds of local stations were formed. The absence of a written constitution in Great Britain results in its approach being much like that of U.S. Supreme Court Justice Frankfurter's, both viewing freedom as important, along with order, justice, and other values. But in Britain, without judicial review of constitutionality, it is left to the lawmakers to balance those values. Concern about the growing power of British trade unions to interfere with the content of news-papers and the mails, as well as about the effects of the Official Secrets Act, has generated a movement for the codification of rights. Unions in 1977 refused to deliver the mails of a struck plant and several times refused to print papers with ads or stories of which they disapproved. In Canada the presence of a controlling federal bill of rights was at the heart of the bitter resistance by Quebec to the Constitution instituted in 1982.

3. Similarly in the 1920s in Europe, labor governments for the first time took power and regulatory social legislation was adopted, but totalitarian movements arose to offer a populist counterattack to liberal reforms. Large private enterprises came to dominate the press, and critics sought to control "irresponsible" media, particularly in the new technology of broadcasting.

4. The Marxist utopia is the freeing of all activity from resource constraints.

5. American newspapers are natural monopolies because they are so heavily advertiser supported; they would not be so if their readers paid most of the cost. The reason there are three broadcasting networks, not one, is the limit on the amount of advertising each broadcaster can carry. If the most successful network could add advertising minutes indefinitely, it would drive out the other networks. But as it is, there is too much advertising to fit on one or even two networks.

6. *Miami Herald Publishing Co. v. Tornillo*, 418 US 241, 41 L. ed. 2nd 730, 94 S.Ct. 2831. Lee Bollinger, in "Freedom of the Press and Public Access: Toward a Theory of Partial Regulation of the Mass Media," *University of Michigan Law Review* 75 (1976): 1, argues that regulating some media and not others may be a good idea, even though the Supreme Court was wrong in basing broadcast regulation on a premise of special scarcity. This is a Frankfurtian brief for accepting the dangers of congressional experimentation.

7. In countries where cable television is operated by a government PTT rather than by private entrepreneurs, separation of carrier and content may make both economic and political sense.

8. *Home Box Office, Inc., v. FCC*, 567 F 2d 9, 185 US App. D.C. 142 (1977).

9. The Corporation for Public Broadcasting has recently been permitted a limited experiment running some ads. This barrier may be giving way.

10. *Frost v. Railroad Commission of California*, 271 US 583, 70 L.ed. 1101, 46 S.Ct. 605; *Washington ex rel Stimson Lumber Co. v. Kuykendall* 275 US 207, 72 L.ed. 241, 48 S.Ct. 41. Cf. *Stephenson v. Binford,* 287 US 251 77 L.ed. 288, 53 S.Ct. 181.

11. In Carterphone Dockets 16942 and 17073 of 1968, the FCC required phone companies to allow a radiophone service to be interconnected with them.

12. The FCC avoided confronting this issue by deferring action until the rates were about to be abandoned anyhow as the press moved over to the use of private lines.

13. Zechariah Chafee, *Free Speech in the United States* (Cambridge: Harvard University Press, 1941), p. 381.

17 Regulating Communications in the 21st Century: New Common Ground

Patricia Hirl Longstaff[1]

There can no longer be much doubt that the various industries known collectively as the communications sector are undergoing profound changes and evolving in ways that are impossible to predict. There is also little doubt that the regulation of these formerly discrete industries must change as they combine and metamorphose into new entities. Because these changes will have an effect on virtually every other human enterprise, the evolution of communications regulation will be one of the most important challenges of the twenty-first century.

As with any pervasive change, new words will creep into conversations to express ideas and things not experienced before, and this seems especially true in areas of changing technology. For example, the merger of computers with communications technology has come to be called "compunications."[2] If a telephone company offers something that looks like a cable television (TV) service, is that a cablephone service? If a broadcaster uses part of its digital spectrum allocation to offer a channel for data services, does that make it a datacaster? What if a cablephone company retransmits the signal of a datacaster?

Such questions are neither frivolous nor far-fetched, and their meaning goes beyond linguistics. A wave of new technology and business mergers has reorganized the communications sector both domestically, within the United States, and internationally, redrawing the boundaries of industries and altering competitive relationships. In the much-touted information age, new products and services are defying old distinctions and definitions. Companies that had been competitors now are cooperating, and those that once cooperated now are competing.

In the face of all this change, legal and policy questions must continue to be analyzed by asking where a service falls with regard to the regulatory boxes established earlier in the twentieth century, when industries such as telephony and broadcasting seemed to be separate industrial species that ought to have separate regulatory systems. In other words, the first question in any public policy analysis has been equivalent to "is it a duck?"

Consider a business that wants to put a color printer in homes and offices to be used with a cable TV service to print out color coupons, advertisements, news articles, or even whole books.[3] Is this a cable service? A publishing service? Will it be subject to the laws regulating cable or the laws (or absence of laws) applicable to publishing? Will the city government, the state public utility commission (PUC), or the Federal Communications Commission (FCC) have jurisdiction? Or should these hybrid technologies remain outside the regulatory process?[4]

If a local telephone company started delivering movies, professional wrestling, and reruns of 1960s sitcoms, it would still look like a telephone company (it will still have lines that go into the home and might also offer "plain old telephone service" [POTS] to the same customers), but it will also look like a cable TV or satellite TV service. In the 1996 Communications Act, Congress decided that, in this situation, telephone companies do not need to seek a local franchise (mandatory for cable). This may have been the right decision, but it begs the question.[5]

Regulatory barriers have also been broken down to allow the local cable company to offer POTS in addition to its standard video fare,[6] and electric companies can offer both POTS and video programming.[7] In one case, a duck took on a second job as a goose, and in the other a sea gull works as both a duck and a goose. Everyone is starting to hang around with ducks, geese, sea gulls, and even hawks. Which should be treated like a duck?[8]

The problems or opportunities, or both, for traditional "media" enterprises and their telecommunications partners and competitors are only part of the story. The law of "cyberspace" is almost wholly uncharted, and scholars studying computer-based communications systems such as the Internet are struggling to determine which of the traditional regulatory models is most appropriate to digital communications, which can be distributed by coaxial cable, fiber-optic lines, twisted copper wire (traditional telephone lines), wireless cable, wireless telephony, or satellite.[9]

This massive reorganization of the communications sector has even called into question fundamental legal and constitutional principles long regarded as firmly settled. As a result, much of the new communications frontier remains outlaw territory.[10] For example, what constitutional rights will be accorded to people who send or receive messages in these new channels? This apparently simple question is complicated by a structural flaw that has developed in building modern communications law: Rights and responsibilities are governed not so much by what one says but what channel one says it in.[11]

The present system of constitutional protections is based on three regulatory models built for print, broadcast, and common carriers (telephone and postal). Attempts to apply these models to new technologies (and even to old ones in the face of digitization and improvements to the efficient use of spectrum) has become a nightmare for all involved. Under the current system, information distributed on paper has the highest level of constitutional protection and very little government regulation. The same information distributed using the electromagnetic spectrum in an over-the-air system has much less constitutional protection and a lot more regulation. Distribution by a wire-based system moves into an uncharted frontier, especially if, like cable TV operators, the distributor is both a sender of information and the owner of the channel.

According to Hollywood westerns, in the absence of rules on the frontier, the big guys usually win, but many policymakers (and small players) think this the wrong outcome where communications are concerned.[12] And without an adequate regulatory force in the field, the development of the new territory may be slowed by fear—fear that on the part of communications companies could lead to reluctance to introduce new products or invest in new infrastructure before the rules are clear.[13]

Regulators must deal also with consumers' fears in the debates on the privacy of data,[14] government eavesdropping,[15] and the cost of access to the new information wonderland.[16] Anxiety about regulation has been cited as one of the major brakes on the continuing commercialization of the evolving U.S. communications and computer technologies.[17]

The theoretical framework proposed here may help the various industries bridge part of the vast cultural and regulatory differences between themselves and the new industries with which they are coming into contact. For example, telephone companies have seen themselves as "partners" with government in providing universal telephone service and, until recently, were accustomed to seeking regulatory approval for even the smallest change in the ways they do business. This procedure is absolutely antithetical to the view that newspapers have of their own relationship to government and will be a serious impediment to any joint ventures or business activities between these industries in the future.

The proposed framework does not advocate form or vilify any particular technologies or those who operate them. Governments everywhere are swamped by trade associations representing newspapers, broadcasters, telephone companies, and cable companies as well as all the new and hybrid technologies. These associations will point with justifiable pride to the contributions their members may make to the future of civilization while painting rival technologies as forces of evil. Such an approach could lead to what is commonly known as regulatory gridlock, and, while it could leave regulators unable to move, it could also result in an absence of the predictability so desperately needed. Regulatory paralysis would put many crucial questions into the courts, where judges must make decisions with little to guide them other than laws made back when ducks were ducks.[18]

Of course, it would be naive, and probably counterproductive, to expect the existing regulatory apparatus to change overnight. The slow pace of change in the law is sometimes said to be one of its strengths, especially in the face of great social or technical change. Justice Holmes put the case succinctly: "It cannot be helped ... the law is always behind the times."[19] Clearly, change is necessary, but precipitous change would make the problems faced by this evolving communications sector even worse. Manipulation targeting toward the pressure points of the system, however, could help move change in the desired direction(s). A long acknowledged and major function of the law is to "maintain adaptability" and to redefine relations between individuals and groups as the conditions of life change.[20]

The current systems of communications regulation evolved as new technologies were added to the regulatory agenda, so an evolutionary process that would enable all participants to evolve and adapt to the new technological environment would seem to make more sense than one involving the massive bloodshed (in this instance, financial hemorrhaging) associated with revolutionary change. An evolutionary process would also allow for mid-course corrections and adaptations to circumstances still unforeseeable. Policymakers will not necessarily be relegated to being spectators during this process. By going "back to the basics," they can focus on the things about communications that will stay put and will not be scattered by the winds of change.[21]

What is proposed here does not in any way dictate particular outcomes for any policy question nor mandate that policymakers in all jurisdictions make the same choices. But it does provide a universal framework for these discussions and makes international coordination more efficient when that is deemed appropriate.

Information Theory

A valid scientific theory seldom if ever offers the solution to the pressing problems which we repeatedly state. It seldom supplies a sensible answer to our multitudinous questions.

Rather than rationalizing our ideas, it discards them entirely, or, rather it leaves them where they were. It tells us in a fresh new way what aspects of our experience can profitably be related and simply understood.   —John R. Pierce

Science as a Basis for Law

One of the hallmarks of the legal systems of most countries is a passion for equal justice under the law. Two cases with essentially the same facts ought to end with the same result. Attributes of the parties themselves irrelevant to the issues should not, in theory, control the outcome. The goal of equal justice enhances the predictability of the law and allows citizens and businesses to plan their affairs. Laws of commerce that are hard to predict can distort or even paralyze activity in a market economy Laws of science attempt to predict how people (and all other forms of matter in the universe) will behave under certain conditions. Much of jurisprudence is based on the predictions of scientific disciplines known as the "social" sciences—sociology, anthropology, and political science. For example, much of the criminal justice system is based on assumptions about how people will react to the threat of imprisonment or various efforts at rehabilitation.

The so-called "hard" sciences—physics, chemistry, biology—also are used as the basis for laws and regulations to predict desired (or undesired) outcomes. For example, the regulation of nuclear reactors would not be useful were it not based on nuclear physics.

Information theory is not generally taught in high schools or liberal arts colleges, and many readers will not be familiar with the field. Yet it is one of the theoretical underpinnings for the advancements in telecommunications and computers that have led to the modern communications revolution. Here, the structure of information theory will be used, but not the underlying mathematics. Those interested in the mathematical basis of the theory may consult Claude Shannon's original work.[22]

Foundations of Information Theory

Information theory cannot point to any one academic birthplace. Its roots are in many areas, primarily physics and mathematics. Like most scientific theories, it did not come to attention outside academic circles until it became useful in engineering and technology, that is, until someone could use it to make something or to make something work. It has been used to analyze subjects as

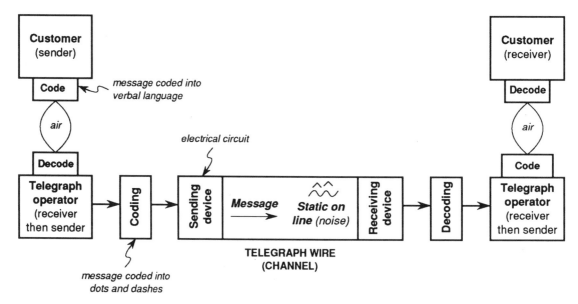

Figure 17.1   General model of communication

diverse as weapons delivery, cybernetics, psychology, and even art.[23] It is useful in so many areas because it describes every communications process, from the intercellular to the interstellar.

Every communication can be broken down to a basic model, all the elements of which may be present on many levels or at many stages of the process (see figure 17.1).

In some cases, the message is stored during or between communication transactions. For example, messages are stored in books, on computer disks, and, of course, in the human brain. Communication has also been analyzed into "substance, process, and format."[24] These concepts are not inconsistent with the Shannon model but are ways to describe various ways the parts of the model work together. For example, "format" describes how coding and the channel work together (e.g., a book is coded into a written language then printed on paper as its channel). All complex modern systems of communication—radio, television, satellite communication, cable, and wireless phones and computers—are refinements or elaborations on these concepts.

For example, information theory can be seen in action (although it was not yet identified as such) in the work of Samuel F. B. Morse. In 1832, Morse pioneered the use of a coded electrical signal to send information over long distances. Because this system could send only a "click" to the machine at the other end of the wire, the letters of words being transmitted were coded as a series of short and long pauses between clicks, a system that became known as Morse Code. This system illustrates the basic elements of any communication:

Sender: The one attempting to send a message to another (in this case, the person wanting to send a telegram).

Receiver: The one who perceives the message, whether or not the intended receiver (such as the person[s] who read a telegram).

Encoding: The process (for example, changing words into dots and dashes) that codes the message so that it can be used in a particular channel.

Sending device: A machine that puts the coded message into the channel. (The "device" can be the key the telegraph operator presses to open and close the electric circuit, which creates the clicks at the other end.)

Receiving device: A machine that takes the coded message out of the channel. (The device can be the sounder at the other end that makes the clicks.)

Decoding: The process that changes the coded message back into the original words. (The operator at the receiving end translates the dots and dashes back into the language used by the sender.)

Channel: The medium (over-the-air or wire) through which the message travels. (The telegraph line through which electrical current flows is a channel.)

Message: Changes or variations in what goes through the channel, not to be confused with "content," which is a combination of message and the information the receiver brings to the message. (In a telegraph system, the breaks in the current that moves through the wire are the message.)

Noise: Other messages or signals in the channel that make it difficult to sort out the one the receiver wants to receive. (Extraneous static or breaks in the signal caused by forces other than the telegraph operator are perceived as noise.)

In the case of the telegraph, at least three communication processes occur. The sender (customer) communicates with the telegraph operator, who communicates with the operator at the other end, who communicates with the person for whom the message is intended. If the receiver decides to send a message in response, the process takes place in reverse, with the receiver becoming the sender (see figure 17.2).

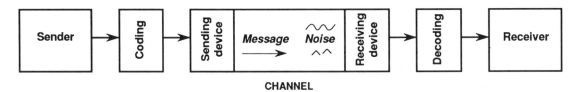

CHANNEL

Figure 17.2   Model of telegraph communications

The technology of communications improved steadily during the first half of the twentieth century, but the foundations (i.e., the basic structure and the mathematics) upon which communications were based remained essentially unexamined until the Second World War, when finding a way to predict the position of moving enemy airplanes and ships became critical to delivering ordnance. This need required the use of messages received by radar devices to predict the position of the enemy craft detected, and this predictive function was developed by applying mathematics. The problem was solved independently in Russia, by A. N. Kolmogoroff, and in the United States, by Norbert Wiener. In both efforts, a system was devised to separate out the "noise" the radar received from the signal made by the movement of the vessel in order to plot the vessel's likely course.[25] At about the same time, the mathematician Claude E. Shannon was developing mathematical theories that were to become the foundation for the computer language of binary digits (ones and zeroes) and the basis of modern digital communications.

These two bodies of work have been used to build communications systems that can encode messages from known patterns and transmit them accurately and swiftly in the presence of noise. Accuracy and speed allow more messages to be sent in the same amount of time, increasing the efficiency of both human and mechanical input into the communication process. This efficiency is generally discussed as "bandwidth" and can be understood as a measure of how large the channel is and how fast messages can move in it, like water flowing through a pipe: The bigger the pipe, the more water will flow through it per second. For example, if a traditional phone line constructed of paired-copper wire and using analog technology can transmit X amount of information per second but a line constructed of fiber-optic cable and using digital technology can transmit a million times X amount of information in the same amount of time, the latter system is said to have greater bandwidth.[26]

As more communications systems become digital, the basic similarities among communications technologies will be more apparent, making it increasingly difficult to posit any relevant difference among a message delivered over coaxial cable, fiber-optic cable, or by satellite. A byte is a byte is a byte.

Information theory is not to be confused with "information policy" (at least at this point), a term applied to a broad range of issues including privacy and intellectual property rights. Nor should it be confused with the social science known as "communications theory," which is only tangentially related in subject matter.[27]

At this juncture, defining what is meant by "regulation" for the purposes of this discussion is important. The term is used here to mean any government limitation on the choices of persons who control any of the various components of a communications process.[28] It applies equally to limitations imposed by the judicial, legislative, or administrative branches of government at any level, from international regulatory bodies to those of the smallest village.

Under the current regulatory scheme of most nations, it is not always immediately clear which part of the communications process is being regulated, and in many cases governments have attempted to classify regulation of messages as regulation of channels to make the regulations more politically or constitutionally palatable. But it is possible in all cases for regulators and courts to determine what is being regulated by asking which of the elements is being limited. For example, a regulation of violence on television may be characterized as a regulation of the channel (i.e., the airwaves) but, instead, it is a regulation of the sender because the channel is not limited by the regulation, only the senders' activities and choices are circumscribed.

Several other issues of definition need to be dealt with at this point. First, the terms *media* and *medium* are here avoided where possible. In communications regulatory circles, these terms are generally applied to businesses that both are senders of messages and have some control of the channel(s) through which the messages are sent, i.e., broadcast and cable. The dictionary defines "medium" as:

> 2. A substance through which a force acts or an effect is transmitted; as, air is the common medium of sound; surrounding or enveloping substance or element; environment; also, the condition on which any event or action occurs; necessary means of motion or action. 3. That through or by which anything is accomplished, conveyed, or carried on; an intermediate means or channel; instrumentality; as, an advertising medium.[29]

These definitions contain not only the concept of "channel" (i.e., the thing or process that enables a message to get from the sender to the receiver) but also elements of coding or message, or both. For that reason, the terms media and medium are not used in order to keep those concepts separate here.

Also, for the present level of analysis, definitional boundaries between communications and computation are avoided.[30] Computers can be used for many purposes in the communication process, including encoding, sending and receiving equipment, and storing. In some respects, computation can be used to increase the speed or efficiency of any part of the communication process, except (at least as far as is now known) of the human beings who are the ultimate senders and receivers. Because they have become so closely intertwined, separating computer ducks from communications geese has become impossible. There are a lot of deese and gucks. The only reason in the past that anyone has tried to solve this taxonomic riddle is because the regulatory systems of most countries are charged with regulating communications, not computation. Here it is assumed that at this point in the evolutionary process, communications and computation are inextricably intertwined and that computation can be used at any point in modern communications systems, and, like complex biological systems, can be a part of ducks or geese or birds not yet known.

Applying a Framework of Information Theory to Issues of Communications Policy Senders

Not only human beings send messages (e.g., a neutron star sends a signal to announces its presence and the type of star it is, and a dog barks at the door to announce its desire to go out), but here senders are assumed to be persons, either natural or corporate.[31] A sender is the ultimate source of a message, the one whose actions started the communication. These actions do not need to be purposeful. Indeed, everyone sends thousands of unintended messages every day, in dress, walk, and facial expressions, all of which allow others to perceive important information. In most cases, however, senders exercise some choice. According to information theory, if senders have *no* choice their messages would convey no meaning, because the message would be absolutely predictable. For example, if I always send only one message (e.g., "wolf"), my receiver(s) will soon not perceive any information coming from me, because they are certain of what I will say. Any restriction on the choices of the sender increases the certainty (and decreases the uncertainty) of the receiver, and it also diminishes the amount of possible information sent in any message. This is called entropy, and it is a useful concept for discussion of the regulation of senders or the coding used for communications because it indicates that limiting the senders' choices will decrease the information available in the system.[32]

This concept has implications for the discussion of free speech and the flow of messages across borders.

In the United States, government regulation of senders is extremely rare, because most restrictions on senders' choices strike at the heart of the freedom of expression guaranteed by the First Amendment. In other countries government regulation of senders can take many forms, including the most extreme: imprisoning or even killing senders to prevent them from sending messages.

Censorship

Regulation of senders might single out a group and limit them by prohibiting them from sending certain messages or *any* messages. In the United States, the landmark case of *Near v. Minnesota* constrained the government's ability to impose prior restraints on the sending of most messages, particularly those involving discussion of political matters.[33] However, messages concerning the safety of troops in times of war,[34] obscenity,[35] certain advertising messages,[36] and matters of national security[37] all can be stopped by court order.

Access by Senders

Senders' choices can be reduced also by regulating the sender's ability to transmit in particular channels (e.g., licensing access for broadcasters and cable companies), regulating time periods when a message can enter a channel (e.g, specifying times for protest marches), or regulating the coding of the message (e.g., the language it must be sent in). In the United States, this type of regulation, when characterized as a restriction on the "time, place, and manner," has been subjected to a lower form of constitutional scrutiny.[38] The application of such regulations may vary according to the channel used. For example, in the United States messages judged to be "indecent" may be sent only at certain times of the day (the "safe harbor" hours) in a broadcast channel but may be distributed at any time in print.[39] Similarly, certain kinds of advertising for legal products are prohibited from broadcast and cable channels (e.g., tobacco and alcohol) but allowed in print. These regulations are said to protect children (one group of potential receivers) by restricting their access to messages that may harm them. These regulations on broadcasters have been justified by regulators on the ground that broadcast frequencies have been deemed a "scarce resource," and licensees must accept restrictions in their choices in the public interest.[40]

Over the years, some have urged that senders should have a First Amendment right of access to private or semipublic channels which the owner of the channel should not be able to "censor." This argument was rejected specifically by the Supreme Court with regard to newspapers but accepted to a limited extent for broadcast.[41]

Nondiscrimination in allowing senders and receivers access is a hallmark of the channels known as common carrier systems (e.g., telephone companies). These channels must give access to the system to anyone who pays the tariff approved by the government, and the channel owners have no control over the content of messages sent in their channel.[42] Telephone companies, however, have been allowed to deny senders access to "900" services (i.e., the caller pays the toll), which are "adult entertainment" messages, because these services were held not to be common carrier services. Is the telephone company more than a channel in 900 services? In this case, the telephone company has taken on the functions of both an intermediary sender and a channel, much as a newspaper does when it publishes (or fails to publish) "letters to the editor." Senders' and receivers' choices are being limited in such cases, but since neither a phone company nor a newspaper is the government, their actions to restrict senders' and receivers' choices are not subject to constitutional scrutiny.[43]

Responsibility for Messages

The responsibilities of both primary and intermediary senders for libel and violation of laws such as copyright when using new channels are far from settled, and some predictability in these areas will be necessary for the development of new information services. In libel cases, U.S. court decisions indicate that the level of responsibility that will be imposed for intermediary senders "on line," e.g., Internet access providers, depends on whether they make decisions about what to send in their system, which is said to make them then look like a publisher or broadcaster more than a common carrier. Having asserted power over messages in the channel, intermediary senders must also accept responsibility for them. The responsibility of intermediary senders for violations of copyright by on-line senders and receivers remains murkier.[44]

Forced Speech

In some cases, the government has taken it upon itself to force senders who own or control the channel to send particular messages to receivers who have not specifically requested them. All these regulations limit the choices of senders who own or control channels by requiring them to use part of their resources for the benefit of government or other senders or receivers.[45] For example, the government has required broadcasters and cablecasters to send certain messages intended for children[46] and to send campaign messages of congressional candidates[47] as well as responses made by unendorsed candidates.[48]

These regulations are inconsistent with the rule (at least for oral and print communications) that the First Amendment does not allow government to force anyone to speak.[49] Like the rules limiting access already discussed, the rules for forced speech by broadcasters have been justified on the grounds that because broadcasting is done through licensing use of the electromagnetic spectrum, in return for the privilege of the license to broadcast government can demand certain speech.[50] At least one commentator has suggested that candidates for office must be given similar access to computer-based communications networks.[51]

The same rules apply to cable TV (which is not limited by the spectrum, because it uses a wire technology) under the fiction that a physical (or economic) limit exists on the number of lines that might come into a home or office, so that local government must ration this limited public resource, giving government the right to make demands on the owners of the channel and the senders in it.

Multichannel communications systems have been required to carry the messages of broadcast channels in order to save broadcasters from extinction in a competitive and evolving marketplace. The Supreme Court has upheld this forced speech and condoned regulations that force one channel to carry the messages of others to preserve a variety of channels.[52] Thus, cable systems were forced to carry all the broadcast signals in their market, and similar requirements for direct broadcast satellites have also been considered. The application of these principles to channels such as print and the Internet remain unclear.

Receivers

A receiver is an identifiable entity that becomes aware of a message. As in the case of senders, receivers need not be human. A dog becomes aware of a message when scolded by its owner and may "learn" from the message to change its behavior. But here receivers are assumed to be people or legal entities. Like sending, the act of receiving need not be purposeful. Human beings and corporations become aware of messages not intended for them and which they had no intention of receiving. Yet overhearing a conversation in the employees' cafeteria is nonetheless receiving a message, even if the receiver were to take steps not to hear it by, for example, moving away from the speakers. Direct regulation of receivers is rare, because it would require laws that would place physical limits on the ability to perceive. Regulation of the equipment required to receive messages (e.g., satellite dishes) is more common. In addition to being technologically difficult, the restriction of choices of receivers (like regulation of senders) strikes directly at the heart of freedom of expression.

The Right Not to Receive

There is an interesting line of U.S. cases that appear to give individuals rights *not* to receive messages. For example, the Supreme Court held that U.S. citizens have the right to have their children *not* receive messages that are indecent (at least not by public communications channels).[53] Some cases have upheld laws that forbid sending *any* message through a particular channel (e.g., the use of sound trucks in residential neighborhoods) in order to protect receivers from communications they perceive as "noise."[54] An interesting example of this is the regulation of "junk fax" (where the receiver often must pay for the unwanted message). Similar regulation has been debated for "junk cellular" messages (unsolicited messages sent to cell phones) and "spam" (unsolicited e-mail).

The Right to Receive

On the other hand, some cases give receivers the right to receive certain messages. For example, adults have the right to receive indecent messages if they choose to do so.[55] Receivers, however, do not generally have the right to demand that certain messages be sent by a particular sender without the sender agreeing to some contractual obligation. For example, radio listeners who enjoy classical music cannot demand that a particular broadcaster provide or retain that programming.[56]

The "rights" of receivers are also debated with regard to public access to a given channel or level of information. Unlike the laws that force broadcasters to send certain information because it is "good for" receivers, the proposals in this area appear to mandate that certain channels or information be available to receivers at low or no cost if the receivers *choose* to receive it. These regulations generally restrict suppliers' choices in the system (such as senders, channels, encoders, and so on) by demanding that they use some of their resources to insure that access is available. This issue arises again in the discussion of channels and universal services (see below).

Much regulation of senders and channels is, at least ostensibly, for the benefit of receivers. This is a predictable public policy, given that receivers are more numerous in a point-to-multipoint channel and are also voters. But senders and their trade associations are undeniably important parts of the political process and can be expected to continue to assert their own rights under the Constitution.

One difficult part of many of these debates is separating the function of sending from that of acting as a channel, because the public policy, regulatory authority, and constitutional parameters may differ for each. Cable, for example, operates as a sender and as a channel for other senders. A regulatory analysis may be different for activities that involve operation as a channel (carrying the messages of other senders) and as a sender (being the source of the message sent). Separating them this way enables the courts and policymakers to arrive at the same answers for all similarly situated entities (natural or corporate), regardless of which or how many of the various parts of the communications process they engage in.

Devices for Sending and Receiving

Consumer devices for sending and receiving are the site of the human interface with modern communications systems. Such devices are, for the people who use them, the "face" of a communications system. Experience has shown that the interface must be easy to use and require low maintenance—that is, the devices must be "user friendly." Their primary function is to translate messages from the format assumed in the channel back into a format or code that is understandable, enjoyable, or both, to the human beings using the system. The equipment employed by both the sending and receiving entities must use the same operating specifications and the same coding and decoding (codec) system. Because the devices are not always distributed by the same companies, someone needs to decide what the *standards* will be for the entire system.

This decision can be rendered by government fiat, or each communications firm might develop unique standards for its own new technologies (both equipment and coding systems) and then wait to see which of the competing technologies survives the rigors of the marketplace. This winner-take-all rule can be illustrated by the battles for dominance in video and audio tape. VHS

(Video Helical Scan) and audiocassettes eventually emerged as the preferred code or storage devices, and because mass communications devices are valuable only if they are ubiquitous, the alternative systems (Betamax and eight-track tape) did not survive in the mass market. This rule for choosing communications codes or channels, or both, can be seen either as the survival of the fittest or as a waste of resources for both senders and receivers who invested in the losing technology. It can lead to resistance in suppliers and consumers, may hinder the introduction of new technology, and may also explain why regulators are sometimes asked to act as referees or to decide a fight before it takes place by setting mandatory standards.

When should government impose standards for coding or sending and receiving equipment, thereby limiting the choices of the marketplace and giving a potential windfall to one of the competing standards? Presumably, the public policy to be furthered by any such activity is the ubiquitous availability of the technology made possible by enhanced consumer confidence in its viability and a reduction of wasted resources that would otherwise go into the losing technology. New technologies, however, that fail to meet government standards will be "frozen out." Further, government standards-setting allows suppliers with access to political power to influence the standards that will be set in order to promote their own products and keep competitors at bay.

But on what basis should public officials favor one set of coding and sending/ receiving over another, and at what point in the development of the technology should a decision be made? If a standard is selected too soon, the technology may not have developed to its full potential and other countries may leap ahead in their use of the system. If the standard is set too late, many resources will be lost to the forces of competition and the technology may not be strong enough to fight off new competitors.[57]

One measure of any system is its *efficiency*: how much information can the competing coding systems accurately deliver within a given time and with given resources.[58] Another measure is its *adaptability*: the system must change as outside forces affecting it change (e.g., competitive forces, consumer education and needs, innovations in the product and process within the industry).

Messages and Substance

Because Shannon developed information theory outside the journalistic or entertainment "media," the concepts of "content" or "meaning" were different for information theory.[59] In information theory, a "message" is a coded token (something that stands for something else) that moves through the channel and has no meaning for anyone until decoded. The messages in a channel using a binary digital system are a meaningless series of ones and zeroes unless the receiver knows how they were coded.

What the receiver actually perceives has been called "meaning" or "content," but here the term "substance" is used, to avoid any suggestion that messages might contain anything separate from the coding and the information already possessed by the receiver. Thus, substance = coded messages + information already possessed by the receiver. If I code a message into French and attempt to convey something about snow to someone who does not know French and lives near the equator, the "substance" received will be quite different from the same message sent to a person in Paris. This example assumes that no two people perceive a message in exactly the same way. This difference in the effect of messages is well documented in communications literature.[60]

Unfortunately, many public policymakers and courts continue to act as if messages are like bullets: Whoever they are aimed at will perceive message as "truth," regardless of previous knowledge and experience. Although research in communications has shown definitively that the "bullet theory" is false, it is the basis for most censorship laws. A more informed view of the communications process might result in greater success for attempts to mold public opinion or public morals.

Messages may be said to have economic value. In most cases, the substance of the message is critical to this value, and the value may diminish with time so that the message will have no value at all if it does not reach the intended receiver in the appropriate time. Stock quotes, for example, are most valuable when sent in "real time," i.e., as trades are being made. Error-free, timely delivery of messages and other "quality-of-service" issues are also on the regulatory agenda.

But because neither messages nor substance can be a person whose choices can be limited, neither can be regulated directly under the definition of regulation used here, that is, restricted choice. But both can be affected by the regulation of choices (or a lack of them) for anyone participating in the communication process.

Encoding and Decoding

A code is a set of agreements between potential communicators that establishes significance for certain words, gestures, electronic signals, or other ways in which messages are sent. Language is a code whereby two or more people agree in advance that particular sounds (or letters representing those sounds) signify a specific thing or concept. In Morse Code a certain number and arrangement of dots and dashes denote a specific letter of the alphabet. In analog broadcasting, sounds and pictures are encoded using certain wavelengths and frequencies of the electromagnetic spectrum, then decoded into sounds and pictures again by receiving devices in homes, offices, and cars. Digital messages are coded into a series of ones and zeroes.

Code Agreement

In all forms of communication, agreement must be reached in advance. Mass communications channels require coordination between senders and receivers on a large scale, a job that has customarily fallen to government or other large institutions. For example, in the United States the more intricate rules of the code known as English (formal grammar, spelling, punctuation) are taught in schools sometimes along with the language codes of other cultures to assure that U.S. citizens will be able to communicate accurately with one another and with other people in a global marketplace.

In more complex technological systems, the coding is closely linked to the sending, receiving, and channel equipment used. Coding of a broadcast signal, for example, is dependent on the equipment used by the broadcast stations and the receiving devices used by consumers. It would not pay to code a signal in digital form if the consumers' receiving devices "understand" only code for analog. These coding functions are closely tied in the regulatory setting, particularly in the area of standards previously discussed.

One criterion important for a successful coding system is *security*. In many cases, messages are coded to deny access to them. Only those who know the code can decode them, as in messages sent by intelligence operatives who do not want other countries' operatives to read them. Security is critical for selling access to information sent to many potential receivers. Information, like all other economic goods and services, has no value unless it is a scarce resource. For example, information sent to subscribers by cable for "premium" channels is encoded so that only those with the appropriate decoders can receive it. Similar coding techniques are used for messages sent by the many new satellite- and telephone-based services, whose commercial value depends on the sender's or channel's control over distribution of the code or, more often, of the decoding devices.[61] For the sake of security, governments have been asked to make receiving coded messages (and selling codes or devices that allow decoding) a crime, because, as with stealing a copy of a movie at a video store or a copy of a book from a library, unauthorized receivers can "steal" access to these messages.[62]

These issues need to be addressed with diminishing regard for traditional concepts of "media" and increasing consideration for what kinds of laws are realistically enforceable in a world where digital coding allows messages to move with great speed within and between channels. Like all the issues discussed, message theft can only be effectively dealt with across all channels and across international borders.

Noise

Regulation of message coding and channel allocation is often undertaken to decrease the presence or effect of noise in a channel. Noise can lessen the clarity of the message or even distort it.[63] The problem is easy to visualize: Think of trying to talk to someone right next to you in the midst of a very exciting football game. The channel (the surrounding air) is so filled with messages that people must talk louder than the ambient noise level in order for a message to reach the intended receiver. Talking where there is less noise requires less energy and results in more accurate transmission of the message.

In the context of information theory, the concept of noise can be applied to all forms of communication in all channels. In this broad sense, noise can be defined as unwanted signals in the channel which are not part of the sender's message. Radio and telephone receivers hiss or crackle in certain atmospheric conditions, when natural electromagnetic fluctuations join messages of human origin in the channel. When broadcasting video images, noise is perceived as "snow" in the picture. Similarly, when two radio programs or telephone conversations are sent in the same channel, the receiver may have difficulty separating the message from the noise. Messages encoded using digital, rather than analog, technology are somewhat less affected by electronic noise in the channel, but the problem is perennial.

In addition to decreased efficiency (requiring more power of the sender or more time for decoding by the receiver), noise in the channel can cause errors in the communication, i.e., the receiver receives a message different from that sent. These errors may be merely irritating (missed letters in the transmission of text) or may create big problems (errors in the numbers received in a banking transaction).

Although little public (or private) interest has centered on the presence of noise in a communications channel, regulation that could lead to its reduction has generally been welcomed by senders, receivers, and channel owners alike, even if it were to some extent to reduce their choices. Noise reduction was the basis for regulation of the broadcast industry and is the stated purpose of many quality-of-service regulations for telephony and cable at all levels of government.[64] New questions that will be presented to regulators with regard to noise include: How much regulation of noise is justifiable in a market-driven industry, where companies can compete on the basis of quality?[65] Should regulation of the various options for coding signals be judged on the basis (among other things) of the ability of their code to reduce noise or to reduce the effect of noise on the message?

In some cases, one person's noise is another person's message. Several members of an audience shouting down a speaker with whom they disagree is one example. Of two contending parties, which has the right to send a message in a channel that neither of them has exclusive right to use? Such contests are ordinarily decided by the speaker with the greater power of amplification. To avoid escalation of amplification, this battle might be reformulated as a discussion of noise or of the rights of senders and receivers in particular channels.

Channels

The use of information theory to structure public policy may be needed most for the debates over the relative rights and responsibilities of those who own or control the many channels through which messages flow today and will flow tomorrow. If, as many predict, the companies that distribute information on paper (newspapers, magazines, books) soon will distribute that same information by wire (cable or telephone or both) or over the air (by wireless cable or satellite), does it make sense to deprive them (and other senders) of the constitutional protection they enjoyed when they used forest products and public streets as their channel for distribution?[66] Should some channels be required to offer universal, low-cost access while others are allowed to distribute the same messages on an ability-to-pay basis? Should the government prefer one channel over another by offering it special protection from competitors, subsidizing research and development, or giving it special tax breaks?

These questions have been (and will continue to be) debated in judicial, legislative, and regulatory arenas. Unfortunately, debate continues to center on the question "is it a duck?" Again, focussing on what people or firms do in the communications process rather than on the technology used may be the most productive way to proceed.

Channels have at least two characteristics that offer a basis for rationalized regulatory treatment: the number of potential senders or receivers, or both, in the channel and the potential of the channel for interactivity. One channel may exhibit a variety of possibilities for these characteristics. For example, both telephone and cable lines can be interactive (as in POTS or Internet services) or noninteractive (e.g., cable "channels" and fax services).[67] Interactivity does not necessarily require a communications system to be centralized in the way the telephone system has been. The "brains" of the system can be distributed in the equipment located close to the senders or receivers (e.g., computer networks). According to Ithiel de Sola Pool:

> There is no reason to assume that the communications network of the future will be a single large organization with a central brain. Having a hierarchical structure governed by a central brain is only one was to organize complex systems. A human being is organized that way; so is a nation-state. But the capitalist economy is not, nor is the complex system of scientific knowledge, nor is the ecological system of the biosphere. For an uncentralized system to function, there must be some established ways of interconnecting the parts other than by command; the interconnections may be managed by conventions, habits, or Darwinian process.[68]

If a decentralized system or a system of competition among channels were chosen, certain rules of the game would need to be evolved by some combination of the marketplace and government regulation. For channels that operate as networks, de Sola Pool saw these rules as falling into three categories: interconnection, technical standards for interface with the channel(s), and a directory system.[69] Organizing consensus on these issues will be one of the great policy challenges of the next century, especially if global interconnectivity is the goal.

Many channels can be used for a wide variety of distribution schemes to let senders reach different numbers of receivers: *point-to-point* (one sender to one receiver, e.g., the Postal Service or POTS); *point-to-multipoint* (one to many, e.g., broadcast, cable, print, and postal); *multipoint-to-point* (many to one, e.g., credit card verification systems); and *multipoint-to-multipoint* (many to many, e.g., videoconferencing and computer bulletin boards). Both wired and wireless technologies can be used for all these types of channels and will, in many places, compete directly for customers. Justifying different regulatory treatment for channels that essentially do the same thing in every way that matters to those using them will become increasingly difficult.

An innovative approach to channel regulation was seen in the FCC's rules for the service known as "video dialtone."[70] This service would have offered access to broadband services, whereby customers could have sent or received video messages just as they do audio messages. Customers could have ordered a variety of video services sent by telephone lines. The service was originally thought to require the large bandwidth of fiber-optic cables, but evidence suggested it could have been implemented in a limited way over regular copper wires by using sophisticated message-compression techniques. Because, unlike a cable system, broadband does not rely on a limited number of "channels" nor look like broadcast or telephone service, the new technology required new ways of thinking. The FCC broke down this kind of communication process into its components to create three possible types of service:

> Essentially, channel service, video dialtone, and cable service form a hierarchy relating to the degree of control an entity has over the content being transported. When providing channel service the telephone company acts purely as a conduit, not interacting in any way with the transported content. Video dialtone envisions the provider contributing to and enhancing the content by providing non-programming services and gateways. Finally, cable service itself is distinguished by an entity's ability to have complete editorial control over content, as well as control over the selection and pricing of programming.[71]

According to this scheme, the functions of channel and sender are separated and treated differently. Even though the market for video dialtone did not materialize as quickly as was hoped, its regulation was a significant step in the direction of developing a rational, broadly applicable foundation for all communications regulation.

Cable television offers another interesting case history of a regulatory muddle caused by an attempt to place a new technology into existing legal boxes. It is a classic example of a new bird that everyone tries to call by old names. Attempts to regulate cable TV were initially justified by the FCC (and upheld by the courts) because cable was "reasonably ancillary" to the authority of the FCC to regulate broadcasting.[72] Cable TV looked like a duck, but defining it as duck-like became a problem when the FCC attempted to mandate that cable systems provide public-access channels. The Supreme Court found that if cable were like broadcasting, it could not be regulated as a common carrier nor made to provide nondiscriminatory access to the channel.[73] Ironically, government could not mandate access for the public but could mandate access for cable's competitors, the broadcasters.

Some proposals have called for government itself to set up systems for access to information. For example, the government of the state of Kansas has set up the Information Network of Kansas (INK) to provide citizens with access by computer and modem to public information of government agencies and to develop information bases for which the INK will charge access fees.[74] As in the case of municipally owned cable systems, this situation puts government into direct competition with commercial senders and channels (e.g., newspapers, broadcasters, commercial cable systems, computer-based information systems) and poses a significant problem for government regulation of the communications industry: It is not clear how one sender or channel can regulate all the others.

Ownership and Control of Channels

Ownership of the channels of communications is a common regulatory concern owing to government's distrust of concentrations of power in key components of the economy, which dates back to the breakup of the industrial empires of the late nineteenth century in the United States. This fear of concentration has been even greater in communications than in most other economic sectors because of the political and social power of communications channels. Evidence of this can be seen in the unwillingness of regulators to depend on antitrust laws to prevent competitive abuses, preferring instead to pass specific regulations about who can (and cannot) own the various channels. FCC rules determined the number of broadcast stations any person or corporation may own in a given market and in the country as a whole.[75]

Other rules prohibit companies from operating both newspapers and broadcast stations in any given market and telephone companies from operating cable TV services in markets where they provide POTS.[76,77] Little regulatory activity has occurred regarding cross-ownership by telcos and newspapers or broadcasters, because, until recently, no one (including the companies themselves) thought of them as competitors.

But competition between channels appears inevitable, and the battles waged by the publishing industry in the early 1990s, to keep telcos out of the information and advertising businesses, suggest how intense that competition is liable to be. Newspaper publishers asked Congress to enact legislation to reinstate the restrictions on the Bell operating companies (BOCs) enforced as part of the antitrust settlement that broke up the Bell system.[78] The settlement divested

AT&T of the operating companies and restricted their entry into a number of businesses, including the potentially lucrative area of information services; in 1991, the federal court lifted this restriction.[79] The publishing industry has argued that the danger of monopolistic practices by the BOCs remains so great that the BOCs should be kept out of information services until other potential players in the field are strong enough to offer significant competition, and it argues that monopolization of this channel of communications would result in fewer choices for receivers.

Government regulations have historically encouraged the existence of a variety of sources of information, i.e., a variety of senders and channels for messages on any given subject. The publicly stated purpose of these regulations has not been to protect senders or channels but to justify protection for receivers by assuring them access to as many messages as possible.

Constitutional Treatment of Channels

In 1983, while most of the communications world rested comfortably in its niches, Ithiel de Sola Pool made impassioned pleas for freedom of speech in the new media:

Perhaps the continued existence of one forum for uninhibited debate would be enough to assure a ferment of opinions and ideas. If so, it would suffice that free speech in the traditional media continued unaffected by the regulations applied to the new media. That, however, is not the case. The new media are not only competing with the old media for attention, but are also changing the very system under which the old media operate.[80]

New channels continue to fight for equal protection under law. In deciding the extent of constitutional rights that will be afforded cable TV, one Supreme Court opinion framed the issue as whether cable is like a newspaper or a broadcaster, when in many respects it not like either yet shares fundamental aspects of a communications system with both.[81] Cable, newspaper, or broadcaster, all are point-to-multipoint channels through which messages (primarily news and entertainment) flow from senders who have gathered and edited them for distribution to many receivers simultaneously. In many communities, similar messages about local news travel through several channels at the same time and *exactly* the same message sent by the broadcaster is sent by the cable operator distributing the broadcast signal on its system. Yet messages sent in these different channels may receive different levels of constitutional protection.[82]

The genesis of different treatment was the law's perception of a print–broadcast dichotomy. This perception was focussed on the differences between the two channels and might (had regulation stayed at the level of codes and noise) have been consistent with constitutional law regarding the print media. Once Congress had its hand in the regulation of broadcast channels, however, it was not long before government was regulating the broadcast senders as well.

Broadcast technology is based on sending and receiving messages coded by using variations in the length or frequency of an electromagnetic wave. If all broadcasters tried to send messages on the same wavelength or frequency, the noise that would result would lead to chaos so that no receivers would be able to sort out the messages they wanted to receive. In the early days of radio, when such chaos was a real possibility, Congress established a regulatory scheme to allocate space on the spectrum to broadcasters to prevent them from interfering with one another's transmissions.[83] Owing to the nature of the electromagnetic spectrum and the earth's atmosphere, coding was regulated and each option for coding (broadcasting on a certain frequency) created a separate "channel." Because Congress and the FCC allocated only a small part of the spectrum for commercial use, the number of channels in any geographic area became a scarce resource, necessitating choice between competing applicants for a license in the same locality.

Given this power to choose, criteria for choice had to be developed, which led directly to government's power to demand that certain messages be sent (public service programming, children's programming, political advertising) or not sent (indecent messages, certain advertising for legal products and services). The Supreme Court approved this regulatory scheme, even though it would not have been constitutional for the print media. The Court accepted the argument that the spectrum is a "scarce resource" that belongs to the public, and therefore the public can demand certain speech (and refraining from speech) in return for the license.[84] Government-created scarcity is the legal basis also for government control over cable TV and the telephone industry (both assumed to be "natural" monopolies). This propensity of government to create local monopolies (thus, a scarcity of choice for consumers) has often been justified as necessary to stimulate the introduction of new technology, which would give the monopoly provider a chance to recoup high up-front costs.

Government licensing of channels (i.e., of printing presses, thus effectively regulating the content of newspapers and books) in England and its colonies was one of the sparks of the American Revolution. History teaches that when government can license channels, it can regulate the senders who are the licensees of those channels.[85] Communications firms may be glad to get the chance to operate under the monopoly (or restricted-entry) status conferred by their licenses or franchises and only later comprehend the price government will attempt to extract for the privilege. That price became clear to broadcasters when they saw that the print media (with which broadcasters are fierce competitors for local advertising) derived economic advantages from not coming under the same forced (or restrained) speech obligations that both increase broadcasters' costs and eliminate some sources of potential revenue. For example, broadcasters can be forced to air a response (at no charge) from someone personally attacked on the station[86] while the same requirement of a newspaper is unconstitutional *even though* most U.S. communities may have only one newspaper but a number of broadcasters.[87]

The application of constitutional principles need not be limited by technological "facts" no longer in existence, such as the scarcity of certain communications channels or "natural" monopolies. A focus on the rights of all senders, receivers, and channels would be more broadly applicable and would keep the courts and the Constitution out of the business of bird-naming.

Universal Service

Once government has given a channel some kind of monopoly or franchise in the form of a license or other authority to do business (with entry restrictions for potential competitors in that channel), it generally attempts to make sure that all citizens have access to the channel. In broadcast, the FCC bent over backward to establish and nurture services in rural areas. In metropolitan areas, the FCC has given special preference to broadcast services aimed at underserved groups, such as racial and cultural minorities. Such efforts to promote rural and multicultural broadcasting have been seriously undermined when the economic facts of life for broadcasters were transformed by changes in the U.S. economy, by new broadcast technology, and by competition from cable TV and other information and entertainment services.[88]

For public policy decision makers, the question will inevitably become one of the lengths to which government must go to protect broadcasters from new competition by eliminating the public-service obligations that add to their costs or by government supplying subsidies in the form of tax breaks or grants.

Should all citizens have access to free (that is, advertiser-supported), over-the-air broadcasts of news and entertainment (as the National Association of Broadcasters asserts in the case that upheld the Must-Carry rules[89]), or should questions regarding universal service be asked more broadly? For example, should government assure that all citizens have access to a certain minimum level of information at no cost to them from the channel(s) that can most efficiently deliver the information? If so, how should government compensate the owners of the channels for public use of their facilities? When this question was posed with regard to the channel known as telephone service, the government decided to compensate telephone companies for universal service obligations by protecting them from competition and allowing part of the revenue from profitable areas to subsidize service in unprofitable areas. Thus, rates higher than actual costs were charged to business, long-distance, and urban customers to subsidize service to households, and local and rural customers. This scheme created a monopoly supplier of an important service, requiring regulations to be put in place to assure adequate service and "reasonable" rates for consumers while also guaranteeing a reasonable rate of return to the company. As technology and regulators started to push the telecommunications envelope, making it possible for companies outside "the system" to deliver point-to-point audio,[90] the deal previously struck to assure universal service began to unravel, and it shows no sign of being knit back together soon.[91]

Many regulators and consumer advocates want government to assure that all citizens have access to all the channels of information that advocates believe will be critical for individual and organizational success in the next century. But they want government also to encourage competition in the communications sector and to make sure that communications will never again be dominated by a few companies. Regulators on all levels of government have let it be known that they want competition *and* universal service.[92] Clearly, a new paradigm for regulation is needed if both of these goals are to be accomplished.[93]

Because these critical communications services will be available through a variety of technologies, the regulation and responsibilities for providing government-mandated services will need to fall evenly on all vendors, regardless of which service they have historically been associated with (and regardless of the responsibilities and privileges associated with that service). In an era when many wired and wireless channels will provide point-to-point communications that are (so far as consumers are concerned) exactly the same as the service provided by the telephone company, continuation of the system in which universal service regulation is applied only to "telephone" companies will be counterproductive.

Fairness and predictability would be brought back to the system if all channels of information were treated as potential sources of citizen enlightenment and entertainment and as potential monopolists, with the power to threaten the underpinnings of a market economy. It is not the purpose here to suggest the form this new regulatory scheme might take, but to frame the access issues broadly enough to encompass all the problems and opportunities the evolution of the communications industry presents. New laws and regulations can be constructed by asking what kind of channel it is (e.g., point-to-multipoint, interactive) and what kinds of channels it competes with, not what kind of technology it uses (or used to use).

Conclusion

A regulatory system that begins by defining these basic parts of the communication process (i.e., sender, receiver, channel, coding, noise, and message), and then proceeds to regulate (restrict choices) for those engaging in one or more of these parts, could bring a measure of uniformity and predictability to the application of the law both for traditional and emerging communications technologies. Such an approach will not foreclose different treatment of similar activity, but difference could be determined by public policy goals, not according to historical technological distinctions.

With a clearer picture of the information needs of the twenty-first century, government might choose to impose universal service or mandated access obligations on certain channels (at public expense), if these obligations can be characterized as "public goods" or are not available owing to market failures. But, like so many of the policy dilemmas in the modern communications sector, the right time to make these regulations remains a question, because how much or what type of information infrastructure will be provided in the new competitive environments is not known. Such questions seem to argue for an evolutionary approach to policymaking in this area.

Evolution might occur in several ways. For example, new laws or regulations might be drafted broadly, to set up case-by-case development of specifics by regulatory bodies—an approach that offers the advantage of flexibility in a changing environment but allows stakeholders less confidence in their ability to predict how the law will work in new cases. This approach would put much of the decision making into the hands of courts reviewing these regulations, unless an administrative process or specialized alternative dispute mechanism were put in place. Another option, one that offers more predictability, might be to attempt to set out many specifics in advance within a detailed law, on the assumption that policymakers have the information necessary to make specific rules.

The framework proposed here could be used by any court, legislative body, or regulatory agency that finds it necessary to rationalize or harmonize the regulatory, common law, or constitutional principles applicable to new communications technologies emerging and converging in the global marketplace. Gradual, evolutionary implementation of these communications elements as a foundation for regulation would facilitate discussion of the kinds of issues posed here on a global scale, given that not all countries may need to deal with them at the same time or with the same priorities.

As in all evolving systems, making long-term predictions about where the communications sector will go is not possible, but the goals of flexibility, adaptability, and fairness seem destinations all the people along for the ride will need to agree on. The hard part will be taking the first steps away from systems to which many have grown accustomed, when ducks were ducks and everyone knew the rules.

Notes

1. The views expressed here owe much to the work of many people, but especially to that of Claude Shannon, Anthony G. Oettinger, Ithiel de Sola Pool, M. Ethan Katsh, and John R. Pierce, all of whom have seen communications as larger than any particular technology.

2. See chapter 5.

3. A joint venture to deliver a similar service was announced in 1993 by Hewlett Packard and Time Warner. See "The Media Business," *The New York Times*, Oct. 12, 1993, D15.

4. This may be the best option where freedom of expression is concerned. "Those freedoms that are neither challenged nor defined are the most secure." See A. Bickel, "The Uninhibited, Robust, and Wide-Open First Amendment," in *Where Do You Draw the Line?*, edited by Victor Cline (Provo, Utah: Brigham Young University Press, 1974), 65.

5. Telephone video services, however, had not materialized by the end of 1990s. For an early and comprehensive discussion, see Robert L. Pettit and Christopher J. McGuire, "Video Dialtone: Reflections on Changing Perspectives in Telecommunications Regulation," *Harvard Journal of Law and Technology* 6 (Spring 1993), 343–362.

6. In the late 1990s, several cable companies began either to upgrade their systems to include fiber-optic cables and telephony switches or announced their intentions to provide mobile, point-to-point communications service via digital personal communications systems (PCS) that will compete directly with local phone services.

7. For a description of electric utilities that, as of March 1998, have announced plans to offer local telecommunications services, see Rachael King, "Exercise in Utility," *tele.com* (March 1998), 69–73.

8. James Walter Grudus has suggested that this regulatory dilemma can be solved with a new framework based on competition and separate regulation for information transmission and information services. This view is not inconsistent with the proposal made here. See Grudus, "Local Broadband Networks: A New Regulatory Philosophy," *Yale Journal of Regulation* 10, 1 (1993), 89–145.

9. See I. K. Gotts and A. D. Rutenberg, "Navigating the Global Information Superhighway: A Bumpy road Ahead," *Harvard Journal of Law and Technology* 8 (1995), 275–344; Henry H. Perritt, Jr., "Tort Liability, the First Amendment, and Equal Access to Electronic Networks," *Harvard Journal of Law and Technology* 5, 6 (1992), 65–151.

10. In his now classic book describing the communication revolution as it is being developed in the Media Lab at the Massachusetts Institute of Tecyhnology (MIT), Stewart Brand wrote that because technology always moves faster than the law, all new technologies are outlaw areas and all are all dynamitge. See Brand, *The Media Lab: Inventing the Future at MIT* (New York: Penguin, 1987), 213.

11. For a detailed discussion, see the Committee on Commerce, Science, and Transportation, U.S. Senate, *Print and Electronic Media: The Case for First Amendment Parity* (Washington, D.C.: U.S. Gov't Printing Office, 1983).

12. Although the Telecommunications Act of 1996 increased limits on broadcast ownership, Congress and the FCC have continued to make efforts to avoid concentration of ownership by broadcasters by limiting the number of stations that can be owned in any particular market and in the country as a whole, and they have gone to some lengths to make it possible for minorities to own stations. 47 CFR 73.3555 and 73.4140. In the telephone business, this policy is evident in the Modified Final Judgment (MFJ), which attempted to control the activities of the units of the former Bell system. See Richard A. Hindman, "The Diversity Principle and the MFJ Information Services Restriction: Applying Time-Worn First Amendment Assumptions to the New Technologies," *Catholic University Law Review* 38, 2 (1989), 471–510.

13. The new rules will be developed by legislation and by court cases that will interpret both new and existing legislation as well as the common law. It is assumed that stakeholders will endeavor to choose the forum most likely to recognize their interests.

14. For example, many state regulators have been faced with claims of "privacy" violation with the introduction of "caller ID" (identification). For a survey of this and related issues, see Anne Wells Branscomb, *Who Owns Information: From Privacy to Public Access* (New York: Basic Books, 1994); and Thomas E. McManus, *Telephone Transaction-Generated Information: Rights and Restrictions* (Cambridge, Mass.: Harvard University Program on Information Resources Policy, P-90-5, May 1990).

15. The Federal Bureau of Investigation (FBI) met with resistance when it requested special regulations to allow it to eavesdrop on calls encoded by the proposed technology, called the Clipper Chip. See Paul Wallich, "Clipper Chip Runs Aground," *Scientific American* 269, 2 (August 1993), 116; and Kirsten Scheurer, "The Clipper Chip: Cryptography Technology and the Constitution," *Rutgers Computer and Technology Law Journal* (Spring 1995), 263–292.

16. Many people, including the Clinton administration, think that charging users too much for access to the information highway would create an underclass of information "have-nots" and that government must step in to insure something like universal access to at least a minimum amount of information. See *The National Information Infrastructure: Agenda for Action* (Washington, D.C.: National Telecommunications and Information Administration, Report No. PB93-231272, 1993); but see Benjamin M. Compaine, "Information Gaps: Myth or Reality," in *Issues in New Information Technology*, edited by Benjamin M. Compaine (Norwood, N.J.: Ablex Publishing Corp., 1988).

17. See *The National Information Infrastructure: Agenda For Action*; and, for an industry perspective, see the National Critical Technologies Panel, *Second Biennial Report* (Washington, D.C.: U.S. Gov't Printing Office, January, 1993).

18. At the same time, the courts are struggling to come to grips with what the new technology will mean to the practice of law. Given that the court system is based on the processing and storage of information, the new technologies pose a challenge to old systems, because the need for efficiency has become a paramount concern. A system that has depended on (even revered) the written word is adapting to a new computer-based "literacy." For a comprehensive and insightful discussion of this change and its effect on the law, see M. Ethan Katsh, *The Electronic Media and the Transformation of the Law* (New York: Oxford University Press, 1989).

19. Oliver Wendell Holmes, *Collected Legal Papers* (Boston: Little, Brown, 1921), 231.

20. Iredell Jenkins, *Social Order and the Limits of the Law* (Princeton, N.J.: Princeton University Press, 1980), 9.

21. The metaphor was coined by Anthony G. Oettinger in a lecture at Harvard University in 1994.

22. See Claude E. Shannon, "A Mathematical Theory of Information," *Bell System Technical Journal* 27 (1948), 379–423, 623–56; see, also, Anthony Liversidge, "Interview, Claude Shannon," *Scientific American* (January 1990), 22–22B.

23. See John R. Pierce, *An Introduction to Communication Theory, Symbols, Signals and Noise* (New York: Dover Publications, 1980.)

24. See Oettinger, chapter 5,

25. Wiener's most famous work, *Cybernetics* (Cambridge, Mass.: Technology Press, 1948), deals with communication and control.

26. The term originated in broadcast regulation, where a communication is sent using stretches of the electromagnetic "spectrum" called "bands." Technologies that transmit more information per second generally require a larger portion of the spectrum. The spectrum may be regarded as a tape measure which has been rolled out, and space along it must be allocated to distinct communicators so they will not interfere with one another. Some communicators will need smaller bands than others because of the technology they are using. For example, radio transmitters need smaller bands than television transmitters, because television must send enough messages in its signal to send both video and audio to receivers. A wire-based system does not use airwaves, so the technology used will, in effect, determine the length of the tape and, therefore, how much information can be sent per second.

27. See, e.g., Wilbur Schramm, "The Unique Perspective of Communication: A Retrospective View," *Journal of Communication* 33, 3 (1983), 6–17; and Hanno Hardt, *Communication History and Theory in America* (New York: Routledge, 1992).

28. Certainly, "regulation" is a much broader concept, which includes government-created rights as well as restrictions, but in this paper it has been limited to simplify matters for those without legal training.

29. *Webster's New International Dictionary of the English Language*, 2nd ed. (Springfield, Mass.: G & C Merriam Co., 1961).

30. This battle has been fought (apparently to a stalemate) in the FCC proceedings known as *Computer I, II*, and *III*. See Alfred Sikes, "After Computer III: Picking up the Pieces at the FCC," *Public Utilities Fortnightly* 126, 4 (August 1990).

31. An interesting problem will arise with the development of artificial intelligence and computer-generated messages not designed by human intelligence. For an accessible review of this area, see Daniel Crevier, *AI: The Tumultuous History of the Search for Artificial Intelligence* (New York: Basic Books, 1993).

32. See Pierce, *An Introduction to Communication Theory, Symbols, Signals and Noise*, especially chapter five.

33. 283 US 697, 75 L.Ed. 1357, 51 S. Ct. 625 (1930).

34. Ibid.

35. *Roth v. United States* 354 U.S. 476 (1957).

36. *Central Hudson Gas & Electric Corp. v. Public Service Commission of New York* 447 U.S. 557 (1980). See, e.g., Ronald K. L. Collins and David M. Skover, "Commerce and Communication," *Texas Law Review* 71, 4 (March 1993), 697–746; and Charles G. Geyh, "The Regulation of Speech Incident to the Sale or Promotion of Goods and Services: A Multifactor Approach," *University of Pittsburgh Law Review* 52, 1 (1990), 1–73.

37. See, e.g., David L. Sobel, "Free Speech and National Security," *Bill of Rights Journal* 20 (December 1987), 5.

38. See Laurence Tribe, Chapter Twelve, Sections 12 to 23, *American Constitutional Law*, 2nd ed. (New York: Foundation Press, 1988).

39. See Jeremy Lipshultz, "Conceptual Problems of Broadcast Indecency Policy and Application," *Communications and the Law* 14, 2 (1992), 3–29.

40. *Red Lion Broadcasting Co. v. FCC* 395 U.S. 367 (1969).

41. *Red Lion v. FCC* 395 US 367 (1969); *Miami Herald v. Tornillo* 418 US 241 (1974).

42. 47 USC 202(a) (1988).

43. The constitution prohibits only infringement on free speech by government. Private firms and individuals are not covered by this prohibition, although their activities that affect speech may be limited by other laws.

44. See Jonathan Rosenoer, *Cyberlaw: The Law of the Internet* (New York: Springer Publishing, 1995).

45. For an overview of the compelled speech doctrine, see David W. Ogden, "Is There a First Amendment Right to Remain Silent?" *Federal Bar News and Journal* 40, 6 (1993), 368–373.

46. Congress has set limits on the amount of advertising contained in programming aimed primarily at children, which can be not more than 10.5 minutes per hour on weekends and not more than 12 minutes per hour on weekdays. In addition, the renewal of television broadcast licenses depend on a showing that the licensee has "served the educational and informational needs of children." 47 USC 303a and 303b.

47. FCC regulations require broadcasters to sell advertising time to candidates at their "lowest unit cost" and forbids them from altering the advertising, even if it may offend many viewers or contains indecent or libelous material. 47 USC 315.

48. If a station endorses a candidate for office, it must allow all other candidates for that office to respond at no charge. 47 C.F.R. 73.1930.

49. See *West Virginia State Board of Education v. Barnette*, 319 U.S. 241 (1943) (mandatory flag salutes by school children prohibited); *Miami Herald v. Tornillo* 418 U.S. 241 (1974) (forced publication on public issues by newspapers prohibited); *Pacific Gas and Electric v. P.U.C. of California*, 475 U.S 1 (1986) (forced publication of consumer information in utility newsletter prohibited).

50. In *Red Lion v. FCC*, 395 U.S. 367 (1969), the Supreme Court used this rationale to uphold the Fairness Doctrine, which required broadcasters to air information on both sides of issues of public importance and to give free time for response to those attacked in the coverage of controversial issues. This doctrine was subsequently repealed. See Thomas W. Hazlett, "The Rationality of U.S. Regulation of the Broadcast Spectrum," *Journal of Law and Economics* 33, 1 (1990), 133–175.

51. Angela J. Campbell, "Political Campaigning in the Information Age: A Proposal for Protecting Political Candidate's Use of On-Line Computer Services," *Villanova Law Review* 38, 2 (1993).

52. *Turner Broadcasting System, Inc. v. FCC* __ U.S. __, 117 S.Ct. 1174, 137 L.Ed. 369 (1997).

53. FCC v. Pacifica Foundation, 438 U.S. 726 (1978) (indecent radio broadcast); see also, *Roman v. Post Office*, 397 U.S. 728 (1970) (indecent material sent via postal system).

54. *Kovacs v. Cooper*, 336 U.S. 77 (1949).

55. *Action for Children's Television v. FCC*, 852 F.2d 1332 (D.C.Cir 1988) (messages via broadcast); *Sable Communications of California v. FCC*, 492 U.S. 115, 109 S.Ct. 2829, 106 L.Ed.2d 93 (1989)(messages via telephone); *Cruz v. Ferre* 755 F.2d 1415 (1985) (messages via cable) and *Janet Reno v. American Civil Liberties Union*, 1997 LW 348012 (messages via the Internet).

56. *FCC v. WNCN Listeners Guild*, 450 U.S. 582, 101 S.Ct. 1266, 67 L.Ed.2nd 521 (1981).

57. For a discussion of the effect of competition and cooperation in the communications sector, see P. H. Longstaff, *Competition and Cooperaton: From Biology to Business Regulation* (Cambridge, Mass.: Harvard University Program on Information Resources Policy, P-98-4, October 1998).

58. Here information theory would measure entropy, the tendency of open systems to move toward disorganization.

59. He was employed by Bell Laboratories, a common carrier environment in which the emphasis was on efficient and effective conveyance of other people's messages without regard to their substance.

60. See, e.g., Sally Jackson, *Message Effects Research: Principles of Design and Analysis* (New York: Guilford Press, 1992).

61. Devices previously considered decoders are rapidly taking on other functionality. For example, the cable box used to decode cable signals in the home is being redesigned to allow subscribers to participate in interactive services, such as on-line information services and computer bulletin boards, thus making a TV with a cable box look a lot like a personal computer with a modem. See "Cable Converters Entering New Era," *Broadcasting and Cable* (June 14, 1993), 79, The agreements necessary to set up the appropriate coding, however, have not yet been worked out, and representatives of the cable and consumer electronics industries are hoping to come to a meeting of the minds before the FCC steps in. "Working Toward Compatibility," *Broadcasting and Cable* (June 14, 1993), 92.

62. See David L. Abney, "The Judicial Outlook on Signal Piracy," *Communications and the Law* 8, 3 (1986), 3–19.

63. In this context, "accuracy" of the message does not mean its substance. A message is accurately received if the coded tokens (words, bytes) are received in the same way they were transmitted.

64. 47 CFR 63 (telco); 47 CFR 76(k) (cable).

65. For a discussion of government regulation of quality in a competitive market, see David J. Goodman, "Government Regulation and Innovation," in *Information Technology: Public Issues*, edited by Raymond Plant et al. (New York: St. Martins Press, 1988), 65.

66. See, e.g., William Glaberson, "Creating Electronic Editions, Newspapers Try New Roles," *The New York Times*, Aug. 16, 1993, 1.

67. With the addition of switching capability to cable systems.

68. Ithiel de Sola Pool, *Technologies of Freedom* (Cambridge, Mass.: Harvard University Press, 1983), 229–230.

69. Ibid., 230.

70. Telephone Company–Cable Television Cross-Ownership Rules, Sections 63.54–58, Second report and Order, Recommendations to Congress, and Second Further Notice of Proposed Rulemaking, 7 F.C.C.R. 5781 (1992).

71. Pettit and J. McGuire, "Video Dialtone: Reflections on Changing Perspectives in Telecommunications Regulation," 348.

72. *US v. Southwestern Cable Co.* 392 US 157 (1968).

73. *FCC v. Midwest Video Corporation* 440 US 689 (1979). For an overview of cable regulation in this area, see E. Dana Roof et al., "Structural Regulation of Cable Television: A Formula for Diversity," *Communications and the Law* 15, 2 (1993).

74. Kansas Statutes 74-9301

75. 47 CFR 73.3555. These limits were somewhat eased to allow broadcast companies to control more stations, therefore giving them an opportunity to lower their costs of operation through economies of scale thus achieved. Apparently, the fear that broadcasters will garner too much economic and political power has been replaced by the realization that they are no longer the only (or even the most powerful) show in town.

76. 47 CFR 73.3555(d).

77. 47 CFR 63.54-58 But see *Chesapeake and Potomac Telephone Company of Virginia, et al., v. US et al.*, 830 F. Supp. 909 (D.C. Eastern Dist. Virginia, Aug. 24, 1993).

78. See, e.g., "A New Bill on the Baby Bells," *The New York Times*, May 8, 1992, D16; and Rob Seitz, "All About Information Services: Phone Companies Join Their Rivals in the Facts Business," *The New York Times*, June 7, 1992, 3–10.

79. *US v. Western Electric Co.* 767 F. Supp. 308 (D.D.C. 1991); see also, *US v. Western Electric Co.* 900 F. 2d 283 (D.C. Cir. 1990) and *MCI Communications Corp. v. US.* 498 US 911 (1990).

80. Pool, *Technologies for Freedom*, 22.

81. In an order denying a request to enjoin enforcement of a law that requires cable operators to carry the signal of local broadcasters, Justice Rehnquist stated: "Although we have recognized that cable operators engage in speech protected by the First Amendment ... we have not decided whether the activities of cable operators are more akin to that of newspapers or wireless broadcasters." *Turner Broadcasting System, Inc. et al. v. FCC et al.* 113 S.Ct. 1806, at 1808 (1993), 123 L.Ed.2d 642, at 645.

82. See, generally, Donald E. Lively, "Modern Media and the First Amendment: Rediscovering Freedom of the Press," *Washington Law Review* 67, 1992, 599–624.

83. Radio Act of 1927, recodified in the Communications Act of 1934.

84. *Red Lion v. FCC* 395 US 367 (1969).

85. In the 1980s, many local governments became so enamored of the power to license the media that they attempted to license news racks, claiming there were too many on the street and that they had to be limited. These attempts were struck down as unconstitutional on the basis of the long tradition in the law that protects the print media. *Lakewood v. Plain Dealer* 468 US 750 (1988).

86. 47 CFR 73.1920.

87. *Miami Herald v. Tornillo* 418 US 241 (1974).

88. See, e.g., *Notice of Proposed Rulemaking (Regarding Ownership Restrictions)*, MM Docket No. 91–140; *Notice of Inquiry, in the Matter of Review of the Policy Implications of the Changing Video Marketplace*, MM Docket No. 91–221, Adopted July 11, 1991; Florence Setzer and Jonathon Levy, *Broadcast Television in a Multichannel Marketplace*, Office of Plans and Policy, Working Paper No. 26, June 1991.

89. *Turner Broadcasting System, Inc. v. FCC* 117 S.Ct. 1174, 137 L.Ed. 369 (1997).

90. Interestingly, network television was one of the first competitors to break the Bell System monopoly. It was among the first to ask the FCC for permission to construct its own system to transmit programming to local affiliates. The exact same messages were being regulated under two different parts of the Communications Act, merely because they were transmitted on two different parts of the spectrum. FCC Report and Order, Docket 11164, "Amendment of Part 4 of the Commission's Rules and Regulations Governing Television Auxiliary Broadcast Stations" (Video II), Aug. 4, 1958, 44 FCC 1354.

91. For a fascinating inside view of the beginning of the end of the Bell monopoly, see Peter Temin, *The Fall of the Bell System* (Cambridge and New York: Press Syndicate of the University of Cambridge, 1987).

92. Both are expressed as goals in *The National Information Infrastructure: Agenda For Action*, which does not, however, acknowledge that they may be mutually exclusive because, in theory, competition will reduce prices to cost and thus leave no money in the system to subsidize users who cannot pay the full cost of service, e.g., rural users (with high cost for outside plant) or people with low incomes.

93. See P. H. Longstaff, *Telecommunications Competition and Universal Service: The Essential Tradeoffs* (Cambridge, Mass.: Harvard University Program on Information Policy Resources Policy, P-96-2, May 1996).

18 FCC Reform: Does Governing Require a New Standard?

William H. Read and Ronald Alan Weiner

The fundamental—even perennial—national issue in telecommunications is: Should the federal government economically regulate the telecommunications industry? And if so, how?

The Telecommunications Act of 1996 (the "1996 Act"), the first major revision of the United States's basic communications law in more than sixty years, seems to accept the need for continuing regulation and the established means for undertaking it.[1] The 1996 Act keeps in place the Federal Communications Commission (FCC), the specialized regulatory agency created by the 1934 Communications Act, amended but not replaced by the new law.[2] The 1996 Act also keeps in place the "public interest" standard under which the Commission operates.

This report offers a new option that might be considered should Congress wish to visit the issue of whether the government should economically regulate the telecommunications industry. This option would hasten the demise of administrative agency regulation of communications by amending the public interest standard of the 1934 Communications Act through incorporation of pro-competitive antitrust doctrine.[3] A public interest standard based on competitiveness may be appropriate to conditions of technological abundance and convergence, such as those that have replaced the communications scarcity and media separation of an earlier era and that gave rise to administrative agency regulation.

Although recommendations to abolish the FCC may make headlines, and proposals to cut its budget may appeal to budget-balancing members of Congress, the option presented here recognizes that the agency has important responsibilities in any transition to full competition and that it offers reform by removing the agency's political discretion to define the public interest in any manner it sees fit by mere majority vote.

Background: Arguments and Issues

Since the late 1960s, at least among academics, technological convergence has been said to be occurring in the sciences of communications and computing.[4] More recently, in the 1990s, this convergence has been the subject of articles in the business and trade press:

The telephone, television and computer are merging into a single intelligent box..., a telecomputer ... which will be linked to the rest of the world by high-capacity smart wires.[5]

Some observers have predicted that the "telecomputer" will be widely available and in use by the end of the 1990s.[6] The introduction of convergent technologies linked by "smart wires" is perceived as profound, because it erodes technological boundaries that have long separated historically distinct industries of telephony, computing, broadcasting, cable television, and consumer electronics. President Clinton has predicted that this technological revolution will bring an economic and social development equal to the one that accompanied the introduction of the railroads in the nineteenth century.[7]

Technology Meets Regulation

The question of how government will adapt to this new condition of abundance and digital unity in communications has prompted public debate.[8] The Clinton administration's response was to establish an Information Infrastructure Task Force, with committees on telecommunications, information policy, and applications, this last with responsibility for implementing recommendations of Vice-President Gore's *National Performance Review* (also called *Reinventing Government*) in the area of information technology (also called "the information superhighway").

Vice-President Gore believed that the FCC should be empowered to "create a unified regulatory scheme" that would somehow combine a flexible regulatory environment with free and open markets.[9] In an era when technologies are converging and when the declining costs of computing are enabling decentralization in communications networks, it indeed makes sense to argue for a policy of free and open markets. But did it make sense to argue at the same time for some sort of new "unified regulatory scheme"? Given that economists justify economic regulation as a surrogate for competition, how can new regulation bring the American consumer the benefits of converging technologies through free and open markets? Does not regulation impede competition? These questions were significant as Congress contemplated a revision of the Communications Act.

The traditional agenda of federal regulation of communications has produced such results as the FCC's inflexible zoning system for the spectrum, which has slowed the introduction of new technologies and become an entry barrier to a communications service in need of spectrum. Given the continuing advances of converging technologies, a regulatory scheme that both divides various communications firms and circumscribes the services they offer may be arbitrary, if not obsolete.[10]

As the FCC implements the provisions of the new law, what is now needed is not regulation based on precedents under the public interest standard but, rather, an amended standard. This standard would be based on the competitive principles of antitrust law, not on the limited resource principles of regulatory law. Put another way, the conditions of scarcity and inflexibility in communications are changing to conditions of abundance and versatility. With the costs of communications and computing declining, abundance increases; with spreading acceptance of digital formats, versatility abounds. These technological imperatives produce a convergence that, in turn, creates new choices. Video programming offers an example: Consumers at home no longer rely solely on over-the-air television (TV) for video programming; cable TV and video-cassette recorders (VCRs) are widely available. From a technological standpoint, telephone companies are capable of entering the home video market, as are multimedia computer companies. The true public interest would be to see many competing firms in the market, not regulation of some already in this market nor regulation preventing those wishing to enter it.

Thus, the federal communications act today might be amended to reflect the following intent: *The public interest is best served when the private communications system functions in competitive markets and therefore any regulatory economic intervention should be premised on the principles of antitrust law.*

The Public Interest

The 1934 Act[11] established the FCC[12] and gave it broad jurisdiction to regulate "interstate and foreign communication by wire or radio," including common carriers (discussed in this section) and radio broadcasting (discussed in the following section). Over-the-air and cable television did not yet exist, nor computers, over which the FCC has no jurisdiction.[13]

The 1934 Act, which consolidated federal regulation of communication into one agency,[14] had its legal origin in the late 1800s, when Congress focussed on railroad regulation and the public interest standard.[15] The regulation that evolved, using the public interest standard, covered two related activities: (1) government-granted monopolies, such as railroads, telephone companies, and electric utilities, and (2) public resources made available to private entities for private gain, including again railroads, telephone, and electric companies that used public land. In 1910, wireless, as radio was then called, was added to this list when Congress amended the Interstate Commerce Act to bring interstate and foreign wire and wireless communication under federal jurisdiction.[16] The Radio Act of 1912, which followed the sinking of the *Titanic*, represented the first comprehensive radio legislation.[17] It adopted, among other things, the international distress signal.[18]

The 1934 Act requires that the FCC shall determine "whether the public interest, convenience, and necessity will be served by the granting of [broadcast] facility construction permits and station licenses."[19] The law provides that "No [wireline common] carrier shall undertake the construction of a new line or of an extension of any line ... unless there shall first have been obtained from the Commission a certificate that the present or future public convenience and necessity require or will require the construction...."[20] Although the key words in the statute vary for broadcasters and common carriers, the Supreme Court has rejected efforts to distinguish between the terms.[21] Indeed, although both the agency and the courts have struggled to interpret what Congress meant by those words, given they are not defined in the 1934 Act, there is no doubt that "the statutory standard ... leaves wide discretion and calls for imaginative interpretation."[22]

Problems of statutory construction are common in administrative law, but the review in this paper of FCC decisions leaves no doubt that the Commission has so tortured the public interest standard through its applications in both broadcast and common carrier regulation that, in the view of the authors, the public interest of the United States in communications might be better served by an amended standard.[23] The review begins by examining how the FCC has defined the public interest in allocating access to the radio spectrum.

Spectrum Scarcity

The regulatory rationale for broadcast regulation is the scarcity of frequencies: "The radio spectrum simply is not large enough to accommodate everybody," Justice Frankfurter observed in 1943.[24] Spectrum's "inherent physical limitation"[25] has been considered justification for federal imposition on broadcasters of public service obligations in return for the "free and exclusive use of a limited and valuable" public resource.[26]

The scarcity rationale, which supports regulation of broadcasting in the public interest, has yielded many problems, not least among them the lack of scarcity. In 1927, the United States was served by fewer that 600 AM radio stations. No FM stations, TV stations, cable TV, low-power TV, video cassettes, or electronic publishing existed then, nor any of the other current or planned technological alternatives that undermine the scarcity rationale—and in the 1990s, there are eight times as many AM radio stations on the air as were operating in 1927.

In 1927, Congress, apprehensive that a few special interests might monopolize the radio frequencies, passed the Radio Act to safeguard the public interest.[27] The public interest standard that has governed broadcasting since then has become controversial, mainly because, coupled with the scarcity rationale, it was used to justify extensive government intrusion into the First Amendment rights of broadcast journalists, exceeding anything imposed on "the platform or the press."[28] Of all the intrusions, the most despised was the Fairness Doctrine, which provoked forty years of controversy.[29]

The Fairness Doctrine

The Fairness Doctrine, which was abolished by the FCC on August 7, 1987,[30] imposed twin public interest obligations on broadcasters licensed to use specific frequencies of the "scarce" spectrum:

Broadcast licensees are required to provide coverage of vitally important controversial issues of interest in the community served by the licensees and to provide a reasonable opportunity for the presentation of contrasting viewpoints on such issues.[31]

The evolution and demise of the Doctrine reveals the problematic state of the public interest standard. The slippery slope first began in 1929, when the Federal Radio Commission[32] discussed the obligation of broadcasters to provide equal time to political candidates as set forth in section 18 of the Radio Act.[33] The Commission said:

> It would not be fair, indeed it would not be good service to the public to allow a one-sided presentation of the political issues of a campaign. In so far as a program consists of discussion of public questions, public interest requires ample play for the free and fair competition of opposing views, and the commission believes that the principle applies not only to addresses by political candidates but to all discussion of issues of importance to the public.[34]

The Doctrine became an FCC policy in 1949,[35] and in 1969, in *Red Lion Broadcasting Co. v. FCC*,[36] the Supreme Court upheld the constitutionality of the personal attack component of the Doctrine. The Court's approval of the Doctrine as a necessary regulation of spectrum scarcity has frequently been cited as justifying regulation of broadcast content. Justice White, writing for a unanimous Court, determined that Congress, when it amended the Communications Act in 1959,[37] had intended to include the Fairness Doctrine in the public interest standard:

> [The] language makes it very plain that Congress, in 1959, announced that the phrase "public interest," which had been in the Act since 1927, imposed a duty on broadcasters to discuss both sides of controversial public issues. In other words, the amendment vindicated the FCC's general view that the Fairness Doctrine inhered in the public interest standard.[38]

The implication here—that, according to the Supreme Court, unless the public interest standard could be eliminated, the Fairness Doctrine could not be eliminated—made it difficult for the FCC later to revisit the Doctrine. Thus, to abolish it, the FCC had to determine that the media marketplace had changed drastically since the *Red Lion* decision and that the Doctrine no longer served the public interest.[39] Although the FCC's 1985 Fairness Report[40] challenged the Doctrine on both the scarcity rationale and the First Amendment rights of broadcasters, the Commission had to avoid the appearance of not following the teachings of *Red Lion*. The public interest standard was therefore reinterpreted to mean that the Doctrine inhibited, rather than encouraged, dissemination of information.

The year after the issuance of the Fairness Report, the U.S. Court of Appeals for the District of Columbia held that Congress had not codified the Fairness Doctrine in its 1959 amendment to the Communications Act.[41]

With the demise of the Fairness Doctrine, the broadcast industry was relieved of a despised regulation, but the FCC made it clear that broadcasters were still required to observe other programming obligations:

> The fact that government may not impose unconstitutional conditions on the receipt of a public benefit does not preclude the Commission's ability, and obligation, to license broadcasters in the public interest, convenience, and necessity.... The Commission may still impose certain conditions on licensees in furtherance of this public interest obligation. Nothing in this decision, therefore, is intended to call into question the validity of the public interest standard under the Communications Act.[42]

Broadcast Deregulation

While continuing to acknowledge that it was mandated by Congress to regulate in the public interest, the FCC in the 1980s, under then Chairman Mark S. Fowler, assumed a new agenda—deregulation of the broadcast industry. Fowler viewed the economic efficiency of broadcast licensees and voluntary discretion in programming as better ways than regulation to serve the public interest. In a seminal article, Fowler and his legal advisor, Daniel L. Brenner, stating that the historic justifications for regulation did not withstand close scrutiny, advocated allowing broadcasters to respond to public demand.[43] Support for their thesis could be found in economics, especially among economists who advocated marketplace solutions. As Ronald Coase noted as early as 1959,[44] all resources are scarce, and the ideal way to allocate them is not through regulation but by a market-based system that uses prices to ensure that scarce resources go to those who will make the best use of them.[45]

Fowler went further, contending that the FCC second-guessed business judgment and that this discouraged risk-taking and innovation by entrepreneurs.[46] The Fowler Commission, acting on this new agenda, took steps to deregulate both ownership and operation of broadcast stations. Restrictions on multiple ownership were relaxed,[47] "trafficking" rules that limited alienation of licenses were eliminated,[48] and restrictions on the content of programs were eliminated.[49]

These regulatory changes reflected Fowler's belief that the marketplace best serves the public interest.[50] The argument can be made, however, that a revised public interest standard failed to address the fundamental challenge—to reassess the power of the FCC when the FCC implements the public interest standard.

Counter Arguments: Regulation, Reregulation, and Deregulation

An Illegitlmate Standard

Professor William Mayton has argued that the public interest standard used by the FCC is illegitimate in that it "implicates a derangement of constitutional structure, a structure put in place to assure that government power is used circumspectly."[51] This powerful argument draws on the precedent of deregulation of the press in 1694 by the "Regulations of Printing Acts."[52] In the words of Blackstone, "The press properly became free, in 1694; and has ever since so continued."[53] In modern times, given technological convergence among media, the argument is compelling that the power the FCC holds under the public interest standard should be held unconstitutional. According to Professor Mayton, all media should be free. The law that governs the press, he argued, should be precedent for the electronic media, to the benefit of American democracy.[54]

A second point by Mayton with respect to FCC power is that, when read correctly, the 1934 Act does not delegate an open-ended public interest power to the FCC.[55] Mayton is not alone in contending that Congress did not delegate general power to the FCC to regulate broadcasting in the public interest. Professor Jaffe has argued that

[T]he use of "public interest" in the statute did not manifest a congressional intent to give the Commission general powers to "regulate" the industry or to solve any "problems" other than the problem of [radio] interference which gave rise to the legislation.[56]

In 1940, in its first decision concerning FCC power under the 1934 Communications Act, the Supreme Court agreed:

[T]he Act does not essay to regulate the business of the licensee. The Commission is given no supervisory control of the programs, of business management or of policy.[57]

But three years later, the Court opened the public interest door to expanded FCC powers. In *NBC v. United States*,[58] Justice Frankfurter combined different parts of the 1934 Act to describe broad FCC authority: "[T]he 'public interest' to be served under the Communications Act is thus the interest of the listening public in the 'larger and more effective use of the radio.'"[59]

Read together, *NBC v. United States*[60] and *Red Lion Broadcasting Co. v FCC*[61] legitimated expansive powers for the FCC under the public interest standard. Since these decisions were handed down, much has changed—so much that efforts have been under way, starting as far back as 1976, to rewrite the Communications Act.[62] At the same time, given these changing conditions, the FCC has been working to redefine the public interest—yet the issue is not one of redefinition but, as Professor Mayton argued, reassessment.

Telecommunications Reregulation

When the Communications Act became law in 1934, there were three parts to the paradigm for regulating telephone and telegraph companies:

- The utility had a protected franchise based on the economic concept of natural monopoly.
- It was quarantined from entering competitive markets.
- Government would thoroughly regulate the company's prices, business practices, and conditions of service.[63]

As recently as 1984, this model helped shape the thinking of government decision makers. That year, the U.S. District Court in Washington, D.C., began regulating the regional Bell telephone companies, following the AT&T Divestiture Decree, which created these companies.[64] The model has been significantly altered by both the FCC and state public service commissions, which have adopted alternative forms of regulation by implementing rate-freeze or price-cap regulation.[65] The model was further eroded when the U.S. District Court in Alexandria, Virginia, agreed with Bell Atlantic that the federal government had imposed an unconstitutional quarantine on one of its telephone companies (Chesapeake & Potomac) by banning such companies from entering the cable TV business in the same area in which they provided telephone service.[66] The Court held that the ban infringed on the company's First Amendment rights, thus indirectly challenging the inferior constitutional protection the Supreme Court afforded electronic speech in *Red Lion*.[67]

The principal reason for this evolution of the model, culminating in the 1996 Act, has been the changing conditions in communications, which have led to increasing competition, which in turn, has led commentators and regulators to see economic efficiency as a primary goal of telecommunications regulation.[68] One commentator has argued that the FCC has changed its focus from the goal of universally available and affordable residential telephone service to economic efficiency: "The federal redistributory or *equity* goal," he contends, "has become "secondary to the pursuit of economic *efficiency* through reliance on a change in markets and competition."[69]

The FCC first adopted these concepts of efficiency and competition in telecommunications in a series of decisions that began in 1956 with telephone accessory equipment and culminated in 1968 in *Carterfone* and the FCC's decision to open the public telecommunications network to equipment provided by vendors other than telephone companies.[70] In the area of long-distance telephone, the Commission adopted a similar policy by opening the market to new entrants.[71] It also encouraged the entry of new technologies into the marketplace, such as direct broadcast satellites and cellular telephones.[72] Finally, it relaxed some quarantine restrictions on telephone companies to allow them to enter the competitive markets of "enhanced," i.e., computerized, services and "customer premises," i.e., terminal, equipment.[73]

Regulate Structure or Performance

All the Commission's actions were initiated pursuant to the public interest standard, which on the one hand enabled the Commission to adopt freedom of entry positions based on convergence of technology, while on the other hand it allowed the Commission to segregate segments of the industry and restrict participants in one area from entering another. For example, cellular telephony was authorized as an unregulated duopoly, with one franchise reserved for the local telephone company and the other allocated by the Commission to a competitor.[74] In effect, the Commission substituted formal control of market structure for deregulation of price and quality. Increasingly, regulation of structure was replaced by that of performance as more in the public interest.

At the same time that it was placing increased reliance on marketplace forces, accompanied by structural controls on entry to the market, the FCC was also placing heightened emphasis on antitrust law.[75] An example was the 1982 staff report of the Office of Policy and Plans entitled *Measurement of Concentration in Home Video Markets*,[76] which argued that when local video markets (broadly defined) are reasonably competitive, the FCC's goals are realized.[77]

The FCC was hardly embracing the consumer welfare model of antitrust law. To do that would have meant avoiding the imposition of structural regulations that raised barriers to market entry, vertical integration, and efficient exploitation of economies of scale. It was permissible, the Commission implicitly reasoned, for regulation, at times, to restrain trade. The public interest standard could accommodate such an outcome. One jurist, Judge Posner of the Seventh Circuit, reflected on this curious situation:

> If the Commission were enforcing the antitrust laws, it would not be allowed to trade off a reduction in competition.... Since it is enforcing the nebulous public interest standard instead, it is permitted, and maybe even required, to make such a tradeoff—at least we do not understand any of the parties to question the Commission's authority to do so.[78]

The issue was not the Commission's authority; "the nebulous public interest standard" is just that—nebulous. The question then, is how the standard should be defined in light of changing conditions in communications.

Regulation and Competition

Where regulation is concerned, less presumably is better and competition presumably is best.[79] This theme was heard often in the mid-1980s, when Washington was filled with calls for regulatory reform and deregulation; and the FCC, under Republican control, interpreted the public interest to mean more competition and less regulation. Intellectually, the theme was fed by the "Chicago School" of economists, who challenged much regulation as being economically without merit.[80] The success of the Japanese in international business reinforced the view that the competitiveness of the American economy had been weakened, in part at least by too much regulation.

The FCC, apparently caught up in this "regulatory failure" theory, sought to promote less restrictive means of favoring competition. Arguably, what the Commission created was "regulated competition." Congress did not help, for example, by enacting first cable TV regulation legislation in 1984[81] and then, just eight years later, reregulating the industry.[82] The reregulation bill left implementation to the FCC, and when the Commission rolled back cable rates, not only did the industry howl but the planned Bell Atlantic–TCI merger collapsed, dealing a setback to the Clinton administration's ambitions for an information superhighway built by converging industries with private monies.[83]

"Our mission was to protect the public against unreasonable prices, while promoting business," Reed Hundt, the FCC chairman, commented after the decision.[84] The regulatory tool can be a difficult instrument to use in attempting to achieve these twin reasonabilities. Classical regulation often fails, as Justice Breyer has argued, because of a fundamental mismatch between the tool and the evil it is intended to fix.[85] A more appropriate tool in communications might be antitrust law rather than precedents of the FCC that apply the ill-defined public interest standard. This tool can be made available by amending the 1934 Act to define the public interest in pro-competitive, antitrust terms.

By adopting the antitrust approach, Congress could correct a continuing omission, place a safeguard against infringement on the First Amendment rights of the growing electronic media, and at last come to grips with the fundamental question of the FCC's authority. Put another way, Congress could correct a problem described this way by former FCC General Counsel Henry Geller:

> [In effect, Congress has said to the FCC] Here is a new field, communications; we have no idea how it will develop so we leave it to you to do the best you can in the public interest.[86]

In the late 1990s, the nation knows how the field of communications has developed and may develop further. By defining the public interest in communications in antitrust terms, the nation can have both reasonable prices and business progress.

The Antitrust Perspective

The United States telephone industry has been shaped more by antitrust law than by any aspect of federal or state regulation.[87]

No event in the history of communications jurisprudence better reinforces this statement than the 1982 AT&T Divestiture.[88] AT&T, with assets worth more than those of General Motors, Ford, Chrysler, General Electric, and IBM combined, was divested in an effort to separate the competitive aspects of AT&T's business from the remaining elements of the Bell monopoly.[89] Changes in the telecommunications market brought about by the settlement of the government's antitrust suit against AT&T represented a dramatic impact of antitrust law on the industry.

Even in instances in which divestiture infused competition into the communications market, the anticompetitive restrictions of the "public interest" standard has remained prohibitive.[90] Incorporating the pro-competitive theory of antitrust law into the standard might encourage uniformity of outcomes in the governance of communications.

Before examining the value that a pro-competitive standard would offer both the communications industry and consumers, this paper looks at the history and nature of the various antitrust laws and the relationship of those laws to regulated industries.

In theory, application of the antitrust laws serves the interest of the public and the industry by prohibiting the exercise of market failures, curbing cartel-like behavior, and promoting vigorous competition.[91] Would such outcomes be better served in the communications industry by the application by the FCC of antitrust standards rather than the ill-defined public interest standard? Under what kind of policy initiative are the consumer-oriented ends of quality, access, and reasonable pricing most likely to meet the market ideals of robust competition and independence from constant and inefficient government intrusion?

The time may have come to streamline the public interest standard of the 1934 Act or replace it with a competitive model that could assure that the public interest truly is served by incorporating antitrust principles into the working definition of the public interest standard.[92] The next two sections discuss regulated industries in which comparable deregulation has been instituted, and present, in more detail, how an antitrust regime could be administered.

Traditional Regulation of Natural Monopolies

In contrast to the antitrust laws, economic regulation of an industry is intended as a surrogate for competition in which one firm has a natural monopoly over public goods.[93] Historically, the justification for economic regulation has been that the regulatory scheme protects the public interest because market failures prevent the market from serving the public interest.

One of the earliest examples of government regulation came from state regulatory initiatives aimed at controlling the dominant railroad monopoly and its discriminatory market abuses. In 1877, the Supreme Court, in the case of *Munn v. Illinois*, upheld the right of a state to regulate pricing and licensing requirements that directly affected railroad practices.[94] The rationale was that certain activities uniquely affected the public interest and must therefore be constrained to maintain the public good. The assumption is that the public interest will be served if consumers can be assured least-cost purchasing of a service. Government regulation strives toward this end through approximating least cost and determining regulated pricing.[95]

Regulated markets reveal quite a different story. Traditional government regulation of the "natural monopolies" has often resulted in a failure to meet consumer needs.[96] The corollary of regulation been a trend toward the emergence of deregulation, often as a result of pro-competitive policy. This trend may be attributed to the belief that competition is more capable of bearing beneficial economic implications in a post-industrial international marketplace.[97]

Further, given advances in technologies, a regulation justifiable in 1934 may no longer be warranted in the late 1990s. After trucks and planes were invented, railroads were no longer a natural monopoly.

Deregulation of Natural Monopolies

The airline industry was deregulated in 1978.[98] Although initially unregulated, Congress created the Civil Aeronautics Board in 1938,[99] on the theory that, like the railroad and other common carrier transportation industries, air transportation should be viewed as a public utility.[100] Before deregulation, the airline industry had an inefficient regulatory structure, which ultimately led to high rates for consumers and low profits for the industry.[101] The early policies on which regulation was predicated contributed to these market inefficiencies.[102] Regulations included assigning airline companies specific markets, controlling schedules, and uniform consumer price setting. The Airline Deregulation Act of 1978 attempted to curb market imperfections by increasing entry opportunities for new airlines and introducing greater flexibility and discretion for individual airlines to lower and raise fares.[103] The Civil Aeronautics Board was eliminated in 1985, although many of its administrative functions were transferred to the Department of Transportation (DOT).[104]

The impact of deregulation on the airline industry was, and is likely to remain, debatable.[105] Whether the industry actually was deregulated is in question. Although it is too early to assess the substantive long-term effects of deregulation, many short-term consequences have occurred. The introduction of intense competition into the market resulted in an overall expansion of service options at reduced prices for consumers.[106] The sudden increase in supply outpaced the demand, leading to a number of highly publicized bankruptcies and mergers.[107] Ticket prices for consumers have slowly begun to increase again as the industry has reverted to a concentrated oligopolistic structure.[108]

The absence of any antitrust jurisdiction in the hands of a specialized airline agency that could effectively monitor day-to-day business operations is notable. This is not to imply that airlines do not need to consider antitrust issues, for these are necessarily part of any business with substantial market power. Antitrust enforcement would be more vigorous, thus a more effective deterrent to anticompetitive activities, were a centralized antitrust jurisdiction to exist within a *specialized* administrative agency.

What does exist is the ability of the DOT to authorize antitrust immunity for certain actions, for example, the DOT's approval and grant of antitrust immunity for a commercial cooperation and integration agreement between Northwest and KLM airlines.[109] Although this agreement can be seen as pro-competitive, it exemplifies the type of authority that threatens to inhibit the antitrust presence, which can artificially stimulate competition. Rather than grant antitrust exemptions, the focus of the overseeing federal agency might better be on whether the proposed activity would have an anticompetitive impact and, hence, violate antitrust standards.

The airline industry is not the only regulated market to experiment with deregulation without abandoning antitrust immunity and like exemptions. Throughout the latter half of the twentieth century, railroads experienced little economic success, especially in passenger service. The industry was originally regulated by the Interstate Commerce Commission in an attempt to minimize competition, provide universal service, and protect agricultural product shippers from exploitation by the railroad cartels.[110] In response to growing competition to the railroads from airlines and motor carriers, Congress passed the Railroad Revitalization and Regulatory Reform Act of 1976[111] and soon afterward the Staggers Rail Act of 1980,[112] intending to intensify competition and allow for greater pricing discretion by individual carriers.

The effects have been similar to those of airline deregulation. The railroads' ability finally to abandon costly and unprofitable markets[113] they had previously been obligated to serve[114] was a significant benefit. Once again, deregulation was not accompanied by adequate active antitrust supervision where previously there had been a regulatory framework.

Without the worry of having a special industry agency to monitor antitrust concerns, and to no one's surprise, monopolistic concentration of market power has evolved within the modern railroad industry.[115] The Interstate Commerce Commission's authority to immunize mergers of rail carriers from antitrust review when it finds the merger to be consistent with public interest is noteworthy.[116]

There are lessons to be learned from the regulation of the airline and railroad industries. Economists, lawyers, and industry insiders have offered suggestions about how to modify the structure of deregulation to ensure market conditions that properly balance the goals of service, quality, efficiency, and competition.[117] While scholars debate the economic implications of regulation, the message of the airline experience seems to have been lost. That message seems to be that more attention to the initial structuring of the deregulatory scheme may be needed.[118]

Market inconsistencies and variables such as technological development and international competition add to the difficulty of structuring a regulatory framework for the communications industry. Absolute and instantaneous deregulation is neither competitively advantageous nor politically tolerable. The most practical strategy for those who oppose the current regulatory process may be to fortify gradual deregulation by superimposing strictly enforced antitrust principles on the regulatory system. This approach would offer the advantage of maintaining government and judicial oversight of anticompetitive conduct through the application of existing antitrust laws. A means would thus exist to guard against the market imperfections associated with deregulation.

Stated another way, antitrust policies should be vigorously enforced to ensure that, after deregulation, market conditions would be in place that would benefit consumers and industry players equally. This would best be achieved through granting to the administrative agency with the most specialized knowledge of the particular industry an antitrust jurisdiction that would include the power to enjoin potential anti-competitive activities, rather than, as is now the case, the power to grant such ventures antitrust immunity.[119] The remedy for such an antitrust violation? Partial, if not complete, reregulation, until the anti-competitive influences have been alleviated.

Through the incorporation of antitrust principles into the public interest standard, many fringe applications of antitrust exemptions and defenses would be intrinsically truncated.[120] Related antitrust concerns of time, cost, and extensive discovery would be comparably diminished by agency review as opposed to full-blown litigation. A similar functional strategy would serve the communications industry well.

A delicate blending of the competitive goals and industrial freedom of the antitrust laws and of the business sector's fear of reregulation offers the greatest potential to facilitate convergence of the public interest with market stability. Of no regulated industry is this truer than communications, in which for reasons already discussed, the existing regulatory structure has become obsolete. The antitrust influence within the industry is historically well established and pervasive.[121] The FCC, under the leadership of Chairman Reed Hundt, has already started to undertake the types of analysis that must be applied in antitrust cases,[122] for example, in its September 1994 decision approving the AT&T–McCaw merger, in which the Commission stated:

We now address the competitive impact of the proposed merger in each of the markets we have identified. In each market we must examine, the issue is whether the proposed merger will violate antitrust policies. In the case of a proposed merger, we are particularly mindful of Section 7 of the Clayton Act, which generally proscribes mergers "where in any line of commerce in any section of the country" the effect of the merger may be "substantially to lessen competition, or to tend to create a monopoly."[123] We also take care to examine the proposed merger for equally serious but less broad-sweeping violations of antitrust principles, such as theft of confidential information, tie-in sales, unjustified price discrimination, and other abuses of market power.[124] The principal way in which the commentators allege that the proposed merger will violate antitrust principles is by abuses which, it is said, will flow from the combination of McCaw's "bottleneck" cellular exchange and AT&T's power in other markets. In general, after careful consideration of the voluminous antitrust arguments made by all parties, we conclude that the competitive component of our statutory public interest standard will be satisfied by the imposition of two major conditions on our approval of the proposed merger:

(1) that AT&T shall not discriminate in favor of McCaw and against its other customers for cellular network equipment under existing contracts; and

(2) that AT&T and McCaw shall each take appropriate steps to prevent third parties' proprietary data from falling into the other's hands.

Antitrust Enforcement upon Regulated Industries

Inevitably, in any regulatory structure that seeks to protect monopolies in order to serve the public interest, some antitrust issues will exist. In theory, antitrust laws act as a check on anticompetitive behavior by persons with market power to ensure competition and avoid such evils as predatory pricing and tying.[125]

The conflict between command and control regulations and general antitrust laws has been met with guarded protection of the regulated industries through judicially crafted immunity exceptions to antitrust enforcement, but, because such protection offers an attractive opportunity to abuse the regulatory system, the public interest might be better served by a government regime that would emphasize open competition and discretionary pricing in conjunction with active antitrust enforcement, without the illusory protection that immunity doctrines have historically provided.[126] This is not to say that the communications industry has not been largely shaped and influenced by the antitrust laws.[127] Yet, although the history of the communications industry reflects episodes of active antitrust enforcement, pervasive application of different immunity doctrines has led to an equal amount of exception from the antitrust laws.

Ins and Outs of Enforcement and Competition

Inclusionary Antitrust Enforcement and Competitive Sustenance

When competitors enter into agreements whereby their conduct interferes with interstate commerce, the agreement is considered a horizontal restraint.[128] Section 1[129] of the Sherman Act[130] concerns market behavior, such as agreements to restrict output or to increase prices in order to limit or exclude competition. Such cartel behavior implicates Section 1 by restricting the normal supply and demand functions of the marketplace.[131] Violations of Section 1 have rarely come into court. Unlike other antitrust provisions, such as exclusive dealings and vertical agreements, the conduct prohibited by this provision has not been relevant to a communications market in which competition has been severely restricted by the natural monopoly structure that resulted from the public utility regulatory scheme.[132]

Section 2[133] of the Sherman Act[134] prohibits predatory and exclusionary conduct by one firm with market power, or which attempts to gain market power, against actual or potential competitors. Examples include monopolization,[135] attempts to monopolize, or any conspiracy to monopolize.[136] The concerns of Section 2 go beyond size in itself. In the seminal case of *United States v. Aluminum Company of America*,[137] Judge Learned Hand emphasized that offending firms required not just market power[138] but also anticompetitive conduct.[139] Unlike Section 1 of the Sherman Act, this provision has been the basis of a good deal of antitrust litigation within the communications industry.[140]

One common arrangement is the "tie-in" (also called a tying arrangement), which occurs when a sale of goods is conditioned on the buyer's purchase of other additional goods or services from the same seller.[141] Tying arrangements are prohibited by Sections 1 and 2 of the Sherman Act[142] and by Section 3[143] of the Clayton Act.[144] Tying problems among regulated industries are typically attempts by a firm to bypass regulation by leveraging its market power into related but unregulated markets.[145]

In the communications industry, application of antitying enforcement was evident as early as 1962, in the case of *United States v. Loew's, Inc.* Loew's, a motion picture distributor, conditioned the sale of its more popular films on the additional sale of a block of films with less appeal. Such a coercive effect is precisely what the antitrust laws are intended to eliminate from the market place. Telephony, in particular, lends itself to frequent tying scrutiny, because the market lines and boundaries of offered products and services are often unclear.[146]

There are many other antitrust laws and concepts that communications firms are commonly accused of violating but which immunity has, by and large, protected them from prosecution. Two frequently cited complaints are predatory pricing[147] and monopoly leveraging.[148] Were a new or revised antitrust standard of the kind discussed here incorporated into the public interest, convenience, and necessity standard of the 1934 Act, these antitrust theories would play a more significant role in the regulation of the communications industry.[149] Application of these competition-promoting laws would require more than instituting a suitable antitrust archetype into existing communications law. As discussed, communications firms have, for the most part, been immune to antitrust jurisprudence. For a new governing regime to achieve optimum market conditions, restrictions on antitrust enforcement would need to be removed. Removing them would not in any way restrict traditional antitrust oversight of industry behavior by the Department of Justice (DOJ) and others,[150] but were the legal environment purged of overly complicated procedural defenses, antitrust standards might become better focused on actual anticompetitive effects and less attentive to impedance by inefficient governance.

Exclusionary Jurisprudence and the Suppression of Competition

The degree to which the current (late 1990s) regulatory scheme displaces the application of antitrust principles largely depends the pervasiveness of the regulation in question. This is, in one way, a matter of jurisdiction: When do the courts have jurisdiction to enforce antitrust principles against a regulated industry, and when does the relevant agency have sole territorial province to dictate antitrust approval? Can, at times, regulations and antitrust enforcement coexist?

Congress or the courts or both have in some instances granted express antitrust immunity to a specific industry.[151] Congress did it with the communications industry, at least as applied to consolidations and mergers of telephone companies that the FCC considered within the public interest.[152] Other actions may not be similarly exempt from antitrust enforcement,[153] nor has statutory exemption played a significant role in modern legal history.[154]

Express Immunity

Explicit antitrust immunity has been granted to the communications industry in a number of areas, generally out of the belief that the industry was a natural monopoly and a product to which all should have universal access, and thus competition was trumped by the public interest standard.[155] The communications industry has often been viewed as a public utility in the sense that the entire economy works better if there is a global communications network. As previously discussed, technological advances have changed the common perception that the market cannot accommodate competition. Many of the express antitrust immunity provisions that exist today, however, may instead impede the public interest and inhibit development of the information superhighway, as well as other goods and services eagerly awaited by consumers.

The case of *ITT World Communications, Inc. v. New York Tel. Co.* affirmed the FCC's exclusive jurisdiction over rate-making issues within the telecommunications industry.[156] Rate matters were foreclosed from other parties wishing to assert antitrust jurisdiction. Congress expressly gave the Commission exclusive jurisdiction over mergers of telephone and telegraph companies.[157] Regulatory approval of such a merger, typically granted on the basis of the vague, if not arbitrary, public interest standard, creates antitrust immunity for communications firms.

Pervasive Regulation

Courts may grant implied immunity to an entire industry function if two conditions are met:

1. If antitrust enforcement would directly interfere with Congressionally approved regulatory action that approved the conduct in question ... and;
2. If the pervasiveness of regulatory control by one agency over the conduct of an industry is such that Congress is assumed to have determined competition to be an inadequate means of vindicating the public interest.[158]

The courts have gone as far as to allow a defense of acting in the public interest. In *Southern Pacific Communications v. AT&T*,[159] it was held that when AT&T makes telephone interconnecting determinations on the basis of the public interest standard, it would be contrary to public policy to subject AT&T to antitrust liability.[160] Two further supplementary methods by which courts can exempt the communications industry from antitrust enforcement are the *Noerr-Pennington* and state action doctrines.[161]

The Noerr-Pennington Doctrine

Noerr-Pennington provides antitrust immunity to a firm or firms even if competitors individually or in combination petition the government with the intent of influencing the decision-making process of an agency. This case is frequently cited as a defense to allegations that continual tariff filings to the FCC are attempts to restrain competition through delay and complication tactics. In 1991, MCI Communications successfully used the *Noerr-Pennington* defense when confronted by allegations from competitor TeleStar that MCI's petitioning activities before the Commission were actually a subversive attempt to impede TeleStar's petition for a license.[162]

If, on the other hand, efforts by competitors to petition and influence the government are illusory, the defense is voided. Such efforts have been appropriately labeled the "sham" exception to the *Noerr-Pennington* defense.[163] When Litton Systems sued AT&T claiming that AT&T's tariff filings, which required the use of special interface devices when connecting competing terminal equipment to AT&T lines, were intended only to inhibit competition, AT&T asserted the *Noerr-Pennington* defense. Even though the FCC initially allowed the tariff to go into effect without questioning its reasonableness, a jury found AT&T's actions to be in bad faith. On appeal, this verdict was affirmed, because the court agreed that AT&T had no bona fide expectation that the challenged tariff was reasonable. AT&T had monopolized the telephone terminal equipment market, and the sham exception to the *Noerr-Pennington* doctrine was applied.[164]

The State Action Doctrine

The state action defense to antitrust enforcement potentially provides incidental immunity to the communications industry in a complex manner. Broadly speaking, this judicial doctrine exempts certain state actions, such as regulations promulgated by state legislatures or state public utility commissions, from the scope of the *federal* antitrust laws.

The state action doctrine was introduced in the landmark case of *Parker v. Brown*, in which a California statute mandated that raisin producers set their levels for prices and output according to standards established by the industry.[165] The plaintiff, a producer who wished to bypass the regulations and set his own levels, challenged the law as violating the Sherman Act and, therefore, as preempted by federal law. The court, while recognizing the conflict, refused to preempt the state law and instead said that the purpose of the Sherman Act was not to prohibit states from regulating their domestic economies. In essence, the dichotomy the court found was between the Sherman Act (and other federal antitrust laws), intended to restrain *private* individual acts that adversely affect competition, and *public* actions by the states. The court made it clear that states cannot simply give blanket protection from antitrust laws to a particular industry within the state's economy. The theoretical foundation on which the court rests its holding is economic federalism, and inherent in a federal system of government is a license for states to regulate their own economies, however inefficient their regulations may be.

In 1985, the Supreme Court decided, in *Southern Motor Carriers Rate Conference, Inc. v. United States*, that a defendant can use state action as a defense to an antitrust suit by claiming that state policy sanctioned its activities.[166] In this case, a state statute that required a regulatory commission to set interstate common carrier rates was challenged by the federal government as a price-fixing scheme. The rate bureaus claimed that the statute authorized them—although admittedly, it did not expressly compel them—to agree on joint rate making. As with the entry of telcos into cable television, the rate bureaus had submitted proposals to the state public service commission and had received approval.

The actions were held to be immune under the state action doctrine even though the activities of the rate bureaus were not, in the strict sense, compelled by the state. Instead, the Court articulated a two-prong standard whereby a regulatory action is presumed to be state action, thus immune from antitrust liability, (1) if the activity is "clearly articulated and affirmatively expressed as state policy," and (2) if the actor is a private party relying on state regulation and it can demonstrate that its anticompetitive conduct was "actively supervised" by the state.[167] While expressly rejecting a "compulsion" requirement because it reduces the "range of regulatory alternatives available to the State,"[168] the Court made sure to resurrect the federalism notion that was the foundation of the *Parker* decision, noting that "the *Parker* decision was premised on the assumption that Congress, in enacting the Sherman Act, did not intend to compromise the State's ability to regulate their domestic commerce."[169]

Shortly after this opinion was rendered, this highly deferential standard was criticized as abstract and too easily satisfied.[170] The deference to state flexibility was fleeting. In 1988, the theoretical underpinnings of antitrust federalism were dealt a blow in *Patrick v. Burget*, when the Supreme Court elected to interpret the concept of "active supervision" strictly.[171] The Court held that for active supervision to exist, the State must "have and exercise ultimate control over the challenged anticompetitive conduct.... [T]he mere exercise of some state involvement or monitoring does not suffice."[172] Active supervision will exist only if the regulatory agency has statutory authority to review the substance of the peer review process, not just the proceedings. The Court's analysis focused on two elements: (1) whether the state agency had the statutory authority to exercise active supervision and, (2) if so, whether the state's involvement reached the level of "active supervision." Once again, the Court failed to address the question of what level of activity by the state is necessary to immunize private actions undertaken pursuant to state regulatory schemes.

This latest reshaping of the state action doctrine left other questions unanswered. The effects of the 1988 decision will take time to materialize, but the momentum is clear. The basic concept of federalism, which was the theoretical foundation of both the Sherman Act and the original *Parker* doctrine, has significantly deteriorated. For private parties that rely on state regulatory approval to protect them from federal antitrust enforcement, more is now demanded than ever before, although just what is needed remains to be clarified by the Court.

Motions to dismiss by private parties in communications that raise state action immunity probably should be denied, except in cases in which states actually supervise the communications industry. In line with this thinking, industry participants would not be able to neglect antitrust enforcement merely because regulatory approval was initially granted to permit a certain activity. One of the main reasons for the questionable success of much antitrust enforcement is abuse of such defenses and immunities by regulated industries, including the communications sector.[173]

As the status of the state action doctrine shows, simplicity is greatly needed in the application of antitrust jurisprudence. Tedious manipulation of the state action defense by the private sector over the years has obscured the goals of efficiency and competition. Unencumbered antitrust enforcement may be needed to mold economic and jurisprudential pedagogy into market actuality.

Summary

The doctrinal application of the state action defense to an antitrust allegation is still available to communications firms that act pursuant to state legislative or regulatory mandates. Although such arguments have rarely been made in recent antitrust cases, the doctrine remains potentially fruitful for achieving the preemption of the antitrust laws as they affect the communications industry. In conjunction with explicit statutory exemptions, implied antitrust immunity, and the *Noerr-Pennington* doctrine, the state action defense insulates all but the smallest percentage of anticompetitive activity in the communications marketplace.

In attempting to embark on a new governing standard that would emphasize open markets the better to satiate both public and private interests, these shields to effective antitrust enforcement must necessarily be alleviated. A redefinition of the public interest standard premised on pro-competitive findings would be counterintuitive to continuing to allow communications firms to raise regulation as a defense in an antitrust lawsuit.[174]

A New Option for Administrative and Jurisdictional Composition

The FCC serves a useful function in maintaining order in the communications industry, but, as explained in the previous chapters, the premises that have supported the cradle-to-grave regulation of the industry through proscribed natural monopolies are being forced into extinction by rapid technological progress. Antitrust principles may offer a common-sensical solution to governing an industry in which technological converging resources offer the greatest hope of advancement.

Swift Congressional Fiat

For a new option, no monumental government restructuring may be needed. The current (late 1990s) regulatory framework, which apportions authority to both the FCC and state public utility commissions, would probably remain remarkably unchanged.

In particular, nothing might be needed that would alter or amend the jurisdiction of the states, and antitrust jurisdiction would endure with the DOJ, the

Federal Trade Commission (FTC), the state attorneys general, and private third parties. All that might be needed would be to amend the wording of the public interest standard of the 1934 Act.[175] In doing so, Congress would simply be codifying the broad holding of the D.C. Circuit's opinion in the 1980 case of *United States v. FCC*, in which the court held that consideration of competitive issues is a necessary part of the FCC's determinations pursuant to the public interest standard.[176] The Commission discharges its antitrust responsibilities when it "seriously considers the antitrust consequences of a proposal and weighs those consequences with other public interest factors."

Congressional amendment of the 1934 Act to incorporate the competitive concepts of antitrust laws in the relevant public interest standards could dramatically facilitate the reality of greater consumer choice at competitive prices in communications.[177] Although other legislative suggestions might merit attention, none is so wonderfully simple. The amended section might read:

> Competition in communications best serves the national interest. Therefore the Federal Communications Commission shall act in the public interest, convenience and necessity with respect to radio frequency licenses, and in the public convenience and necessity with respect to wireline common carriers by refraining from regulation where such regulation impedes competition. Competition shall be defined in accordance with the principles of federal antitrust law.

This passage would not foreclose the possibility of the FCC initiating formal rule-making procedures to refine precisely how the amended section might be interpreted and applied. Thus, the FCC and industry competitors would have both an opportunity to voice opinion and to shape policy. By introducing competition while vigorously reinforcing and affirming the interests of the general public, this compromise could benefit all interested parties.

Antitrust Jurisdiction

Although the FCC has no congressionally authorized antitrust jurisdiction, for the proposed administrative system to function little would be needed to transfer such authority to it because the FCC would never litigate antitrust allegations. Antitrust jurisdiction would remain with the DOJ and the FTC. The only amount of antitrust jurisdiction needed to be instituted at the Commission would be enough to review the activities of communications firms in order to insure a finding of "no anticompetitive effect." The FCC's Competition Division, which is already staffed with economists and lawyers with a strong mix of antitrust and telecommunications experience, would review licensing or prior approval circumstances or both, which are governed solely by the public interest standard. In short, the purpose of the FCC review would be legislatively to define the public interest standard with the pro-competitive concepts employed by the antitrust laws.

Such a "screening" function would provide quality agency review of questionable anticompetitive activities without unduly restraining industry behavior. Just as important, no party seeking to bring an antitrust action against a communications firm would be precluded from doing so merely because of the Commission's heightened antitrust capacity. The FCC, being a specialized agency, could vastly enhance competition through its ability to have rule-makings and make general policy. Transaction-specific agencies, such as the DOJ and FTC, typically act only on specific instances of isolated conduct, so the roles of the FCC and DOJ would naturally complement each other. The FCC's "finding" would offer persuasive evidence in federal antitrust litigation but in and of itself would not be binding.

Administrative Operation

Any finding of "anticompetitive effect" (hence, in violation of the public interest) would be afforded an automatic right of review by an oversight bureau to be created by Congress. After exhausting all administrative avenues of review, the disproved applicant might choose to petition the federal court for judicial review, and such appeals could be litigated by the DOJ, representing the federal government. Like other judicial trials reviewing the actions of a federal agency, deference would be given to the Competition Division because of both its specialized insight and the technical nature of the subject matter.[178]

Such a procedure would more than adequately equip the FCC with the authority needed to review the competitive impact of any proposed industry development without undermining the antitrust jurisdiction of the DOJ. Keeping general-purpose bodies like the DOJ and the courts in the equation would balance the administration of the laws, thus guarding against any threat of "regulatory capture."

No alteration to the antitrust laws would be necessary. Firms competing in the communications marketplace would simply be regarded as having non-regulated status in relation to practices and activities falling within the gamut of the public interest competitiveness standard of the amended statutory authority.

This treatment would effectively de-immunize the communications industry from antitrust scrutiny, previously estopped. Approval by the Competition Division of the FCC would not act as a form of implied immunity but might be asserted at trial as evidence of good faith and procedural compliance. This might be comparable to the traditional relationship between regulatory approval and antitrust law. In allowing a tariff to go into effect, the FCC does not contend that the tariff is needed to make the regulatory scheme work;[179] thus, antitrust immunity is never insured by federal agency approval.[180]

Conclusion

Competition is, undoubtedly, in the public interest. The Supreme Court has foreclosed inquiry into whether competition and the public interest are compatible: In *National Society of Professional Engineers v. United States*, the Court stated that the antitrust laws reflect a judgment by the legislature that competition is in the public interest because it will ultimately result in lower consumer prices, higher-quality goods and services, and a consistently productive economic environment.[181] Addressing the Sherman Act in particular, the Court observed:

Even assuming occasional exceptions to the presumed consequences of competition, the statutory policy precludes inquiry into the question whether competition is good or bad.[182]

Even if antitrust law cannot guarantee an ideal economic market, the ancillary benefits still greatly outweigh whatever slight imperfections may exist. As the Supreme Court remarked in *Brown Shoe Co. v. United States*:[183]

. . . we cannot fail to recognize Congress' desire to promote competition through the protection of viable, small, locally owned businesses. Congress anticipated that occasional higher costs and prices might result from the maintenance of fragmented industries and markets. It resolved these competing considerations in favor of centralization.[184]

Although the Court expressly rejected the assertion that the public interest standard conflicts with the pro-competitive standard of antitrust laws, the multitude of regulations and antitrust exemptions has severely limited their application to the communications industry.[185] A new option may be needed, one that can finally provide boundaries—best defined by incorporating pro-competitive antitrust concepts into the Communications Act of 1934—to the public interest standard.[186] The large body of antitrust jurisprudence could guide a standard that has long been the target of cynical debate.

More important, as a vehicle for progress, the new option might permit the private and public sectors to unite in an effort to assert America's technological prowess in the global communications market, and at the same time, provide consumers with quality goods and services at fair prices in an open and competitive market.

Consideration of FCC reform need not necessarily be limited to modest options, such as budget cutting, nor to radical ones, such as abolition. Instead, Congress might better define the standard under which the Commission administers its responsibilities, offering agency reform oriented toward procompetitive results.

Notes

1. S. 652, The Telecommunications Act of 1996.

2. 47 U.S.C. Sections 214(a), 307(a), 309(a) (1976).

3. Id.

4. See, generally, Oettinger, Berman, and Read, *High and Low Politics: Information Resources* (1977).

5. George Gilder, *Forbes* (April 13, 1992).

6. Lippman, MIT Media Lab, Video, September 1993.

7. President William J. Clinton, "Technology for America's Economic Growth," Feb. 22, 1993.

8. For example, Peter W. Huber, *Issues in Science and Technology*, Fall 1993; and American Enterprise Institute for Public Policy Research project prospectus on "Telecommunications Deregulation," February 1993.

9. "Gore Rides the Highway," *Washington Technology*, Jan. 13, 1994.

10. See Kellogg, Thorne, and Huber, *Federal Telecommunications Law* (1992).

11. 47 U.S.C. 35 (1934).

12. Id. at 151.

13. Television was not mentioned in the Act, however the service uses radio frequencies. The FCC asserted jurisdiction over Cable Television. *Cable Television Report and Order*, 36 F.C.C. 2d 143 (1972).

14. Jurisdiction of wire and radio communication had been split among three federal agencies: the Federal Radio Commission, the Interstate Commerce Commission,

and the Postmaster General. See Head, *Broadcasting in America*, 3rd ed. at 133 (1976).

15. *Munn v. Illinois*, 94 U.S. 113 (1877). The Supreme Court held that states may regulate the use of private property when the use was "affected with the public interest."

16. 36 Stat. 539 (1910).

17. Pub. L. No. 62-264, 37 Stat. 302 (1912).

18. Id. at section 4.

19. 47 U.S.C. section 309(a).

20. 47 U.S.C. Section 214(a).

21. *Interstate Commerce Commission v. Railway Labor Executives Assn.*, 315 U.S. at 376 (1942).

22. *Federal Communications Commission v. RCA Communications, Inc.*, 346 U.S. at 86, 90 (1953).

23. See, e.g., Federal Power Commission, 16 U.S.C. sections 797(g), 800(a) (1982); Interstate Commerce Commission, 49 U.S.C. section 1(18) (1976).

24. *National Broadcasting Co. v. United States*, 319 U.S. 190, 213 (1943).

25. *CBS v. Democratic National Comm.*, 412 U.S. at 101 (1973).

26. *Office of Communication of United Church of Christ v. Federal Communications Commission*, 359 F.2d 994, 1003 (D.C. Cir. 1966).

27. See, generally, Deregulation of Radio, 73 F.C.C. 2d 457.

28. *Supra* at note 25.

29. 47 C.F.R. sections 73.1910, 76.209 (1987).

30. *Syracuse Peace Council*, Memorandum Opinion and Order, 2 F.C.C. rcd. 5043 (1987).

31. *In re Inquiry into Section 73.1910 of the Commission's Rules and Regulations Concerning the General Fairness Doctrine Obligations of Broadcasting Licensees*, 102 F.C.C. 2d 143, 146 (1985).

32. Federal Radio Act, Pub. L. No. 690632, 44 Stat. 1162 (1927).

33. Id. at section 18.

34. *Great Lakes Broadcasting Company*, 3 F.R.C. Ann.Rep. at 33.

35. *In the Matter of Editorializing by Broadcast Licensees*, 13 F.C.C. 1246 (1949).

36. 395 U.S. 367 (1969).

37. Pub. L. No. 86-274, 73 Stat. 557 (1959).

38. 395 U.S. at 380.

39. See 1987 *Syracuse, supra*, note 30.

40. *Fairness Reports, supra*, note 31.

41. *Telecommunications Research and Action Center v. FCC*, 801 F.2d 501 (D.C. Cir. 1986).

42. 1987 *Syracuse, supra* note 30, at para. 80.

43. Mark S. Fowler and Daniel L. Brenner, *A Marketplace Approach to Broadcast Regulation*, 60 Tex. L. Rev. 207, 207–257 (1982).

44. Coase, *The Federal Communications Commission*, 2 J. L. & Econ. 1, 14 (1959).

45. Fowler and Brenner, *supra*, note 43, at 221.

46. Fowler, *Foreword*, 32 Cath. U.L. Rev. 523, 524–26 (1983).

47. *In re Amendment of Section 73.3555 of the Commission's Rules, the Broadcast Multiple Ownership Rules*, 4 F.C.C. Rec. 1741 (1988).

48. *In re Amendment of Section 73.3597 of the Commission's Rules (Applications for Voluntary Assignments or Transfers of Control)*, 55 Rad. Reg. 2d 1081 (1982).

49. *In re Deregulation of Radio*, 84 F.C.C. 2d 968 (1981); *In re the Revision of Programming and Commercialization Policies*, 98 F.C.C. 2d 1076 (1991).

50. Fowler's philosophy and policy were controversial. See, e.g., Sunstein, *Preferences and Politics*, Phil. & Pub. Affairs 3, 28–29 (1991); Comment, *Deregulating Commercial television: Will the Marketplace Watch Out for Children?*, 34 Am. U. L. Rev. 141, 143 (1984); Comment, *Radio Deregulation and the Public Interest: Office of Communication of the United Church of Christ v. Federal Communications Commission*, 4 Cardozo Arts & Enter. L.J. 169 (1985).

51. William Mayton, *The Illegitimacy of the Public Interest Standard at the FCC*, 38 Emory L.J. 715 (1989).

52. *Parliament's Remonstrances Against the Renewal of the Licensing Act*, XI H.C. Jour. 305–06.

53. 4 Blackstone, Commentaries 152 n(a).

54. See *Lovell v. City of Griffin*, 303 U.S. 444, 451–52 (1938); *Schneider v. State*, 308 U.S. 147, 164 (1939); *Grosjean v. American Press Co.*, 297 U.S. 233, 245–48 (1936); *Near v. Minnesota*, 283 U.S. 697, 713–16 (1931).

55. Mayton, *supra* note 51, at 763.

56. Jaffe, *The Illusion of the Ideal Administration*, 86 Harv. L. Rev. 1183, 1192 (1954).

57. Federal Communications Commission v. Sanders Brothers Radio Station, 309 U.S. 470, 475 (1940).

58. *Supra*, note 24.

59. Id. at 216.

60. Id.

61. *Supra*, note 36.

62. See Krasnow, Longley, and Terry, *The Politics of Broadcast Regulation*, 240–69 (3d ed. 1982).

63. Kellogg, *supra*, note 10, at 1–2.

64. *United States v. American Telephone & Telegraph Co.*, 552 F.Supp. 131 (D.D.C. 1982), *aff'd*, 103 S.Ct. 1240 (1983).

65. Although price cap regulation is preferred by telecommunications companies to the more comprehensive rate-of-return regulation, it is not without problems. See Braeutigam and Panzar, *Effects of the Change from Rate-of-Return to Price-Cap Regulation*, 83 Am. Econ. Rev. Papers & Proc. 191 (1993).

66. *Chesapeake & Potomac Tel. Co v. United States*, 1993 U.S. Dist. LEXIS 11822 (E.D. Va. Aug. 24, 1993).

67. *Supra*, note 37.

68. See, e.g., Baumol and Sidak, *Toward Competition in Local Telephony* (1994).

69. Noam, *Federal and State Roles in Telecommunications: The Effects of Deregulation*, 36 Vand. L.R. 949, at 950. (1983).

70. See *Hush A Phone Corp. v. United States*, 238 F.2d 266 (D.C. Cir. 1956); *Use of the Carterphone Device*, 13 F.C.C. 2d 420 (1968); *Proposals for New or Revised Classes of Interstate and Foreign Message Toll Telephone Service (MTS) and Wide Area Telephone Service (WATS)*, 56 F.C.C. 593 (1975), *aff'd sub nom. North Carolina Util. Comm'n v. Federal Communications Commission*, 552 F.2d 1036 (4th Cir.), *cert. denied*, 434 U.S. 874 (1977) (equipment registration decision); *Use of the Carterfone Device in Message Toll Tel. Serv.*, 13 F.C.C. 2d 420 (1986); *Jordaphone Corp. v. United States*, 18 F.C.C. 644 (1954); *Use of Recording Devices in Connection with Tel. Serv.*, 11 F.C.C. 1033 (1947).

71. The FCC began cautiously in its *Allocation of the Frequencies in the Bands Above 890 Mz*, 27 F.C.C. 359 (1959), but ten years later, in *Microwave Communications, Inc.*, 18 F.C.C. 2d 953 (1969), it put federal regulation on a successively liberalized road to market entry.

72. 90 F.C.C. 2d 676 (1982); 86 F.C.C. 2d 469 (1981).

73. *Amendment of Section 64.702 of the Commission's Rules and Regulations, Third Computer Inquiry* (CC No. 85-220), Notice of Proposed Rulemaking, 50 Fed. Reg. 33581, at para. 141 (August 20, 1985), Report and Order, 104 F.C.C. 2d 958 (1986).

74. See *An Inquiry into the Use of the Bands, 825–845 MHz & 870–890 MHz for Cellular Communications Sys.*, 86 F.C.C. 2d 469 (1981).

75. See Botein, *New Communications Technology: The Emerging Antitrust Agency*, 4 Comm. & Ent. L.J. 685 (1981).

76. Levy and Setzer, *Measurements of Concentration in Home Video Markets 81*, Office of Plans and Policy, Dec. 23, 1982.

77. Id.

78. Schurz, 982 F.2d at 1049 (citing *Federal Communications Commission v. National Citizens Comm. for Broadcasting*, 436 U.S. 775 [1978]); *Federal Communications Commission v. Pacifica Found.*, 438 U.S. 726 (1978); *National Broadcasting Co. v. United States, supra*, note 24.

79. See Breyer, *Regulation and Its Reform* (1982).

80. See, e.g., Stigler, *The Theory of Economic Regulation, 2 Bell J. Econ. & Mgmt. Sci.* (1971).

81. Pub. L. No. 98-549, 98 Stat. 2779 (1984).

82. Pub. L. No. 102-385, 106 Stat. 1460 (1992).

83. *Supra*, notes 7, 9.

84. *The Wall Street Journal*, March 2, 1994, A12.

85. Breyer, *supra*, note 79.

86. Henry Geller, *A Modest Proposal to Reform the Federal Communications Commission* (1974).

87. Kellogg, Thorne, and Huber, Telecommunications Law, *supra*, note 10.

88. *Supra*, note 64.

89. See Harry M. Shooshan III, *Disconnecting Bell: The Impact of the AT&T Divestiture* (1984), vii.

90. See section on "The Public Interest," starting on p. 493 (discussion of the negative effects of the public interest standard).

91. See Joseph F. Brodley, *The Economic Goals of Antitrust: Efficiency, Consumer Welfare, and Technological Progress*, 62 N.Y.U. L.Rev. 1020 (1987), which asserts that, contrary to populist debate by economic scholars, antitrust laws encompass noneconomic goals, such as serving the public interest and promoting fair competition, and assure the purely economic objectives of market efficiency.

92. *Supra*, note 11.

93. A "natural monopoly" is a market structure in which one firm can satisfy the demand in a market at a lower cost than two or more firms could. See Marshall Howard, *Antitrust and Trade Regulation* (1984) and F. M. Scherer, *Market Structure* (3rd ed.)

94. *Supra*, note 15.

95. See Kenneth M. Parzych, *Public Policy and the Regulatory Environment* (1993).

96. Again, the failure of the government and the courts to provide adequately and consistently a definition of "public interest" accounts for why the standard is nearly impossible to claim as satisfied.

97. See Carol Tucker Foreman, *Regulating for the Future: The Creative Balance* (1991).

98. Air Transportation Regulatory Reform Act of 1978, Pub.L. No. 95-504, 92 Stat. 1705.

99. Civil Aeronautics Act, ch. 601, 52 Stat. 973 (1938) (codified at 49 U.S.C. ss 1301–1542)(1980).

100. See George W. James, *Airline Economics* 169 (1982); Paul S. Dempsey, *Airline Deregulation and Laissez-Faire Mythology: Economic Theory in Turbulence*, 56 J.Air L. & Com. 305, 309–312 (1990); *see also*, Paul S. Dempsey, *The Rise and Fall of the Civil Aeronautics Board—Opening Wide the Floodgates of Entry*, 11 Transp. L.J. 91, 95 (1979).

101. Elizabeth E. Bailey and David Graham, *Deregulating the Airlines* (1985). Although standard services were provided to a number of smaller markets, which would be considered inefficient in an economy of scale rationale.

102. See Parzych, *supra*, note 95, 176–180.

103. 49 U.S.C. section 1301 *et seq.*

104. Transportation Act of 1940, Title 49, generally.

105. The vast quantity of materials written since the deregulation of the airline industry are exemplary of the different schools of economic and regulatory theorists. Because this was the first major regulated industry to undergo massive deregulation, it has provided a fertile ground for all commentators interested in criticizing and examining its development and the consequences. Whether deregulation ultimately is successful is not likely to deter critics of deregulation as an alternative public policy.

106. David G. Monk, *The Lessons of Airline Regulation and Deregulation: Will We Make the Same Mistakes In Space?* 57 J. Air L. & Com. 715 (1992).

107. *Supra*, note 106, 179.

108. Paul S. Dempsey, *The Social and Economic Consequences of Deregulation: The Transportation Industry in Transition*, 18 (1989).

109. See *Acquisition of Northwest Airlines by Wings Holdings, Inc.*, D.O.T. Order No. 93-1-11, at 1 (1993); also, James T. McKenna, *Northwest-KLM Package Challenges Competition*, Aviation Wk. & Space Tech., Feb. 15, 1993, at 31.

110. Interstate Commerce Act, 49 U.S.C. section 1 *et seq.*

111. 45 U.S.C. 821 (1976).

112. 49 U.S.C. Sections 10101.

113. Although this might bring to mind concerns of universal service in the telecommunications market, technological advances have made the provision of near-universal service more cost-efficient than ever before.

114. See Parsych, *supra*, note 95, 175–178.

115. Id. at 177.

116. See *Penn Central Merger & N. & W. Inclusion Cases*, 389 U.S. 486 (1968).

117. See, e.g., Bruce B. Wilson, *Railroads, Airlines, and the Antitrust Laws in the Post-Regulatory World: Common Concerns and Shared Lessons*, 60 Antitrust L.J. 711 (1991); Michael E. Levine, *Airline Deregulation: A Perspective*, 60 Antitrust L.J. 687 (1991); Richard D. Cudahy, *The Coming Demise of Deregulation*, 10 Yale J. on Reg. 1 (1993); Abner J. Mikva, *Deregulating Through the Back Door: The Hard Way to Fight A Revolution*, 57 U. Chi. L. Rev. 521 (1990).

118. See p. 514, "A New Option for Administrative and Jurisdictional Composition."

119. The granting of antitrust jurisdiction should be only enough to review industry activities. It is meant as a supplemental device by which the FCC may coordinate its actions with existing antitrust jurisdiction of the Department of Justice (DOJ),

the Federal Trade Commission (FTC), state attorneys general, and private parties while not subtracting any antitrust jurisdiction from these groups. While all of these potential players in antitrust litigation will retain their current roles, the FCC would merely act as a "screening bureau" for industry activities. See Chapter Five.

120. See p. 509 summarizing the various antitrust exemptions and defenses available to regulated industries.

121. See, generally, p. 502 discussion of antitrust influence on the communications industry.

122. The FCC, in the *Cable Competition Report*, the *AT&T–McCaw* decision, and the *TV Ownership NPRM*, has addressed issues such as mergers, product and geographic market definition, and identifying barriers to entry.

123. 15 U.S.C. section 18.

124. "Market power is the power to force a purchaser to do something that he would not do in a competitive market.... It has been defined as the ability of a single seller to raise price and restrict output." *Eastman Kodak Co. v. Image Technical Services, Inc.*, 112 S. Ct. 2072, 2080–81 (1992).

125. See p. 504 discussing predatory pricing principles associated with Section 2 of the Sherman Act.

126. This is not to say that regulations and antitrust cannot coexist. The theory of "contestable markets" argues that the appropriate market structure consists of competition for control of a market rather than within one. Under such a notion, pricing within the market is influenced by both actual and potential competition. See, e.g., Morrison and Winston, *Empirical Implications and Tests of the Contestability Hypothesis*, 30 J.L. & Econ. 53 (1987).

127. See discussion at p. 502.

128. See, generally, Sullivan and Harrison, *Understanding Antitrust and Its Economic Implications* (1988).

129. "Every contract, combination in the form of trust or otherwise, or conspiracy, in restraint of trade or commerce among the several States, or with foreign nations, is declared to be illegal. Every person who shall make any contract or engage in any combination or conspiracy hereby declared to be illegal shall be deemed guilty of a felony, and, on conviction thereof, shall be punished by fine not exceeding one million dollars, or by imprisonment not exceeding three years, or by both said punishments, in the discretion of the court." 15 U.S.C. Section 1 (1983).

130. 26 Stat. 204, ch. 647 (1890), *codified at* 15 U.S.C. section 1 *et seq.*

131. *Society of Professional Engineers v. United States*, 435 U.S. 679 (1978).

132. Such antitrust provisions stand to become increasingly relevant, however, as the natural monopoly structure gives way to open competition in the near future. Faced with multiple market entrants vying for previously protected market shares, the dominant firms may be tempted to enter into violative agreements in order to fend off new competitors.

133. "Every person who shall monopolize, or attempt to monopolize, or combine or conspire with any other person or persons, to monopolize any part of the trade or commerce among the several States, or with foreign nations, shall be deemed guilty of a felony, and, on conviction thereof, shall be punished by fine not exceeding one million dollars if a corporation, or, if any other person, one hundred thousand dollars, or by imprisonment not exceeding three years, or by both said punishments, in the discretion of the court." 15 U.S.C. Section 2 (1983).

134. *Supra*, note 128.

135. Monopolization has been defined by the Supreme Court in *United States v. Grinnell Corp.*, 384 U.S. 563, 570–71 (1966) as consisting of two elements: (1) the possession of monopoly power in the relevant market; and (2) the willful acquisition or maintenance of that power as distinguished from the growth or development of a superior product, business acumen or historic accident.

136. See Sullivan and Harrison, *supra*, note 128, 207.

137. 148 F.2d 416 (2d Cir. 1945).

138. Market power has been explained and defined in a myriad of ways since the inception of antitrust jurisprudence. The context-based analysis is fact-sensitive and subject to different economic probes. The Supreme Court, in *U.S. v. Du Pont de Nemours & Co.*, 351 U.S. 377, 391–92 (1956), defined it as "the power to control prices or exclude competition." See, generally, Landes and Posner, *Market Power in Antitrust Cases*, 94 Harv. L.Rev. 937 (1981).

139. This second element is even more slippery than the concept of market power. Although no singular standard has evolved, it seems to require a minimum of conduct that, independent of competitive merit, has as its primary purpose the predatory elimination of competition. The Supreme Court, in *United States v. Grinnell*, 384 U.S. 563 (1966), stated that such behavior must exhibit a "willful acquisition or maintenance of that power as distinguished from growth or development as a consequence of a superior product, business acumen, or historic accident." Id. at 570–571.

140. See, e.g., *Phonetele, Inc. v. AT&T*, 664 F.2d 716 (9th Cir. 1981); *TV Signal Co. v. AT&T*, 1980–1 Trade Cas. (CCH) para. 63,242 (8th Cir. 1980); *MCI Communications Corp. v. AT&T*, 708 F.2d 1081 (7th Cir. 1983); *Mid-Texas Communications Sys. v. AT&T*, 615 F.2d 1372 (5th Cir. 1980); *Six-twenty-nine Productions, Inc. v. Rollins Telecasting, Inc.*, 365 F.2d 478 (5th Cir. 1966); *Northeastern Tel. Co. v. AT&T*, 651 F.2d 76 (2d Cir. 1981), *cert denied*, 455 U.S. 973 (1982).

141. *Supra*, note 10, 185.

142. *Supra*, notes 131 and 135.

143. "It shall be unlawful for any person engaged in commerce, in the course of such commerce, to lease or make a sale or contract for sale of goods, wares, merchandise, machinery, supplies, or other commodities, whether patented or unpatented, for use, consumption, or resale within the United States or any Territory thereof or the District of Columbia or any insular possession or other place under the jurisdiction of the United States, or fix a price charged therefor, or discount from, or rebate upon, such price, on the condition, agreement, or understanding that the lessee or purchaser thereof shall not use or deal in the goods, wares, merchandise, machinery, supplies, or other commodities of a competitor or competitors of the lessor or seller, where the effect of such lease, sale, or contract for sale or such condition, agreement, or understanding may be to substantially lessen competition or tend to create a monopoly in any line of commerce." 15 U.S.C. Section 3 (1983).

144. 15 U.S.C. Section 14 (1976).

145. *Jefferson Parrish Hospital District No. 2 v. Hyde*, 466 U.S. 2 (1984). See also Kaplow, *Extension of Monopoly Power Through Leverage*, 85 Colum. L.Rev. 515 (1985).

146. *Supra*, note 10, 141.

147. Commonly understood as occurring when one firm with market power and the possibility of recoupment reduces its prices with the intent not to compete for customers but to injure or destroy a competitor.

148. When a firm that competes in several markets and has monopoly power in one but not another leverages the monopoly power in one market to gain a competitive advantage in a market in which no monopoly power exists. See *United States v. Griffith*, 334 U.S. 100 (1948).

149. *Supra*, note 132.

150. *Supra*, note 121.

151. Examples include insurance, railroads, agriculture, and fisheries. See Sullivan and Harrison, *supra*, note 132, 52–55.

152. Section 221(a) of the 1934 Act, *supra*, note 11: "If the Commission finds that the proposed consolidation, acquisition, or control will be of advantage to the persons to whom service is to be rendered and in the public interest, it shall certify to that effect; and thereupon any Act or Acts by Congress making the proposed transaction unlawful shall not apply...."

153. See *Mid-Texas*, 615 F.2d at 1378 n.3 ("The existence of an explicit exemption in one part of the Act does not provide authority for the proposition that other

actions not directly covered are impliedly exempt."); *Industrial Communications Systems, Inc. v. Pacific Tel. & Tel. Co.*, 505 F.2d 152, 156 (9th Cir. 1974).

154. The statutory exemption referred to has rarely been used since the 1920s. Yet the exemption exists as a matter of law, therefore enforcement of the statute by a court may be only a matter of a party premising its case upon the exemption.

155. See, generally, David C. Hjelmfelt, *Antitrust And Regulated Industries*, 218–223 (1985).

156. 381 F.Supp. 113 (S.D.N.Y. 1974).

157. 47 U.S.C. Sections 221, 222 (1983).

158. *United States v. AT&T*, 461 F.Supp. 1314, 1322 (D.D.C. 1978).

159. 740 F.2d 980 (D.C. Cir. 1984).

160. Section 201(a) of the 1934 Act (47 U.S.C. Section 201(a) (1976)).

161. *Eastern R.R. Presidents Conference v. Noerr Motor Freight, Inc.*, 363 U.S. 127 (1961); *UMW v. Pennington*, 381 U.S. 657 (1965).

162. *TeleStar, Inc. v. MCI Communications Corp.*, 1991–2 Trade Cas. (CCH) 69,654 (10th Cir. 1991).

163. 365 U.S. at 149.

164. See, generally, *Litton Systems, Inc. v. AT&T Co.*, 700 F.2d 785 (2d Cir. 1983).

165. 317 U.S. 341 (1943).

166. 471 U.S. 48 (1985).

167. Id. at 60.

168. See note 166, at 61.

169. Id. at 56.

170. See M. Shawn McMurray, *The Perils of Judicial Legislation: The Establishment and Evolution of the Parker v. Brown Exemption to the Sherman Antitrust Act*, 20 N. Ky. L.Rev. 249 (1993).

171. 486 U.S. 94 (1988).

172. Id. at 101.

173. This is not to imply, however, that when and where states do actually "supervise" the communications industry, there should not be a defense. Then again, this would not be an issue at all if the states did not interfere with the industry.

174. Again, this concept extends only to activities directly related to the new standard. The traditional exemptions would still be available in areas of regulation that have not yet incorporated the antitrust doctrines.

175. *Supra*, note 11.

176. 652 F.2d 72, 88 (D.C. Cir. 1980) (en banc).

177. Id.

178. See *Chevron, U.S.A., Inc. v. natural Resources Defense Council, Inc.*, 467 U.S. 837 (1984).

179. *Phonetele, Inc. v. AT&T*, 664 F.2d 716, 733 (9th Cir. 1981).

180. See, e.g., United States v. RCA, 358 U.S. 334 (1959), in which the DOJ brought an antitrust action against swapping TV stations in different cities by NBC and Westinghouse even though prior approval of the exchange had been granted by the FCC.

181. 435 U.S. 679, 695 (1978).

182. Id. at 695.

183. 370 U.S. 294 (1962).

184. Id. at 344.

185. See *Sound, Inc. v. AT&T*, 631 F.2d 1324 (8th Cir. 1980).

186. *Supra*, note 11.

19 Cybercommunities and Cybercommerce: Can We Learn to Cope?

Anne Wells Branscomb

At a meeting of lawyers in New York City on "Business and Legal Issues on the Internet and On-line Services," Kent Stuckey, General Counsel of Compu-Serve, announced that he had invented two phrases appropriate to this new electronic environment. They are *vuja-de* and *prestalgia.* The first, of course the opposite of déjà-vu, is the feeling that, Wow, I've never been here before, isn't this new and interesting! *Prestalgia*, the opposite of nostalgia, is the longing to live in the future now.

A good place to start this journey is to look at what I prefer to call "the Networld" rather than Cyberspace. Cyberspace is where you are when you are communicating through a computer, but the Networld is a universe of cyber-spaces or new frontiers where netizens are homesteading, building fences, and establishing new on-line social environments—what I call "cyber-communities." Indeed, netizens who populate these cybercommunities are making the rules of the information superhighways and establishing a new area of netlaw to apply in their own cyberspaces.

Umberto Eco has defined the differences in "religions" in the Networld. The Macintosh world, he says, is "cheerful, friendly, conciliatory—here everyone has a right to salvation"—in other words, Catholic.[1] The DOS world, he says, is really Protestant, even Calvinistic: "To make the system work you need to interpret it yourself." The Windows world is more Anglican: "big ceremonies in the cathedral but with the possibility of returning to DOS to fiddle with things." People like to carry into the Networld metaphors with which they are familiar. Indeed, we like to hope that we won't have to change very much to live there.

Politics has also come to the Networld. Vice President Gore has become the champion of computer networking both nationally and globally, and he held the first on-line press conference in 1993, whereupon the *New York Times* con-ferred upon him the title "First Citizen in Cyberspace." Jock Gill, the White

House computer guru who set up President Clinton's e-mail system (which responded to messages through the United States Postal Service, or what the computer cognoscenti call "snail-mail") refers to himself as "the Digital Postmaster General." Then, in early 1995, Newt Gingrich, leader of the House of Representatives, got carried away with the potential of the new technology and proposed what even he acknowledged was "a nutty idea," giving tax credits to the poor to enable them to buy laptop computers. The Library of Congress did come through with its new database, *Thomas*, named for Thomas Jefferson, whose entire library became the foundation of the Library of Congress collections when its first collection was destroyed by fire in the War of 1812. *Thomas* makes available on-line the database, all the legislation enacted by the 103rd Congress and all the pending legislation, together with all resolutions and actions taken by the 104th Congress. *Thomas* was accessed a million times in its first six weeks of operation. To complete the loop, in February 1995 presidential hopeful Lamar Alexander was the first candidate to announce his availability on-line on the America Online (AOL) service. Washington insiders, asked about the new political opportunities in cyberspace, commented that it was not that they did not recognize that this was a new ballpark—they do, but they don't like it![2]

The availability of cellular telephones and laptop computers has changed the way business executives do business. These new technologies have changed our working and eating habits, even our social customs, as when dealing with secretaries on-line, rather than face to face. In fact, secretaries may become a dying breed as professionals take on more and more of their own wordprocessing and on-line communication.

The art world is also found in abundance in the Networld—from the Louvre to little-known local artists. The Louvre has its own home page. Indeed, very clear images of the new discoveries of the cave drawings were on the World Wide Web (WWW or "the Web") shortly after they were discovered. But less well-known sources of art also are making their way onto the Web, and even those of us who thought we had no talent for art are finding that with new software like "Paintbrush" we may have talents we might have never realized without these new tools.

Entertainment is everywhere—even birthday parties on-line, avoiding the need to supply refreshments or clean up afterward. The Jack Daniels distillery, however, hopes that its 145th birthday party for founder Jack will prompt you to purchase its products for your real-world celebrations.

There are many new cyberspaces coming on-line on the Web—a new Cybertown or a virtual city on the Web—where we find an information center directing viewers to a cyberbroadcasting center; a library with cross-references to many interesting materials available on-line in other cyberspaces; an education center, of course; a business district to which entrepreneurs of all kinds are invited to set up shop; a darker side of Cybertown, where the nonconformists may hide out in the "cyberhood"; and even an electronic zoo.

More important perhaps than these graphical sites on the Web are the "cyber-communities" that have been developing over the last decade through computer-mediated text. The WELL (Whole Earth 'Lectronic Link), one of the earliest, founded in 1985 in Marin County, includes not just subscribers and participants in the Bay Area of San Francisco but also computer pioneers all over the country. They gather on-line to share their interests, their politics, their joys and sorrows as well as aspirations for the future of the Networld. Howard Rheingold, in his book *The Virtual Community*, described how these on-line communities can become very supportive, helping members who are dying of cancer, saving the lives of people stricken with heart attacks, sharing the concerns of baby boomers about their entry into the "parenting" years, and meeting people from all over the world.[3]

The inhabitants of the WELL suffered a traumatic experience several years ago when one of their members expunged all his messages from the on-line discussion and then committed suicide. The community arose not only with remorse but also outrage that he had removed himself from on-line memory. That memory was, they alleged, a community property from which one of the group had no right to remove material that had already been entered into it.

Another such community is the LambdaMOO, a virtual-reality environment set up by Xerox Parc for professionals interested in experimenting with multimedia and interactive services. Here the participants were confronted with what they considered to be outrageous behavior on-line—one male user's taking control of a female persona on-line and committing what was considered to be "virtual rape." Outraged participants in the group argued at length over what should be done to the perpetrator. After much deliberation about what constituted "due process" on-line, the group decided that the accused was guilty as charged and should be "toaded." In fairy tale terms, that means turned into a frog—in cyberspace terms, thrown out of the LambdaMOO.

Special discussion groups have been set up for women, because they have, for the most part, found this universe of predominantly young male computer-literate users quite hostile. Recently, however, polls show that women as well as minorities are coming on-line in greater and greater numbers, so that the universe of users is beginning to reflect more nearly the real-world population, albeit the more affluent portion of that population. CompuServe has SIGs, or "special interest groups."

Both Prodigy and AOL also offer specialized services for special interests, only some of which can be characterized as true "cybercommunities." However, the Web pages seem to be cultivating cult or tribal loyalty, and many Usenet groups have developed into on-line communities with their own rules of behavior or "netiquette." Newcomers are invited to read the FAQ, or "Frequently Asked Questions," before attempting to participate in group discussion. Last, of course, all the major corporations are developing internal e-mail services and establishing their own protocols to govern their use. IBM's "profs" system is one of the oldest, and a doctoral thesis has already explored several dozen different electronic streams active within it. Clearly, netizens like to tailor their own cyberspaces to suit their own needs and interests.

What are some of the advantages that we have come to recognize in the Networld of electronic computer-mediated communication? First and foremost is the global reach to the far corners of the earth, thus facilitating the rapidly developing global marketplace, substituting information for gold bars as the coin of the realm, as Walter Wriston, former CEO of Citicorp, early recognized.[4] Such computer-mediated communication is readily available to anyone with the money to buy a computer, a modem, and the right software and who has the expertise to use them. The electronic environment is quite innovative, making possible interactive exchanges and, for the first time in the history of communication messages, making possible not just one-to-one or one-to-many but many people interacting with many others in the same electronic spaces.

Thus, group activity on-line is becoming the new challenge as well as opening new opportunities for experimentation. So far, it has been largely unregulated, and, although there are not many cybercops yet, they are not just sitting in the wings and watching (or lurking); those that do exist are becoming quite active. Recently, the Secret Service raided 120 sites where pedophiles were using AOL services to exchange illegal images and to solicit explicit sexual encounters with young children.[5] This sort of raid does soothe our fears that cyberspace activities may get out of hand and reassures us that abusive behavior on-line that spills over into the real world can be curtailed through existing law-enforcement mechanisms.

On-line communication is less intrusive than other mediums of exchange. Junk mail is not extensive yet, and cybercitizens have expressed outrage when "electronic junkmail" has reached their e-mail boxes.

On-line communication is more egalitarian than television or newspapers, or at least is purported to be, so opportunity beckons, and business and lawyers as well as individuals are scrambling to be the first in cyberspace. Home pages are proliferating all over the Web. On the other hand, not everyone is as confident as the computer pioneers were in the mid-1980s that computer-mediated communication will be democratizing, increasingly providing autonomy over information to individual users. Some fear that just the opposite will be the case. Indeed, James Beniger, writing for a conference on "public space" last spring at the Annenberg School for Communication at the University of Pennsylvania, expressed concern that the Web would be dominated by the corporate logos of well-known, well-heeled corporate enterprises much as global television advertising is dominated by multinationals.[6]

Which scenario will play itself out in the Networld remains to be seen, but that is only one of the concerns that have come to the fore. The rapid growth of the Internet and other on-line services is exhausting the capabilities of all of us to keep up with the changes. The rapid development of the technology is equally daunting. A cartoon I recently ran across expressed the consternation with which many of us meet each new announcement of "progress." Windows 95, it declared, was named that because it causes us to throw our old computers out the window.[7]

Other concerns include a real antipathy to advertising from long-time users of the Internet, a heritage of sharing of information, which, along with ease of copying made possible by the new technology, has led us to ignore the legal protection offered by the copyright laws to proprietary information. Pornographic images are cropping up, leaving us concerned about protecting our children from exposure to objectionable material as they "surf" the net. Anonymity and pseudonymity, which have been not just tolerated but encouraged in many on-line services and environments, especially the computer game rooms and virtual reality environments, can have real-world consequences injurious to innocent parties who cannot identify the culprits. Indeed, we are in a state of confusion about whose jurisdiction such abuses come under and whether we can govern cyberspaces at all.

What troubles many users is the lack of similarity between programs, the generally unfriendly user environment, or incompatible user interfaces. Such incompatibility is due largely to the necessity for software designers to make their programs as different as possible in order to have something original that can be protected under the copyright law or something earth-shakingly non-obvious and new that can be protected by a patent. On the other hand, we simple-minded users want something as friendly and familiar as possible. Many of us do not like icons that make us feel like children of Egypt trying to learn hieroglyphics.

Of course, we could all throw in the towel and let Microsoft software become the industry standard. I have heard knowledgeable computer professionals admit that they would welcome such standardization. However, to bow to a hugely powerful monopoly would be contrary to the tradition of antitrust laws and to a dedication to the competitive market to satisfy our needs.

Somehow, we have not thought through the necessity to encourage software programmers to develop standardized building blocks that are as reliable and trustworthy as the interchangeable parts we use in our industrial machinery. If we are to rely upon artificial intelligence for our working tools and use programs that can threaten life and limb, then we will have to develop new legal tools that encourage, rather than discourage, similarity.

The new browsers for the Web are making it easier for many of us to enter the Networld comfortably and to wend our way around its various new electronic malls and Web pages. The Web on the Internet offers the opportunity to develop a true marketplace of information where competent users can insert whatever information product or advertise whatever product or service they desire. We are, therefore, on the threshold of one of the more exciting experiments in history—the development of an entirely new way of marketing, bartering, or giving away information. What we are doing is forging the infrastructure of an information economy. We have not yet untangled ourselves from the strictures of our industrial economy nor adjusted our economic thinking to the needs of information economies. The village market in the town square evolved into a larger community of independent merchants and, later, into even larger shopping malls of nationally advertised products, so that there has always been a "fair" or "agora" or place where buyers and sellers meet. Market day was when those who had something to sell and those who had something to buy gathered to exchange commodities and, at the same time, to exchange thoughts and opinions. The Web offers such a global marketplace to which any and all can contribute. Yahoo, one of the more popular indexing sites, offers information about 266 electronic malls as well as many thousands of companies that offer services on the Web.

Much of the Web looks quite familiar, filled with corporate names we recognize—IBM and Eastman Kodak are prominent. The challenge of the electronic marketplace is to attract purchasers, subscribers, or adherents to one's merchandise, service, or political persuasion. A review of pioneering Web pages of corporate enterprises suggests that many a lure is being devised to do so. Lures often come in the form of free information in exchange for looking in on a Web page, such as the Eastman Kodak's images, free for the taking, or Godiva's recipes, free for downloading. In economic terms, the lure constitutes paying prospective customers for devoting time to review the offerings of the merchandiser. Since time is the one inelastic commodity in today's electronic market, it does not seem unreasonable to provide compensation for its use.

This ploy is not unlike the practice of corporations that offer premium discount coupons for purchasing a product. It is clear that tradeoffs are being devised to accommodate the need to attract customers in the electronic environment as well. Time Warner may have a different strategy with its innovative home page, the *Pathfinder*, where "hot spots" direct the user to various locations throughout the vast information resources offered by the Time Warner empire. *HotWired*, for example, offers all its contents free but seeks to capture an ID for each "hit," thus making it possible to "sell" subscribers to advertisers by recording which sites the subscribers find attractive.

Apprehensive academics with whom I am acquainted refuse to enter the *HotWired* home pages for fear of being "captured" and "sold" to advertisers. Most of us are curious enough to see what *HotWired* is offering on-line that we forego protection and willingly offer our e-mail addresses for verification and capture and, no doubt, future sale to others. In a more perfect world, the law of privacy might require that a statement be made up front as to the nature of the ID being captured and what use will be made of it, so that the identified person could make a knowledgeable choice about what they are giving up to obtain the information on the *HotWired* home pages.

Should we seek to place a legal requirement on all of those merchants who offer free information in exchange for releasing our names, addresses, and preferences that they disclose any future intended reuse of that information? Should they be required to seek our permission for reuse? Should they be required to offer a realistic and simple way of opting out of such reuse, short of being denied access to the information? Perhaps the user should be given the option of exchanging free use of the information offered or charged a price for access if the user is unwilling to have personal data disclosed to third parties. Clearly, an information service that puts its wares on-line without a charge is seeking some other manner of compensation, such as advertisers who will pay for access to their subscribers.

Some of the trends in advertising on the Internet are becoming apparent. Advertisers are either offering information as bait, such as the Classic Car site, which not only provides a listing of classic cars for sale worldwide but also announces classic car rallies and provides travel diaries, such as that of "The Classic Car in Africa." Some sites offer new classification and cross-reference services similar to the yellow pages but vastly superior.

Other service providers are beginning to serve as intermediaries in the role of critics evaluating sites or offering "knowbots," knowledge robots that can roam the hidden byways and backwoods of the Networld in search of just the information that meets special interests and needs. Many sites are catering to herding instincts and attempting to attract viewers to their Web pages in much the same way that readers are attracted to magazines that address special interests in print.

The more forward-looking companies with a presence on the Web seem to be searching for viable ways to charge for distributing information on-line, because no one is making much money on the Web, except the makers of Netscape, whose stock soared on the day of its first offering, more than doubling from an offering of $28 to $75 before settling down at $58.25, over night making its CEO the newest and youngest multimillionaire.[8]

Prodigy, the first to start out with advertising on most of its pages, offended the pioneer computer literati, who had come to look upon the Internet as a very special place to call their own and where advertising was prohibited by the "acceptable use policies" put in place by government funding for research purposes. Now that commercial interests have overwhelmed the pioneers with their concerns about making a profit and their reliance upon advertising techniques to market their wares, netizens have been rising up in anger to protest the dispatch of advertising material directly into e-mail accounts. One irate user suggested that "Private businesses should exist in a global yellow pages to which one can refer as one needs. To receive any unsolicited advertising in my file would be enough for me to pitch the computer out."

Well, that may have been hyperbole for emphasis. But when two lawyers in Phoenix spammed (which is like throwing a piece of spam at a fan) the Usenet groups on the Internet with thousands of e-mail messages advertising their services to immigrants seeking green cards, the user constituency went berserk in protest.[9] Canter and Siegel's voicemail was stuffed to overflowing. Their e-mail box "flamed" with angry responses. One clever software programmer designed a "cancelmoose," a program that can be deployed to seek out and destroy Canter and Siegel messages. Eventually, Canter and Siegel's service provider curtailed service. Apparently without success, Canter and Siegel have sought lawyers in Phoenix to represent them in filing suit against the service provider based upon First Amendment considerations.

They made enough profit out of their efforts, however, to seek yet another time to "spam" thousands of news groups earlier this year. This time, by more devious methods, they posted ads from a third party's site but with a return address to their own e-mail box. The ploy was detected early in its use, and the service provider cut off access to the Internet before too much opposition could be generated.[10]

Clearly, unsolicited advertising is considered a no-no by many long-time residents of the Networld. One of them suggested that receiving the Canter and Siegel ads was like having your mailbox stuffed with thousands of letters with postage due![11] Clearly, the Networld differs from the real world, and real costs associated with junk e-mail may be considered unacceptable. Clearly, advertisers must be careful as they enter the Networld to try to understand its culture. Advertisers can interact with existing user groups without offending them while seeking to attract more outsiders to these sites. Here are a few suggestions found on-line:[12]

(i)   Learn what is acceptable

(ii)   Post only to appropriate forums

(iii)   Keep messages short and snappy

(iv)   Avoid sensationalism

(v)   Create your own forum

(vi)   Interact with the on-line community

(vii)   Be creative and captivating

(viii) Avoid deception and annoyance

Every society has taboos. Ours now prohibits advertising tobacco and hard liquor on television. There are already twenty-two breweries and seven distilleries on the Web, so we have to ask ourselves, "Is cyberspace more like television or magazines—or so different that it requires writing new regulations for cyberspace? Should we seek to prohibit advertisers from dispatching unsolicited advertising material into our e-mail accounts? our postal boxes? our telephone voicemail?"

There would seem to be no crying economic need for advertisers or politicians or nonprofit organizations to impose their positions upon unwilling receivers, either by telemarketing or by e-mail, if we recognize that people in their roles as citizen, contributor, or consumer have ample opportunities to seek out what is of special interest to them. Perhaps such an "option" carries with it the economic burden of providing equitable access to the electronic agora through centralized communications centers or strategically placed public computer terminals.

There is no reason why the private sector might not be prompted to place public terminals where they can attract consumers to the electronic markets. Already there are electronic cafés, which provide sophisticated software to access electronic information services to customers sipping cappuccino or herbal tea. Such access could also be provided in beer halls, shopping centers, schools, hospitals, or wherever the computer-literate population of the future might care to obtain access to the electronic marketplace. If the private sector is to be relied upon to offer the publicly accessible terminals, the opportunity for the equivalent of redlining in real estate is apparent. The terminals will probably be installed in the more affluent neighborhoods, just as the newer interactive cable systems are being installed in affluent suburbs as a priority over poorer neighborhoods absent a requirement that all of the franchised service area be wired. The size of the World Wide Web, and its thousands, even millions, of opportunities to communicate alternatives, may not make possible a global public space into which ideas and opinions might flow. The Web is not the broadcasting environment of the 1950s, 1960s, or 1970s in the United States, where only four alternative channels were available on television and a president might commandeer them all for a visit with his constituents. Thus, we might ask what price we may be paying for the lack of "public space" if we require and achieve a relatively strong level of personal privacy and personal autonomy over information sources coming into and out of our information domains.

Another area of consternation is copyright protection for valuable information assets. Copying is so easy in the Networld that many of us think nothing of downloading an article or an image and re-posting it to our on-line discussion group. But there is an order-of-magnitude difference between copying something to share with two or three friends and posting it to your closest one hundred thousand correspondents on-line in a news or Listserv group. Authors and publishers are justifiably concerned. The copies are as good as the originals. Many authors and publishers hesitate to permit their writings to be incorporated into on-line services. Protection of proprietary claims is one of the most troubling areas from a legal standpoint, generating both case law in the courts and government white papers proposing to tweak the copyright law a little here and there to stem the tide of unauthorized copying. In *Playboy v. Frena*, a bulletin board operator was found to have infringed *Playboy*'s copyright despite protestations by the operator that he had no knowledge that one of the bulletin board's subscribers had uploaded the images.[13] In *U.S. v. LaMacchia*, on the other hand, a District Court Judge in Boston refused to find an MIT student guilty of an old statute prohibiting use of transmission lines for nefarious purposes for providing a space into which users could both upload and download copyrighted software, because Congress has not specifically found such behavior to be a crime.[14] The National Information Infrastructure (NII) white paper released by the working group responsible for recommendations to facilitate the use of computerized communication recommends a change approving a criminal offense without specific intent if the value of the software transmitted is valued at $5,000 or more.[15]

Here we have a conflict of positions ranging from those like John Perry Barlow, who think that we are beating a dead horse to try to modify copyright law to fit computer communication, to those long-standing copyright and patent lawyers, who defend their turf with a vengeance that defies understanding.[16] Clearly, the law is in a state of flux, both domestically and internationally, and it is not clear yet how the law will come out with respect to protection of information assets. Some see encryption of all transactions as the solution, others, digital cash, which could be used to make small purchases of information to be downloaded with a secure payments system record as the outcome. Already, however, efforts to set up a secure system for making payments online using MasterCard and Visa accounts has been compromised within a few weeks by a group of Frenchmen using 120 personal computers and a couple of parallel linked supercomputers. Two students at Berkeley with an interest in cryptography discovered the flaw in Netscape's security by using much less burdensome means.

Bugs in the software are a problem that will not go away in the near future. Small glitches, like the mathematical error that Intel sought to minimize, can become quite burdensome and costly, leading to unexpected and unreliable results. The software industry must mature substantially before we, as users, will be willing to rely upon this new technology, unless we can be assured that our transactions are not being tracked, our credit cards stolen, and that the programs can deliver certifiably reliable information and systems software.

Another area that has led to much consternation on-line among users and among lawyers seeking to understand the on-line environment is the conflict between anonymity and accountability. Clearly, there has been a great deal of exchange of anonymous messages on the Internet, and according to the well-circulated cartoon from the *New Yorker*, "On the Internet nobody knows you are a dog." Well, that was true when all was in text. But it is less true on the Web, where it is obvious that you are a cat if your image is featured on the White House home page. Consequently, the problem of anonymity may diminish, but it will not go away as users hasten to adorn home pages with images as well as text, audio, and video segments.

There is a long-standing heritage of anonymous political material since the issuance of the *Federalist Papers* as anonymous writings. Women authors have sought to hide their gender for fear that readers would not seek out a woman author. Whistle blowers may be reluctant to sound off their complaints unless their identity is protected from those who would seek retribution for disclosures about alleged wrongdoing. The Supreme Court in the *McIntyre v. Ohio Election Commission* case, confirmed that anonymous political speech is protected by the First Amendment.[17] However, this does not necessarily mean that all anonymous communications are also clothed with immunity from accountability. In 1976, in *Buckley v. Valeo*, the Supreme Court upheld a requirement that political contributions over $100 be identified as to source.[18] So there is sufficient room within the precedents to tailor the requirements for identification within the Networld to provide a measure of accountability without offending the First Amendment. This area is likely to be troublesome and fraught with confrontation, because many netizens consider anonymity a right and in many cybercommunities pseudonyms are a well established practice, rather than the exception.

Should we expect human behavior to be different on-line from what it is in the real world? Interestingly enough, the disappearance of face-to-face or voice-to-voice encounters seems to have peeled off a layer of civilization, and sometimes behavior on-line seems more brutal and frank and sometimes more hurtful. Cases are beginning to come into the courts in an attempt to determine where the responsibility should reside for abusive behavior of users. We have significant cultural differences concerning identification and accountability for behavior, but many of the developing cybercommunities will want to decide for themselves what kind of electronic environment they choose to navigate. So long as their behavior does not spill out into real-world impacts, there is no reason why they should not be given a certain amount of autonomy. Many cybercommunities will resist any effort of the outside world to make them conform to standards with which they do not agree, and the technology permits bypassing most controls if the user is determined to do so and willing to pay the price to reach another site or node on the global network.

Traffic in pornographic images has become a major topic of discussion, as mentioned earlier, because parents have discovered their children "surfing" the alt.sex Usenet groups where such material is easily identifiable. The Carnegie Mellon study of traffic in pornographic images has been criticized by social scientists. They challenge the methodology was flawed, resulting in grossly inflated percentages of pornographic images as being accessed.[19] Such criticism does not diminish the genuine concern that has been expressed about the availability and ease of access to such images. The Senate passed a bill prohibiting the posting of obscene images,[20] whereas the House passed a bill guaranteeing more open access according to individual tastes.[21]

The Amateur Action Bulletin Board case now going through the courts raises some important questions. The proprietors of the bulletin boards (BBS) were convicted for sending what were determined to be obscene images from California into Memphis, Tennessee, and face prison sentences. The question that may be determined on appeal is, whose standards should apply, those of the local community (deep in the Bible Belt) or those of the "virtual community" of adult subscribers to the Amateur Action Bulletin Board. Or is there a generic standard that may be applied to determine what is objectionable and no longer protected by the First Amendment? Having seen a number of the images transmitted on Amateur Action, I will not be surprised if the Supreme Court Justices, should the case reach them, may look on them as Justice Potter Stewart did other pornographic images, saying he wasn't sure he could describe obscenity but he knew it when he saw it. They may look and say, "This is obscene," thus changing the standard from local community standards to a generic norm.

Nonetheless, however the litigation and legislation are decided, information providers are scurrying around to design technical means for identifying material that users may consider objectionable, so that the users may maintain more control over their own information traffic. The real question is, "Can we protect the children?" As we all know, that which is prohibited to our children often becomes the most attractive to find, and determined young computer users will find ways around most restrictions.

I suspect that the problem is self-correcting. If college students spend too much time downloading images from the Internet, they will probably flunk their courses. Parents and professors worry about Web addiction. It does not really create a major problem, except to the afflicted, unless users playing games or exploring the virtual-reality realms use up so much of the space for traffic that they clog the information highways, restricting traffic for more important files being transferred, such as heavy traffic between hospitals and research facilities. Indeed, the Australians used this as an excuse to block many sexually explicit news groups.

Information privacy is one of the major problems confronting on-line communication. Most of us say we are concerned about it, but most of us do not know what we mean. Transaction-generated information is the most troublesome, because information is being collected about our travels, state of health, and purchases. A couple of years ago, I started purchasing copper pots for a new house I was building in Colorado. Only a few weeks had gone by before a catalog of copper pots appeared in my mail. Clearly, someone was watching. This example is a benign one, even a useful identification of my tastes that permitted marketers to target my particular interests, but it leaves me apprehensive that I have no control over where my name, address, and transaction-generated information are sold and to whom and for what purposes. When computers first came into our lives we were worried about Big Brother, the government, looking over our shoulders and invading our private lives. Today, we are discovering that Big Brother is Big Business, which is the real "snooper" robbing us of the seclusion and privacy to which we feel we are entitled.

In order to rationalize the concerns about privacy, I have started dividing them into specialized categories, such as seclusion (the right to avoid unwanted intrusions), secrecy (the right to avoid unwanted disclosures), autonomy (the right to control one's own information environment), and confidentiality (the right to release personal information with the expectation that it will not be disclosed to third parties without our knowledge or consent). It is important that we specify what is objectionable, so that we may identify legal and technical and social means of satisfying our various concerns.

The real difficulty is the lack of parity between consumer and marketer, although many direct marketers are beginning to understand that marketing methods of protecting our privacy is good business strategy. Some are offering opportunities to opt out of selling our names to other businesses. Surprisingly, the only areas where we have expressed sufficient concern to obtain legal protection are in those of video privacy—two laws protecting us from disclosure of our viewing habits on cable television and in video rental stores. A third federal law seeks to have state legislatures provide opportunities for citizens to opt out of being included in motor vehicle records sold to businesses.

The determination not to release information without the assurance that it will not be sold, exchanged, or otherwise released without permission will, I expect, eventually become the norm, rather than the exception. Recently, an individual in the Virginia suburbs of Washington, D.C., filed suit under a Virginia statute against *U.S. News and World Report* for transferring his name and address, without his permission, to the *Smithsonian* magazine for the purpose of soliciting his subscription.[22] For individuals to have to bear the burden of litigation is a severe deterrent to obtaining general relief for an entire population.

Citizens in the real world and netizens in the Networld are increasingly militant in claiming what they perceive to be their rights to maintain autonomy over their own information environments. Strategies include a variety of methods: (i) curtailing service by information providers where behavior contravenes standards set forth in terms of service; (ii) designing technical means so the user can filter or destroy objectionable e-mail; (iii) "flaming" those who fail to live up to the "netiquette" set forth for particular cybercommunities; (iv) expelling users who exhibit intolerable behavior; or (v) migrating into other cyberspaces and leaving the objectionable parties behind.

We have a long way to go to facilitate navigation around the Internet and the World Wide Web, but we are beginning to see pointers and gateways to help us locate where we want to be. The most popular locator, Yahoo, had 44,000 entries in early September. Gateways from one Web page to another are becoming common. Cross-posting from one entrepreneur to another is the name of the game. Getting as many others to point to your home page has become a must.

In summary, the bad news is that not everybody has a computer or a modem, nor are we all computer literate. Digital cash is not secure yet but promises to become so very soon. Few cyberlaws are in place, and much global confusion exists about what the law on-line is or should become. Privacy concerns have not yet been adequately addressed. *But* the future looks promising.

The good news is that almost everyone wants a home page, and theoretically everyone can have one. Even without one, a user can surf the Web to one's heart's content and every taste can be satisfied. There will be a mixture of political, social, and commercial activities on-line, just as in the real world. Fortunately, unlike the real world, cyberspaces are expandable, so cybercommunities will continue to proliferate. This is a healthy trend, unless it leaves us too divided into our various constituencies to reach consensus about mutual problems.

What does the future hold? For one thing, many questions concerning global governance of the global Networld. The controls of the network, contrary to the popular notion that the Internet is uncontrollable, are at the interconnection points and in the hands of network managers. That is where the borders of the information highways exist. As a consequence, there are many doubts about how we will govern ourselves within these boundaries, how we will interact, and, especially, how the Networld dovetails with the real world. Can national boundaries be maintained and patrolled, and can undesirable information kept out? Should these borders be controlled?

One scenario of the future describes a situation in which all of us democratically sit at our computer consoles sending and receiving "perfect" information, so that we are all tuned into the same Networld. Given such perfect information, an information marketplace, a marketplace of ideas, should function to permit consensual decisions without the intervention of governments at all. Neal Stephenson, in his fascinating but troubling science fiction novel *Snow Crash*, describes a more sinister world where governments like the United States are so insignificant that the U.S. president is no longer recognizable as an important world figure.[23] Instead, large commercial consortia finance their own armed agents to maintain order in physical spaces under their control, and our individual "avatars" move comfortably throughout the virtual world, interacting with one another on-line in a manner that seems to merge real and virtual worlds into a seamless Web.

Whether either or these scenarios will become the reality or another yet to be determined will arrive depends upon those of us who reside in the real world but are exploring and learning how to live in the Networld.

Notes

1. "[Analogy] The Software Schism," in "Readings," *Harper's Magazine*, January 1995, 33. The magazine noted, "From 'La Bustina di Minerva,' a column by Umberto Eco, in the September 30, 1994, issue of the Italian journal *L'Espresso*. Eco's column was anonymously translated into English and posted on the Internet in October."

2. Alicia Mundy, "Politicians in Cyberspace: Presidential Hopefuls Are Bypassing the Pundits and the Press by Putting Up Their Own Web Sites; World Wide Web on the Internet," *MediaWeek*, July 10, 1995, 20.

3. Reading, Mass.: Addison-Wesley, 1993.

4. *Twilight of Sovereignty* (N.Y.: Scribner's, 1992).

5. Peter H. Lewis, "Company Says Electronic Mail Was Opened to Find Pornography," *The New York Times*, Sept. 13, 1995, A-16.

6. Annenberg Scholars Conference on Public Space, March 1–4, 1995.

7. *Pittsburgh Post-Gazette*, Sept. 24, 1995, © 1995 Rogers—*Pittsburgh Post-Gazette*.

8. See "Spinning a Golden Web," *People*, Sept. 11, 1995, 74.

9. 104 *YALE L.J.* 1639, *1658, n69 Cyberspace Upstarts Propose Etiquette Rules for Infobahn, *Atlanta Journal & Constitution*, June 14, 1994, at E3.

10. Ibid.

11. Ibid.

12. Mstrange@Fondrola.Net.

13. Playboy enterprises, Inc. v. Frena, 839 F. Supp. 1552 (M.D. Fla. 1993).

14. U.S. v. David LaMacchia, 871 F. Supp. 535 (U.S.D.C. Mass. 1995).

15. Ronald H. Brown, Information Infrastructure Task Force, *Intellectual Property and the National Information Infrastructure*, The Report of the Working Group on Intellectual Property Rights, Bruce Lehman, Assistant Secretary of Commerce and Commissioner of Patents and Trademarks, Chair, September 1995.

16. John Perry Barlow, "The Economy of Ideas: A Framework for Rethinking Patents and Copyrights in the Digital Age (Everything You Know about Intellectual Property is Wrong)," *Wired* 2, 3 (March 1995), 84–90.

17. McIntyre v. Ohio Election Commission, (93 986 April 95) 63 U.S. LAW WEEK 4279.

18. Buckley v. Valeo, 424 U.S. 1 (1976).

19. Marty Rimm, "Marketing Pornography on the Information Superhighway: A Survey of 917,410 Images, Descriptions, Short Stories and Animations Downloaded 8.5 Million Times by Consumers in over 2,000 Cities in Forty Countries, Provinces, and Territories," 83 GEO. L.J. [June 1995].

20. S. 314 Exon Amendment, adopted June 14, 1995, 104th Cong. 1st Sess.

21. H.R. 1555, Cox-Wyden Amendment, adopted August 4, 1995.

22. C. Bruce Knecht, "Junk-Mail Hater Seeks Profits from Sale of His Name," *Wall Street Journal*, Oct. 13, 1995, B1.

23. New York: Bantam, 1993.

20   Cyberrules: Problems and Prospects for On-Line Commerce

Debora Spar

In societies, as in games, rules matter. They set the boundaries of permissible behavior, clarify the terms of interaction, and lay the groundwork for recognizing victors and punishing losers. In both competitive games and civil societies, rules are intended to prevent interaction from degenerating into chaos. They provide some sense of security and predictability, informing participants of what is permissible and what is not. Even in their breach, rules are critical, because they define a violation and arrange for its punishment. When rules break down, interaction of any sort becomes a much riskier and uncertain venture. Witness the child who sulks off the playground because someone "broke the rules" or, infinitely more tragic, the chaos of Somalia, Rwanda, and the former Yugoslavia.

In business transactions as well, rules matter. Indeed, as in games more narrowly or societies more broadly defined, rules ease and facilitate commercial interaction. Despite the occasional sense of operating in uncharted or unordered territories, business for the most part operates in an environment where rules prevail. These rules can be formal, such as contract law, laws of incorporation, and antitrust. Or they can be informal, incorporating norms of commerce such as upholding a deal or paying bills within thirty days. In either case, and most frequently in tandem, these rules describe the environment in which business occurs. By clarifying what is and is not permissible, they facilitate exchange between the transacting people or firms and enable the parties to exchange goods and services with a shared concept of what this exchange entails and a shared confidence that the terms of the exchange will be met. Without this confidence, commercial transactions are liable to decline. Like children frustrated by an anarchic game or motorists reluctant to drive on a road without rules, firms may be wary of transacting unless they have some reasonable information about the basic rules of their exchange: who owns the goods or services being exchanged (property rights); how the exchange will be compensated (means of exchange); and how the terms of the deal will be structured and ensured (security and enforcement).

So basic and pervasive are these rules that they often go unnoticed by the businesses that rely upon them. Indeed, until a contract is broken or property stolen, most business executives pay little explicit attention to the underlying rules of their game. That is the beauty of rules: They aim to make the structure of the game so transparent and secure that the players can dedicate the bulk of their energies to mastery and technique. But if the rules are changing or inchoate or unknown, the game is liable to falter. This is true for sports and societies. It is true also, in many cases, for commerce.

Recently, though, an area of business with few established rules has attracted a tremendous amount of commercial interest and enthusiasm. Since the late 1980s, the Internet has been growing at a staggering pace, doubling in size each year and expanding its user base in 1995 at a rate of roughly 10 to 20 percent a month. With managers scrambling to push their businesses on-line, the Net has become the focus of vast media and commercial attention. Headlines describe its explosion as but the start of an Information Revolution (capitals optional, but generally preferred) that promises to change the conduct of commerce dramatically.

Clearly, change is underway. But what is often overlooked in the excitement about this change is the importance of rules. Before the Internet can truly attract and support the wide-scale commercial enterprises its adherents foresee, it must first provide businesses with the basic rules of commerce. These should include, eventually, a common conception of property rights, a system for setting and securing the means of electronic exchange, and a mechanism for enforcing both property rights and secure exchanges.

In the mid-1990s, most of these rules are still fluid and evolving. The legal status of electronic property rights remains ambiguous, as do the legal and practical issues surrounding on-line exchange. Enforcement authority is limited on the Internet, and few agencies exist with either the power or the predisposition to punish violators of the norms of on-line conduct.

This state of affairs, I suggest, cannot survive forever. Though portions of the Internet may remain rugged and unruled, other portions—most of them—will eventually develop their own rules and norms. The rules may vary markedly from area to area and may be governed by a host of potential authorities—governments, businesses, independent sysops, or possibly even no one at all. But there will, over time, be rules. And there will, in particular, be rules that adhere to and support commercial transactions—rules that will allow on-line ventures to run their businesses with some stability, security, and certainty.

This paper explores the prospects for "cyberrules" and the processes by which such rules are likely to emerge. I start with one simple assumption—that rules matter—and one corollary—that they matter particularly for commercial transactions. My normative claims are exceedingly limited. I by no means suggest that governments or their bureaucrats ought necessarily to rush into cyberspace. Nor, on the other hand, do I share many analysts' view that cyberspace should necessarily remain open, unregulated, and free for all. Indeed, I say very little about what form of cyberspace is most desirable or what role governments ought to play in shaping its evolution. Rather, my concern is restricted to describing what I see as an inevitable aspect of on-line development: There will be rules in cyberspace, and the shape and makers of these rules will in time affect how we go on-line and what we do there.

My definition of "rules" is deliberately kept open and inclusive. Rules, in my view, encompass far more than the explicit rules and regulations of any particular state. They include international agreements, commonly accepted practices, cultural norms, and businesses' standard operating procedures. They include, in short, the "rules of the game"—standards that define what is permissible and acceptable and that, in one form or another, can effectively be enforced and maintained on-line.

My goal is not to describe how such rules should evolve or who should mastermind their creation, but, rather, to examine cyberspace from a rules-based perspective, exploring how law and order and security and standards are evolving along the cutting edge of the electronic frontier.

From Science to Sales: The Commercial Evolution of the Internet

Someday the Internet may become an information superhighway, but right now it is more like a 19th-century railroad that passes through the badlands of the Old West. As waves of new settlers flock to cyberspace in search of free information or commercial opportunity, they make easy marks for sharpers who play a keyboard as deftly as Billy the Kid ever drew a six-gun. Old hands on the electronic frontier lament both the rising crime rate and the waning of long-established norms of open collaboration.
—Paul Wallich[1]

The Internet got its start in the late 1960s as a communications infrastructure called ARPANET, run by the Department of Defense and its Advanced

Research Project Agency (ARPA). Consisting of a series of links joining together discrete computer networks, the ARPANET was an experiment in "internetworking," designed to give university research scientists an opportunity to create a solid "network of networks" to facilitate the exchange of scientific and military information and save the costs of replicating computer capabilities at multiple sites. Taking advantage of recent developments in computer technology, and trying also to make the system impervious to nuclear attacks or natural disasters, the developers of the ARPANET structured the system in a highly decentralized manner.

Over time, this decentralized network of networks became known as the Internet. Following the model of the national telephone system (and even employing many of its connections), the Internet's pathways remained out of sight and mind to its users. No one needed to know how messages moved from one site to another, only that they got there securely. Unlike the telephone system, however, the architecture of the Internet allowed any single user to broadcast a message simultaneously to any site on the network. This possibility reflected the Internet's scientific purpose: to enable an elite corps of researchers to share critical information. Given this purpose, the Internet's founders saw no need to restrict access to the system or to embed within it any means for controlling the flow of information. On the contrary, in the late 1960s and early 1970s, before the advent of the personal computer, it was reasonable to conclude that anyone with the technical means to access the Internet would be from the very scientific or engineering community that the system was designed to serve.

For roughly twenty years, this community quietly flourished on-line. Expanding rapidly from just four host computers in 1969 to nearly two thousand by 1985, the Internet became a common mode of communication among university researchers, government scientists, and a handful of outside computer engineers. Funding for the creation and maintenance of the system's infrastructure came from the National Science Foundation (NSF), which during the course of the 1980s took responsibility from the Department of Defense. As computer use expanded and then exploded in the 1970s and 1980s, so too did the Internet grow. Academics from outside the hard sciences began to communicate via e-mail, as did the increasing legions of software writers and computer company employees.

As discussions grew to incorporate new entrants, electronic bulletin boards were formed, and for the first time, people began to "meet" in cyberspace. Still, the culture of the Internet remained akin to that of a small, like-minded community. Users were overwhelmingly computer-literate, highly educated, and scientifically minded. Many were hackers, and commerce had no place in their slowly expanding community. Indeed, NSF policy explicitly discouraged any use of the Internet for nonscholarly purposes.[2]

By the late 1980s, this policy had effectively disappeared. Aware of the growing commercial interest in the Net, as well as its own budgetary limits, the NSF began slowly to privatize it. Initially, private firms just provided infrastructural services to the Net's established user base. Then in 1989, commercial service providers emerged, offering Internet access to a wide new range of private and commercial customers. In 1990, the Internet was officially opened to commercial ventures. As a result, the Net was transformed. In the early 1980s the Internet community consisted only of about 25 linked scientific and academic networks. By 1995, when the last piece of the NSF backbone was retired in favor of higher-speed, privately owned backbones, the Net had grown to include over 44,000 networks extending to 160 countries and including 26,000 registered commercial entities.[3] Extending far beyond academe and the Defense Department, users numbered somewhere between 40 and 50 million in 1995, and were increasing by an estimated 10 to 20 percent a month.

More than just a quantum increase in numbers, the entrance of the "newbies" meant a fundamental change in the culture of the Internet and the community it had spawned. Arriving on-line primarily through servers such as Prodigy or America Online, these new users understandably had little interest in the research questions that had bound previous users together. The newbies were also largely unfamiliar with much of the Internet's specific protocol or with the systems that sat at its foundation. Cyberspace for the newbies was simply an adventure—an opportunity to meet people, gain information and, ironically perhaps, recreate a sense of small-town intimacy and immediacy. But many newcomers also came to cyberspace for profit—to explore the potential of a vast new realm and stake a claim in the technology that promised to revolutionize the nature of transactions. As a result, the Internet's relatively new business district—the *.com* domain—quickly swelled to become the largest sector of the Net, and the transformation of commerce seemed well underway.

Uses and Users

Amidst all this enthusiasm, it might easily be supposed that nearly all commercial enterprises had moved their entire businesses on-line, from Time

Warner to IBM to the local flower shops. But as of mid-1996, commercial uses of the Internet remain relatively narrow and well defined. Essentially, the Internet remains just a conduit for sending and receiving bits of information. As such, it can serve business either as a means of delivering information about other tangible goods or as a means of directly transmitting information-based, intangible goods.

In the first case, use of the Internet has no effect on the good being sold or the means of its delivery: A raincoat purchased from L. L. Bean's home page is still a raincoat and will still arrive by truck or plane—that is, by an inherently mechanical means. Because of the nature of what they sell, tangible goods firms cannot transmit their products electronically. Instead, going on-line entails using the electronic medium of the Net to interact with existing customers and entice new ones. The difference lies less with the product or its production than with the way in which it is sold and marketed: the services that surround the commercial process.

Accordingly, most companies that produce tangible goods have seized upon the Internet largely as a means of providing customer support and low-cost advertising. The pioneers in this area are computer manufacturers, whose commerce on the Net emerged quite naturall from their communication on the Net.[4] Silicon Graphics, for instance, the multibillion-dollar leader in work-stations, uses e-mail to share problem-solving techniques with its customers and distributors, saving the company an estimated $5 million a year in reduced service calls.[5]

Other on-line pioneers included retailers such as the Internet Shopping Network and Timberland. In many ways, their conversion to electronic commerce is more telling than that of the computer manufacturers: Seeing computers sold and serviced on the Net, after all, is hardly a shock, given that the people who buy workstations are among the oldest travelers on the Internet. Cubic zirconium and hiking boots, however, are a different matter, because they are hardly the "techie" products initially expected in cyberspace. And yet, increasingly, there they are, along with the full range of products from such retailers as Crate & Barrel, Sharper Image, Neiman Marcus, Sara Lee, and a host of other mail-order firms lining up in cybermalls.

But however large they grow, the malls will always be constrained by their physical incompatibility with electronic commerce, because the products they sell—the raincoats, jewelry, and boots—are entirely tangible. The Internet may affect the ways in which these goods are sold, or serviced, or marketed, but it does little to alter the underlying nature of the business.

By contrast, electronic commerce in *intangible* goods raises the prospect of a fundamental shift in the nature of exchange. Unlike tangible goods, intangible products such as software and financial services themselves consist largely of information. So long as commerce was based primarily on tangible exchanges, providers of intangible products were compelled to convert their bits to atoms, packaging inherently intangible products into tangible forms. Thus, financial service providers built banks and provided tellers, while software creators put information on plastic disks and wrapped them in brightly colored boxes. Now, however, the Internet, as an electronic conduit for information, offers these providers the opportunity to discard tangible packaging and return to their basic intangible product. This change is radical, and it presents business with tempting new opportunities.

Consider the sale of software. Like computer manufacturers, the firms in the $80-billion software industry are ideally situated for doing business on-line. Their employees and customers both tend to be technically sophisticated and to own the physical conduits—the terminals—that connect them to the Net. Unlike computer firms, though, software producers can actually distribute and service their product electronically. Using the Internet, they can allow customers to download directly the software and manuals they desire. They can also provide customers with databases of support information and answer electronically their most common questions. Through these means, providers can significantly lower their costs of distribution and technical support.[6] Over time, on-line sales have the potential to restructure the software industry alto-gether, because the electronic medium allows software creators to reintegrate the distribution function previously ceded to other firms. Or as Laurent Pacalin, Director of Worldwide Electronic Distribution for Oracle Corporation, a leader in database software, observed, on-line distribution allows the software com-pany to "leapfrog the box-pushers and deal directly with the customers."[7] And so the "box-pushers," like many intermediaries, may be left behind, their packaging rendered obsolete by direct electronic exchange.

Similar changes are likely to befall publishing companies, whose products of information and text lend themselves quite naturally to electronic commerce. As with software, on-line "distribution" promises to reduce publishers' costs by significantly eliminating paper, printing, binding, warehousing, and circulation. It also offers publishing firms novel ways of mixing and manipulating the product they offer. With the rapid development of digitally based multimedia technology, "published" information need not consist only of text and still photos. Instead, on-line publishing can allow "readers" to mix together sound, video, and text-based information. Magazines can invite any "reader" with a terminal to interact directly with authors, or to receive only certain types of stories. Already, on-line magazines such as *HotWired* have emerged to take advantage of this evolving electronic format, armed with the philosophy that just as "television wasn't radio with pictures, the Net isn't magazines with buttons.... Instead, this is a new medium demanding new thinking, new content."[8]

As in the software industry, much of the new thinking demanded by on-line publishing focuses on new ways of packaging the published content. The old way was relatively simple. Publishers put the content—book, magazine, or newspaper—between two tangible covers and left it to the reader to move sequentially through the enclosed information. For those who did not want to read all of the text, tables of contents or indexes served as a road map and allowed for nonsequential choosing or skimming. But that was the extent of the options. With electronic publishing no such constraints exist. Instead, the very structure of the medium encourages users to move from topic to topic, article to article, with little concern for linear order. This structure also encourages the growth of new intermediaries to wade through the barrage of on-line information and retrieve and customize it for specific groups or individual users. Consequently, even as electronic publishing threatens to destroy some segments of the existing industry, it promises to create others. The repackaging of the product will undoubtedly bring about a massive restructuring of the industry.

A similar restructuring is probable also in the financial services industry. If electronic commerce progresses as its adherents expect, it will have a profound impact on banks and brokerage services. Again, the source of change lies in the intangibility of the product being sold, and the impetus for change is sharply reduced cost. If banks and other financial service providers ultimately sell information, and if they can sell this information electronically, they will have less need for the tangible trappings that have surrounded their business in the past. Or as Shikhar Ghosh, Chairman of Open Market, notes, "Banking is a pure information business ... so why invest in furniture, buildings, vice presidents?"[9] Indeed, why not move to a model of business based on transactions, rather than relationships? Under the current system, people bank with a bank. They choose an institution and route their transactions through it. If, however, banks truly move their business to the Internet, the nature of this relationship may be subject to change. Because the processing costs for moving money electronically are negligible, on-line banking implies that customers will be able to open and close accounts effortlessly. Banks may then find themselves competing on new ground, developing different means for wooing and maintaining their traditional customers.

What this means for the banking industry, and for the myriad businesses linked to the current banking and financial systems, is unclear. At a minimum, though, it means that commercial interaction may be pushed further away from a personal or relations-based mode of exchange and closer to a purely transaction-based mode. This, after all, is one of the more compelling commercial prospects of the Internet: to make individual transactions accessible, immediate, and inexpensive.

Put into a historical perspective, this transformation is even more profound than many current analysts have noted. Historically, the evolution of commerce has depended on and coincided with the evolution of institutions to secure the means and rules of exchange. Because transacting—giving away one good in exchange for another—is inherently risky and costly, institutions and relationships have emerged over time to mediate these risks and costs and allow for exchange to proceed. The history of these relationships and institutions surrounds the history of commercial evolution. It begins with primitive exchanges (three pigs for a cow) that rest almost everywhere on personal familiarity and are limited to the scope of a trader's immediate circle of contacts. Driving the need for familiarity is the risk inherent in the transaction: If the cow dies the following morning, the unfortunate purchaser wants some recourse to the seller, and the best means for assuring that is to know precisely the identity and location of the seller. Security comes also from the knowledge that the traders will transact again, thereby reducing the likelihood that either will succumb to the temptation to cheat the other.[10] For interaction to progress beyond the limited bounds of familiarity, the traders (and their society) must develop institutions that allow them to replace personal ties with more formal and impersonal ones. As societies develop such formal ties, commerce expands beyond the community and economic growth ensues. The nature of the ties—such as private property, contract law, a common currency, and a means of enforcement—is to reduce the cost of transactions and ensure security in the absence of a long-term personal relationship. As transactions become more complicated (overseas purchasing, foreign investment, corporate mergers, futures trading, junk bonds) so, too, must the rules evolve, reducing the risks and costs that remain inherent in exchange.

What the Internet does, particularly for intangible products, is to push this commercial evolution into its next, electronic phase. Moving ever further away from the personal relationships of primitive commerce, it promises to reduce business to its most basic component: the transaction. Theoretically at least, the technological prowess and open architecture of the Net should allow millions of users to transact with one another anonymously, immediately, internationally, and inexpensively. This is the radical commercial promise of the Internet.

Yet, what those who make this promise often neglect to consider is that even this radically new form of commerce will demand and require a supporting set of rules. Like successful commerce in any other space or time, it will need rules of property, rules of payment, and rules of security. It will need some entity to ensure the sanctity of possession and the security of exchange. It will need some means to punish those who cheat, or steal, or trespass. At the moment, most of the rules and rulers remain in their infancy.

The Rules of Exchange

"It's business on a lawless frontier."   —Michael Wolff, Internet author[11]

Once upon a time, the Internet had rules. In its earliest days, the Net was very much a community of like-minded individuals who developed clear codes of conduct and working norms of behavior. Their rules were rarely written or even explicit, but they did not have to be, because they were widely observed by all those traveling on the Net. Just as early automobile drivers developed the rules of the road, so the early Internet users developed their own norms of behavior. They created symbols to express emotions such as joy [:-)] and sorrow [:-(]. They created rules, such as Don't-change-the-subject and Read-the-FAQ-file, and they even created a language of sorts, with expressions such as "FAQ," "flame," and "spam."[12]

Despite its reputation as the untamed realm of hackers, the early Net was actually an organized, orderly community. The strength of its rules was powerfully demonstrated in 1994, when a now infamous pair of Arizona lawyers posted an advertisement for their services on hundreds of electronic bulletin boards, bombarding many uninterested users with multiple copies. Seeing the advertisement as a violation of the Net's then-existing norm against private commerce and "junk-mail," thousands of users "flamed" the lawyers' office with a torrent of hate mail and cyber-threats. With this spontaneous response they demonstrated not only the power of on-line norms but also the ability of the Internet community to monitor and enforce these norms, punishing violations with on-line's closest approximation of force.

Since the lawyers' venture, however, the norms have themselves come under attack, besieged by an onslaught of newcomers. These newcomers are by no means bad for the Net; indeed, they (even the derided newbies) are the ones with both the mass and the power to alter how the Net is used and what it can do. But because they come from beyond the scientific and engineering communities, and particularly because they want to use the Internet as a means of conducting business as well as correspondence, their participation breaks the existing rules and demands new ones. In particular, mass participation on the Internet requires at least three sets of rules: rules of property rights, rules of currency, and rules of enforcement.

Property Rights

All economic systems are based on a shared understanding of property rights. Developed usually over decades or even centuries of evolution, these rights clarify the basis of ownership and exchange. They provide a consistent way of defining who owns what and how these possessions can be transferred from one owner to another. In the basic example above, for instance, property rights establish that Person A owns the cow and is willing to exchange it for the three pigs. Without well-accepted rules of property, the exchange either would not occur or would be exceedingly costly. Someone else could always just take the cow by force or stealth. Property rights reduce the costs of exchange by clarifying ownership and providing some means for punishing those who violate it. They define not only possession but also theft.

In modern market economies, property rights also provide the incentives that drive innovation and growth. If property is communal or property rights ill defined, no one in the community has an incentive to produce anything more than can be consumed. What creates the incentive, and thus what drives technological and economic progress, is a system that clearly defines private property and enables the owner of this property to appropriate it for individual benefit.[13] Without the ability to appropriate rents from private property, few people in any community would be willing to invest in specialization, or technological advance, or even a particularly hard day's work. To generate these types of investments, communities and economies must therefore create and preserve rules of private property.[14] And as economies evolve, they must ensure that their property rights evolve as well.[15]

This connection between property rights and commerce applies with full force to the Internet. For even if electronic commerce fundamentally transforms the nature of business, it does not eliminate business's basic need for an infrastructure that clarifies ownership and allows owners to reap the economic rewards of their possessions. At the moment, however, there is only a limited system of on-line property rights. The Net instead approximates a free-for-all in which information is often regarded as a public good and common practice is "what's yours is mine."[16] This norm of sharing was eminently reasonable in the early days of the Net, when its purpose lay in facilitating communication among researchers. As a norm for commercial activity, sharing is less reasonable. It simply will not work, because few entrepreneurs have a long-term interest in sharing their product. They may want to advertise the product on the Net, they may even want to sell it directly on the Net, but they also want to make money from it—to appropriate the rents of ownership and recoup the costs of investment and innovation. So long as all information on the Net is treated as common property, this cannot be done.

What makes the issue of on-line ownership so troublesome is that ownership almost always refers to information, to bits rather than atoms. And despite a spate of recent developments, owning bits is still difficult, because most legal systems are based primarily on tangible rather than intangible property. The most generally applicable laws, those of copyright and intellectual property, are relatively underdeveloped and often contentious. They also vary dramatically across countries.

To understand the extent of the problem, consider the three industries described earlier: software, publishing and financial services. In each the product being sold is essentially information: text and ideas. On the Internet, these goods can be disseminated and reproduced at extremely low costs, which presumably gives the author of the text or the originator of the ideas new ways of distributing the work. It also potentially denies them the proceeds from this work. For once information is transmitted into the vast and anonymous realm of cyberspace, it can be endlessly copied and altered—inexpensively and without detection. That is why the Internet is such an exciting development for people who want to access information. That is also why it demands caution by firms in the business of selling information. No firm that creates property wants to leave this property untended and unprotected in an accessible public space. Yet this is precisely the dilemma that information-based firms face as they consider the move toward electronic commerce.

Understandably, then, firms that deal in the business of information are approaching the Net with caution. The Recording Industry Association and the Walt Disney Company both initially held back, worried that their products might be not only misappropriated but also actually changed or misrepresented on-line.[17] Similarly, the Smithsonian Institution has limited electronic reproduction of its artistic works, reasoning that "at least for now ... cyberspace is a chaotic wild west frontier full of highway bandits and subject to only the roughest kind of vigilante justice."[18]

At the root of the problem for all these companies is the inapplicability of existing copyright law to electronic commerce. Even in the United States, where copyright laws are arguably the most advanced, "original works of authorship" are defined as "fixed in a *tangible* medium of expression ... from which they can be perceived, reproduced or otherwise communicated."[19] Even though the central statute governing copyright law was explicitly amended in 1980 to cover software programs, its extension to electronic transmission remains vague.

According to Bruce Lehman, commissioner of the U.S. Patent and Trademark Office, "Existing copyright law doesn't make it clear that it is a violation of the copyright owner's rights to distribute a protected work over the Internet."[20] Or as Nicholas Negroponte puts it, "All copyright law is essentially a Gutenberg artifact, bound to paper and constructed in ignorance of the digital age."[21] So long as this digital gap exists, anyone who makes intellectual content available on the Internet will be risking that their content—their intellectual property—will be broadly distributed without their consent and with little, if any, economic return. For anyone or any firm that makes a living from intellectual property, these risks are simply too large. Even those who do not intend to profit from their intellectual property may want to retain control; actors, for instance, might not want their faces or voices clipped from one movie and inserted into another, nor might authors want their words rearranged to serve others' themes or purposes. But under the existing norms of electronic commerce, firms have no secure means to prevent these practices, so the Internet remains a "lawless frontier," where intellectual property is potentially up for grabs and ownership lies often in possession.

There is, of course, a fairly obvious way to solve the problem of property rights. If this problem is the absence of law, then a solution may rest—historically has often rested—with the creation of law by a central government. In cyberspace, that law would come, most probably, from an extension of existing copyright law. Because copyright already deals with intangible products such as

Spar

ideas, and because it provides for the commercialization of intellectual property, its extension into cyberspace would seem to make a great deal of sense. By guaranteeing owners of intellectual property that their information and ideas would remain "theirs" on-line, copyright law should allow information-based firms to move more confidently on to the Internet. Accordingly, lawmakers in Washington have recently been tinkering with the statutes of copyright law. In September 1995, a working group convened under the auspices of the White House Infrastructure Task Force recommended changes in the language of the 1976 copyright law to include transmission explicitly as a form of distribution. The working group also endorsed a "fair use" provision that would limit any noncommercial use of intellectual property that damages the legal owner of the property.

If enacted as law, the working group's provisions will do a lot to protect the property of firms that transact in cyberspace. But they still won't do nearly enough. First, copyright law is already among the most intricate and esoteric areas of law. Courts vary widely in their interpretation of existing statutes, and even in their understanding of the laws' intent. The extension of these laws into a whole new realm of commerce is almost certain to create great clouds of ambiguity and uncertainty, leaving courts and litigants to fumble toward new definitions of private property and property rights. Second, because the laws are national, they will have only a limited influence on the international transactions that proliferate on the Internet. Even if the laws stop a Cincinnati-based firm from covertly downloading a U.S.-based competitor's software or textbook or database, they may not stop the same firm, or any other, from routing the download through a computer in Bangkok or the Netherlands. Third, even if the laws were applied at the global level (and there is talk of doing so under the auspices of the new World Trade Organization), the laws still do not provide the means for a commercial provider to determine whether its information has been altered or copied in cyberspace. The laws also provide no technical solution to the problems involved in tracing on-line violations. Even if a firm suspects that its product has been stolen, how can it find the thief, especially if all transactions can be routed through multiple sites and untraceable user-ID's?

There is also another problem concerning any legal or governmental solution: The Net does not want it. Ideologically, the Net is still composed of those who see information as the ultimate public good, something that fundamentally transcends the realm of private property. Quoting Thomas Jefferson, for instance, *Wired* magazine recently commented that "ideas should freely spread from one to another over the globe, for the moral and mutual instruction of man, and improvement of his condition.... Inventions ... cannot, in nature, be a subject of property."[22] Though often less eloquently expressed, the notion of public information permeates the Internet. So does the more radical belief that governmental intervention anywhere on-line represents an unacceptable invasion of privacy, even of freedom. As commercial interests enter the Internet community, such sentiments may easily be diluted, especially given that commercial providers stand to benefit from the extension of law into cyberspace. A strong disinclination toward regulation seems likely to remain on-line for some time, as indicated by a leading industry consultant's claim that "the federal government has the unique power to do things really badly really fast."[23]

Who, then, will write the rules for protecting intellectual property in an electronic age? One possibility is that no one will, and that the rules will remain in their present vague and inchoate form. If so, then electronic commerce is liable to stagnate. It may not, like CB radio, almost overnight go from technological hot-shot to toy, but neither will it become a significant forum for commercial activity. Instead, the Net will remain much as it is right now—a beehive of activity and experimentation, a channel for mass communication and correspondence, but a channel in which information is exchanged only for free, rather than for profit. This would not necessarily be a bad fate for the Net, but it would be quite different from the scenario that most Internet adherents currently foresee.

A second possibility is that these same adherents will themselves create the rules of electronic commerce. Facing a void of legal rules and definitions, they will adopt practices and develop technological means that work to preserve their property on-line and ensure some means of recouping their investments. These practices and technologies will not, of course, have the status of law, but over time they may become the standards of electronic commerce, much as the customs and practices developed by medieval merchants eventually became commercial law in Europe.

This is not to imply that firms can, by themselves, create laws of intellectual property. They cannot, because they have neither the legal mandate nor the physical means of enforcement. At some point, governments are likely to be essential to the process, especially insofar as they retain the ability to punish those who would break the rules. But in the search to protect their own property interests on-line, firms and entrepreneurs may begin to create the procedures that become the basis of law. Every time, for instance, a firm pays for software on-line, or reimburses electronic authors for copies of their work, the firm is establishing a precedent of electronic ownership. Similarly, every time firms limit their distribution to a well-defined list of customers, they reinforce the right of property and create some technical means for securing such a right. Even the most sophisticated technical system, of course, cannot operate in a legal void, and ultimately distribution channels can only be secured in an environment where unauthorized access is clearly defined and punishable as a violation of law. As this law evolves, however, corporations, rather than state agencies, may shoulder the bulk of the development.

Means of Exchange

If firms become the creators of on-line property rights, they will be acting not out of direct interest in the rules of electronic commerce but rather from a defensive, almost instinctual interest in preserving property. Their concern will probably lie not with the system of property rights per se, but with the specific cases of their own property and their own means of financial preservation. By contrast, a second area of on-line rules—the rules and means of exchange—is explicitly about the rules themselves and is already compelling firms to venture directly into the rulemaking business.

As described above, property rights are the foundation of any market-based system. They are the fundamental institution, the rules of the road upon which any economic exchange depends. The means of exchange are more prosaic and tangible. Rather than defining the rules in any significant way, they provide the means by which they operate.

In most economic systems, the means of exchange is money: Currency of one form or another is widely accepted as payment for transactions. Though the form of currency has evolved over time—from shells to gold to coin, cash, and checks—the rules and processes surrounding it have remained largely the same. Typically, currency is issued by a central government that retains a monopoly over its creation and backs it with fractional reserves of gold, precious metals, or other countries' currencies. Even when the currency is not directly backed by a tangible asset, the government's management of its supply creates a value based on confidence (that the government will always accept it as a store of value) and scarcity (that there is never quite enough to go around).

In contrast to the rules of property, which must change to meet the demands of electronic commerce, these existing rules of money could probably function quite well as a means of conducting electronic exchange. Even in cyberspace, consumers can order goods priced in dollars (or yen or marks), charge them to a credit card, and let banks intermediate the financial transaction. Nothing intrinsic to electronic commerce forces the existing means of exchange to adapt. There are no technical obstacles to routing and recording even nontraditional transactions through this well-established route, no new demand for financial oversight or regulation.

Instead, the source of change lies with the vast financial opportunities that electronic commerce appears to present. Specifically, it lies with the instantaneous and nonphysical nature of electronic transactions. If electronic purchases become commonplace, they will probably include such minute transactions, dubbed "micropurchases," as buying an article from the *Atlantic Monthly* or browsing through three minutes of the *New York Times*. The cost of processing such services through the traditional route would overwhelm the price of the service itself; for small on-line entrepreneurs, cost could even doom the business from the start. But if payment could occur electronically and instantly, then the cost of transacting would plummet, allowing commercial activity to flourish on-line. As an added benefit, electronic exchange potentially could function like cash, allowing both buyer and seller to maintain anonymity. With a wallet full of "e-cash," buyers could browse quickly and anonymously in cyberspace. Without needing to rely on credit cards, bank tellers, and checkbooks, they could save both time and money. This is many observers' seductive vision of Internet commerce—fast, cheap, and completely anonymous.

Technologically, the creation of electronic money rests with the issuance of an anonymous electronic note. An institution sells electronic money to its customers, coding the e-cash onto a wallet-size card or transmitting it directly to another on-line merchant. It debits the amount of the e-money, plus a small transaction fee, from the customer's old-fashioned account. Three aspects of this process are critical: (1) that electronic transfers remain anonymous; (2) that they remain secure; and (3) that transaction fees remain minimal. In the past, similar requirements were met by agencies of a central government. Governments printed the currency, allowed it to circulate anonymously, punished those who stole or copied it, and covered their expenses through taxes. On the Internet, however, no central authority establishes the means of exchange. National governments have shown little interest, because e-cash raises troubling questions for them and their law enforcement agencies. How, for instance, will e-cash expand the possibilities of tax evasion and money laundering? And how will governments track the assets of individuals or the trading balances of states? If e-cash proliferates, it is liable to allow many aspects of economic activity to escape the scrutiny of government agencies. With these issues looming, government agencies have little incentive to play any role in the creation of e-cash.

For private firms, however, the incentives are great. First, there is the simple cost-cutting potential of electronic payment. Many firms, and particularly banks, have a considerable interest in cutting the costs of intermediate transactions and moving directly to electronic payment systems. Several institutions, such as Citibank and Wells Fargo, already employ proprietary software systems that allow customers to do their banking on-line. As banks and other financial systems increasingly compete in new and fluid ways, such payment systems could well become critical to their success.

The real prize, though, will probably come from pushing electronic payment out of proprietary networks and into the broader reaches of cyberspace. Eventually, the value of e-cash, like the value of any currency, will be determined by the market's demand for it. To increase demand, the currency must be widely accepted. In the past, governments ensured acceptance simply by proclaiming their currency "legal tender." In the future, the game may become significantly more competitive. Firms that establish the most accessible and secure means of exchange will capture the market of all those seeking to conduct electronic transactions beyond internal borders. Success in this game will breed further success, because the acceptability of a currency increases its attractiveness to other users.

Accordingly, the race to develop the means of electronic exchange has already become one of the most spirited competitions in cyberspace. Much of this race is about technology, and winning will entail the refinement of encryption algorithms and secure "electronic wallets." But because technology alone cannot support a full-fledged system of electronic exchange, the race is also about rules. If payment systems are ever to proliferate along the Internet, they will probably require a trusted entity to oversee and regulate their use. The issue—much broader than the widely publicized threat of credit card theft—is the confidence with which any major financial institution can hope to approach the Internet. Many such institutions already engage in electronic commerce, moving vast sums of money through their own internal networks or via external proprietary networks such as SWIFT (the Society for Worldwide Interbank Financial Telecommunication). But performing these transactions in a closed and controlled network is very different from allowing them to occur across the conspicuously public spaces of the Internet. If such firms are to move onto the broader reaches of the Net, they will need some means of recourse. They will need, at a minimum, to know that some identifiable and credible entity is backing the value of their money and preventing widespread fraud and abuse. Historically, these tasks have fallen to governments. On the Internet, private firms might well find themselves performing equivalent functions, creating and maintaining the rules of electronic exchange. In the process, they are likely to stumble on a third critical area of rules: rules of security and enforcement.

Security and Enforcement

Rules of security and enforcement are, to a large extent, the crux of the matter for Internet commerce, and perhaps even for the broader reach of Internet communication. Yet rules are only as good as the capacity to enforce them. Without enforcement, rules are meaningless—words or notions without either compliance or commitment.

In cyberspace, rules of enforcement will be particularly important for the maintenance of property rights and the establishment of the means of exchange. For property rights to function on-line, the rights must not only be clear but also secured and enforced: Knowing that the information (software, book, financial data) is legally yours does no good if others can easily access it and use it without fear of punishment. Similarly, the entire concept of electronic payment rests with the ability to make these payments secure: to guarantee that no one can steal or counterfeit electronic cash and that any possible perpetrators will be traced, apprehended, and punished.

Ensuring the security of property and transactions is an age-old problem, one that has generally been solved by the coercive powers of an outside authority. Often coercion issues from the state: Modern governments, for instance, consistently retain the power to punish and imprison those who steal others' property or counterfeit currency. In other instances, coercion comes from private forces. The Sicilian Mafia and the Cali cocaine cartel, for example, both employ extensive private security forces to ensure that the intricate rules of their games are upheld. In still other cases, property rights are upheld by embedded community norms, such as those of an Israeli kibbutz. In all of these cases, some entity ultimately determines whether the rules have been broken and how the perpetrator should be punished. Despite their obvious differences, the modern state, the Mafia, and the kibbutz all share certain key characteristics: They are governed by an accepted set of rules and norms, and they have the means and the authority to enforce the rules of their realms.

The Internet, as said earlier, has no central authority. As information travels along the complex network of networks, it passes through many different computers and sorters, with separate packets potentially crossing various international borders. This far-flung and unpredictable architecture, which is precisely what makes the Internet such a powerful and impervious medium, also turns enforcement of any sort into a particularly thorny problem. The open structure of the system means, inherently, that there is no central point of control—there is, to put it colloquially, "no *there* there."

This architectural resistance to authority poses no problem for many of the Internet's uses and users. Indeed, for many functions—anonymous chatting, cross-border advertising, "underground" information—it is a tremendous, really unprecedented boost. For commercial users, though, the lack of control is more problematic, particularly with regard to issues of property rights and the means of exchange. Before firms transfer large chunks of their valuable information on-line, and before they employ novel systems for electronic payment, they will need some guarantee that their property and their payment will be safe in cyberspace. But the decentralized structure of the Internet makes such guarantees difficult to offer or enforce. No policing agency controls the multiple point of access, and no government has defined precisely what constitutes theft or how an anonymous "thief" could be traced, identified, or apprehended on-line. Even if governments were to define precisely the rules of cyberspace, and even if they somehow managed to establish the means of catching cyber-criminals, on-line enforcement would still be plagued by the overwhelming issue of national borders. In cyberspace, information can cross borders instantly and imperceptibly, but laws, and their enforcement, remain creatures of the tangible realm, attached to the territory from whence they are issued. As a result, the prospects for on-line enforcement remain uncertain.

Conclusions

As stated at the outset, this paper is about rules. Beginning with the assumption that rules matter, I have tried to describe the extent to which the absence of rules may hinder the development of commerce on the Internet and the kinds of rules that need to emerge before commerce can reach its full on-line potential.

The topics of "rules" and "Internet" may strike some, initially, as unrelated. Because the Internet developed as an open and free-wheeling community, it has grown to pride itself on its very lack of rules and absence of authority. But, as I have suggested, there actually were rules, very strong and well-developed rules, in the early days of the Internet. And there will have to be new rules developed and enforced as the Net evolves to incorporate a new and very different base of users.

So long as rules are seen in their broadest sense, including norms and practices as well as formal laws, most observers would probably agree (even begrudgingly) that rules of some sort are necessary in cyberspace, and that enforcement mechanisms of some sort must also accompany them. Where disagreement lies is over the content of the rules and, especially, the nature and identity of the enforcer.

This last section offers a brief description of a range of possibilities for ruling the Net. My aim is not to not to suggest which one is most likely, or even most desirable. Rather, I want only to explore what the range of options looks like, what advantages and disadvantages each contains, and how a movement toward any one of them would affect the subsequent evolution of the Internet.

The first possibility is that Internet users will continue to eschew any type of formal rules or government-sanctioned authority in cyberspace. This appears to be the outcome predicted and desired by groups such as the Electronic Frontier Foundation, which argue that "governments of the Industrial World . . . are not welcome among us [and] have no sovereignty where we gather."[24] If this view prevails, and if centralized authorities are effectively banished from cyberspace, the Internet of the future may resemble in some ways the Internet of the recent past. It will be primarily a medium for the free flow of information, a channel for open and anonymous communication, and a realm in which a handful of informal rules emerge slowly, piecemeal, and without any real penalty for their violation. Insofar as information is generally regarded as a public good, the Internet will not be a realm particularly well-suited to commerce—which to those espousing this view may not be a bad outcome.

A second and very different possibility is that the cross-national structure of the Internet will eventually demand an international system of regulation and enforcement. This view is popular with many international civil servants already working to develop a suitable framework for ruling the Internet. In the spring of 1996, for instance, the Geneva-based World Intellectual Property Organization (WIPO) completed a draft treaty for a series of amendments to the Berne convention that aims to expand international copyright convention to include electronic transmissions. As with most international agreements, the WIPO treaty suggests a delicate balance between international and national governments. An international body would act to develop and arbitrate a set of global rules, while actual enforcement of the rules would remain in the hands of national governments. As expressed by its supporters, this approach to cyberspace has many advantages. It makes the rules explicit, applies them across the breadth of the Internet, and taps an appropriate enforcer. As with most international agreements, however, effectiveness depends on the commitment of its members. If users around the world disregard the treaty's provisions, or if governments fail to enforce them, WIPO, or any other international organization, can do little in its defense.

Accordingly, many national governments have recently moved to strengthen their own controls over cyberspace. In 1996, the U.S. government passed the contested Communications Decency Act; Germany upheld its decision to prosecute the U.S.-based company CompuServe for the transmission of pornographic materials; and China made clear its desire to establish a closed and patrolled national service called Intranet. Although none of these measures deals directly with the commercial uses discussed here, they nevertheless describe a model that could be applied to property rights and means of exchange. The model is an obvious one, even a fairly common one. As technology creates new means of interaction, governments step in to rule and regulate these areas of interaction, using their traditional powers of coercion to ensure that the rules are upheld. Even in the age of cyberspace, this model is compelling. It is clear, it is transparent, and it fits well with the expectations and sensibilities of most citizens—especially those who might bristle at the thought of either cyberanarchy or international regulation.

Yet, as stressed throughout this discussion, the traditional model of government-as-enforcer does not readily translate to cyberspace. Detecting violations, tracing violators, and dealing with crimes that can cross borders all are problems that defy easy solutions. In addition, the most far-reaching attempts to rule and police cyberspace have been greeted, at least in the United States, with nearly complete derision. The Communications Decency Act has been criticized not only as unconstitutional but also as unenforceable. The Clipper chip—a 1993 proposal of the National Security Agency (NSA) that would have enabled the government to eavesdrop on all electronic transmissions—was denounced by those who saw it as an unconstitutional invasion of privacy. Thus, although national governments remain, potentially at least, the obvious source for the creation and enforcement of on-line rules, any steps toward increasing government's power in this sphere are bound to be fraught with both political and technological barriers.

Which brings me to the fourth and final possibility for on-line enforcement. This is the possibility that firms, rather than governments, will begin to establish the rules of cyberspace. Recall that firms have perhaps the most to gain from going on-line. Yet before they make this leap en masse, firms will need to have in place the basic rules of the game: rules of property, security of exchange, and means of enforcement. If neither national nor international governments are well positioned to make and enforce these rules, then business entities might begin to fill the vacuum.

Already, evidence suggests that such a movement is underway. Rather than lobbying governments to create and support the rules of Internet commerce, firms such as Microsoft, America Online, and Open Market are effectively writing the rules themselves. Specifically, they are using both technology and organizational structure to support enforceable systems of property rights and secure exchange.

To a large extent, these firms are relying on technology to provide the security that commerce demands and governments cannot yet provide. Two approaches in particular are generating considerable interest: encryption and firewalls. With advanced encryption systems, firms can protect both property and exchange. They can guarantee that information and payment are genuine and that they are received only by a certain user, or group of users. With firewalls, firms can physically enclose their corner of the Internet, restricting access to their commercial interactions and, as necessary, to their intellectual property.

These technologies become potentially even more powerful when coupled with a business model that creates, in effect, an enforcer. Already, early forms of enforcement exist in on-line service providers such as America Online and CompuServe. Even though these providers thus far have limited themselves only to minimal services (access and navigation), they could easily move to the much higher value-added services associated with rules and rulemaking. They could, for instance, provide access only to certain groups, or cluster their users into communities linked by similar interests or needs. Armed with the appropriate tracking and billing technologies, service providers could potentially perform the crucial functions of intermediation and enforcement. They could track their users, bill them, and pay their content providers. They could also guarantee both users and providers that violations of the rules would be punished, probably by expulsion from the service provider's community. In effect, these firms could create and enforce the rules of commerce in their own orderly and well-defined corners of cyberspace.

In many ways, this last possibility is the most attractive to proponents of Internet commerce. If firms can establish and support commercial communities, then they can have the orderly and rule-bound commerce that many desire without the governmental involvement that many fear. Yet, as with the other possibilities for ruling the Net, this one has its obstacles and drawbacks. It allows for the firms that write the rules to become exceedingly powerful and to control vast amounts of data. It also pushes these firms into the potentially uncomfortable position of enforcer. Most seriously, the scenario described by private rulemaking—one of walls and guards and tracked purposes—is the precise opposite of the open market and universal access that have characterized the Internet to date. It is also apparently at odds with the free-flowing democracy that mass electronic communication is often thought to foster. Insofar as private firms develop and enforce the rules of Internet commerce, they may simultaneously constrain, or at least restrict, the options for open and noncommercial interaction.

For the purposes of this paper, I will not be so foolhardy as to suggest which of these four possibilities represents the most viable path for the evolution of on-line rules.[25] My point instead is to suggest that rules will matter greatly in cyberspace. Each of the paths I have described carries its own set of costs and benefits, winners and losers. Each would shape the subsequent evolution of the Internet in a different way and establish different balances of power among society's competing groups. They will define what the game is about and who gets to play it. Real power will reside with the marshals of the new frontier—not those with the fanciest wizardry or the hottest site, but those who rule the Net.

Notes

1. "Wire Pirates," *Scientific American* 270, 3 (March 1994), 90.

2. The NSF's acceptable-use policy statement read in part: "NSFNET Backbone Services are provided to support open-research and education in and among U.S. research and instructional institutions, plus research arms of for-profit firms when engaged in open scholarly communication and research. *Use for other purposes is not acceptable.*" Cited in Michael Sullivan Trainor, *Detour: The Truth About the Information Superhighway* (San Mateo, Calif.: IDG Books, 1995), 175. (Emphasis added.)

3. Philip Einer-DeWitt, "Welcome to Cyberspace: What Is It? Where Is It? And How Do We Get There?" *Time* 145, 12 (Spring 1995), Special Issue, "Welcome to Cyberspace," 4; Sullivan-Trainor, 175.

4. In 1994, for example, three of the leading U.S. computer manufacturers—Sun Microsystems, Silicon Graphics, and Digital—estimated that between 70 and 90 percent of their customers already had access to e-mail over the Internet. See Lisa Thorell, "Doing Business on the Internet. Case Studies: DEC, Silicon Graphics, and Sun," *Internet World* 5, 5 (July–August 1994), 53.

5. Ibid.

6. Product distribution costs alone (disk duplication, diskettes, manuals, and shipping costs) typically account for 20 percent of a software firm's costs. For more on the possibilities of on-line distribution, see George Lawton, "Software Distribution Through the Internet," *Software Magazine* 3 (March 1995), 29.

7. Notes from personal interview by Jeffrey Bussgang, Jan. 31, 1995, p. 19.

8. Quoted from *HotWired*'s "welcome" message to subscribers (April 1995).

9. "Open Market," Harvard Business School Case N9-195-205.

10. This can be represented more formally as the familiar observation that cooperation is more easily achieved when interaction is iterated over time.

11. Jared Sandberg, "Computer Experts See Hackers Gaining an Upper Hand in Fight Over Security," *Wall Street Journal*, Jan. 24, 1995, B-4.

12. A "FAQ" (frequently asked question) file contains answers to questions that many people ask when first joining a discussion. FAQs exist to prevent on-line discussions from bogging down by repeated introduction of the same topics. "Flame," both a verb and a noun, refers to the extremely harsh criticism (generally too harsh for real life) to which Internetters often subject one another. "Spam," also a verb and a noun, refers to unsolicited e-mail inappropriately flooding mailboxes.

13. Marxists, of course, would insist that the communal state represents the natural and desirable condition of economic organization. With a handful of exceptions, though, it is exceedingly difficult in the 1990s to find evidence of the long-term viability of an economic system based on communal rights.

14. The argument of this section draws extensively on the work and writings of Douglass C. North. See, in particular, North, *Structure and Change in Economic History* (N.Y.: W.W. Norton & Company, 1981); and North and Robert P. Thomas, *The Rise of the Western World: A New Economic History* (Cambridge: Cambridge University Press, 1973).

15. In this context, it is interesting to note that at every major junction in the evolution of capitalism, the transformation of commerce has coincided with and been facilitated by a change in the structure of property rights and the incentives they create. Hunters and gatherers became farmers once they developed the means to protect "their" lands; feudal lords turned to commerce once they were allowed to own and

bequeath property; and oceanic exploration flourished once the kings of Europe offered bounties for discovery and cleared the seas of pirates. Where property rights fail to develop, economic growth stagnates, as is the case in the less-developed world. Insufficient property rights can also explain the demise of Soviet-style commerce, where property rights were clear (all in the hands of "the people") but did not establish the incentives necessary to fuel economic growth. What allowed the system to grow, by contrast, was a rigid structure of state-controlled disincentives (coercion). Once the coercive apparatus declined, so too did any substantial economic activity.

16. Anne Wells Branscomb, *Who Owns Information? From Privacy to Public Access* (N.Y.: Basic Books, 1994), 6.

17. See Otis Port, "Halting Highway Robbery on the Internet," *Businessweek* (Oct. 17, 1994), 212; and Max Frankel, "Cyberights," *The New York Times Magazine*, Feb. 12, 1995, 26.

18. Ralph Blumenthal, "Thieves in the Idea Marketplace," *The New York Times*, Feb. 11, 1995, 1–13.

19. Copyright Act of 1976, as cited in Dorothy E. Denning and Herbert S. Lin, *Rights and Responsibilities of Participants in Networked Communities* (Washington, D.C.: National Research Council, National Academy Press, 1994), 87. (Emphasis added.)

20. Quoted in "Writing Copyright Law for an Information Age," *The New York Times*, July 7, 1994, D-4.

21. Nicholas Negroponte, "A Bill of Writers," *Wired* (May 1995), 224.

22. Quoted in "The Economy of Ideas," *Wired* (March 1994), 88.

23. Peter Huber, quoted in Paul Andrews, "Cyber-Thinkers Ask Government to Stay Off the Digital Highway," *Seattle Times*, 23 Aug. 1995, A3 [NEXIS].

24. John Perry Barlow, "A Declaration of the Independence of Cyberspace," quoted in Catherine Yang, "Law Creeps onto the Lawless Net," *Businessweek* (May 6, 1996), 58.

25. I have been foolhardy elsewhere, however. See Spar and Jeffrey J. Bussgang, "Ruling the Net," *Harvard Business Review* (May–June 1996); see also Spar and Bussgang, "Ruling Commerce in the Networld," *Journal of Computer-Mediated Communication* 2, 1, a special issue on "Emerging Law on the Electronic Frontier," edited by Anne Wells Branscomb, Harvard University Program on Information Resources Policy (June 1996) [on-line].

21   Political Gridlock on the Information Highway

W. Russell Neuman, Lee McKnight, and Richard J. Solomon

In this chapter we present a long-term view of the evolution of information and communications technologies and services and draw from this what we hope is an elegantly simple conclusion: that the time has come for an Open Communications Infrastructure (OCI). OCI promises to break the political gridlock surrounding information and communications technologies and speed us along on the information highway, toward the information-intensive society of the 21st century.

The Clash of the Titans

Historical Precedent in Economic Conflict

Economic historians may counsel less scholarly enthusiasm and more realism for the continual process of economic change. Large-scale economic turf wars, they are prone to point out, are in more than ample supply. In American history the festering tensions between the industrial North and the agricultural South in the 19th century culminated in the Civil War, which was as much about agricultural economic independence as about slavery (Walton, 1994). Following the Civil War, the expansion West was marked by a battle between two agricultural sectors—the cattle ranchers versus the farmers (Degler, 1967), the narrative engine of more than a few Western motion pictures. In the 1890s the battle lines shifted to the forces of gold versus the forces of silver culminating in the election of 1896 (Friedman, 1963).

The 19th century witnessed technological change in the nature of networks with the transition from roads and canals to railroads. After the turn of the century, technological change continued, from railroads to motorized trucking and ultimately air transport. In communications there was the introduction of the telegraph and fifty years later the transition from telegraph to telephone. These developments brought into being what we have come to know as the era of the Robber Barons. The railroads were the first large-scale exemplar of corporate capitalism. The centralized economic power of these new corporate entities was unprecedented. The capacity of the government to respond to abuse and exercise legislative oversight followed a predictable lag of several decades. Significant legislation affecting the nature of networks includes the Interstate Commerce Commission of 1888, the Sherman Anti-Trust Act of 1890 and the Clayton Act of 1914.

In the 1990s, we are experiencing a pace of technical change like that for communications and transportation in the middle to late 19th century. The wild era of post-Civil War political economy rewarded aggressive and quick-witted economic entrepreneurship. This predictably led to abuses through a period of economic restructuring. Federal authorities only belatedly recognized the dramatic character of change, and still more slowly responded to the resulting political and economic distortions. We expect that drama to play again in the 1990s and the 21st century. Same play. New characters. Modern dress.

In the following sections we develop this argument, and propose an historically self-conscious approach for appropriate, balanced and realistic public policy for Open Communications Infrastructure. But first, the players and the play should be formally introduced.

The Players

The would-be Robber Barons of the 1990s have considerable financial resources with which to expand and protect their empires. Table 21.1 sketches the rough outlines of the industrial sectors as they stand now on the eve of convergence. The core industries represent about $500 billion a year in gross revenues in the United States alone. As two-way electronics allows penetration into the neighboring turf of retailing and information services, the estimate is conservatively doubled to about one trillion dollars a year, roughly 20% of the American gross domestic product. The other 80% of the economy is directly affected by the technical and market changes in information and communications systems, as we see, for example, when manufacturers turn to information technology in their effort to engineer new efficiencies into their manufacturing cycles. It is not difficult to see why corporate boards, CEOs and strategic plan-

Table 21.1 Converging industrial sectors of the information economy: Revenues pre-convergence (1993)

Industrial sector Industry	(in billions)	
Publishing	$124	
Newspapers		45
Magazines		22
Books		18
Direct mail		27
Information services		12
Broadcasting	63	
Radio		10
TV		29
Cable		25
Satellite		1
Telecommunications	134	
Local		83
Long distance		51
Computers and data networks	53	
Hardware		28
Software		20
Data networks		5
Theatrical motion pictures		5
Consumer electronics		20

Source: Weller and Hingorani, 1994

ners are attracted to the idea of having a significant portion of this enormous pie become their proprietary electronic real estate.

The Playing Field

There is a significant difference between the era of Gould, Morgan and Carnegie and the present day. For most of the 1800s there was no federal regulatory tradition, which had yet to be invented. Now there is not only a tradition but many turf-conscious bureaucracies and a fully elaborated ideology of government oversight for most of the far-flung communications industries. It may prove easier to invent new public policy instruments than to reinvent or redirect existing ones.

In the current policy debate, one frequently hears a plea for a level playing field. All we want, telephone, cable or publishing executives are wont to claim, is to tip the playing field back to level, to correct the imbalance which currently favors the other guy. There are several problems with such a metaphor. First, there are dozens of industrial sectors involved in this political struggle. It is hard to imagine a field tipped in twelve directions at once. Second, the appearance of the direction of the tip depends on where you stand. As with the grass on the other side of the fence, each player eyes the turf of the competitors with special anxiety. It is not just self-serving cynicism; the combatants come to view these inequities with both considerable emotion and sincerity.

Perhaps a better metaphor is the Ptolemaic model of heavenly motion. As human measurement of the movement of the sun, the planets and the stars improved, medieval astronomers stuck to their geocentric model, of course, but invented little subtheories to explain the anomalies. They observed brief periods of retrograde motion and posited that planets moved not in a given orbit but in a tiny sub-orbit around an invisible object in the original orbit. After a while there were orbits around orbits around orbits—an unbelievably unwieldy and unlikely contraption. An astute astronomer might have sensed that the time was right for a paradigm shift.

Ultimately, of course, the heliocentric model of planetary motion resolved the problem and reintroduced a model of striking and refreshing scientific simplicity. In the pages ahead we will make such an argument with regard to the current state of telecommunication regulation and the need for creating an Open Communications Policy as a new paradigm.

For our current purposes, however, we want only to demonstrate the Ptolmeic character of the current system. After a century of laws written to regulate grain elevators and railroads which were edited to incorporate telegraphy, telephony, radio, television, satellites and computers, each embellished by a litigious century of accumulating case law, we have an awkwardly uneven playing field of Ptolemaic complexity—a playing field only a lawyer could love.

The accumulated inequities of the playing field are easy to demonstrate. Table 21.2 illustrates several examples of the current array of regulatory distinctions ranging from subsidy to a variety of circumscriptions. These regulatory distinctions for the most part reflect the logic of the moment when these industries first emerged as identifiable business sectors. The earliest was the post office. It

Table 21.2 Regulatory models of information industries: Government provision, subsidy, rate, and content Regulation

	Provision	Subsidy	Rate reg	Content reg
Publishing				
Newspapers	×			
Magazines	×			
Books		×		
Recorded music		×		
Motion Pictures				
Broadcasting				
Radio		×		×
Television	×			×
Cable			×	
Satellite				
Advertising				
Media				
Promotion				
Direct Mail		×		
Information services				
Consumer electronics				
Postal services		×		
Telecommunication			×	
Computation				
Hardware				
Software				

made sense for the government to both provide service and to encourage the free flow of information and a national sense of community in spite of physical isolation across a sparsely populated continent, by subsidizing the conveyance of newspapers, books and magazines. The early days of newspapers were marked by robust competition with over a dozen dailies available in many larger cities. No need for regulation in such a market, indeed the political tradition of the independence of the fourth estate and the First Amendment itself would seem to preclude it.

Broadcasting is rate-regulated with provisions guaranteeing lowest possible advertising rates for political ads; and content-regulated through the prohibition of "offensive" content and requirements for children's programming. The regulation of radio and television broadcasting content was based on the "public trustee" principle. The rationale was that since the public airwaves were provided to competing commercial broadcasters without charge, although there was no need to regulate profits among competing broadcasters, there was nevertheless a public trustee obligation to abide by publicly determined content guidelines. Broadcasters who violate the content rules can be reprimanded, fined and ultimately have their right to broadcast revoked.

Cable television systems were originally not regulated at all at the federal level because they do not use the radio spectrum. As their market penetration and economic importance rose in the 1960s, at the behest of the broadcasting industry, the Federal Communications Commission simply declared that cable was "ancillary" to broadcasting and thus subject to FCC regulation—a declaration of authority ultimately sustained by the courts (Kellog, Thorne, and Huber, 1992). Given that cable service, unlike broadcasting, requires access to utility poles, cable companies are subject to contractual and regulatory constraints from local and state authorities. This local authority, however, was severely restricted by the Cable Communications Act of 1984. Through the act the increasingly wealthy cable industry gained through the act so much power and independence from competition and rate regulation that the resultant rise in cable rates generated one of the most curious legislative turnabouts—the Cable Act of 1992 which attempted to roll back and reregulate cable rates. In this curious political history nobody got around to regulating cable's potentially offensive content. The logic was that broadcasting through the airwaves is somehow "invasive" and available to all without charge. Cablecasting requires the customer to proactively order and pay for the service and thus one can simply disconnect in the event of perceived offense.

Because telephone service was judged to be a natural monopoly, the government agreed in 1913 to forbid new competition against AT&T. In return AT&T accepted federal rate regulation as a guard against the prospect of monopolistic tariffs. With the tradition of common carriage, however, telephone carriers, unlike broadcasters, were not responsible for the content of what was carried over the system. This precludes the use of content-oriented regulation. The need for telephonic content regulation started to gain supports in the 1980s as commercial adult-oriented services sprang up, and both federal and local regulators decided to promulgate rules for restricted access to these kinds of services.

The absurdity of the current system can be illustrated by examining the possible regulatory constraints on a single message as it might pass through different media of mass communication. For example, established copyright laws work well with the established print model, but break down with electronic publishing. Computers can alter text in an electronic form through a simple computer program, but it is unclear if a computer is guilty of copyright infringement. Can a computer author copyrighted material? (Pool, 1983) It turns out that whether the message is transmitted electronically or in print, it matters a great deal to the courts and regulators. It may be of little consequence, however, to the sender or receiver, except for the regulatory impediments. Eliminating this uneven playing field, which distorts and inhibits communication, is a principal reason for adopting the Open Communications Infrastructure regulatory model.

The Rhetoric of Gridlock

We have witnessed an interesting transition in the rhetoric of competition among the communications industries over the last several decades. We identify three stages.

The first stage, spanning much of the first half of the twentieth century, might be characterized as one of sectoral independence. Each communications industry had its turf and the boundaries were clear-cut. There was some competition across sectors—for example among publishers, broadcasters and telephone yellow pages for advertising revenues—but the focus of competition was within each sector (magazines versus magazines, one radio station versus another). The measures of industrial success and failure were industry specific—Nielsen ratings, circulation figures, telephone penetration. The rhetoric was low-key, even polite.

The second stage emerged in the 1980s, reflecting a growing recognition of the prospects of meaningful cross-sectoral conflict and competition. It was also characterized by a rush to the barricades. The impulse was to protect sectoral boundary lines. One of the most intriguing was the standoff between the newspaper industry and the telephone industry. Newspapers derive 30% of their income from the sale of classified advertising and they recognized that the use of dial-up information services and computer bulletin boards threatened significant inroads into this income stream. The American Newspaper Publishers Association (now renamed the Newspaper Association of America) set up high-level committees to plot strategy and to lobby Congress for protection. Basically, they argued that if telephone companies were permitted in the information service business such a development would put newspapers out of business. Similarly, the Regional Bell Operating Companies (RBOCs) were to be kept out of long distance and manufacturing businesses, for fear of the consequences they would produce for their competitors. The politics was intense and the rhetoric zero-sum, but largely out of public view.

The third stage, the battle of survival, follows a shift of strategies by which the sectoral players acknowledged that there was going to be a technological shift and that an advanced electronic network would be built. But now each sector claims that they alone are qualified to build it. Each claims there is no need for the competitor's network. Each claims a better technological platform to get the job done, and each also claims the other will function as a monopolist. The telephone company, the cable company and the computer network company each imagine a single high-capacity network of the future connecting every firm and every household. It would be wasteful, they argue, to build more than one network. It is true, of course, that advanced technology permits virtually all of the services under discussion to be provided by a single network. The battle for survival is imagined to be over who will ultimately own this single, universal, high-capacity network, forcing all the others to do business on its turf. Because each of the major players dreams of owning this great engine of economic power, they are inclined to argue for the "special efficiencies" of the single-network model but warn of the evil intentions of the others.

Examples abound. AT&T Executive Vice President Robert Kavner gave a keynote address at the 1994 trade show of the consumer electronics industry. Stay away from the cable industry for the provision of interactive services, he warned. "They will act as gatekeepers restricting what goes into homes over the emerging information highway. Working with the cable industry is like picnicking with a tiger, you might enjoy the meal, but the tiger always eats last. The cable industry threatens the very existence of the consumer electronics industry because of cable's stranglehold control on the set top box" (Carlson, 1994). A month later the cable industry filed an FCC filing asking that Pacific Telesis (PacTel) be forbidden from offering advanced services on its proposed $16-billion high-speed video and data superhighways. Why? Because the construction would be unfairly subsidized by telephone customers paying higher phone bills. PacTel responded, "They are trying to use the regulatory process to impede competition in their marketplace, at the same time they are trying to get into our marketplace." "This is about survival," they added (Adelson, 1994).

The survival of many firms in many information industries is now threatened as market share, technology, service design and network architecture shift seemingly minute to minute. New cross-sectoral research standards, production, distribution and marketing alliances are announced daily, while others are renounced quietly. And the battle does not stop at the water's edge, but is instead fueled by global communication links.

The War's Second Front

Thus far we have characterized the clash of the titans primarily as a battle of domestic industrial groups seeking economic dominance. Still, we live in an age of increasingly interpenetrated national economies and multinational corporations. Goods, services and people cross international boundaries with increasing ease, speed and frequency. Regional economic integration in Europe and the Americas takes on new significance. The communications revolution is both one of the central causes of globalized economics and the central playing field on which economic competition among nations takes place. In the information age, if one nation or region manages to attain significant control of the electronic playing field, it will have achieved a remarkable competitive advantage. Such questions attract considerable attention in Europe, Asia and North America. Analysts in each region alternatively fantasize about the prospect of their own success in seizing dominance and fret over the dire possibility that others will.

American Freestyle vs. Coordinated Efforts in Japan and Europe

Concerns about the American communications infrastructure are deepened by the realization that extraordinarily well-financed coordinated plans for system enhancement are being undertaken in Europe and Asia. As early as 1972 the Japanese government circulated *The Information Society: A Year 2000 Japanese National Goal*. It outlined a stepwise plan of advanced techniques for manufacturing semiconductors, building national data networks and database technologies. In 1981 NTT put forward a plan for an Information Network System (INS). In 1984, the Ministry of International Trade and Industry (MITI) announced a complementary plan for advanced communications systems in model cities. In 1985, the New Telecommunications Law established a dramatic new process for deregulatory reform and system development. In 1987 the Private Sector Vitality Act provided additional tax preferences and interest-free loans for telecommunications infrastructure development and research projects.

These coordinated policies and their recent revisions are expected to result in a $250-billion dollar investment in Japanese infrastructural development. Many other projects have sought to improve Japanese competitiveness in related electronics industries such as semiconductors, and in some cases have succeeded.

The European situation is similar. In this case the seminal document is the French *Nora-Minc Report* of 1980 which called for massive enhancement of the French network, expansion of telephone penetration with the highest percentage of digital switching and the largest packet-switched network in the world. There were parallel projects in England and the establishment of a new independent government agency, OFTEL, whose mission is to promote advanced telecommunications development. In Germany the Witte Report *Restructuring of the Telecommunications System* was released in 1987; it was followed by the restructuring of the Bundespost and the opening of a number of markets to competition. Plans for privatization of Deutsche Telekom are progressing. By 1997, the most modern network in the world will be installed throughout the former East Germany, with the hope that this advanced information infrastructure will rapidly raise the living standards and quality of life in the region.

These national initiatives are coordinated with European Community (EC) efforts, including the European Strategic Programme for Research in Information Technology (ESPRIT), Advanced Communications Technologies and Services (ACTS, formerly known as Research in Advanced Communications in Europe, or RACE), and the Special Telecommunications Action for Regional Development (STAR) as well as with the industry-initiated Eureka program for advanced video technologies. These projects have yet to demonstrate their effectiveness in bringing new products to market. Nonetheless, European industry has been encouraged to serve an integrated European market through the harmonization of European standards and cross-border research-and-development collaboration.

American Policy Paralysis

How can American industry and citizens respond to these challenges? Should a partially revised law dating from the 1930s continue as the guiding policy statement for communications into the 1990s, given the policy paralysis we currently face? Is the Telecommunications Act of 1996 a sufficiently radical reform to move the United States beyond policy gridlock?

Stalemate at a New Level

As a worst-case scenario, we may find that the telcos, the broadcasters, the cable industry, the private radio and consumer electronics manufacturers, the computer companies and the publishers, although they all have their eyes on their neighbor's markets, opt to stick with what they know best and protect their cash flow, sunk costs and existing plant, and choose to challenge and undercut the deal of 1996. In the wake of the Telecommunications Act of 1996 litigiousness is rampant and ingenious new forms of legal foot-dragging are invented. Meanwhile, the administration and Capitol Hill continue to be paralyzed by intense cross-pressures.

Under this scenario, new technical standards committees proliferate as their function shifts from setting standards to preventing them. Each vendor continues to believe it can outmaneuver all the others into adopting its own proprietary technology as the accepted technical standard for interconnection, and to that end resists cooperative efforts. The FCC bows to industry pressure and attempts to conduct technical tests to pick the best technology on "objective technical criteria." The testing process is conducted and controlled by industry consortia because the FCC lacks funding. The tests take forever and the test results are ambiguous. Half of the vendors take the FCC to court to demonstrate that the tests are unfair. None of the tests has any relevance anyway, because by the time the testing is completed a new generation of technology has been developed.

In a less stark scenario, we may find that the 1996 act provides for a modest step forward and, despite the efforts of some industry stalwarts, the technology prevails. The local exchange companies lose their battle against bypass. Local television and radio broadcasters lose their local monopolies as satellite and terrestrial spectrum, coaxial, twisted pair and fiber wireline each come to offer equivalent services.

There are three problems with this version of the future. First, it significantly delays the development of an advanced intelligent network, with the attendant disadvantages to economic efficiency and productivity. Second, it builds an interoperable network out of pieces explicitly designed not to work that way, leading to inefficiencies and operational awkwardness. Third, and perhaps most important, policy gridlock threatens to hold American companies back from the cutting edge, and effectively abandons the field of integrated communications to Europe and Japan.

Does the United States have a game plan? Until the presidential executive order establishing the United States Advisory Council on the National Information Infrastructure (NII), industrial policy was indirectly set under the rubric of defense R&D (McKnight and Neuman, 1995). With the publication of *The National Information Infrastructure: Agenda for Action* by a Clinton administration task force, the United States did have some specific goals, among them: (1) prompt private-sector investment via tax and regulatory policy, (2) extend the "universal service" concept to ensure that information resources are available to all at affordable prices, (3) act as a catalyst to promote technological innovation and new applications, (4) promote seamless and interactive user-driven operation of the NII, (5) ensure information security and network reliability.

Together with the Telecommunications Act of 1996, the NII initiative should be a complete and effective game plan. But our concern is that the NII initiative retreated to the background as the Telecommunications Act threatens to result in more regulation, rather than less.

A Case Study in Political Economics

Political economy is the interdisciplinary study of the interaction of political and economic systems. Much of the work in this field focuses on how market failures of various sorts may require explicit intervention of the polity to protect the environment, provide a social welfare safety net, constrain monopolistic practices and the like. Or from the other direction, scholars may study how economic incentives and influences distort an otherwise open process of political decision making.

We put forward a strategic policy position we call Open Communications Infrastructure, the case for which, we feel, is forcefully made by the case study itself.

To put our position in perspective, we draw on the vocabulary of international relations, which organizes much of its scholarship over the last century around the polarities of idealism and realism. Very briefly summarized, the idealists emphasize the potential of extranational institutions and international law to promote international cooperation and reduce the likelihood of military means for resolving differences among nations. Realists, in contrast, a somewhat more cynical lot, argue that international conflict is fundamentally inevitable, and that a naive faith in well-intentioned diplomacy is likely to be counter-productive and may lead one to misperceive the motives and intentions of likely adversaries.

The industrial policy debate can be usefully understood through the lens of these polarities. Both the free marketeers and the industrial policy makers each have a mirror-image realist and idealist world view. Free marketeers have an unshakable faith in the mechanism of the marketplace to allocate resources efficiently. And they have an equally unshakable cynicism about the ability of government experts to pick winners and allocate resources. Industrial policy makers, on the other hand, see themselves as realists in their view of the marketplace. They view industrialists as astute profiteers who would distort the marketplace to maximize profit and restrict competition were they permitted. The job of government is to hold these players in check, and industrial policy advocates exhibit faith and enthusiasm about the ability of government agents to effectively perform that role.

We characterize ourselves as being close to the neorealists in outlook, deeply cynical students as a result of our study of this dramatic transformation of the communications industry and its roots in the last century and a half of government–industry interactions. However, we have little faith in either would-be regulators or would-be industrialists to lead us to the information highway promised land. Put bluntly, given the opportunity, both would screw it up.

Regulatory systems work best when the industrial and technological structure is stable, the inputs and outputs easily measured, and the public welfare goals are clearly identified. None of these properties is evident in our case.

Markets work best when competitive entry and exit is easy, competitive services are straightforwardly comparable, costs and prices are evident and comparable, scale and scope economies are limited, and buyer and seller have equivalent expertise. None of these properties is evident in our case.

Furthermore, the likely compromise of a half-regulated and half-competitive system of communications networks may actually be worse than either by itself. In our view these halfway proposals for reform threaten to build in the worst of both worlds, as the economic distortions of the regulatory process and the regulatory distortion of the competitive process diminish the effectiveness of both while dramatically slowing down the pace and incentives for technical progress. We use the term *halfway* to characterize these sorts of mixed proposals. Most of the proposals and analyses we have seen thus far appear to fall into the halfway trap. Halfway proposals by design only reach halfway to their conflicting goals. They are trying laboriously and mightily to untie the Gordian Knot one strand at a time. It will never work.

The policy gridlock must be cut dramatically by means of a clear and distinct policy initiative. Such an initiative posits that regulators are ill-equipped to micromanage such fast-moving technical developments. It posits as well that industrialists who for the most part have enjoyed a century and a half of near-monopolistic profitability will do everything they can to recapture and monopolize the new network structure. Some media executives seem to perceive it as something akin to a natural right, others perhaps simply as sound business practice. In any case a laissez-faire approach of leaving the transition to "market forces" alone is a recipe for disaster.

There is a role for proactive government involvement in managing the transition from a regulated to a truly competitive system, but it requires the policy makers to abandon the regulation of entry and exit, of prices, and of mandated services at the outset and to focus on nurturing and protecting meaningful competition.

Open Communications Infrastructure

Because this study draws together historical and economic analysis and the explicit advocacy of a policy position in the communications policy domain, it seems appropriate here at the outset to signal where we are headed. In the spirit of the communications field where virility is measured by the obscurity of one's acronyms, we feel compelled to develop an acronym which captures the character of our argument. In public presentations over the last several years we have come to rely on the phrase "Open Communications Infrastructure." "Open" captures the spirit of our call to move quickly away from a regulated common-carriage system to a competitive, privatized, interconnected system of systems. Our proposal would reflect a traditional and conservative slant if we went no further. But "infrastructure" emphasizes the public character of this evolving network and the need for close public scrutiny, proactive government involvement and safeguards for protection against market failure and the underallocation of resources for public goods. The term "communications" in the middle of our phrase, as its root meaning suggests, is the common element that by its nature links the otherwise disparate terms "open" and "infrastructure" together. The nature of the evolving technology in this domain, we argue, is best served by privatized and competitive provision, but the nature of communications, the commons, the agora, the public space is inherently and

Table 21.3 Five regulatory traditions

Paradigm	Public role	Private role
Public ownership	Ownership and management of monopoly system	Manufacturing only
Common carriage	Heavy regulation of entry, exit, tariff and management procedures	Ownership and management of monopoly system
Open communications infrastructure	Regulation focuses on maintenance of competition and spectrum allocation	Ownership and management of competitive system
Public trustee	Light regulation of procedure, initial regulation of entry	Ownership and management of quasi-competitive system
Laissez-faire	Minimal regulation of business practice	Ownership and management; level of competition not determined

inevitably public and, unlike the provision of cardboard boxes or canned peas, requires special attention. The conjuncture of these two domains in communications policy, we assert, requires a new approach.

Table 21.3 outlines four traditional models for regulation in the communications field arrayed from the most active to the least active role for government. In reviewing that array, it seems most appropriate to position OCI near the middle. Most of the world's nations saw fit to provide postal, telecommunications and broadcasting systems as government monopolies. The United States was one of the few nations with a private broadcasting system (less than 20% of the world's nations, most of them in Latin America, had private broadcasting systems until the 1970s). The United States was virtually alone in its choice for a private telecommunications system. As the pressures of technology and globalization exert pressure on nations to move toward private provision, one might imagine that the American experience and regulatory tradition would prove to be a comparative advantage. Not necessarily. It depends on whether the historical traditions of the Postal Telegraph and Telephone mindset or of the common carrier and public trustee mindset will be the most difficult to break through.

Common carriage, as we have noted, puts both federal and local government in the role as arbiter of rates, guarantor of universal service and general overseer of means and methods. It is a delicate and often frustrating mechanism for both parties—the regulators and the regulated. The system infrastructure is horrendously complex, and regulators are heavily dependent on information provided by the communications companies to determine rules and tariffs.

The public trustee model derives from the American experience in private broadcasting. The logic dictates that private vendors in limited competition can provide better service than a publicly managed system. However, since the spectrum is a public resource, in order to maintain their access to a public resource, broadcasters would need to demonstrate their responsiveness to the public "interest, convenience and necessity" at regular intervals. For much of the history of American radio and television broadcasting, station managers conducted pro forma audience surveys, filled out forms about news and public affairs programs, ran editorials, and kept technical logs as part of a sham process of oversight. Virtually no stations lost their licenses for failing to serve the public interest. A few lost licenses for illegal behavior and blatant disregard of technical regulations. But the public trustee tradition does provide a model for content regulation as regulators keep a close eye out for violations of decency, political access and right-of-reply regulations. It is a curious mix of legally limited competition, based on the presumption of spectrum scarcity, cyclical bureaucratic attention to content rules of varied vintage and a codified disregard for the underlying economics. Proponents of deregulation are unlikely to tout the Public Trustee concept as the model of the future, but it does offer a useful exemplar of the difficulty of an heterogeneous system by which regulators are charged with monitoring only a narrowly specified set of behaviors of an otherwise unregulated collection of oligopolists.

The laissez-faire model is the ideal to which all policy analysts might otherwise aspire, relying on the marketplace and open competition to hold down prices, spur innovation and maintain service quality. Were it only so easy. The problem, of course, is the diversity and perversity of market failures—anticompetitive collusion, incomplete market information, distorting transaction costs, and a variety of non-economic social and political goals underresourced by market allocation. These market failures become especially difficult to unravel, given the peculiar characteristics of networks, in particular, their positive network externalities, the critical importance of interfaces and their diversity of use.

Reminiscent of the Robber Baron era, we focus on the issue of anticompetitive collusion and put forward a new paradigm of regulation which sets as its goal the maintenance and protection of competition. We identify a series of private mechanisms to deal with incomplete market information and distorting transaction costs. We set aside the issue of other social goals as an issue best addressed as a matter common to all sectors and not limited to communications.

Perhaps our strongest case is our critique of the halfway evolution of partially regulated communications systems—the worst possible combination of unstructured quasi-random regulation and quasi-unregulated monopolists.

The central elements of the OCI model are:

1. *Open Architecture*   The future of the network is digital. Voice, text, data and images will be transported by electrons and photons in digital format. Some messages will require extensive bandwidth, others will not. All communications systems, spectrum-based or wireline-based, have the potential for two-way interconnectivity. Some applications such as broadcast-style video may be predominantly one-way, but there is no reason to design the architecture so that two-way communication is precluded (as is true in today's radio, television and cable delivery systems). At the heart of this approach is flexibility, or the design of a system that facilitates interconnection among different systems and services at present and as they develop over time. By emphasizing interconnectivity and interoperability, incentives in innovation shift from trying to protect licensing revenues by means of a proprietary technical communications standard or inherited spectrum allocation to the economies of scale in efficient manufacturing and service provision.

2. *Open Access*   The currently dominant model of communications economics is based on a presumption that limited spectrum and inefficiencies of the competitive provision of wireline communications services require legal barriers to competitive entry, and regulatory oversight of the legally designated monopolists. The premise is outmoded. The critical turning point has occurred first in voice telephony, and will occur in radio within two years and in video in a similar time frame. Ironically, we see the turning point first in Eastern Europe and the Third World, where the need for building telecommunications is most urgent. Wireless access to the local loop turns out, in many cases, to be fully competitive with wireline provision, but the use of wireless access to the network has other properties, especially in cellular and microcellular applications.

   The critical property, we argue, is the lack of steep economies of scale in service provision. To offer universal wireline service, from the outset, one must wire every street on every block. To offer cellular service one can start at small scale. For fewer customers, fewer cells are required. As service demand expands, the number of cells expands gradually and efficiently, without requiring additional bandwidth. Another property, of course, is mobility and the flexibility of personalized communication service. In this way, the promise of Open Communications Infrastructure is an unanticipated artifact of cellular and Personal Communications Network (PCN) technology. Wireless access to the local loop makes open competition in provision of local exchange service a meaningful prospect.

3. *Universal Access* The principal element of the Kingsbury Commitment in 1913 was a horse-trade. Vail was willing to put the entire AT&T network under the control of federal common carrier regulation in return for protection from further competition. However, part of the deal was Vail's commitment to deliver on universal service, with cost averaging, and for the most part, the system he built delivered as promised.

The deregulation of communications at this juncture raises fears that less privileged and more remote communities will be deprived of access. The fear is that competitive provision will lead to the decline of universal service. Critics, for example, point to the deregulation of airlines and the resultant changes in the cost and quantity of service to remote areas. However, it is at this point that the transportation–communications parallel breaks down. The economies of scale in providing airplanes and airports are still considerable (as many of us who have shared the services of a pilot and copilot with one or two other passengers in a small plane might attest.) Wireless works the other way. In fact, wireless is much more efficient than wireline for low-density applications in rural areas. Furthermore, direct satellite provision offers additional avenues for service extension and system redundancy. Universal access is a natural component of Open Communications Infrastructure.

4. *Flexible Access* An interconnected and interoperable network of telecommunications, broadcasting and electronic publishing breaks down a number of traditional distinctions. In OCI, one can make a call on the cable, send a fax over the radio and watch television from the telephone line. The format will be digital. The bandwidth will be adjusted according to the demands of the user and the character of the communications. A teenager may not require high speed and sophisticated data communications to manage her bank account, so the terminal can be simple and inexpensive, and the demand on the network small and economical. Viewers casual about

the quality of the picture and the release date of the movies they watch on TV can opt for the least expensive display, lower bandwidth provision and older movies on an advertising-supported "free" channel or lower-cost pay-per-view. Viewers who are video aficionados with the latest equipment may demand the most sophisticated high-bandwidth signal and recently released programming. Such distinctions need not be legislated: A truly competitive market will provide more diversity than the law could imagine. But the fundamental flexibility and interoperability in communications architecture is not an inevitable outgrowth of current market dynamics. The role of public policy in defining the nature of the market is critical.

The Telecommunications Act of 1996

There is no doubt that the Telecommunications Act of 1996 presents a landmark piece of legislation for the 21st century. Unfortunately, although the rhetoric is right, the rules are wrong. It regulates more than it deregulates. It delays and constrains competition rather than encouraging it. It is a landmark of micromangement. By accumulating each powerful lobby's request to tilt the playing field to its relative advantage, the act inadvertently introduces a new level of government interference in virtually all forms of electronic communication. It became, in the lingo of the Beltway, a classic Christmas tree—a bill to which each industry group attached its own self-serving ornament.

The act is intended to "provide for an orderly transition from regulated markets to competitive and deregulated telecommunications markets consistent with the public interest, convenience, and necessity." In reality that translates into inventing a whole new class of regulations to manage the transition to deregulation. The size of the bill alone gives away the real story—over one hundred pages of detailed prohibitions and regulations. The term deregulation appears twice. The term regulation (or cognate such as regulatory) 202 times. There are 353 specific references to the Federal Communications Commission, including 94 cases of the "Commission shall" and 30 cases of the "Commission may." There are 80 formal proceedings the Commission must initiate.

The rhetorical means of the act is laudable:

- To promote competition in provision of local telephone service.
- To promote competition in provision of long distance telephone service.
- To promote competition in provision of multichannel television service.

But the act's language sets up complex rules and timetables for setting up additional rules and procedures to guide and regulate the transition to those end states. This is, we argue, attempting to untie the knot one strand at a time.

The act consistently changes which rules apply depending on which actor is providing service. The very titles of the act reflect the different rules proposed for telephone, broadcast, cable, computer network, satellite and public utility providers. Broadcasters (may) get free spectrum for ancillary use (including telecommunications) but telephone companies are expected to bid at auction. The rules about obscene or indecent communications via computer network are different from broadcast, from cable and from telecommunications services. The VChip provisions apply to television but not video over the Internet.

The act requires the Commission to make numerous decisions about the existence or absence of effective competition, the fairness of prices, possible discrimination among vendors, possible cross-subsidy between different types of communications services, the technical viability of interoperability, the physical location of telecommunications switching facilities, the character of communications content, and the impact of regulation on market behavior.

Time and time again, the act substitutes political muscle for public interest in determining policy. Take for example the definition of effective competition for deregulation of cable television. Multichannel television competition from a telephone company counts as effective competition but the same service provided by satellite does not. Why? Well, if one counted competition from satellite broadcasting in the United States in 1996, virtually all markets would qualify as effectively competitive because of the existence of DirectTV and PrimeStar multichannel direct broadcast satellite service offerings.

The act introduces the idea of competition in local telecommunications with great grandeur, but local competition was already underway in a dozen states under a variety of local deregulatory experiments.

Will the public interest in universal service be adequately protected in the act? A complicated fund for providing competitive service for regions not likely to get competition (and hence, lower rates) is embodied. Just how, or who benefits from this, and what it does for those left out of the information revolution due to lack of money, lack of education or lack of interest is quite unclear. Assumptions that competition will lower costs without pushing margins to the razor edge were clearly behind the grand overview of the bills in the past several years, but a more compelling problem has arisen in the meantime: How does either the industry or the government finance future telecom infrastructure if carriage approaches zero cost as capacity approaches infinity, and markets for carrying bits contract due to new technologies rather than expand? This is not conventional wisdom for conventional economics. The act may be too much too late.

The questions at the moment are: 1) whether the deals struck will remain acceptable to a confused Congress and a perplexed administration during a particularly strident election year; 2) whether the large long distance firms (AT&T, MCI, Sprint) have sufficient market presence to withstand the assault from equally powerful new competitors without the albatross of obsolete plant as they enter the competitors' local market, which has a similar set of technical burdens. It is likely that a new, though perhaps not as comprehensive, bill may be crafted in the near future. If new deals cannot be struck among these companies, different arrangements will be proposed by a future administration and a different Congress. The sweet smell of success may turn sour quite quickly unless some miracle creating new markets, new jobs and new money appears rather rapidly.

The Clinton administration, in spite of its unhappiness with provisions with regard to cable television rate deregulation and purportedly with matters relating to universal service and attacks on freedom of speech, needed a bill to demonstrate its continued leadership in national and global information infrastructure development. It felt it had to confirm its ability to work effectively with the Republican leadership of the House and Senate on matters important to the business community. The long distance carriers, recognizing they had been outmaneuvered by the local telephone firms in gaining the confidence and support of key Republican Senators and Congresspersons, chose finally not to fight a battle which might lead to greater estrangement with the Republican leadership. Externalities, in the final denouement, carried the day; change was inevitable, and the mood was a bill passed either now or never. With the potential markets and technology curves equally confusing to all, whatever entrepreneurial spirit was emerging in a formerly wholly monopolistic, quite non-market-oriented set of industries took over and, working in unusual secrecy with the House-Senate conference committee (which finally limits lobbying opportunities to only the most connected players), reconciled a bill that even Clinton could not find enough political strength to veto, despite some clauses which were anathema the Democratic Party's long history.

The principal failure of the act is the clear lack of understanding shown of the real progress being made toward development of the National Information Infrastructure, through the incredibly rapid expansion of internetworked small and distributed computer processing—the Internet. The Internet's main feature—a "bug" to those who like things to be orderly and predictable—is that it is uncontrollable, even chaotic. Its novel and radical applications, evolving open protocols, growth of users and traffic, and, most important, its unpredictable change have become a global driving force for information infrastructure. It is both scary (as the Chinese government has demonstrated by its regressive laws) and exhilarating (as the stock market has indicated by multiples in the stratosphere for certain companies with marginal products and negative income flows).

For example, on the Internet:

- traffic can shift suddenly

- services can change suddenly

- new technology and potential de facto standards can be introduced by anyone, as long as they work

- the only effective governing body is the all-volunteer body of experts called the Internet Engineering Task Force, which deals with technical protocol design and maintenance

- a residual coordinating power remains with the U.S. Government, through R & D programs of the Department of Defense Advanced Research Projects Agency and the National Science Foundation—but both of these agencies are by nature averse to regulatory policymaking. Due to pressure from the formerly dominant computer and telecom firms, the federal government is easing out of one area after another related to the "governance" of the Internet. At the same time, the Federal Communications Commission and the Federal Trade Commission are increasingly questioning how their traditional regulatory activities are being affected by the growth of the Internet. Instead of direction being taken up by the old-line conventional firms, the past few years have shown even more chaos and more radically innovative ideas coming from small firms (becoming big firms overnight), such as Netscape, Newbridge, Sun, Cisco, Intel, Cascade and Microsoft. A decade ago, who would have predicted that such firms would dominate with power and ideas? What have AT&T, IBM, DEC contributed that shifted the path of information infrastructure in comparison with what the new giants on the block have done? From one cynical point of view, the old firms contributed the laid-off personnel that helped direct the new leading companies.

The lack of understanding in Congress and among the special-interest lobbying groups may be the biggest surprise of the early years of the next millennium.

The delay and equivocalness that will certainly emerge from certain lawsuits because of the act's contradictory provisions cannot be avoided in the U.S. political process. While older vested interests and the jobs they entail may realize they bought a devil's bargain, telecommunications lawyers and consultants are not threatened by the legislation in any way, and can look forward to a prosperous and fruitful future under any scenario.

The Law of Unintended Consequences

Another likely effect of the act is that it surely will have significant, recursive effects on technology, market development and policy practices: the Law of Unintended Consequences. In this, the recursive nature of digital computers themselves—that a stored-program device, as Alan Turing understood from the very beginning some 60 years ago, can define its own instructions, its own Cyberspace, so to speak—is a natural outgrowth of a chaotic system under no one's control.

It is unlikely that the technical, economic and policy distortions introduced by the Telecommunications Act of 1996 will inhibit the rapid development of the National and Global Information Infrastructure, but the realization of universal service and its social benefits for education and health care, to name a few areas, are unlikely to be either equitable or substantive without some major modifications in the near future. It certainly was not the intention of the bill's drafters to spread the new wealth, but the public has yet to be heard from. As with other concerted public movements in the past, ranging from the original pressures to regulate and rein in the railroads and telecom firms in the past century, to anti-monopoly actions in this century, and the very powerful, and more popular than ever grassroots movement for environmental protection and change, telecommunications is sure to be affected by the reaction of its customers to the new provisions. Unlike some other industries who labor and profit in quiet sectors, communications deals with everyone, all the time and in insidious ways. The actors cannot hide.

But aside from the potential unintended consequences of the act, there are the obvious embodied flaws: Parts of the act include unconstitutional, and to some, unconscionable abridgments of the freedom of speech, the press, religion and the right to petition the government for a redress of grievances. The history of the laws to protect speech (and it has been noted that the First Amendment is but a local ordinance in Cyberspace) indicates that courts in all democratic countries take a narrow view of government interference in such rights, because through bitter experience democratic citizenry do not trust their governments. Such lack of trust extends to the denizens of government bureaucracies themselves who know how much power can corrupt. Arguments about speech simply will not go away because of ill-conceived legislation. Indeed, since the act was passed, the level of "obscene" speech on the Net has probably increased as netizens feel compelled to challenge the act's restrictions.

One unintended consequence of the act is that the legal separation and traditional treatment of the printed press, broadcasting and telecommunications may have collapsed in a new framework that pretends to provide a consistent treatment for all media. This was the key point Ithiel de Sola Pool made in his landmark study, *Technologies of Freedom* (Pool 1983). As we noted, how does one categorize "multicasting" under the new law? Another unintended result: If the separate treatment of broadcasting and telecommunications no longer stands up to legal scrutiny, then if government intrusion into private communications between individuals and groups is to be sanctioned, the effects of the act may be either incredibly repressive, or if thrown out by the courts, a useless exercise.

In the Internet community, it is said that "the Internet treats censorship as a broken connection and works around it." It is important to understand that this is more than an allusion; the Internet Protocol (IP) does exactly that, and programming servers to extend the route around within Web software is trivial. Even a grade-school student can learn how. Perhaps another unintended consequence of the act is to raise the status of technical prodigies to political heroes. Who said government doesn't know how to incent educational goals and create new jobs?

The futile attempt in the Congress to pander to an ill-informed public about the real, but far from pervasive or intrusive, dangers of on-line pornography is one pertinent example of how far Congressional and press attention was removed from the critical question of whether the cross-sectoral deals struck in the act will really serve to "provide for an orderly transition from regulated markets to competitive and deregulated telecommunications markets consistent with the public interest, convenience, and necessity."

More appropriate than the provisions of the act for governing the requirements of an information-intensive society would be a new policy framework for an Open Communications Infrastructure. This new framework would make no regulatory distinction between wired and wireless networks or between content and conduit. Only such a unified policy framework is capable of supporting social and economic needs as well as sustaining technical development in the years to come. This act falls far short of this goal.

Conclusion

It is a perilous venture to write of future communications policy scenarios when the daily papers, politicians and lobbyists assure us that peace is at hand, that all issues will be resolved within days. We think not. For, as we have argued, neither the myopic advocates for incremental changes to the status quo nor the breathless futurists and cyberspace libertarians have adequate understanding of three words: Open Communications Infrastructure. One side would have us inch forward (or backward) on the information highway; the other would have us wander, lost in cyberspace without a map or any shared understanding of the rules of the road.

In putting forth the model of Open Communications Infrastructure as an American alternative, we feel we play to the strengths of American business and the American political tradition. We feel the choice is to wait hopefully for it to happen by itself, if it does happen, or to make it happen. The central goals are clear:

- Fully competitive provision of all local and national communications services.
- Lifting all distinctions between:
  - wireline and wireless communications services.
  - narrowband and broadband.
  - broadcast and switched communications services.
  - content and conduit.

The development of an intelligent and forward-looking American communications policy for the next century will require a great deal of further research and analysis. Our purpose here is to put a proposal on the table for further discussion. This chapter develops the case for a proactive approach to revitalizing the American communications infrastructure as forcefully as our resources and capacities permit. It is the product of independent academic research. It is not the final word, but is, we hope, the beginning of a debate.

References

Adelson, Andrea, 1994. "Cable Group Opposes Pactel Data Proposal." *New York Times.* February 10.

Carlson, Jim. 1994. "AT&T Executive Attacks Cable Industry as War Over Interactive TV Heats Up." *Wall Street Journal.* January 10.

Degler, Carl N. 1967. *The Age of the Economic Revolution, 1876–1900.* Glenview, IL: Scott Foresman.

Friedman, Milton, and Ann J. Schwartz. 1963. *A Monetary History of the United States.* Princeton: Princeton University Press.

Kellog, Michael K., John Thorne, and Peter Huber. 1992. *Federal Telecommunications Law.* Boston: Little Brown.

McKnight, Lee and W. Russell Neuman. 1995. "Technology Policy and National Information Infrastructure," in Drake, William, ed. *The New Information Infrastructure: Strategies for U.S. Policy.* New York: Twentieth Century Fund Press.

Pool, Ithiel de Sola. 1983. *Technologies of Freedom.* Cambridge: Harvard University Press.

Walton, Gary M., and Hugh Rockoff, 1994. *History of the American Economy.* Fort Worth, TX: Dryden.

Weller, Timothy N. and Seema R. Hingorani, 1994. "Information Superhighway: Putting the Pieces Together." Donaldson, Lufkin, and Jenrette.

22   Information Resources in the 21st Century

Benjamin M. Compaine and William H. Read

The phase "The Information Age" has become commonplace. Our political and business leaders use it in their speeches; scholars write about it in books, journals, and learned articles; there have even been *New Yorker* cartoons about it. One shows a moving van in front of suburban Midwestern home, with an excited homemaker telling her neighbor: "We're moving to California to be part of the Information Age."

For the fictitious homemaker in the cartoon, the Information Age started in the mid-1980s. And for each of us there was a personal beginning: Perhaps the day when the first computer-generated inventory report came in the interoffice mail, or we booked an airline trip through a computerized reservation system, or used an automatic teller machine. Among younger readers the beginning may well have been Pac Man or one of the other popular interactive electronic games.

Was the invention of the computer the beginning? Perhaps. Peter Drucker, the noted management theorist, has suggested that the new age began with the GI Bill, the landmark legislation that opened higher education to the masses. In this view, the new age is really about what Julian Simon called "The Ultimate Resource"—human intellect. Sociologist Daniel Bell embraced both views, arguing that an emerging information society was structured around both new technology and expanding knowledge resources. In his writings on "The Post-Industrial Society," Bell credited his Harvard colleague Anthony G. Oettinger with providing fundamental new insights regarding the new technology.

In the late 1960s, Tony Oettinger offered an almost heretical concept: Computing and communications, he said, are scientifically and technologically unified. While a few scientists at AT&T's Bell Labs or IBM's Watson Labs might have agreed, certainly the executives of their parent organizations would not. No, they would have contended, their individual businesses were rooted in distinct and separable technologies. Later, Oettinger offered another almost heretical insight: Convergent computer and communications technologies were destined to become versatile and abundant resources. To those who would listen (and back then, there were not many), Oettinger asserted that the consequences of his insights would be profound. He forecast that substantial industrial instability would follow, as industrial lines of demarcation blurred, entry barriers lowered, the power of suppliers eroded and that of consumers increased, and that the problems and opportunities brought on by these fundamental changes would have far-reaching economic and social effects.

This was the intellectual capital out of which the articles in this volume have come. While it is perhaps unfair to many others to anoint Oettinger as the "father of the information age," he was certainly there at its dawn. And the chapters of this book, reflecting either his own words or works more or less in the same spirit, attest to the accuracy of the basic insights Oettinger recognized at the beginning of the merger of computers and communications.

The remainder of this brief summary chapter is intended to review what has occurred in the information-technology arena since the early 1970s—not coincidently spanning the time of the activities of the Harvard Program on Information Resources Policy. Much of what has been covered can be categorized as providing support for three broad trends that the program articulated in the early 1970s:

- technological convergence;
- technological abundance and versatility;
- industrial and political realignments

Technological Convergence

When industrial leaders like Bell Labs' William Baker entered the telephone business, they did not even use the word *computer*, because there were none. And when computers did arrive, the phone companies found them useful for things like billing and payroll. Telephone engineers focused most of their attention on what is called "circuit switching," for without it a telephone network was not economically feasible. Switches allow for the sharing of circuit resources, and the more efficient the sharing the more affordable the network becomes to its users.

The first switches were operated by humans—telephone operators at a switchboard. Next came mechanical switches, which permitted direct dialing. And then electronic switches, which enabled new functionality in the network —things like speed dialing, call waiting, voice mail, and more. These so-called intelligent services were based on digital technology and data communication. The telephone switch had become a computer.

As all this was occurring in telephony, the computer industry, then led by IBM, was learning to link remote terminals to mainframes, and to build data networks, and ultimately networks of networks integrated with a standard "internet" protocol.

When one speaks of "voice over the Internet" or "frame relay data communication," one assumes the convergence of computing and communications technology. Indeed, there is even a trade magazine called *Computer Telephony*. Examples of convergence abound and their impact can be perceived as either ordinary or extraordinary depending on the individual.

For example, telephones on airplanes made their debut in 1984. At first there would be two or three phones in the front or back of the plane. For many travelers they were useful. But the quality was poor and connections were regularly broken in midstream. The technology was analog. And they were expensive to use.

A decade later there was generally a phone for each row of seats. In some cases one per seat. The technology was digital. The intelligent network allowed users to receive calls at their seats. The quality was equal to a good landline connection.

Is a high-quality connection from a plane moving at 480 nautical miles per hour at 31,000 feet remarkable? It depends on your perspective. For an eight-year-old calling her Dad from the plane, there is nothing remarkable about it. To her, calling from the plane is as natural and as simple as calling from home (or the car!): It's just the way it is. So is having the VCR or one hundred channels of television. For many young adolescents, there is no distinction between what is broadcast and what is cable, which are analog and which may be digital. They matter-of-factly get e-mail, or create reports with research material gathered from the Web and written in HTML using a word-processing program.

Convergence is all around us, but we don't always recognize it. Computer–communications convergence is a powerful force for change.

Technological Versatility and Abundance

Electrical engineers were traditionally taught about communications channels and how these channels, through wire or wireless, could—and should—be optimized for specialized purposes. Engineers wanted optimization, because the theory held that inefficiency would otherwise result. Thus, for example, AT&T (which not incidentally was once in the wireless radio broadcasting business) dedicated itself to building a nationwide wireline network optimized for telephony. RCA, the Radio Corporation of America, committed itself to optimizing a broadcasting network, as did others. That pattern of optimizing networks for a single purpose endured for a half-century, and great companies and industries emerged using this model.

With the advent of electronic technology, the possibility arose of using channels for more than one purpose—data under voice, for example. A keen observer of these new possibilities with an understanding of converging communications and electronic technology now understands that, in the 21st century, channels dedicated to single purposes are yielding to a multipurpose environment. Moreover, digital technology is, for most applications, superior to analog, and with it comes not just greater versatility but, like the "green revolution" in agriculture resources of the 20th century, the transformation of information resource scarcity to abundance. We already see substantial trends in this direction, whether in Moore's Law, seven-cent-a-minute long-distance telephone rates, or one hundred-channel cable-television systems combined with high-speed Internet access.

The implications of versatility and abundance can be summed up in one word, "options." For forty years, most television viewers had a choice of three or four networks and perhaps a handful of local, hard-to-tune-in, independent UHF stations. Cable and satellite, fiber optics and digital compression have given most households today the option to watch 60 to 200 channels. A critic may quibble with the quality of many: full-time shopping channels, constant reruns of black and white comedies from the 1960s, Hollywood films that never made it to the theater. But it also includes multiple all-news and public-affairs channels; networks catering to various ethnic and language groups; interests in science, learning, technology, comedy. There are channels catering to children ("free" with advertiser support or "pay" without advertising—more options). There are channels with all sports, all the time. Channels that try to cater to a female audience, to various religious perspectives and family values. There is something, it seems, for anyone to like—and to dislike. Video has become what we were used to with the magazine rack or the library.

The Internet, of course, is all about options. Read the local newspaper on paper or online? Listen to classic hits on the radio or from a Web site? Get the news from a traditional news service or from an alternative source? Call an associate or send e-mail? Fax from your fax machine or fax via a service on the Net? Watch the evening news or read it or listen to it from the Web? Watch TV to unwind tonight or "chat" on line with friends or with total strangers in a "chat room?"

Industrial and Political Realignments

In the political realm, the role of information technologies is growing. In the revolution of the mullahs that overthrew the Shah of Iran in 1979, the government controlled the broadcast facilities directly and the press indirectly. But the opposition forces headquartered in Paris used the modern direct-dial phone system the Shah had installed as part of his modernization policies, thus allowing them to bypass the communications controls other authoritarian regimes typically employed. They used cheap and easily duplicated audio cassettes to smuggle in and distribute their message to the masses. They used photocopying machines to bypass the controlled printing presses.[1]

During the uprising in Tiananmen Square in China in 1989, it was widely reported that the students used faxes to distribute their positions and events to the news media and to communicate with the expatriate Chinese community abroad. The latter, in turn, were able to monitor the live accounts from CNN in China that were not available locally and thus fax back news available in San Francisco, but not blocks away from where the demonstrators were located.

Now, the Internet has taken its place among the applications of information technologies. Here is how one report started:

As rebellions broke out across Indonesia ... protesters did not have tanks or guns. But they had a powerful tool that wasn't available during the country's previous uprisings: the Internet.

Bypassing the government-controlled television and radio stations, dissidents shared information about protests by e-mail, inundated news groups with stories of President Suharto's corruption, and used chat groups to exchange tips about resisting troops. In a country made up of thousands of islands, where phone calls are expensive, the electronic messages reached key organizers. "This was the first revolution using the Internet," said W. Scott Thompson, an associate professor of international politics at the Fletcher School of Law and Diplomacy at Tufts University.[2]

Information technology has played a substantial role in the formation and disaggregation of capital in the last decades of the twentieth century:

The rise and fall and rise of IBM;

the emergence of Microsoft and Intel;

not one, but two divestitures by what was once the world's largest tele-communications company, AT&T;

the failed proposed merger of MCI with British Telecom and MCI's merger deal with WorldCom;

the rise of MCI itself;

the failed alliance between US West and Time-Warner;

an aborted merger between Bell Atlantic and Tele-Communications, Inc and, at this writing, an announced merger between AT&T and the same TCI;

megamergers by Bell Atlantic and SBC;

privatization of government-owned telephone and broadcasting companies around the world;

the decreasing distinction among the insurance, banking, and securities industries.

The list of examples of industrial realignments in the information industry is long and growing.

The implications of these realignments may be positive and negative—and often both at once. The 1990s hegemony of Microsoft with its Windows operating system raised antitrust concerns, as did Intel's strong hold on the microprocessor environment. Both companies may have been able to extract monopoly-like profits, raising prices for all consumers and perhaps stifling innovation. But Windows and the Intel family of CPUs also brought a degree of standardization and compatibility to the personal computer world that created efficiencies and no doubt enhanced productivity over a more chaotic alternative.

Media realignments that were hyped to create multimedia synergies may have similarly mixed effects. And the alliance of Microsoft and the television network NBC produced a cable/Internet hybrid called MSNBC. Its long-term prospects, as might be expected, are unclear. Initially designed to provide news and information as both a cable service and via a Web site, we would expect its form to be fluid as it evolves. But at one level MSNBC (as one of many possible ventures that could have been cited) was an example of a new outlet for content, avenue for advertisers, and option for consumers.

But what can happen to turn a plus to a minus? In 1998 an attempt to bring synergy to the media after the merger of Time-Warner with Cable News Network was an embarrassing premiere of a new program that brought together *Time* magazine with CNN. A sloppily reported major "exposé" (since recanted by CNN) about the supposed use of nerve gas by U.S. troops in Laos during the Vietnam War lead to magnifying the errors with the same sloppy facts in a *Time* magazine article. In the end, this realignment yielded a story doubly short on facts but promoted twice as much as it might have been in the past.[3]

Indeed, when we start to talk about resources that had once been scarce now being abundant, we set the stage for uncertainty and instability. When alternatives to the traditional forms—newspapers, broadcast television, circuit-switched phone calls—become routinely available, the old, stable relationships and economics are subject to new challenges, threats and opportunities.

A paper published by two of the Program on Information Resources Policy's analysts, John LeGates and John McLaughlin, surveyed the information-industry landscape and came up with a list that asked public and private policy-makers to question basic assumptions of their business/regulatory models.[4] Information businesses and, when appropriate, their regulators, need to ask:

- Is there a need for uniformity in telephone markets?

- Is computer communications increasing the productivity of service jobs or automating them out of existence?

- What are the business implications of relocating "electronic smarts" in "computer as network vs. network as computer?"

- As political power has shifted from rural America to the urban/suburban majority, can telephone companies continue to count on public support for their monopolies and subsidies?

- With information workers comprising as much as fifty percent of the work force, will regulators find themselves continually refereeing the struggle among suppliers rather than protecting users?

- With information technology getting cheaper and faster, and information resources substituting for other more expensive resources, how far will the information revolution go?
- Given the dynamics of information supply, how can businesses prudently plan for the future?
- As information products and services evolve from scarcity to abundance, what is the proper role of government oversight?

These questions were proposed in 1989. The answers to many have evolved since then. Others, such as the last one, are still unresolved and, as Neuman et al. suggest in chapter 21, still the source of substantial debate.

Much of the best policy research seeks to identify the big questions, and to provide insights into the issues and the stakeholders. Some prescribes solutions; other research, much of which is reflected in this volume, has focused the attention of decision makers—both private and public—on what is at stake in a world of industrial instability in the age of information. Whether a business thrives, merely survives, or dies in the early decades of the 21st century may depend in large part on its understanding and application of information resources.

The Internet: The Merging of all Trends?

Convergence, abundance, blurring of boundaries, and realignments have been the themes of this volume. And all are reflected in the "overnight" blossoming of the Internet. Of course, the quotes around "overnight" are there to suggest that there is far more to it. Not only does the basis of the Internet go back to 1968, but the many forces and trends that allowed it to explode into prominence in the mid-1990s were the aggregation of decades of smaller, often individually unremarkable developments.

Tony Oettinger and his colleagues didn't "predict" the Internet or the World Wide Web. But they did make plain that forces were emerging that would allow something like it to emerge, later if not sooner. For example, in the early 1980s, the program explained to those who asked why the various products generally called videotext were premature: The technology, regulation and economic pieces were not ready. But a decade later the pieces were maturing, making the World Wide Web the success it was becoming at the end of the 1990s.[5]

The convergence of computers and communications is seen dramatically in the use of the Internet. The stand-alone personal computer of the 1980s has given way to the networked computer—even if only temporarily networked by a dial-up modem connection—at the start of the 21st century. The digital way described in chapters 6 and 8 has been part of the trend toward the abundance of telecommunications and computer resources that have become affordable to a mass audience, as modems reach speeds through digital tricks that could have never happened with analog signals. Computer power, random access memory and mass storage in 1980 were neither technologically advanced enough nor economically feasible to make accessible the graphical displays and relatively fast downloads that made the Web work fifteen years later. We could have had the Web in 1980 if we could have all been equipped with minicomputers that cost six figures and been able to afford dedicated leased telephone lines.

The Internet is also a lesson in realignments. An opportunist telecommunications company, WorldCom, built on the new way, swallowed up MCI, which itself had challenged the first force, AT&T. Compaq, which didn't exist when Digital Equipment Corporation was approaching its zenith of influence and profit, ingested DEC with barely a hiccup.

The Internet has brought a new reality to the notion of blurring boundaries. Can one publish a "news*paper*" if the content is available only online? With audio and video programing available real time, what becomes the boundary between what we used to call "television" and data processing? To run a television or radio station requires a license from the Federal Communications Commission. These licenses are almost impossible to obtain, other than by buying an existing one for millions (or hundreds of millions) of dollars. But anyone with $10,000 worth of equipment (and that cost will decrease) can transmit a video stream over the Internet. No license, no equal time or right of reply requirements, thank you. These "broadcasters" do not need to entice cable operators to make room for them on their systems. And they have access to a global audience for either highly targeted content (aficionados of falconry, for example) or mass-interest subjects, such as the hot musical group of the moment.

Government regulators are discovering that, whether they like it or not, they have little domestic control over many contentious issues, including indecency, gambling, and encryption.

While the specifics of who would win and who would lose, or what the exact timing of these changes would be, were not part of the mission of Oettinger and his colleagues, the coming together of the pieces that have contributed to the Internet becoming a mass medium today is seen in the themes of the research covered in this volume and that was evident, as William Baker noted in the Foreword, as early as the late 1960s. Nor should there be any doubt that the Internet of yesterday (when these words were written) and the Internet of today (when these words are read) will bear much resemblance to the Internet of tomorrow. It may be more useful to think of the Internet, in the words of John McLaughlin, "as being one more way-station on the road to the versatile and abundant digital future."

The Value of Good Thinking

We have entered into this new Age of Information—or whatever label one prefers—much as our forefathers entered the Industrial Age. They "energized" the means of production, and nothing—socially, economically, politically— was ever the same. Today we are "informationalizing" everything, because our convergent technological information resources are becoming more and more abundant and more and more versatile.

In Washington, as well as in state and foreign capitals, the political consequences of this new age are being felt. Everywhere, the shape and performance of the information infrastructure are being rethought. New economic theories are being offered to account for "increasing returns" of information businesses, and the consequences of virtual communities are on our social agenda.

In times of uncertainty, created by great technological change, it is critical that good minds continue to think about these things.

Notes

1. Majid Tehranian, "Iran: Communication, Alienation, Revolution," *InterMedia*, March 1979, pp. 6–12.

2. David L. Marcus, "Indonesia Revolt was Net Driven," *The Boston Globe*, May 23, 1998, p. A1.

3. "CNN Retracts Report That U.S. Used Nerve Gas," *The New York Times*, July 3, 1998, Online from Dow Jones Interactive Publications Library, http://interactive.wsj.com.

4. John LeGates and John McLaughlin, *Forces, Trends and Glitches in the World of Communications*, P-89-2, (Cambridge, Mass.: Program on Information Resources Policy, Harvard University, 1989).

5. Depending on one's perception, the Web may or may not have been a "success" circa 1999. Information providers—whether traditional publishers or players—were not making much, if any, money. On the other hand, thousands of Internet service providers, manufacturers of modems, routers, hubs, and other hardware, and telecommunications carriers, not to mention consultants, newsletter publishers, and conference organizers, had found the Internet quite remunerative. A few sites and businesses—bookseller Amazon.com most prominently—found opportunity on the Web, as have providers of corporate intranets and others who were able to provide services such as customer support. (Such is the nature of this business that by the time this book is in print Amazon.com may be a giant in bookselling—or may have been bought up or even gone out of business. Developments on the Internet move faster than conventional books can be published.)

About the Editors and Authors

Benjamin M. Compaine has experienced the information business as both a researcher and as a manager. He was an executive director of the Program on Information Resources Policy from 1979–1986. He is the author, coauthor, or editor of eight books. His best-known book is *Who Owns the Media?* Other books include *Issues in New Information Technology* and *Understanding New Media*. He has taught at Pennsylvania State University and at Temple University, where he was the Bell Atlantic Professor of Telecommunications. From 1986 to 1994 he was president and chief executive of Nova Systems Inc., a developer of management information tools. A graduate of Dickinson College, he received his M.BA. from Harvard University and Ph.D. from Temple University.

William H. Read is Professor of Information Policy and Management at the School of Public Policy at the Georgia Institute of Technology. He is the author or coauthor or editor of five books, including *The Information Revolution: Its Current and Future Consequences* and *America's Mass Media Merchants* (1977) and more than two dozen monographs and articles. He is a member of the editorial board of the *Federal Communications Law Journal*. He has been honored with the Federal Communications Bar Association's Distinguished Service Award, the highest honor given by the nation's communications attorneys. Read's public service includes positions at the White House, the U.S. Department of Commerce, and the U.S. Information Agency.

Daniel Bell is professor of social sciences, Emeritus at Harvard University. He coined the term "post-industrial society" in his landmark book, *The Coming of Post-Industrial Society*. (1973). In the 1970s he was chairman of the Commission on the Year 2000 of the American Academy of Arts and Sciences.

Anne Wells Branscomb was a communications attorney and a Research Affiliate of the Harvard Program. Her last book was *Who Owns Information?* (1995). She was an Inaugural Fellow of the Gannett Center for Media Studies at Columbia University. Her law degree was from George Washington University. She also held degrees from Harvard and the University of North Carolina.

Derrick C. Huang is director of marketing at Siemens Telecom Networks. Previously he managed network solutions marketing, market development, and new product introduction for Broadband Networks at Nortel. He has a Ph.D. in computer science from Harvard University and degrees in physics from Harvard and National Taiwan University.

Martin C. Libicki is a senior policy analyst at the RAND Corporation. His studies include *Information Technology Standards: Quest for the Common Byte* (1995), and *The Mesh and the Net: Speculations on National Security in the Age of Free Silicon* (1994).

Patricia Hirl Longstaff is associate professor at the Newhouse School of Public Communications, Syracuse University. Previously she was a communications lawyer. She is the author of many articles on communications regulation and coauthor of *Mass Communications Law in Minnesota* (1992) and *Law and the Media in the Midwest* (1984). She earned an M.P.A. at Harvard.

Robert W. Lucky is corporate vice president of applied research at Bellcore, a telecommunications software and consulting company. Before joining Bellcore in 1992, he was executive director of the communications sciences research division at Bell Laboratories. He is the author of a textbook on data communications, as well as a collection of essays, *Lucky Strikes Again*, and a popularized science book about information, *Silicon Dreams*.

Lee McKnight is Edward R. Murrow Professor of International Communications at The Fletcher School of Law and Diplomacy and Tufts University. He is coeditor of *Internet Economics* (1997).

John F. McLaughlin was an executive director of the Program on Information Resources Policy for fifteen years. There he was the key architect of the Information Business Map. Previously he spent sixteen years with the federal government, where he founded the Postal Service's Office of Strategic Planning. He also served with the Federal Aviation Agency's Research and Development Service. He holds degrees from Princeton and MIT.

Vincent Mosco is professor of communication at Carleton University, Ottawa. He is the author of four books and editor or coeditor of seven books on telecommunication policy, mass media, computers, and information technology. His most recent book is *The Political Economy of Communication: Rethinking and Renewal* (1996). He serves as a consultant to the Canadian and U.S. governments on telecommunications policy and social impacts. International Council. He received his Ph.D. in sociology from Harvard University.

W. Russell Neuman is professor of communications at the Annenberg School, University of Pennsylvania, where the directs the Program in Information and Society. He is the author of *The Future of the Mass Audience.* He has held faculty and research positions at MIT, Tufts, and Harvard.

Eli M. Noam is professor of finance and economics at Columbia University Graduate School of Business and is founder and director of the Columbia Institute for Tele-Information. Among this many books are *Telecommunications Regulation: Today and Tomorrow* and *The Dynamics of Telecommunications Policies in Europe and the United States.* He served as commissioner with the New York State Public Service Commission. He received an A.B., Ph.D. (Economics), and J.D. from Harvard.

Anthony G. Oettinger is Gordon McKay Professor of Applied Mathematics, professor of information resources policy, and a member of the Faculty of Government at Harvard University. He founded the Harvard Program on Information Resources Policy in 1972 to create useful knowledge, both competent and impartial, on controversial information matters. In the White House, among the many organizations he has served, Professor Oettinger was a consultant to the president's Foreign Intelligence Advisory Board (1981–90), the National Security Council (1975–81) and the Office of Science and Technology (1961–73). He chaired the Massachusetts Cable Television Commission (1975–79). He received his undergraduate and Ph.D. degrees from Harvard.

Ithiel de Sola Pool was one of the preeminent and most influential political scientists of his time. For many years he was the Sloan Professor of Political Science at MIT. *Technologies of Freedom,* completed in 1983, shortly before he died, continues to stand as a landmark work on the joining of technology and policy. He was the coeditor (with Wilbur Schramm) of the classic *Handbook of Communication* (1974) and wrote *Forecasting the Telephone: A Retrospective Technology Assessment* (1983).

Jerome S. Rubin was the president and CEO of Mead Data Central at the time it pioneered the LEXIS and NEXIS online information retrieval systems. Subsequently he was chairman of the Professional Information and Book Publishing Group of Times Mirror, Inc. Since 1995 he has been advisory managing partner. He is the chairman of the MIT Media Lab's News in the Future consortium. His undergraduate and law degrees are from Harvard University.

Richard J. Solomon is associate director of the Research Program on Communications Policy at MIT.

Debra Spar is associate professor at Harvard Business School. Her publications include *The Cooperative Edge: The Internal Politics of International Cartels* (1994), *Iron Triangles and Revolving Doors: Cases in U.S. Foreign Policymaking* (coauthor, 1991), and *Beyond Globalism: Remaking American Foreign Economic Policy*. She previously taught at the University of Toronto and in the government department at Harvard. She received a B.S. from the School of Foreign Service, Georgetown, and her M.A. and Ph.D. from Harvard.

Ronald Alan Weiner is an attorney with the law firm Macey, Wilensky, Cohen, Wittner & Kessler in Atlanta, Georgia. He received his law degree from Georgia State University.

Janet Wikler is senior vice president and director of strategic planning for Simon & Schuster, a subsidiary of Viacom. She has been involved in the publishing business since 1968 and has been involved with applying new technologies to publishing since 1977. She has a B.A. in English, an M.S. in education, and an M.B.A., all from the University of Pennsylvania.

Index